Wrightslaw: Special Education Law

Third Edition

Peter W. D. Wright, Esq.

Pamela Darr Wright, MA, MSW

Harbor House Law Press, Inc.
Hartfield, Virginia

Wrightslaw: Special Education Law, Third Edition by Peter W. D. Wright and Pamela Darr Wright

Library of Congress Cataloging-in-Publication Data
Wright, Peter W. D. and Pamela Darr Wright
Wrightslaw: Special Education Law, Third Edition
p. cm.
Includes bibliographic references and index.

1. Law — special education — United States. 1. Title
   2. Special education — parent participation — United States.
   Library of Congress Control Number: 2022930518

Print Edition:
 ISBN: 10: 1-892320-17-7
 ISBN: 13: 978-1-892320-17-9

E-book Edition
 ISBN: 1-892320-18-5
 ISBN: 13: 978-1-892320-18-6

10 9 8 7 6 5 4 3 2 1

Cover Design by Farrukh Khan, UpWork.com. https//www.upwork.com/freelancers/-01fc3d97402a5ce02
Printed in the United States of America by McNaughton-Gunn

Printing History
 First Edition November 1999
 Second Edition March 2007
 Third Edition March 2023

Disclaimer
Law is always evolving. The information in this book is general information. The publisher and authors are not engaged in rendering legal or other professional services. For legal advice about a specific set of facts, you should consult with an attorney.

The purpose of this book is to educate and inform. While every effort has been made to make this book as accurate as possible, there may be errors. The authors regret any errors that may have occurred and are happy to rectify them in future printings of this book.

Bulk Purchases
Harbor House Law Press books are available at discounts for bulk purchases, academic sales or textbook adoptions. For information, contact Harbor House Law Press, P. O. Box 480, Hartfield VA 23071. Please provide the title of the book, ISBN number, quantity, how the book will be used, and date needed.
 Toll Free Phone Orders: (877) LAW IDEA or (877) 529-4332
 Toll Free Fax Orders: (800) 863-5348
 Internet Orders: https://www.wrightslaw.com/store/

We dedicate this book to our parents, Virginia Bowen Darr, Robert William Darr, Penelope Ladd Wright, and Thomas W. D. Wright.

From these remarkable people, we inherited our passion and commitment to make the world a better place for all children.

We also dedicate this book to Diana Hanbury King and Roger Saunders, who taught Peter how to read, write, spell, and do arithmetic.

This book is also dedicated to Debra Pratt, our office manager and steady rock for 25+ years.

Other Books by Pete and Pam Wright

Wrightslaw: IDEA 2004

Wrightslaw: From Emotions to Advocacy, 2nd Ed.

Wrightslaw: All About IEPs

Wrightslaw: All About Tests and Assessments, 2nd Ed.

Year in Review Series

Wrightslaw: Special Education Legal Developments and Cases 2019

Wrightslaw: Special Education Legal Developments and Cases 2018

Wrightslaw: Special Education Legal Developments and Cases 2017

Wrightslaw: Special Education Legal Developments and Cases 2016

Wrightslaw: Special Education Legal Developments and Cases 2015

TABLE OF CONTENTS

---

1 While IDEA begins at Section 1400 and ends at Section 1482, in this Table of Contents, we have included and hyperlinked the five most common IDEA statutes used by readers They are sections 1400, 1401, 1412, 1414, and 1415.

---

2   Section 794 of Title 29 is the key statute known as the Section 504 statute.

CHAPTER 1

Introduction

In 1997, when we posted the first articles on a simple website called Wrightslaw.com, information about special education legal issues was hard to find, and subscriptions to legal journals were remarkably expensive.

In 1999, when we published the first edition of *Wrightslaw: Special Education Law*, we hoped "ordinary people" would realize that special education law and advocacy is not as difficult as thought and that more people would begin to advocate for children with disabilities.

In 2006, as we wrote the Introduction for the second edition of *Wrightslaw: Special Education Law*, we reflected on the increased demand for training in special education law and advocacy.

Twenty-five years have passed since we posted the first articles on Wrightslaw and published the first book about special education law. We are thankful that "ordinary people" continue to rely on our website and books. How do we account for this?

When it became clear that many schools were failing to provide children with disabilities with a free appropriate education to "prepare them for further education, employment and independent living,"[1] parents, educators, related service providers, lay advocates, and lawyers turned to advocacy.

School psychologists, school social workers, related services providers, and teachers who chose to work in special education because they wanted to help children with disabilities and their families faced hard choices. After years in the trenches, many of these professionals realized that ignorance, bureaucratic indifference, and overt hostility toward families of special needs children was preventing them from following their dreams. They used their knowledge, skills, and experience within the system to become effective advocates for special needs children and their families.

Most attorneys who have entered this field on behalf of children, did so after advocating for their own special needs children. When they encountered unexpected obstacles and outright resistance, they decided to use their knowledge and skills to help others.

Who Should Read This Book?

If you are the **parent of a child with a disability**, you represent your child's interests. To effectively advocate for your child, you need to learn about your child's rights and your rights and responsibilities under IDEA, Section 504 of the Rehabilitation Act, and the ADA and how these laws affect your child's education.

If you work as a **teacher, related services provider, or school administrator**, IDEA, Section 504, and ADA have a profound impact on you and your job. You may receive conflicting information and advice about these laws. You need to know what the laws actually say and how they are enforced locally and nationally.

---

1   20 U.S.C. § 1400(d) - the "purpose" of the **Individuals with Disabilities Education Act.**

If you **teach courses in special education, school psychology, school administration, or education law**, your students need to know how to find correct answers to their legal questions. The students need to learn how these laws impact their future careers and service to others.

If you are an **employee of a state department of education**, you may be responsible for investigating complaints, collecting data, or other activities to improve educational results for children with disabilities. You need to know the requirements in IDEA, Section 504, ADA, FERPA, and McKinney-Vento that affect your work.

If you are an **attorney or an advocate who represents children with disabilities**, you need this book on your desk, in your briefcase, and you need the **E-book edition (adobe.pdf)** on your computer so you can access the useful embedded hyperlinks throughout this book.

Since the publication of the Second Edition of this book in 2006, some statutory and regulatory changes were made to IDEA, Section 504, ADA, and McKinney-Vento. In recent years, Section 504 and the ADA have had a much greater impact on education, from preschool through graduate school, including professional licensing exams. We incorporate those impacts into this book.

What to Expect in This Book?

Wrightslaw: Special Education Law, Third Edition provides the full text of the statutes and regulations relating to the education of students with disabilities, from preschool through graduate school and licensing exams. You'll find answers to questions like these:

What do the laws say about child find? Are children who attend private schools, religious schools, and charter schools eligible for special education and related services?

What do the laws say about evaluations, reevaluations, and parental consent? What do the laws say about evaluating a child before a change of placement?

What do the laws say about Individualized Education Programs? Section 504 Plans? Who is entitled to accommodations?

Can the school refuse to provide an IEP or a Section 504 Plan to a child who is making good grades? What do the laws say about parental access to educational records?

What do the laws say about least restrictive environment and inclusion? What do the laws say about a child's placement? When a child moves to a different jurisdiction, can the receiving school terminate the IEP?

What do the laws say about bullying at school? Restraint and seclusion?

What do the laws say about compensatory education? Who makes decisions about compensatory education for children's lost learning during the pandemic?

What do the laws say about suspensions and expulsions? Is a child with a disability entitled to educational services after being suspended or expelled?

Do IDEA and Section 504 use the same definition of a "free appropriate public education"? Who enforces IDEA? Who enforces Section 504 of the Rehabilitation Act?

If a child has a disability and an IEP, is the school required to provide the child with physical education?

If a child has an Individualized Health Care Plan, is the school required to follow the plan? Are colleges or institutions of higher education required to provide the accommodations and modifications in a child's IEP or Section 504 Plan?

Is an IEP or a Section 504 Plan better for a child with special needs?

How this Book is Organized

Wrightslaw: Special Education Law, Third Edition has expanded to include other laws that affect special education for children with disabilities. This book includes

- Individuals with Disabilities Education Act (IDEA)
- Section 504 of the Rehabilitation Act of 1973 (Section 504)
- American with Disabilities Act of 1990 (ADA)
- Family Educational Rights and Privacy Act (FERPA)
- McKinney-Vento Homeless Assistance Act and
- portions of the United States Code, Federal Rules of Civil Procedure, and the U.S. Constitution.

As you learn about these laws and the interplay between them, don't be surprised if you feel confused and frustrated. *You aren't alone.* If you are patient, put in the time, and do your homework, the pieces of this puzzle will fall into place.

Wrightslaw: Special Education Law, Third Edition includes ten chapters. The first four chapters provide a comprehensive overview of special education law and how the laws evolved. You may be tempted to jump in and search for a specific legal issue or concept. Put on the brakes!

Finish Chapter 1 and continue through the end of Chapter 4. Be sure to skim the Index. Why? The first four chapters include concepts and terms that may not be repeated in later chapters. **You need to learn these concepts now.**

In **Chapter 2: The History of Special Education Law and Litigation**, you'll read the story about how public education and special education evolved. Several landmark cases led Congress to enact Public Law 94-142 in 1975. That law is now known as the Individuals with Disabilities Education Act (IDEA). This chapter includes the history of Section 504 of the Rehabilitation Act of 1973—with sit-ins and demonstrations—and its relationship with the Americans with Disabilities Act (ADA).

Chapter 3 is about Statutes, Regulations, the Commentary, and Caselaw. As you master the concepts in this chapter, you'll develop the skills to do your own legal research. You'll learn how special education law evolves through the caselaw generated by the U.S. Courts of Appeals and the Supreme Court of the United States (SCOTUS). This chapter includes the Tutorial: **How to Use Google Scholar as your Legal Research Tool**. Google Scholar is a free accessible search engine that allows you to search opinions of state appellate and supreme courts, U.S. District Courts, U.S. Courts of Appeal, and decisions from the U.S. Supreme Court (SCOTUS).

Chapter 4 is your Overview of IDEA, Section 504, and the ADA. In this chapter, you'll see how each law is organized, the key sections in IDEA, and the essential elements of Section 504 and the ADA. You'll learn how these statutes relate to each other when applied to educational issues, from preschool through higher education.

Chapter 5 includes the full text of the Individuals with Disabilities Education Act (IDEA) published in the United States Code beginning at 20 U.S.C. § 1400, with extensive footnotes, cross-references, hyperlinks, and strategies.

Chapter 6 contains the full text of the IDEA Regulations published in the Code of Federal Regulations beginning at 34 CFR Part 300.

Chapter 7 contains key text from Section 504 of the Rehabilitation Act of 1973 published in the United States Code, beginning at 29 U.S.C. § 701, and the **Section 504 Regulations** published in 34 CFR Part 104.

Chapter 8 contains the key text from Americans with Disabilities Act As Amended (ADA) published in the United States Code, beginning at 42 U.S.C. § 12101, and the **ADA Regulations** published in 28 CFR Part 35 and Part 36.

Chapter 9 includes relevant portions of other laws including the **Family Educational Rights and Privacy Act (FERPA)** beginning with 20 U.S.C. § 1232g and the **McKinney-Vento Homeless Assistance Act** which starts at 42 U.S. Code § 11431 and other legal authorities frequently cited in disability litigation. These include 28 U.S.C. §§

1331, 1343, 1441, 2201, 2202 and 42 U.S.C. § 1983 relating to a "Federal Question," "Civil Rights," "Removal of civil actions," "Creation of Remedy," "Further Relief," and "Civil action for deprivation of rights." Chapter 9 also includes specific rules from the **Federal Rules of Civil Procedure (FRCP)** and portions of the **First, Fourth, and Fifth Amendments to the Constitution** that address freedom of speech, unreasonable searches and seizures, and the right to due process of law.

Chapter 10, Selected Topics in Special Education Law answers questions about topics that generate misinformation and/or topics where the correct answer depends on whether the question arises under IDEA, Section 504, and/or the ADA. Some topics are complex (i.e., discipline, suspension, and expulsion), while others are not addressed in any special education law (i.e., Individual Health Care Plans). The topics are listed below and are hyperlinked to Chapter 10.

Selected Topics

Academic Content Standards	Enforcement	Placement, Change of
Assistive Technology	Evaluations	Placement, Continuum
Bullying & Harassment	FAPE	Related Services
Charter Schools	Grades	Restraint and Seclusion
Child Find	Individualized Health Care Plans	Section 504 v IEP
COVID & Compensatory Ed.	Least Restrictive Environment	Supplementary Aids & Services
Discipline	Military children	Transition
Eligibility	PE/Adaptive PE	Transition to Higher Ed.

Strategies to Develop Expertise in Special Education Law

The special education laws have different purposes and are enforced differently. This inevitably leads to confusion and consternation among parents, educators, related service providers, administrators, and to many advocates and attorneys.

Ignorance of the law can be as damaging as the child's disabilities. You need to understand the benefits of and differences between the statutes. IDEA is the statute that governs special education for children with disabilities. Section 504 and the ADA are civil rights statutes. When you have a question about a child's rights or protections, the answer will often depend on whether the question arises under IDEA, Section 504, and/or the ADA.

Although statutes and regulations are fairly static, caselaw is always evolving. You will learn more about this concept in Chapter 3, in the discussion about the 13 appellate courts that sit below the Supreme Court of the United States (SCOTUS) which are called "U.S. Courts of Appeal."

Tip: Download your state's special education regulations. Print a copy of the regulations in order to cross reference this book with your state regulations and vice versa.

The *Wrightslaw Year in Review* books[2] from 2015 through 2019 will help you understand the evolution of caselaw. Each Year in Review book contains all special education decisions issued by all U.S. Courts of Appeal and SCOTUS during the specific calendar year.

To learn more about special education law and advocacy and remain current about new cases and issues, subscribe to **The Special Ed Advocate**, the free online newsletter published by Wrightslaw.[3]

---

2   https://www.wrightslaw.com/store/index.html#yir

3   https://www.wrightslaw.com/

Strategies to Help You Use the E-book Edition

In the E-Book edition (PDF) of *Wrightslaw: Special Education Law, 3rd Ed.*, the page numbers in the Index are hyperlinked to pages within the book. The hyperlinks in the PDF edition allow you to click a link and go directly to a website on the Internet or to a specific location in the book. The embedded hyperlinks are not visible until you move your cursor over the text and the cursor changes into a hand. (see below)

The embedded link is marked with a < **left arrow and a right arrow** >, so that when you see text **between these arrows, you are alerted that the text is a hyperlink.** For example, <this will take you to the beginning of chapter Five> and <this will take you to our website, Wrightslaw dot com.>

The example below begins with **subsection "1400(d) Purposes"** located in the **Individuals with Disabilities Education Act (IDEA)** at the beginning of Chapter 5. We added a **left arrow and a right arrow,** <   >.

   <**§1400(d) Purposes**. The purposes of this chapter are– >

   (1)(A) to ensure that all children with disabilities have available to them a free appropriate public education that emphasizes special education and related services designed to meet their **unique needs and prepare them for further education, employment, and independent living;**[4]

In this example, the two symbols, < **and** >, indicate that the text between the arrows <is an embedded hyperlink>. When you click on it, you will jump to the "Purpose" of IDEA in Chapter 5. To quickly return to this page, use either Command F or Control F,[5] insert simply the left arrow < in your search box and the first entry (of many), will be to this page.

If the text is a URL, the link does not begin or end with an <arrow>. All 350+ URLs in this book are hyperlinked. On the date of publication, all hyperlinks were retrieved, checked, and were working. Over time, some websites are likely to move articles or other resources so you can expect to find broken links.[6]

At the end of each chapter, you will find **Quick Links** to the chapters. With the **E-book (PDF) edition**, you can use these Quick Links to navigate to the beginning of other chapters.

Depending on your keyboard and operating system, you may increase your options to move quickly through this book. You can use do a full search of the book for a specific word or phrase. ["Command" or "Control" or "Alt" + F] If you are searching for a phrase, you may need to use quotation marks around the phrase. When you use the "thumbnails" and "sidebar," you can also move quickly through the book.

With some keyboards and operating systems, using the "page up," "page down," "home," and "end" keys, and sometimes in combination with your "option" and / or "control" or ""function" keys, you can increase your options to move quickly through the book.

We know some readers are impulsive and will quickly jump to a specific statute, section, or regulation without reading the earlier chapters, including this one. If you take this path, you will miss the information in this chapter about

---

4 **The Purposes of IDEA in Section 1400(d) is the mission statement of this law.** When drafting IEP goals and objectives, keep this "mission statement" in mind.

5 This depends on whether you are using a Windows or Mac computer. This is the search / find feature.

6 If you find typographical, grammatical, other errors, or broken links, please send an email to us at <typo@wrightslaw.com.> In subsequent reprints of this book, we can correct them.

<embedded hyperlinks> to locations within and outside of this book and similarly important information in the other early chapters.

Since a law book is primarily a resource book and is not usually read from cover to cover, some readers may not be aware of relevant information in other locations in this book. For this reason, we deliberately repeat ourselves on some topics and issues. If you are reading this book and have a sense that you read something similar earlier in this book, you probably did.

For example, IDEA applies to the child whose disability adversely affects educational performance, so the child needs special education and related services. If a child has a disability but is not eligible for an IEP under IDEA, the child is likely to be eligible for a Section 504 Plan and protection from discrimination under Section 504 and the ADA.

Although statutes and regulations are fairly static, caselaw is always evolving. You will learn more about this concept in Chapter 3, in the discussion of the 13 appellate courts that sit below the Supreme Court of the United States (SCOTUS) called "U.S. Courts of Appeal."

The Wrightslaw Year in Review books from 2015 through 2019 will help you understand how caselaw evolves. Each Year in Review book contains all special education decisions issued by all U.S. Courts of Appeal and SCOTUS during that calendar year.

Updates

After this book is published, any later changes in statutes or regulations will be posted on the Wrightslaw website at: https://www.wrightslaw.com/lawbook.update/

In Summation

In this Introduction, you learned who this book is written for, what to expect, how the book is organized, strategies to develop expertise in special education law, and strategies to use the E-book edition of this book.

In the next chapter, you can relax as you read the story about how public education and special education evolved. You'll learn about the landmark cases that led Congress to enact Public Law 94-142 in 1975 and you'll read the fiery history of Section 504 of the Rehabilitation Act of 1973, including sit-ins and demonstrations.

End of Chapter 1 - Introduction

Hyperlinks to Chapters

Ch. 01 Introduction	Ch. 06 IDEA Regulations
Ch. 02 History	Ch. 07 Section 504
Ch. 03 Overview of Law, Courts, Research	Ch. 08 ADA
Ch. 04 Overview of IDEA, Section 504, ADA	Ch. 09 Other laws
Ch. 05 IDEA (US Code)	Ch. 10 Selected Topics

CHAPTER 2

History of Special Education Law and Litigation

In these days, it is doubtful that any child may reasonably be expected to succeed in life

if he is denied the opportunity of an education.[1]

To understand the battles being fought today for children with disabilities, you need to understand the history and traditions associated with public schools and special education.

In this chapter, you will learn about the evolution of public education and special education, the impact of several landmark cases, and the circumstances that led Congress to enact Public Law 94-142, the law known as the Individuals with Disabilities Education Act (IDEA).

Common Schools Teach Common Values

During the 19th and early 20th centuries, Waves of poor, non-English speaking immigrants poured into the United States. Citizens feared that these new immigrants would bring class hatred, religious intolerance, crime, and violence to America. Social and political leaders searched for ways to "reach down into the lower portions of the population and teach children to share the values, ideals, and controls held by the rest of society."[2]

Horace Mann, an educational reformer, believed that when children from different social, religious, and economic backgrounds are educated together, they learn to accept and respect each other. Mann proposed that communities establish "common schools" to socialize children and to improve interpersonal relationships, and social conditions.[3]

Many poor children attended school sporadically, quit early, or didn't enroll in school at all. For Dr. Mann's plan to work, all children had to attend school. Public school authorities lobbied for compulsory school attendance laws and the power to prosecute parents legally if they failed to send their children to school.[4]

---

1   *Brown v. Board of Education*, 347 U.S. 483, 493 (1954)

2   Church, Robert L. (1976) *Education in the United States,* page 81 (New York: The Free Press)

3   Cremin, Lawrence A. (1967) *The Transformation of the School: Progressivism in American Education,* **1876**-1957, pages 183-194 (New York: Knopf)

4   Sperry, David, Philip T. K. Daniel, Dixie Snow Huefner, E. Gordon Gee. (1998) *Education Law and the Public Schools: A Compendium,* pages 139-145 (Norwood, MA: Christopher-Gordon Publishers, Inc.); Cremin, pages 182-226

Early Special Education Programs

The first special education programs were delinquency prevention programs for "at risk" children who lived in urban slums. School districts designed manual training classes to supplement their general education programs. By 1890, hundreds of thousands of children were learning carpentry, metal work, sewing, cooking and drawing in manual classes. Early special education programs also focused on the "moral training" of African-American children.[5]

A few special schools and special classes for children with disabilities existed in 19th century America. They gradually evolved during the 20th century.[6] Programs for children with specific learning disabilities, sometimes called congenital word blindness, strephosymbolia,[7] brain injury, minimal brain damage," and other terms) became more common in the 1940's and 1950's.[8] Private special education programs were rare and expensive. For most children with disabilities, special education programs were simply not available. There was no federal law requiring states to educate children with disabilities.

1954 - *Brown v. Board of Education*

In 1954, the U.S. Supreme Court issued a landmark civil rights decision in *Brown v. Board of Education*.[9]

In *Brown*, school children from four states argued that segregated public schools were inherently unequal and deprived them of equal protection of the laws. The Supreme Court found that African-American children had the right to equal educational opportunities and that segregated schools "have no place in the field of public education." The Court wrote:

> Today, education is perhaps the most important function of state and local governments. Compulsory school attendance laws and the great expenditures for education both demonstrate our recognition of the importance of education to our democratic society. It is required in the performance of our most basic public responsibilities, even service in the armed forces. It is the very foundation of good citizenship. Today it is a principal instrument in awakening the child to cultural values, in preparing him for later professional training, and in helping him to adjust normally to his environment. In these days, it is doubtful that any child may reasonably be expected to succeed in life if he is denied the opportunity of an education. Such an opportunity, where the state has undertaken to provide it, is a right that must be made available to all on equal terms.[10]

> We come then to the question presented: Does segregation of children in public schools solely on the basis of race, even though the physical facilities and other "tangible" factors may be equal, deprive the children of the minority group of equal educational opportunities? We believe that it does.[11]

---

5   Cremin, pages 182-226

6   *See,* for example, *History of the Vineland Training School* at: https://en.wikipedia.org/wiki/Vineland_Training_School, Perkins School for the Blind at: https://www.perkins.org/our-history, and The American School for the Deaf at: https://www.asd-1817.org/about/history--cogswell-heritage-house.

7   On July 25, **1925** Dr. Samuel T. Orton presented a paper about "Strephosymbolia" and "Congenital Word Blindness" (now known as dyslexia), at the American Neurological Association's Annual Meeting.

8   Hallahan, Daniel P. and Cecil D. Mercer (2001) *Learning Disabilities: Historical Perspectives.* Learning Disabilities Summit: Building a Foundation for the Future at: https://files.eric.ed.gov/fulltext/ED458756.pdf citing early work by Orton, Fernald, Cruickshank and Kirk.

9   *Brown v. Board of Education,* 347 U.S. 483 (1954) https://www.wrightslaw.com/law/caselaw/ussupct.brown.bd.ed.htm

10   *Id.,* at 493

11   *Id.,* at 493

In *Brown*, the Supreme Court described the emotional impact that segregation has on children, especially when segregation "has the sanction of the law:"

> To separate them from others of similar age and qualifications solely because of their race generates a feeling of inferiority as to their status in the community that may affect their hearts and minds in a way unlikely ever to be undone . . . Segregation of white and colored children in public schools has a detrimental effect upon the colored children. The impact is greater when it has the sanction of the law; for the policy of separating the races is usually interpreted as denoting the inferiority of the Negro group. A sense of inferiority affects the motivation of a child to learn. Segregation with the sanction of law, therefore, has a tendency to [retard] the educational and mental development of Negro children and to deprive them of some of the benefits they would receive in a racially integrated school system.[12]

After the decision in *Brown*, parents of children with disabilities brought lawsuits against school districts for excluding and segregating their children. These parents argued that by excluding their children, schools were discriminating against the children because of their disabilities.

1965 - Elementary and Secondary Education Act (ESEA)

In 1965, Congress enacted Public Law 89-10, the Elementary and Secondary Education Act (ESEA) to address the inequality of educational opportunities for underprivileged children. This legislation sought to provide disadvantaged students with access to a quality education.[13] In 1966, Congress amended the ESEA[14] and established a grant program to help states pay for programs to educate handicapped children.

1970 - Education of the Handicapped Act (EHA)

In 1970, as a part of the ESEA, Congress enacted the Education of the Handicapped Act (EHA) (Public Law 91-230).[15] The purpose of this law was to help states initiate, develop, expand, and improve programs to educate handicapped children at the preschool, elementary and secondary school levels.

These early special education programs were grant programs with no requirements about how funds were to be used or whether the programs improved the education of children with disabilities. The EHA did not require schools to provide children with disabilities with a "Free Appropriate Public Education" and did not prohibit schools from suspending and expelling children to avoid paying to educate them. Dyslexia was included in the 1970 definition of specific learning disabilities.[16]

1972 - *PARC* and *Mills*

During the early 1970s, two cases were catalysts for change: *Pennsylvania Assn. for Retarded Children (PARC) v. Commonwealth of Pennsylvania*,[17] and *Mills v. Board of Education of District of Columbia*.[18]

According to Pennsylvania statutes, if a child was deemed to be "uneducable," the school was not responsible for providing any educational services. *PARC* challenged the exclusion of children with mental retardation (intellectual

12 *Id.*, at 494

13 1965 - Public Law 89-10 - https://www.govinfo.gov/content/pkg/STATUTE-79/pdf/STATUTE-79-Pg27.pdf#page=1

14 1966 - Public Law 89-750 - https://www.govinfo.gov/content/pkg/STATUTE-80/pdf/STATUTE-80-Pg1191.pdf#page=1

15 1970 - Public Law 91-230 - https://www.govinfo.gov/content/pkg/STATUTE-84/pdf/STATUTE-84-Pg121.pdf#page=55

16 *See* page 177 of EHA

17. *Pennsylvania Assn. for Retarded Children v. Commonwealth*, 334 F. Supp. 1257 (E. D. Pa, 1971) and 343 F. Supp. 279 (E. D. Pa. 1972)

18 *Mills v. Board of Education of District of Columbia*, 348 F. Supp. 866 (D. DC 1972)

disabilities)[19] from public schools. On May 5, 1972, the *PARC* court issued its Opinion, Order. and Injunction.[20] The exclusion language was deleted from the statute. Educational placement decisions must include parental participation and a means to resolve disputes.[21]

Mills[22] involved the practice of suspending, expelling, and excluding children with disabilities from the District of Columbia public schools. The school district's primary defense in *Mills* was the high cost[23] of educating children with disabilities:

> The genesis of this case is found (1) in the failure of the District of Columbia to provide publicly supported education and training to plaintiffs and other "exceptional" children, members of their class, and (2) the excluding, suspending, expelling, reassigning and transferring of "exceptional" children from regular public school classes without affording them due process of law.[24]

Relying on the Due Process Clause of the U.S. Constitution, Judge Waddy wrote:

> The inadequacies of the District of Columbia Public School System whether occasioned by insufficient funding or administrative inefficiency, **certainly cannot be permitted to bear more heavily** on the "exceptional" or handicapped child than on the normal child.[25]

1972 - Congressional Investigation - Expulsion of Handicapped Children

After the decisions in *PARC* and *Mills*, Congress investigated how children with disabilities were educated and found that children with disabilities were routinely expelled and suspended from public schools because of the cost to educate these children. Congress also found that "the educational needs of millions of children with disabilities were not being fully met . . ."[26] and they were not receiving an appropriate education:

> Yet, the most recent statistics provided by the Bureau of Education for the Handicapped estimated that of the more than 8 million children . . . with handicapping conditions requiring special education and related services, only 3.9 million such children are receiving an appropriate education. **1.75 million handicapped children are receiving no educational services at all,** and **2.5 million handicapped children are receiving an inappropriate education.**[27] (emphasis added)

> The long-range implications of these statistics are that public agencies and taxpayers will spend billions of dollars over the lifetimes of these individuals to maintain such persons as dependents and in a minimally acceptable lifestyle. **With proper education services, many would be able to become productive citizens, contributing to society instead of being forced to remain burdens.**[28]

---

19 Pursuant to **Rosa's Law,** mental retardation is now known as "intellectual disabilities" - *see* statutory revision to 20 U.S.C. § 1401(3).

20 *PARC*s 1972 decision is located at: located at: https://www.leagle.com/decision/1972622343fsupp2791570.

21 *PARC* 1972, 343 F. Supp at 303-306

22 The full text of *Mills* is available at: https://www.leagle.com/decision/19721214348fsupp86611090.xml

23 Financial cost is often the primary defense used by school districts in special education cases before the U.S. Supreme Court.

24 *Mills* at 868

25 *Id.* at 876

26 20 U.S.C. § 1400(c)(2)

27 *United States Code Congressional and Administrative News* 1975 (U.S.C.C.A.N. 1975) at 1433

28 *Id.* at 1433

There is no pride in being forced to receive economic assistance. Not only does this have negative effects upon the handicapped person, but it has far-reaching effects for such person's family.[29]

Parents of handicapped children all too frequently are not able to advocate for the rights of their children because they have been erroneously led to believe that their children will not be able to lead meaningful lives . . . It should not . . . be necessary for parents throughout the country to continue utilizing the courts to assure themselves a remedy . . ."[30]

1973 - The Rehabilitation Act of 1973

In 1973, H.R. 8070[31] was passed by a unanimous vote of Congress and signed into law as The Rehabilitation Act of 1973, Public Law 93-112.[32] The purpose was:

To replace the Vocational Rehabilitation Act, to extend and revise the authorization of grants to States for vocational rehabilitation services, with special emphasis on services to those with the most severe handicaps, to expand special Federal responsibilities and research and training programs with respect to handicapped individuals, to establish special responsibilities in the Secretary of Health, Education, and Welfare and for other purposes.

Section 504 of The Rehabilitation Act is a civil rights statute that prohibits "discrimination under any program or activity receiving Federal financial assistance." The law has been revised several times. The essence of Section 504 is in the regulations provided in <Chapter 7.> In May, 2022, the Office for Civil Rights announce plans to revise the Section 504 regulations.

1974 - Family Educational Rights and Privacy Act (FERPA)

On August 21, 1974, Congress enacted Public Law 93-380,[33] the <Family Educational Rights and Privacy Act (FERPA).> This law required schools to "establish appropriate procedures for the granting of a request by parents for access to their child's school records within a reasonable period of time, but in no case more than forty-five days after the request has been made."

Parents shall have an opportunity for a hearing to challenge the content of their child's school records, to insure that the records are not inaccurate, misleading, or otherwise in violation of the privacy or other rights of students, and to provide an opportunity for the correction or deletion of any such inaccurate, misleading, or otherwise inappropriate data contained therein.

You will find FERPA in the United States Code at 20 U.S.C. § 1232g and in <Chapter 9> of this book.

1975 - Public Law 94-142: The Education for All Handicapped Children Act of 1975

On November 19, 1975, Congress amended the 1970 Education for Handicapped Act (EHA) and enacted **Public Law 94-142**,[34] known as **The Education for All Handicapped Children Act of 1975**. Congress intended that all children with disabilities would "have a right to education, and to establish a process by which State and local educational agencies may be held accountable for providing educational services for all handicapped children."[35]

---

29   *Id.* at 1433

30   *Id.* at 1433

31   https://www.congress.gov/bill/93rd-congress/house-bill/8070/all-actions?overview=closed#tabs

32   https://www.congress.gov/93/statute/STATUTE-87/STATUTE-87-Pg355.pdf

33   https://www.govinfo.gov/content/pkg/STATUTE-88/pdf/STATUTE-88-Pg484.pdf

34   https://www.wrightslaw.com/idea/law/PL94-142.pdf

35   *United States Code Congressional and Administrative News* 1975 (U.S.C.C.A.N. 1975) at 1427

Initially, the law focused on ensuring that children with disabilities had access to an education and due process of law. As with EHA, Congress included the word "dyslexia" and addressed concepts such as "written prior notice," "independent educational evaluations" (IEE), due process hearings, and "least restrictive environment" (LRE).

Congress stated that the "removal of handicapped children from the regular educational environment occurs **only when** the nature or severity of the handicap is such that education in regular classes with the use of supplementary aids and services cannot be achieved satisfactorily."[36] This new landmark legislation created an elaborate system of legal checks and balances called "**procedural safeguards**" to protect the rights of children and their parents.[37]

1977 - Section 504 of the Rehabilitation Act of 1973 / The Regulations

Section 504 is a civil rights statute that prohibits "discrimination under any program or activity receiving **Federal financial assistance**."[38] When a law is passed, federal agencies issue regulations to clarify the definitions, meanings, and how the law will be enforced. After this law went into effect, the Department of Health, Education, and Welfare (HEW) delayed the process because of opposition from "hospitals, universities, state and county governments" that would be affected by the regulations.

Later, "HEW set up a task force with no representation from the disability community to 'study' them. It became clear, through delays and leaks from inside, that the regulations were being seriously weakened in coverage, enforcement, and the whole integration mandate."

These delays led to sit-ins in several cities. The highly publicized **28 day sit-in** at HEW's San Francisco federal building involved more than 150 people with disabilities and led to a dramatic Congressional hearing. A television newscaster reported on the third day, that "the squeeze is on, hot water has been turned off on the fourth floor, where the occupation army of cripples has taken over."[39]

At a victory speech on April 30, 1977, activist Kitty Cone said that the disability community had "written a new page in American history . . . We showed strength and courage and power and commitment . . . that we the shut-ins, or the shut-outs, we the hidden, supposedly the frail and the weak, that we can wage a struggle at the highest level of government and win."[40]

The 504 Sit-In is the longest nonviolent occupation of a federal building in U.S. history. HEW issued the Section 504 regulations on April 28, 1977.[41, 42]

The Section 504 regulations require school districts to provide a "**free appropriate public education**" (FAPE) to all qualified students with a disability within the district's jurisdiction, regardless of the nature or severity of the disability.

---

36   Public Law 94-142 at 89 STAT. 781

37   Many of the "procedural safeguards" contained in 20 U.S.C. § 1415 were taken almost verbatim from District Court Judge Waddy's Order in *Mills v. D.C.*

In 2005, the **National Council on Disability (NCD)**, a federal agency, commissioned this author to write a comprehensive Policy Paper about the Burden of Proof issues that were pending before the U.S. Supreme Court in *Schaffer v. Weast*. The Policy Paper was filed with the Court as the NCD's official position. *See IDEA Burden of Proof: On Parents or Schools?* https://www.wrightslaw.com/ncd/wright.burdenproof.pdf. The history of the *Mills* case and Judge Waddy's unique rulings were discussed in depth. *Mills*, more so than *PARC*, established the initial foundation and structure of our special education statute in effect today.

38   29 U.S.C. § 794

39   At 8:27 in the video available at: https://vimeo.com/channels/504sitin

40   https://www.nytimes.com/2021/03/26/obituaries/kitty-cone-overlooked.html

41   https://dredf.org/504-sit-in-20th-anniversary/short-history-of-the-504-sit-in/   Author: Kitty Cone

42   Judith Heumann, who later became the Head at the Office of Special Education and Rehabilitative Services (OSEP) at the U.S. Department of Education (USDOE) had a primary role in the organization of the sit-in.
    https://en.wikipedia.org/wiki/504_Sit-in

In Section 504, FAPE means providing regular or special education and related aids and services designed to meet the student's individual educational needs **as adequately as the needs of nondisabled students are met**.[43] Section 504 provides protections to all children with disabilities, including children who are not eligible for IEPs. The Section 504 definition of FAPE is different[44] from the Individuals with Disabilities Education Act (IDEA) definition of FAPE.[45]

1990 - The Americans with Disabilities Act

In 1990, the Americans with Disabilities passed. The ADA was based on the success of Section 504's nondiscriminatory requirements on entities that receive federal financial assistance. The ADA extended provisions in Section 504 to the private sector, including private schools, daycare centers, and others serving individuals with disabilities.

ADA Title II applies to public schools, and **ADA Title III applies to private schools** and services, including day care and nursery schools.

The ADA regulations were developed by different federal agencies, depending on the Title. The Equal Employment Opportunity Commission (EEOC), Department of Justice (USDOJ), Department of Transportation (USDOT), and the Federal Communications Commission (FCC) created regulations for their areas of responsibility.

In 1999, pursuant to the ADA, the U.S. Supreme Court issued the decision in *Olmstead v. L.C. by Zimring* (527 U.S. 581)[46] which held that the unjustified segregation of persons with disabilities is discrimination because it is not the most integrated setting.[47]

1997 - Individuals with Disabilities Education Act (IDEA 97)

After Congress passed the special education law in 1975, they amended and renamed the law several times. In the "Handicapped Children's Protection Act of 1986,"[48] Congress reversed the impact of a prior denial of attorneys fees by SCOTUS in *Smith v. Robinson*[49] and expressly authorized awards of attorneys fees to parents who prevail in special education due process hearings. Congress also revised the law to include services for "Infants and Toddlers with Disabilities,"[50] known as "Part C services."

In 1990, Congress expanded the definition of a "child with a disability" to include autism.[51, 52]

---

43   Section 504 definition of FAPE is at 34 CFR § 104.33

44   See Chapter 10, <Selected Topics - FAPE>

45   The IDEA definition of FAPE is at 20 U.S.C. § 1401(9) and 34 CFR § 300.17

46   https://www.law.cornell.edu/supct/pdf/98-536P.ZO

47   Jonathan Zimring is an attorney in Georgia who also represented the parents in the Cobb County IEE case discussed in Chapter 5 in conjunction with the IEE statute.

48   Public Law 99-372 - https://www.govinfo.gov/content/pkg/STATUTE-100/pdf/STATUTE-100-Pg796.pdf

49   *Smith v. Robinson*, 468 U.S. 992 (1984)

50   Public Law 99-457 - https://www.govinfo.gov/content/pkg/STATUTE-100/pdf/STATUTE-100-Pg1145.pdf

51   20 U.S.C. § 1401(3) Prior to this change in 1990, a child with autism was not eligible for an IEP under federal law. However, some state

52   In Virginia, prior to that change in 1990, there were two cases where school districts successfully argued in court that autism was a medical condition and not covered under this law, thus the children were denied IEPs. Some states included autism and "autistic-like" characteristics within the state's definition of "developmental disabilities" and "other health impaired," enabling the children to obtain special education services. In Virginia, until the above statutory change, this author always avoided the "autism" label. Instead, the testimony and reports from evaluators and expert witnesses often noted that the child had a "pervasive developmental disorder" with "autistic-like" characteristics.

In **1997**, Congress made **significant revisions,** including an emphasis on discipline and educational outcomes (Public Law 105-17).[53]The name was changed to the Individuals with Disabilities Education Act of 1997 and the law became known as **"IDEA 97"** to differentiate it from earlier versions.

2000 - NCD - Back to School on Civil Rights: IDEA Compliance Report

In 2000, the **National Council on Disability (NCD)** published *Back to School on Civil Rights*, the long-awaited report on the **enforcement** of the Individuals with Disabilities Education Act since the law was enacted.[54, 55]

Findings

- **Every State was out of compliance** with IDEA requirements to some degree; in the sampling of states studied, noncompliance persisted over many years.

  - 90 percent of states and territories fail to adequately supervise local education agencies (school district's) education of students with disabilities.

  - 88 percent of states do not comply with requirements to provide services to assist a student's transition from school to post-education activities.

  - 36 states failed to ensure that children with disabilities are educated in regular classrooms.

  - 45 states failed to ensure that local school authorities adhered to nondiscrimination laws.

- **Federal efforts to enforce the law** over several administrations **were inconsistent, ineffective and lacked any real teeth**.

- The Department of Education consistently **failed to impose sanctions on states that refused to comply with the law**, including withholding funds and referring states to the Department of Justice for legal action.

- **Enforcing the law was the burden of parents** who too often must invoke formal complaint procedures and due process hearings, including expensive and time-consuming litigation, to obtain the appropriate services and supports that their children were entitled under the law.

- Even parents with significant resources were hard-pressed to prevail over state education agencies (SEA) and local education agencies (LEA) when they, or their publicly financed attorneys choose to be resistant.[56]

Recommendations

The National Council on Disability urged Congress to amend IDEA and provide the **Department of Justice** with **independent authority to investigate and litigate** against school districts or states where pattern and practice violations of IDEA exist.[57]

---

53   Public Law 105-17 - https://www.wrightslaw.com/idea/law/PL105-17.pdf

54   https://ncd.gov/publications/2000/Jan252000

55   https://www.wrightslaw.com/law/reports/IDEA_Compliance_0.html

56   See the September 211, 2022, federal court class-action complaint filed against the VA DOE and Fairfax County alleging that parents prevail in less than 2% of cases because the Virginia Department of Education "carefully curated a group of twenty-two (22) hearing officers who nearly always rule in favor of school districts and against parents." *Chaplick v. Fairfax County Bd. of Ed. and VA DOE* at:
     https://www.wrightslaw.com/law/pleadings/2022.0921.complaint.chaplick.v.virginia.doe.pdf

57   https://www.wrightslaw.com/law/reports/IDEA_Compliance_6.htm

2001 - No Child Left Behind (NCLB)

In 2001, the Elementary and Secondary Education Act of 1965 was reauthorized and named "**No Child Left Behind (NCLB).**" The primary purpose was "to ensure that **all children** have a fair, equal, and significant opportunity to obtain a high-quality education and reach, at a minimum, proficiency on challenging State academic achievement standards and state academic assessments."[58] The law focused on reading and teachers being "highly qualified."

In 2015, Congress repealed NCLB and replaced it with the "Every Student Succeeds Act" (ESSA).

2004 - Individuals with Disabilities Education Act (IDEA)

On December 3, 2004, Congress reauthorized IDEA again. The amended statute became known as "**IDEA 2004**" to differentiate it from the prior **IDEA 97**. (In this book, we refer to this current law as "IDEA.") The IDEA statute is in the United States Code (U.S.C.), Title 20, beginning at Section 1400, and is cited as 20 U.S.C. § 1400. (The full text is Chapter 5 in this book.) The special education regulations issued by the USDOE are published in Volume 34 of the Code of Federal Regulations (CFR) beginning at Section 300, the first regulation is cited as 34 CFR § 300.1. (The full text is Chapter 6 in this book.)

In the reauthorized IDEA, Congress increased the focus on **accountability and improved outcomes** by emphasizing reading, early intervention, transition, further education, and research-based instruction. IDEA contained requirements for "highly qualified" teachers and defined "core academic subjects." When Congress repealed NCLB in 2015, they eliminated the goal that all children would be proficient in reading by the end of grade 3 and removed the "core academic subjects" and "highly qualified teacher" portions from NCLB and IDEA.

The primary purposes of the Individuals with Disabilities Education Act of 2004 are:

- to provide an education that meets a child's **unique needs** that prepares the child for **further education, employment, and independent living,** and
- to **protect the rights** of children with disabilities and their parents.[59]

Congress did not make the changes recommended by the National Council on Disability to improve the enforcement of IDEA by shifting enforcement to the U. S. Department of Justice.

2008 - ADA Amendments Act

In 2008, after several SCOTUS rulings that narrowed the ADA's definition of a disability, Congress revised and reauthorized the ADA and broadened the definition of disabilities to include conditions such as asthma, diabetes, epilepsy, and other episodic conditions.

2015 - Every Student Succeeds Act (ESSA)

In 2015, Congress reauthorized the Elementary and Secondary Education Act (ESEA) of 1965 and renamed the law as "Every Student Succeeds Act of 2015." In response to intense lobbying, Congress watered down the Purpose, eliminated the requirements for "highly qualified teachers," and removed the goal that all children would be proficient readers by the end of grade 3.[60]

ESSA requires states to establish goals for the performance of children with disabilities that are consistent with the goals and standards for nondisabled children. States are also required to improve graduation rates, reduce

---

58   Quote from 20 U.S.C. § 6301 of the No Child Left Behind Act of 2001 that was repealed in 2015 and replaced with ESSA.

59   20 U.S.C. § 1400(d)(1)

60   20 U.S.C. § 6301, as amended by ESSA on December 10, 2015.

drop-out rates, and report the progress of children with disabilities on state and district assessments.[61] Given the failure to enforce IDEA for decades, we are skeptical about how the government will enforce ESSA.

2016 – "Denied" in Texas

On September 9, 2016, a story broke in Texas that rocked the world of special education beyond that state's borders. *Denied: How Texas Keeps Thousands of Children Out of Special Education,*[62] is a series of articles by investigative reporter Brian M. Rosenthal and published in *The Houston Chronicle.*

The investigation began when Rosenthal wanted an answer to this question: *Why is Texas last in America – by far – in the percentage of children receiving special education services?* The national average was 14 percent but only 8.5 percent of students in Texas received special education services.

Rosenthal discovered that twelve years earlier, the Texas Education Agency (TEA) quietly set a "benchmark" directing all 1,200 Texas school districts to limit special education enrollments to 8.5 percent. Over the next decade, the number of children receiving special education services dropped to 8.5 percent as hundreds of thousands of children were denied special education services. Students with emotional problems and English Language Learners were among the first to be denied. The cap saved Texas billions of dollars.

Not surprisingly, Rosenthal's articles triggered an investigation by the USDOE. In 2018, after a 15-month investigation, the USDOE found that the TEA violated IDEA by failing to maintain its prior year's financial support for children with disabilities.[63] After the USDOE withheld $33.3 million from the TEA, the TEA sued the USDOE.

An Administrative Law Judge upheld the USDOE. TEA appealed to the U.S. Court of Appeals for the Fifth Circuit. The Fifth Circuit upheld the decision in *Texas Education Agency v. US Dept. of Education*, 908 F.3d 127 (2018).[64]

TEA submitted a Corrective Action Response (CAR) to the USDOE's Office of Special Education Programs (OSEP) to address their "noncompliance by failing to properly implement IDEA requirements" in several areas. After a site visit to "monitor TEA's implementation of the State's Corrective Action Response (CAR)," the director of OSEP sent a letter to the TEA on October 19, 2020[65] and advised that "OSEP cannot determine, in the absence of additional and up-to-date information, whether these actions have been sufficient" to fully address any of the requirements for improving special education across the state. See also the Disability Rights Texas article.[66]

On June 24, 2021 OSEP sent TEA another letter to advise that the state "needs assistance."[67]

On March 21, 2022 the *Killeen Daily Herald* newspaper reported that OSEP was encouraging Texas parents to "share their special education experiences" directly:

> Amid continuous reports of special education violations in the Lone Star State, the U.S. Department of Education has created a way for Texas families to share their special education experiences directly with the federal agency.

---

61   *See* 20 U.S.C. § 1412(a)(15) and 20 U.S.C. § 6311(c)(4)(A)(i)

62   https://www.houstonchronicle.com/denied/1/

63   https://www.npr.org/sections/ed/2018/01/11/577400134/texas-violates-federal-law-education-department-finds

64   https://www.wrightslaw.com/law/caselaw/2018/5th.usdoe.v.tea.pdf

65   https://www2.ed.gov/fund/data/report/idea/partbdmsrpts/tx-b-2020-dmsletter.pdf

66   https://www.disabilityrightstx.org/en/news/feds-cannot-determine-whether-texas-has-made-progress-fixing-special-ed-violations/

67   https://sites.ed.gov/idea/files/TX-aprltr-2021b.pdf

Families willing to share their special education stories with the Department of Education's Office of Special Education Programs may do so by emailing TXinquiry@ed.gov.[68]

This appears to be the first instance that the USDOE has requested parents to contact the agency directly about their "special education experience" with any state.

2017 - Supreme Court of the United States (SCOTUS)

In 2017, SCOTUS reversed decisions from two U.S. Courts of Appeal and issued **two unanimous pro-child** rulings in *Fry v. Napoleon Comm. Sch. Dist.*,[69] and *Endrew F. ex rel. Joseph F. v. Douglas Cnty. Sch. Dist. RE-1, 580 U.S. 386*[70]

Fry v. Napoleon Comm. Sch. Dist., 580 U.S. 154 (2017)

Ehlena Fry had a severe type of cerebral palsy that affected her legs, arms, and body. Her pediatrician urged her parents to obtain a service dog to help Ehlena live as independently as possible.

> In October 2009, Ehlena's parents acquired Wonder, a Goldendoodle that was specially trained to help Ehlena with balance, retrieve dropped items, open and close doors, turn on lights and perform many other tasks . . .

> Respondents Napoleon Community Schools and Jackson County Intermediate School District refused to permit E.F. to attend school with her service dog . . . As a result, E.F. was forced to attend school without her prescribed service dog from October 2009 to April 2010.

> After months of mediation, the school allowed Wonder to accompany Ehlena for a 'trial period' but did not allow Wonder to work. Instead, ". . . the school required the dog to remain in the back of the room during classes, forbade the dog from assisting E.F. with many tasks he had been trained to do, and banned the dog from accompanying and assisting her during recess, lunch, computer lab, library time and other activities. After the trial period, the School District refused to permit Wonder to accompany E.F. to school."[71]

> Ehlena's parents brought this suit under the ADA and Section 504 of the Rehabilitation Act (504), not under the IDEA because the ADA is an anti-discrimination statute that requires public entities to make reasonable modifications to rules, policies or practices. IDEA provides limited rights and protections and does not guarantee 'equal' educational opportunities.

> Because service animals are essential to ensuring equal access for many people with disabilities, the Department of Justice interpreted the statute's "reasonable modifications" language to require that "individuals with disabilities shall be permitted to be accompanied by their service animals in all areas . . . where members of the public . . . are allowed to go," <28 CFR § 35.136(g).>

The decision in *Fry* clarified the requirements when parents must "Exhaust" their administrative remedies before filing suit in court. "We hold that **exhaustion is not necessary when the gravamen** of the plaintiff's suit is something other than the denial of the IDEA's core guarantee — what the Act calls a 'free appropriate public education.'" [72, 73, 74]

---

68 https://kdhnews.com/news/education/dept-of-education-asks-for-texas-special-ed-input/article_19438e50-a973-11ec-ad6f-dfb4fe04c7ba.html

69 580 U.S. 154, 137 S. Ct. 743, 197 L. Ed. 2d 46 (2017)

70 580 U.S. 386, 137 S. Ct. 988, 197 L. Ed. 2d 335 (2017)

71 Petition for Certiorari at https://www.wrightslaw.com/law/pleadings/fry.petition.cert.2015.10.pdf

72 https://www.wrightslaw.com/law/art/fry.napoleon.504.service.dog.htm

73 *Fry v. Napoleon Comm. Sch.*, 137 S. Ct. 743, 197 L. Ed. 2d 46, 580 U.S. 154 (2017)

74 https://www.wrightslaw.com/law/caselaw/2017/ussupct.fry.napoleon.15-497.pdf

Endrew F. ex rel. Joseph F. v. Douglas Cnty. Sch. Dist. RE-1, 580 U.S. 386 (2017)

Endrew F. is a child with autism and ADHD. His disabilities affected his cognitive functioning, language and reading skills, and social abilities, including his ability to communicate his emotions and needs.

Drew attended a public school in Douglas County, Colorado from preschool through fourth grade where he received special education through Individualized Education Programs (IEPs). Drew's parents contended that he did not make academic progress in second grade, third grade or fourth grade. His IEPs suggested that he did not make the progress needed to receive educational benefit and a free, appropriate public education (FAPE).

At the end of fourth grade, Drew's parents withdrew him from the public school and placed him in a private school that specialized in educating children with autism. The parents requested that the school district reimburse them for his tuition. An Administrative Law Judge held that Douglas School District provided a program in which Drew made "some progress" so the parents were not entitled to reimbursement for their son's education.

On appeal, a federal judge held that the IEPs "... were sufficient to show a pattern of, at the least, minimal progress" and added that a public school is only required to provide a "basic floor of opportunity" ... [and] "some educational benefit."

In 2015, the Court of Appeals for the Tenth Circuit affirmed the district court's decision that IDEA requires "some educational benefit" that "must merely be more than *de minimis*" and that under this minimal standard, the IEP developed for Drew's fifth grade year was adequate. The parents appealed to the U.S. Supreme Court.

The ruling from the Tenth Circuit widened the split among circuits about the level of educational benefit school districts must provide to children with disabilities. The question presented to the Supreme Court is whether the "educational benefit" provided by a school district must be "merely more than *de minimis*" or "*meaningful*" to satisfy the requirements for a free appropriate public education (FAPE).

In 2017, the Supreme Court issued a unanimous decisions that rejected the "*de minimis*" standard and adopted a standard that is "markedly more demanding than the 'merely more than the *de minimis*' test applied by the 10th Circuit." The decision focused on the child's potential and the need to provide opportunities to meet challenging objectives.

Endrew F. is significant because it redefined "Free Appropriate Public Education" (FAPE) and how to determine if a child has or has not received FAPE. Chief Justice Roberts wrote:

> The IEP must aim to enable the child to make progress. After all, the essential function of an IEP is to set out a plan for pursuing academic and functional advancement.

> A focus on the particular child is at the core of the IDEA. The instruction offered must be specially designed to meet a child's unique needs through an individualized education program.

> An IEP is not a form document. It is constructed only after careful consideration of the child's present levels of achievement, disability, and potential for growth.

> ... a student offered an educational program providing 'merely more than *de minimis*' progress from year to year can hardly be said to have been offered an education at all ... The IDEA demands more. It requires an educational program reasonably calculated to enable a child to make progress appropriate in light of the child's circumstances.[75, 76]

The decision by Chief Justice Roberts did not reverse *Board of Education v. Rowley*, 458 U.S. 176 (1982) but clarified the word "appropriate" and that a different standard must be used when children with disabilities are not fully mainstreamed. The IEP team must look at the child's unique needs to develop an IEP that is "pursuing academic and functional advancement."

---

75   *Endrew F. v. Douglas County Sch. Dist.*, 580 U.S. 386 (2017), 137 S. Ct. 988; 197 L. Ed. 2d 335

76   https://www.wrightslaw.com/law/caselaw/2017/ussupct.endrew.douglas.15-827.pdf

For more about *Endrew F.*, *Rowley*, and FAPE, turn to Chapter 10: Selected Topics about a <"Free Appropriate Public Education (FAPE)>."

The full text of the decisions in *Fry* and *Endrew F.* and the transcripts of remarks by Justice Kagen and Chief Justice Roberts are in the 2017 edition of **Wrightslaw Year in Review.**[77]

2018 - NCD Report Series

On February 7, 2018, the National Council on Disability (NCD)[78] published a five-part series titled *The Individuals with Disabilities Education Act Report*.[79] This was 18 years after its comprehensive *Back to School on Civil Rights - IDEA Compliance Report,* published in 2000, which recommended that the U.S. Department of Justice investigate violations of special education law by states and school districts. The 2018 report addressed ongoing enforcement problems and focused "on significant issues of concern raised in our previous reports that have yet to be resolved."

The five reports are:

Broken Promises: the Underfunding of IDEA;[80]

English Learners and Students from Low-Income Families;[81]

Federal Monitoring and Enforcement of IDEA Compliance;[82]

Every Student Succeeds Act and Students with Disabilities,[83] and

The Segregation of Students with Disabilities[84]

NCD concluded that the USDOE's Office of Special Education Programs (OSEP) continued to pass the buck on enforcing IDEA. OSEP **does not**:

- use its authority to withhold funds when states do not comply with the law;
- refer cases to the U.S. Department of Justice for enforcement;
- have a formal process for parents to file complaints about IDEA violations; or
- require states to provide their findings of school district non-compliance.

2020-2022 - The COVID Pandemic

When the COVID pandemic hit in March 2020, schools went into lockdown. Children were separated from their teachers, isolated from their classmates, and expected to attend class remotely. Remote learning is not a good way for children to learn. Parents and experts worried about learning loss and regression. The risks of learning loss and regression were greater for children with disabilities who had IEPs and Section 504 plans to address their unique needs.

In early 2022, the National Assessment of Educational Progress (NAEP), commonly known as the **Nation's Report Card**, tested fourth graders in reading and math and compared their scores to fourth grade reading and math scores in 2019 before the pandemic.[85]

77 https://www.wrightslaw.com/store/2017law.html

78 https://www.ncd.gov/

79 https://www.ncd.gov/publications/2018/individuals-disabilities-education-act-report-series-5-report-briefs

80 https://www.ncd.gov/sites/default/files/NCD_BrokenPromises_508.pdf

81 https://www.ncd.gov/sites/default/files/NCD_EnglishLanguageLearners_508.pdf

82 https://www.ncd.gov/sites/default/files/NCD_Monitoring-Enforcement_Accessible.pdf

83 https://www.ncd.gov/sites/default/files/NCD_ESSA-SWD_Accessible.pdf

84 https://www.ncd.gov/sites/default/files/NCD_Segregation-SWD_508.pdf

85 https://www.nationsreportcard.gov/highlights/ltt/2022/

The *New York Times* reported that the test results showed the "pandemic's devastating effects on schoolchildren, with the performance of 9-year-olds in math and reading dropping to the levels from two decades ago."[86]

The *Wall Street Journal* stated "The drops in test scores were roughly four times greater among the students who were the least proficient in both math and reading."

> If students are poor readers at the beginning of fourth grade, the learning gap between their peers begins to compound across subjects, prompting increased frustration and falling self-confidence . . . third-graders who lack proficiency in reading are four times more likely to drop out of high school . . . While some children will become stronger and more resilient adults, many who fall behind academically at this age will continue to lag, leaving them at risk for increased struggles across their lifetime.[87]

See also <COVID and Compensatory Education in Chapter 10: Selected Topics.>

2023 - Supreme Court of the United States (SCOTUS)

Perez v. Sturgis Public Schools

On October 3, 2022, the U.S. Supreme Court granted certiorari in **Perez v. Sturgis Public Schools**.[88]

The statement of facts in the U.S. District Court Complaint[89] allege that the school district failed to provide Miguel Perez, "a 23-year-old deaf individual" with a "qualified sign language interpreter at any point during his educational career . . . From 2004 to 2016, the District engaged in an ongoing practice of failing to provide Miguel with the auxiliary aids and services necessary for him to participate in and receive the benefits of Sturgis Public Schools and otherwise discriminated against Miguel solely because he is deaf."

During those twelve years, in lieu of a "qualified sign language interpreter" the school district provided Perez with an "educational assistant" who "did not know sign language . . . had no credentials whatsoever . . .[and] invented her own system of signing." As a result, Perez "cannot read or write." The complaint alleged intentional violations of Section 504, the ADA, the Michigan "Persons with Disabilities Civil Rights Act"[90] and sought damages pursuant to a Jury Trial.

The case began when Perez requested a special education due process hearing, alleging violations of IDEA and Section 504, seeking dollar compensatory damages. The hearing officer dismissed the ADA claim and the parties then, without litigation and testimony, "settled his IDEA claim in full." Perez then filed the federal court complaint "to obtain a remedy the IDEA could not provide: money damages for his past harm." The district court dismissed Perez's ADA lawsuit because he did not exhaust his non-IDEA claims and "accepted a settlement before the administrative hearing." The Sixth Circuit affirmed.

Miguel Perez asserts that this "conflicts with precedent from the First, Third, Ninth, and Tenth Circuits . . . [and] defies common sense."[91]

---

86 "The Pandemic Erased Two Decades of Progress in Math and Reading" (New York Times, 9/01/22)
https://www.nytimes.com/2022/09/01/us/national-test-scores-math-reading-pandemic.html

87 Reading and Math Scores Plummeted During Pandemic, New Data Show (Wall Street Journal, 9/01/22)
https://www.wsj.com/articles/education-departments-first-pandemic-era-trend-data-show-worst-reading-math-declines-in-decades-11662004860

88 Case No. 21-887

89 https://www.wrightslaw.com/law/scotus/sturgis/2018.1002.complaint.by.perez.us.district.ct.pdf

90 M.C.L. 37.1101 *et seq.*

91 *See* Petition for Certiorari - https://www.wrightslaw.com/law/scotus/sturgis/2021.1213.perez.petition.for.certiorari.pdf

SCOTUS Blog[92] reports the issues as: "(1) Whether, and in what circumstances, courts should excuse further exhaustion of the Individuals with Disabilities Education Act's administrative proceedings under Section 1415(l) when such proceedings would be futile; and (2) whether Section 1415(l) requires exhaustion of a non-IDEA claim seeking money damages that are not available under the IDEA."

This case is expected to clarify the 2017 ruling in *Fry* and may affect the "favorable public policy" of settlement agreements since the IDEA issues were settled and not litigated.

Documents, briefs, and other updates on this case, including the date of Oral Argument and the Opinion[93] of the Court will be available on the SCOTUS docket,[94] the SCOTUS blog,[95] and the Wrightslaw SCOTUS/Sturgis page[96] that will have a current update and links to the briefs and Opinions.[97]

In Summation

In this chapter, you learned about the impact of racial and disability discrimination decisions on the evolution of special education law and how investigations and demonstrations affected anti-discrimination laws. You examined the significance of two recent SCOTUS decisions and learned about another SCOTUS case to be heard in 2023.

In **Chapter 3**, you will learn about the relationships between statutes, regulations, and caselaw, how to do legal research and find relevant caselaw, statutes, regulations, commentary, and legal citations. You learned about legislative intent, judicial interpretations, and how law evolves.

To further develop your skills in legal research, you will be learn how to use the "Legal Information Institute" maintained by the Cornell Law School, Google Scholar and PACER,[98] in order to read actual federal court complaints, briefs, motions, docket sheets, witness lists, jury instructions, and other documents filed in the courthouse.

End of Chapter 2

---

92   https://www.scotusblog.com/case-files/cases/perez-v-sturgis-public-schools/

93   The Opinion in this author's 1993 *Florence County Sch. Dist. IV v. Carter*, 510 U.S. 7 (1993) case was issued on November 9, 1993, approximately 24 months after the favorable ruling from the Fourth Circuit. (950 F.2d 156 (1991)). In *Perez v. Sturgis*, the Sixth Circuit's ruling was issued on June 25, 2021. A decision in this case will probably be issued sometime in 2023.

94   https://www.supremecourt.gov/search.aspx?filename=/docket/docketfiles/html/public/21-887.html

95   https://www.scotusblog.com/case-files/cases/perez-v-sturgis-public-schools/

96   https://www.wrightslaw.com/law/art/2022.perez.sturgis.scotus.htm

97   https://www.wrightslaw.com/law/scotus/sturgis/

98   The Public Access to Court Electronic Records website is maintained by the Administrative Office of the U.S. Courts and open to the public.

Hyperlinks to Chapters

Ch. 01 Introduction	Ch. 06 IDEA Regulations
Ch. 02 History	Ch. 07 Section 504
Ch. 03 Overview of Law, Courts, Research	Ch. 08 ADA
Ch. 04 Overview of IDEA, Section 504, ADA	Ch. 09 Other laws
Ch. 05 IDEA (US Code)	Ch. 10 Selected Topics

CHAPTER 3

Statutes, Regulations, Commentary, Citations, Caselaw, Courts, Legal Research, Acronyms and Abbreviations

In this chapter, you will learn about statutes, regulations, the commentary to the regulations, caselaw,[1] and the relationships between them. You will learn about legislative intent and how law evolves through judicial interpretations from the U.S. Courts of Appeal and the U.S. Supreme Court (SCOTUS). You will also learn how to do legal research. At the end of this chapter is a table of common <Acronyms and Abbreviations.>

When you need answers to your questions about legal rights and responsibilities, you need to do your own legal research! One purpose of this book is to bridge the gap between the law and your understanding of the language within it.

In this book, you will read the law. In the beginning, this is more difficult than reading articles about the law or having the law explained to you. As you continue to read, you will become accustomed to the language and structure of the law. The law will become more meaningful to you. When you learn how the law is organized, you can quickly find the law that is relevant to your questions.

Statutes

Congress first publishes a law as an "Act" in the *Statutes at Large*. Statutes[2] published in the *Statutes at Large* have sections (sections 1, 2, 3, 4, etc.) and subsections such as (a), (b), (c), (d), etc. When an "Act" is signed by the President and becomes law, it is copied and pasted by the Government Printing Office (GPO) into the *United States Code* (U.S.C.). The **numbering system** used to categorize an *Act* in the *Statutes at Large* **is different** from the system used in the *United States Code*. You should use the **U.S.C. as your reference**.[3] The "United States Code" is often referred to as the "U.S. Code" and abbreviated as either "U.S.C." or "USC."

When the Act is published in the U.S.C., it is organized into 53 subject Titles. Each Title represents a major subject area. **Title 20 is "Education," Title 29 is "Labor,"** and **Title 42 is "The Public Health and Welfare."** As you

---

1 Is it caselaw, case-law, or case law? Depends on who you ask. Black's Law Dictionary and the Chicago Manual of Style use caselaw, but Merriam Webster Dictionary uses case law. When referring to this concept, the Cornell Legal Information Institute uses one word. A "Bluebook" tutorial uses two words.

https://www.lawprose.org/lawprose-lesson-213-caselaw-one-word-or-two/

2 Statutes are laws passed by federal, state, and local legislatures.

3 For example, the law about IEPs is in Section 614 of the Act and in Title 20 of the United States Code in Section 1414, subsection d, and is cited as 20 U.S.C. § 1414(d).

will learn later and in depth, these three titles, which are **the focus** of this book, include the **Individuals with Disabilities Education Act, Section 504 of The Rehabilitation Act,** and **the Americans with Disabilities Act**.

The **Individuals with Disabilities Education Act (IDEA)** is located in Title 20 of the United States Code and begins at Section 1400 and continues to Section 1482. That first section is cited as 20 U.S.C. § 1400. Section 1400 has four subsections: a, b, c, and d.

The official United States Code (U.S.C.) published by the Government Printing Office (GPO) is not cross-referenced to regulations or caselaw. Two companies publish versions of the U.S.C. annotated with cross references to regulations and caselaw regarding particular code sections. The United States Code Annotated (U.S.C.A.) is published by West Publishing and the United States Code Service (U.S.C.S.) is issued by LexisNexis.

Regulations[4]

Regulations clarify, expand on, supplement and explain the United States Code. Regulations have **the force of law.** The U.S. Department of Education (USDOE) develops and publishes the federal regulations for IDEA and Section 504 related to public schools.[5] The ADA regulations are published by the U.S. Department of Justice (USDOJ). The USDOE, USDOJ, and the States[6] must ensure that their regulations are consistent with the United States Code (U.S.C.). While state statutes and regulations may provide more rights and specific procedures than federal laws, **they may not take away rights that are guaranteed by federal law.** If a state law or regulation is in direct conflict[7] with a federal law, the federal law controls, pursuant to <the **"Supremacy Clause"** of the U.S. Constitution.>[8]

Before a federal agency publishes regulations, the agency must publish the proposed regulations in the *Federal Register* (FR)[9] and solicit comments from citizens about the proposed regulations. After reviewing the comments, revising the proposed regulations, the agency, in this instance, the USDOE publishes the Final Regulations in a document known as the Analysis and Commentary, typically referred to as **"The Commentary."**

The USDOE maintains a database[10] of **"Dear Colleague[11] Letters," "Policy Letters,"** and **"Policy Support Documents"** issued before 2001[12] and from 2001 through the present.[13] Many are also available on our Wrightslaw website and can be found by entering the word "colleague" into our Google search engine. Over time, some have been removed from the USDOE's website, but many are still available. The IDEA regulations, Section 504 regulations and ADA regulations are in Chapter 6, 7, and 8 of this book. Chapter 9 includes relevant portions of the Family Educational Rights and Privacy Act (FERPA) and the McKinney-Vento Homeless Assistance Act.

---

4   Regulations are issued by federal agencies, such as USDOE, states and state departments of education, and other agencies.

5   Other federal agencies publish Section 504 regulations specific to their area of responsibility, such as the Federal Communications Commission (FCC) for telecommunication issues.

6   State statutes must also be consistent with federal law and are impacted by the "Supremacy Clause."

7   In some instances, IDEA **does permit a state law or regulation to vary** from the federal statute. That variance is identified and permitted by the express words in the statute. *See* 20 U.S.C. § 1412(a)(1)(B)(i) regarding students aged 21 and the sixty day timeline to determine initial eligibility at <20 U.S.C. § 1414(a)(1)(C)(i)(I).>

8   "This Constitution, and the Laws of the United States . . . shall be the supreme Law of the Land; and the Judges in every State shall be bound thereby . . ." U.S. Const. art. VI, cl. 2.

9   Cited as 71 Fed. Reg. 46681 (August 14, 2006). The first page begins on 466681. It is 307 pages long.

10   https://sites.ed.gov/idea/policy-letters-policy-support-documents/

11   https://search.usa.gov/search?utf8=%E2%9C%93&affiliate=ed.gov&query=colleague

12   https://sites.ed.gov/idea/files/pre-2001-osep-policy-documents-8-26-2020.pdf

13   https://sites.ed.gov/idea/policy-guidance/

Commentary to the Regulations

On June 21, 2005, the USDOE published proposed IDEA regulations for public comment and input in the Federal Register. The USDOE held hearings around the country and received proposed changes.

On August 14, 2006, the USDOE published the **Final Regulations in the *Federal Register*** in the **"Analysis and Commentary."** **The Commentary** is 307 pages long and provides many comments received about the proposed regulations, what changes were made, and **the rationale for those changes**.

In earlier reauthorizations of the Individuals with Disabilities Education Act, the USDOE published a Question and Answer Appendix to the Regulations that answered questions about IEPs, consent, evaluations and other issues. In 2006, the USDOE did not publish an Appendix of questions and answers, but the Commentary provides answers to common questions, definitions, and discussions of legal terms in the IDEA statute and regulations. The Commentary often clarifies the "plain meaning" of a legal term or phrase in the Regulations. When you are doing legal research or are looking for the answer to a specific question, the Commentary is a valuable resource.

For an example, the USDOE was asked to clarify the meaning of "comparable services" for a child with an IEP who moves to another jurisdiction. USDOE responded, **"We do not believe it is necessary to define 'comparable services'** in these regulations because the Department interprets 'comparable' to have the plain meaning of the word, which is 'similar' or 'equivalent.'"** So, **USDOE defined the term.**[14] This is why you need to be familiar with, and know how to use the Commentary. Confusing terms and legal phrases in a statute are often copied and pasted into the Regulations by the USDOE because it does not want to define or explain a term that Congress used in the law.

Terms, definitions, and requirements are described and explained in plain language. When you read the discussion about a regulation in the Commentary, the comments from the USDOE will help you understand why USDOE did or did not clarify a vague term or requirement. The Commentary will also help you understand the different perspectives and how these interpretations influenced a regulation.

Vague terms, language, and legal requirements are not unusual in law. When Congress uses muddled language, this permits a proposed Bill to be voted out of legislative committee for a vote by the full legislative body. That legislative body shifts the burden to define and clarify the law to the courts.

You will find "The Commentary" as a single adobe.pdf file and as seven smaller individual adobe.pdf files linked in the "Wrightslaw Law Library" under the "IDEA" portion.[15]

Analysis and Commentary by topic

- Definitions / Regs 1-100 (pages 46547 through 46579)
- ESY, LRE, etc / Regs 101-230 (pages 46579 through 46629)
- Evaluations / Regs 300-311 (pages 46629 through 46661)
- IEPs / Regs 320-328 (pages 46661 through 46688)
- Procedures / Regs 501-520 (pages 46688 through 46713)
- Discipline / Regs 530-537 (pages 46713 through 46730)
- Monitoring / Regs 600-815 (pages 46730 through 46743)

---

14 71 Fed. Reg. 46681 (August 14, 2006)

15 https://www.wrightslaw.com/idea/commentary.htm

Legal Citations

References to law are called legal citations. Legal citations are standardized formats that explain where you will find a statute, a section in the U.S. Code, a regulation, or a case.

When you see a legal citation such as 20 U.S.C. § 1400 *et seq.*[16] the term "*et seq.*" means beginning at Section 1400 and continuing thereafter. A case is cited by volume number, name of case reporter, page number, and year. For example 950 F.2d 156 (4th Cir. 1991) and 510 U.S. 7 (1993) are the citations for the author's Shannon Carter case, as published in Volume 950 of the Federal Reporter, 2nd Series, at page 156 in 1991 and in Volume 510 of the United States Supreme Court Reports at page 7 in 1993.

The "Findings and Purposes" of IDEA are in Section 1400 of Title 20 of the United States Code. The legal citation for Findings and Purposes is 20 U.S.C. § 1400. You can refer to Findings and Purposes as "20 U.S.C. § 1400" or "Section 1400." In *Wrightslaw: Special Education Law, 3rd Ed.*, legal citations do not include the Title number. For example, the full legal citation for the law about IEPs is 20 U.S.C. § 1414(d). As a rule, we use a simpler format for citations, such as Section 1414(d). For the definition of a "child with a disability," we use Section 1401(3).

If you are citing a statute or regulation in a document, you **must pay close attention to the parentheses,** the subsections, and whether the first subsection is a number or a letter, upper or lower case. Most statutes in IDEA use lower case letters as the first subsection. That subsection (a) is followed by the digit one, then two, etc.

In The Rehabilitation Act located in Title 29, a key statute is 29 U.S.C. § 794, which contains subsections a, b, c, and d. Thus the first subsection is cited at <29 U.S.C. § 794(a).> However, the very next statute is 794a, written and cited as <29 U.S.C. § 794a.> One statute has parentheses after the digit four and the other statute does not, thus they are different statutes, but at first glance, they look the same.

Judicial Interpretations, Courts, and Caselaw

Evolving Caselaw

In this book, you will learn how legal decisions about IDEA, Section 504, and the ADA cause these laws to evolve. As explained in Chapter 1, a single word in the law, deliberately vague, can set the stage for future litigation. The use of deliberately vague words is common in all legislation and is not limited to special education and disability issues.

While statutes and regulations are fairly static, **caselaw is always evolving.**

Since the Education for All Handicapped Children Act (Public Law 94-142) was enacted in 1975, the law has changed and evolved. Special education litigation usually begins with a **special education due process hearing.**

In some states, the <request for the hearing, the due process request notice> is filed with the state department of education. In other states,[17] the request is filed with the "Office of Administrative Hearings," which is completely independent of the state department of education. The individual who presides over the hearing is usually known as a "Hearing Officer" or as an "Administrative Law Judge" (ALJ). In "Single-Tier" states,[18] the losing party can appeal directly to state court or federal court. In a "Two-Tier" state, the losing party must first appeal to their State Department of Education to request that a "Review Officer" or "Review Panel" be appointed. After a "Review Decision" is issued, the losing party can appeal to federal court or to their state court. North Carolina recently changed to a Single-Tier system.[19]

---

16 *Et seq.*, is a Latin abbreviation of et sequentia meaning "and the following ones" and is typically italicized. This is a legal term indicating that a writer is citing a page or section and the pages or sections that follow. IDEA continues through Section 1482.

17 CA - https://www.dgs.ca.gov/OAH/Case-Types/Special-Education/Services/Page-Content/Special-Education-Services-List-Folder/Requesting-a-SE-Hearing
    NC - https://www.oah.nc.gov/
    TX - https://www.soah.texas.gov/individuals-disabilities-education-act-special-education

18 All but six states are "Single-Tier" states.

19 See North Carolina statute § 115C-109.6(h2). Impartial due process hearings at:
    https://www.ncleg.gov/EnactedLegislation/Statutes/HTML/BySection/Chapter_115C/GS_115C-109.6.html

U.S. District Courts

State courts and federal courts are different judicial systems. Most special education appeals are filed in federal court because, if a <**"Federal Question"**> is the basis of the dispute, a case filed in state court can be "removed" by the defendant to federal court.

The U.S. District Court judge must follow the law in prior decisions issued by the Court of Appeals for that judicial district and decisions issued by SCOTUS, but is not required to follow decisions issued by other Circuits.

The losing party in the federal court case can then appeal from the U.S. District Court to the U.S. Court of Appeals for that Circuit.

U.S. Courts of Appeal

There are thirteen Circuit Courts of Appeals.[20] One is a "Federal Circuit" for specialized appeals. The other 12 are regional for the 94 federal judicial districts. Most states have only one judicial district, but some[21] have as many as four U.S. District Courts (judicial districts). Virginia includes an Eastern District and Western District Court. Appeals from either of those two courts must be filed with the Fourth Circuit, which also handles appeals from Maryland, North Carolina, South Carolina, and West Virginia.

Table	States in Each Circuit
1st Circuit	MA, ME, NH, RI, PR
2nd Circuit	CT, NY, VT
3rd Circuit	DE, NJ, PA, USVI
4th Circuit	MD, NC, SC, VA, WV
5th Circuit	LA, MS, TX
6th Circuit	KY, MI, OH TN
7th Circuit	IL, IN, WI
8th Circuit	AR, IA, MN, MO, ND, NE, SD
9th Circuit	AK, AZ, CA, HI, ID, MT, NV, OR, WA
10th Circuit	CO, KS, NM, OK, UT, WY
11th Circuit	AL, FL, GA
DC Circuit	Washington, DC

When the Court of Appeals in your Circuit issues a decision, that decision is binding on all states under the jurisdiction of that Circuit, but it is not binding in other Circuits or states.

Special education law evolves primarily through the **caselaw created by the Courts of Appeal.**[22]

---

20   Circuit Map - https://www.uscourts.gov/sites/default/files/u.s._federal_courts_circuit_map_1.pdf

21   California, New York, and Texas

22   See the evolution of caselaw about the "exhaustion of administrative remedies" mandated in 20 U.S.C. § 1415(l) and interpreted in the 2017 SCOTUS *Fry* case and upcoming ***Perez v. Sturgis Public Schools*** SCOTUS decision expected in 2023 and discussed in Chapter 2.

Beginning in 2015, Harbor House Law Press has published the *Wrightslaw Year in Review* books[23] that contain all special education legal decisions issued by the United States Courts of Appeal for each year, i.e., 2015, 2016, 2017, 2018 and 2019. The 2017 book includes the **two SCOTUS decisions** issued that year.

Wrightslaw Year in Review **casebooks will help you understand how caselaw is evolving.** When you are familiar with the five key sections in IDEA and review the *Wrightslaw Year in Review* books in chronological order, you will better predict special education legal outcomes in the future.

Supreme Court of the United States (SCOTUS)

Over time, rulings within one Circuit conflict with rulings in another Circuit. This creates a **"Split between Circuits."** In Rule Ten of the "Rules of the Supreme Court of the United States," the Court explains that:

> A petition for a writ of certiorari will be granted only for compelling reasons. . . . [Such as when] a United States court of appeals has entered a decision **in conflict** with the decision of another United States court of appeals.
>
> . . .
>
> A petition for a writ of certiorari is **rarely granted** when the asserted error consists of erroneous factual findings or the misapplication of a properly stated rule of law[24]

The losing party at the U.S. Court of Appeals can file a "Petition for a Writ of Certiorari," to request that SCOTUS grant the petitioner the right to proceed with an appeal before SCOTUS. Of the approximate 8,000 Petitions received each year, SCOTUS grants Writs in about 80 cases.

All state and federal courts must follow rulings issued by SCOTUS. If Congress disagrees with a decision issued by SCOTUS, Congress may revise the law to change the impact of the decision. For example, several rulings by SCOTUS triggered Congress to revise the ADA.

Legal Interpretations

Law is subject to different interpretations. Attorneys and judges may interpret a section of the law differently, depending on their perspectives. If you read an article about special education law, the interpretations and conclusions are likely to represent the opinions of the author. If you read the law and regulations on your own, you will form your own ideas, interpretations, and conclusions about the law and the impact it is likely to have on you.

Compelling facts may cause a judge to want to rule in one direction, even if the ruling is contrary to current caselaw. The decision-maker in this situation may find and use unique facts in the case to create an exception to general caselaw. "Exceptions to the rule" decisions cause the body of law to change and grow.

Over time, if most courts agree on an interpretation, a majority rule evolves. A minority rule may also develop. If a majority rule does not develop, the legal issue becomes more confusing. Courts of Appeal in different circuits may issue conflicting rulings, which, as discussed above leads to a "split among circuits" and may result in a final, "law of the land," ruling from SCOTUS.

Legislative Intent

When you read SCOTUS decisions, you will see that the Justices often refer to legislative history and legislative intent. Legislative intent is usually found in Committee Reports, transcripts of debates in the *Congressional Record*, and other sources.

Before Congress passes a new law, it holds hearings and takes testimony to help make decisions about the purpose of the law and how to accomplish that purpose.

---

23   https://www.wrightslaw.com/store/index.html#yir

24   https://www.supremecourt.gov/ctrules/2019RulesoftheCourt.pdf

When Congress passes a law ("The Act"), it will begin with the "Findings of Congress" that caused Congress to pass the law. These Findings may take several pages of text. The legislative history and content of the discussions by individual Senators and Representatives may be published in the United States Code Congressional and Administrative News (U.S.C.C.A.N.), and available in the public domain.

You will find a wealth of information at the website for Congress.[25]

Legal Research

When you research a special education legal issue, you should study:

- United States Code
- Federal and State Regulations
- USDOE's Analysis and Commentary about the IDEA
- Judicial decisions and caselaw

When you have questions about a legal issue, **start first with the United States Code** section related to your issue. Next, read the **federal regulation** that discusses and/or clarifies the issue. Then read your **state regulation**. If the answer remains unclear, read the "The Commentary" published in the *Federal Register*[26] to determine any disputed issues about the regulation. Expect to read the Code and regulation several times.

Next, look for cases about your legal issue. When you find cases, read the earlier decisions first, then move on to the more recent decisions. If you know the case was appealed, read the earlier decision that was appealed and reversed (or appealed and affirmed). When you read early decisions, you will see how law on that issue is evolving.

Depending on the issue and clarity of the decisions you read, you may decide to search that term, statute, or legal issue in other states and circuits. Reading decisions about your issue will give you a different perspective on how it is perceived. For every court that takes the position that a law is clear, another court is likely to interpret the law differently and write a different opinion. This is the nature of law.

Legal Research - United States Code (USC), Congressional Record, Federal Register, and more

The "GovInfo" website[27] provides access to many legal documents including federal court opinions, the U.S.C., the Regulations, the Congressional Record, Federal Register, and more. The Office of the Law Revision Counsel of the United States House of Representatives provides a website[28] with links to the complete federal law with each title of the US Code. The key titles in special education law are: Title 20 (IDEA), Title 29 (Section 504), and Title 42 (ADA).

Legal Research - Legal Information Institute

To find sections of the United States Code (U.S.C.) and regulations in the Code of Federal Regulations (CFR) that are not in this book, we recommend the **"Legal Information Institute" maintained by the Cornell Law School.**[29] At that website, you will find links to the U.S.C., the CFR, the Rules of Court for U.S. District Courts and Circuit Courts of Appeals, and the U.S. Constitution, including its Articles and Amendments.

You can use the Legal Information Institute to view the history and evolution of a statute, and to see if any statutes, sections, or regulations in this book have been revised since the book was published. It includes the date the law was first published in the U.S. Code along with the dates and nature of later revisions.

---

25   https://www.congress.gov/

26   This is cited as Fed. Reg. and also as FR with volume, page number and date. Both citation formats are used.

27   https://www.govinfo.gov/

28   https://uscode.house.gov/

29   https://www.law.cornell.edu/lii/get_the_law

Assume you want to find the legal definition of a "child with a disability" in IDEA. The legal citation for this definition in the Code is at <20 U.S.C. § 1401(3)> and in the regulations at <34 CFR § 300.8.> If you enter the following URL on the Cornell's Legal Information Institute's website, your search will take you to that statute, with the definitions used in IDEA. The definitions are in alphabetical order and the third one listed is the definition of a "child with a disability."

https://www.law.cornell.edu/uscode/text/20/1401

On the "Notes" tab at the top of that page, you will see "Amendments" to the Code in regard to this definition. It references the year, 2015, and lists paragraphs below that year. You will see that amendments were made to paragraphs 4, 8(A), 10, and 18 in 2015. Paragraphs (3)(A)(i) and (30)(C) of section 1401 were amended in 2010.

To see if any changes have been made to the law about evaluations, eligibility, and IEPs, located at 20 U.S.C. § 1414, change the above URL so that **the last four numbers are 1414.**

https://www.law.cornell.edu/uscode/text/20/1414

Under the "Amendments" tab, you will see that one change was made in 2015, which is incorporated into this book.

For the definition of a "child with a disability" in the **Code of Federal Regulations (CFR)** issued by the U.S. Department of Education (USDOE) located at 34 CFR § 300.8 at the Cornell Legal Information Institute, enter the following URL:

https://www.law.cornell.edu/cfr/text/34/300.8

At the end of this regulation, you will see references to the Federal Register as "FR" with the volume number, the letters "FR", page number, and date the regulation was published and incorporated into the CFR. This regulation was first published in the Federal Register in Volume 71, and begins on page 46753 and is referenced in the Legal Information Institute as 71 FR 46753.[30] It was placed into the CFR on August 14, 2006 and revisions were made on October 30, 2007 and July 11, 2017. The Federal Register (FR) entry is hyperlinked so that you can review the link and the changes made to the regulation. The August 14, 2006, document is also known as "**The Commentary**" which we discussed earlier.

Legal Research - Google Scholar[31]

Google Scholar is a free accessible search engine that indexes the full text of federal and state legal decisions. Google Scholar allows you to search published opinions of state appellate and state supreme courts since 1950, opinions from U.S. District Courts and Courts of Appeal since 1923, and decisions from the U.S. Supreme Court since 1791.

The Google Scholar page **initially defaults** to a search for "Articles" such as peer-reviewed papers, theses, books, abstracts, technical reports, and scholarly articles available on the Internet. Adjacent to that "bullet point," to the right, you will want to click on the **"Case law" bullet.**

Click **"Case law"** then "Select courts." When the Courts page opens, go to the right column, **Federal courts**, select the State and Federal District Courts in your state and the Court of Appeals for your desired Circuit (such as 2nd or 9th Circuit), then click "Done" at the bottom.

A screen will instruct you to "Please enter a query in the search box above." Insert the following text, word for word, with quotation marks "individuals with disabilities education act." To limit your search to this year, add it, such as 2023. Your search query should read: "individuals with disabilities education act" 2023 (or another year, or not include any year). When you press "enter" or "return," Google Scholar will do a full-text search of all cases in its database from your selected courts that have the words in your query and the year, i.e., 2023.

---

30   The proper legal citation for this entry is "71 Fed. Reg. 46,753 (August 14, 2006)" in legal briefs and pleadings.

31   https://scholar.google.com/

A tab on the right side of the screen allows you to sort cases by the date issued in chronological order, with the most recent at the top of the page. When you click each link, you will see the full text of the case. The cases in Google Scholar include embedded clickable citation links to cases referenced in the decision.

If you edit your search query by deleting the year, you will find all cases issued by the selected courts that contain the phrase "individuals with disabilities education act." You can edit the desired courts to include U. S. District Courts and Courts of Appeal nationwide.

You can change your search query to find cases that have other terms, including dyslexia, autism, Section 504, restraint, damages, retaliation, "individualized educational program," "IEP," "independent educational evaluation," "IEE," "Americans with Disabilities Act," etc.

You must **use quotation marks** around your search terms to avoid being flooded with cases that have words that are not relevant to your search.

At the bottom of the page that provided your list of cases are the words "**Create Alert.**" If you click on that box and enter your email address, you will receive an emailed link to **future decisions**[32] from your selected courts.

You can also search for the name of an individual, an administrator, an expert witness, a Judge, a school district, and even an educational methodology. In Chapter 4's discussion about "procedural violations" is an example of a <Google Scholar search for cases containing "procedural violations.">

Legal Research - Leagle[33]

Leagle provides decisions from trial courts and appellate courts nationwide. It also includes a lawyer directory. Using the "Advanced Search" feature, you can enter a phrase, "Individuals with Disabilities Education Act" and find all cases that have that phrase in the decision. You can narrow the search down to specific dates and locations. Leagle is similar to Google Scholar. One may include cases not found by the other. It may be useful to use both caselaw search services.

Leagle's main page explains: "Our library is comprehensive and contains over 5 million published and unpublished cases since 1950 . . . [and the] Leagle Lawyer directory contains over 150,000 lawyer listings in every area of practice."

Elsewhere on their website, they report:

> Leagle, Inc. is a leading provider of copies of primary caselaw from all Federal courts and all State higher courts. Our collection is up to date within 24 hours of release of opinions from the courts and is also complete historically for all time for Federal courts and back to 1950 for state appellate and supreme courts. We add Slip Opinions daily, and Advance Sheets and Bound Volume copies as they become available. Our materials are fully copyrighted by Leagle, Inc.

> Our policy is to post court decision text exactly as it appears in released court documents. Note that cases marked "Do Not Publish" or similarly, by the courts, indicate the decision is not to be used as legal precedent, however the decision is still available for public access.

Legal Research - PACER

The Administrative Office of the U.S. Courts created **PACER**, the **"Public Access to Court Electronic Records"** website. PACER allows the general public, the press, anyone, to view legal documents, federal court complaints, briefs, court orders, legal decisions, jury instructions, exhibits, motions, and other documents filed in lawsuits.

---

32 If you also search the Google "Articles" for specific terms, words, and phrases, such as autism, dyslexia, seclusion, etc. and provide your email address, you will also receive alerts as articles are published that contain your search term.

33 https://www.leagle.com/leaglesearch

PACER has several fee levels, depending on whether you are an attorney filing legal pleadings in a case, a non-attorney representing yourself, pro-se, or an individual who wants to review case files. Most readers are interested in a "Case Search Only" account. To use PACER, you must register with PACER[34] and provide a credit card number for the minimal search fee and ten cents per page for retrieved documents.

PACER's policy is that "Case information is available through PACER 24 hours a day, including weekends and holidays. Each court maintains its own case information. If you know the district or circuit in which the case is filed, search that court directly.[35] If you do not know where the case is filed, use the PACER Case Locator."

In the PACER image below, in order to search for a federal case in which you know both the court and the case number, first click on the window labeled "Region," in the lower left, using the arrow down, scroll past the Circuit Courts of Appeal, to the state name and district, and division, if any, such as eastern, western, northern southern, and click on the specific court.. Then insert the number of the case in the box marked Case Number. Usually that is all of the information that you need to enter in order to find a case.

Once the case is found, you will typically want to click on the "Docket" and scroll through document for the names of the attorneys and entry number for specific pleadings and Orders entered.

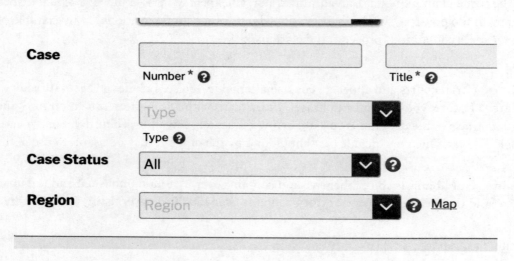

To view any documents in the court's file, click on it and you can view it online or download it to your computer.

34 https://pacer.uscourts.gov/register-account/pacer-case-search-only

35 https://pacer.uscourts.gov/file-case/court-cmecf-lookup

Acronyms and Abbreviations

Special education law uses many acronyms and abbreviations that are confusing to those new to this topic. You might want to "screen shot" this table and print it out for future use as you proceed through this book. The most common are listed below in alphabetical order.

Table: Acronyms and Abbreviations

ADA	Americans with Disabilities Act	LD	Learning Disability
ADD/ADHD	Attention Deficit (Hyperactive) Disorder	LEA	Local Education Agency
ADR	Alternative Dispute Resolution	LEP	Limited English Proficient
ALJ	Administrative Law Judge	LRE	Least Restrictive Environment
BIP	Behavioral Intervention Plan	NCLB	No Child Left Behind
CFR	Code of Federal Regulations	OCR	Office for Civil Rights
ESSA	Every Student Succeeds Act	OSEP	Office of Special Education Programs
ESY	Extended School Year	RTI	Response to Intervention
FAPE	Free Appropriate Public Education	SCOTUS	Supreme Court of the United States
FBA	Functional Behavioral Assessment	SEA	State Education Agency
FERPA	Family Educational Rights and Privacy Act	SLD	Specific Learning Disability
HO	Hearing Officer	SRO	State Review Officer
IDEA	Individuals with Disabilities Education Act	SRBI	Scientifically Based Reading Instruction
IEE	Independent Educational Evaluation	USC	United States Code
IEP	Individualized Educational Program	USDOE	United States Department of Education
IFSP	Individualized Family Service Plan	USDOJ	United States Department of Justice

In Summation

In this chapter, you learned about statutes, regulations, commentary, legal citations, caselaw, and legal research. You learned about legislative intent, judicial interpretations, and how law evolves.

In **Chapter 4,** we will provide you with an overview of the three main laws that affect children and students with special needs and the educators who work with them. After you review that chapter, you will have a greater understanding of IDEA, Section 504, and the ADA.

End of Chapter 3

Hyperlinks to Chapters

Ch. 01 Introduction	Ch. 06 IDEA Regulations
Ch. 02 History	Ch. 07 Section 504
Ch. 03 Overview of Law, Courts, Research	Ch. 08 ADA
Ch. 04 Overview of IDEA, Section 504, ADA	Ch. 09 Other laws
Ch. 05 IDEA (US Code)	Ch. 10 Selected Topics

CHAPTER 4

Overview of IDEA, Section 504, and the ADA

Quicklinks To[1]

    <IDEA Overview>
    <Section 504 Overview >
    <ADA Overview >

This chapter provides an overview of the statutes that directly affect children and adults with special needs in educational settings, from nursery school through graduate school. These statutes are the **Individuals with Disabilities Education Act (IDEA), Section 504 of the Rehabilitation Act of 1973,** and the **Americans with Disabilities Act.**

As background, the **United States Code** is broken down into **Titles.** The **Titles specific to this book** are **Title 20, Title 29,** and **Title 42.**

Title 20, "Education" contains 80 chapters.[2] Our interest is in Chapter 33,[3] sections 1400 through 1482, which is <IDEA.>

Title 29, "Labor" contains 32 chapters.[4] Our interest is in Chapter 16,[5] which contains sections 701 through 797, including **The Rehabilitation Act of 1973**[6] and the law of <**Section 504.**>[7]

Title 42, "Public Health and Welfare" contains 161 chapters.[8] Our interest is in Chapter 126[9] titled **Equal Opportunity for Individuals with Disabilities** and contains sections 12101 through 12213. Title 42 includes the <**Americans with Disabilities Act.**>

---

1 **Wrightslaw Note**: Per the information provided in Chapter 1, this book contains **embedded hyperlinks.** Those who have the **E-book (adobe.pdf version)**, can click on the link and go directly to the webpage or location in this book. Embedded hyperlinks are marked with a <, left pointing arrow, and a > right pointing arrow. All URLs are hyperlinked and do not have arrows.

2 https://www.law.cornell.edu/uscode/text/20

3 https://www.law.cornell.edu/uscode/text/20/chapter-33

4 https://www.law.cornell.edu/uscode/text/29

5 https://www.law.cornell.edu/uscode/text/29/chapter-16

6 29 U.S.C. § 701 *et seq.*

7 29 U.S.C. § 794

8 https://www.law.cornell.edu/uscode/text/42

9 https://www.law.cornell.edu/uscode/text/42/chapter-126

In 2004, Congress enacted **Public Law 108-446**[10] which became known as **IDEA 2004**. It modified the "Purpose"of the law to also prepare the "child with a disability" for "further education" such as "post-secondary education."[11] It placed greater emphasis on "transition services" and ensured that children who move from one jurisdiction to another are provided a "comparable IEP." [12] The 2004 revision incorporated the 2001 No Child Left Behind Act into IDEA.

Because it is no longer necessary to differentiate the 1997 version (IDEA 97) from the 2004 version (IDEA 2004), **we refer to the current version of the law as IDEA. The full text of the IDEA statute and its federal regulations are in Chapters 5 and 6** of *Wrightslaw: Special Education Law, 3rd Ed.*, beginning with 20 U.S.C. § 1400 and 34 CFR § 300.1, respectively.

Purposes: IDEA, Section 504, and the ADA

The purpose[13] of IDEA differs from the purposes of Section 504 and the ADA.

The purpose[14] **of IDEA**, as explained in Chapter 1, "is to ensure that all children with disabilities have available to them a free appropriate public education that emphasizes special education and related services designed to meet their unique needs and prepare them for further education, employment, and independent living."

The purpose[15] of Section 504 of the Rehabilitation Act of 1973 is to protect the rights of individuals with disabilities in programs and activities that receive Federal financial assistance. In educational settings, individuals with disabilities must be provided with accommodations and modifications so they can access educational programs and activities. They may not be discriminated against for reasons related to their disability. More detail and specifics about The Rehabilitation Act and Section 504 is provided later in this chapter.

The purpose[16] **of the Americans with Disabilities Act Amendments Act of 2008** (ADA, sometimes referenced as **ADA AA**), is to prohibit discrimination against individuals with disabilities in many settings, including public schools, private schools, daycare, restaurants, lodging, transportation, and more, whether or not an entity receives federal funds. The college student who suffers from an <episodic condition> such as asthma or diabetes, and the toddler in a private day care facility or nursery school who has problems being potty trained, are both protected. Protections apply to children, students, and individuals in public educational facilities or in private schools and other settings.

Overview of the Individuals with Disabilities Education Act

When Congress revised and reauthorized the law in 2004, it added the phrase "prepare for further education"[17] in its purpose. Congress developed timelines to determine a child's eligibility for an IEP, focused on accountability and improved outcomes, and required "comparable IEPs"[18] for children who move.

IDEA states that schools should use "proven methods of teaching and learning" based on "replicable research."[19] Many schools use educational methods that are not research-based. Pressure from litigation is forcing school dis-

---

10 https://www.wrightslaw.com/idea/law/PL108-446.pdf

11 "Post-secondary education" is within "Definitions." *See* "Transition Services" at 20 U.S.C. § 1401(34).

12 20 U.S.C. § 1414(d)(2)(C)

13 20 U.S.C. § 1400(d) - to prepare the children "for further education, employment, and independent living" and "to ensure that the rights of children with disabilities and parents of such children are protected . . . ."

14 <20 U.S.C. § 1400(d)(1)(A)>

15 <29 U.S.C. § 794(a)>

16 <42 U.S.C. § 12101(b)>

17 20 U.S.C. § 1400(d)(1)(A)

18 20 U.S.C. § 1414(d)(2)(C)

19 20 U.S.C. § 1400(c)(4)

tricts to adopt research-based methods of teaching. IDEA also includes a sixty-day timeline[20] to determine initial eligibility for special education services and requirements for infants and toddlers with disabilities.[21]

The Individuals with Disabilities Education Act of 2004 is divided into five parts:

Part A – General Provisions (Sections 1400 – 1409)

Part B – Assistance for Education of All Children with Disabilities (Sections 1411 – 1419)

Part C – Infants and Toddlers with Disabilities (Sections 1431 – 1444)

Part D – National Activities to Improve Education of Children with Disabilities (Sections 1450 – 1482)

Part E – National Center for Special Education Research (Section 9567)

Parents, advocates, attorneys, and educators will refer most often to the following five sections of Part A and Part B:

Section 1400 – Findings and Purposes

Section 1401 – Definitions

Section 1412 – State Eligibility (the Catch-all Section)

Section 1414 – Evaluations, Eligibility Determinations, Individual Education Programs, Educational Placements

Section 1415 – Procedural Safeguards

IDEA is not a complicated or difficult statute to understand. You need to master the purpose of the law in Section 1400(d). You also need to be familiar with the definitions, especially the definition of a "child with a disability" in Section 1401. You need to know the law about evaluations and IEPs in Section 1414 and about procedures and discipline in Section 1415.

Part A – General Provisions

Part A of the Individuals with Disabilities Education Act of 2004 includes Sections 1400 through Section 1409 of Title 20 of the United States Code (U.S.C.). Section 1400 describes the Findings and Purposes of the law. Legal definitions, in alphabetical order, are in Section 1401. Section 1403 advises that states are not immune from suit if they violate IDEA. Section 1408 is about paperwork reduction.

Section 1400: Findings & Purposes

The most important section in the Individuals with Disabilities Education Act is Section 1400 which describes the Findings and Purposes of the law. **The purpose in subsection (d) is the mission statement of this law.**

Findings

The history and findings that led Congress to pass IDEA is in Section 1400(c). In 1975, when Congress enacted the Education for All Handicapped Children Act (Public Law 94-142), fewer than half of all children with disabilities were receiving an appropriate education. At Section 1400(c)(2), the law explains that millions of children with disabilities were "excluded entirely from the public school system."[22] Initially, the law focused on ensuring that children had access to an education and due process of law.

---

20   20 U.S.C. § 1414(a)(1)(C)

21   20 U.S.C. § 1431

22   20 U.S.C. § 1400(c)(2)

In the Findings of IDEA, Congress explained that:

(1) Disability is a natural part of the human experience and in no way diminishes the right of individuals to participate in or contribute to society. **Improving educational results for children** with disabilities is an essential element of our national policy of ensuring equality of opportunity, full participation, **independent living, and economic self-sufficiency**[23] for individuals with disabilities.[24]

Congress found that the "implementation of this chapter has been impeded by low expectations, and an insufficient focus on applying replicable research on proven methods of teaching and learning for children with disabilities."[25]

In 2004, Congress reported that almost "30 years of research and experience demonstrated"[26] that special education would be more effective by:

having high expectations for such children and **ensuring their access to the general education curriculum in regular classrooms, to the maximum extent possible** . . . in order to meet the challenging expectations that have been established for all children; and be prepared to lead productive and independent adult lives **to the maximum extent possible.**[27]

Congress wanted "to ensure that such children benefit from such efforts and that special education can become a service for such children rather than a place where such children are sent."[28] Congress stressed the need to use "scientifically based early reading programs, positive behavioral interventions and supports,[29] and early intervening services to reduce the need to label children as disabled before addressing the learning and behavioral needs of such children."[30]

Purposes

The most important section in IDEA is Purposes in Section 1400(d). The main purposes are:

to ensure that all children with disabilities have available to them a free appropriate public education that emphasizes special education and related services designed to **meet their unique needs** and **prepare them for further education, employment, and independent living,**" and "to ensure that the **rights of children** with disabilities **and parents** of such children **are protected** . . . ."[31]

Purposes is the mission statement of IDEA. When you are developing an IEP, use this mission statement as your long-term goal. You want the child prepared for further education, employment and independent living, to be economically self-sufficient and to have the best chance for independent living. When working on IEP goals and objectives, keep this mission statement in mind.[32]

---

23 When reading the "Purpose" of this law in the next subsection "d," keep the "independent living and **economic self-sufficiency**" in mind as one of the purposes of this law.

24 20 U.S.C. § 1400(c)(1)

25 20 U.S.C. § 1400(c)(4)

26 In IDEA 97, this phrase was "over 20 years."

27 20 U.S.C. § 1400(c)(5), *see also* the Least Restrictive Environment (LRE) in Section 1412(a)(3).

28 20 U.S.C. § 1400(a)(5)(C)

29 *See* the "Special factors" in the IEP statute at 20 U.S.C. § 1414(d).

30 20 U.S.C. § 1400(a)(5)(F)

31 20 U.S.C. § 1400(d)(1)

32 The legal citation for the IDEA regulation that contains the purpose of this law is 34 CFR § 300.1.

Section 1401: Definitions

Section 1401 of IDEA contains thirty-five legal definitions in alphabetical order. Included are the definitions of Assistive Technology Devices and Services, Child with a Disability,[33] Related Services, Specific Learning Disability, Supplementary Aids and Services, and Transition Services. After 2004, several definitions were removed or revised. In 2015, after No Child Left Behind (NCLB) was replaced with the Every Student Succeeds Act (ESSA), the definitions for "core academic subjects" and "highly qualified teacher" were removed from both statutes. "Child with a Disability" and "limited English proficient" were revised.

Assistive Technology Device and Assistive Technology Service

The first definition in IDEA is **Assistive Technology Device** which includes almost all devices that are "used to increase, maintain, or improve functional capabilities of a child with a disability." It does not include a device that is surgically implanted such as a cochlear implant.[34]

Assistive Technology Service is broad and includes "any service that **directly assists a child** with a disability in the selection, acquisition, or use of an assistive technology device," and the "purchasing, leasing, or otherwise providing for the acquisition of assistive technology devices by such child . . . [and] selecting, designing, fitting, customizing, adapting, applying, maintaining, repairing, or replacing assistive technology devices."[35]

Child with a Disability[36]

If you are a parent, the most important definition is likely to be "child with a disability." Your child's classification as a "child with a disability" determines whether your child is eligible for special education and related services under IDEA. In 2010. pursuant to "Rosa's Law," subsection 3 of section 1401, replaced the words "mentally retarded" with "intellectual disabilities."

A child with a disability is *not* automatically eligible for special education and related services under IDEA. The key phrase is "who, by reason thereof, *needs special education and related services*," and that the disability adversely affects educational performance.

If a child has a disability but does not need "special education and related services," the child will not be eligible under IDEA but may be eligible for a Section 504 Plan and the protections, right of access, and freedom from discrimination under Section 504 and the ADA. The IDEA definition of a child with a disability in the regulations[37] is much more comprehensive in describing a child with a disability than the definition in the U.S. Code at section 1401(3).[38]

Free Appropriate Public Education (FAPE)

A "free appropriate public education" (FAPE) is defined as special education and related services that are provided at public expense, meet state standards, are appropriate, and are provided in conformity with an IEP.[39] Because the definition of the word "appropriate" is vague, the term has been litigated extensively since the law was enacted.

In *Board of Education v. Rowley*, 458 U.S. 176 (1982), SCOTUS concluded that the child with a disability **is not entitled to the "best" education, nor to an education that maximizes the child's potential.**

---

33   Subsection 3 was revised in 2010 to omit "mental retardation" and replace it with "intellectual disabilities" pursuant to "Rosa's Law." Public Law 111-256. URL is: https://www.govinfo.gov/content/pkg/PLAW-111publ256/pdf/PLAW-111publ256.pdf

ESPN story about Rosa - https://www.espn.com/espnw/news-commentary/story/_/id/13287823/meet-little-girl-wiped-government-use-r-word

34   20 U.S.C. § 1401(1)

35   20 U.S.C. § 1401(2)

36   <20 U.S.C. § 1401(3)>

37   The definition of a "Child with a Disability" in the regulations at <34 CFR § 300.8>.

38   The definition of a "Child with a Disability" in the statute is at <20 U.S.C. § 1401(3)>.

39   20 U.S.C. § 1401(9)

In 2017, SCOTUS issued the unanimous *Endrew F.* decision which has had significant positive impact on the quality of Individual Education Programs (IEPS) for children with disabilities. This is discussed in more depth in Chapter 10, Selected Topics, under the heading of FAPE. Chief Justice Roberts wrote that FAPE is based on the quality of the IEP which "is not a form document. It is constructed only after careful consideration of the child's present levels of achievement, disability, and **potential for growth**."

He explained that the old *Rowley* standard was applicable to children with disabilities who are fully integrated in a mainstream, full inclusion setting, but that it is not necessarily applicable in other settings. The Court did not reverse the 1982 *Rowley* decision, but clarified that a different standard needs to be used with children with disabilities who are not fully mainstreamed.

Related Services

Related services are "designed to enable a child with a disability . . . to benefit from special education"[40] and include transportation, physical therapy, occupational therapy and more.

Special Education

IDEA defines "special education" as "specially designed instruction, at no cost to the parents, to meet the unique needs of a child with a disability . . ."[41] It encompasses a range of services and may include one-on-one tutoring, intensive academic remediation, services in the general education classroom, and 40-hour Applied Behavioral Analysis (ABA) programs. Special education is provided in different settings, including the child's home.

Specific Learning Disability[42]

In "Definitions," a specific learning disability (SLD, often referred to as LD) is "a disorder in 1 or more of the basic psychological processes involved in understanding or in using language, spoken or written, which disorder may manifest itself in the imperfect ability to listen, think, speak, read, write, spell, or do mathematical calculations . . . [and] includes such conditions as . . . dyslexia." The word "dyslexia" has been in this statute since 1975[43] and was included in the 1970 predecessor at page 177 of Public Law 91-230.[44]

The determination about whether a child has a "specific learning disability" and is entitled to an IEP is affected by the "Evaluation" language in 20 U.S.C. § 1414(b). Schools "shall not be required to take into consideration whether a child has a severe discrepancy between achievement and intellectual ability . . ." to find a child eligible for special education services as a child with a specific learning disability.[45] The requirement to find a discrepancy between intellectual ability and educational achievement was removed. Its use was not prohibited and some school districts continue to use it in determining the presence of SLD.

Supplementary Aids and Services[46]

Supplementary aids and services are "provided in regular education classes . . . to enable children with disabilities to be educated with nondisabled children to the maximum extent . . . in accordance with section 1412(a)(5)."[47, 48]

---

40   20 U.S.C. § 1401(26)

41   20 U.S.C. § 1401(29)

42   20 U.S.C. § 1401(30)

43   **Dyslexia and SLD are also in the ADA** at 28 CFR §§ 35.108(b)(2) + 36.105(b)(2)

44   https://www.govinfo.gov/content/pkg/STATUTE-84/pdf/STATUTE-84-Pg121.pdf#page=55

45   20 U.S.C. § 1414(b)(6)

46   20 U.S.C. § 1401(33)

47   This is the **"Least Restrictive Environment"** (LRE) statute.

48   Supplementary aids and services are provided in general education classes so children with disabilities can be educated with their non-disabled peers and participate in extra curricular and non-academic settings. *See* 34 CFR §§ 300.42, 300.107, and 300.117. Compare "supplementary aids and services" with "related services" in 20 U.S.C. § 1401(26).

Transition Services[49]

The definition of "transition services" clarifies that transition is "a results-oriented process" to improve "the academic and functional achievement of the child with a disability." The goal of transition is to facilitate the child's transition from school to employment and further education. Transition services must be based on "the individual child's needs, taking into account the child's strengths, preferences, and interests."

Part B – Assistance for Education of All Children with Disabilities

Part B[50] governs special education and related services for children with disabilities between the ages of 3 and 21. For most readers, **the most important sections in Part B are Section 1412, Section 1414, and Section 1415.**

Section 1412 includes child find, least restrictive environment, unilateral placements, reimbursement, state and district assessments, and more.

Section 1413 addresses the eligibility of Local Educational Agencies (LEA) and includes Charter Schools and LEA compliance efforts by the SEA.

Section 1414 describes requirements for initial evaluations, parental consent, reevaluations, eligibility, IEPs, and educational placements.

Section 1415 describes the procedural safeguards designed to protect the rights of children and their parents. These safeguards include the right to examine educational records, to obtain an **independent educational evaluation (IEE),** and the legal requirements for prior written notice, procedural safeguards notice, due process complaint notice, **due process hearings**, resolution sessions, mediation, attorneys' fees, **discipline**, and exhaustion of administrative remedies.

Section 1412: State Eligibility ("Catch-All Section")

Section 1412 about State Eligibility is often called the "Catch-All" statute because it includes child find, least restrictive environment, transition to preschool programs, equitable services for children in private schools, unilateral placements in private programs, tuition reimbursement, participation in assessments, accommodations guidelines, and alternate assessments.[51] Although Extended School Year (ESY) is not referenced in Section 1412 or 1414, the ESY regulation at 34 CFR § 300.106 cites Section 1412 as the legal authority for the ESY requirement.

This section provides that a state must make assurances to the USDOE that "the state has in effect policies and procedures" to meet the conditions of IDEA[52] pursuant to the "State's Plan."

Free Appropriate Public Education (FAPE)

To receive federal funds, states must provide assurances to the U.S. Department of Education that they have policies and procedures in place to ensure that all children with disabilities receive a free appropriate public education.

The right to a free appropriate public education extends to children with disabilities who have been suspended or expelled from school.[53] Section 1412 opens with this requirement, which was designed to ensure that states could not suspend / expel children with disabilities for financial reasons, as happened routinely prior to 1975.

---

49   20 U.S.C. § 1401(34)

50   Part C is for "Infants and Toddlers with Disabilities."

51   20 U.S.C. § 1412

52   20 U.S.C. § 1412(a)

53   20 U.S.C. § 1412(a)(1)(A)

Child Find

Child find requires school districts to identify, locate, and evaluate all children with disabilities, including children who are home schooled, homeless, wards of the state, and children who attend private schools, and determine which children are and are not receiving special education and related services.[54]

"Nothing in this chapter requires that children be classified by their disability so long as each child who has a disability listed in Section 1401 of this title and who, by reason of that disability, needs special education and related services is regarded as a child with a disability under this subchapter."[55] **Classification by label is not required in the federal law.**

Least Restrictive Environment (LRE), Inclusion, and Mainstreaming

"To the maximum extent appropriate, children with disabilities . . . are educated with children who are not disabled." Removal from regular education "occurs only when the nature or severity of the disability of a child is such that education in regular classes with the use of supplementary aids and services cannot be achieved satisfactorily."[56]

LRE is often referred to as mainstreaming or inclusion. However, the terms are not synonymous. Mainstreaming a child typically means placing the child into a regular education classroom where the child may or may not receive supports. An inclusion placement may be for social benefit but the child is "not expected to learn the same material."[57]

Pursuant to the regulations, the placement is to be as close to the child's home as possible, preferably in the school the child would attend if non-disabled.[58]

The LRE for a child may be a private school that specializes in educating children with a specific disability. See the discussion in the next chapter about LRE and this author's Florence County Sch. Dist. IV v. Shannon Carter SCOTUS case. This concept also applies to Section 504 and the ADA.[59]

Transition from Early Intervention Programs

Children who transition from Part C programs must "experience a smooth and effective transition . . . [and by] the third birthday of such a child" either an Individualized Family Service Plan (IFSP) or an IEP "has been developed and is being implemented . . ."[60]

Children in Private Schools

"Such services to parentally placed private school children with disabilities may be provided to the children on the premises of private, including religious, schools, to the extent consistent with law."[61]

Child Find

"Child Find" requires school districts to report data about the number of children who are evaluated, found eligible, and provided services. These requirements also apply to children who attend private and religious schools in thedis-

---

54   20 U.S.C. § 1412(a)(3)(A)

55   20 U.S.C. § 1412(a)(3)(B)

56   20 U.S.C. § 1412(a)(5)

57   http://www.differencebetween.net/language/words-language/difference-between-mainstreaming-and-inclusion/

58   34 CFR § 300.116

59   42 U.S.C. § 12182(b)(1)(B); 28 CFR §§ 35.130(d) and 36.203; 34 CFR §§ 104.4(b)(2) and 104.43(d)

60   20 U.S.C. § 1412(a)(9)

61   20 U.S.C. § 1412(a)(10)(A)(i)(III)

trict.[62] Children with disabilities who attend private schools are entitled to equitable services.[63] The law provides for equitable participation of children who attend private schools and consultation between public and private school officials.

Private School Tuition Reimbursement

If a parent removes their child from a public school program and places the child into a private program, the parent may be reimbursed for the costs of the private program. The hearing officer / administrative law judge must determine that the public school did not provide FAPE to the child "in a timely manner"[64] and that the parent provided the school with the required ten business day advance notice of their intent to remove the child from the public school,[65] and that the private program is appropriate.

If you are a parent and plan to request tuition reimbursement, you need to be familiar with this federal statute and regulations, your state statute and regulations, and local state and federal caselaw about reimbursement. You should also read the **Rules of Adverse Assumptions** and expect that you may require a special education due process hearing to recover the tuition. Before you actually remove your child from a public school program, you must put the school district on notice so that the school can cure your objections and provide your child with FAPE. [66, 67]

State Educational Agency (SEA) is Responsible for General Supervision

The SEA is responsible for all educational programs for children with disabilities in the State and for ensuring that educational programs "meet the educational standards of the State educational agency."[68]

Participation in State and District Assessments

Congress requires that "All children with disabilities are included in all general State and districtwide assessment programs . . . with appropriate accommodations and alternate assessments where necessary and as indicated in their respective individualized education programs."[69] States and districts must issue reports to the public about state and district assessments, alternate assessments, and the performance of children with disabilities on these assessments.[70]

Overidentification of Minority Children

Congress found that "African-American children are identified as having intellectual disabilities and emotional disturbance at rates greater than their White counterparts. . . . [and] that schools with predominately White students and teachers have placed disproportionately high numbers of their minority students into special education."[71]

Congress required States to develop "policies and procedures to prevent the inappropriate over identification or disproportionate representation by race and ethnicity as children with disabilities . . ."[72]

---

62   20 U.S.C. § 1412(a)(10)(A)(ii)

63   20 U.S.C. § 1412(a)(10)(A)(ii)(II)

64   20 U.S.C. § 1412(a)(10)(C)

65   Parents must provide advance notice of their intent to remove the child. It is our recommendation that this notice be in writing using our "Letter to the Stranger" model. *See* https://www.wrightslaw.com/advoc/articles/tactics.ltr.stranger.htm

66   20 U.S.C. § 1412(a)(10)(C)

67   Some courts have found that advance payment of a deposit for private school tuition prior to the ten-business day notice violates the intent of this law, and a subsequent loss of the right to reimbursement of private school tuition. Read Chapter 21, *Wrightslaw: From Emotions to Advocacy*. To increase the odds of a successful outcome, assume that the worst will happen and prepare for it in advance with a paper trail.

68   20 U.S.C. § 1412(a)(11)(A)

69   20 U.S.C. § 1412(a)(16)(A)

70   20 U.S.C. § 1412(a)(16)(D)

71   20 U.S.C. § 1400(c)(12)(E)

72   20 U.S.C. § 1412(c)(24)

Mandatory Medication Prohibited

IDEA prohibits school personnel from requiring a child to obtain a prescription for a controlled substance such as Ritalin, Adderal, etc., in order to attend school, receive an evaluation, or receive special education.[73]

Section 1413: Local Educational Agency Eligibility

Section 1413 includes requirements for school district (LEA) and charter school eligibility. IDEA includes requirements about purchasing instructional materials, records of migratory children, and early intervening services.

Services to Children Who Attend Charter Schools

"[C]harter schools that are public schools of the local educational agency" must serve children with disabilities who attend charter schools in the same manner as children who attend other public schools, and must provide supplementary services and related services on site at the charter school.[74]

Local Educational Agency Compliance

The SEA is responsible for supervising the LEAs. If an LEA fails to comply with IDEA, then this section authorizes the SEA to reduce funds and take other steps.[75] *See also* 20 U.S.C. § 1412(a)(11) about the SEA's responsibilities.

Early Intervening Services

School districts may use a portion of their Part B funds to provide early intervening services for students who need academic and behavioral assistance but **have not been identified** as needing special education services. Funds may also be used for professional development so teachers have the knowledge and skills to deliver scientifically based academic and literacy instruction.[76]

Section 1414: Evaluations, Eligibility, Individualized Education Programs, and Educational Placements

Section 1414 is the **second most important section**[77] in IDEA and is about Evaluations, Consent, Reevaluations, Eligibility, IEPs, IEP Meetings, and Educational Placements. Section 1414 contains six subsections:

(a) - Evaluations, Parental Consent, Reevaluations
(b) - Evaluation Procedures
(c) - Additional Requirements for Evaluation and Reevaluations
(d) - Individualized Education Programs (IEPs)
(e) - Educational Placements
(f) - Alternative Means of Meeting Participation

Initial Evaluations

Parents, state departments of education, state agencies, and school district staff may request an initial evaluation of a child to determine eligibility for an IEP.[78] IDEA requires that initial evaluations and eligibility be completed **within 60 calendar days of receiving parental consent**[79] **unless** a state has statutes or regulations with shorter or longer timelines. A number of states do have longer timelines.

---

73   20 U.S.C. § 1412(c)(25)

74   20 U.S.C. § 1413(a)(5)

75   20 U.S.C. § 1413(d); *see also* 20 U.S.C. § 1412(a)(11) about the SEA's responsibilities.

76   20 U.S.C. § 1413(f)

77   Purpose at 20 U.S.C. § 1400(d) is the most important statute in this law.

78   20 U.S.C. § 1414(a)(1)(B)

79   20 U.S.C. § 1414(a)(1)(C)

You need to check your state regulations to determine the timeline. The clock does not begin to run from **the date of the parent's request, but from the date of consent**. A letter requesting that a child be evaluated and that "this letter is my consent" should be sufficient. The use of consent forms provided by a school district is not required in the law.[80]

Parental Consent

The school must obtain informed parental consent before conducting an initial evaluation.[81] If the parent does not consent to an initial evaluation, or does not respond to a request to provide consent, subject to state law, the district may or may not pursue a due process hearing against the parent.[82]

Parental consent for an evaluation is not consent for the child to receive special education services.[83] The school must obtain informed parental consent **before providing special education services**. If the parent does not consent to special education services, the district **may not pursue** a due process hearing against the parent. If the parent refuses consent for services, the district has not violated the IDEA, and is not required to convene an IEP meeting or develop an IEP for the child.[84] The regulations provide more detail about consent.[85]

Reevaluations

The school is not required to reevaluate a child more often than once a year, unless the parent and school agree to more frequent evaluations. The school is required to evaluate at least every three years, unless the parent and school agree that a reevaluation is unnecessary.[86] The school must reevaluate if the child's educational needs change or if the child's parent or teacher requests a reevaluation.[87]

IDEA requires the IEP to include "a statement of the child's present levels of academic achievement and functional performance."[88] If a child has not been evaluated for a year or more, the IEP team will not have current information about the child's present levels of academic achievement and functional performance on which to base the IEP.

Under federal law, the 60 day timeline for initial evaluations does not apply to reevaluations, however, some state regulations provide a timeline for the reevaluation process.

Evaluation Procedures

The school **shall "use a variety of assessment tools** and strategies to gather relevant functional, developmental, and academic information" about the child. Information from evaluations will be used to determine the content of the child's IEP and to help the child make progress in the general education curriculum.[89]

---

80   See 34 CFR §§ 300.508 and 300.509 and the Federal Register at 71 Fed. Reg. 46699 (August 14, 2006) noting that the "use of model forms should not be required" in regard to filing a state complaint or request for a Due Process Hearing.

81   20 U.S.C. § 1414(a)(1)(D)(i)(I)

82   20 U.S.C. § 1414(a)(1)(D)(ii)(I)

83   20 U.S.C. § 1414(a)(1)(D)(ii)(II)

84   20 U.S.C. § 1414(a)(1)(D)(ii)

85   34 CFR § 300.300

86   It is important to have ongoing continuous educational achievement test data. Three years is too long to wait to assess change and progress.

87   20 U.S.C. § 1414(a)(2)

88   20 U.S.C. § 1414(d)(1)(A)(i)

89   20 U.S.C. § 1414(b)(2)(A)

The school shall **"not use any single measure or assessment as the sole criterion"**[90] for determining if a child is eligible for special education services. The children shall be assessed **"in all areas** of suspected disability."[91] Assessments **shall provide relevant information to determine the child's educational needs.**[92]

The school must ensure that assessments are not: **"discriminatory on a racial or cultural basis** . . . are provided and administered in the language and form most likely to yield accurate information on what the child knows and can do academically, developmentally, and functionally . . . [and] are administered by trained and knowledgeable personnel."[93, 94]

When a child transfers to a new school district, the receiving district must complete assessments "as expeditiously as possible, to ensure prompt completion of full evaluations."[95]

Eligibility and Educational Need

IDEA requires a team of qualified professionals and the child's parent to determine "whether the child is a child with a disability . . . and [to determine] the educational needs of the child."[96] The school shall give the parents a copy of the evaluation report and documentation of eligibility.

If the school team decides that a child with a disability is not eligible for special education services under IDEA, or if the parent disagrees with the school's classification or label, the parent should consider obtaining a comprehensive psycho-educational evaluation from an expert in the private sector.[97] Even if not eligible for an IEP, the child may be eligible for a **"Section 504 Plan"** and the protections of Section 504 and the ADA. To learn more about both, see the discussion in this Chapter about Section 504 and the ADA and take our quiz - **"*What's Your 504 IQ?*"**[98]

Lack of Appropriate Instruction

A child shall **not** be found eligible for an IEP **if the child's problems are due to "lack of appropriate instruction** in reading, including in the essential components of reading instruction, . . . lack of instruction in math, or limited English proficiency."[99]

Experts in learning disabilities have reported that some children identified as having specific learning disabilities are "victims of poor teaching." Nearly all children[100] can learn to read if taught appropriately, but many children do not receive appropriate instruction because their "teachers are not adequately prepared."

The essential components of reading instruction were defined in **No Child Left Behind (NCLB)** and located at 20 U.S.C. § 6368. However, **NCLB was replaced by Every Student Succeeds Act (ESSA).**

The legal definition of the "essential components of reading instruction" is now at 29 U.S.C. § 3272(8).[101]

---

90   20 U.S.C. § 1414(b)(2)(B)

91   *See* our discussion in Chapter Five.about the *Timothy O. v. Paso Robles Sch. Dist.* case where the school failed to evaluate, in all areas, a child with autism.

92   20 U.S.C. § 1414(b)(3)

93   In California, the use of IQ testing to determine eligibility of "black children" for an "EMR placement" is limited pursuant to *Larry P. v. Riles*, 495 F. Supp. 626 (ND CA 1979), affirmed by the Ninth Circuit at 793 F. 2d 969 (9th Cir. 1984)

94   20 U.S.C. § 1414(b)(3)

95   20 U.S.C. § 1414(b)(3)(D)

96   20 U.S.C. § 1414(b)(4)

97   See Independent Educational Evaluation (IEE) at <20 U.S.C. § 1415(b)(1)> and 34 CFR § 300.502.

98   https://www.wrightslaw.com/info/test.504.iq.htm

99   20 U.S.C. § 1414(b)(5)

100   Lyon, G. Reid and Jack M. Fletcher. "Early Warning System." Education Next, Summer 2001: Vol. 1, No 2 / https://www.educationnext.org/early-warning-system/

101   29 U.S.C. § 3272(8) Essential components of reading instruction "means explicit and systematic instruction in - (A) phonemic awareness; (B) phonics; (C) vocabulary development; (D) reading fluency, including oral reading skills; and (E) reading comprehension strategies." *See* https://www.law.cornell.edu/uscode/text/29/3272#8 Another portion of that law also explains that "a youth . . . [who] has English reading, writing, or computing skills at or below the 8th grade level on a generally accepted standardized test" is characterized as "basic skills deficient." 29 U.S.C. § 3102(5)(A)

Identifying Children with Specific Learning Disabilities

The school "shall not be required to take into consideration whether a child has a severe discrepancy between achievement and intellectual ability"[102] to determine if the child has a specific learning disability and needs special education services. The school district may use Response to Intervention (RTI)[103] to determine the child's response to scientific, research-based intervention as part of the evaluation process.[104] The legal definitions of "scientifically based reading research,"[105] and the "essential components of reading instruction" were previously included in NCLB and were subsequently moved as a part of ESSA.

Learning disabilities and dyslexia are neurobiological in origin and can be identified prior to a student entering school. "[E]vidence from studies based on functional brain imaging that reveals the activity of the brain while someone reads. These studies indicate a pattern of brain organization in poor readers that differs from that seen in nonimpaired readers." Lyon and Fletcher reported that:

> Functional brain imaging, conducted while a child reads words, is also being used to show how intensive teaching can influence the brain's reading circuitry. Imaging occurs before and after intervention, during which children significantly improve in reading ability. It appears that after intervention, brain activation patterns shift to the normative profile seen in nonimpaired readers.[106]

The Comprehensive Test of Phonological Processing can be administered to a four year old child. The "wait to fail" models and beliefs that the child "will grow out of it" have been disproven by science for decades. Children with dyslexia and learning disabilities need intensive early intervention, as experienced by this author, who received intensive intervention in the 1950's using the Orton-Gillingham Approach.

According to Nancy Duggan of Decoding Dyslexia, MA,[107] "reading fluency is a core skill that our students need to be successful independent learners . . . if students are not identified as dyslexic early, it will take longer for them to learn reading fluency, and explicit instruction is needed for these students to develop the skills of reading fluency."[108]

FAPE must be available to a child "even though the child has not failed or been retained in a course or grade, and is advancing from grade to grade."[109] Waiting to evaluate and waiting for the child to fail, postpones the necessary remediation and teaching of reading skills to a child.

Delays in providing specialized instruction to children who struggle to read damages them. Children learn to read in K-3rd grade. After 3rd grade, children must read to learn. Children who are not proficient readers by the end of 3rd grade are unlikely to be proficient.

Additional Requirements for Evaluations and Reevaluations

Information from evaluations and reevaluations shall be used to determine "the educational needs of the child" and "the present levels of academic achievement and related developmental needs of the child."

---

102 20 U.S.C. § 1414(b)(6)(A)

103 <20 U.S.C. § 1414(b)(6)> and 34 CFR § 300.307

104 For more articles, publications and other resources about Response to Intervention, go to:
https://www.wrightslaw.com/info/rti.index.htm

105 It was moved to 20 U.S.C. § 1033(2)

106 Lyon, G. Reid and Jack M. Fletcher. "Early Warning System." Education Next, Summer 2001: Vol. 1, No 2 /
https://www.educationnext.org/early-warning-system/

107 http://www.decodingdyslexiama.org/

108 Personal communication; See also Doe v. Cape Elizabeth Sch. Dist. 832 F.3d 69 (1st Cir. 2016) in our *Wrightslaw Year in Review* book where the Court of Appeals talked about the importance of assessing reading fluency. In ruling for the child, the Court scolded the District Court because it did not "make an independent judgment as to Jane's reading fluency deficit."

109 <34 CFR § 300.101(c)(1)>

The school must review private sector evaluations and information provided by the parents.[110]

IDEA includes language that allows school personnel to decide whether "no additional data are needed" to detemine the child's educational needs or eligibility.[111] If the IEP team and other qualified professionals decide they **do not need** "to determine whether the child continues to be a child with a disability and to determine the child's educational needs," the school can notify the parents that they do not intend to reevaluate. The school must provide the reasons for this decision. Under these circumstances, the parent must specifically request a reevaluation.[112] This language appears to be at odds with the requirement that the school must reevaluate "at least once every three years."[113]

The school must evaluate the child before **terminating the child's eligibility for special education services**. The school is not required to evaluate when the child graduates from high school with a <**"regular diploma"**>[114] or "ages out" of special education.[115] However, if the child graduates with a regular diploma or is no longer eligible for services because of age, the school **must provide the child** with a summary of "academic and functional performance" and recommendations to help the child meet postsecondary goals.[116]

Individualized Education Programs (IEPs)[117]

Present Levels of Academic Achievement and Functional Performance

The child's IEP must include a statement of the child's present levels of **academic achievement and functional performance** that includes how the child's disability affects the child's involvement and performance in the general education curriculum.[118, 119, 120] This is frequently referred to as PLOP, PLAAFP, PLEP, and PLP.

Measurable Goals

The child's IEP must include "a statement of measurable annual goals"[121] to address the child's present levels of academic achievement and functional performance. Imagine embarking on a weight loss program without knowing your weight or how many pounds you want to lose. If you fail to measure your weight at periodic intervals, will you meet your goals? To measure progress, you must have data, accumulated over time. For IEP goals and objectives, learn how to write "SMART IEPs."[122]

---

110   20 U.S.C. § 1414(c)(1)(a)(i)

111   20 U.S.C. § 1414(c)(4)

112   20 U.S.C. § 1414(c)(4))

113   20 U.S.C. § 1414(a)(2)(B)(ii)

114   Regular high school diploma is defined at 34 CFR § 300.102(a)(3)(iv)

115   20 U.S.C. § 1414(c)(5)

116   20 U.S.C. § 1414(c)(5)(B)

117   <20 U.S.C. § 1414(d)> - Sometimes the letter "P" in IEP is erroneously referred to as a "Plan." In Texas, this is known as an "ARD Committee" for "Admission, Review, and Dismissal."

118   **Per the Commentary, academic achievement** "generally refers to a child's performance in academic areas (e.g., reading or language arts, math, science, and history)." *See* Commentary in 71 Fed. Reg. 46662 (August 14, 2006) URL for the IEP portion of the Commentary is: https://www.wrightslaw.com/idea/comment/46661-46688.reg.320-328.ieps.pdf

119   **Per the Commentary, academic achievement** "generally refers to a child's performance in academic areas (e.g., reading or language arts, math, science, and history)." *See* Commentary in 71 Fed. Reg. 46662 (August 14, 2006) URL for the IEP portion of the Commentary is: https://www.wrightslaw.com/idea/comment/46661-46688.reg.320-328.ieps.pdf

120   20 U.S.C. § 1414(d)(1)(A)(i)(I)(aa)

121   20 U.S.C. § 1414(d)(1)(A)(i)(II)

122   To learn how to write IEPs with goals and objectives that are Specific, Measurable, use Action words, that are Realistic and Time specific, read Chapter 11, SMART IEPs, in *Wrightslaw: From Emotions to Advocacy*.
https://www.wrightslaw.com/bks/feta2/feta2.htm

The child's IEP must include "a statement of the special education and related services and supplementary aids[123] and services, based on peer-reviewed research to the extent practicable, to be provided to the child . . . and a statement of program modifications or supports **for school personnel** that will be provided for the child." This is needed most often with children who present severe behavioral challenges to the teacher and school district.

Educational Progress

The IEP must include "a description of how **the child's progress** toward meeting the annual goals . . . will be measured and **when periodic reports** on the progress the child is making toward meeting the annual goals (such as through the use of quarterly or other periodic reports, concurrent with the issuance of report cards) **will be provided.**"[124]

Appropriate Accommodations and Alternate Assessments

IDEA contains language about "individual appropriate accommodations" on state and district testing and requirements for alternate assessments. Your child's IEP must include "a statement of any individual appropriate accommodations that are necessary to measure the academic achievement and functional performance of the child on State and districtwide assessments . . . ."[125]

If the IEP Team recommends that your child take an **alternate assessment, the team must include a statement about** "why the child cannot participate in the regular assessment" and **why** "the particular alternate assessment selected is appropriate for the child."[126]

Transition Services

Transition services[127] are to begin "not later than the first IEP to be in effect when the child is 16, and updated annually thereafter . . . [and include] **appropriate measurable postsecondary goals** based upon age appropriate transition assessments related to training, education, employment, and, where appropriate, independent living skills . . . and the transition services (including **courses of study**)[128] needed to assist the child in reaching these goals."[129]

IEP Team Meetings

A member of the IEP team **may be excused** from attending an IEP meeting if the member's area of curriculum or service will not be discussed or modified and if the parent and school agree. An IEP team member may also be excused from an IEP meeting that involves their area of curriculum or service if they submit input in writing and **the parent's consent is in writing.**[130]

Children Who Transfer Schools

If the child transfers to a district in the same state or another state, the receiving school must provide **comparable services** to those in the sending district's IEP until they develop and implement a new IEP.[131] If the child moves during the summer to a new school district, since there must be an IEP at the beginning of each school year, the new school must provide the child with appropriate services.[132]

---

123 The definitions of related services and supplementary aids and services are located in 20 U.S.C. § 1401.

124 20 U.S.C. § 1414(d)(1)(A)(i)(III)

125 20 U.S.C. § 1414(d)(1)(A)(i)(VI)

126 20 U.S.C. § 1414(d)(1)(A)(i)(VI)(bb)

127 20 U.S.C. § 1401(34)

128 In The Commentary, this phrase includes **Advanced Placement** courses. 71 Fed. Reg. 46668 (August 14, 2006) https://www.wrightslaw.com/idea/comment/46661-46688.reg.320-328.ieps.pdf

129 20 U.S.C. § 1414(d)(1)(A)(i)(VIII)

130 20 U.S.C. § 1414(d)(1)(C)

131 20 U.S.C. § 1414(d)(2)(C)

132 *See* the USDOE's letter on this subject in the next Chapter related to <Section 1414(d)(2)(C).>

Developing the IEP

In developing the IEP, the IEP team *shall* (i.e. must) consider:

the child's strengths

the parent's concerns for enhancing the child's education

the results of the initial evaluation or most recent evaluation

the child's academic, developmental, and functional needs[133]

The IEP team *shall* **consider special factors** for children:

whose behavior impedes learning[134, 135]

who have limited English proficiency

who are blind or visually impaired

who are deaf or hard of hearing[136]

whether the child needs assistive technology and services

Reviewing and Revising IEPs

The child's IEP **must be reviewed at least once a year**[137] to determine if the child is achieving the annual goals. In addition, the IEP team must revise the IEP to address:

any lack of expected progress

results of any reevaluation

information provided by the parents

anticipated needs

If the parent and school decide to amend or modify the IEP that was developed at an annual IEP meeting, and they do not want to convene another IEP Team meeting, they may revise the IEP by agreement. The IEP Team must create a written document to amend or modify that annual IEP. This document must describe the changes or modification in the IEP and note that, by agreement of the parties, an IEP meeting was not convened.[138, 139] The parent should be provided with a copy of the revised IEP.

Multi-Year IEPs

As a "Pilot program" and "Demonstration" project, this portion of the IEP law permits a state to implement an IEP to last for three years, subject to the submission of a proposal to the USDOE.[140] No state has used this three year IEP option and requested approval of such a proposal. IEP review dates must be based on "natural transition points." If implemented, parents have the right to opt-out of this program and can request a review of the IEP without waiting for the natural transition point. This three-year IEP option is not in effect in any state.

---

133   20 U.S.C. § 1414(d)(3)(A)

134   20 U.S.C. § 1414(d)(3)(B)(i) - "shall" mandates **Behavioral Intervention Plans (BIP).**

135   *See* the footnotes for "special factors" in the next chapter. There have been a number of cases where a Court found the failure to have an appropriate **Functional Behavioral Assessment (FBA)** resulted in a flawed **Behavioral Intervention Plan (BIP)** and thus the child **was denied FAPE and entitled to Compensatory Education** dating back to the initial BIP. For more about "**Special Factors,**" *see* Chapter 7, titled "Special Factors" in *Wrightslaw: All About IEPs.*".

136   20 U.S.C. § 1414(d)(3)(B)(iv) - must consider the child's communication needs.

137   20 U.S.C. § 1414(d)(4)(A)(i)

138   However, an amendment to an IEP **cannot** "take the place of an annual IEP Team meeting." *See* Commentary in 71 Fed. Reg 46685 (August 14, 2006).

139   20 U.S.C. § 1414(d)(3)(D)

140   20 U.S.C. § 1414(d)(5)

Failure to Meet Transition Objectives

For a student in transition, if an agency, such as Vocational Rehabilitation Services drops the ball and does not provide appropriate services, the school district must convene an IEP meeting to develop alternative strategies.[141]

Children with Disabilities in Adult Prisons

If "a child with a disability"[142] is incarcerated in an adult prison or jail, the youngster is **still entitled to FAPE** unless a "bona fide security interest or compelling penological interest . . . cannot otherwise be accommodated."[143]

Placement Decisions

Parents are members of the team that decides the child's placement. Decisions about the child's placement cannot be made until after the IEP team, which includes the parent, reaches consensus about the child's needs, program, and goals.[144]

See also Section 1400(c)(5)(C) where Congress explained that special education is "**a service for such children rather than a place** where such children are sent."

Although the law is clear on this issue, the child's "label" or eligibility category often drives decisions about services and placement, leading school personnel to determine the child's placement before the IEP meeting. These unilateral actions prevent parents from "meaningful participation" in educational decision-making for their child. The word **"placement" typically refers not to the physical place,** i.e., classroom where the child is located, but instead **to the nature of the program**.

For example, moving a child from the **LD self-contained classroom at East End** Elementary School **to the same** LD self-contained classroom **at West End** Elementary School **is not usually, in caselaw, considered a change in placement.** However, moving the child from the LD self-contained classroom at East End Elementary School into the **LD Resource** classroom at East End, **a change of program,** is considered to be a change of placement.[145]

Alternative Means of Meeting Participation

School meetings do not have to be face-to-face. So long as the parent and school district agree, meetings may be by phone or video conferences.[146]

Section 1415: Procedural Safeguards

Section 1415 describes the safeguards[147] designed to protect the rights of children with disabilities and their parents. These safeguards include the right to participate in all meetings, to examine all educational records, and to obtain an Independent Educational Evaluation (IEE) of the child. Section 1415 includes requirements for prior written notice, procedural safeguards notice, mediation, resolution sessions, due process hearings, the two-year statute of limitations, appeals, discipline, and age of majority.

---

141 20 U.S.C. § 1414(d)(6)

142 20 U.S.C. § 1401(3)

143 20 U.S.C. § 1414(d)(7)

144 20 U.S.C. § 1414(e)

145 For more, *see* the footnote to Section 1414(e) in the next chapter.

146 20 U.S.C. § 1414(f)

147 20 U.S.C. § 1415

Prior Written Notice (PWN)

If the school district proposes to change or refuses to change the identification, evaluation, or educational placement of a child, the school must provide the parent with written notice.[148]

The content of the "prior written notice" must:[149]

- describe the action proposed or refused
- explain why the school proposed or refused to take action
- describe each evaluation procedure, assessment, record, or report used as a basis for the proposed or refused action
- provide sources the parent can contact to obtain assistance
- describe other options considered and why these options were rejected
- **describe the factors that were relevant** to the school's proposal or refusal[150]

Due Process Complaint Notice

The party who requests a due process hearing must provide a detailed notice to the other party that includes identifying information about the child, the nature of the problem, facts, and a proposed resolution.[151]

The Due Process Complaint Notice can be a letter[152] to request a due process hearing that includes the required components.[153] A due process hearing may not be held until after this DP complaint notice has been filed. For several DP request letters that favorably affected the outcome of their cases, please *see* the North Carolina "Brody" letter[154] and the Ohio "James" letter[155] on our website, written using our "Letter to the Stranger"[156] format.

Procedural Safeguards Notice

The Procedural Safeguards Notice[157] provides parents with specific information about their rights and protections. This includes an Independent Educational Evaluation (IEE), prior written notice, the right to examine all educational records, notice of the time period (statute of limitations) within which "to make a complaint," mediation, due process, current educational placement, discipline, private placement reimbursement, and attorneys' fees.[158]

Independent Educational Evaluation (IEE)

Parents have a right to obtain an Independent Educational Evaluation[159] of their child. School districts often attempt to restrict the parent's choice to a list of approved evaluators selected by the district. In 2004, the Office of

---

148 20 U.S.C. § 1415(b)(3)

149 20 U.S.C. § 1415(c)(1)

150 The U.S. Department of Education published a Model Prior Written Notice Form at: https://www.ed.gov/policy/speced/guid/idea/modelform-notice.pdf

151 20 U.S.C. §§ 1415(b)(7) and 1415(c)(2)

152 Use of a state's model form to request a special education due process hearing is not required. See 34 CFR §§ 300.508 and 509, and the Federal Register at 71 Fed. Reg. 46699 (August 14, 2006) noting that the "use of model forms should not be required" in regard to filing a state complaint or request for a Due Process Hearing. https://www.wrightslaw.com/idea/comment/46688-46713.reg.501-520.procedures.pdf

153 To write persuasive letters, read Chapter 24, "Letter to the Stranger," in *Wrightslaw: From Emotions to Advocacy*.

154 https://www.wrightslaw.com/advoc/stranger/brody.html

155 https://www.wrightslaw.com/advoc/ltrs/strngr.joejames.htm

156 https://www.wrightslaw.com/advoc/articles/Letter_to_Stranger.html

157 20 U.S.C. § 1415(d)

158 The U.S. Department of Education published a **Model Procedural Safeguards Form** at: https://www.ed.gov/policy/speced/guid/idea/modelform-safeguards.pdf

159 20 U.S.C. § 1415(b(1)

Special Education Programs issued a policy letter to clarify that parents have **the right to choose their independent evaluator.**[160] If the school district refuses to provide an IEE, it must request a special education due process hearing against the family to prove that their last evaluation is appropriate.

For more, *see* the ***Cobb County Sch. Dist. v. DB*** case in the footnote to Section 1415(b)(1) in the next chapter. At the conclusion of this hotly contested case, the school district paid parent's attorney over **$300,000.00 in attorney's fees** and had to provide the IEE. If you use the Google search engine on our website searching against "IEE," you will find many articles about IEEs.

Mediation

The ability to use mediation to resolve disputes is provided in IDEA. Mediation must be voluntary and may not be used to deny or delay a parent's right to a due process hearing. It must be conducted by a qualified, impartial mediator.[161]

Mediation is a confidential process in which the parties meet with a disinterested party in an effort to resolve their dispute. A successful mediation requires the parties to discuss their views and differences frankly. Before entering into mediation, both parties should understand their rights and the law.

A due process hearing does not have to be pending for a party to request mediation.

Discussions during mediation are confidential. If the case is not settled, confidential disclosures and admissions may not be used as evidence in a subsequent trial.[162]

Written Settlement Agreements

Prior to the revisions in IDEA in 2004, when a party breached or failed to honor a mediation agreement, the other party had to file a civil lawsuit under a breach of contract theory in order to enforce the agreement. Pursuant to Section 1415(e)(2)(F)(iii), a party can use the power of a federal or state court to enforce the agreement.[163]

Due Process Hearings

Many pre-trial procedures and timelines for due process hearings are included in IDEA, including the resolution session,[164] due process complaint notice, amended complaint notice, statute of limitations and timelines. If you will be involved in a special education due process hearing, be sure that you are familiar with the federal regulations specific to due process hearings[165] and your state's due process regulations and trial procedures.

Statute of Limitations

The statute of limitations (SOL) to present a complaint is usually two years,[166] however, the special education regulations in some states provide a shorter timeline. If a due process hearing may be on your horizon, you need to know the statute of limitations in your state.

Review your state's regulations and statutes to determine your SOL. To confirm that your understanding is correct, contact your State Department of Education / State Education Agency (SEA) to request information about your SOL. **Do not rely on one source of information.** You must have independent verification about your state's SOL.

IDEA includes detailed procedural requirements for pretrial matters in due process hearings. You should assume that your state has special education laws and regulations specific to procedural matters and that they may differ from what you see in IDEA. **Failure to carefully research and comply with your state's laws and regulations can be fatal to a pending case.**

---

160   *See* "Letter to Parker" https://www.wrightslaw.com/info/test.eval.choice.osep.htm

161   20 U.S.C. § 1415(e)

162   20 U.S.C. § 1415(e)(2)(G)

163   20 U.S.C. § 1415(e)(2)(F)

164   20 U.S.C. § 1415(f)(1)(B)

165   They begin at <34 CFR § 300.507>.

166   20 U.S.C. § 1415(b)(6)(B)

Other Procedures and Timelines

If the school did not provide prior written notice[167] to the parents previously, the school must send that notice within 10 days. After receiving the due process complaint notice, the other party must file a response that specifically addresses the issues raised in the complaint within 10 days.[168] If the notice is insufficient, the receiving party must complain to the hearing officer within 15 days.

The hearing officer must determine if the complaint is sufficient within 5 days.[169] A party may amend its due process complaint notice **only if the other party consents** in writing or the Hearing Officer / Administrative Law Judge (ALJ) consents and the other party is given the opportunity to resolve the dispute by using a resolution session.[170] This requirement is similar to the <"12(b)(6)" Motion to Dismiss> proceeding in the Federal Rules of Civil Procedure (FRCP)[171] and is addressed at the end of Chapter Nine.

Resolution Session

After the school district receives the parent's due process complaint notice, it is required to convene a resolution session within 15 days, even if the Notice is insufficient.[172] The resolution session provides the parties with an opportunity to resolve their dispute before a due process hearing. For that session, the school district must send the "relevant member or members of the IEP team" who have knowledge about the facts in the parent's complaint and a district representative who has decision-making authority (settlement authority). The school board attorney may not attend the resolution session **unless** an attorney accompanies the parent.

The parent and the district may agree to waive the resolution session or use mediation. If the district has not resolved the complaint to the parents' satisfaction within 30 days of receiving the Complaint, the due process hearing can be held.[173]

"Five-Day Rule"[174]

The law requires that evaluations and recommendations be disclosed **five business days** before a due process hearing.[175] Most state statutes, regulations, and standards of practice, require that all exhibits, exhibit lists, and witness lists be disclosed at least 5 business days before a hearing.

Failure to comply with these requirements about disclosure **usually results in dismissal** of the plaintiff / petitioner's case.[176, 177]

---

167   20 U.S.C. § 1415(c)(2)(B)(i)(I)

168   20 U.S.C. § 1415(c)(2)(ii)

169   20 U.S.C. § 1415(c)(2)(D)

170   20 U.S.C. § 1415(c)(2)(E)

171   FRCP Rule 12 - https://www.law.cornell.edu/rules/frcp/rule_12

172   20 U.S.C. § 1415(f)(1)(B)

173   20 U.S.C. § 1415(f)(1)(B)(ii)

174   20 U.S.C. § 1415(f)(2)

175   20 U.S.C. § 1415(f)(2)

176   Our video of a special education due process hearing - **Surviving Due Process:** *Stephen Jeffers v. School Board,* is available on DVD. It takes you through a due process hearing, from initial preparations to testimony by the final witness. See direct examination and dramatic cross-examination of witnesses, objections, arguments between counsel, and rulings by the hearing officer. **Surviving Due Process** is based on an actual case litigated in Virginia and is available for purchase from our online store at: https://www.wrightslaw.com/store/dpdvd.html for $19.95.

177   In all types of civil litigation, failure to comply with a requirement of this nature typically results in dismissal of the case. This is not unique to special education matters as courts and quasi-judicial administrative agencies seek to lower their caseload of active cases. As an attorney in active practice, this author ensured that the list of witnesses, list of exhibits, and copies of the exhibits, were prepared several weeks prior to the scheduled hearing date. Early preparation for litigation increases the odds of a favorable settlement.

Substantive v. Procedural Issues

IDEA clarifies that "a decision made by a hearing officer shall be made on substantive grounds based on a determination of whether the child received a free appropriate public education."[178] Examples of substantive issues include determining if the child has a disability that adversely affects educational performance (eligibility) or if the child received a free appropriate education (FAPE).

Allegations that a school district **violated a procedural rule or timeline are usually not considered** unless it directly impeded the child's right to FAPE, impeded the parent's opportunity to participate, or, most significantly, "**caused a deprivation of educational benefits.**"[179] Examples of procedural issues that are typically not considered are delays in scheduling evaluations, convening meetings, or not having all appropriate personnel at an IEP meeting. A failure to evaluate for an extended period of time is often considered to deprive the child of an educational benefit.

In many cases, an allegation of a procedural violation is a significant part of the parent's case. To find cases in your state and your Circuit, and nationwide, use **Google Scholar,**[180] select the appropriate courts, and enter as your search terms the following, exactly, with the quotation marks: **"individuals with disabilities education act" "1415(f)(3)(E)"**

The U.S.C. citation of **"1415(f)(3)(E)"** is that portion of the US Code that references procedural violations. Your Google search will be limited to cases that include the above two quotes. Using those two search terms, a recent search of all state and federal courts found 490 cases. In the 90 days before the search, there were four cases specific to this issue. Two decisions were in favor of the school district and two were in favor of the child and parents, with the Court finding a procedural violation which resulted in a denial of FAPE.

A search without putting quotations around the subsection, 1415(f)(3)(E), resulted in 5,540 cases found, because hundreds of cases referenced the number "1415" which was too broad a search. A search without any quotations around any of the search terms resulted in 11,800 cases found. Very few were about special education procedural violations.

Minimum Standards for Hearing Officers[181]

IDEA requires that hearing officers be knowledgeable about the law, federal and state regulations, and caselaw. Hearing officers must also have the knowledge and ability to "conduct hearings and write decisions in accordance with appropriate standard legal practice."[182]

Attorneys' Fees

Parents who prevail in litigation can recover attorneys' fees from school districts.[183] Settlement of a case in favor of a child is not sufficient for an award of attorneys' fees, unless award expressly included attorneys' fees in the settlement document. Under IDEA, school districts may recover attorneys' fees from the parent or the parent's attorney if the complaint is frivolous, unreasonable, or filed for an improper purpose, or to harass, cause unnecessary delay, or needlessly increase the cost of litigation. This is very rare and occurs usually when a parent, who is unfamiliar with the law, files a "pro se" case, or when the attorney or lay advocate representing the child has a personal vendetta against the school district. Our series of *Wrightslaw Year in Review* books have a number of cases about parents who recovered attorneys fees from school districts.

---

178   20 U.S.C. § 1415(f)(3)(E)(i)

179   20 U.S.C. § 1415(f)(3)(E)(ii)(III)

180   The mechanics of using Google Scholar are discussed in **Chapter 3, about Legal Research**.

181   In many states the procedures and operation of special education due process hearings is maintained by a state officer or agency, often known as the

182   20 U.S.C. § 1415(f)(3)(A)(iv)

183   20 U.S.C. § 1415(i)(3)(B)

Stay-Put / Pendency[184]

The subsection "Maintenance of Current Educational Placement" is generally known as either the "Stay-Put" or "Pendency" statute.[185] Except in discipline matters, while a special education due process is pending, the child is to stay-put in the "then current educational placement of the child." This is a requirement that the LEA maintain a placement, but, pursuant to caselaw, parents are not required to keep their child in that placement, such as in a typical tuition reimbursement case.

Discipline[186]

"Placement in Alternative Educational Setting" is the subsection title for **Discipline,** which is located in Section 1415(k). It includes requirements for disciplinary placements in interim alternative educational settings, manifestation determinations, placements, appeals, and authority of the hearing officer.

As you learned in the "History" portion of Chapter 2, prior to this law being passed in 1975, children with disabilities were either not allowed to attend school or they were regularly suspended and expelled from school, usually for financial reasons. Too often, the school district could not afford to install ramps or elevators for children in wheelchairs, or for children with "hidden handicaps" provide qualified speech language therapists, Orton-Gillingham or other reading tutors or other qualified staff.

The first subsection of IDEA about a State's responsibilities is located in Section 1412(a)(1) and explains that, **even if a child is suspended or expelled from school, the child is still entitled to FAPE.**[187]

Section 1415(k) is long and detailed. The key to understanding "Discipline" in special education begins with the concept known as "**Manifestation Determination**" and whether the child's

- conduct in question was caused by, or had a direct and substantial relationship to, the child's disability; or
- if the conduct in question was the direct result of the LEAs failure to implement the IEP.[188]

IDEA allows schools to place a child with a disability into an interim alternative setting **if the child violates a code of student conduct and the child's behavior was not a manifestation of the child's disability.**[189]

School officials may suspend the child for up to 10 days. If the school removes a child for 10 days or more,[190] regardless of the severity of the child's misconduct (i.e., violation of a code of conduct v. possession of a weapon), the school **must continue to provide the child with FAPE.**[191] The child should continue to receive educational services, participate in the general education curriculum, and make progress on the IEP goals. The child will receive "as appropriate, functional behavioral assessment, behavioral intervention services and modifications" to prevent the behavior from reoccurring.[192]

If the LEA, "the parent, and relevant members of the IEP Team make the determination that the conduct **was a manifestation of the child's disability,** the IEP Team **shall** conduct a functional behavioral assessment and implement a behavioral intervention plan."[193] If the child already has a behavior intervention plan, the IEP Team shall modify the plan to address the child's behavior.[194]

---

184   20 U.S.C. § 1415(j)

185   Different circuit courts have used one or the other in a discussion about this statute. It goes by different names in different parts of the country dependent upon a particular Court of Appeals.

186   20 U.S.C. § 1415(k)

187   20 U.S.C. § 1412(a)(1)(A)

188   20 U.S.C. § 1415(k)(1)(E)

189   20 U.S.C. § 1415(k)

190   A removal for more than 10 consecutive school days, or a series of removals that total more than 10 school days constitute a change of placement. *See* 34 CFR § 300.536(a).

191   20 U.S.C. § 1415(k)(1)

192   20 U.S.C. § 1415(k)(1)(D)

193   20 U.S.C. § 1415(k)(1)(F)(i)

194   20 U.S.C. § 1415(k)(1)(F)(ii)

If the child carries a dangerous weapon to school, knowingly possesses or uses illegal drugs at school, or inflicts serious bodily injury upon another person while at school, the school may remove the child to an interim alternative placement for not more than 45 school days.[195] The school must continue to provide the child with FAPE.

Illegal drugs, dangerous weapons, and bodily injury (substantial risk of death, extreme physical pain,) as applied to discipline issues in IDEA, are defined.[196]

To prevent zero-tolerance abuses and refusal to exercise discretion in decisions about discipline, Congress added language in the law that school personnel "consider any unique circumstance on a **case-by-case basis**" in determining whether to change a child's placement.

Exhaustion of Administrative Remedies

Section 1415(l), is titled "Rule of Construction" but is better known **as the "Exhaustion" statute**. Before filing a lawsuit in court in a typical special education dispute, you must first exhaust your administrative remedies, i.e., file and proceed with a special education due process hearing. After that process has been exhausted, you can then file suit in court. This section also explains that your rights are not limited to those under IDEA and that you can also proceed forward with alleged violations of the Constitution and other Federal laws protecting the rights of children with disabilities."[197]

Section 1415(l) was the subject of the 2017 SCOTUS case, *Fry v. Napoleon Comm. Sch.,* authored by Justice Kagan who explained "We hold that **exhaustion is not necessary** when the gravamen of the plaintiff's suit is something other than the denial of the IDEA's core guarantee - what the Act calls a 'free appropriate public education.'"[198] Since *Fry*, there have been a number of decisions where cases were dismissed because the court held that the parents failed to exhaust administrative remedies, and in doing so, cite *Fry* as the authority. At the same time, many courts have said that exhaustion is not necessary if the relief sought is something that could not be provided under IDEA.

The full text of *Fry* and the "Transcript of the Announcement" of the *Fry* Opinion by Justice Kagan are in the 2017 edition of the *Wrightslaw Year in Review* book at pages 83 and 96 respectively. More about this issue is in the footnotes to Section 1415(l) in Chapter 6.

Section 1415(l) also the subject of the *Perez v. Sturgis Public Schools*[199] case pending before the U. S. Supreme Court with a decision expected in 2023.

Transfer of Parental Rights at Age of Majority

Section 1415(m) explains that when a "child with a disability reaches the age of majority"[200] the legal rights that the parents have are transferred to the child. In almost all states, the age of majority is the child's 18th birthday. Under a "Special rule" there are provisions in the law for the parents to continue to represent the interests of the child after the child reaches the age of majority.[201]

Section 1416 - Monitoring, State Plans, and Enforcement

This is used by the USDOE against a SEA. It requires States to file state plans, and provides the enforcement procedure, and withholding of funds to be used by the USDOE against an SEA.[202]

---

195   20 U.S.C. § 1415(k)(1)(G)

196   20 U.S.C. § 1415(k)(7)

197   20 U.S.C. § 1415(l)

198   *Fry v. Napoleon Comm. Sch.,* 580 U.S. 154 (2017), 137 S. Ct. 743, 197 L. Ed. 2d 46

199   https://www.wrightslaw.com/law/scotus/sturgis/

200   20 U.S.C. § 1415(m)

201   20 U.S.C. § 1415(m)(2)

202   20 U.S.C. § 1416(e)

Section 1417 - Administration, Instructional Content, and Model Forms

This section explains that the Federal Government is not authorized to "mandate, direct, or control a State, local educational agency, or school's **specific instructional content**, academic achievement standards and assessments, curriculum, or program of instruction."[203] The USDOE was required to develop and **publish model forms** for IEPs, IFSPs, Notice of Procedural Safeguards and Prior Written Notice.[204] We encourage you to download, print, and read these "Model Forms."

Individualized Education Program (IEP): https://www.wrightslaw.com/idea/law/model.iep.form.pdf

Procedural Safeguards Notice: https://www.wrightslaw.com/idea/law/model.safeguard.form.pdf

Prior Written Notice: https://www.wrightslaw.com/idea/law/model.pwn.form.pdf

Section 1418 - Program Information

States "shall provide data . . . to determine if **significant disproportionality** based on race and ethnicity is occurring in the State . . ."[205] **The focus relates to the identification, placement, and disciplinary actions of children with disabilities.** Pursuant to the preceding Section 1416, the monitoring is to focus on "(C) Disproportionate representation of racial and ethnic groups in special education and related services, to the extent the representation is the result of inappropriate identification."[206]

Section 1419 - Preschool Grants

This section provides preschool grants to assist States in providing special education and related services, to children with disabilities aged 3 through 5, inclusive; and, at the State's discretion, to 2-year-old children with disabilities.

Part C - Infants and Toddlers with Disabilities

Part C governs early intervention services for infants and toddlers under the age of 3, with some exceptions. Part C includes Section 1431 through Section 1444 of Title 20 of the United States Code.

Section 1431 - Findings and Policy

Congress stressed that there is an "urgent and substantial need . . . to recognize the significant brain development that occurs during a child's first 3 years of life . . ."[207] [and that there is an] "urgent and substantial need to maximize the potential for individuals with disabilities to live independently in society."[208]

It is the policy of the United States to provide financial assistance to States to develop and implement a **statewide, comprehensive, coordinated, multidisciplinary, interagency system that provides early intervention services** for infants and toddlers with disabilities and their families."[209]

Section 1432(4) - Definitions - Early Intervention Services

Early intervention services must be designed to meet the child's developmental needs, including physical, cognitive, communication, social and emotional, and adaptive areas, and must be provided by qualified personnel.[210] Many

---

203   20 U.S.C. § 1417(b)

204   20 U.S.C. § 1417(e)

205   20 U.S.C. § 1418(d)(1)

206   20 U.S.C. § 1416(a)(3)(C)

207   20 U.S.C. § 1431(a)(1)

208   20 U.S.C. § 1431(a)(3)

209   20 U.S.C. § 1431(b)

210   20 U.S.C. § 1432(4)

school districts offer one-size-fits-all school-based programs that are not "designed to meet the developmental needs" of a particular infant or toddler. Early intervention services "are provided at no cost except where a federal or State law provides for payments by families, including a schedule of sliding fees . . ."[211]

Section 1432(5) - Definitions - Infant or Toddler with a Disability

An infant or toddler with a disability is "an individual under 3 years of age who needs early intervention services because the individual is experiencing developmental delays, as measured by appropriate diagnostic instruments and procedures"[212] in one or more areas of development. At the state's discretion,[213] an infant or toddler with a disability may also include "at-risk infants and toddlers" and children who previously received early intervention services until they enter kindergarten or elementary school.

Section 1433 - General Authority for Early Intervention Programs

States are required to provide "early intervention services for infants and toddlers with disabilities and their families."[214] Part C describes the minimum requirements for those programs. States must have policies to ensure that early intervention services are based on scientifically based research. The evaluation of the child must be timely, comprehensive and multidisciplinary and must include "a family-directed identification of the needs of each family." States must have comprehensive child find systems and public awareness programs and must maintain central information directories about early intervention services, resources, and experts, and demonstration programs.[215]

States must also have comprehensive systems of personnel development, including training for paraprofessionals and primary referral sources, policies and procedures to ensure that personnel are appropriately and adequately trained, and that early intervention services are provided in natural environments.[216]

States may continue to provide early intervention services to young children with disabilities until they enter or are eligible to enter kindergarten.[217] These early intervention services must "include an educational component that promotes school readiness and incorporates pre-literacy, language and numeracy skills."[218]

Section 1436 - Individualized Family Service Plan (IFSP)

The legal requirements for Individualized Family Service Plans (IFSPs)[219] are similar to the requirements for Individualized Education Programs,[220] but with some important differences. The assessment and program development process includes a "family-directed assessment" of the family's resources, priorities, and concerns. Individualized Family Service Plans must include "measurable results or outcomes expected to be achieved . . . including pre-literacy and language skills" and the "criteria, procedures, and timelines" that will be used to measure the child's progress. IDEA requires that the IFSP include "a statement of specific early intervention services based on peer-reviewed research . . . necessary to meet the unique needs" of the child and family.

211 20 U.S.C. § 1432(4)(B)

212 20 U.S.C. § 1432(5)(A)

213 20 U.S.C. § 1432(5)(B)

214 20 U.S.C. § 1433

215 20 U.S.C. § 1435(a)

216 20 U.S.C. § 1435(a)(8)

217 20 U.S.C. § 1435(c)

218 20 U.S.C. § 1435(c)(2)

219 20 U.S.C. § 1436

220 The IEP statute is 20 U.S.C. § 1414(d). Note that an IFSP is a "Plan" and an IEP is a "Program."

Section 1439 - Procedural Safeguards

The protections and safeguards for young children with disabilities and their parents in the Procedural Safeguards section of Part C[221] are similar to those in Part B, but with some important differences. Parents of young children have a right to accept or decline any early intervention service without jeopardizing their right to other early intervention services. The law includes a procedure to protect the rights of the child when the parents are not known or cannot be found by appointing an individual to act as a surrogate for the parents.

Part D – National Activities to Improve Education of Children with Disabilities

Part D is organized into four subparts. **Subpart 1** about State Personnel Development Grants includes purpose, definition of personnel, eligibility, applications, and how funds may be used. **Subpart 2** about Personnel Preparation focuses on improving educational outcomes and results by improving teacher training, and professional development. **Subpart 3** describes requirements for Parent Training and Information Centers and Community Resource Centers. **Subpart 4** contains General Provisions.

Section 1450 - Findings

Findings in Part D, Section 1450, describes the critical need for adequately trained personnel and for "[h]igh quality, comprehensive professional development programs . . . to ensure that the persons responsible for the education or transition of children with disabilities possess the skills and knowledge necessary to address the educational and related needs of those children."[222] It also provides for parent training.[223]

Section 1462 - Personnel Development

Section 1462 about Personnel Development to Improve Services and Results for Children with Disabilities focuses on the need to ensure that all teachers "have the necessary skills and knowledge, derived from practices that have been determined, through **scientifically based research,** to be successful in serving those children"[224]

Section 1471 - Parent Training and Information Centers (PTI) and Parent Resource Centers (CPRC)

The Education Department shall award grants to at least one parent organization in each state for a Parent Training and Information Center. The purpose of these Centers is to help parents learn about their children's disabilities and educational needs, **their legal rights** and responsibilities, how to communicate effectively with school personnel, and how to participate in educational decision-making.[225]

The Education Department may also award grants to parent organizations that do not meet the criteria for a PTI but focus on helping under-served parents. For example, a center may focus on helping low-income parents, parents with limited English proficiency, and parents with disabilities.

End of the IDEA Overview

---

221   20 U.S.C. § 1439

222   20 U.S.C. § 1450(6)

223   20 U.S.C. § 1450(11)

224   20 U.S.C. § 1462(a)(2)

225   20 U.S.C. § 1471(b)

Quicklinks To[226]

> <IDEA Overview>
> <Section 504 Overview >
> <ADA Overview >

Overview of the Rehabilitation Act of 1973 and Section 504

The Rehabilitation Act and Section 504 within it, is a civil rights law that prohibits discrimination against individuals with disabilities. **It impacts educational and other settings t**hat receive federal financial assistance. In the educational setting, it is intended to ensure that children with disabilities have equal access to an education. These children may receive accommodations and modifications. **The purpose of Section 504 is quite different from IDEA.**

History of The Rehabilitation Act of 1973

After Public Law 93-112[227] was passed on September 26, 1973, it was known[228] as the "**Rehabilitation Act of 1973.**" The law consists of **Five "Titles"** with the focus and purpose related to the vocational rehabilitation of "handicapped individuals." The first four Titles address vocational rehabilitation, research, federal responsibilities and grants, and administration. The last one, "**Title V - Miscellaneous,**" includes five "Sections."[229] The fifth and last section is "**Section 504 - Nondiscrimination under Federal grants.**"

Section 504 consists of a single sentence:

> No otherwise qualified handicapped individual in the United States, as defined in section 7(6),[230] shall, solely by reason of his handicap, be excluded from the participation in, be denied the benefits of, or be subjected to discrimination under any program or activity receiving Federal financial assistance.

The Rehabilitation Act of 1973 was passed two years before IDEA's predecessor, the Education for All Handicapped Children Act of 1975. After the **Section 504 regulations were signed** in 1977, "Section 504" began to have an impact in various settings. It was the impetus for the **1990 Americans with Disabilities Act (ADA).** In 1992, the Rehabilitation Act of 1973 was amended to reaffirm the "precepts" of the ADA. As noted in the legislative history:

> The 1992 Amendments revised the Rehabilitation Act's findings, purpose, and policy provisions to incorporate language acknowledging the discriminatory barriers faced by persons with disabilities, and recognizing that persons with disabilities have the right to "enjoy full inclusion and integration in the economic, political, social, cultural, and educational mainstream of American society." 29 U.S.C. 701(a)(3) as amended.
>
> . . .
>
> The statement of purpose and policy is a reaffirmation of the precepts of the Americans with Disabilities Act, which has been referred to as the **20th century emancipation proclamation for individuals with disabilities**.

---

226   **Wrightslaw Note**: Per the information provided in Chapter 1, this book contains **embedded hyperlinks.** Those who have the **E-book (adobe.pdf version)**, can click on the link and go directly to the webpage or location in this book. Embedded hyperlinks are marked with a <, left pointing arrow, and a > right pointing arrow. All URLs are hyperlinked and do not have arrows.

227   https://www.govinfo.gov/content/pkg/STATUTE-87/pdf/STATUTE-87-Pg355.pdf

228   It was previously known as the "Vocational Rehabilitation Act."

229   Those sections were about existing laws, employment, architectural barriers, and federal contracts.

230   The words "section 7(6)" have been replaced with the words, "705(20) of this title." This defines the "individual with a disability" as "any individual who (A) has a physical or mental impairment which for such individual constitutes or results in a substantial impediment to employment; and (B) can benefit in terms of an employment outcome from vocational rehabilitation services provided pursuant to subchapter I, III, or VI."

It is the Committee's intent that these principles guide the policies, practices, and procedures developed under all titles of the [Rehabilitation] Act.[231]

While amending the Section 504 regulations, the U.S. Department of Justice wrote in a "Notice of Proposed Rulemaking:

Title II [of the ADA][232] and section 504 are generally understood to **impose similar requirements**, given the similar language employed in the ADA and the Rehabilitation Act and the congressional directive that the ADA be construed to grant **at least as much protection** as provided by the regulations implementing the Rehabilitation Act.[233]

However, in the ADA's early years, SCOTUS issued decisions in several cases that narrowly construed the ADA's **definition of disabilities.** To offset the adverse impact of those decisions, **Congress amended the ADA in 2008, and broadened the definition of those protected by the law.** It ensured that **episodic conditions** such as asthma, diabetes, epilepsy, and other similar conditions of an episodic nature were included.

Section 504's definition of a disability in <29 U.S.C. § 705(20)> **actually uses, and incorporates by reference, the definition in the ADA** at <42 U.S.C. § 12102.> A change in the ADA, Section 12102, automatically changes it in Section 504. A legal decision about the ADA definition of disability in Section 12102 is directly applicable to a the definition of a disability in Section 504. Disability as defined in Section 504 **is the definition** provided in the ADA.

Section 504 and the ADA

The ADA is based on Section 504 and Section 504 is based on the ADA. Each law incorporates the other by reference. Section 504 - Nondiscrimination is a single section within **The Rehabilitation Act of 1973,** located at 29 U.S.C. § 794. It has few subsections, details, and lacks specificity.[234] It is conceptually much harder to assess specific scenarios. It incorporates by reference much of the Americans with Disabilities Act (ADA) and requires one to go back and forth between Section 504, its regulations and the ADA statute and regulations to fully understand a legal issue.

As you read decisions involving either Section 504 or the ADA, or both, and whether the individual has a disability and is entitled to protections, remember that **ADA cases and decisions have a direct impact on 504 cases and decisions, and visa versa.**

Section 504 revolves around the concept of "Nondiscrimination" and whether the individual qualifies for protection. In **29 U.S.C. § 794 - Nondiscrimination**, the law opens with "No otherwise qualified individual with a disability in the United States, as defined in <**section 705(20)**> of this title, **shall**, solely by reason of her or his disability, **be excluded from the participation in, be denied the benefits of, or be subjected to discrimination** under any program or activity receiving Federal financial assistance . . . ."[235]

---

231   S. Rep. 102–357 at 14 (Aug. 3, 1992); H.R. Rep. 102–822 at 81 (Aug. 10, 1992)

232   Title II of the ADA applies to "Public Services" including public schools. It does not apply to private schools, which are governed by Title III.

233   https://www.ada.gov/regs2016/504_nprm.html#_ftn3

234   Continuing the contrast, IDEA's Section 1414 about evaluations, eligibility, and IEPs, has 6 subsections. For IEPs in Section 1414(d), there are 7 subsections, each one containing additional subsections. IDEA's Section 1415 about procedural safeguards, due process hearings, court, discipline, etc., has 15 subsections.

235   <29 U.S.C. § 794(a)>

The law is impacted by the entity's receipt of federal financial assistance[236] and whether the individual is eligible for the protections of Section 504. Eligibility is determined by the language **"as defined in section 705(20) of this title"** and reads:

29 U.S.C. § 705 - Definitions
(20) Individual with a disability

> **(A) In general.** Except as otherwise provided in subparagraph (B), the term **"individual with a disability"** means any individual who -
>
> > (i) has a physical or mental impairment which for such individual constitutes or results in a substantial impediment to employment; and
> >
> > (ii) can benefit in terms of an employment outcome from vocational rehabilitation services provided pursuant to subchapter I, III, or VI.
>
> **(B) Certain programs; limitations on major life activities.** Subject to subparagraphs (C), (D), (E), and (F), the term **"individual with a disability"** means, for purposes of sections 701, 711, and 712 of this title, and subchapters II, IV, V,[237] and VII of this chapter, any person who has a disability **as defined in section 12102** of title 42.[238, 239]

In subsection B (above), the term **"individual with a disability"** means, <"for purposes of" Subchapter V>[240] "any person who has a disability as defined in section 12102 of title 42," which is the **definition** of <"Disability" in the Americans with Disabilities Act,> is incorporated by reference here in Section 504.

To fully master the definition of a disability as defined by Section 504 and ADA concerning public entities, be aware that **the ADA statute is the starting point and provides an overview definition**. Look first at <42 U.S.C. § 12102> and then <34 CFR § 104.3(j)> and <28 CFR § 35.108>, the Section 504 and the ADA regulations respectively. As discussed later in this Chapter, the ADA "Definition" has four subsections: "disability," "major life activities," being "regarded as having an impairment," and "rules of construction."

Unlike IDEA, the essence of Section 504 is in the regulations and policy statements from the Office for Civil Rights (OCR) of the USDOE, the caselaw, and its interaction with ADA.

Section 504 **does not require** a public school to provide an IEP that is designed to meet a child's unique needs and provide the child with educational benefit. Under Section 504, the child may be entitled to a Section 504 Plan, (discussed later in this chapter). Under Section 504, fewer specific procedural safeguards are available to the child with a disability and the child's parents than under IDEA. However, in some instances, Section 504 may provide greater remedies and protections than those available to an IDEA child with an IEP. <Chapter 7> contains the text of selected sections from **The Rehabilitation Act of 1973** and the **Section 504 regulations** published by the U.S. Department of Education in Title 34 of the Code of Federal Regulations at Part 104.

Parents, teachers, administrators, advocates, and special education attorneys should have a copy of "**Parent and Educator Resource Guide to Section 504 in Public Elementary and Secondary Schools**" published by OCR and available at the USDOE's OCR website[241] and, as a backup, from Wrightslaw.[242]

---

236   Entities who do not receive any form of federal funds, and private entities such as private schools, daycare centers. graduate schools, and other, non-public school educational facilities, although not impacted by Section 504, may not discriminate based on Title III in the ADA and the ADA regulations in Part 36. Public schools are covered by Title II in the ADA statute and the ADA regulations in Part 35. **Entities "controlled" by religious organizations are exempt from the ADA**.

237   Subchapter V is the "Rights and Advocacy" portion of Chapter 16 and can be viewed at:
https://www.law.cornell.edu/uscode/text/29/chapter-16/subchapter-V

238   29 U.S.C. § 705(20)(B) is the definition of an individual with a disability in Section 504.

239   42 U.S.C. § 12102 is the definition of an individual with a disability in the ADA.

240   Subchapter V "of this chapter" is 29 U.S.C. § 794

241   https://www2.ed.gov/about/offices/list/ocr/docs/504-resource-guide-201612.pdf

242   https://www.wrightslaw.com/law/ocr/sec504.guide.ocr.2016.pdf

We did not include the full text of the Act in this book, but included the key provisions of the law that apply to children and adults in preschool, daycare, public / private educational settings and higher education. We focus on four sections in "General Provisions," and two sections in Subchapter V that cover "Rights and Advocacy," and, **29 U.S.C. § 794,** which is known as "**Section 504 of The Rehabilitation Act of 1973.**"

In Chapter 7, you will find the key sections and related federal regulations for The Rehabilitation Act and Section 504. Chapter 8 has the key sections and related federal regulations of the Americans with Disabilities Act (ADA).

The Rehabilitation Act of 1973 and Section 504 of that Act are **interrelated with** the ADA. Each "incorporates by reference" portions of the other's statutory language. A later change of a word or phrase by Congress in one law automatically changes that word or phrase in the other law without further revision required.

This overview of The Rehabilitation Act and Section 504, as they apply in educational scenarios, provides the critical sections in the U.S. Code and regulations from the CFR with a summary of each.

Sections of The Rehabilitation Act of 1973

Title 29 of the United States Code[243] has thirty-two chapters covering "Family and Medical Leave," "Employee Polygraph Protection," "Migrant Worker Protection" and more. We focus **only on Chapter 16** titled Vocational Rehabilitation[244] which includes **The Rehabilitation Act of 1973** and consists of **approximately 100 sections** about issues such as employment, independent living and vocational rehabilitation.

Chapter 16 begins with **"General Provisions"** which has 18 sections. In Chapter 7 of this book, you will find 4 of the 18 sections of the "General Provisions"[245] and 2 of the 11 sections from subchapter V.[246]

"Section 504" of The Rehabilitation Act of 1973 is a **single section**[247] in subchapter V of Chapter 16 of Title 29.

The Rehabilitation Act of 1973 - General Provisions

29 U.S.C. § 701 - Findings and Purpose

In Section 701, Congress found that "millions of Americans have one or more physical or mental disabilities and the number of Americans with such disabilities is increasing . . . ." "[T]he goals of the Nation properly include the goal of providing individuals with disabilities with the tools necessary to . . . achieve equality of opportunity, full inclusion . . . and **economic and social self-sufficiency . . . .**"[248]

Congress wants the Federal Government to play "a leadership role in promoting the employment of individuals with disabilities, especially individuals with significant disabilities, and . . . to ensure, to the greatest extent possible, that youth with disabilities and students with disabilities **who are transitioning from** receipt of special education services under the **Individuals with Disabilities Education Act** (20 U.S.C. § 1400 *et seq.*), and receipt of services under **section 794**[249] of this title have **opportunities for postsecondary success**.

---

243 https://www.law.cornell.edu/uscode/text/29

244 https://www.law.cornell.edu/uscode/text/29/chapter-16

245 29 U.S.C. §§ 707, 702, 705, 712

246 29 U.S.C. §§ 794, 794a

247 <29 U.S.C. § 794>

248 *See* 29 U.S.C. § 701(a)(6)(B). In IDEA at 20 U.S.C. § 1400(c) Congress emphasized economic self-sufficiency.

249 Section 794 of Title 29 is the actual "Section 504 of the Rehabilitation Act" statute. (29 U.S.C. § 794)

29 U.S.C. § 702 - Rehabilitative Services Administration

Several federal agencies are charged with monitoring the Rehabilitation Act depending on the agency, (transportation, communication, etc.) Education is governed by 29 U.S.C. § 702 - Rehabilitative Services Administration, which states that there "is established in the Office of the Secretary in the Department of Education a Rehabilitation Services Administration which shall be headed by a Commissioner . . . ."[250] Section 504 regulations are specific to each agency.

29 U.S.C. § 705 - Definitions

The 42 definitions in 29 U.S.C. § 705 are listed in alphabetical order. Significant definitions in this book include (3) Assistive technology terms, (9) Disability, (16) Impartial hearing officer, (18) Independent living services, **(20) Individual with a disability,** (21) Individual with a significant disability, (37) Student with a disability, and (42) youth with a disability.[251]

As noted previously, **Subsection 20** explains that the term "**individual with a disability**" means . . . any person who has a disability as defined in section 12102 of title 42" [of the ADA].[252]

In **Subsection 37,** the "term '**student with a disability**' means an individual with a disability who . . . is eligible for, and receiving, special education or related services **under [IDEA]** . . . **or** (II) is an individual with a disability, for purposes of **section 794**[253] of this title."

29 U.S.C. § 712 - Information clearinghouse

The Information clearinghouse requires the Secretary of Education to establish an "Office of Information and Resources for Individuals with Disabilities"[254] to provide information and data about "the location, provision, and availability of services and programs for individuals with disabilities."

The Rehabilitation Act of 1973 - Subchapter V - Rights and Advocacy

"Rights and Advocacy" in Title 29, Chapter 16, Subchapter V,[255] contains eleven sections. Two sections directly related to this book are **Sections 794 and 794a. The first one, 794, is the essence of Section 504.** It establishes that there shall be "Nondiscrimination." The next section, 794a, provides the right to remedies and attorneys fees.

29 U.S.C. § 794 - Nondiscrimination under Federal grants and programs.

This section is virtually unchanged from its original language[256] in 1973 and **in subsection (a),** states that:

No otherwise qualified individual with a disability in the United States, as defined in section 705(20) of this title, shall, **solely by reason of her or his disability, be excluded from** the participation in, be denied the benefits of, or **be subjected to discrimination** under any program or activity receiving **Federal financial assistance** or under any program or activity conducted by any Executive agency or by the United States Postal Service.

---

250   29 U.S.C. § 702(a)

251   An example of the definitions we excluded from this book are "competitive integrated employment" and "construction."

252   Pursuant to 29 U.S.C. § 705(20)(F) excluded are those who have ". . . pedophilia, exhibitionism, voyeurism . . . or other sexual behavior disorders . . . ."

253   Section 504 of the Rehabilitation Act of 1973.

254   29 U.S.C. § 712(c)

255   https://www.law.cornell.edu/uscode/text/29/chapter-16/subchapter-V

256   At: https://www.govinfo.gov/content/pkg/STATUTE-87/pdf/STATUTE-87-Pg355.pdf

go to page 394 of The Act for Section 504 as originally written by Congress in 1973. *See* the history of Section 504 in Chapter 2.

The head of each such agency shall promulgate such regulations as may be necessary to carry out the amendments to this section . . . .[257]

The regulations provide greater specificity in determinating whether there is a violation. Section 794 of "Section 504" is followed immediately by Section 794a about "Remedies and attorney fees."[258]

29 U.S.C. § 794a - Remedies and attorney fees[259]

Subsections (a) and (b) incorporate by reference the Civil Rights Act of 1964[260] and authorize "a reasonable attorney's fee as part of the costs."[261]

Section 504 Rehabilitation Act Regulations

The **essence of Section 504 is in its regulations and the Part 35**[262] **regulations for the ADA**. Chapter 7 of this book contains selected regulations for Section 504 issued by the USDOE and Chapter 8 contains the ADA regulations.

The Section 504 regulations are located in Title 34 of the Code of Federal Regulations (CFR) beginning at 34 CFR Part 104.[263] They are broken down into Subparts A through G and two appendices, A and B, that provide an "Analysis of Final Regulation," and Guidelines.

Subpart A - General Provisions

34 CFR § 104.1 - Purpose explains that the "purpose of this part is to effectuate section 504 of the Rehabilitation Act of 1973, which is **designed to eliminate discrimination on the basis of handicap** in any program or activity receiving Federal financial assistance."

34 CFR § 104.2 - Application notes that this "Part 104" applies to **each recipient of Federal financial assistance** from the Department of Education and to the program or activity that receives such assistance.

<34 CFR § 104.3 - Definitions> include Federal financial assistance, handicapped person, physical or mental impairment, major life activity, qualified handicapped person, and more.

34 CFR § 104.4 - "Discrimination Prohibited" repeats the language in 29 U.S.C. § 794 and explains in **104.4(b)(1)** that a recipient of federal funds **may not:**

> **(b)(1)**
>
> **(i)** Deny a qualified handicapped person the opportunity **to participate in or benefit** from the aid, benefit, or service;
>
> **(ii)** Afford a qualified handicapped person an opportunity to participate in or benefit from the aid, benefit, or service that is **not equal** to that afforded others;
>
> **(iii)** Provide a qualified handicapped person with an aid, benefit, or service that **is not as effective** as that provided to others;
>
> . . .
>
> **(vii) Otherwise limit** a qualified handicapped person in the enjoyment of any right, privilege, advantage, or opportunity enjoyed by others receiving an aid, benefit, or service.[264]

---

257   29 U.S.C. § 794(a)

258   Pay attention to the parentheses, **794 and 794a are two different statutes**. The first subsection of each statute is 794(a) and 794a(a)!

259   29 U.S.C. § 794a(a)

260   *See* 42 U.S.C. Chapter 21 at: https://www.law.cornell.edu/uscode/text/42/chapter-21

261   29 U.S.C. § 794a(b)

262   Part 36 Regulations of the ADA apply to private entities and other, similar public entities.

263   https://www.law.cornell.edu/cfr/text/34/part-104

264   34 CFR § 104.4(b)(1)

In the next subsection at **104.4(b)(2),** the aids, benefits, and services "must afford handicapped persons **equal opportunity** to obtain the same result, to gain the same benefit, or to reach the same level of achievement, in the most integrated setting appropriate to the person's needs."[265]

34 CFR § 104.7 - Designation of responsible employee requires that the agency must have a Section 504 Coordinator and adopt "grievance procedures that incorporate appropriate due process standards and that provide for the prompt and equitable resolution of complaints alleging any action prohibited by this part."
The above regulations are in <**Subpart A of Part 104 of the Section 504 regulations**.>

Subpart B - Employment Practices [not included][266]
<Subpart C - Accessibility>

34 CFR § 104.21 - Discrimination prohibited. - No qualified handicapped person shall, because a recipient's facilities are **inaccessible to or unusable by handicapped persons,** be denied the benefits of, be excluded from participation in, or otherwise be subjected to discrimination under any program or activity to which this part applies.

34 CFR § 104.22 - Existing facilities explains that, in the above regulation, when each part of a program or activity "is viewed in its entirety, it is readily accessible to handicapped persons," but is not required that "every part of" its facilities be "accessible to and usable by handicapped persons."

<Subpart D - Preschool, Elementary, Secondary, and Adult Education>

Subpart D[267] of Part 104, applies to **preschool, elementary, secondary, and adult education** programs and activities that receive federal financial assistance.

34 CFR § 104.32 - Location and notification requires pubic schools[268] to locate and identify "every qualified handicapped person residing in the recipient's jurisdiction who is not receiving a public education" and advise them of their rights under Section 504. This **"child find"** regulation is consistent with IDEA's "child find" requirement at <20 U.S.C. § 1412(a)(3).>

34 CFR § 104.33 - Free appropriate public education (FAPE) is different from the FAPE requirement in IDEA. The 504 regulation explains that FAPE is "the provision of **regular or special education and related aids and services** that (i) are designed to meet individual educational needs of handicapped persons **as adequately** as the needs of nonhandicapped persons are met." Implementation of an IEP developed in accordance with IDEA is one means "of meeting the standard."[269] It explains that a "free education" means one that is without cost "except for those fees that are imposed on non-handicapped persons . . . ."

"If a public or private residential placement is necessary to provide a [FAPE] ". . . the placement, **including non-medical care and room and board**, shall be provided **at no cost** to the person or his or her parents or guardian."[270]

34 CFR § 104.34 - Educational setting is similar to the <**"Least Restrictive Environment" (LRE) of IDEA**>[271] in that it mandates that the recipient of federal funds "shall educate . . . each qualified handicapped person . . . with persons who are not handicapped to the maximum extent appropriate to the needs of the handicapped person." Similar to the language in IDEA about LRE, it allows for a more restrictive setting if the "use of supplementary aids and services cannot be achieved satisfactorily." Like IDEA, for an alternate setting, it "shall take into account the proximity of the alternate setting to the person's home."

---

265   34 CFR § 104.4(b)(2)

266   Subpart B is not included in this book, but is available on the Internet at:
https://www.law.cornell.edu/cfr/text/34/part-104/subpart-B.

267   Omitted **Subparts B and C** are about employment and accessible facilities.

268   The phrase, "public schools," in the context of Section 504 and the ADA means all "preschool, elementary, secondary, and adult education programs and activities that receive federal financial assistance."

269   34 CFR § 104.33(b)(2)

270   34 CFR § 104.33(c)(3). In IDEA, *see* 20 U.S.C. § 1412(a)(10)(B)

271   20 U.S.C. § 1412(a)(5)

In **nonacademic settings**, "In providing or arranging for the provision of nonacademic and extracurricular services and activities, including meals, recess periods, . . . a recipient shall ensure that handicapped persons **participate with nonhandicapped persons in such activities and services to the maximum extent appropriate** to the needs of the handicapped person in question."

34 CFR § 104.35 - Evaluation and placement establishes that a child who "**needs or is believed to need** special education **or** related services" **must** be evaluated before "taking any action with respect to the [child's] initial placement" and any "**subsequent significant change in placement.**" This may be critical in **behavioral discipline issues** when a school is considering suspension or expulsion. i.e., a significant change in **placement of the person** in regular or special education and any **subsequent significant change in placement.**[272]

The regulation describes the criteria for tests, personnel administering the evaluations, and assurance that the placement decision is in accord with the prior regulation and is the LRE.

Reevaluations are required to be consistent with this regulation and may be accomplished by following the reevaluation procedures in <IDEA at 20 U.S.C. § 1414(a)(2).>

34 CFR § 104.36 - Procedural safeguards requires "the identification, evaluation, or educational placement" of the student. This includes notice, an opportunity to examine records, and the right to an impartial hearing. Again, as with the preceding regulation, compliance with 20 U.S.C. § 1415 in IDEA will meet this requirement.

34 CFR § 104.37 - Nonacademic services is previously addressed in 34 CFR § 104.34(b), applies to "Educational Services, "but this regulation provides more detail and requirements. It mandates that "non-academic and extracurricular services and activities [are provided] in such manner as is necessary to afford handicapped students **an equal opportunity for participation** in such services and activities."

It explains that "physical education courses . . . [etc., and] intramural athletics shall provide . . . equal opportunity for participation" and addresses "activities that are separate or different from those offered to nonhandicapped students . . ."

34 CFR § 104.38 - Preschool and adult education mandates that any recipient that provides such services, including day care, may not exclude "qualified handicapped persons" and shall take into account their needs.

34 CFR § 104.39 - Private education establishes that private schools cannot discriminate. The individual must be provided with FAPE, as defined by Section 504, subject to the school, if necessary, making minor adjustments. The school "may not charge more for . . . [FAPE] except to the extent that any additional charge is justified by a substantial increase in cost to the recipient."

<Subpart E - Postsecondary Education>

Subpart E, about higher education begins with information about admissions and recruitment.

34 CFR § 104.42 - Admissions and Recruitment explains that colleges and universities "may not apply limitations upon the number or proportion of handicapped persons who may be admitted." The admission tests are to be accessible and "accurately reflect the applicant's aptitude or achievement level." The school may not make a "**preadmission inquiry**" about presence of a disability.

34 CFR § 104.43 - Treatment of students requires the facility to provide "**an equal opportunity** for the participation of qualified handicapped persons [and] **may not, on the basis of handicap, exclude** any qualified handicapped student from any course, **course of study,**[273] or other part of its education program or activity."

---

272   In **discipline**, a "handicapped" child's removal from regular classes via an alternate placement, suspension, or expulsion can be a "significant change in placement" which **mandates an evaluation "before** taking any action." *See also* the determination as to whether an individual is covered, per the ADA at 42 U.S.C. § 12102(4) "shall be construed in favor of broad coverage" and includes "episodic" conditions and even someone who may not have a disability, but is "regarded as having a disability."

273   In the IDEA Commentary about IEPs, this phrase includes "**advanced placement courses**" for college bound students with IEPs.

34 CFR § 104.44 - Academic adjustments permits "[m]odifications [that] may include changes in the length of time permitted for the completion of degree requirements, substitution of specific courses required for the completion of degree requirements, and adaptation of the manner in which specific courses are conducted."

"Students with impaired sensory, manual, or speaking skills" are to be provided with educational auxiliary aids. However, "[r]ecipients need not provide attendants, individually prescribed devices, readers for personal use or study, or other devices or services of a personal nature."

Colleges and universities are **not required to implement** or base their "academic adjustments" on the student's prior **public school Section 504 Plan or IEP**, which have no required legal basis in higher education. Some facilities may choose to honor those documents, but they are not required to do so. However, a student may require course modifications and accommodations.

Course examinations shall represent "the student's achievement in the course, rather than reflecting the student's impaired sensory, manual" or speaking skills.

It is **not discriminatory** to maintain academic requirements that "**are essential to the instruction . . . or to any directly related licensing requirement.**"

In subsequent regulations 104.45 and 104.46, Section 504 requires that **if either housing or financial aid** is provided to those who are not handicapped, then it must be comparable for the handicapped. The requirements for providing "Nonacademic services" in **34 CFR § 104.47** is similar to the requirement in prior regulation 34 CFR § 104.37 with additional language about "Social organizations." "[F]raternities, sororities**, or similar organizations shall . . . not permit discrimination."

Subpart F - Health, Welfare, and Social Services

Subpart F goes beyond educational settings and applies to hospitals and social service agencies. Subpart F includes **34 CFR § 104.51 through 104.54** which requires that such entities "shall provide appropriate auxiliary aids to persons with impaired sensory, manual, or speaking skills, where necessary to afford such persons an equal opportunity to benefit from the service in question" and requires that "institutionalized individuals" shall be "provided an appropriate education."

34 CFR § 104.52(c) mandates emergency treatment for hearing impaired individuals. "A hospital that provides health services or benefits shall establish a procedure for effective communication with persons with impaired hearing for the purpose of providing emergency health care."

Title 34 of the Code of Federal Regulations, Part 104, ends with a single regulation in Subpart G.

Subpart G - Procedures

34 CFR § 104.61 - Procedures explains that: "The procedural provisions applicable to title VI of the Civil Rights Act of 1964 apply to this part. These procedures are found in §§ 100.6-100.10 and part 101 of this title."

End of the Overview of the Rehabilitation Act of 1973 and Section 504

Quicklinks To[274]

<IDEA Overview>
<Section 504 Overview >
<ADA Overview >

Overview of The Americans with Disabilities Act (ADA)

The ADA prohibits discrimination against individuals with disabilities in a number of settings, public and private, including nursery schools, public and private schools, colleges, universities and on professional licensing exams.[275]

The determination about whether an individual qualifies for protections under ADA **is much broader than IDEA,** is based on "broad coverage," and includes an "impairment that is episodic or in remission . . . if it would substantially limit a major life activity when active."[276]

Although the ADA is not identical to Section 504 of the Rehabilitation Act of 1973, it **was based on Section 504.** Sections of the ADA and Section 504 incorporate the other, by reference. Depending on specific factual scenarios, some courts have said that the laws mirror each other while other courts differentiated between the two. The issue is often fact specific.

As background, the Rehabilitation Act of 1973 was passed before the ADA was enacted. Section 504 has been amended several times and **is the basis** for the later **1990 Americans with Disabilities Act (ADA).**[277] The 1990 amendments to the ADA (Public Law 101-336) consisted of three initial preliminary sections and Five Titles with Subtitles and Subparts.[278]

In 2008, Congress amended the ADA (Public Law 110-325) in response to several rulings from the U.S. Supreme Court. Congress stated that the high court wrongly "interpreted the term 'substantially limits' to require a greater degree of limitation than was intended" and added that the "Act may be cited as the **ADA Amendments Act of 2008.**" However, rather than refer to this law as ADA AA, or ADAAA, as it has been described in some publications, we refer to the current law, with its 2008 amendments, as **ADA.**

This book does not include **the complete Act.** We focus on the key provisions that apply to children and adults in preschool, daycare, public / private educational settings and higher education. For example, **Title I** about "Employment" is not included in this book.[279]

This book includes portions of Title II about public schools, Title III about private schools and services, including **day care and nursery schools, and five sections from Title IV - "Miscellaneous Provisions."**[280]

---

274   **Wrightslaw Note:** Per the information provided in Chapter 1, this book contains **embedded hyperlinks.** Those who have the **E-book (adobe.pdf version),** can click on the link and go directly to the webpage or location in this book. Embedded hyperlinks are marked with a <, left pointing arrow, and a > right pointing arrow. All URLs are hyperlinked and do not have arrows.

275   42 U.S.C. § 12101(a)(3)

276   42 U.S.C. § 12102

277   The Act as passed by Congress is 191 pages long. Title V begins at page 133. Section 504 begins at page 142

278   That July 26, 1990, document is available at:
https://www.govinfo.gov/content/pkg/STATUTE-104/pdf/STATUTE-104-Pg327.pdf

279   Title I is not included as it pertains to employers and employees. Those sections, 42 U.S.C. §§ 12111 through 12117, are available at: https://www.law.cornell.edu/uscode/text/42/chapter-126/subchapter-I

280   Most are not education related. All sections - 42 U.S.C. §§ 12201-12213 are located and available at: https://www.law.cornell.edu/uscode/text/42/chapter-126/subchapter-IV

In addition to private clubs, schools and entities **"controlled" by religious organizations are exempt** from the ADA.[281]

If a school or other entity receives federal financial assistance, it is subject to Section 504.

As with Section 504, the **bulk of the ADA "law" exists primarily** in the regulations and caselaw.

The ADA regulations for Title II, III, and IV are contained in **Title 28 of the Code of Federal Regulations**. The regulations for Title II, "Public Services," including public schools, are in **28 CFR Part 35**. The regulations for private entities, including private schools, state bar exams, nursery schools, etc. are in **28 CFR Part 36**.

Differences between Title II, Part 35 and Title III, Part 36

Title II of the ADA statute and the Part 35 regulations prohibit discrimination on the basis of disability by **public entities"**[282] including **public schools**. **Title III and the Part 36 regulations prohibit** "discrimination on the basis of disability by covered **public accommodations"**[283] which include a "nursery, elementary, secondary, undergraduate, or postgraduate private school, or other place of education . . . [and] a day care center."[284]

The regulations for each Part are almost identical as they apply to a public school, a private school, or private setting. For example, the definition of "disability" in both Parts of the CFR incorporate the definition of a disability[285] in the U.S. Code, but also provide more detail and specificity. The statute is the starting point, but the details are in the regulations. **The two disability definition regulations** are in the regulations at <28 CFR § 35.108> and <28 CFR § 36.105>. If you compare these regulations, you will see that they are identical except that the phrase "public accommodation" is replaced by "public entity."

In subsection (f)(3) of the above two regulations, the last portion about establishing liability is slightly different in that one references Title II and discrimination by a public entity[286] and the other references Title III and discrimination by a "public accommodation."[287]

Enforcement of Title II and Title III **violations are different**.

The ADA Statute - Overview of Definitions

As you review a factual and legal scenario to determine whether the ADA applies, and if so, to what extent, start with <42 U.S.C. § 12101 - **Findings and Purpose**.> Then review the "**Definition of Disability**" located at <42 U.S.C. § 12102> which is applicable to **Title II and Title III**.

"Definition of Disability" has four subsections: "disability," "major life activities," being "regarded as having an impairment," and "rules of construction." To master this definition, as defined by the ADA, use the statute as your starting point. Next review the regulation in either 28 CFR Part 35 or Part 36, depending on whether a public entity or private entity is involved.

---

281   <42 U.S.C. § 12187>

282   28 CFR § 35.101 - Purpose of Part 35

283   28 CFR § 36.101 - Purpose of Part 36

284   28 CFR § 36.104(10) - Definitions

285   <42 U.S.C. § 12102>

286   28 CFR § 35.108(f)(3)

287   28 CFR § 36.105(f)(3)

In Section 12102, the **first subsection**[288] explains that **disability means**, with respect to an individual -

- (A) a physical or mental **impairment that substantially limits** one or **more major life activities** of such individual;
- (B) a **record** of such an impairment; or
- (C) **being regarded as** having such an impairment.

The definition has three prongs. **Any one of the above three,** standing alone, is sufficient for liability.

The **second subsection**[289] clarifies that "**Major life activities**" "include, but are not limited to . . . learning, reading, concentrating, thinking, communicating, and working." This also "includes the operation of a major bodily function," such as neurological issues and functions of the brain.

The definition is not intended to be limiting, but is to be construed broadly.

The **third subsection of the disability definition** is "**Regarded as having such an impairment,**"[290] which means that the issue is not whether the individual was disabled at the time of any alleged discrimination, but whether the person was regarded as having a disability **at the time** of the discrimination.

Subsection four provides "**Rules of Construction**"[291] which explains that the definition of disability shall be "construed in favor of **broad coverage**" and includes "**episodic conditions**" and "**without regard to the ameliorative effects of mitigating measures**" such as cochlear implants, prosthetics, medication, hearing aids, assistive technology, accommodations [292] or other means of mitigating the impact of the disability, other than ordinary eyeglasses and contact lenses.

For example, the student in a higher education setting who suffers from an episodic condition such as asthma or diabetes and the toddler in a day care facility or nursery school who has difficulty being potty trained are both protected.[293] These protections apply to children, students, and individuals in public schools and private schools.

Qualified Individual with a Disability - Title II and Part 35

Title II and Part 35, the statute and the regulation, contain another "Disability" definition at <42 U.S.C. § 12131(2)> and <28 CFR § 35.104.> The definitions are identical and state that "The term '**qualified individual with a disability**' means an individual with a disability who,** with or without reasonable modifications to rules, policies, or practices, the removal of architectural, communication, or transportation barriers, or the provision of auxiliary aids and services, **meets the essential eligibility requirements** for the receipt of services or the participation in programs or activities provided by a public entity."

Title II, III, and IV in Educational Settings

For our purposes, **three "Titles" in the ADA** apply to educational settings:

Title II - Public Services includes public schools;
Title III - Public Accommodations and Services Operated by Private Entities includes private schools and universities; and
Title IV - Miscellaneous Provisions

---

288   42 U.S.C. § 12102(1)

289   42 U.S.C. § 12102(2)

290   42 U.S.C. § 12102(3)

291   42 U.S.C. § 12102(4)

292   42 U.S.C. § 12102(4)(E)

293   42 U.S.C. § 12181(7)(J) and (K)

Title II begins with the definition of a "**Public Entity**" followed by "The term 'qualified individual with a disability' means an individual with a disability who . . . meets the essential eligibility requirements for the receipt of services or the participation in programs or activities provided by a public entity."[294] It then explains that "no qualified individual with a disability **shall, by reason of such disability, be excluded** from participation in or be denied the benefits of the services, programs, or activities of a public entity, or be subjected to discrimination by any such entity."[295]

The next section[296] describes how ADA violations will be enforced. "The remedies, procedures, and rights set forth **in section 794a of title 29**[297] **shall be the remedies,** procedures, and rights this subchapter provides to any person alleging discrimination on the basis of disability in violation of section 12132 of this title."[298]

Title III - "**Public Accommodations and Private Entities**" initially defines a "private entity" as "any entity other than a public entity"[299] and includes hotels, restaurants, movie theaters, auditoriums, stores, parks, zoos, places of recreation, "a nursery, elementary, secondary, undergraduate, or postgraduate private school, or other place of education; . . . and a day care center," places of exercise, recreation and other establishments.[300]

The next part of Title III explains that, as a general rule, "[n]o individual shall be discriminated against** on the basis of disability **in the full and equal enjoymen**t of the goods, services, facilities, privileges, advantages, or accommodations of any place of public accommodation by any person who owns, leases (or leases to), or operates a place of public accommodation."[301]

Title III explains that **it is discrimination to deny the person an opportunity "to participate in or benefi**t from the goods, services, facilities, privileges, advantages, or accommodations of an entity." If the "benefit" provided is **unequal, that is discrimination** and typically a "separate benefit" is also discriminatory.[302]

Similar to the **"Least Restrictive Environment" (LRE)**[303] in IDEA, the ADA emphasizes that "goods, services, facilities, privileges, advantages, and accommodations shall be afforded to an individual with a disability in the **most integrated setting** appropriate to the needs of the individual."[304]

Title III provides "**Specific prohibitions**" and notes that "discrimination includes—

(i) the imposition or application of **eligibility criteria that screen out or tend to screen out an individual** . . . [and]
(ii) **a failure to make reasonable modifications** in policies, practices, or procedures, when such modifications are necessary . . . ."[305]

An exception to the failure to make a reasonable modification is if the entity can "demonstrate that making such modifications would **fundamentally alter**[306] the nature of such goods, services, facilities, privileges, advantages, or accommodations."[307]

---

294   42 U.S.C. § 12131(2)

295   42 U.S.C. § 12132

296   42 U.S.C. § 12133

297   This incorporates by reference 29 U.S.C. § 794 - The Rehabilitation Act of 1973.

298   42 U.S.C. § 12133

299   42 U.S.C. § 12181(6)

300   42 U.S.C. § 12181(6) and (7)

301   42 U.S.C. § 12182(a)

302   42 U.S.C. § 12182(b)(1)(A)

303   20 U.S.C. § 1412(a)(5)

304   42 U.S.C. § 12182(b)(1)(B)

305   42 U.S.C. § 12182(b)(2)(A)

306   Whether the modification or accommodation would "fundamentally alter" the program is a major issue in many ADA cases.

307   42 U.S.C. § 12182(b)(2)(A)(ii)

ADA also prohibits the "**failure to remove architectural barriers** . . . where such removal is readily achievable."[308]

Exceptions are direct threats to health and safety that cannot be "eliminated by a modification of policies, practices, or procedures or by the provision of auxiliary aids or services."[309]

Private schools "**controlled by religious organizations" are exempted** from the ADA.[310]

Enforcement of the ADA

Enforcement of Title II and Title III violations are different. While **enforcement of Title II against Public Services is through Section 504** of the Rehabilitation Act of 1973, **enforcement of Title III is through the statutory provisions in the Civil Rights Act.**[311]

For **discrimination by a public entity in violation of Title II,** such as a public school, the "remedies, procedures, and rights set forth in section 794a of title 29[312] **shall be** the remedies, procedures, and rights this subchapter provides to any person alleging discrimination on the basis of disability in violation . . ." of this title.[313] In other words, a Title II violation is handled pursuant to a Section 504 lawsuit. A private citizen can file a complaint in federal court seeking enforcement, but, as noted above, 29 U.S.C. § 794a provides the remedies and procedures. If the defendant is a public school, depending upon the "gravamen"[314] of the case and relief sought, the plaintiff may have to exhaust their administrative remedies pursuant to IDEA.[315]

For **discrimination by a private school**, nursery school, or other "covered public accommodation" in **violation of Title III**, either the Attorney General or a private citizen can file a complaint in federal court seeking enforcement of this statute.[316] Unlike most IDEA disputes, since the defendant is not a public school, the plaintiff does not have to exhaust administrative remedies.[317]

The law explains that if the Attorney General believes that an individual or a group are engaged in a practice or pattern of discrimination, or that a person has been discriminated against, "the Attorney General may commence a civil action in any appropriate United States district court."[318] In a footnote to <42 U.S.C. § 12181(7)(K)>, noting that a day care center is covered, is a link to the U.S. District Court Complaint filed by the U.S. Department of Justice in its lawsuit against Chesterbrook Academy, a day care center in New Jersey. The Complaint and November, 2019 Settlement Agreement are on the Wrightslaw website.

In a lawsuit filed by an individual or by the Department of Justice, the court may grant "equitable relief that such court considers to be appropriate" including an injunction and a requirement that a policy or practice be modified and may order monetary damages.[319]

Title III of the ADA mandates that "Any person that offers examinations or courses related to applications, licensing, certification, or credentialing for secondary or postsecondary education, professional, or trade purposes shall

---

308   42 U.S.C. § 12182(b)(2)(A)(iv)

309   42 U.S.C. § 12182(b)(3)

310   <42 U.S.C. § 12187>

311   42 U.S.C. § 12188 and 42 U.S.C. § 2000a through 2000a-6, located at:
https://www.law.cornell.edu/uscode/text/42/chapter-21/subchapter-II

312   Section 504 of the Rehabilitation Act

313   <42 U.S.C. § 12133 - Enforcement of Title II>

314   *See* the SCOTUS 2017 *Fry* case discussed in the Chapter 5 footnote to 20 U.S.C. § 1415(l)

315   20 U.S.C. § 1415(l)

316   <42 U.S.C. § 12188 - Enforcement of Title III>

317   <20 U.S.C. § 1415(l) - Exhaustion of Administrative Remedies>

318   42 U.S.C. § 12188(b)

319   42 U.S.C. § 12188(b)(2)

offer such examinations or courses in a place **and manner accessible to persons with disabilities** or offer alternative accessible arrangements for such individuals."[320]

Frequent examples are prospective attorneys taking **State Bar Exams** and medical students taking the **United States Medical Licensing Examination (USMLE)**. *See* the footnote to <42 U.S.C. § 12189> in regard to the NY Bar Exam *Bartlett* case ruled on by Justice Sotomayor and the December, 2019 *Ramsay* medical student case.

Title IV - Miscellaneous Provisions explains that "[n]othing in this chapter shall be construed to require an individual with a disability **to accept an accommodation**, aid, service, opportunity, or benefit which such individual chooses not to accept."[321] **A state is not immune** under the eleventh amendment to the Constitution of the United States from an action in Federal or State court of competent jurisdiction for a violation of this chapter.[322]

It is unlawful for anyone to "coerce, intimidate, threaten, or interfere" with anyone who has "made a charge, testified, assisted, or participated in any manner in an investigation."[323]

End of Overview about the Americans with Disabilities Act

In Summation

This Chapter 4 includes an overview of IDEA, Section 504, and the ADA. **Chapter 5** includes the full text of the Individuals with Disabilities Education Act of 2004 with our comments and footnotes.

Quicklinks To

<IDEA Overview>
<Section 504 Overview >
<ADA Overview >

End of Chapter 4 - Overview of IDEA, 504, ADA, Selected Topics

---

320 42 U.S.C. § 12189

321 42 U.S.C. § 12201

322 42 U.S.C. § 12202

323 42 U.S.C. § 12203

Hyperlinks to Chapters

Ch. 01 Introduction	Ch. 06 IDEA Regulations
Ch. 02 History	Ch. 07 Section 504
Ch. 03 Overview of Law, Courts, Research	Ch. 08 ADA
Ch. 04 Overview of IDEA, Section 504, ADA	Ch. 09 Other laws
Ch. 05 IDEA (US Code)	Ch. 10 Selected Topics

CHAPTER 5

Individuals with Disabilities Education Act
20 U.S.C. § 1400 *et seq.*

Part A / Subchapter I - General Provisions[1]

<20 U.S.C. § 1400. Short Title; Findings; Purposes>
<20 U.S.C. § 1401. Definitions>
20 U.S.C. § 1402. Office of Special Education Programs
20 U.S.C. § 1403. Abrogation of State Sovereign Immunity
20 U.S.C. § 1404. Acquisition of Equipment; Construction or Alteration of Facilities
20 U.S.C. § 1405. Employment of Individuals with Disabilities
20 U.S.C. § 1406. Requirements for Prescribing Regulations
20 U.S.C. § 1407. State Administration
20 U.S.C. § 1408. Paperwork Reduction
20 U.S.C. § 1409. Freely Associated States

< Part B / Subchapter II - Assistance for Education of All Children with Disabilities>[2]

20 U.S.C. § 1411. Authorization; Allotment; Use of Funds; Authorization of Appropriations
<20 U.S.C. § 1412. State Eligibility>
20 U.S.C. § 1413. Local Educational Agency Eligibility
<20 U.S.C. § 1414. Evaluations, Eligibility Determinations, IEPs, and Educational Placements>
<20 U.S.C. § 1415. Procedural Safeguards>
20 U.S.C. § 1416. Monitoring, Technical Assistance, and Enforcement
20 U.S.C. § 1417. Administration
20 U.S.C. § 1418. Program Information
20 U.S.C. § 1419. Preschool Grants

---

1   Subchapter I is known as Part A of IDEA.

2   Subchapter II is known as Part B of IDEA.

<Part C / Subchapter III[3] - Infants and Toddlers with Disabilities>

20 U.S.C. § 1431. Findings and Policy

20 U.S.C. § 1433. General Authority

20 U.S.C. § 1434. Eligibility

20 U.S.C. § 1435. Requirements for Statewide System

<20 U.S.C. § 1436. Individualized Family Service Plan>

20 U.S.C. § 1437. State Application and Assurances

20 U.S.C. § 1438. Uses of Funds

20 U.S.C. § 1439. Procedural Safeguards

20 U.S.C. § 1440. Payor of Last Resort

20 U.S.C. § 1441. State Interagency Coordinating Council

20 U.S.C. § 1442. Federal Administration

20 U.S.C. § 1443. Allocation of Funds

20 U.S.C. § 1444. Authorization of Appropriations

<Part D / Subchapter IV[4, 5] - National Activities to Improve Education of Children with Disabilities>

20 U.S.C. § 1450. Findings

Part A - State Personnel Development Grants

20 U.S.C. § 1451. Purpose; Definition of Personnel; Program Authority

20 U.S.C. § 1452. Eligibility and Collaborative Process

20 U.S.C. § 1453. Applications

20 U.S.C. § 1454. Use of Funds

20 U.S.C. § 1455. Authorization of Appropriations

Part B - Personnel Preparation, Technical Assistance, Model Demonstration Projects, and Dissemination of Information

20 U.S.C. § 1461. Purpose; Definition of Eligible Entity

20 U.S.C. § 1462. Personnel Development to Improve Services and Results for Children with Disabilities

20 U.S.C. § 1463. Technical Assistance, Demonstration Projects, and Scientifically Based Research

20 U.S.C. § 1464. Studies and Evaluations

20 U.S.C. § 1465. Interim Alternative Educational Settings, Behavioral Supports, and School Interventions

20 U.S.C. § 1466. Authorization of Appropriations

Part C - Supports to Improve Results for Children with Disabilities

20 U.S.C. § 1470. Purposes

20 U.S.C. § 1471. Parent Training and Information Centers

20 U.S.C. § 1472. Community Parent Resource Centers

---

3   Subchapter III is known as Part C of IDEA.

4   Subchapter IV is known as Part D of IDEA.

5   After § 1450, **this subchapter, Part D, (Subchapter IV) contains four subparts**: A, B, C, and D, which can be confusing.

20 U.S.C. § 1473. Technical Assistance for Parent Training and Information Centers

20 U.S.C. § 1474. Technology Development, Media Services; and Instructional Materials

20 U.S.C. § 1475. Authorization of Appropriations

Part D - General Provisions

20 U.S.C. § 1481. Comprehensive Plan for Subparts 2 and 3

20 U.S.C. § 1482. Administrative Provisions

HyperLinks to Specific Sections in IDEA

20 U.S.C. § 1400	Findings and Purposes	20 U.S.C. § 1415	Procedural Safeguards
20 U.S.C. § 1401	Definitions	20 U.S.C. § 1415(b)(1)	Indep. Educ. Eval. IEE
20 U.S.C. § 1412	State Responsibilities	20 U.S.C. § 1415(f)	Due Process Hearing
20 U.S.C. § 1414(a)	Evaluations	20 U.S.C. § 1415(j)	Stay-Put / Pendency
20 U.S.C. § 1414(d)	IEPs	20 U.S.C. § 1415(k)	Discipline

The Individuals with Disabilities Education Act of 2004
Part A – General Provisions[6]

Part A of the Individuals with Disabilities Education Act, General Provisions, includes Sections 1400 through Section 1409 of Title 20 of the United States Code (U.S.C.). Section 1400(d) is the most important section in IDEA. It describes the purpose of the law. Next, Section 1401, includes the legal definitions in alphabetical order. Section 1403 advises that states are not immune from suit if they violate IDEA. Section 1406 describes the requirements and timelines for the federal special education regulations.

20 U.S.C. § 1400. Congressional Findings and Purposes

20 U.S.C. § 1401. Definitions

20 U.S.C. § 1402. Office of Special Education Programs

20 U.S.C. § 1403. Abrogation of State Sovereign Immunity

20 U.S.C. § 1404. Acquisition of Equipment; Construction or Alteration of Facilities

20 U.S.C. § 1405. Employment of Individuals with Disabilities

20 U.S.C. § 1406. Requirements for Prescribing Regulations

20 U.S.C. § 1407. State Administration

20 U.S.C. § 1408. Paperwork Reduction

20 U.S.C. § 1409. Freely Associated States

---

6   **Wrightslaw Note**: Part A of the Individuals with Disabilities Education Act, General Provisions, includes Sections 1400 through Section 1409. For most readers, Section 1400(d) is the most important statute in IDEA. since it describes the purpose of the law. Section 1401 includes the legal definitions in alphabetical order. Section 1403 advises that states are not immune from suit if they violate IDEA. Section 1406 describes the requirements and timelines for the federal special education regulations.

20 U.S.C. § 1400 - Short Title; Findings; Purposes[7]

(a) Short Title.[8] This title may be cited as the 'Individuals with Disabilities Education Act.'

(b) Omitted.

(c) Findings. Congress finds the following:

(1) Disability is a natural part of the human experience and in no way diminishes the right of individuals to participate in or contribute to society. Improving educational results for children with disabilities is an essential element of our national policy of **ensuring equality of opportunity, full participation, independent living, and economic self-sufficiency**[9] for individuals with disabilities.

(2) Before the date of enactment of the Education for All Handicapped Children Act of 1975 (Public Law 94-142), the educational needs of millions of children with disabilities were not being fully met because–

(A) the children did not receive appropriate educational services;

(B) the children **were excluded entirely from the public school system** and from being educated with their peers;

(C) **undiagnosed disabilities** prevented the children from having a successful educational experience; or

(D) a **lack of adequate resources** within the public school system forced families to find services outside the public school system.[10]

(3) Since the enactment and implementation of the Education for All Handicapped Children Act of 1975, this title has been successful in ensuring children with disabilities and the families of such children access to a free appropriate public education and in improving educational results for children with disabilities.

(4) However, the implementation of this title has been impeded by **low expectations, and an insufficient focus on applying replicable research on proven methods of teaching and learning** for children with disabilities.[11]

(5) Almost **30 years of research**[12] and experience has demonstrated that the **education of children with disabilities can be made more effective** by-

(A) having **high expectations** for such children and ensuring their **access to the general education curriculum** in the regular classroom, to the maximum extent possible, in order to-

---

7 **Wrightslaw Overview**: As noted in the above title, this section describes the findings that led Congress to pass the Education for All Handicapped Children Act of 1975 (Public Law 94-142) which is now the Individuals with Disabilities Education Act of 2004. The mission statement of the law and the most important statute in this book is Section 1400(d), the Purpose of the law! It is "to ensure that all children with disabilities have available to them a free appropriate public education that emphasizes special education and related services designed to meet their unique needs and prepare them for further education, employment and independent living" and "to ensure that the rights of children with disabilities and parents of such children are protected . . ."

When you have questions about a confusing term or section in the law, re-read Section 1400, especially Purposes in Section 1400(d). This will help you understand how the confusing portion fits into the overall purpose of the law.

8 The **Overviews, footnotes, and bold formatting** in the law were inserted by the authors and are not a part of the statutes and regulations.

9 **Independent living and economic self-sufficiency** are long term goals for our children with special needs.

10 Before Congress passed the Education for All Handicapped Children Act (Public Law 94-142) in 1975, more than one million handicapped children were excluded from school. Initially, the law focused on ensuring that children had access to an education and due process of law. When Congress reauthorized the Individuals with Disabilities Education Act (IDEA) law in 1997, they emphasized accountability and improved outcomes while maintaining the goals of access and due process. In the 2004 reauthorization of IDEA, Congress increased the focus on accountability and improved outcomes by bringing IDEA into conformity with the Elementary and Secondary Education Act of 1965 (ESEA).

11 IDEA addresses poor educational outcomes for children with disabilities by requiring "proven methods of teaching and learning" based on "replicable research." "Research based methods" are also referred to as "evidence-based." Pressure from litigation, legal rulings requiring schools to use research based methods, and ESSA are forcing school districts to adopt evidence-based teaching methods backed by research.

12 In the prior version, IDEA 97, this read "Over 20 years of research." This law was passed in 2004. When a new version is published, perhaps in the next few years, we should expect this to be revised.

(i) **meet developmental goals** and, to the maximum extent possible, the **challenging expectations that have been established for all children**; and

(ii) be **prepared to lead productive and independent adult lives**, to the **maximum extent possible**;

(B) **strengthening the role and responsibility of parents** and **ensuring that families** of such children **have meaningful opportunities to participate in the education**[13] of their children at school and at home;

(C) **coordinating this title** with other local, educational service agency, State, and Federal school improvement efforts, including improvement efforts under the **Elementary and Secondary Education Act of 1965**,[14] in order to ensure that such children benefit from such efforts and that **special education can become a service for such children rather than a place where such children are sent**;[15]

(D) providing appropriate special education and related services, and aids and supports in the regular classroom, to such children, whenever appropriate;

(E) supporting **high-quality, intensive preservice preparation and professional development** for all personnel who work with children with disabilities in order to ensure that such personnel have the skills and knowledge necessary to improve the academic achievement and functional performance of children with disabilities, including the use of **scientifically based instructional practices**, to the maximum extent possible;

(F) providing incentives for whole-school approaches, **scientifically based early reading programs, positive behavioral interventions and supports**,[16] and **early intervening services**[17] to **reduce the need to label children as disabled** in order to address the learning and behavioral needs of such children;[18]

(G) focusing resources on teaching and learning while reducing paperwork and requirements that do not assist in improving educational results; and

(H) supporting the development and use of technology, including **assistive technology devices and assistive technology services**,[19] **to maximize accessibility** for children with disabilities.

(6) While States, local educational agencies, and educational service agencies are primarily responsible for providing an education for all children with disabilities, it is in the national interest that the Federal Government have a supporting role in assisting State and local efforts to educate children with disabilities in order **to improve results for such children and to ensure equal protection of the law.**

---

13 This language supports parental observation of children in the classroom.

14 The Elementary and Secondary Education Act of 1965 (ESEA) is the federal law that was enacted to help schools educate disadvantaged children. When the ESEA was reauthorized in 2001, it was named "No Child Left Behind" (NCLB). In 2015, Congress repealed NCLB and replaced it with the Every Student Succeeds Act (ESSA), and deleted the requirements related to "highly qualified" and "core academic subjects." IDEA "incorporates by reference" some sections in ESEA which address the "improvement efforts under the ESEA." This incorporation by reference may be a direct reference to the legal citation of a section in ESEA or, via a copy and paste, may use the exact terms, language or definitions.

15 **Special education is a service, not a place.** Special education is not the classroom in the trailer or the special education school across town. Pursuant to the least restrictive environment (LRE) requirement in 20 U.S.C. § 1412(a)(5), special education services should be delivered in general education settings except "when the nature or severity of the disability of the child is such that education in regular classes with the use of supplementary aids and services cannot be achieved satisfactorily." When school personnel view special education as a "place," they fail to evaluate the child's unique needs and how the school can meet these needs.

16 *See* the "**special factors**" in the IEP statute at <20 U.S.C. § 1414(d)(3)(B)(i)> for the requirement that "the IEP Team shall (i) in the case of a child whose behavior impedes the child's learning or that of others, consider the use of positive behavior interventions and supports, and other strategies, to address that behavior."

17 Early intervening services (EIS) are for children "who have not been identified as needing special education or related services, but who need additional academic and behavioral support to succeed in a general education environment." *See* 20 U.S.C. § 1413(f)(1).

18 Many school districts refuse to evaluate or provide special education services until after a child fails. This **"wait to fail"** model has tragic results. The neurological "window of opportunity" for learning to read begins to close during elementary school. Late remediation is more difficult and carries a high price tag, emotionally and economically.

19 Assistive technology devices and services are defined in 20 U.S.C. § 1401 and in the <u>Assistive Technology Act</u> at 29 U.S.C. § 3002. The IEP team "**shall consider** whether the child needs assistive technology devices and services." 20 U.S.C. § 1414(d)(3)(B)(v).

(7) A more equitable allocation of resources is essential for the Federal Government to meet its responsibility to **provide an equal educational opportunity** for all individuals.

(8) Parents and schools should be given expanded **opportunities to resolve their disagreements in positive and constructive ways.**

(9) Teachers, schools, local educational agencies, and States should be relieved of **irrelevant and unnecessary paperwork** burdens that do not lead to improved educational outcomes.

(10)

(A) The Federal Government must be responsive to the growing needs of an **increasingly diverse society**.

(B) America's **ethnic profile is rapidly changing**. In 2000, 1 of every 3 persons in the United States was a member of a **minority group** or was **limited English proficient**.

(C) Minority children comprise an increasing percentage of public school students.

(D) With such changing demographics, recruitment efforts for special education personnel should focus on **increasing** the participation of **minorities in the teaching profession** in order to provide appropriate role models with sufficient knowledge to address the special education needs of these students.

(11)

(A) The **limited English proficient population is the fastest growing in our Nation**, and the growth is occurring in many parts of our Nation.

(B) Studies have documented apparent **discrepancies in** the levels of **referral and placement of limited English proficient children in special education**.

(C) Such discrepancies pose a special challenge for special education in the referral of, assessment of, and provision of services for, our Nation's students from **non-English language** backgrounds.

(12)

(A) Greater efforts are needed to **prevent** the intensification of problems connected with **mislabeling and high dropout rates among minority children with disabilities.**

(B) More minority children continue to be served in special education than would be expected from the percentage of minority students in the general school population.

(C) **African-American children** are **identified as having intellectual disabilities and emotional disturbance** at rates greater than their White counterparts.

(D) In the 1998-1999 school year, African-American children represented just 14.8 percent of the population aged 6 through 21, but comprised 20.2 percent of all children with disabilities.

(E) Studies have found that schools with predominately White students and teachers have placed **disproportionately high numbers of their minority students into special education**.

(13)

(A) As the number of **minority students** in special education **increases,** the number of **minority teachers** and related services personnel produced in colleges and universities **continues to decrease**.

(B) The **opportunity for full participation** by minority individuals, minority organizations, and Historically Black Colleges and Universities in awards for grants and contracts, boards of organizations receiving assistance under this title, peer review panels, and training of professionals in the area of special education is essential to obtain greater success in the education of minority children with disabilities.

(14) As the graduation rates for children with disabilities continue to climb, providing **effective transition services** to promote **successful post-school employment or education** is **an important measure of accountability** for children with disabilities.

(d) Purposes. The purposes of this title are—

(1)

(A) to ensure that all children with disabilities have available to them a free appropriate public education that emphasizes special education and related services designed to meet their **unique needs and prepare them for further education,**[20] **employment, and independent living;**[21]

(B) to ensure that the **rights of children** with disabilities **and parents** of such children **are protected**; and

(C) to assist States, localities, educational service agencies, and Federal agencies to provide for the education of all children with disabilities;

(2) to assist States in the **implementation of a statewide**, comprehensive, coordinated, multidisciplinary, interagency system of **early intervention services** for infants and toddlers with disabilities and their families;

(3) to ensure that educators and parents have the **necessary tools to improve educational results** for children with disabilities by supporting system improvement activities; coordinated research and personnel preparation; coordinated technical assistance, dissemination, and support; and technology development and media services; and(4) to **assess, and ensure the effectiveness of, efforts to educate children with disabilities.**[22]

20 U.S.C. § 1401 - Definitions[23]

(1) Assistive Technology Device.[24]

(A) In General. The term 'assistive technology device' means any item, piece of equipment, or product system, whether acquired commercially off the shelf, modified, or customized, that is used to increase, maintain, or improve functional capabilities of a child with a disability.

(B) Exception. The term does not include a medical device that is surgically implanted, or the replacement of such device.[25]

(2) Assistive Technology Service. The term 'assistive technology service' means any service that **directly assists a child** with a disability in the selection, acquisition, or use of an assistive technology device. Such term includes–

(A) the evaluation of the needs of such child, including a functional evaluation of the child in the child's customary environment;[26]

(B) purchasing, leasing, or otherwise providing for the acquisition of assistive technology devices by such child;

(C) selecting, designing, fitting, customizing, adapting, applying, maintaining, repairing, or replacing assistive technology devices;

(D) coordinating and using other therapies, interventions, or services with assistive technology devices, such as those associated with existing education and rehabilitation plans and programs;

---

20   Section 1400(c)(14) describes "effective transition services to promote successful post-school employment or education." The definition of "transition services" is ". . . to facilitate the child's movement from school to post-school activities, including post-secondary education . . ." 20 U.S.C. § 1401(34)

21   **Section 1400(d)(1)(A) is the mission statement of IDEA.** The purpose of special education is to prepare children with disabilities for further education, employment, and independent living. **This is the most important statute in this book.**

22   IDEA requires that all children with disabilities participate in all state and district assessments, with appropriate accommodations as determined by the IEP team.

23   **Wrightslaw Overview**: These definitions in the U.S. Code are supplemented by the definitions in the Code of Federal Regulations which begin at 34 CFR § 300.4 and continue to § 300.45. Read both sets of definitions carefully. Pay close attention to the definitions of child with a disability, free appropriate public education, least restrictive environment (LRE), IEP, related services, special education, and specific learning disability. The definitions are in alphabetical order. A definition may take you to another section of the law that provides additional information on the subject. With the regulations in the next chapter, the definitions are more detailed. We encourage you to read both carefully. The definitions in the regulations have the <"force of law.">

24   See also Universal Design at 20 U.S.C. § 1401(35) and <Selected Topics Assistive Technology in Chapter 10.>

25   *See* regulations <34 CFR §§ 300.5,> 300.6, <300.34(b),> and <300.113 about assistive technology devices, **hearing aids**> and **cochlear implants**.

26   An assistive technology evaluation may be conducted in the child's home, a customary environment for a child.

(E) training or technical assistance for such child,[27] or, where appropriate, the family of such child; and

(F) training or technical assistance for professionals (including individuals providing education and rehabilitation services), employers, or other individuals who provide services to, employ, or are otherwise substantially involved in the major life functions of such child.

(3) Child With A Disability.[28, 29]

(A) In General. The term '**child with a disability**' means a child–

(i) with intellectual disabilities,[30] hearing impairments (including deafness), speech or language impairments, visual impairments (including blindness), serious emotional disturbance (referred to in this title as 'emotional disturbance'), orthopedic impairments, autism, traumatic brain injury, other health impairments, or specific learning disabilities; and

(ii) **who, by reason thereof needs special education and related services.**[31, 32]

(B) Child Aged 3 Through 9. The term '**child with a disability**' for a child aged 3 through 9 (or any subset of that age range, including ages 3 through 5),[33] may, at the discretion of the State and the local educational agency, include a child–

(i) experiencing developmental delays, as defined by the State and as measured by appropriate diagnostic instruments and procedures, in 1 or more of the following areas: physical development; cognitive development; communication development; social or emotional development; or adaptive development; and

(ii) who, by reason thereof, needs special education and related services.[34, 35]

(4) Core Academic Subjects. - Repealed[36] in 2015 pursuant to ESSA that replaced NCLB.

(5) Educational Service Agency. The term '**educational service agency**' means a regional public multiservice agency-authorized by State law to develop, manage, and provide services or programs to local educational agencies; and recognized as an administrative agency for purposes of the provision of special education and related services provided within public elementary schools and secondary schools of the State; and includes any other public institution

---

27   Children with disabilities need to be taught how to use technology devices and services to increase and improve their ability to function independently in and out of school. Technology devices include, but are not limited to, dictation software, text readers, and computerized speaking devices. Parents, teachers, and other professionals also need training to use the technology.

28   The USDOE's definition of a "child with a disability" in the regulations is much more comprehensive. *See* <34 CFR § 300.8> in the next chapter of this book.

29   Many states have forms and checklists on their website to assist in answering questions about eligibility, IEEs, Discipline, etc. *See* https://www.dpi.nc.gov/districts-schools/classroom-resources/exceptional-children/federal-regulations-state-policies#forms

30   In 2010, pursuant to "Rosa's Law," the words "mental retardation" were deleted throughout IDEA and replaced with "intellectual disabilities."

31   A child with a disability is not automatically eligible for special education and related services under IDEA. The key phrase is "who, by reason thereof, needs special education and related services." The disability must "**adversely affect**" educational performance. A child can advance steadily from grade to grade, without failing grades, and still be classified as a child with a disability. *See* 34 CFR § 300.101(c). If a child has a disability but does not need special education services, the child may be eligible for protections under Section 504 of the Rehabilitation Act. *See* more about Section 504 in this book in Chapter 7 and at: https://www.wrightslaw.com/info/sec504.index.htm.

32   Classification by disability, **is not required** prior to providing an IEP. *See* 20 U.S.C. § 1412(a)(3)(B)

33   Part C describes early intervention services for infants and toddlers with disabilities under three years of age and their families.

34   School districts may provide special education services to children with developmental delays, whether or not the child has a specific disability label. If a child between the ages of 3 and 9 has a developmental delay but has not been found eligible for services under Section 1401(3)(A)(i), this section may open the door to special education services. The requirement that schools provide services to young children with developmental delays is intended to address their needs for early intervention services.

35   If a child only needs a related service, then depending on the state regulations, the child may or may not be eligible for an IEP. 34 CFR § 300.8. However, related services are mandated under Section 504. *See* Chapter 7 in this book.

36   This term is included in Chapter 28 of Title 20 at 20 U.S.C. § 1021(3). https://www.law.cornell.edu/uscode/text/20/1021.

or agency having administrative control and direction over a public elementary school or secondary school.

(6) Elementary School. The term '**elementary school**' means a nonprofit institutional day or residential school, including a public elementary charter school,[37] that provides elementary education, as determined under State law.

(7) Equipment. The term '**equipment**' includes–

(A) machinery, utilities, and built-in equipment, and any necessary enclosures or structures to house such machinery, utilities, or equipment; and

(B) all other items necessary for the functioning of a particular facility as a facility for the provision of educational services, including items such as instructional equipment and necessary furniture; printed, published, and audio-visual instructional materials; telecommunications, sensory, and other technological aids and devices; and books, periodicals, documents, and other related materials.

(8) Excess Costs. The term '**excess costs**' means those costs that are in excess of the average annual per-student expenditure in a local educational agency during the preceding school year for an elementary school or secondary school student, as may be appropriate, and which shall be computed after deducting-

(A) amounts received–

(i) under part B;

(ii) under part A of title I of the Elementary and Secondary Education Act of 1965; and

(iii) under part A of title III of that Act; and

(B) any State or local funds expended for programs that would qualify for assistance under any of those parts

(9) Free Appropriate Public Education. The term '**free appropriate public education**'[38] means special education and related services that–[39]

(A) have been provided at public expense, under public supervision and direction, and without charge;

(B) meet the standards of the State educational agency;

(C) include an appropriate preschool, elementary school, or secondary school education in the State involved; and

(D) are provided in conformity with the individualized education program required under Section 1414(d) of this title.

(10) Highly Qualified. Repealed in 2015 pursuant to ESSA replacing NCLB.

(11) Homeless Children. The term '**homeless children**' has the meaning given the term 'homeless children and youths' in Section 11434a of title 42.[40, 41]

(12) Indian. The term '**Indian**' means an individual who is a member of an Indian tribe.

(13) Indian Tribe. The term '**Indian tribe**' means any Federal or State Indian tribe, band, rancheria, pueblo, colony, or community, including any Alaska Native village or regional village corporation (as defined in or established under the Alaska Native Claims Settlement Act (43 U.S.C. 1601 et seq.)).

---

37 For more information about charter schools, *see* 34 CFR § 300.209.

38 See the discussion in Chapter 10 about <FAPE in "Selected Topics"> and Chief Justice Roberts' Opinion in the ***Endrew F.*** SCOTUS case.

39 **Best is a four letter word!** Parents **must never ask the school to provide what is "best"** for their child or that they want a program to **maximize** their child's potential. Evaluations from experts in the private sector should **never** recommend "the best program" or "most ideal," or even use the word, "ideally," with regard to the child. Courts have held that children with disabilities are entitled to an "appropriate" education, not the "best" education. Use the terms "appropriate" or "minimally appropriate."

40 Homeless children "lack a fixed, regular, and adequate nighttime residence . . . [are] sharing the housing of other persons . . . living in motels, hotels, trailer parks, or camping grounds . . . [or are] living in cars, parks, public spaces, abandoned buildings, substandard housing, bus or train stations, or similar settings." (42 U.S.C. § 11434a(2))

41 *See* Chapter 9 for information about the McKinney-Vento Homeless Assistance Act statute which begins at 42 U.S.C. § 11431.

(14) Individualized Education Program; IEP. The term '**individualized education program**' or '**IEP**' means a written statement for each child with a disability that is developed, reviewed, and revised in accordance with Section 1414(d) of this title.[42]

(15) Individualized Family Service Plan. The term '**individualized family service plan**' has the meaning given the term in Section 1436 of this title.

(16) Infant or Toddler With A Disability. The term '**infant or toddler with a disability**' has the meaning given the term in Section 1432 of this title.[43]

(17) Institution of Higher Education. The term '**institution of higher education**'–

(A) has the meaning given the term in Section 1001 of this Title; and

(B) also includes any community college receiving funding from the Secretary of the Interior under the Tribally Controlled Colleges or Universities Assistance Act of 1978.

(18) Limited English Proficient. The term '**limited English proficient**' has the meaning given the term "**English learner**" in Section 8101 of the Elementary and Secondary Education Act[44] of 1965 [20 U.S.C. 7801].[45, 46]

(19) Local Educational Agency.

(A) In General. The term '**local educational agency**' means[47] a public board of education or other public authority legally constituted within a State for either administrative control or direction of, or to perform a service function for, public elementary schools or secondary schools in a city, county, township, school district, or other political subdivision of a State, or for such combination of school districts or counties as are recognized in a State as an administrative agency for its public elementary schools or secondary schools.

(B) Educational Service Agencies and Other Public Institutions or Agencies. The term includes –

(i) an educational service agency; and

(ii) any other public institution or agency having administrative control and direction of a public elementary school or secondary school.

(C) BIA Funded Schools.[48] The term includes an elementary school or secondary school funded by the Bureau of Indian Affairs, but only to the extent that such inclusion makes the school eligible for programs for which specific eligibility is not provided to the school in another provision of law and the school does not have a student population that is smaller than the student population of the local educational agency receiving assistance under this title with the smallest student population, **except that the school shall not be subject to the jurisdiction of any State educational agency** other than the Bureau of Indian Affairs.

---

42   The legal requirements for IEPs, IEP teams, meeting attendance, when IEPs must be in effect, reviewing and revising IEPs, placements, and alternative ways to participate in IEP meetings are in 20 U.S.C. § 1414(d).

43   "An individual under 3 years of age who needs early intervention services because the individual (i) is experiencing developmental delays, as measured by appropriate diagnostic instruments and procedures in 1 or more of the areas of cognitive development, physical development, communication development, social or emotional development, and adaptive development; or (ii) has a diagnosed physical or mental condition that has a high probability of resulting in developmental delay; and . . ." (*See* 20 U.S.C. § 1432 in Part C of IDEA for the full text of this definition.)

44   Known as ESEA.

45   An individual "who is aged 3 through 21 . . . who was not born in the United States or whose native language is a language other than English; . . . who is a Native American or Alaska Native, or a native resident of the outlying areas; and . . . who comes from an environment where a language other than English [is primary] . . . or who is migratory . . . and whose difficulties . . . may be sufficient to deny the individual - (i) the ability to meet the challenging State academic standards; [and] (ii) the ability to successfully achieve in classrooms where the language of instruction is English . . ." 20 U.S.C. § 7801(20)

46   This is an example of "incorporation by reference" in which this is the definition used in Section 8101. If Section 8101 is changed in the future, the definition here will change automatically. However, if that definition did not incorporate by reference ESEA, but copied and pasted the words of Section 8101 from ESEA, then a change in Section 8101 would not change the definition in IDEA.

47   In Hawaii and the U.S. Virgin Islands, the State Educational Agency (SEA) also serves as the LEA because there are no separate LEAs under the state SEA.

48   *See* the footnote to 20 U.S.C. § 1411(h) about the egregious *Stephen C. v. Bureau of Indian Education* case.

(20) Native Language. The term 'native language', when used with respect to an individual who is limited English proficient, means the language normally used by the individual or, in the case of a child, the language normally used by the parents of the child.

(21) Nonprofit. The term 'nonprofit', as applied to a school, agency, organization, or institution, means a school, agency, organization, or institution owned and operated by 1 or more nonprofit corporations or associations no part of the net earnings of which inures, or may lawfully inure, to the benefit of any private shareholder or individual.

(22) Outlying Area. The term 'outlying area' means the United States Virgin Islands, Guam, American Samoa, and the Commonwealth of the Northern Mariana Islands.

(23) Parent. The term 'parent' means–**(A)** a **natural, adoptive, or foster parent of a child** (unless a foster parent is **prohibited** by State law[49] from serving as a parent);

(B) a guardian (but not the State if the child is a ward of the State);

(C) an individual acting in the place of a natural or adoptive parent **(including a grandparent, stepparent, or other relative) with whom the child lives,** or an individual who is legally responsible for the child's welfare; or

(D) except as used in Sections 1415(b)(2)[50] and 1439(a)(5), an individual assigned under either of those sections to be a **surrogate parent**.[51]

(24) Parent Organization. The term 'parent organization' has the meaning given the term in Section 1471(g) of this title.

(25) Parent Training and Information Center. The term 'parent training and information center' means a center assisted under Section 1471 or 1472 of this title.

(26) Related Services.[52]

(A) In General. The term 'related service' means transportation, and such developmental, corrective, and **other supportive services**[53] (including speech-language pathology and audiology services, interpreting services, psychological services, physical and occupational therapy, recreation, including therapeutic recreation, social work services, school nurse services **designed to enable a child with a disability** to receive a free appropriate public education as described in the individualized education program of the child, counseling services, including rehabilitation counseling, orientation and mobility services, and medical services, except that such medical services shall be for diagnostic and evaluation purposes only) as may be required to assist a child with a disability **to benefit from special education**, and includes the early identification and assessment of disabling conditions in children.[54]

---

49 If you are a foster parent, some states allow you to assume the role of a parent at public school special education eligibility and IEP meetings, however that is not true in all states. Be sure to check the definition of parent and role of a foster parent and if a surrogate parent can act in that capacity in your state.

50 20 U.S.C. § 1415(b)(2) explains that there shall be "Procedures to protect the rights of the child whenever the parents of the child are not known, the agency cannot, after reasonable efforts, locate the parents, or the child is a ward of the State, including **the assignment of an individual to act as a surrogate** for the parents . . ."

51 The definition of "parent" includes natural, adoptive, and foster parents, guardians, individuals who act in the place of a parent, individuals who are legally responsible for the child, and surrogate parents. *See* 34 CFR § 300.519 for the definition of "surrogate parent." *See also* 20 U.S.C. § 1415(b)(2).

52 **Definitions of many related services** are in <34 CFR § 300.34(c).> Related services may also be a major component of Section 504 in that a child who qualifies for the protections of Section 504 and / or the ADA, may be entitled to "Related Services" if needed to provide the child with FAPE. *See* 34 CFR § 104.33.

53 SCOTUS held that "clean intermittent catheterization" (CIC), pursuant to this statute is a "supportive service required to assist a handicapped child to benefit from special education." *Irving Indep. Sch. Dist. v. Tatro*, 468 U.S. 883 (1984).

54 Related services are services the child needs **to benefit from special education**. Compare the definition of "related services" to "supplementary aids and services" in 20 U.S.C. § 1401(33). Related services and supplementary services may include one-on-one tutoring or remediation of academic skills. The law does not require a child to be placed in a special education class before receiving related services including tutoring or academic remediation.

(B) Exception. The term does not include a medical device that is surgically implanted, or the replacement of such device.[55]

(27) Secondary School. The term 'secondary school' means a nonprofit institutional day or residential school, including a public secondary charter school,[56] that provides secondary education, as determined under State law, except that it does not include any education beyond grade 12.

(28) Secretary. The term 'Secretary' means the Secretary of Education.

(29) Special Education. The term 'special education' means **specially designed instruction**,[57] at no cost to parents, to meet the **unique needs** of a child with a disability, including–

(A) instruction conducted in the classroom, in the home, in hospitals and institutions, and in other settings;[58] and

(B) instruction in physical education.

(30) Specific Learning Disability.

(A) In General. The term 'specific learning disability' means a disorder in 1 or more of the basic psychological processes involved in understanding or in using language, spoken or written, which disorder may manifest itself in the imperfect ability to listen, think, speak, read, write, spell, or do mathematical calculations.[59]

(B) Disorders Included.[60] Such term **includes** such conditions as **perceptual disabilities, brain injury, minimal brain dysfunction, dyslexia,**[61] **and developmental aphasia**.

(C) Disorders Not Included. Such term does not include a learning problem that is primarily the result of visual, hearing, or motor disabilities, of intellectual disabilities, of emotional disturbance, or of environmental, cultural, or economic disadvantage.

(31) State. The term 'State' means each of the 50 States, the District of Columbia, the Commonwealth of Puerto Rico, and each of the outlying areas.[62]

---

55   The exclusion of surgically implanted medical devices tracks the exception in the definitions of "Assistive Technology Device" and "Assistive Technology Service." While school districts are not responsible for surgically implanting devices, they may be responsible for corrective and supportive services. For example, schools may have to provide audiology services to operate, adjust and map cochlear implant devices. *See* 34 CFR § 300.34.

56   For more information about charter schools, *see* 34 CFR § 300.209.Charter schools must comply with IDEA.

57   The definition of "specially designed instruction" is in <34 CFR § 300.39(b)(3)> and was clarified by Chief Justice Roberts in the March 22, 2017 **Endrew F.** SCOTUS decision. *See* our 2017 **Wrightslaw Year in Review** book.

58   Special education encompasses a range of services and may include one-on-one tutoring, intensive academic remediation, and 40-hour Applied Behavioral Analysis (ABA) programs. Special education is provided in a variety of settings, including the child's home.

59   For more about specific learning disabilities, the elimination of the requirement to use a "discrepancy" formula, and Response to Intervention, *see* 20 U.S.C. § 1414(b)(6).

60   The terms used to describe these specific learning disabilities are those used during the 1970's when Congress enacted Public Law 94-142. The term "minimal brain dysfunction" is now known as "Attention Deficit Disorder." "**Dyslexia**" is a language based learning disability in reading, writing, spelling, and/or math. From a legal perspective, dyslexia is a learning disability that adversely affects educational performance. The word "dyslexia" has been in the statute since 1970 in the <EHA> and repeated again in 1975. **Dyslexia and SLD are also in the ADA** at 28 CFR §§ 35.108(b)(2), 36.105(b)(2).

61   **Dyslexia was initially known as "Strephosymbolia" and "Congenital Word Blindness"** and began to receive public attention on July 25, 1925 when Dr. Samuel T. Orton presented a paper at American Neurological Association's Annual Meeting. His monograph **"Strephosymbolia"** is available from the **"Academy of Orton-Gillingham Practitioners and Educators"** at: https://www.ortonacademy.org/resources/helpful-books-dvds/.

In February, 1929 Dr. Orton published an article in the Journal of Educational Psychology about "The 'Sight Reading' Method of Teaching Reading, as a Source of Reading Disability." The sight method, i.e., whole language, "may give rise to far reaching damage" to a child's "emotional life." https://www.wrightslaw.com/advoc/articles/1929.orton.samuel.sightreading.causesdisability.pdf

In the 1930's, Dr. Orton joined forces with psychologist / educator Anna Gillingham to create the **Orton-Gillingham Approach**. This "Approach" was used by Diana Hanbury King (https://www.wrightslaw.com/info/king.diana.tribute.htm) in the 1950's to teach co-author, Pete Wright, how to read, write, spell and do arithmetic.

62   Outlying areas are defined at 20 U.S.C. § 1401(22).

(32) State Educational Agency. The term 'State educational agency'[63] means the State board of education or other agency or officer primarily responsible for the State supervision of public elementary schools and secondary schools, or, if there is no such officer or agency, an officer or agency designated by the Governor or by State law.

(33) Supplementary Aids and Services. The term 'supplementary aids and services' means aids, services, and other supports that **are provided in regular education classes** or other education-related settings **to enable children** with disabilities **to be educated with nondisabled children** to the maximum extent appropriate in accordance with Section 1412(a)(5)[64] of this title.[65]

(34) Transition Services. The term 'transition services' means a coordinated set of activities for a child with a disability that–

(A) is designed to be within a results-oriented process, that is **focused on improving the academic and functional achievement of the child** with a disability **to facilitate the child's movement from school to post-school activities,** including post-secondary education, vocational education, integrated employment (including supported employment), continuing and adult education, adult services, independent living, or community participation;

(B) is **based on the individual child's need**s, taking into account the child's **strengths, preferences, and interests**; and

(C) includes instruction, related services, community experiences, the development of employment and other post-school adult living objectives, and, when appropriate, acquisition of daily living skills and functional vocational evaluation.[66]

(35) Universal Design. The term 'universal design' has the meaning given the term in Section 3002 in title 29.[67]

(36) Ward of the State.

(A) In General. The term 'ward of the State' means a child who, as determined by the State where the child resides, is a foster child, is a ward of the State, or is in the custody of a public child welfare agency.[68]

(B) Exception. The term **does not** include a foster child who has a foster parent who meets the definition of a parent in paragraph (23).

20 U.S.C. § 1402 - Office of Special Education Programs[69]

(a) Establishment. There shall be, within the Office of Special Education and Rehabilitative Services in the Department of Education, an Office of Special Education Programs, which shall be the principal agency in the

---

63   In Hawaii and the U.S. Virgin Islands, the State Educational Agency (SEA) serves, in practice, as the LEA, since there are no separate LEAs under the state SEA.

64   This is the **"Least Restrictive Environment"** (LRE) section.

65   Supplementary aids and services **are provided in general education classes** so children with disabilities can be educated with their non-disabled peers and participate in extra curricular and non-academic settings. *See* 34 CFR §§ 300.42, 300.107, and 300.117. Compare "supplementary aids and services" with "related services" in 20 U.S.C. § 1401(26).

66   The definition of transition services includes a "results-oriented process" that improves "the academic and functional achievement of the child with a disability" and facilitates the child's transition from school to employment and further education. Transition services are based on the individual child's needs and strengths.

67   The key concept in Universal Design, often called Universal Design for Learning, is that new curricular materials and learning technologies will be flexible to accommodate the unique learning styles of a wide range of individuals, including children with disabilities. Examples include accessible websites, electronic versions of textbooks and other materials; captioned and/or narrated videos; word processors with word prediction; and voice recognition. *See* the Early Childhood Technical Assistive Center at: http://ectacenter.org/topics/atech/udl.asp. The definition of universal design is in the Assistive Technology Act at 29 U.S.C. § 3002(19).

68   *See also* 20 U.S.C. § 1401(23) for the expanded definition of "parent" and 20 U.S.C. § 1414(a)(1)(D)(iii) about parental consent for children who are wards of the state.

69   **Wrightslaw Overview**: This section authorizes the USDOE, Office of Special Education Programs (OSEP) as the principal agency to administer the IDEA. The Secretary selects the Director who reports directly to the Assistant Secretary for Special Education and Rehabilitative Services.

Department for administering and carrying out this title and other programs and activities concerning the education of children with disabilities.

(b) Director. The Office established under subsection (a) shall be headed by a Director who shall be selected by the Secretary and shall report directly to the Assistant Secretary for Special Education and Rehabilitative Services.

(c) Voluntary and Uncompensated Services. Notwithstanding Section 1342 of title 31, United States Code, the Secretary is authorized to accept voluntary and uncompensated services in furtherance of the purposes of this title.

20 U.S.C. § 1403 - Abrogation of State Sovereign Immunity

(a) In General. A State **shall not be immune** under the 11th amendment to the Constitution of the United States from suit in Federal court for a violation of this title.[70]

(b) Remedies. In a suit against a State for a violation of this title, remedies (including remedies both at law and in equity) are available for such a violation to the same extent as those remedies are available for such a violation in the suit against any public entity other than a State.

(c) Effective Date. Subsections (a) and (b) apply with respect to violations that occur in whole or part after October 30, 1990.

20 U.S.C. § 1404 - Acquisition of Equipment; Construction or Alteration of Facilities

(a) In General. If the Secretary determines that a program authorized under this title will be improved by permitting program funds to be used to acquire appropriate equipment, or to construct new facilities or alter existing facilities, the Secretary is authorized to allow the use of those funds for those purposes.

(b) Compliance With Certain Regulations. Any construction of new facilities or alteration of existing facilities under subsection (a) shall comply with the requirements of–

(1) appendix A of part 36 of title 28, Code of Federal Regulations (commonly known as the 'Americans with Disabilities Accessibility Guidelines for Buildings and Facilities'); or

(2) appendix A of subpart 101-19.6 of title 41, Code of Federal Regulations (commonly known as the 'Uniform Federal Accessibility Standards').

20 U.S.C. § 1405 - Employment of Individuals with Disabilities

The Secretary shall ensure that each recipient of assistance under this title **makes positive efforts** to employ and advance in employment qualified individuals with disabilities in programs assisted under this title.

20 U.S.C. § 1406 - Requirements for Prescribing Regulations[71]

(a) In General. In carrying out the provisions of this title, the Secretary[72] shall issue regulations under this title only to the extent that such regulations are necessary to ensure that there is compliance with the specific requirements of this title.

(b) Protections Provided to Children. The Secretary may not implement, or publish in final form, any regulation prescribed pursuant to this title that–

(1) violates or contradicts any provision of this title; or

---

70   State departments of education (SEAs) are responsible for supervising school districts (LEAs) and enforcing IDEA. *See* 20 U.S.C. § 1412(a)(11).and 20 U.S.C. § 1416(e). In Chapter 9, see our discussion about <*C.B. v. Chicago Public Schools*, a Section 1983 lawsuit> against a school board attorney and special education director and their potential loss of immunity. Discovery has commenced in preparation for a jury trial seeking dollar damages. .

71   **Wrightslaw Overview**: The U.S. Department of Education is responsible for developing the federal special education regulations. After the Department publishes proposed regulations, there is a public comment period. Comments may be made in writing or at public meetings. After reviewing the comments, the Department publishes the Final Regulations. The federal special education regulations are published in the Federal Register (FR) and in the Code of Federal Regulations (CFR) beginning at 34 CFR Part 300. The 2006 regulations or any subsequent amendments or reauthorizations may not lessen the protections in effect on July 20, 1983. The full text of the Code of Federal Regulations for IDEA is in the next chapter of this book.

72   This section of IDEA authorizes the U.S. Dept. Of Education (USDOE) to issue the special education regulations. However, pursuant to the **Supremacy Clause of the U.S. Constitution**, neither the USDOE **nor States may take away rights** provided by federal law.

(2) procedurally or substantively **lessens the protections provided to children** with disabilities under this title, as embodied in regulations in effect on July 20, 1983 (particularly as such protections related to parental consent to initial evaluation or initial placement in special education, least restrictive environment, related services, timelines, attendance of evaluation personnel at individualized education program meetings, or qualifications of personnel), except to the extent that such regulation reflects the **clear and unequivocal intent of Congress** in legislation.[73]

(c) Public Comment Period. The Secretary shall provide a public comment period of not less than 75 days on any regulation proposed under part B or part C on which an opportunity for public comment is otherwise required by law.[74]

(d) Policy Letters and Statements. The Secretary **may not** issue policy letters or other statements (including letters or statements regarding issues of national significance) that–

(1) violate or **contradict any provision of this title**; or

(2) establish a rule that is required for compliance with, and eligibility under, this title without following the requirements of Section 553 of title 5, United States Code.

(e) Explanation and Assurances. Any written response by the Secretary under subsection (d) regarding a policy, question, or interpretation under part B shall include an explanation in the written response that–

(1) such response is provided as informal guidance and is not legally binding;

(2) when required, such response is issued in compliance with the requirements of Section 553 of title 5, United States Code; and

(3) such response represents the interpretation by the Department of Education of the applicable statutory or regulatory requirements in the context of the specific facts presented.

(f) Correspondence From Department of Education Describing Interpretations of This Title.

(1) In General. The Secretary **shall**, on a **quarterly basis, publish in the Federal Register**, and **widely disseminate** to interested entities through various additional forms of communication, a **list of correspondence** from the Department of Education received by individuals during the previous quarter that describes the interpretations of the Department of Education of this title or the regulations implemented pursuant to this title.

(2) Additional Information. For each item of correspondence published in a list under paragraph (1), the Secretary shall–

(A) identify the topic addressed by the correspondence and shall include such other summary information as the Secretary determines to be appropriate; and

(B) ensure that all such correspondence is issued, where applicable, in compliance with the requirements of Section 553 of title 5, United States Code.

20 U.S.C. § 1407 - State Administration

(a) Rulemaking. Each State that receives funds under this title **shall–**

(1) ensure that any State rules, regulations, and policies relating to this title **conform to the purposes of this title;**

(2) identify in writing to local educational agencies located in the State and the Secretary **any such rule, regulation, or policy** as a State-imposed requirement that is **not required** by this title and Federal regulations; and

(3) **minimize the number of rules**, regulations, and policies to which the local educational agencies and schools located in the State are subject under this title.

---

73 The USDOE may not publish regulations that lessen the protections provided in the 1983 regulations, unless this reflects the clear and unequivocal intent of Congress.

74 After proposed regulations are published in the Federal Register, the public may comment. The USDOE held live hearings around the country for the 2006 IDEA regulations. Many comments are discussed in the Commentary. URL: https://www.wrightslaw.com/idea/commentary.htm

(b) Support and Facilitation.

State rules, regulations, and policies under this title **shall support** and facilitate local educational agency and school-level system **improvement designed to enable children with disabilities to meet the challenging State student academic achievement standards.**[75]

20 U.S.C. § 1408 - Paperwork Reduction

(a) Pilot Program.

(1) Purpose. The purpose of this section is to provide an opportunity for States to identify ways to **reduce paperwork burdens** and other administrative duties that are directly associated with the requirements of this title, in order to increase the time and resources available for instruction and other activities aimed at improving educational and functional results for children with disabilities.

(2) Authorization.

(A) In General. In order to carry out the purpose of this section, the Secretary is authorized to grant waivers of statutory requirements of, or regulatory requirements relating to, part B for a period of time not to exceed 4 years with respect to not more than 15 States based on proposals submitted by States to reduce excessive paperwork and noninstructional time burdens that do not assist in improving educational and functional results for children with disabilities.

(B) Exception. The Secretary **shall not waive** under this section any statutory requirements of, or regulatory requirements relating to, **applicable civil rights requirements**.

(C) Rule of Construction. Nothing in this section shall be construed to–

(i) affect the right of a child with a disability to receive a free appropriate public education under part B; and

(ii) permit a State or local educational agency to waive procedural safeguards under Section 1415 of this title.

(3) Proposal.

(A) In General. A State desiring to participate in the program under this section shall submit a proposal to the Secretary at such time and in such manner as the Secretary may reasonably require.

(B) Content. The proposal shall include–

(i) a list of any statutory requirements of, or regulatory requirements relating to, part B that the State desires the Secretary to waive, in whole or in part; and

(ii) a list of any State requirements that the State proposes to waive or change, in whole or in part, to carry out a waiver granted to the State by the Secretary.

(4) Termination of Waiver. The Secretary shall terminate a State's waiver under this section if the Secretary determines that the State–

(A) needs assistance under Section 1416(d)(2)(A)(ii) of this title and that the waiver has contributed to or caused such need for assistance;

(B) needs intervention under Section 1416(d)(2)(A)(iii) of this title or needs substantial intervention under Section 1416(d)(2)(A)(iv) of this title; or

(C) failed to appropriately implement its waiver.

(b) Report.

Beginning 2 years after the date of enactment of the Individuals with Disabilities Education Improvement Act of 2004, the Secretary shall include in the annual report to Congress submitted pursuant to Section 3486 of this title information related to the effectiveness of waivers granted under subsection (a), including any specific recommendations for broader implementation of such waivers, in—

---

75 The State Education Agency (SEA) shall assist local school districts, i.e., the LEAs, to improve the education of children with disabilities so they are able to meet the state's achievement standards (in place for all children, including those without disabilities.)

(1) **reducing** –

    (A) **the paperwork burden** on teachers, principals, administrators, and related service providers; and

    (B) noninstructional time spent by teachers in complying with part B;

(2) enhancing longer-term educational planning;

(3) **improving positive outcomes** for children with disabilities;

(4) promoting collaboration between IEP Team members; and

(5) **ensuring satisfaction of family members.**

20 U.S.C. § 1409 - Freely Associated States

The Republic of the Marshall Islands, the Federated States of Micronesia, and the Republic of Palau shall continue to be eligible for competitive grants[76] administered by the Secretary under this title to the extent that such grants continue to be available to States and local educational agencies under this title.

End of Part A

HyperLinks to Specific Sections in IDEA

20 U.S.C. § 1400	Findings and Purposes	20 U.S.C. § 1415	Procedural Safeguards
20 U.S.C. § 1401	Definitions	20 U.S.C. § 1415(b)(1)	Indep. Educ. Eval. IEE
20 U.S.C. § 1412	State Responsibilities	20 U.S.C. § 1415(f)	Due Process Hearing
20 U.S.C. § 1414(a)	Evaluations	20 U.S.C. § 1415(j)	Stay-Put / Pendency
20 U.S.C. § 1414(d)	IEPs	20 U.S.C. § 1415(k)	Discipline

---

76   Grants are available to these islands in the Pacific Rim.

Part B - Assistance for Education of All Children with Disabilities[77, 78]

20 U.S.C. § 1411. Authorization; allotment; use of funds; authorization of appropriations

<20 U.S.C. § 1412. State eligibility>

20 U.S.C. § 1413. Local educational agency eligibility

<20 U.S.C. § 1414. Evaluations, eligibility determinations, IEPs, and educational placements>

<20 U.S.C. § 1415. Procedural safeguards>

20 U.S.C. § 1416. Monitoring, technical assistance, and enforcement

20 U.S.C. § 1417. Administration

20 U.S.C. § 1418. Program information

20 U.S.C. § 1419. Preschool grants

20 U.S.C. § 1411 - Authorization; Allotment; Use of Funds; Authorization of Appropriations.[79]

(a) Grants to States.

(1) Purpose of Grants.

The Secretary shall make grants to States, outlying areas, and freely associated States, and provide funds to the Secretary of the Interior, to assist them to provide special education and related services to children with disabilities in accordance with this part.

(2) Maximum amount. The **maximum amount** of the grant **a State may receive** under this section–

(A) for fiscal years 2005 and 2006 is–

(i) **the number of children with disabilities** in the State who are receiving special education and related services–

(I) aged 3 through 5 if the State is eligible for a grant under Section 1419 of this title; and

(II) aged 6 through 21; multiplied by

(ii) 40 percent of the average per-pupil expenditure in public elementary schools and secondary schools in the United States; and

(B) for fiscal year 2007 and subsequent fiscal years is–

(i) the number of children with disabilities in the 2004-2005 school year in the State who received special education and related services–

(I) aged 3 through 5 if the State is eligible for a grant under Section 1419 of this title; and

(II) aged 6 through 21; multiplied by

---

77 **Wrightslaw Overview: Part B of IDEA**, Assistance for Education of All Children with Disabilities, governs special education for children between the ages of 3 and 21 and includes Sections 1411 through Section 1419 of Title 20 of the United States Code.

78 **Wrightslaw Note:** For most readers, **the key sections of IDEA in Part B are Section 1412, Section 1414, and Section 1415.** **Section 1412** includes child find, least restrictive environment, unilateral placements, reimbursement, and state and district assessments. **Section 1414** describes requirements for evaluations, reevaluations, consent, eligibility, IEPs, and placements. **Section 1415** describes the rules of procedure designed to protect the rights of children with disabilities and their parents. These safeguards include the right to examine educational records and obtain an independent educational evaluation, and the legal requirements for prior written notice, procedural safeguards notice, due process complaint notice, due process hearings, resolution sessions, mediation, attorney's fees, and discipline.

79 **Wrightslaw Overview:** Section 1411 provides funding formulas, ratios, definitions, and requirements. It provides an optional Local Educational Agency (LEA) Risk Pool in 20 U.S.C. § 1411(e)(3) that allows states to reserve up to 10% of funds for "risk pools" to address the "high need children" with disabilities. Funds in the risk pool may not be used for litigation expenses. The Regulations for Section 1411 begin at 34 CFR § 300.700 through § 300.717.

(ii) 40 percent of the average per-pupil expenditure in public elementary schools and secondary schools in the United States; adjusted by

(iii) the rate of annual change in the sum of–

(I) 85 percent of such State's population described in subsection (d)(3)(A)(i)(II); and

(II) 15 percent of such State's population described in subsection (d)(3)(A)(i)(III).

(b) Outlying Areas and Freely Associated States, Secretary of the Interior.

(1) Outlying Areas and Freely Associated States.[80]

(A) Funds Reserved. From the amount appropriated for any fiscal year under subsection (i), the Secretary shall reserve not more than 1 percent, which shall be used–

(i) to provide assistance to the outlying areas in accordance with their respective populations of individuals aged 3 through 21; and

(ii) to provide each freely associated State a grant in the amount that such freely associated State received for fiscal year 2003 under this part, but only if the freely associated State meets the applicable requirements of this part, as well as the requirements of Section 1411(b)(2)(C) of this title as such section was in effect on the day before the date of enactment of the Individuals with Disabilities Education Improvement Act of 2004.

(B) Special Rule. The provisions of Public Law 95-134, permitting the consolidation of grants by the outlying areas, shall not apply to funds provided to the outlying areas or the freely associated States under this section.

(C) Definition. In this paragraph, the term '**freely associated States**' means the Republic of the Marshall Islands, the Federated States of Micronesia, and the Republic of Palau.

(2) Secretary of the Interior. From the amount appropriated for any fiscal year under subsection (i), the Secretary shall reserve 1.226 percent to provide assistance to the Secretary of the Interior in accordance with subsection (h).

(c) Technical Assistance.

(1) In General. The Secretary may reserve not more than 1/2 of 1 percent of the amounts appropriated under this part for each fiscal year to provide technical assistance activities authorized under Section 1416(i) of this title.

(2) Maximum amount. The maximum amount the Secretary may reserve under paragraph (1) for any fiscal year is $25,000,000, cumulatively adjusted by the rate of inflation as measured by the percentage increase, if any, from the preceding fiscal year in the Consumer Price Index For All Urban Consumers, published by the Bureau of Labor Statistics of the Department of Labor.

(d) Allocations to States.

(1) In General. After reserving funds for technical assistance, and for payments to the outlying areas, the freely associated States, and the Secretary of the Interior under subsections (b) and (c) for a fiscal year, the Secretary shall allocate the remaining amount among the States in accordance with this subsection.

(2) Special Rule for use of Fiscal Year 1999 Amount. If a State received any funds under this section for fiscal year 1999 on the basis of children aged 3 through 5, but does not make a free appropriate public education available to all children with disabilities aged 3 through 5 in the State in any subsequent fiscal year, the Secretary shall compute the State's amount for fiscal year 1999, solely for the purpose of calculating the State's allocation in that subsequent year under paragraph (3) or (4), by subtracting the amount allocated to the State for fiscal year 1999 on the basis of those children.

(3) Increase in Funds. If the amount available for allocations to States under paragraph (1) for a fiscal year is equal to or greater than the amount allocated to the States under this paragraph for the preceding fiscal year, those allocations shall be calculated as follows:

---

80 'State' means each of the 50 States, the District of Columbia, the Commonwealth of Puerto Rico, and each of the outlying areas. *See* the definitions at 20 U.S.C. § 1401(31).

(A) Allocation of Increase.

(i) In General. Except as provided in subparagraph (B), the Secretary shall allocate for the fiscal year-

(I) to each State the amount the State received under this section for fiscal year 1999;

(II) 85 percent of any remaining funds to States on the basis of the States' relative populations of children aged 3 through 21 who are of the same age as children with disabilities for whom the State ensures the availability of a free appropriate public education under this part; and

(III) 15 percent of those remaining funds to States on the basis of the States' relative populations of children described in subclause (II) who are living in poverty.

(ii) Data. For the purpose of making grants under this paragraph, the Secretary shall use the most recent population data, including data on children living in poverty, that are available and satisfactory to the Secretary.

(B) Limitations. Notwithstanding subparagraph (A), allocations under this paragraph shall be subject to the following:

(i) Preceding Year Allocation. No State's allocation shall be less than its allocation under this section for the preceding fiscal year.

(ii) Minimum. No State's allocation shall be less than the greatest of-

(I) the sum of-

(aa) the amount the State received under this section for fiscal year 1999; and

(bb) 1/3 of 1 percent of the amount by which the amount appropriated under subsection (i) for the fiscal year exceeds the amount appropriated for this section for fiscal year 1999;

(II) the sum of—

(aa) the amount the State received under this section for the preceding fiscal year; and

(bb) that amount multiplied by the percentage by which the increase in the funds appropriated for this section from the preceding fiscal year exceeds 1.5 percent; or

(III) the sum of—

(aa) the amount the State received under this section for the preceding fiscal year; and

(bb) that amount multiplied by 90 percent of the percentage increase in the amount appropriated for this section from the preceding fiscal year.

(iii) Maximum. Notwithstanding clause (ii), no State's allocation under this paragraph shall exceed the sum of-

(I) the amount the State received under this section for the preceding fiscal year; and

(II) that amount multiplied by the sum of 1.5 percent and the percentage increase in the amount appropriated under this section from the preceding fiscal year.

(C) Ratable Reduction. If the amount available for allocations under this paragraph is insufficient to pay those allocations in full, those allocations shall be ratably reduced, subject to subparagraph (B)(i).

(4) Decrease in Funds. If the amount available for allocations to States under paragraph (1) for a fiscal year is less than the amount allocated to the States under this section for the preceding fiscal year, those allocations shall be calculated as follows:

(A) Amounts Greater than Fiscal Year 1999 Allocations. If the amount available for allocations is greater than the amount allocated to the States for fiscal year 1999, each State shall be allocated the sum of-

(i) the amount the State received under this section for fiscal year 1999; and

(ii) an amount that bears the same relation to any remaining funds as the increase the State received under this section for the preceding fiscal year over fiscal year 1999 bears to the total of all such increases for all States.

(B) Amounts Equal to or Less than Fiscal Year 1999 Allocations.

(i) In General. If the amount available for allocations under this paragraph is equal to or less than the amount allocated to the States for fiscal year 1999, each State shall be allocated the amount the State received for fiscal year 1999.

(ii) Ratable Reduction. If the amount available for allocations under this paragraph is insufficient to make the allocations described in clause (i), those allocations shall be ratably reduced.

(e) State Level Activities.

(1) State Administration.

(A) In General. For the purpose of administering this part, including paragraph (3), Section 1419 of this title, and the coordination of activities under this part with, and providing technical assistance to, other programs that provide services to children with disabilities–

(i) each State may reserve for each fiscal year not more than the maximum amount the State was eligible to reserve for State administration under this section for fiscal year 2004 or $800,000 (adjusted in accordance with subparagraph (B)), whichever is greater; and

(ii) each outlying area may reserve for each fiscal year not more than 5 percent of the amount the outlying area receives under subsection (b)(1) for the fiscal year or $35,000, whichever is greater.

(B) Cumulative Annual Adjustments. For each fiscal year beginning with fiscal year 2005, the Secretary shall cumulatively adjust

(i) the maximum amount the State was eligible to reserve for State administration under this part for fiscal year 2004; and

(ii) $800,000, by the rate of inflation as measured by the percentage increase, if any, from the preceding fiscal year in the Consumer Price Index For All Urban Consumers, published by the Bureau of Labor Statistics of the Department of Labor.

(C) Certification. Prior to expenditure of funds under this paragraph, the State shall certify to the Secretary that the arrangements to establish responsibility for services pursuant to Section 1412(a)(12)(A) of this title are current.

(D) Part C. Funds reserved under subparagraph (A) may be used for the administration of part C, if the State educational agency is the lead agency for the State under such part.

(2) Other State Level Activities.

(A) State Level Activities.

(i) In General. Except as provided in clause (iii), for the purpose of carrying out State-level activities, each State may reserve for each of the fiscal years 2005 and 2006 not more than 10 percent from the amount of the State's allocation under subsection (d) for each of the fiscal years 2005 and 2006, respectively. For fiscal year 2007 and each subsequent fiscal year, the State may reserve the maximum amount the State was eligible to reserve under the preceding sentence for fiscal year 2006 (cumulatively adjusted by the rate of inflation as measured by the percentage increase, if any, from the preceding fiscal year in the Consumer Price Index For All Urban Consumers, published by the Bureau of Labor Statistics of the Department of Labor).

(ii) Small State Adjustment. Notwithstanding clause (i) and except as provided in clause (iii), in the case of a State for which the maximum amount reserved for State administration is not greater than $850,000, the State may reserve for the purpose of carrying out State-level activities for each of the fiscal years 2005 and 2006, not more than 10.5 percent from the amount of the State's allocation under subsection (d) for each of the fiscal years 2005 and 2006, respectively. For fiscal year 2007 and each subsequent fiscal year, such State may reserve the maximum amount the State was eligible to reserve under the preceding sentence for fiscal year 2006 (cumulatively adjusted by the rate of inflation as measured by the percentage increase, if any, from the preceding fiscal year in the Consumer Price Index For All Urban Consumers, published by the Bureau of Labor Statistics of the Department of Labor).

(iii) Exception. If a State does not reserve funds under paragraph (3) for a fiscal year, then–

(I) in the case of a State that is not described in clause (ii), for fiscal year 2005 or 2006, clause (i) shall be applied by substituting 9.0 percent for 10 percent; and

(II) in the case of a State that is described in clause (ii), for fiscal year 2005 or 2006, clause (ii) shall be applied by substituting 9.5 percent for 10.5 percent.

(B) Required Activities. Funds reserved under subparagraph (A) shall be used to carry out the following activities:

(i) For monitoring, enforcement, and complaint investigation.

(ii) To **establish and implement the mediation process** required by section 1415(e) of this title, including providing for the cost of mediators and support personnel.

(C) Authorized Activities. Funds reserved under subparagraph (A) may be used to carry out the following activities:

(i) For support and direct services, including technical assistance, personnel preparation, and professional development and training.

(ii) To support paperwork reduction activities, including expanding the use of technology in the IEP process.

(iii) To assist local educational agencies in providing positive behavioral interventions and supports and appropriate mental health services for children with disabilities.

(iv) To improve the use of technology in the classroom by children with disabilities to enhance learning.

(v) To support the use of technology, including technology with universal design principles and assistive technology devices, to maximize accessibility to the general education curriculum for children with disabilities.

(vi) Development and implementation of transition programs, including coordination of services with agencies involved in supporting the transition of children with disabilities to postsecondary activities.

(vii) To assist local educational agencies in meeting personnel shortages.

(viii) To support capacity building activities and improve the delivery of services by local educational agencies to improve results for children with disabilities.

(ix) **Alternative programming** for children with disabilities who have been expelled from school, and services for children with disabilities **in correctional facilities**,[81] children enrolled in State-operated or State-supported schools, and children with disabilities in **charter schools**.

(x) To support the development and provision of appropriate accommodations for children with disabilities, or the development and provision of alternate assessments that are valid and reliable for assessing the performance of children with disabilities, in accordance with Sections 6311(b) and 6361 of this title.

(xi) To provide technical assistance to schools and local educational agencies, and direct services, including direct student services described in section 6303b(c)(3) of this title to children with disabilities, to schools or local educational agencies implementing comprehensive support and improvement activities or targeted support and improvement activities under section 6311(d) of this title on the basis of consistent underperformance of the disaggregated subgroup of children with disabilities, including providing professional development to special and regular education teachers, who teach children with disabilities, based on scientifically based research to improve educational instruction, in order to improve academic achievement based on the challenging academic standards described in section 6311(b)(1) of this title.

---

81   *See* Section 1414(d)(7) which mandates that an incarcerated adult with an IEP is still entitled to FAPE unless there is "a bona fide security or compelling penological interest that cannot otherwise be accommodated."

(3) Local Educational Agency Risk Pool.[82]

(A) In General.

(i) Reservation of Funds. For the purpose of assisting local educational agencies (including a charter school that is a local educational agency or a consortium of local educational agencies) in addressing the needs of high need children with disabilities, each State shall have the option to reserve for each fiscal year 10 percent of the amount of funds the State reserves for State-level activities under paragraph (2) (A)–

(I) to establish and make disbursements from the high cost fund to local educational agencies in accordance with this paragraph during the first and succeeding fiscal years of the high cost fund; and

(II) to support innovative and effective ways of cost sharing by the State, by a local educational agency, or among a consortium of local educational agencies, as determined by the State in coordination with representatives from local educational agencies, subject to subparagraph (B)(ii).

(ii) Definition of Local Educational Agency. In this paragraph the term 'local educational agency' **includes a charter school** that is a local educational agency, or a consortium of local educational agencies.

(B) Limitation on Uses of Funds.

(i) Establishment of High Cost Fund. A State shall not use any of the funds the State reserves pursuant to subparagraph (A)(i), but may use the funds the State reserves under paragraph (1), to establish and support the high cost fund.

(ii) Innovative and Effective Cost Sharing. A State shall not use more than 5 percent of the funds the State reserves pursuant to subparagraph (A)(i) for each fiscal year to support innovative and effective ways of cost sharing among consortia of local educational agencies.

(C) State Plan for High Cost Fund.

(i) Definition. The State educational agency **shall establish the State's definition of a high need child with a disability**, which definition shall be developed in consultation with local educational agencies.

(ii) State Plan. The State educational agency shall develop, not later than 90 days after the State reserves funds under this paragraph, annually review, and amend as necessary, a State plan for the high cost fund. Such State plan shall–

(I) establish, in coordination with representatives from local educational agencies, a definition of a high need child with a disability that, at a minimum—

(aa) addresses the financial impact a high need child with a disability has on the budget of the child's local educational agency; and

(bb) ensures that the cost of the high need child with a disability is greater than 3 times the average per pupil expenditure (as defined in Section 7801 of the this title) in that State;

(II) establish eligibility criteria for the participation of a local educational agency that, at a minimum, takes into account the number and percentage of high need children with disabilities served by a local educational agency;

(III) develop a funding mechanism that provides distributions each fiscal year to local educational agencies that meet the criteria developed by the State under subclause (II); and

(IV) establish an annual schedule by which the State educational agency shall make its distributions from the high cost fund each fiscal year.

(iii) Public Availability. The State shall make its final **State plan publicly available not less than 30 days before the beginning of the school year**, including dissemination of such information on the State website.

---

82   Funds in the risk pool may be disbursed for "innovative, effective ways of cost sharing" by districts and consortiums of districts. Funds in the risk pool may not be used to support litigation.

(D) Disbursements from the High Cost Fund.

(i) In General. Each State educational agency shall make all annual disbursements from the high cost fund established under subparagraph (A)(i) in accordance with the State plan published pursuant to subparagraph (C).

(ii) Use of Disbursements. Each State educational agency shall make annual disbursements to eligible local educational agencies in accordance with its State plan under subparagraph (C)(ii).

(iii) Appropriate Costs. The costs associated with educating a high need child with a disability under subparagraph (C)(i) are only those costs associated with providing direct special education and related services to such child that are identified in such child's IEP.

(E) Legal Fees. The disbursements under subparagraph (D) **shall not support legal fees, court costs, or other costs associated with a cause of action** brought on behalf of a child with a disability to ensure a free appropriate public education for such child.

(F) Assurance of a Free Appropriate Public Education.- Nothing in this paragraph **shall be construed–**

(i) to limit or condition the right of a child with a disability who is assisted under this part to receive a free appropriate public education pursuant to Section 1412(a)(1) of this title in the least restrictive environment pursuant to Section 1412(a)(5) of this title; or

(ii) to authorize a State educational agency or local educational agency **to establish a limit on what may be spent on the education of a child with a disability.**

(G) Special Rule for Risk Pool and High Need Assistance Programs in Effect as of January 1, 2004. Notwithstanding the provisions of subparagraphs (A) through (F), a State may use funds reserved pursuant to this paragraph for implementing a placement neutral cost sharing and reimbursement program of high need, low incidence, catastrophic, or extraordinary aid to local educational agencies that provides services to high need students based on eligibility criteria for such programs that were created not later than January 1, 2004, and are currently in operation, if such program serves children that meet the requirement of the definition of a high need child with a disability as described in subparagraph (C)(ii)(I).

(H) Medicaid Services not Affected. Disbursements provided under this paragraph shall not be used to pay costs that otherwise would be reimbursed as medical assistance for a child with a disability under the State medicaid program under title XIX of the Social Security Act.

(I) Remaining Funds. Funds reserved under subparagraph (A) in any fiscal year but not expended in that fiscal year pursuant to subparagraph (D) shall be allocated to local educational agencies for the succeeding fiscal year in the same manner as funds are allocated to local educational agencies under subsection (f) for the succeeding fiscal year.

(4) Inapplicability of Certain Prohibitions. A State may use funds the State reserves under paragraphs (1) and (2) without regard to–

(A) the prohibition on commingling of funds in Section 1412(a)(17)(B) of this title; and

(B) the prohibition on supplanting other funds in Section 1412(a)(17)(C) of this title.

(5) Report on Use of Funds. As part of the information required to be submitted to the Secretary under Section 1412 of this title, each State shall annually describe how amounts under this section–

(A) will be used to meet the requirements of this title; and

(B) will be allocated among the activities described in this section to meet State priorities based on input from local educational agencies.

(6) Special Rule for Increased Funds. A State may use funds the State reserves under paragraph (1)(A) as a result of inflationary increases under paragraph (1)(B) to carry out activities authorized under clause (i), (iii), (vii), or (viii) of paragraph (2)(C).

(7) Flexibility in Using Funds for Part C. Any State eligible to receive a grant under Section 1419 of this title may use funds made available under paragraph (1)(A), subsection (f)(3), or Section 1419(f)(5) of this title to develop and implement a State policy jointly with the lead agency under part C and the State educational agency to provide early intervention services (which shall include an educational component that promotes school readiness and incorporates preliteracy, language, and numeracy skills) in accordance with part C to children with disabilities who are eligible for services under Section 1419 of this title and who previously received services under part C until such children enter, or are eligible under State law to enter, kindergarten, or elementary school as appropriate.

(f) Subgrants to Local Educational Agencies.

(1) Subgrants Required. Each State that receives a grant under this section for any fiscal year shall distribute any funds the State does not reserve under subsection (e) to local educational agencies (including public charter schools that operate as local educational agencies) in the State that have established their eligibility under Section 1413 of this title for use in accordance with this part.

(2) Procedure for Allocations to Local Educational Agencies. For each fiscal year for which funds are allocated to States under subsection (d), each State shall allocate funds under paragraph (1) as follows:

(A) Base Payments. The State shall first award each local educational agency described in paragraph (1) the amount the local educational agency would have received under this section for fiscal year 1999, if the State had distributed 75 percent of its grant for that year under Section 1411(d) of this title as Section 1411(d) of this title was then in effect.

(B) Allocation of Remaining Funds. After making allocations under subparagraph (A), the State shall–

(i) allocate 85 percent of any remaining funds to those local educational agencies on the basis of the relative numbers of children enrolled in public and private elementary schools and secondary schools within the local educational agency's jurisdiction; and

(ii) allocate 15 percent of those remaining funds to those local educational agencies in accordance with their relative numbers of children living in poverty, as determined by the State educational agency.

(3) Reallocation of Funds. If a State educational agency determines that a local educational agency is adequately providing a free appropriate public education to all children with disabilities residing in the area served by that local educational agency with State and local funds, the State educational agency may reallocate any portion of the funds under this part that are not needed by that local educational agency to provide a free appropriate public education to other local educational agencies in the State that are not adequately providing special education and related services to all children with disabilities residing in the areas served by those other local educational agencies.

(g) Definitions. In this section:

(1) Average per Pupil Expenditure in Public Elementary Schools and Secondary Schools in the United States. The term 'average per-pupil expenditure in public elementary schools and secondary schools in the United States' means–

(A) without regard to the source of funds–

(i) the aggregate current expenditures, during the second fiscal year preceding the fiscal year for which the determination is made (or, if satisfactory data for that year are not available, during the most recent preceding fiscal year for which satisfactory data are available) of all local educational agencies in the 50 States and the District of Columbia; plus

(ii) any direct expenditures by the State for the operation of those agencies; divided by

(B) the aggregate number of children in average daily attendance to whom those agencies provided free public education during that preceding year.

(2) State. The term 'State' means each of the 50 States, the District of Columbia, and the Commonwealth of Puerto Rico.

(h) Use of Amounts by Secretary of the Interior.[83]

  (1) Provision of Amounts for Assistance.

    (A) In General. The Secretary of Education shall provide amounts to the Secretary of the Interior to meet the need for assistance for the education of children with disabilities on reservations aged 5 to 21, inclusive, enrolled in elementary schools and secondary schools for Indian children operated or funded by the Secretary of the Interior. The amount of such payment for any fiscal year shall be equal to 80 percent of the amount allotted under subsection (b)(2) for that fiscal year. Of the amount described in the preceding sentence–

      (i) 80 percent shall be allocated to such schools by July 1 of that fiscal year; and

      (ii) 20 percent shall be allocated to such schools by September 30 of that fiscal year.

    (B) Calculation of Number of Children. In the case of Indian students aged 3 to 5, inclusive, who are enrolled in programs affiliated with the Bureau of Indian Affairs (referred to in this subsection as the "BIA") schools and that are required by the States in which such schools are located to attain or maintain State accreditation, and which schools have such accreditation prior to the date of enactment of the Individuals with Disabilities Education Act Amendments of 1991, the school shall be allowed to count those children for the purpose of distribution of the funds provided under this paragraph to the Secretary of the Interior. The Secretary of the Interior shall be responsible for meeting all of the requirements of this part for those children, in accordance with paragraph (2).

    (C) Additional Requirement. With respect to all other children aged 3 to 21, inclusive, on reservations, the State educational agency shall be responsible for ensuring that all of the requirements of this part are implemented.

  (2) Submission of Information. The Secretary of Education may provide the Secretary of the Interior amounts under paragraph (1) for a fiscal year only if the Secretary of the Interior submits to the Secretary of Education information that–

    (A) demonstrates that the Department of the Interior meets the appropriate requirements, as determined by the Secretary of Education, of Sections 1412 (including monitoring and evaluation activities) and 1413 of this title;

    (B) includes a description of how the Secretary of the Interior will coordinate the provision of services under this part with local educational agencies, tribes and tribal organizations, and other private and Federal service providers;

    (C) includes an assurance that there are public hearings, adequate notice of such hearings, and an opportunity for comment afforded to members of tribes, tribal governing bodies, and affected local school boards before the adoption of the policies, programs, and procedures related to the requirements described in subparagraph (A);

---

83   The U.S. Department of the Interior and the Bureau of Indian Education (BIE) are defendants in an egregious case (*Stephan C. v. BIE*) as reported by the Washington Post on January 12, 2017. The Post reported that "Havasupai Elementary School does not teach any subjects other than English and math, according to the complaint; there is no instruction in science, history, social studies, foreign language, or the arts. There aren't enough textbooks or a functioning library or any after-school sports teams or clubs, according to the complaint. There are so many and such frequent teacher vacancies that students are allegedly taught often by non-certified staff, including the janitor, or they are taught by a series of substitutes who rotate in for two-week stints. The school shuts down altogether for weeks at a time."

"The school has no system for evaluating or serving children with disabilities, who comprise about half of the student body, according to the complaint. And school officials are so incapable of meeting the needs of students with special needs that they often require those children to be educated at home, attending school as little as three hours per week." https://tinyurl.com/y999wfyg / There is a webpage devoted to this "landmark lawsuit" at: http://unitefornativestudents.org/.

The District Court, in Case # 3:17-cv-08004, entered Summary Judgment for the defendants. On March 16, 2022, the Ninth Circuit, in Case # 21-15097, court reversed and remanded the case to the District Court. The Ninth Circuit explained that **all of the students are entitled to compensatory education**, even if they are no longer enrolled in a BIE school.

Oral argument before the Ninth Circuit was held on February 9, 2022 and the ruling was entered five weeks later. **Video of the argument** is available at: https://www.ca9.uscourts.gov/media/video/?20220209/21-15097/

(D) includes an assurance that the Secretary of the Interior will provide such information as the Secretary of Education may require to comply with Section 1418 of this title;

(E) includes an assurance that the Secretary of the Interior and the Secretary of Health and Human Services have entered into a memorandum of agreement, to be provided to the Secretary of Education, for the coordination of services, resources, and personnel between their respective Federal, State, and local offices and with State and local educational agencies and other entities to facilitate the provision of services to Indian children with disabilities residing on or near reservations (such agreement shall provide for the apportionment of responsibilities and costs, including child find, evaluation, diagnosis, remediation or therapeutic measures, and (where appropriate) equipment and medical or personal supplies as needed for a child to remain in school or a program); and

(F) includes an assurance that the Department of the Interior will cooperate with the Department of Education in its exercise of monitoring and oversight of this application, and any agreements entered into between the Secretary of the Interior and other entities under this part, and will fulfill its duties under this part.

(3) Applicability. The Secretary shall withhold payments under this subsection with respect to the information described in paragraph (2) in the same manner as the Secretary withholds payments under Section 1416(e)(6) of this title.

(4) Payments for Education and Services for Indian Children with Disabilities Aged 3 Through 5.

(A) In General. With funds appropriated under subsection (i), the Secretary of Education shall make payments to the Secretary of the Interior to be distributed to tribes or tribal organizations (as defined under Section 450b of title 25) or consortia of tribes or tribal organizations to provide for the coordination of assistance for special education and related services for children with disabilities aged 3 through 5 on reservations served by elementary schools and secondary schools for Indian children operated or funded by the Department of the Interior. The amount of such payments under subparagraph (B) for any fiscal year shall be equal to 20 percent of the amount allotted under subsection (b)(2).

(B) Distribution of Funds. The Secretary of the Interior shall distribute the total amount of the payment under subparagraph (A) by allocating to each tribe, tribal organization, or consortium an amount based on the number of children with disabilities aged 3 through 5 residing on reservations as reported annually, divided by the total of those children served by all tribes or tribal organizations.

(C) Submission of Information. To receive a payment under this paragraph, the tribe or tribal organization shall submit such figures to the Secretary of the Interior as required to determine the amounts to be allocated under subparagraph (B). This information shall be compiled and submitted to the Secretary of Education.

(D) Use of Funds. The funds received by a tribe or tribal organization shall be used to assist in child find, screening, and other procedures for the early identification of children aged 3 through 5, parent training, and the provision of direct services. These activities may be carried out directly or through contracts or cooperative agreements with the BIA, local educational agencies, and other public or private nonprofit organizations. The tribe or tribal organization is encouraged to involve Indian parents in the development and implementation of these activities. The tribe or tribal organization shall, as appropriate, make referrals to local, State, or Federal entities for the provision of services or further diagnosis.

(E) Biennial Report. To be eligible to receive a grant pursuant to subparagraph (A), the tribe or tribal organization shall provide to the Secretary of the Interior a biennial report of activities undertaken under this paragraph, including the number of contracts and cooperative agreements entered into, the number of children contacted and receiving services for each year, and the estimated number of children needing services during the 2 years following the year in which the report is made. The Secretary of the Interior shall include a summary of this information on a biennial basis in the report to the Secretary of Education required under this subsection. The Secretary of Education may require any additional information from the Secretary of the Interior.

(F) Prohibitions. None of the funds allocated under this paragraph may be used by the Secretary of the Interior for administrative purposes, including child count and the provision of technical assistance.

(5) Plan for Coordination of Services. The Secretary of the Interior shall develop and implement **a plan for the coordination of services for all Indian children with disabilities residing on reservations** covered under this title. Such plan shall provide for the coordination of services benefiting those children from whatever source, including tribes, the Indian Health Service, other BIA divisions, and other Federal agencies. In developing the plan, the Secretary of the Interior shall consult with all interested and involved parties. The plan shall be based on the needs of the children and the system best suited for meeting those needs, and may involve the establishment of cooperative agreements between the BIA, other Federal agencies, and other entities. The plan shall also be distributed upon request to States, State educational agencies and local educational agencies, and other agencies providing services to infants, toddlers, and children with disabilities, to tribes, and to other interested parties.

(6) Establishment of Advisory Board. To meet the requirements of Section 1412(a)(21) of this title, the Secretary of the Interior **shall establish**, under the BIA, an advisory board composed of individuals involved in or concerned with the education and provision of services to Indian infants, toddlers, children, and youth with disabilities, including Indians with disabilities, Indian parents or guardians of such children, teachers, service providers, State and local educational officials, representatives of tribes or tribal organizations, representatives from State Interagency Coordinating Councils under Section 1441 of this title in States having reservations, and other members representing the various divisions and entities of the BIA. The chairperson shall be selected by the Secretary of the Interior. The advisory board shall–

(A) assist in the coordination of services within the BIA and with other local, State, and Federal agencies in the provision of education for infants, toddlers, and children with disabilities;

(B) advise and assist the Secretary of the Interior in the performance of the Secretary of the Interior's responsibilities described in this subsection;

(C) develop and recommend policies concerning effective inter– and intra-agency collaboration, including modifications to regulations, and the elimination of barriers to inter– and intra-agency programs and activities;

(D) provide assistance and disseminate information on best practices, effective program coordination strategies, and recommendations for improved early intervention services or educational programming for Indian infants, toddlers, and children with disabilities; and

(E) provide assistance in the preparation of information required under paragraph (2)(D).

(7) Annual Reports.

(A) In General. The advisory board established under paragraph (6) shall prepare and submit to the Secretary of the Interior and to Congress an annual report containing a description of the activities of the advisory board for the preceding year.

(B) Availability. The Secretary of the Interior shall make available to the Secretary of Education the report described in subparagraph (A).

(i) **Authorizations of Appropriations.** For the purpose of carrying out this part, other than Section 1419 of this title, there are authorized to be appropriated–

(1) $12,358,376,571 for fiscal year 2005;

(2) $14,648,647,143 for fiscal year 2006;

(3) $16,938,917,714 for fiscal year 2007;

(4) $19,229,188,286 for fiscal year 2008;

(5) $21,519,458,857 for fiscal year 2009;

(6) $23,809,729,429 for fiscal year 2010;

(7) $26,100,000,000 for fiscal year 2011; and

(8) such sums as may be necessary for fiscal year 2012 and each succeeding fiscal year.

20 U.S.C. § 1412 - State Eligibility.[84]

(a) In General. A **State is eligible for assistance** under this part for a fiscal year **if the State submits a plan that provides assurances** to the Secretary **that the State has in effect policies and procedures** to ensure that the State meets **each of the following conditions:**

(1) Free Appropriate Public Education.

(A) In General. A **free appropriate public education is available to all children with disabilities** residing in the State between the **ages of 3 and 21, inclusive**, including children with disabilities **who have been suspended or expelled** from school.[85]

(B) Limitation. The obligation to make a free appropriate public education available to all children with disabilities does not apply with respect to children–

(i) aged 3 through 5 and 18 through 21 **in a State** to the extent that its application to those children would be **inconsistent with State law** or practice, or the order of any court, respecting the provision of public education to children in those age ranges; and

(ii) aged 18 through 21 to the extent that State law does not require that special education and related services under this part be provided to children with disabilities who, in the educational placement **prior to their incarceration in an adult correctional facility–**

(I) **were not actually identified** as being a child with a disability under Section 1401 of this title; or

(II) **did not have an individualized education program** under this part.[86]

(C) State Flexibility. A State that provides early intervention services in accordance with part C to a child who is eligible for services under Section 1419 of this title, is not required to provide such child with a free appropriate public education.[87]

(2) Full Educational Opportunity Goal. The State has established a goal of providing full educational opportunity to all children with disabilities and a detailed timetable for accomplishing that goal.

(3) Child Find.

(A) In General. All children with disabilities residing in the State, including children with disabilities who are **homeless children** or are **wards of the State** and children with disabilities **attending private schools**, regardless of the severity of their disabilities, **and who are in need of special education and related services, are identified, located, and evaluated** and a practical method is developed and implemented to determine which children with disabilities are currently receiving needed special education and related services.[88]

---

84   **Wrightslaw Overview:** Section 1412 is often called the "Catch-All" statute because it includes a variety of diverse topics including **child find, least restrictive environment (LRE)**, transition to preschool programs, equitable services for children in private schools, unilateral placements, **tuition reimbursement**, and assessments. Section 1412(a)(3) describes requirements for child find. Section 1412(a)(5) describes requirements for educating children with disabilities in the least restrictive environment **(LRE).**

Section 1412(a)(10) explains services that must be provided to children who attend private schools and requirements about consultation with private schools and equitable services for children who attend private schools. It contains the requirements for unilateral placements by parents and tuition reimbursement. Section 1412(a)(11) clarifies that **the state is ultimately responsible for programs operated by local school districts** and ensuring that children with disabilities receive a free appropriate education. Section 1412(a)(16) includes requirements about state assessments, **accommodation guidelines,** and alternate assessments. Section 1412(a)(23) includes requirements about access to instructional materials. Section 1412(a)(25) describes the prohibition on mandatory medication. The **Regulations for Section 1412 begin at <Section 300.100>** and continue to Section 300.198.

85   All children who are eligible for special education services under IDEA are entitled to a free appropriate public education (FAPE), including children who have been suspended or expelled from school. Before Congress enacted Public Law 94-142, millions of children with disabilities were not allowed to attend public schools. (*See* Findings in Section 1400(c) and Discipline in Section 1415(k)).

86   *See also* 20 U.S.C. § 1414(d)(7) about adult children with IEPs incarcerated in an adult facility and whether or not FAPE is still required, depending on "penological interest" such as security.

87   *See* 20 U.S.C. § 1432(4)(B) which describes early intervention services that "are provided at no cost except where a Federal or State law provides for a system of payments by families, including a schedule of sliding fees."

88   Child find requires school districts to identify, locate, and evaluate all children with disabilities. *See also* 20 U.S.C. § 1412(a)(10) regarding child find and students who attend private schools. This includes consultations with private school officials.

(B) Construction. Nothing in this chapter requires that children be classified by their disability so long as each child who has a disability listed in Section 1401 of this title and who, by reason of that disability, needs special education and related services is regarded as a child with a disability under this part.[89]

(4) Individualized Education Program. An individualized education program, or an individualized family service plan that meets the requirements of Section 1436(d) of this title, **is developed, reviewed, and revised for each child with a disability** in accordance with Section 1414(d) of this title.

(5) Least Restrictive Environment.[90, 91]

(A) In General. To the maximum extent appropriate,[92] **children with disabilities**, including children in public or private institutions or other care facilities, **are educated with children who are not disabled**, and special classes, separate schooling, or other removal of children with disabilities from the regular educational environment **occurs only when** the nature or severity of the disability of a child is such that education in regular classes[93] with the use of supplementary aids and services cannot be achieved satisfactorily.

(B) Additional Requirement.

(i) In General. A **State funding mechanism shall not result in placements that violate the requirements** of subparagraph (A), and a State shall not use a funding mechanism by which the State distributes funds on the basis of the type of setting in which a child is served that will result in the failure to provide a child with a disability a free appropriate public education according to the unique needs of the child as described in the child's IEP.

(ii) Assurance. If the State does not have policies and procedures to ensure compliance with clause (i), the State shall provide the Secretary an assurance that the State will revise the funding mechanism as soon as feasible to ensure that such mechanism does not result in such placements.

(6) Procedural Safeguards.

(A) In General. Children with disabilities and their parents are afforded the procedural safeguards required by Section 1415 of this title.

---

89   If the child has a disability that **adversely affects educational performance,** such that the child needs special education and related services, (i.e., the child is eligible for special education services under 20 U.S.C. § 1401(3) of IDEA), the school is **not required to determine the child's "label" or classification** before it provides services.

Too often, schools spend months evaluating the child, not providing special education services, while the child falls further behind. *See also* 20 U.S.C. § 1414(a)(1)(C)(i)(I) about the 60 calendar day timeline between parental consent and completion of the evaluation process. That section provides that states may have timelines that are longer or shorter than 60 days. Check your state's regulations.

90   **Least restrictive environment** is often referred to as the **Inclusion and Mainstreaming** statute, but these concepts are not necessarily the same. Judicial decisions about "mainstreaming," "least restrictive environment" (LRE) and "inclusion" vary, even within the same state. Some districts claim the law requires them to mainstream all children with disabilities, even children who need individualized one-to-one instruction that cannot be delivered in general education classrooms. In other districts, parents must fight to have their disabled child "included" in general education classes.

The law takes a commonsense approach to this issue: children with disabilities should be educated with children who are not disabled "to the maximum extent appropriate." However, children can receive one-to-one or small group instruction outside of regular classes if this is necessary for them to learn. The placement is to be **as close to the child's home as possible**, preferably in the school the child would attend if non-disabled. *See* 34 CFR § 300.116.

91   Since the law was implemented in 1975, there have been many decisions about Mainstreaming, Inclusion, and Least Restrictive Environment. **Listed in chronological order are some of the earlier landmark cases** that have been repeatedly referenced by courts over the years: 1983 - 6th Cir. *Ronckerv. Walter*, 700 F.2d 1058 // 1989 - 5th Cir. *Daniel R.R. v. State Board of Educ.*, 874 F.2d 1036 // 1989 - 4th Cir. *Devries v. Fairfax County Sch. Bd.*, 882 F.2d 876 // 1991 - 11th Cir. *Greer v. Rome City Sch. Dist.*, 950 F.2d 688 // 1993 - 3rd Cir. *Oberti v. Board of Educ.*, 995 F.2d 1204 // 1994 - 9th Cir. *Sacramento City Unif. Sch. Dist. v. Rachel Holland*, 14 F.3d 1398. In *Wrightslaw Year in Review* books, you will find a number of cases in which LRE was a central issue.

92   *See also* the "**integrated setting**" language in Section 504 and the ADA at 42 U.S.C. § 12182(b)(1)(B), 28 CFR § 35.130(d), 28 CFR § 36.203, 34 CFR § 104.4(b)(2), and 34 CFR § 104.43(d).

93   In the author's *Florence County Sch. Dist. IV v. Shannon Carter*, 510 U.S. 7 (1993) case, Shannon attended a residential school where all students had dyslexia and received Orton-Gillingham remediation. Florence County argued that, because all the students had dyslexia, her private school violated the LRE requirement. The Court explained that, since the public school was unable to teach Shannon how to read and Trident Academy did, the LRE placement for Shannon was the placement where she learned to read.

(B) Additional Procedural Safeguards. Procedures to ensure that **testing and evaluation materials and procedures** utilized for the purposes of evaluation and placement of children with disabilities for services under this title will be selected and administered so as **not** to be **racially or culturally discriminatory**. Such materials or procedures shall be provided and **administered in the child's native language or mode of communication**, unless it clearly is not feasible to do so, and **no single procedure shall be the sole criterion** for determining an appropriate educational program for a child.[94]

(7) Evaluation. Children with disabilities are evaluated in accordance with subsections (a) through (c) of Section 1414 of this title.

(8) Confidentiality. Agencies in the State comply with Section 1417(c) of this title (relating to the confidentiality of records and information).

(9) Transition from Part C to Preschool Programs. Children participating in early intervention programs assisted under part C, and who will participate in preschool programs assisted under this part, experience a **smooth and effective transition to those preschool programs** in a manner consistent with Section 1437(a) (9) of this title. By the third birthday of such a child, an individualized education program or, if consistent with Sections 1414(d)(2)(B) and 1436(d) of this title, an individualized family service plan, has been developed and is being implemented for the child. The local educational agency will participate in transition planning conferences arranged by the designated lead agency under Section 1435(a)(10) of this title.

(10) Children in Private Schools.

(A) Children Enrolled in Private Schools by Their Parents.

(i) In General. To the extent consistent with the number and location of **children with disabilities** in the State who are **enrolled by their parents in private elementary schools and secondary schools** in the school district served by a local educational agency, **provision is made for the participation of those children in the program** assisted or carried out under this part by providing for such children special education and related services in accordance with the following requirements, unless the Secretary has arranged for services to those children under subsection (f):

(I) Amounts to be expended for the provision of those services (including **direct services to parentally placed private school children**) by the local educational agency shall be equal to a proportionate amount of Federal funds made available under this part.

(II) In calculating the proportionate amount of Federal funds, the local educational agency, after **timely and meaningful consultation with representatives of private schools** as described in clause (iii), **shall conduct a thorough and complete child find process** to determine the number of parentally placed children with disabilities attending private schools located in the local educational agency.

(III) Such **services to parentally placed private school children with disabilities may be provided to the children on the premises of private, including religious, schools**, to the extent consistent with law.

(IV) State and local funds may supplement and in no case shall supplant the proportionate amount of Federal funds required to be expended under this subparagraph.

(V) Each **local educational agency shall** maintain in its records and **provide to the State educational agency the number of children evaluated** under this subparagraph, the **number of children determined to be children with disabilities** under this paragraph, and the **number of children served** under this paragraph.

---

94 In "**Findings**" at Section 1400(c), Congress described the **over-representation of minority children** and limited English proficient children in special education. These children often do not perform as well on traditional measures of intelligence and educational achievement. The requirements that evaluations shall be administered in the child's native language or mode of communication and that "no single procedure shall be the sole criterion" for determining an appropriate educational program, are attempts to remedy evaluations that caused minority children to be over-represented in special education.

(ii) Child Find Requirement.

(I) In General. The requirements of paragraph (3) (relating to child find) **shall apply with respect to children with disabilities** in the State who are **enrolled in private, including religious, elementary schools and secondary schools.**

(II) Equitable Participation. The child find process shall be designed to **ensure the equitable participation of parentally placed private school children with disabilities** and an accurate count of such children.

(III) Activities. In carrying out this clause, the local educational agency, or where applicable, the State educational agency, shall undertake activities similar to those activities undertaken for the agency's public school children.

(IV) Cost. The **cost of carrying out this clause, including individual evaluations, may not be considered** in determining whether a local educational agency has met its obligations under clause (i).

(V) Completion Period. Such child find process shall be completed in a time period comparable to that for other students attending public schools in the local educational agency.

(iii) Consultation.

To ensure timely and meaningful consultation, a local educational agency, or where appropriate, a State educational agency, **shall consult with private school representatives and representatives of parents of parentally placed private school children with disabilities during the design and development of special education and related services for the children,**[95] including regarding–

(I) the child find process and how **parentally placed private school children suspected of having a disability can participate equitably,**[96] including how parents, teachers, and private school officials will be informed of the process;

(II) the determination of the proportionate amount of Federal funds available to serve parentally placed private school children with disabilities under this subparagraph, including the determination of how the amount was calculated;

(III) the consultation process among the local educational agency, private school officials, and representatives of parents of parentally placed private school children with disabilities, including how such process will operate throughout the school year to ensure that parentally placed private school children with disabilities identified through the child find process can meaningfully participate in special education and related services;

(IV) how, where, and by whom special education and related services will be provided for parentally placed private school children with disabilities, including a discussion of types of services, including direct services and alternate service delivery mechanisms, how such services will be apportioned if funds are insufficient to serve all children, and how and when these decisions will be made; and

(V) how, **if the local educational agency disagrees with the views of the private school officials on the provision of services** or the types of services, whether provided directly or through a contract, the local educational agency **shall provide to the private school officials a written explanation of the reasons why the local educational agency chose not to provide services** directly or through a contract.

---

95 IDEA requires consultation between public school and private school officials and **equitable participation** of children who attend private schools. The consultation process includes a written affirmation, compliance, complaints to the state by private schools, and the provision of equitable services to children who attend private schools. The language about consultation with "private school representatives and representatives of parents of parentally placed private school children" conforms with ESSA at 20 U.S.C. § 6320.

96 "No parentally-placed private school child with a disability has an individual entitlement to receive some or all of the special education and related services that the child would receive if enrolled in a public school." *See* 34 CFR § 300.137 and Commentary in the *Federal Register,* 71 Fed. Reg. 46595 (August 14, 2006). However, some states do require that related services be provided to students in private schools.

(iv) Written Affirmation. When timely and meaningful consultation as required by clause (iii) has occurred, the local educational agency **shall obtain a written affirmation signed by the representatives of participating private schools,** and if such representatives do not provide such affirmation within a reasonable period of time, the local educational agency shall forward the documentation of the consultation process to the State educational agency.

(v) Compliance.

  (I) In General. A **private school official shall have the right to submit a complaint** to the State educational agency that the local educational agency did not engage in consultation that was meaningful and timely, or did not give due consideration to the views of the private school official.

  (II) Procedure. If the private school official wishes to submit a complaint, the official **shall provide the basis of the noncompliance** with this subparagraph by the local educational agency to the State educational agency, and the local educational agency shall forward the appropriate documentation to the State educational agency. If the private school official is dissatisfied with the decision of the State educational agency, such **official may submit a complaint to the Secretary** by providing the basis of the noncompliance with this subparagraph by the local educational agency to the Secretary, and the State educational agency shall forward the appropriate documentation to the Secretary.

(vi) Provision of Equitable Services.

  (I) Directly or Through Contracts. The provision of services pursuant to this subparagraph shall be provided

    (aa) by employees of a public agency; or

    (bb) through contract by the public agency with an individual, association, agency, organization, or other entity.

  (II) Secular, Neutral, Nonideological. Special education and related services provided to parentally placed private school children with disabilities, including materials and equipment, shall be secular, neutral, and nonideological.[97]

(vii) Public Control of Funds. The control of funds used to provide special education and related services under this subparagraph, and title to materials, equipment, and property purchased with those funds, shall be in a public agency for the uses and purposes provided in this title, and a public agency shall administer the funds and property.

(B) Children Placed in, or Referred to, Private Schools by Public Agencies.

(i) In General. Children with disabilities in private schools and facilities are provided special education and related services, in accordance with an individualized education program, at no cost to their parents, if such children are placed in, or referred to, such schools or facilities by the State or appropriate local educational agency as the means of carrying out the requirements of this part or any other applicable law requiring the provision of special education and related services to all children with disabilities within such State.

(ii) Standards. In all cases described in clause (i), the State educational agency shall determine whether such schools and facilities meet standards that apply to State educational agencies and local educational agencies and that children so served **have all the rights** the children would have if served by such agencies.[98]

---

97 Court decisions about whether school districts must provide special education and related services at a child's private school differ around the country. Many courts have held that the public school must make these services available, but that services do not have to be provided at the private school Some states mandate services and transportation from the public school district for the private school child with a disability, including direct services at the private school. Check your own state regulations.

98 If a public school places a child in a private school, the child has the same rights under IDEA as if the child attended a public school.

(C) Payment for Education of Children Enrolled in Private Schools Without Consent of or Referral by the Public Agency.[99]

(i) In General. Subject to subparagraph (A), this part does not require a local educational agency to pay for the cost of education, including special education and related services, of a child with a disability at a private school or facility if that agency made a free appropriate public education available to the child and the parents elected to place the child in such private school or facility.

(ii) Reimbursement for Private School Placement. If the parents of a child with a disability, **who previously received special education**[100] **and related services** under the authority of a public agency, **enroll the child in a private** elementary school or secondary **school without the consent of or referral** by the public agency, a **court or a hearing officer may require the agency to reimburse the parents** for the cost of that enrollment **if** the court or hearing officer finds that **the agency had not made a free appropriate public education available to the child in a timely manner prior to that enrollment**.[101]

(iii) Limitation on Reimbursement. The cost of **reimbursement** described in clause (ii) **may be reduced or denied–**

(I) **if–**

(aa) **at the most recent IEP meeting** that the parents attended prior to removal of the child from the public school, the **parents did not inform the IEP Team that they were rejecting the placement** proposed by the public agency to provide a free appropriate public education to their child, **including stating their concerns and their intent to enroll their child in a private school at public expense; or**[102]

(bb) **10 business days** (including any holidays that occur on a business day) **prior to the removal of the child** from the public school, the **parents did not give written notice** to the public agency of the information described in item (aa);[103]

---

99   This **authorizes private school tuition reimbursement to parents**, depending on the facts of each case. For guidance, *see* Pete Wright's *Shannon Carter* SCOTUS case in 1993 published in 510 U.S. 7 and the 1983 SCOTUS *Burlington* case. There are a number of tuition reimbursement cases in our *Wrightslaw Year in Review* books.

100   In tuition reimbursement cases, frequently known as "Carter" cases, the child must previously have had an IEP. However, *see Forest Grove v. T.A.* 557 U.S. 230 (2009) case in which the U.S. Supreme Court ruled that, even though the child had not received services from the LEA, the child should have been found eligible for an IEP and received services, thus the school could not use this statute as a defense and the parent could sue for reimbursement for the private school tuition.

101   If a parent removes their child from a public school program and places the child into a private program, the parent may be reimbursed for the costs of the private program if a hearing officer or court determines that the public school did not offer FAPE "in a timely manner." However, the parent **must have provided advance notice** to the school district before removing their child.

102   In the 2015 edition of *Wrightslaw: Year in Review*, we feature *Leggett v. DC Pub. Sch.* 793 F.3d 59 (D.C. Cir. 2015), as a "Case of the Year." (https://www.wrightslaw.com/bks/2015law/index.htm) The DC Public Schools failed to "finalize K.E.'s IEP before the school year began, and thus with no assurance that K.E. would get the special-education services she needed, Leggett began exploring alternative placements. She investigated 'literally dozens' of possible schools, but she found only two that appeared to meet K.E.'s needs. One, a local private day school, rejected K.E. on the ground that a 'highly structured, supportive school or therapeutic setting' would better serve her needs. The other, a boarding school in Pennsylvania, accepted her for the upcoming term."

When the parent sued for tuition reimbursement, the hearing officer and the court denied reimbursement because, "the child had no need to be in a residential program," despite finding that DCPS failed to provide FAPE. The Court of Appeals held that it "was DCPS's failure to develop an IEP that forced Leggett's hand." "The regulation expressly requires that 'the placement, including . . . room and board, shall be provided at no cost to the [child] or his or her parents or guardian' if it is 'necessary' to the child's education. 34 CFR § 104.33(c)(3). Because K.E. could not possibly have attended Grier, some three hours from the District, without living there, the school's residential program was clearly 'necessary' and thus reimbursable." **Ms. Leggett represented herself before the Court of Appeals**. *See* https://www.wrightslaw.com/law/caselaw/2015/dccir.pro.se.leggett.tuit.reim.pdf

103   Sample **10 business day notice of removal letters** are in *Wrightslaw: From Emotions to Advocacy*. Any advance payment of a deposit on private school tuition should include a letter to the private school that the parent is prepared to forfeit the deposit if the public school offers FAPE within the ten day period prior to removal.

(II) **if, prior to the parents' removal** of the child from the public school, the public agency **informed the parents**, through the notice requirements described in Section 1415(b)(3) of this title, **of its intent to evaluate the child** (including a statement of the purpose of the evaluation that was appropriate and reasonable), **but the parents did not make the child available for such evaluation**; or

(III) upon a **judicial finding of unreasonableness** with respect to actions taken **by the parents**.

(iv) **Exception**. Notwithstanding the notice requirement in clause (iii)(I), the cost of reimbursement

(I) **shall not be reduced or denied** for failure to provide such notice if–

(aa) the school prevented the parent from providing such notice;

(bb) the parents had not received notice, pursuant to Section 1415 of this title, of the notice requirement in clause (iii)(I); or

(cc) compliance with clause (iii)(I) would likely result in physical harm to the child; and

(II) **may**, in the discretion of a court or a hearing officer, **not be reduced or denied** for failure to provide such notice if–

(aa) the parent is illiterate or cannot write in English; or

(bb) compliance with clause (iii)(I) would likely result in serious emotional harm to the child.

(11) State Educational Agency Responsible for General Supervision.[104, 105]

(A) In General. The State educational agency **is responsible for ensuring** that

(i) the requirements of this part are met;

(ii) all educational programs for children with disabilities in the State, including all such programs administered by any other State agency or local agency–

(I) are under the general supervision of individuals in the State who are responsible for educational programs for children with disabilities; and

(II) meet the educational standards of the State educational agency; and

(iii) in carrying out this part with respect to homeless children, the requirements of subtitle B of title VII of the McKinney-Vento Homeless Assistance Act (42 U.S.C. § 11431 *et seq.*) are met.

(B) Limitation. Subparagraph (A) shall not limit the responsibility of agencies in the State other than the State educational agency to provide, or pay for some or all of the costs of, a free appropriate public education for any child with a disability in the State.

(C) Exception. Notwithstanding subparagraphs (A) and (B), the Governor (or another individual pursuant to State law), consistent with State law, may assign to any public agency in the State the responsibility of ensuring that the requirements of this part are met with respect to children with disabilities who are convicted as adults under State law and incarcerated in adult prisons.

(12) Obligations Related to and Methods of Ensuring Services–

(A) Establishing Responsibility for Services. The Chief Executive Officer of a State or designee of the officer shall ensure that an interagency agreement or other mechanism for interagency coordination is in effect between each public agency described in subparagraph (B) and the State educational agency, in order to ensure that all services described in subparagraph (B)(i) that are needed **to** ensure a free appropriate public education are provided, including the provision of such services during the pendency of any dispute under clause (iii). Such agreement or mechanism shall include the following:

---

104   **State departments of education (SEAs) are responsible for supervising school districts (LEAs).** State complaint procedures are described in 34 CFR §§ 300.151 - 153. Despite this clear language, and 20 U.S.C. § 1403, Abrogation of Sovereign Immunity, some state departments of education view their role as a source of funding, technical assistance and training, and not as an enforcement agency. Some states have argued that they are immune from suit. In a lawsuit by this author against the Virginia DOE, the state unsuccessfully argued a sovereign immunity defense before a U.S. District Court Judge. *See* the footnote to 34 CFR § 300.518(d).

105   *See also* LEA compliance in 20 U.S.C. § 1413(d).

(i) Agency Financial Responsibility. An identification of, or a method for defining, the financial responsibility of each agency for providing services described in subparagraph (B)(i) to ensure a free appropriate public education to children with disabilities, provided that the financial responsibility of each public agency described in subparagraph (B), including the **State medicaid agency**[106] and other public insurers of children with disabilities, shall precede the financial responsibility of the local educational agency (or the State agency responsible for developing the child's IEP).

(ii) Conditions and Terms of Reimbursement. The conditions, terms, and procedures under which a local educational agency shall be reimbursed by other agencies.

(iii) Interagency Disputes. Procedures for resolving interagency disputes (including procedures under which local educational agencies may initiate proceedings) under the agreement or other mechanism to secure reimbursement from other agencies or otherwise implement the provisions of the agreement or mechanism.

(iv) Coordination of Services Procedures. Policies and procedures for agencies to determine and identify the interagency coordination responsibilities of each agency to promote the coordination and timely and appropriate delivery of services described in subparagraph (B)(i).

(B) Obligation of Public Agency.

(i) In General. If any public agency other than an educational agency is otherwise obligated under Federal or State law, or assigned responsibility under State policy pursuant to subparagraph (A), to provide or pay for any services that are also considered special education or related services (such as, but not limited to, services described in Section 1401(1) of this title relating to assistive technology devices, 1401(2) of this title relating to assistive technology services, 1401(26) of this title relating to related services, 1401(33) of this title relating to supplementary aids and services, and 1401(34) of this title relating to transition services) that are necessary for ensuring a free appropriate public education to children with disabilities within the State, such public agency shall fulfill that obligation or responsibility, either directly or through contract or other arrangement pursuant to subparagraph (A) or an agreement pursuant to subparagraph (C).

(ii) Reimbursement for Services by Public Agency. If a public agency other than an educational agency fails to provide or pay for the special education and related services described in clause (i), the local educational agency (or State agency responsible for developing the child's IEP) shall provide or pay for such services to the child.[107] Such local educational agency or State agency is authorized to claim reimbursement for the services from the public agency that failed to provide or pay for such services and such public agency shall reimburse the local educational agency or State agency pursuant to the terms of the interagency agreement or other mechanism described in subparagraph (A)(i) according to the procedures established in such agreement pursuant to subparagraph (A)(ii).

(C) Special Rule. The requirements of subparagraph (A) may be met through–

(i) State statute or regulation;

(ii) signed agreements between respective agency officials that clearly identify the responsibilities of each agency relating to the provision of services; or

(iii) other appropriate written methods as determined by the Chief Executive Officer of the State or designee of the officer and approved by the Secretary.

---

106   USDOE revised 34 CFR § 300.154(d) in 2012 so that school districts do not have to obtain consent each time Medicaid benefits are accessed. This author posted a video about possible future implications of this revision on the **Wrightslaw YouTube video channel**. The video included information about the Five Hundred and Forty Million Dollar whistleblower case in New York filed by a school's speech therapist. She was paid Ten Million as her statutory share based on the recovery. URL - https://youtu.be/mTFmKd9ths4

107   When other public agencies are responsible for providing services, they must comply with this section. Because IDEA focuses on the transition from school to work and further education, state Departments of Vocational Rehabilitation and other agencies may be responsible for providing services.

(13) Procedural Requirements Relating to Local Educational Agency Eligibility.

The State educational agency will not make a final determination that a local educational agency is not eligible for assistance under this part without first affording that agency reasonable notice and an opportunity for a hearing.

(14) Personnel Qualifications.[108]

(A) In General. The State educational agency has established and maintains qualifications to ensure that personnel necessary to carry out this part are appropriately and adequately prepared and trained, including that those personnel have the content knowledge and skills to serve children with disabilities.

(B) Related Services Personnel and Paraprofessionals. The qualifications under subparagraph (A) include qualifications for related services personnel and paraprofessionals that -

(i) are consistent with any **State-approved** or State-recognized **certification, licensing, registration, or other comparable requirements** that apply to the professional discipline in which those personnel are providing special education or related services;

(ii) **ensure that related services personnel** who deliver services in their discipline or profession meet the requirements of clause (i) and **have not had certification or licensure requirements waived** on an emergency, temporary, or provisional basis; and

(iii) allow **paraprofessionals and assistants who are appropriately trained and supervised**, in accordance with State law, regulation, or written policy, in meeting the requirements of this part to be used to **assist in the provision of special education and related services** under this part to children with disabilities.

(C) Qualifications for Special Education Teachers. The qualifications described in subparagraph (A) shall ensure that each person employed as a **special education teacher** in the State who teaches elementary school, middle school, or secondary school -

(i) has obtained **full State certification as a special education teacher** (including participating in an alternate route to certification as a special educator, if such alternate route meets minimum requirements described in section 2005.56(a)(2)(ii) of title 34, Code of Federal Regulations,[109] as such section was in effect on November 28, 2008), or passed the State special education teacher licensing examination, and holds a license to teach in the State as a special education teacher, except with respect to any teacher teaching in a public charter school who shall meet the requirements set forth in the State's public charter school law;

(ii) has not had special education certification or licensure requirements waived on an emergency, temporary, or provisional basis; and

(iii) holds at least a bachelor's degree.

(D) Policy. In implementing this Section, a State shall adopt a policy that includes a requirement that local educational agencies in the State **take measurable steps to recruit, hire, train, and retain personnel who meet the applicable requirements described in this paragraph to provide special** education and related services under this subchapter to children with disabilities.

(E) Rule of Construction. Notwithstanding any other individual right of action that a parent or student may maintain under this part, **nothing** in this paragraph **shall be construed to create a right of action on**

---

108   The requirements about the qualifications of special education teachers changed in 2001 with No Child Left Behind (NCLB) and subsequently changed again in 2015 with Every Student Succeeds Act and the repeal of NCLB. **The earlier terms such as "highly qualified" and "core academic subjects" were removed from IDEA.** *See* 20 U.S.C. § 1401

109   This may be a typographical error in the statute. There is no 34 CFR § 2005.56, however there is a 34 CFR § 200.56 related to **"Highly Qualified Teacher"** and 34 CFR § 300.156 about "Personnel Qualifications." *See* the ESSA regulations which were issued on July 7, 2017 in 82 FR 31707. URL at:

https://www.govinfo.gov/content/pkg/FR-2017-07-07/pdf/2017-12126.pdf#page=24

behalf of an individual student[110] for the failure of a particular State educational agency or local educational agency staff person to meet the applicable requirements described in this paragraph, or to prevent a parent from filing a complaint about staff qualifications with the State educational agency as provided for under this subchapter.

(15) Performance Goals and Indicators. The State-

(A) has established **goals for the performance of children with disabilities** in the State that

(i) promote the purposes of this title, as stated in Section 1400(d) of this title;

(ii) are the same as the State's long-term goals and measurements of interim progress for children with disabilities under section 6311(c)(4)(A)(i) of this title;

(iii) address **graduation rates and dropout rates**, as well as such other factors as the State may determine; and

(iv) are **consistent**, to the extent appropriate, **with any other goals and standards for children** established by the State;

(B) has established performance indicators the State will use to assess progress toward achieving the goals described in subparagraph (A), including measurements of interim progress for children with disabilities under section 6311(c)(4)(A)(i) of this title; and

(C) will annually report to the Secretary and the public on the progress of the State, and of children with disabilities in the State, toward meeting the goals established under subparagraph (A), which may include elements of the reports required under Section 6311(h) of this title.

(16) Participation in Assessments.

(A) In General. All children with disabilities are included in **all** general State and districtwide **assessment programs**, including assessments described under Section 6311 of this title, with **appropriate accommodations and alternate assessments where necessary** and as indicated in their respective individualized education programs.

(B) Accommodation Guidelines. The State (or, in the case of a districtwide assessment, the local educational agency) has developed guidelines for the provision of appropriate accommodations.

(C) Alternate Assessments.[111]

(i) In General. The State (or, in the case of a districtwide assessment, the local educational agency) has developed and implemented guidelines for the participation of children with disabilities in alternate assessments for those children who cannot participate in regular assessments under subparagraph (A) with accommodations as indicated in their respective individualized education programs.

(ii) Requirements for Alternate Assessments. The guidelines under clause (i) shall provide for alternate assessments that -

(I) are aligned with the challenging State academic content standards under section 6311(b)(1) of this title and alternate academic achievement standards under section 6311(b)(1)(E) of this title; and

(II) if the State has adopted alternate academic achievement standards permitted under section 6311(b)(1)(E) of this title, measure the achievement of children with disabilities against those standards.

(iii) Conduct of Alternate Assessments. The State conducts the alternate assessments described in this subparagraph.

---

110   If an educator does not meet this standard, **there is no right to sue the school district on that basis** alone. However, this may be used as evidence to support that the child did not receive FAPE. Parents may file complaints with the SEA about inadequately trained teachers.

111   For more about alternate assessments, *see* the archived 2004 *Toolkit on Teaching and Assessing Students with Disabilities* from the U.S. Department of Education. URL: https://osepideasthatwork.org/federal-resources-stakeholders/tool-kits/tool-kit-teaching-and-assessing-students-disabilities

(D) Reports. The State educational agency (or, in the case of a districtwide assessment, the local educational agency) makes available to the public, and **reports to the public** with the same frequency and in the same detail as it reports on the assessment of nondisabled children, the following:

(i) The number of children with disabilities participating in regular assessments, and the number of those children who were provided accommodations in order to participate in those assessments.

(ii) The number of children with disabilities participating in alternate assessments described in subparagraph (C)(ii)(I).

(iii) The number of children with disabilities participating in alternate assessments described in subparagraph (C)(ii)(II).

(iv) The **performance of children with disabilities on regular assessments and on alternate assessments** (if the number of children with disabilities participating in those assessments is sufficient to yield statistically reliable information and reporting that information will not reveal personally identifiable information about an individual student), compared with the achievement of all children, including children with disabilities, on those assessments.

(E) Universal Design. The State educational agency (or, in the case of a districtwide assessment, the local educational agency) shall, to the extent feasible, use universal design principles in developing and administering any assessments under this paragraph.[112]

(17) Supplementation of State, Local, and Other Federal Funds.

(A) Expenditures. Funds paid to a State under this part will be expended in accordance with all the provisions of this part.

(B) Prohibition Against Commingling. Funds paid to a State under this part will not be commingled with State funds.

(C) Prohibition Against Supplantation and Conditions for Waiver by Secretary. Except as provided in Section 1413 of this title, funds paid to a State under this part will be used to supplement the level of Federal, State, and local funds (including funds that are not under the direct control of State or local educational agencies) expended for special education and related services provided to children with disabilities under this part and in no case to supplant such Federal, State, and local funds, except that, where the State provides clear and convincing evidence that all children with disabilities have available to them a free appropriate public education, the Secretary may waive, in whole or in part, the requirements of this subparagraph if the Secretary concurs with the evidence provided by the State.

(18) Maintenance of State Financial Support.

(A) In General. The State **does not reduce the amount of State financial support for special education** and related services for children with disabilities, or otherwise made available **because of the excess costs** of educating those children, below the amount of that support for the preceding fiscal year.[113]

---

112   The definition of Universal Design is in 20 U.S.C. § 1401(35) and incorporates by reference 29 U.S.C. § 3002(19). "The term 'universal design' means the concept or philosophy of designing and delivering products and services that are usable by people with the widest possible range of functional capabilities, which include products and services that are directly accessible (without requiring assistive technologies) and products and services that are interoperable with assistive technologies." *See also* "ECTA" - http://ectacenter.org/topics/atech/udl.asp.

113   The state may not reduce special education funding because of the cost to educate children with disabilities. A state must continue its "maintenance of financial support" (MFS). In Texas, an ALJ upheld **withholding** of $33,302,428 from TEA for violation of this statute. On appeal by the TEA, the Fifth Circuit upheld the decision to withhold funding. This case is in 2018 edition of *Wrightslaw Year in Review*. See *Texas Education Agency v. U.S. Dept. of Education,* 908 F.3d 127, (5th Cir 2018) links below:

https://www.wrightslaw.com/law/caselaw/2018/usdoe.v.tea.alj.pdf

https://www.wrightslaw.com/law/caselaw/2018/5th.usdoe.v.tea.pdf

(B) Reduction of Funds for Failure to Maintain Support.[114] The Secretary shall reduce the allocation of funds under Section 1411 of this title for any fiscal year following the fiscal year in which the State fails to comply with the requirement of subparagraph (A) by the same amount by which the State fails to meet the requirement.

(C) Waivers for Exceptional or Uncontrollable Circumstances. The Secretary may waive the requirement of subparagraph (A) for a State, for 1 fiscal year at a time, if the Secretary determines that

(i) granting a waiver would be equitable due to exceptional or uncontrollable circumstances such as a natural disaster or a precipitous and unforeseen decline in the financial resources of the State; or

(ii) the State meets the standard in paragraph (17)(C) for a waiver of the requirement to supplement, and not to supplant, funds received under this part.

(D) Subsequent Years. If, for any year, a State fails to meet the requirement of subparagraph (A), including any year for which the State is granted a waiver under subparagraph (C), the financial support required of the State in future years under subparagraph (A) shall be the amount that would have been required in the absence of that failure and not the reduced level of the State's support.

(19) Public Participation. Prior to the adoption of any policies and procedures needed to comply with this Section (including any amendments to such policies and procedures), the State ensures that there are public hearings, adequate notice of the hearings, and an opportunity for comment available to the general public, including individuals with disabilities and parents of children with disabilities.

(20) Rule of Construction. In complying with paragraphs (17) and (18), a State may not use funds paid to it under this part to satisfy State-law mandated funding obligations to local educational agencies, including funding based on student attendance or enrollment, or inflation.

(21) State Advisory Panel.

(A) In General. The State has established and maintains **an advisory panel for the purpose of providing policy guidance** with respect to special education and related services for children with disabilities in the State.

(B) Membership. Such advisory panel shall consist of members[115] appointed by the Governor, or any other official authorized under State law to make such appointments, be representative of the State population, and be **composed of individuals involved in, or concerned with, the education of children with disabilities, including**–

(i) parents of children with disabilities (ages birth through 26);

(ii) individuals with disabilities;

(iii) teachers;

(iv) representatives of institutions of higher education that prepare special education and related services personnel;

(v) State and local education officials, including officials who carry out activities under subtitle B of title VII of the McKinney-Vento Homeless Assistance Act (42 U.S.C. 11431 *et seq.*);

(vi) administrators of programs for children with disabilities;

(vii) representatives of other State agencies involved in the financing or delivery of related services to children with disabilities;

(viii) representatives of private schools and public charter schools;

(ix) not less than 1 representative of a vocational, community, or business organization concerned with the provision of transition services to children with disabilities;

---

114   *See also* 20 U.S.C. § 1416(c) about USDOE withholding funds and enforcement of IDEA against States for these violations.

115   The majority of the members shall be individuals with disabilities, parents, representatives from private and charter schools, child welfare agencies, corrections agencies, and others involved in the education of children with disabilities.

(x) a representative from the State child welfare agency responsible for foster care; and

(xi) representatives from the State juvenile and adult corrections agencies.

(C) Special Rule. A **majority** of the members of the panel **shall** be individuals with disabilities or parents of children with disabilities (ages birth through 26).

(D) Duties. The advisory panel shall–

(i) advise the State educational agency of unmet needs within the State in the education of children with disabilities;

(ii) comment publicly on any rules or regulations proposed by the State regarding the education of children with disabilities;

(iii) advise the State educational agency in developing evaluations and reporting on data to the Secretary under Section 1418 of this title;

(iv) advise the State educational agency in developing corrective action plans to address findings identified in Federal monitoring reports under this part; and

(v) advise the State educational agency in developing and implementing policies relating to the coordination of services for children with disabilities.

(22) Suspension and Expulsion Rates.

(A) In General. The State educational agency examines data, including data disaggregated by race and ethnicity, **to determine if significant discrepancies are occurring** in the rate of long-term suspensions and expulsions of children with disabilities–

(i) among local educational agencies in the State; or

(ii) compared to such rates for nondisabled children within such agencies.

(B) Review and Revision of Policies. If such discrepancies are occurring, the State educational agency reviews and, if appropriate, revises (or requires the affected State or local educational agency to revise) its **policies, procedures, and practices relating to the development and implementation of IEPs, the use of positive behavioral interventions and supports, and procedural safeguards**, to ensure that such policies, procedures, and practices comply with this title.

(23) Access to Instructional Materials.

(A) In General. The State adopts the **National Instructional Materials Accessibility Standard (NIMAS)** for the **purposes of providing instructional materials to blind persons** or other persons with print disabilities, in a timely manner after the publication of the National Instructional Materials Accessibility Standard in the Federal Register.

(B) Rights of State Educational Agency. Nothing in this paragraph shall be construed to require any State educational agency to coordinate with the National Instructional Materials Access Center. If a State educational agency chooses not to coordinate with the National Instructional Materials Access Center, such agency shall provide an assurance to the Secretary that the agency **will provide instructional materials to blind persons or other persons with print disabilities in a timely manner**.

(C) Preparation and Delivery of Files. If a State educational agency chooses to coordinate with the National Instructional Materials Access Center, not later than 2 years after the date of enactment of the Individuals with Disabilities Education Improvement Act of 2004, the agency, as part of any print instructional materials adoption process, procurement contract, or other practice or instrument used for purchase of print instructional materials, shall enter into a written contract with the publisher of the print instructional materials to–

(i) require the publisher to prepare and, on or before delivery of the print instructional materials, provide to the National Instructional Materials Access Center electronic files containing the contents of the print instructional materials using the National Instructional Materials Accessibility Standard; or

(ii) purchase instructional materials from the publisher that are produced in, or may be rendered in, specialized formats.

(D) Assistive Technology. In carrying out this paragraph, the State educational agency, to the maximum extent possible, shall work collaboratively with the State agency responsible for assistive technology programs.

(E) Definitions. In this paragraph:

(i) **National Instructional Materials Access Center**. The term 'National Instructional Materials Access Center' means the center established pursuant to Section 1474(e) of this title.

(ii) **National Instructional Materials Accessibility Standard**. The term 'National Instructional Materials Accessibility Standard' has the meaning given the term in **Section 1474(e)(3)(A)** of this title.[116]

(iii) **Specialized Formats**. The term 'specialized formats' has the meaning given the term in Section 1474(e)(3)(D) of this title.

(24) Overidentification and Disproportionality.[117] The State has in effect, consistent with the purposes of this title and with Section 1418(d) of this title, **policies and procedures designed to prevent the inappropriate overidentification or disproportionate representation by race and ethnicity** of children as children with disabilities, including children with disabilities with a particular impairment described in Section 1401 of this title.

(25) Prohibition on Mandatory Medication.[118]

(A) In General. The State educational agency **shall prohibit** State and local educational agency personnel from **requiring a child to obtain a prescription for a substance covered by the Controlled Substances Act** (21 U.S.C. 801 *et seq.*) **as a condition of attending school, receiving an evaluation** under subsection (a) or (c) of Section 1414 of this title, **or receiving services** under this title.

(B) Rule of Construction. **Nothing** in subparagraph (A) **shall be construed to create a Federal prohibition against** teachers and other **school personnel consulting or sharing classroom-based observations with parents or guardians** regarding a student's academic and functional performance, or behavior in the classroom or school, or regarding the need for evaluation for special education or related services under paragraph (3).

(b) State Educational Agency as Provider of Free Appropriate Public Education or Direct Services. If the State educational agency provides free appropriate public education to children with disabilities, or provides direct services to such children, such agency–

(1) shall comply with any additional requirements of Section 1413(a) of this title, as if such agency were a local educational agency; and

(2) may use amounts that are otherwise available to such agency under this part to serve those children without regard to Section 1413(a)(2)(A)(i) of this title (relating to excess costs).

(c) Exception for Prior State Plans.

(1) In General. If a State has on file with the Secretary policies and procedures that demonstrate that such State meets any requirement of subsection (a), including any policies and procedures filed under this part as in effect

116 The National Instructional Materials Accessibility Standard (NIMAS) provides a system to produce and distribute digital versions of textbooks and other instructional materials that can be converted to accessible formats. IDEA requires that all textbooks and supplemental curricular materials be provided as NIMAS files by mid-December 2006. *See* the National Center on Accessible Educational Materials at: http://aem.cast.org/.

117 In "Findings" at 20 U.S.C. § 1400(c)(12)(C), (E), Congress found that "African-American children are identified as having intellectual disabilities and emotional disturbance at rates greater than their White counterparts. . . [and] schools with predominately White students and teachers have placed disproportionately high numbers of their minority students into special education." States must develop policies and procedures to correct these problems.
Does your state have such "policies and procedures" and enforce compliance with them?

118 **School personnel are prohibited from requiring a child to obtain a prescription** for a controlled substance (i.e., Ritalin, Adderal, etc.) in order to attend school, receive an evaluation, or receive special education services.

before the effective date of the Individuals with Disabilities Education Improvement Act of 2004, the Secretary shall consider such State to have met such requirement for purposes of receiving a grant under this part.

(2) Modifications Made by State. Subject to paragraph (3), an application submitted by a State in accordance with this section shall remain in effect until the State submits to the Secretary such modifications as the State determines necessary. This section shall apply to a modification to an application to the same extent and in the same manner as this section applies to the original plan.

(3) Modifications Required by the Secretary. If, after the effective date of the Individuals with Disabilities Education Improvement Act of 2004, the provisions of this title are amended (or the regulations developed to carry out this title are amended), there is a new interpretation of this title by a Federal court or a State's highest court, or there is an official finding of noncompliance with Federal law or regulations, then the Secretary may require a State to modify its application only to the extent necessary to ensure the State's compliance with this part.

(d) Approval by the Secretary.

(1) In General. If the Secretary determines that a State is eligible to receive a grant under this part, the Secretary shall notify the State of that determination.

(2) Notice and Hearing. The Secretary shall not make a final determination that a State is not eligible to receive a grant under this part until after providing the State–

(A) with reasonable notice; and

(B) with an opportunity for a hearing.[119]

(e) Assistance Under Other Federal Programs.

Nothing in this title permits a State to reduce medical and other assistance available, or to alter eligibility, under titles V and XIX of the Social Security Act[120] with respect to the provision of a free appropriate public education for children with disabilities in the State.

(f) By-Pass for Children in Private Schools.

(1) In General. If, on the date of enactment of the Education of the Handicapped Act Amendments of 1983, a State educational agency was prohibited by law from providing for the equitable participation in special programs of children with disabilities enrolled in private elementary schools and secondary schools as required by subsection (a)(10)(A), or if the Secretary determines that a State educational agency, local educational agency, or other entity has substantially failed or is unwilling to provide for such equitable participation, then the Secretary shall, notwithstanding such provision of law, arrange for the provision of services to such children through arrangements that shall be subject to the requirements of such subsection.

(2) Payments.

(A) Determination of Amounts. If the Secretary arranges for services pursuant to this subsection, the Secretary, after consultation with the appropriate public and private school officials, shall pay to the provider of such services for a fiscal year an amount per child that does not exceed the amount determined by dividing–

(i) the total amount received by the State under this part for such fiscal year; by

(ii) the number of children with disabilities served in the prior year, as reported to the Secretary by the State under Section 1418 of this title.

(B) Withholding of Certain Amounts. Pending final resolution of any investigation or complaint that may result in a determination under this subsection, the Secretary may withhold from the allocation of the affected State educational agency the amount the Secretary estimates will be necessary to pay the cost of services described in subparagraph (A).

---

119   *See* the decisions in the *Texas Education Agency v. USDOE* Administrative Hearing and appeal to the Fifth Circuit in the discussion about <20 U.S.C. § 1412(a)(18).>

120   Title V focuses on improving the health of all mothers and children and funding support for programs for children with special health needs. Title XIX relates to Medicaid. The URLs for each are:
https://www.law.cornell.edu/uscode/text/42/chapter-7/subchapter-V
and https://www.law.cornell.edu/uscode/text/42/chapter-7/subchapter-XIX

(C) Period of Payments. The period under which payments are made under subparagraph (A) shall continue until the Secretary determines that there will no longer be any failure or inability on the part of the State educational agency to meet the requirements of subsection (a)(10)(A).

(3) Notice and Hearing.

(A) In General. The Secretary shall not take any final action under this subsection until the State educational agency affected by such action has had an opportunity, for not less than 45 days after receiving written notice thereof, to submit written objections and to appear before the Secretary or the Secretary's designee to show cause why such action should not be taken.

(B) Review of Action. If a State educational agency is dissatisfied with the Secretary's final action after a proceeding under subparagraph (A), such agency may, not later than 60 days after notice of such action, file with the United States court of appeals for the circuit in which such State is located a petition for review of that action. A copy of the petition shall be forthwith transmitted by the clerk of the court to the Secretary. The Secretary thereupon shall file in the court the record of the proceedings on which the Secretary based the Secretary's action, as provided in Section 2112 of title 28, United States Code.

(C) Review of Findings of Fact. The findings of fact by the Secretary, if supported by substantial evidence, shall be conclusive, but the court, for good cause shown, may remand the case to the Secretary to take further evidence, and the Secretary may thereupon make new or modified findings of fact and may modify the Secretary's previous action, and shall file in the court the record of the further proceedings. Such new or modified findings of fact shall likewise be conclusive if supported by substantial evidence.

(D) Jurisdiction of Court of Appeals; Review by United States Supreme Court. Upon the filing of a petition under subparagraph (B), the United States court of appeals shall have jurisdiction to affirm the action of the Secretary or to set it aside, in whole or in part. The judgment of the court shall be subject to review by the Supreme Court of the United States upon certiorari or certification as provided in Section 1254 of title 28, United States Code.

20 U.S.C. § 1413 - Local Educational Agency Eligibility.[121]

(a) In General - A local educational agency is eligible for assistance under this part for a fiscal year if such agency submits a plan that provides assurances to the State educational agency that the local educational agency meets each of the following conditions:

(1) Consistency With State Policies. The local educational agency, in providing for the education of children with disabilities within its jurisdiction, has in effect policies, procedures, and programs that are consistent with the State policies and procedures established under Section 1412 of this title.

(2) Use of Amounts.

(A) In General. Amounts provided to the local educational agency under this part shall be expended in accordance with the applicable provisions of this part and–

(i) shall be used only to pay the excess costs of providing special education and related services to children with disabilities;

(ii) shall be used to supplement State, local, and other Federal funds and not to supplant such funds; and

(iii) shall not be used, except as provided in subparagraphs (B) and (C), to reduce the level of expenditures for the education of children with disabilities made by the local educational agency from local funds below the level of those expenditures for the preceding fiscal year.

---

121 **Wrightslaw Overview:** Section 1413 includes requirements for **school district (LEA) and charter school eligibility**. This section includes requirements about purchasing instructional materials, records of migratory children, and early intervening services. School districts must provide services to children with disabilities who attend charter schools in the same manner as children who attend other public schools, and must provide supplementary services and related services on site at the charter school. Section 1413(a)(6) describes requirements about access to instructional materials and the option of coordinating with the National Instructional Materials Access Center. Section 1413(f) describes requirements for early intervening services. If a school district does not comply with the law, States can provide direct services.

(B) Exception. Notwithstanding the restriction in subparagraph (A)(iii), a local educational agency may reduce the level of expenditures where such reduction is attributable to–

(i) the voluntary departure, by retirement or otherwise, or departure for just cause, of special education personnel;

(ii) a decrease in the enrollment of children with disabilities;

(iii) the termination of the obligation of the agency, consistent with this part, to provide a program of special education to a particular child with a disability that is an exceptionally costly program, as determined by the State educational agency, because the child–

(I) has left the jurisdiction of the agency;

(II) has reached the age at which the obligation of the agency to provide a free appropriate public education to the child has terminated; or

(III) no longer needs such program of special education; or

(iv) the termination of costly expenditures for long-term purchases, such as the acquisition of equipment or the construction of school facilities.

(C) Adjustment to Local Fiscal Effort in Certain Fiscal Years.

(i) Amounts in Excess. Notwithstanding clauses (ii) and (iii) of subparagraph (A), for any fiscal year for which the allocation received by a local educational agency under Section 1411(f) of this title exceeds the amount the local educational agency received for the previous fiscal year, the local educational agency may reduce the level of expenditures otherwise required by subparagraph (A)(iii) by not more than 50 percent of the amount of such excess.

(ii) Use of Amounts to Carry Out Activities Under ESEA. If a local educational agency exercises the authority under clause (i), the agency shall use an amount of local funds equal to the reduction in expenditures under clause (i) to carry out activities authorized under the Elementary and Secondary Education Act of 1965. [20 U.S.C. § 6301 *et seq*.]

(iii) State Prohibition. Notwithstanding clause (i), if a State educational agency determines that a local educational agency is unable to establish and maintain programs of free appropriate public education that meet the requirements of subsection (a) or the State educational agency has taken action against the local educational agency under Section 1416 of this title, the State educational agency **shall prohibit** the local educational agency from reducing the level of expenditures under clause (i) for that fiscal year.

(iv) Special Rule. The amount of funds expended by a local educational agency under subsection (f) shall count toward the maximum amount of expenditures such local educational agency may reduce under clause (i).

(D) Schoolwide Programs Under Title I of the ESEA. Notwithstanding subparagraph (A) or any other provision of this part, a local educational agency may use funds received under this part for any fiscal year to carry out a schoolwide program under Section 6314 of this title, except that the amount so used in any such program shall not exceed–

(i) the number of children with disabilities participating in the schoolwide program; multiplied by

(ii)

(I) the amount received by the local educational agency under this part for that fiscal year; divided by

(II) the number of children with disabilities in the jurisdiction of that agency.

(3) Personnel Development. The local educational agency **shall ensure that all personnel** necessary to carry out this part **are appropriately and adequately prepared**, subject to the requirements of section 1412(a)(14) of this title and section 2102(b) of the Elementary and Secondary Education Act of 1965 [20 U.S.C. 6612(b)].

(4) Permissive Use of Funds.

(A) Uses. Notwithstanding paragraph (2)(A) or Section 1412(a)(17)(B) of this title (relating to commingled funds), funds provided to the local educational agency under this part may be used for the following activities:

(i) Services and Aids That Also Benefit Nondisabled Children. For the costs of special education and related services, and supplementary aids and services, provided in a regular class or other education-related setting to a child with a disability in accordance with the individualized education program of the child, even if 1 or more nondisabled children benefit from such services.

(ii) Early Intervening Services. To develop and implement coordinated, early intervening educational services in accordance with subsection (f).

(iii) High Cost Education and Related Services. To establish and implement cost or risk sharing funds, consortia, or cooperatives for the local educational agency itself, or for local educational agencies working in a consortium of which the local educational agency is a part, **to pay for high cost special education and related services**.

(B) Administrative Case Management. A local educational agency may use funds received under this part to purchase appropriate technology for recordkeeping, data collection, and related case management activities of teachers and related services personnel providing services described in the individualized education program of children with disabilities, that is needed for the implementation of such case management activities.

(5) Treatment of Charter Schools[122] **and Their Students**. In carrying out this part with respect to charter schools that are public schools of the local educational agency, the local educational agency–

(A) **serves children with disabilities attending those charter schools in the same manner**[123] as the local educational agency serves **children with disabilities in its other schools**, including providing supplementary and related services on site at the charter school to the same extent to which the local educational agency has a policy or practice of providing such services on the site to its other public schools; and

(B) provides funds under this part to those charter schools–

(i) on the same basis as the local educational agency provides funds to the local educational agency's other public schools, including proportional distribution based on relative enrollment of children with disabilities; and

(ii) at the same time as the agency distributes other Federal funds to the agency's other public schools, consistent with the State's charter school law.

(6) Purchase of Instructional Materials.

(A) In General. Not later than **2 years** after the date of enactment of the Individuals with Disabilities Education Improvement Act of 2004, a local educational agency that chooses to coordinate with the National Instructional Materials Access Center, when purchasing print instructional materials, shall acquire the print instructional materials in the same manner and subject to the same conditions as a State educational agency acquires print instructional materials under Section 1412(a)(23) of this title.

(B) Rights of Local Educational Agency. Nothing in this paragraph shall be construed to require a local educational agency to coordinate with the National Instructional Materials Access Center. If a local educational agency chooses not to coordinate with the National Instructional Materials Access Center, the local educational agency shall provide an assurance to the State educational agency that the local educational agency will provide instructional materials to blind persons or other persons with print disabilities in a timely manner.

---

122   For more information about charter schools, *see* 34 CFR § 300.209 and <Selected Topics: Charter Schools in Chapter 10.>

123   Charter schools are to serve children with disabilities in the same manner, as public schools, i.e., they may not discriminate.

(7) Information for State Educational Agency. The local educational agency shall provide the State educational agency with information necessary to enable the State educational agency to carry out its duties under this part, including, with respect to paragraphs (15) and (16) of Section 1412(a) of this title, information relating to the performance of children with disabilities participating in programs carried out under this part.

(8) Public Information. The local educational agency shall make available to parents of children with disabilities and to the general public all documents relating to the eligibility of such agency under this part.

(9) Records Regarding Migratory Children with Disabilities. The local educational agency shall cooperate in the Secretary's efforts under Section 6398 of this title **to ensure the linkage of records** pertaining to migratory children with a disability for the purpose of electronically exchanging, among the States, health and educational information regarding such children.

(b) Exception for Prior Local Plans.

(1) In General. If a local educational agency or State agency has on file with the State educational agency policies and procedures that demonstrate that such local educational agency, or such State agency, as the case may be, meets any requirement of subsection (a), including any policies and procedures filed under this part as in effect before the effective date of the Individuals with Disabilities Education Improvement Act of 2004, the State educational agency shall consider such local educational agency or State agency, as the case may be, to have met such requirement for purposes of receiving assistance under this part.

(2) Modification Made by Local Educational Agency. Subject to paragraph (3), an application submitted by a local educational agency in accordance with this section shall remain in effect until the local educational agency submits to the State educational agency such modifications as the local educational agency determines necessary.

(3) Modifications Required by State Educational Agency. If, after the effective date of the Individuals with Disabilities Education Improvement Act of 2004, the provisions of this title are amended (or the regulations developed to carry out this title are amended), there is a new interpretation of this title by Federal or State courts, or there is an official finding of noncompliance with Federal or State law or regulations, then the State educational agency may require a local educational agency to modify its application only to the extent necessary to ensure the local educational agency's compliance with this part or State law.

(c) Notification of Local Educational Agency or State Agency in Case of Ineligibility.

If the State educational agency determines that a local educational agency or State agency is not eligible under this section, then the State educational agency **shall notify the local educational agency** or State agency, as the case may be, of that determination and shall provide such local educational agency or State agency with reasonable notice and an opportunity for a hearing.

(d) Local Educational Agency Compliance

(1) In General. If the State educational agency, after reasonable notice and an opportunity for a hearing, finds that a local educational agency or State agency that has been determined to be eligible under this section **is failing to comply**[124] **with any requirement** described in subsection (a), the State educational agency **shall reduce or shall not provide any further payments** to the local educational agency or State agency **until** the State educational agency is satisfied that the local educational agency or State agency, as the case may be, is complying with that requirement.

(2) Additional Requirement. Any State agency or local educational agency in receipt of a notice described in paragraph (1) shall, by means of public notice, take such measures as may be necessary to bring the pendency of an action pursuant to this subsection to the attention of the public within the jurisdiction of such agency.

---

124   If a school district fails to comply with the requirements described in Section 1413(a), the State **must eliminate payments** until the district is in compliance. **This requirement is not discretionary.**

(3) Consideration. In carrying out its responsibilities under paragraph (1), the State educational agency **shall consider any decision made in a hearing**[125] **held under Section 1415** of this title that is **adverse** to the local educational agency or State agency involved in that decision.

(e) Joint Establishment of Eligibility

(1) Joint Establishment.

(A) In General. A State educational agency may require a local educational agency to establish its eligibility jointly with another local educational agency if the State educational agency determines that the local educational agency will be ineligible under this section because the local educational agency will not be able to establish and maintain programs of sufficient size and scope to effectively meet the needs of children with disabilities.

(B) Charter School Exception. A State educational agency may not require a charter school that is a local educational agency to jointly establish its eligibility under subparagraph (A) unless the charter school is explicitly permitted to do so under the State's charter school law.

(2) Amount of Payments. If a State educational agency requires the joint establishment of eligibility under paragraph (1), the total amount of funds made available to the affected local educational agencies shall be equal to the sum of the payments that each such local educational agency would have received under Section 1411(f) of this title if such agencies were eligible for such payments.

(3) Requirements. Local educational agencies that establish joint eligibility under this subsection shall–

(A) adopt policies and procedures that are consistent with the State's policies and procedures under Section 1412(a) of this title; and

(B) be jointly responsible for implementing programs that receive assistance under this part.

(4) Requirements for Educational Service Agencies.

(A) In General. If an educational service agency is required by State law to carry out programs under this part, the joint responsibilities given to local educational agencies under this subsection shall–

(i) not apply to the administration and disbursement of any payments received by that educational service agency; and

(ii) be carried out only by that educational service agency.

(B) Additional Requirement. Notwithstanding any other provision of this subsection, an educational service agency shall provide for the education of children with disabilities in the least restrictive environment, as required by Section 1412(a)(5) of this title.

(f) Early Intervening Services.[126]

(1) In General. A local educational agency **may not use more than 15 percent** of the amount such agency receives under this part for any fiscal year, less any amount reduced by the agency pursuant to subsection (a)(2)(C), if any, in combination with other amounts (which may include amounts other than education funds), to develop and implement coordinated, early intervening services, which may include interagency financing structures, for students in kindergarten through grade 12 (with a particular emphasis on students in kindergarten through grade 3) who have **not been identified as needing special education** or related services but **who need additional academic and behavioral support** to succeed in a general education environment.

(2) Activities. In implementing coordinated, early intervening services under this subsection, a local educational agency may carry out activities that include–

---

125   In determining whether a school district is in compliance with the law and whether to withhold funds, the State **shall consider due process decisions that are adverse to the LEA.** This requirement is mandatory.

126   School districts may use **up to 15 percent** of their funds from Part B to develop and implement early intervening services for students who need academic and behavioral assistance but have not been identified as needing special education services. Funds can be used for training so teachers have the knowledge and skills to deliver scientifically based academic instruction and literacy instruction. Funds can also be used to provide students with educational evaluations, services and supports, including scientifically based literacy instruction.

(A) **professional development** (which may be provided by entities other than local educational agencies) for teachers and other school staff to enable such personnel to deliver **scientifically based academic instruction and behavioral interventions**, including **scientifically based literacy instruction,** and, where appropriate, instruction on the use of adaptive and instructional software; and

(B) providing educational and behavioral evaluations, services, and supports, including **scientifically based literacy instruction**.

(3) Construction. Nothing in this subsection shall be construed to limit or create a right to a free appropriate public education under this part.

(4) Reporting. Each local educational agency that develops and maintains coordinated, early intervening services under this subsection shall annually report to the State educational agency on–

(A) the number of students served under this subsection; and

(B) the number of students served under this subsection who subsequently receive special education and related services under this title during the preceding 2-year period.

(5) Coordination with Elementary and Secondary Education Act of 1965. Funds made available to carry out this subsection may be used to carry out coordinated, early intervening services aligned with activities funded by, and carried out under, the Elementary and Secondary Education Act of 1965 if such funds are used to supplement, and not supplant, funds made available under the Elementary and Secondary Education Act of 1965 for the activities and services assisted under this subsection.

(g) Direct Services by the State Educational Agency.

(1) In General. A State educational agency shall use the payments that would otherwise have been available to a local educational agency or to a State agency to provide special education and related services directly to children with disabilities residing in the area served by that local educational agency, or for whom that State agency is responsible, if the State educational agency determines that the local educational agency or State agency, as the case may be–

(A) has not provided the information needed to establish the eligibility of such local educational agency or State agency under this section;

(B) is unable to establish and maintain programs of free appropriate public education that meet the requirements of subsection (a);

(C) is unable or unwilling to be consolidated with 1 or more local educational agencies in order to establish and maintain such programs; or

(D) has 1 or more children with disabilities who can best be served by a regional or State program or service delivery system designed to meet the needs of such children.

(2) Manner and Location of Education and Services. The State educational agency may provide special education and related services under paragraph (1) in such manner and at such locations (including regional or State centers) as the State educational agency considers appropriate. Such education and services shall be provided in accordance with this part.

(h) State Agency Eligibility - Any State agency that desires to receive a subgrant for any fiscal year under Section 1411(f) of this title shall demonstrate to the satisfaction of the State educational agency that –

(1) all children with disabilities who are participating in programs and projects funded under this part receive a free appropriate public education, and that those children and their parents are provided all the rights and procedural safeguards described in this part; and

(2) the agency meets such other conditions of this section as the Secretary determines to be appropriate.

(i) Disciplinary Information

The State may require that a local educational agency include in the records of a child with a disability a statement of **any current or previous disciplinary action** that has been taken against the child and transmit such statement to the same extent that such disciplinary information is included in, and transmitted with, the student records of nondisabled children. The statement may include a description of any behavior engaged in by the child that required disciplinary action, a description of the disciplinary action taken, and any other information that is relevant to the safety of the child and other individuals involved with the child. If the State adopts such a policy, and the child transfers from 1 school to another, the transmission of any of the child's records shall include both the child's current individualized education program and any such statement of current or previous disciplinary action that has been taken against the child.

(j) State Agency Flexibility.

(1) Adjustment to State Fiscal Effort in Certain Fiscal Years. For any fiscal year for which the allotment received by a State under Section 1411 of this title exceeds the amount the State received for the previous fiscal year and if the State in school year 2003-2004 or any subsequent school year pays or reimburses all local educational agencies within the State from State revenue 100 percent of the non-Federal share of the costs of special education and related services, the State educational agency, notwithstanding paragraphs (17) and (18) of Section 1412(a) of this title and Section 1412(b) of this title, may reduce the level of expenditures from State sources for the education of children with disabilities by not more than 50 percent of the amount of such excess.

(2) Prohibition. Notwithstanding paragraph (1), if the Secretary determines that a State educational agency is unable to establish, maintain, or oversee programs of free appropriate public education that meet the requirements of this part, or that the State needs assistance, intervention, or substantial intervention under Section 1416(d)(2)(A) of this title, the Secretary shall prohibit the State educational agency from exercising the authority in paragraph (1).

(3) Education Activities. If a State educational agency exercises the authority under paragraph (1), the agency shall use funds from State sources, in an amount equal to the amount of the reduction under paragraph (1), to support activities authorized under the Elementary and Secondary Education Act of 1965 or to support need based student or teacher higher education programs.

(4) Report. For each fiscal year for which a State educational agency exercises the authority under paragraph (1), the State educational agency shall report to the Secretary the amount of expenditures reduced pursuant to such paragraph and the activities that were funded pursuant to paragraph (3).

(5) Limitation. Notwithstanding paragraph (1), a State educational agency may not reduce the level of expenditures described in paragraph (1) if any local educational agency in the State would, as a result of such reduction, receive less than 100 percent of the amount necessary to ensure that all children with disabilities served by the local educational agency receive a free appropriate public education from the combination of Federal funds received under this title and State funds received from the State educational agency.

20 U.S.C. § 1414 - Evaluations, Eligibility Determinations, Individualized Education Programs, and Educational Placements.[127, 128, 129]

(a) Evaluations, Parental Consent, and Reevaluations.

(1) Initial Evaluations.

(A) In General. A State educational agency, other State agency, or local educational agency **shall conduct a full and individual initial evaluation** in accordance with this paragraph and subsection (b), before the initial provision of special education and related services to a child with a disability under this part.

(B) Request for Initial Evaluation.[130] Consistent with subparagraph (D), either a **parent** of a child,[131] or a State educational agency, other State agency, or local educational agency **may initiate a request for an initial evaluation** to determine if the child is a child with a disability.[132]

(C) Procedures.

(i) In General. Such initial evaluation **shall** consist of procedures–

(I) to determine whether a child **is a child with a disability** (as defined in Section 1401 of this title **within 60 days of receiving parental consent** for the evaluation, **or, if the State** establishes a timeframe within which the evaluation must be conducted, within such timeframe; and

(II) to determine the **educational needs** of such child.[133]

(ii) Exception. The relevant timeframe in clause (i)(I) shall not apply to a local educational agency if–

(I) a child enrolls in a school served by the local educational agency after the relevant timeframe in clause (i)(I) has begun and prior to a determination by the child's previous local educational agency as to whether the child is a child with a disability (as defined in Section 1401 of this title), but only if the subsequent local educational agency is making sufficient progress to ensure a prompt

---

127 **Wrightslaw Overview:** The subsections of Section 1414, (a through f), include requirements for evaluations, reevaluations, eligibility, Individualized Education Programs, and educational placements. **Section 1414(a)** describes requirements for initial evaluations, parental consent, the 60-day timeline to complete evaluations, and limits on reevaluations. **Section 1414(b)** describes evaluation procedures, requirements about determining educational needs, and the discontinuance of the discrepancy model to identify children with specific learning disabilities. **Section 1414(c)** states that schools must consider evaluations and information provided by parents and that schools must reevaluate a child before terminating eligibility.

Section 1414(d) is the law of Individualized Education Programs (IEPs), IEP Team members, meeting attendance, consolidated meetings, and reviewing and revising IEPs. Some states have different names for this process or the steps within the process. An FIE is a "Full and Individual Evaluation," REED is a "review of existing evaluation data," and the ARD committee is the "admission, review, and dismissal" committee. Sometimes the ARD team is the IEP team.

Section 1414(e) clarifies that the parent is a member of any group that makes decisions about a child's educational placement. **Section 1414(f)** describes alternate means of participating in meetings. The **Regulations** about <evaluations start at 300.300> and the **Commentary** in the Federal Register starts at 71 Fed. Reg. 46629 (August 14, 2006). The Regulations about <IEPs starts at 300.320> and the Commentary in the Federal Register begins at 71 Fed. Reg. 46661 (August 14, 2006).

128 https://www.wrightslaw.com/idea/comment/46629-46661.reg.300-311.evals.pdf

129 https://www.wrightslaw.com/idea/comment/46661-46688.reg.320-328.ieps.pdf

130 If a parent requests an evaluation and the LEA refuses, the LEA must provide Prior Written Notice (PWN). *See* 20 U.S.C. § 1415(c)(1) and the Commentary in the *Federal Register*. 71 Fed. Reg. 46636 (August 14, 2006).

131 For sample letters, including a letter to request an evaluation for special education services, *see **Wrightslaw: From Emotions to Advocacy**.*

132 A "child with a disability" is defined in <20 U.S.C. § 1401(3)> and in the Regulations at <34 CFR § 300.8.>

133 IDEA requires the district to complete the initial evaluation and determination of eligibility **within 60 days** of receiving parental *consent* **unless the state has adopted a longer or shorter timeline**. It is the date of the **receipt of consent and *not* the date of the request**. Many states have established timeframes **beyond 60 calendar days. You need to check your state's regulations on this issue**. When federal regulations create a timeline of "days" per <34 CFR § 300.11>, this is **defined as calendar days** and not school days. This statute permits a state regulation to specify an alternative timeline, such as school days, business days, instructional days, or other term. Earlier reauthorizations of IDEA did not include a timeline. Some states have adopted very long timelines, which create delays that prevent children from receiving the services they need. Check your State regulations for the timeline.

completion of the evaluation, and the parent and subsequent local educational agency agree to a specific time when the evaluation will be completed; or

(II) the parent of a child repeatedly fails or refuses to produce the child for the evaluation.

(D) Parental Consent.[134]

(i) In General.

(I) Consent for Initial Evaluation. The agency proposing to conduct an initial evaluation to determine if the child qualifies as a child with a disability as defined in Section 1401 of this title **shall obtain informed consent from the parent**[135] of such child before conducting the evaluation. Parental consent for evaluation **shall not** be construed as consent for placement for receipt of special education and related services.

(II) Consent for Services. An agency that is responsible for making a free appropriate public education available to a child with a disability under this part **shall** seek to obtain **informed consent** from the parent of such child before providing special education and related services to the child.

(ii) Absence of Consent.[136]

(I) For Initial Evaluation. If the parent of such child **does not provide consent for an initial evaluation** under clause (i)(I), or the parent fails to respond to a request to provide the consent, the local educational agency **may pursue the initial evaluation of the child by utilizing the procedures described in Section 1415 of this title**, except to the extent **inconsistent with State law** relating to such parental consent.[137]

(II) For Services. If the parent of such child **refuses to consent to services** under clause (i)(II), the local educational agency **shall not provide special education and related services** to the child by utilizing the procedures described in Section 1415 of this title.

(III) Effect on Agency Obligations. If the parent of such child **refuses to consent to the receipt of special education and related services**, **or the parent fails to respond** to a request to provide such consent

(aa) the local educational agency **shall not** be considered to be in violation of the requirement to make available a free appropriate public education to the child for the failure to provide such child with the special education and related services for which the local educational agency requests such consent; and

(bb) the local educational agency **shall not** be required to convene an IEP meeting or develop an IEP under this section for the child for the special education and related services for which the local educational agency requests such consent.

---

134 The school must obtain parental consent before conducting the initial evaluation. Parental consent for an evaluation is not consent for the child to receive special education services. For information about consent, *see* 34 CFR § 300.9. For information about initial evaluations, *see* 34 CFR § 300.301. The school must obtain informed parental consent before providing such services.

135 The definitions of "parent" and "foster parent" are at 20 U.S.C. § 1401(23) and "ward of the state" is at 20 U.S.C. §1401(36).

136 If the parent does not consent to an evaluation, subject to state law, the district may request a due process hearing against the parent. However, if the parent does not consent to special education services, the district may not pursue a due process hearing against the parent. If the parent refuses consent for services, the district has not violated the IDEA, and is not required to convene an IEP meeting or develop an IEP for the child. *See* the July 19, 2004 letter from Stephanie Lee, Director of OSEP / USDOE to attorney Leigh Manasevit and July 14, 2004 letter from Lee to attorney Howard Fulfrost, at:

https://sites.ed.gov/idea/files/idea/policy/speced/guid/idea/letters/2004-3/manasevit071904eval3q2004.pdf

https://sites.ed.gov/idea/files/idea/policy/speced/guid/idea/letters/2004-3/fulfrost071404eval3q2004.pdf

137 Pursuant to 34 CFR § 300.300(d)(4)(i), if the child is home schooled, or placed in a private school at parent expense, the LEA cannot use due process procedures to force the evaluation.

(iii) Consent for Wards of the State.[138]

(I) In General. If the child is a ward of the State and is not residing with the child's parent, the agency shall make reasonable efforts to obtain the **informed consent from the parent** (as defined in Section 1401 of this title) of the child for an initial evaluation to determine whether the child is a child with a disability.

(II) Exception. The agency shall not be required to obtain informed consent from the parent of a child for an initial evaluation to determine whether the child is a child with a disability if–

(aa) despite reasonable efforts to do so, the agency cannot discover the whereabouts of the parent of the child;

(bb) the rights of the parents of the child have been terminated in accordance with State law; or

(cc) the rights of the parent to make educational decisions have been subrogated by a judge in accordance with State law and consent for an initial evaluation has been given by **an individual appointed by the judge to represent the child**.

(E) Rule of Construction. The **screening of a student by a teacher or specialist** to determine appropriate instructional strategies for curriculum implementation **shall not be considered to be an evaluation for eligibility** for special education and related services.[139]

(2) Reevaluations.[140]

(A) In General. A local educational agency **shall ensure that a reevaluation** of each child with a disability is conducted in accordance with subsections (b) and (c)–

(i) **if** the local educational agency determines that the **educational or related services needs,** including improved academic achievement and functional performance, of the child **warrant a reevaluation**; or

(ii) **if** the child's **parents or teacher requests a reevaluation**.

(B) Limitation.[141] A reevaluation conducted under subparagraph (A) **shall occur**–

(i) not more frequently than **once a year,** unless the parent and the local educational agency agree otherwise; and

(ii) **at least once every 3 years**, unless the parent and the local educational agency agree that a reevaluation is unnecessary.

---

138   If the child is a ward of the state, the school must try to obtain parental consent for an initial evaluation. Exceptions to this requirement are listed. If a judge terminates parental rights or takes educational decision-making rights from the parent, the judge may appoint another individual, such as a probation officer or social worker or other individual, who can make decisions for the child and give consent to an initial evaluation.

139   A "screening" by a teacher or educational diagnostician to determine instructional strategies is not an "evaluation" for eligibility subject to the parental consent requirements for evaluations.

140   The school is not required to reevaluate a child more often than once a year, unless the parent and school agree otherwise. The school shall evaluate at least every three years, unless the parent and school agree that a reevaluation is unnecessary. The school must reevaluate if the child's educational needs change, if the child's parent or teacher request a reevaluation, or the school wants to terminate eligibility for special education pursuant to 20 U.S.C. § 1414(c)(5).

141   Since IDEA requires that the IEP include "a statement of the **child's present levels of academic achievement** and functional performance" (20 U.S.C. § 1414(d)(1)(A)(i)), limits on the frequency of reevaluations are likely to cause difficulties in developing IEPs. If the child has not been evaluated for a year or more, the IEP Team will not have accurate information about the child's present levels of academic achievement and functional performance. If a parent requests a reevaluation and the LEA refuses, as with initial evaluations, the LEA must provide Prior Written Notice (PWN). *See* 20 U.S.C. § 1415(c)(1) and Commentary in the *Federal Register,* 71 Fed. Reg. 46640 (August 14, 2006)

(b) Evaluation Procedures.[142]

(1) Notice. The local educational agency **shall provide notice to the parents** of a child with a disability, in accordance with subsections (b)(3), (b)(4), and (c) of Section 1415 of this title, that describes any evaluation procedures such agency proposes to conduct.

(2) Conduct of Evaluation. In conducting the evaluation, the local educational agency **shall–**

(A) use a **variety of assessment tools and strategies to gather relevant functional, developmental, and academic information**, including **information provided by the parent**,[143] that may assist in determining–

(i) **whether the child is a child with a disability**; and

(ii) the **content of the child's individualized education program**, including information related to enabling the child **to be involved in and progress in the general education curriculum**, or, for preschool children, to participate in appropriate activities;

(B) **not use any single measure or assessment as the sole criterion** for determining whether a child is a child with a disability or determining an appropriate educational program for the child; and

(C) **use technically sound instruments** that may assess the relative contribution of **cognitive and behavioral factors**, in addition to **physical or developmental factors**.

(3) Additional Requirements. Each local educational agency **shall ensure that**

(A) **assessments and other evaluation materials** used to assess a child under this section–

(i) are selected and administered so as **not** to be **discriminatory on a racial or cultural basis**;

(ii) are provided and administered in the language and form most likely to **yield accurate information on what the child knows and can do academically, developmentally, and functionally**, unless it is not feasible to so provide or administer;

(iii) are used for purposes for which the assessments or measures are **valid and reliable**;

(iv) are administered by **trained and knowledgeable personnel**; and

(v) are administered in accordance with any instructions provided by the producer of such assessments;

(B) the child is assessed in **all areas of suspected disability**;[144]

(C) assessment tools and strategies that provide relevant information that directly assists persons in **determining the educational needs** of the child are provided; and

(D) assessments of children with disabilities **who transfer from 1 school district to another school district in the same academic year** are coordinated with such children's prior and subsequent schools, as necessary and **as expeditiously as possible**, to ensure prompt completion of full evaluations.[145]

---

142 The school "shall use a variety of assessment tools and strategies to gather relevant functional, developmental, and academic information" about the child. The school shall "not use any single measure or assessment as the sole criterion" for determining if a child is eligible. **Information from the evaluation is to be used to determine the contents of the child's IEP** and how to help the child make progress in the general education curriculum.

143 If you are a parent, be sure to inform the school **in writing** of all disabilities you suspect. Parents are more likely to obtain a useful evaluation if the evaluators are provided with a written copy of the parental concerns and questions before beginning the evaluation.

144 In *Timothy O v. Paso Robles Unif. Sch. Dist.* (822 F.3d 1105, 1127 ((9th Cir. 2016)), a "Case of the Year" in our 2016 "Year in Review" book, the Ninth Circuit determined that the school district failed to evaluate Luke, a child with autism "in all areas." The court provided a detailed description about autism and the importance of early intervention. The school district concluded that the child with autism was **ineligible for an IEP** "based on **the view of a staff member who opined, after a casual observation**, that Luke did not display signs of autism. This failure to formally assess Luke's disability rendered the provision of a free appropriate education impossible and left his autism untreated for years while Paso Robles's staff, because of a lack of adequate information, took actions that may have been counter-productive and reinforced Luke's refusal to speak."

"Under the IDEA, the school district had an affirmative obligation to formally assess Luke for autism using reliable, standardized, and statutorily proscribed methods. Paso Robles, however, ignored the clear evidence requiring it to do so based solely on the opinion of a school psychologist who did not evaluate the child." The case was remanded back so that the District Court could compute the number of years of compensatory education Luke required and the additional "equitable" remedies and financial reimbursement to award the family.

145 Parents can expedite the transfer of records by requesting in writing that the previous school forward records quickly and by providing copies of their own records to the receiving school.

(4) Determination of Eligibility and Educational Need. Upon completion of the administration of assessments and other evaluation measures–

(A) the **determination of whether the child is a child with a disability** as defined in Section 1401(3) of this title and the **educational needs of the child** shall be made by a team of qualified professionals and the parent of the child in accordance with paragraph (5); and

(B) a copy of the **evaluation report** and the documentation of determination of eligibility **shall be given to the parent**.[146, 147]

(5) Special Rule for Eligibility Determination. In making a determination of eligibility under paragraph (4)(A), a child shall not be determined to be a child with a disability if the determinant factor for such determination is–

(A) **lack of appropriate instruction in reading**,[148] **including in the essential components of reading instruction** (as defined in Section 6368(3) of this title); as such section was in effect on the day before December 10, 2015);

(B) lack of instruction in math;[149] or

(C) **limited English proficiency**.

(6) Specific Learning Disabilities.[150]

(A) In General. Notwithstanding Section 1407(b)[151] of this title, when determining whether a child has a specific learning disability as defined in Section 1401 of this title, a local educational agency **shall not be required**[152] **to take into consideration whether a child has a severe discrepancy between achievement and intellectual ability**[153] in oral expression, listening comprehension, written expression, basic reading skill, reading comprehension, mathematical calculation, or mathematical reasoning.[154]

---

146   If the parent disagrees with the school's decision regarding eligibility or classification of the child's disability, the parent should obtain a comprehensive neuropsychological or psycho-educational evaluation from an expert in the private sector. For more on this topic, read Chapters 8, 10 and 11 in *Wrightslaw: From Emotions to Advocacy*.

147   The evaluation reports are to be provided "at no cost to the parent." 34 CFR § 300.306(a)(2)

148   The "lack of appropriate instruction in reading, including the essential components of reading instruction" was added in 2004 and modified in 2015 in order to be consistent with ESSA. **The essential components of reading instruction are defined as explicit and systematic instruction in - (A) phonemic awareness; (B) phonics; (C) vocabulary development; (D) reading fluency, including oral reading skills; and (E) reading comprehension strategies.** (*See* 20 U.S.C. § 6368(3) and the Commentary to the *Federal Register*, Vol. 71, August 14, 2006, pages 46655 through 46657. The term, "essential components of reading instruction" moved to 29 U.S.C. § 3272(8). https://www.law.cornell.edu/uscode/text/29/3272#8.

149   34 CFR § 300.306(b) explains that the lack of "appropriate" instruction in math, or in reading, is a critical factor in determining if a child is eligible for an IEP.

150   Schools are not required to determine if a child has a severe discrepancy between achievement and intellectual ability nor are schools prohibited from using the discrepancy model. In lieu of a severe discrepancy, a child may be found to exhibit "a pattern of strengths and weaknesses in performance, achievement, or both, relative to age, state-approved grade level standards, or intellectual development . . ." *See* 34 CFR §§ 300.309(a)(2)(ii) and 300.311(a)(5)(ii)(B) and the definition of SLD at <20 U.S.C. § 1401(30).>

151   Section 1407 requires the SEA to assist the LEA to ensure that children with disabilities meet the state's achievement standards.

152   The federal regulation adds that the State "**Must not require the use** of a severe discrepancy . . ." 34 CFR § 300.307(a)(1)

153   In the Commentary, the USDOE explained that it "does not believe that an assessment of psychological or cognitive processing should be required in determining whether a child has an SLD. There is no current evidence that such assessments are necessary or sufficient for identifying SLD. . . In many cases, though, assessments of cognitive processes simply add to the testing burden and do not contribute to interventions." (71 Fed. Reg. 46651 (August 14, 2006))

154   Two regulations related to this section explain that a child may be eligible for services as a child with a specific learning disability "if the child does not achieve adequately for the child's age or to meet State-approved grade-level standards . . ." *See* 34 CFR §§ 300.309, 311. The eligibility requirements for a child with a specific learning disability vary between states. Check your state special education regulations for the requirements in your state.

(B) Additional Authority. In determining whether a child has a specific learning disability, a local educational agency may use a process that determines if the child responds to **scientific, research based intervention**[155] as a part of the evaluation procedures described in paragraphs (2) and (3).[156, 157]

(c) Additional Requirements for Evaluation and Reevaluations.

(1) Review of Existing Evaluation Data. As part of an **initial evaluation** (if appropriate) and as part of **any reevaluation** under this section, the IEP Team and other qualified professionals, as appropriate, **shall** –

(A) **review existing evaluation data** on the child, **including–**

(i) **evaluations and information provided by the parents** of the child;

(ii) **current** classroom-based, local, or State **assessments, and** classroom-based **observations**; and

(iii) **observations** by teachers and related services providers; and

(B) on the basis of that review, and input from the child's parents, **identify what additional data**, if any, **are needed** to determine–

(i) whether the child is a child with a disability as defined in Section 1401(3) of this title, and the **educational needs of the child,** or, in case of a reevaluation of a child, whether the child continues to have such a disability and such educational needs;

(ii) the **present levels of academic achievement and related developmental needs** of the child;

(iii) whether the child **needs** special education and related services, or in the case of a reevaluation of a child, whether the child continues to need special education and related services; and

(iv) **whether any additions or modifications to the special education and related services are needed** to enable the child **to meet the measurable annual goals** set out in the individualized education program of the child **and to participate**, as appropriate, **in the general education curriculum**.

(2) Source of Data. The local educational agency shall administer such assessments and other evaluation measures as may be needed to produce the data identified by the IEP Team under paragraph (1)(B).

(3) Parental Consent. Each local educational agency shall obtain informed parental consent, in accordance with subsection (a)(1)(D), prior to conducting any reevaluation of a child with a disability, except that such informed parental consent need not be obtained if the local educational agency can demonstrate that it had taken reasonable measures to obtain such consent and the child's parent has failed to respond.[158]

---

155 **Response to scientific research-based intervention is also known as RTI** and a **"multi-tiered system of support" (MTSS)** and in New Mexico as **"multi-layered system of support (MLSS).** Schools may use Response to Intervention (RTI) to determine if the child responds to scientific, research-based intervention as part of the evaluation process, but RTI "does not replace the need for a comprehensive evaluation." *See* Commentary in the *Federal Register,* page 46648, discussing 34 CFR § 300.307(a)(2). This is known as the RTI statute. Some states refer to it as SRBI or MTSS and MLSS. This Section 1414(b)(6)(C) is **specific to SLD only and not other disabilities**. It is a subsection of the law about "Evaluation Procedures" to determine if a child has a specific learning disability.

156 The evaluation/eligibility timeline for a specific learning disability may be extended by mutual agreement. *See* 34 CFR § 300.309(c). The child suspected of having a specific learning disability **must be observed** in the regular classroom after the child has been referred for an evaluation. *See* 34 CFR § 300.310(b). The evaluation "may not use any single measure or assessment [such as RTI] as the sole criterion . . ." *See* 20 U.S.C. § 1414(b)(2)(B).

157 Twenty years ago, on January 21, 2011, in response to delayed evaluations, the USDOE said that the "RTI process cannot be used to delay-deny an evaluation for eligibility under IDEA." (https://www.wrightslaw.com/info/rti.osep.memo.0111.pdf) *See* the Wrightslaw YouTube video about RTI and the USDOE's Memorandum at: https://youtu.be/TdM3nC8Sdh8 .

158 Pursuant to 34 CFR § 300.300(d)(4)(i), if the child is in a private school or home school at parent's expense, the LEA cannot use due process procedures to force a reevaluation.

(4) Requirements If Additional Data Are Not Needed.[159] If the IEP Team and other qualified professionals, as appropriate, determine that no additional data are needed to determine whether the child continues to be a child with a disability and to determine the child's educational needs,[160] the local educational agency–

(A) shall notify the child's parents of–

(i) that determination and the reasons for the determination; and

(ii) the right of such parents to request an assessment to determine whether the child continues to be a child with a disability and to determine the child's educational needs; and

(B) shall not be required to conduct such an assessment unless requested to by the child's parents.[161]

(5) Evaluations Before Change in Eligibility.

(A) In General. Except as provided in subparagraph (B), a local educational agency **shall** evaluate a child with a disability in accordance with this section **before determining** that the child is no longer a child with a disability.[162]

(B) Exception.

(i) In General. The evaluation described in subparagraph (A) shall not be required before the termination of a child's eligibility under this part due to graduation from secondary school **with a regular diploma**, or due to **exceeding the age eligibility** for a free appropriate public education under State law.

(ii) Summary of Performance. For a child whose eligibility under this part terminates under circumstances described in clause (i), a local educational agency **shall provide the child with a summary of the child's academic achievement and functional performance**, which shall include **recommendations** on how to assist the child **in meeting the child's postsecondary goals**.[163]

---

159   This language seems to allow the IEP Team, which includes the parents, to decide if "no additional data are needed" to determine eligibility **and** educational needs. It appears to be at odds with the requirement that the school reevaluate "at least once every 3 years." However, if the parents request the three year evaluation, the school is required to "conduct such an assessment."

160   IEP Teams must determine the child's "educational needs" and "present levels of academic achievement and related developmental needs." If a child is not tested at regular intervals, the IEP Team will not have information about the child's educational needs, "present levels of academic achievement" and "related developmental needs."

161   Parents have a right to request an assessment to determine their child's educational needs. To ensure that your request is honored, make your request for an assessment of your child's educational needs in writing.

162   The school must evaluate a child before exiting the child from special education, unless the child meets one of the two exceptions. A certificate of attendance, a special education diploma, or anything other than a "regular diploma" does not relieve the school of the requirement for a reevaluation.

163   If parents or eligible students want the school to provide specific testing for college admissions, they should ensure that such testing is written into the child's transition plan, usually during the junior year.

(d) Individualized Education Programs.[164, 165, 166]

  (1) Definitions. In this title:

    (A) Individualized Education Program.(i) In General. The term **'individualized education program'**[167] **or IEP'** means a written statement for each child with a disability that is developed, reviewed, and revised in accordance with this section and that includes–

      (I) a statement of the child's **present levels of academic achievement**[168] and **functional performance**,[169] including–

        (aa) how the child's disability affects the child's involvement and **progress in the general education curriculum;**

        (bb) for preschool children, as appropriate, how the disability affects the child's participation in appropriate activities; and

        (cc) for children with disabilities who take alternate assessments aligned to alternate achievement standards, a description of benchmarks or short-term objectives;

      (II) **a statement of measurable annual goals, including academic and functional goals,**[170] designed to–

        (aa) meet the child's needs that result from the child's disability to enable the child to be involved in and **make progress in the general education curriculum;** and

        (bb) meet each of **the child's other educational needs** that result from the child's disability;

164 The IEP regulations begin at **<34 CFR § 300.320 and continue through § 300.328.>** In the 1990's and years prior, the IEP regulations included comprehensive question and answer appendices. The question and answer appendix was not included in the most recent regulations (issued in 2006), so you may want to obtain a copy of the *Federal Register's* Commentary to the IEP regulations which begins on page 46661. The Commentary is on the Wrightslaw site at: https://www.wrightslaw.com/idea/commentary.htm

165 The U.S. Department of Education **does not** ". . . encourage public agencies to prepare **a draft IEP prior to the IEP Team** meeting . . . [however, the LEA] should provide the parent with a copy of its **draft proposal**, if the agency has developed one, **prior to the IEP Team meeting** so as to give the parent an opportunity to review the recommendations of the public agency prior to the IEP Team meeting, and be better able to engage in full discussion of the proposals for the IEP. It is not permissible for an agency to have the final IEP completed before an IEP Team meeting begins." *See Federal Register,* 71 Fed. Reg. 46678 (August 14, 2006).

166 **The initial IEP meeting must be held within 30 calendar days** of the child being found eligible and the services must be provided "as soon as possible following development of the IEP." 34 CFR § 300.323(c). The LEA must ensure that the IEP is "accessible to each regular education teacher, special education teacher, related services provider and . . . other providers and [that they are informed of their] "specific responsibilities [and] "the specific accommodations, modifications, and supports that must be provided for the child" 34 CFR § 300.323(c)

167 **The IEP is a "Program" not a "Plan"** in the federal law. However, with regard to infants and toddlers in Section 1436, the IFSP is a "Plan" and not a "Program." Check your state regulations for the correct term in your state. In **Texas** this is known as the **ARD Committee**, for Admission, Review and Discharge.

168 The term "academic achievement generally refers to the child's performance in academic areas (e.g., reading or language arts, math, science, and history.)" *See* Commentary in the *Federal Register,* 71 Fed. Reg. 46661-46662 (August 14, 2006). To learn about your child's standardized test scores in reading and math (i.e., standard scores, percentile ranks, age and grade equivalent scores), read Chapters 10 and 11 about "Tests and Measurements" in *Wrightslaw: From Emotions to Advocacy.*

169 Functional "is a term that is generally understood to refer to skills or activities that are not considered academic or related to a child's academic achievement. Instead 'functional' is often used in the context of routine activities of everyday living." *See* Commentary in the *Federal Register,* 71 Fed. Reg. 46661 (August 14, 2006).

170 To learn how to write IEPs that are **S**pecific, **M**easurable, use **A**ction words, are **R**ealistic and **T**ime specific, read Chapter 11, SMART IEPs, in *Wrightslaw: From Emotions to Advocacy.* (https://www.wrightslaw.com/bks/feta2/feta2.htm).

(III) a description of **how the child's progress** toward meeting the annual goals described in subclause (II) **will be measured**[171] and when **periodic reports** on the progress the child is making toward meeting the annual goals (such as through the use of quarterly or other periodic reports, concurrent with the issuance of report cards) will be provided;

(IV) a statement of the **special education and related services and supplementary aids and services,**[172] based on peer-reviewed research[173] to the extent practicable, to be provided to the child, or on behalf of the child, **and** a statement of the **program modifications or supports for school personnel**[174] that will be provided for the child

(aa) to advance appropriately toward attaining the annual goals;[175]

(bb) to be involved in and make progress in the general education curriculum in accordance with subclause (I) and to participate in **extracurricular and other nonacademic activities**; and

(cc) to be educated and participate with other children with disabilities and nondisabled children in the activities described in this subparagraph;

(V) an explanation of the extent, if any, to which the child **will not participate** with nondisabled children in the regular class and in the activities described in subclause (IV)(cc);

(VI)

(aa) a statement of any individual appropriate accommodations that are necessary to measure the academic achievement and functional performance of the child on State and districtwide assessments consistent with Section 1412(a)(16)(A) of this title; and

(bb) if the IEP Team determines that the child shall take an alternate assessment on a particular State or districtwide assessment of student achievement, a statement of why–

(AA) the child cannot participate in the regular assessment; and

(BB) the particular alternate assessment[176] selected is appropriate for the child;

(VII) the **projected date for the beginning of the services** and modifications described in subclause (IV), and the anticipated **frequency, location, and duration** of those services and modifications; and

(VIII) beginning not later than the first IEP to be in effect **when the child is 16**, and updated annually thereafter–

---

171 The IEP must include measurable annual goals that address the child's "present levels of academic achievement and functional performance." John Willis, evaluator and co-author of *Guide to the Identification of Learning Disabilities*, (Copley Custom Publishing, Acton, MA 1998) advised that "If the team is correctly using curriculum-based assessment as part of Response to Intervention in a Problem-Solving Model, progress on the short-term objectives and annual goals could be measured precisely. This may be something on which parents should insist."

172 These three terms are defined in 20 U.S.C. § 1401, "Definitions."

173 The USDOE explained that "Peer-reviewed research generally refers to research that is reviewed by qualified and independent reviewers to ensure that the quality of the information meets the standards of the field before the research is published. However, there is no single definition . . ." *See* Commentary in the *Federal Register,* 71 Fed. Reg. 46664 (August 14, 2006).

174 Children who present **severe behavioral challenges** must have staff trained in the use of behavior management and the development and use of Functional Behavioral Assessments (FBA) and Behavioral Intervention Plans (BIP). *See* the language that the team **"shall consider" "Special Factors"** in 20 U.S.C. § 1414(d)(3)(B)(i). *Wrightslaw Year in Review* books have a number of cases where the school district failed to develop an appropriate FBA and thus the BIP was flawed, which resulted in the school district being found to have failed to provide FAPE to the child. This often resulted in an award of compensatory education relating back to the date of the initial flawed FBA. Many such cases revealed that the staff were not properly trained and unable to cope with the behavioral special factors presented by the child and thus failed to develop an appropriate FBA and BIP.

175 The U.S. Department of Education has advised school districts that instructional methodology may be written into an IEP. "The Department's longstanding position on about instructional methodology in a child's IEP is that this is an IEP Team's decision. If an IEP Team determines that a specific instructional method is necessary for the child to receive FAPE, the instructional method may be addressed in the IEP. *See* Commentary in the *Federal Register,* 71 Fed. Reg. 46665. (August 14, 2006).

176 An alternate assessment might lead to denial of a regular high school diploma. *See* Commentary in the *Federal Register,* 71 Fed. Reg. 46666 (August 14, 2006).

(aa) appropriate measurable postsecondary goals[177] based upon age appropriate transition assessments related to training, education, employment, and, where appropriate, independent living skills;

(bb) the transition services (including **courses of study**)[178, 179] needed to assist the child in reaching those goals; and

(cc) beginning **not later than 1 year** before the child reaches the age of majority under State law, a statement that the child has been informed of the child's rights under this title, if any, that will transfer to the child on reaching the age of majority under Section 1415(m) of this title.

(ii) Rule of Construction. Nothing in this section shall be construed to require –

(I) that additional information be included in a child's IEP beyond what is explicitly required in this section; and

(II) the IEP Team to include information under 1 component of a child's IEP that is already contained under another component of such IEP.

(B) Individualized Education Program Team. The term 'individualized education program team' or IEP Team' means a group of individuals composed of–

(i) the **parents** of a child with a disability;[180, 181]

(ii) not less than 1 **regular education teacher** of such child (if the child is, or may be, participating in the regular education environment);

(iii) not less than 1 **special education teacher**, or where appropriate, not less than 1 special education provider[182] of such child;

(iv) a **representative of the local educational agency** who–

(I) is qualified to provide, or supervise the provision of, specially designed instruction to meet the unique needs of children with disabilities;

(II) is knowledgeable about the general education curriculum; and

(III) is knowledgeable about the availability of resources of the local educational agency;

(v) an individual who can **interpret** the instructional implications of **evaluation results**, who may be a member of the team described in clauses (ii) through (vi);

(vi) at the discretion of the parent or the agency, **other individuals** who have knowledge or special expertise regarding the child, including related services personnel as appropriate; and

(vii) whenever appropriate, **the child with a disability**.

---

177 "'Post secondary goals' . . . are generally understood to refer to those goals that a child hopes to achieve after leaving secondary school (i.e., high school)." *See* Commentary in the *Federal Register*, 71 Fed. Reg. 46668 (August 14, 2006).

178 Course of study can be "participation in **advanced placement** courses or a vocational education program." *See* Commentary in the *Federal Register*, page 46668.

179 Part B funds can be used for student "participation in transitional programs on college campuses or in community-based settings . . ." *See* Commentary in the *Federal Register*, 71 Fed. Reg. 46668 (August 14, 2006).**In other words, the LEA can pay for community college tuition as a part of the high school student's transition program.**

180 The LEA "must take whatever action is necessary to ensure that the parent understands the proceedings of the IEP Team meeting, including arranging for an interpreter for parents. . ." who are deaf or do not speak English. *See* 34 CFR § 300.322(e).

181 Parents are members of the team and parental participation is a key element. *See* the Wrightslaw Youtube video about the Ninth Circuit's *Doug C. v. Hawaii*, 720 F.3d 1038 (9th Cir. 2013) case where the school convened an IEP meeting in the parent's absence, a major procedural violation. *See* our analysis at: https://www.wrightslaw.com/law/art/dougc.hawaii.pwanalysis.htm and our YouTube video about the case at: https://youtu.be/Hf7vqsmK_ZM .

182 A special education teacher or service provider is "responsible for implementing the IEP" and may be the child's speech pathologist, occupational therapist, or other person, depending on the child's disability and whether the child is receiving speech services, occupational therapy, or other services. *See* Commentary in the *Federal Register*, 71 Fed. Reg. 46675 (August 14, 2006).

(C) IEP Team Attendance.[183]

(i) Attendance Not Necessary. A member of the IEP Team **shall not be required to attend** an IEP meeting, in whole or in part,[184] if the parent of a child with a disability and the local educational agency agree that the attendance of such member is not necessary because the member's area of the curriculum or related services is not being modified or discussed in the meeting.[185]

(ii) Excusal. A member of the IEP Team **may be excused** from attending an IEP meeting, in whole or in part, when the meeting involves a modification to or discussion of the member's area of the curriculum or related services, **if–**

(I) the parent and the local educational agency **consent** to the excusal; and

(II) the member submits, in writing to the parent and the IEP Team, input into the development of the IEP prior to the meeting.

(iii) Written Agreement and Consent Required. A parent's agreement under clause (i) and consent under clause (ii) **shall be in writing**.

(D) IEP Team Transition. In the case of a child who was previously served under part C, an invitation to the initial IEP meeting **shall, at the request of the parent**, be sent to the part C service coordinator or other representatives of the part C system to assist with the smooth transition of services.

(2) Requirement That Program Be in Effect.

(A) In General. At the beginning of each school year, each local educational agency, State educational agency, or other State agency, as the case may be, **shall** have in effect, for each child with a disability in the agency's jurisdiction, an individualized education program,[186] as defined in paragraph (1)(A).[187]

(B) Program for Child Aged 3 Through 5. In the case of a child with a disability aged 3 through 5 (or, at the discretion of the State educational agency, a 2-year-old child with a disability who will turn age 3 during the school year), **the IEP Team shall consider the individualized family service plan** that contains the material described in Section 1436 of this title, and that is developed in accordance with this section, and the individualized family service plan may serve as the IEP of the child if using that plan as the IEP is–

(i) consistent with State policy; and

(ii) agreed to by the agency and the child's parents.[188]

---

183 If parents consent in writing, a member of the IEP Team may be excused from attending an IEP meeting if their area of curriculum or service will not be discussed or modified during the meeting. An IEP Team member may also be excused from an IEP meeting that involves their area of curriculum or service **if they submit input in writing** and **if the parent and school consent**.

184 "An LEA that **routinely excuses IEP Team members** from attending IEP Team meetings **would not be in compliance** with the requirements of the Act and therefore would be subject to the States' monitoring and enforcement provisions." *See* Commentary in the *Federal Register*, 71 Fed. Reg. 46674 (August 14, 2006).

185 The Commentary to the IEP regulations states that "To ensure that all IEP Team members are aware of their responsibilities regarding the implementation of a child's IEP, Section 300.323(d) requires that the **child's IEP be accessible to each regular education teacher**, special education teacher, related services provider, and any other service provider who is responsible for its implementation." See Commentary in the *Federal Register*, 71 Fed. Reg. 4669 (August 14, 2006).

186 IEPs must be in effect at the beginning of the school year for all children with disabilities, including children who are enrolled in private programs. Under IDEA, public schools may be responsible for offering IEPs to students who attend private schools. (*See* 20 U.S.C. § 1412(a)(3), (10) about child find and private schools.) However, if the parent of a child in private school refuses to consent to an evaluation or to special education services, the school is not required to develop an IEP. *See* 20 U.S.C. § 1414(a)(1)(D)(ii)) If the parent refuses to permit the school to evaluate the child, any entitlement to reimbursement for a private school program may be reduced or barred. (20 U.S.C. § 1412(a)(10)(C)(iii)(II)

187 *See* <34 CFR § 300.323(c)> for the **30-day IEP timeline to hold the IEP meeting after initial eligibility**.

188 "The IFSP may serve as the IEP of the child . . . [and the public agency] must provide to the child's parents a detailed explanation of the differences between an IFSP and an IEP . . ." *See* 34 CFR § 300.323(b).

(C) Program for Children Who Transfer School Districts.[189]

   (i) In General.

   (I) Transfer within the Same State. In the case of a child with a disability who transfers school districts within the same academic year, who enrolls in a new school, and who had an IEP that was in effect in the same State, the local educational agency **shall provide such child** with a free appropriate public education, **including services comparable to those described in the previously held IEP**, in consultation with the parents **until such time** as the local educational agency adopts the previously held IEP or develops, adopts, and implements a new IEP that is consistent with Federal and State law.

   (II) Transfer Outside State. In the case of a child with a disability who transfers school districts within the same academic year, who enrolls in a new school, and who had an IEP that was in effect in another State, the local educational agency shall provide such child with a free appropriate public education, **including services comparable to those described in the previously held IEP**, in consultation with the parents **until such time** as the local educational agency **conducts an evaluation**[190] pursuant to subsection (a)(1), if determined to be necessary by such agency, and **develops a new IEP**, if appropriate, that is consistent with Federal and State law.

   (ii) Transmittal of Records. To facilitate the transition for a child described in clause (i)–

   (I) **the new school** in which the child enrolls **shall take reasonable steps** to promptly obtain the child's records, including the IEP and supporting documents and any other records relating to the provision of special education or related services to the child, from the previous school in which the child was enrolled, pursuant to section 99.31(a)(2) of title 34, Code of Federal Regulations; and

   (II) **the previous school** in which the child was enrolled **shall take reasonable steps** to promptly respond to such request from the new school.

(3) Development of IEP.

   (A) In General. In developing each child's IEP, the IEP Team, subject to subparagraph (C), **shall consider**

   (i) the **strengths** of the child;

   (ii) the **concerns of the parents** for enhancing the education of their child;[191, 192]

---

189   If a child with an IEP moves to a new school district, the child is entitled to a "comparable IEP." The Commentary to 34 CFR § 300.323(f) explains that "the Department interprets **'comparable'** to have the plain meaning of the word, which is **'similar' or 'equivalent.'**" *See* Commentary in the *Federal Register,* 71 Fed. Reg. 46681 (August 14, 2006).

If the move occurs during the summer, since there must be an IEP at the beginning of each school year, that new school must provide the child with appropriate services. *See* the USDOE's letter to Attorney Siegel on February 21, 2019. Link is: https://sites.ed.gov/idea/files/osep-letter-to-siegel-02-21-2019.pdf

In the 2/21/2019 letter, the USDOE relied on an older version of the Commentary that was issued for the 1999 regulations for **IDEA 97 as their authority.** Link is: https://www.govinfo.gov/content/pkg/FR-1999-03-12/pdf/99-5754.pdf

190   This evaluation is a new "initial" evaluation, not a reevaluation. A between state move mandates an evaluation by the new school district. *See* the *Federal Register,* 71 Fed. Reg. 46682 (August 14, 2006).

191   In developing the IEP, the IEP Team must consider the parents' concerns about the child's education, including concerns about inadequate progress. Some IEP Teams refuse to accept information from private sector evaluations of the child. The law clearly states that schools shall consider the most recent evaluation on the child.

192   A parent can consent to some services in an IEP and refuse to consent to other services. The agreed upon services must be implemented. *See* 34 CFR §§ 300.300(d)(3), 300.518(c).

(iii) the **results of** the initial evaluation or **most recent evaluation**[193] of the child;[194] and

(iv) the **academic, developmental, and functional needs** of the child.[195]

(B) Consideration of Special Factors.[196] The IEP Team shall–[197]

(i) in the case of a child whose **behavior** impedes the child's learning or that of others, consider the use of **positive behavioral interventions** and supports, and other strategies, to address that behavior;

(ii) in the case of a child with **limited English proficiency**, consider the language needs of the child as such needs relate to the child's IEP;

(iii) in the case of a child who is **blind or visually impaired**, provide for instruction in Braille and the use of Braille unless the IEP Team determines, after an evaluation of the child's reading and writing skills, needs, and appropriate reading and writing media (including an evaluation of the child's future needs for instruction in Braille or the use of Braille), that instruction in Braille or the use of Braille is not appropriate for the child;

(iv) consider the **communication needs** of the child, and in the case of **a child who is deaf or hard of hearing,** consider the child's **language and communication needs,** opportunities for direct communications with peers and professional personnel in the child's language and communication mode, academic level, and **full range of needs**, including opportunities for **direct instruction in the child's language** and communication mode; and

(v) consider whether the child needs **assistive technology devices and services**.

(C) Requirement with Respect to Regular Education Teacher. A regular education teacher of the child, as a member of the IEP Team, shall, to the extent appropriate, participate in the development of the IEP of the child, including the determination of appropriate positive behavioral interventions and supports, and other strategies, and the determination of supplementary aids and services, program modifications, and support for school personnel consistent with paragraph (1)(A)(i)(IV).

(D) Agreement. In making changes to a child's IEP after the annual IEP meeting for a school year, the parent of a child with a disability and the local educational agency **may agree not to convene an IEP meeting** for

---

193   In *Rogich v. Clark County Sch. Dist.* (U.S. District Court, No. 2:17-cv-01541, October 12, 2021), at page 10, the Nevada U.S. District Court judge found in regard to a child with dyslexia, "that the IEP teams did not adequately review the [private] evaluations provided by Plaintiffs nor **meaningfully consider** Plaintiffs' concerns for enhancing the education of their child." Attorney's fees and tuition reimbursement probably cost the Las Vegas LEA in excess of one million dollars. URL is at: https://www.wrightslaw.com/law/caselaw/2021/rogich.v.clark.county.nv.orton.gillingham.pdf

194   Upon request, prior to an IEP meeting, the LEA must permit the parent "to inspect and review any education records." 34 CFR § 300.613(a)

195   The Department of Education published a model Individualized Education Program (IEP) form when the regulations were published. Links to the regulations and model forms are at: https://www.wrightslaw.com/idea/law.htm

196   Chapter 7 in *Wrightslaw: All About IEPs* is devoted exclusively to "Special Factors." https://www.wrightslaw.com/bks/aaiep/index.htm

197   As noted in an earlier footnote, children who present severe behavioral challenges must have staff trained in the use of behavior management and the development and use of Functional Behavioral Assessments (FBA) and Behavioral Intervention Plans (BIP). *See* 20 U.S.C. § 1414(d)(1)(A)(i)(IV). The *Wrightslaw Year in Review* books have a number of cases where the school failed to provide FAPE to a child because of a violation of these two concepts. Staff were not properly trained and were unable to cope with the behavioral special factors presented by the child and failed to develop an appropriate FBA and BIP.

The 2016 edition of *Wrightslaw Year in Review,* features a Second Circuit "Case of the Year" in which the Court focused on the failure to prepare adequate FBAs and BIPs. In *LO v. NYC DOE*, 822 F. 3d 95, 123 (2nd Cir. 2016), the LEA "failed to conduct an FBA for any of the IEPs, despite finding that [the child] possessed behaviors that interfered with learning, which this Court has previously found to constitute a serious procedural violation because it may prevent the CSE from obtaining necessary information about the student's behaviors, leading to their being addressed in the IEP inadequately or not at all." (Decision, page 44-45.) There were three years of procedural violations relating to the BIPs and FBAs. **The student was 20 years old and equitable relief was ordered to extend beyond the 22nd birthday.** Several cases at the District Court level have had similar outcomes.

the purposes of making such changes, and instead may develop a written document to amend or modify the child's current IEP.[198]

(E) Consolidation of IEP Team Meetings. To the extent possible, the local educational agency shall encourage the consolidation of reevaluation meetings for the child and other IEP Team meetings for the child.

(F) Amendments. Changes to the IEP may be made either by the entire IEP Team or, as provided in subparagraph (D), by amending the IEP rather than by redrafting the entire IEP. **Upon request**, a parent shall be **provided with a revised copy of the IEP** with the amendments incorporated.

(4) Review and Revision of IEP.[199]

(A) In General. The local educational agency **shall** ensure that, subject to subparagraph (B), the IEP Team–

(i) reviews the child's IEP periodically, but **not less frequently than annually**,[200] to determine whether the annual goals for the child are being achieved; and

(ii) **revises the IEP as appropriate** to address–

(I) **any lack of expected progress** toward the annual goals and in the general education curriculum, where appropriate;

(II) **the results of any reevaluation** conducted under this section;

(III) information about the child **provided to, or by, the parents**,[201] as described in subsection (c)(1)(B);

(IV) the child's **anticipated needs**; or

(V) other matters.

(B) Requirement with Respect to Regular Education Teacher. A regular education teacher of the child, as a member of the IEP Team, shall, consistent with paragraph (1)(C), participate in the review and revision of the IEP of the child.

(5) Multi-Year IEP Demonstration.[202]

(A) Pilot Program.

(i) **Purpose**. The purpose of this paragraph is to provide an opportunity for States to allow parents and local educational agencies the opportunity for long-term planning by offering the option of developing a comprehensive multi-year IEP, **not to exceed 3 years**, that is designed to coincide with the natural transition points[203] for the child.

(ii) **Authorization**. In order to carry out the purpose of this paragraph, the Secretary is authorized to

---

198   If the parent and school decide to amend or modify the IEP developed at the annual IEP meeting, and do not want to convene another IEP meeting, they may revise the IEP by agreement. The IEP Team must create a written document to amend or modify the IEP. This document should describe the changes or modifications in the IEP and note that, by agreement, an IEP meeting was not convened. The parent should request a copy of the revised IEP.

199   The Commentary to the regulations notes: "The IEP Team is expected to act **in the best interest of the child**. As with any IEP Team meeting, if additional information is needed to finalize an appropriate IEP, there is nothing in the Act that prevents an IEP Team from reconvening after the needed information is obtained, as long as the IEP is developed in a timely manner." *See* Commentary in the *Federal Register*, page 46676.

200   "[A]n amendment to an IEP . . . [cannot] take the place of an annual IEP meeting." *See* Commentary in the *Federal Register*, 71 Fed. Reg. 46685 (August 14, 2006).

201   An evaluation by a private sector evaluator, **must be considered** by the IEP Team.

202   This authorizes a multi-year IEP pilot project. Fifteen states could have applied for approval to use **three-year IEPs**. IEP review dates must be based on "natural transition points." Parents have the right to opt-out of this program. The parent of a child served under a multi-year IEP can have a review of the IEP without waiting for a natural transition point. **Not a single state has adopted this three-year IEP approach. You may disregard it.**

203   *See* 20 U.S.C. § 1414(d)(5)(C) for "natural transition points."

approve not more than 15 proposals from States to carry out the activity described in clause (i).

(iii) Proposal.

    (I) In General. A State desiring to participate in the program under this paragraph shall submit a proposal to the Secretary at such time and in such manner as the Secretary may reasonably require.

    (II) Content. The proposal shall include–

        (aa) assurances that the development of a multi-year IEP under this paragraph is **optional for parents**;

        (bb) assurances that the parent is required to provide informed consent before a comprehensive multi-year IEP is developed;

        (cc) a list of required elements for each multi-year IEP, including–

            (AA) measurable goals pursuant to paragraph (1)(A)(i)(II), coinciding with natural transition points for the child, that will enable the child to be involved in and make progress in the general education curriculum and that will meet the child's other needs that result from the child's disability; and

            (BB) measurable annual goals for determining progress toward meeting the goals described in subitem (AA); and

        (dd) a description of the process for the review and revision of each multi-year IEP, including–

            (AA) a review by the IEP Team of the child's multi-year IEP at each of the child's **natural transition points**;

            (BB) in years other than a child's natural transition points, **an annual review of the child's IEP** to determine the child's current levels of progress and whether the annual goals for the child are being achieved, and a requirement to amend the IEP, as appropriate, to enable the child to continue to meet the measurable goals set out in the IEP;

            (CC) if the IEP Team determines on the basis of a review that the child is not making sufficient progress toward the goals described in the multi-year IEP, a requirement that the local educational agency shall ensure that the IEP Team carries out a more thorough review of the IEP in accordance with paragraph (4) within 30 calendar days; and

            (DD) at the request of the parent, a requirement that the IEP Team shall conduct a review of the child's multi-year IEP rather than or subsequent to an annual review.

(B) Report. Beginning 2 years after the date of enactment of the Individuals with Disabilities Education Improvement Act of 2004, the Secretary shall submit an annual report to the Committee on Education and the Workforce of the House of Representatives and the Committee on Health, Education, Labor, and Pensions of the Senate regarding the effectiveness of the program under this paragraph and any specific recommendations for broader implementation of such program, including

    (i) reducing–

        (I) the paperwork burden on teachers, principals, administrators, and related service providers; and

        (II) noninstructional time spent by teachers in complying with this part;

    (ii) enhancing longer-term educational planning;

    (iii) improving positive outcomes for children with disabilities;

    (iv) promoting collaboration between IEP Team members; and

    (v) ensuring satisfaction of family members.

(C) Definition. In this paragraph, the term 'natural transition points' means those periods that are close in time to the transition of a child with a disability from preschool to elementary grades, from elementary grades to middle or junior high school grades, from middle or junior high school grades to secondary school grades, and from secondary school grades to post-secondary activities, **but in no case a period longer than 3 years**.

(6) Failure to Meet Transition Objectives.

If a participating agency, other than the local educational agency, fails to provide the transition services described in the IEP in accordance with paragraph (1)(A)(i)(VIII), the local educational agency shall reconvene the IEP Team to identify alternative strategies to meet the transition objectives for the child set out in the IEP.[204]

(7) Children with Disabilities in Adult Prisons.[205]

    (A) In General. The **following requirements**[206] shall not apply to children with disabilities who are **convicted as adults** under State law **and incarcerated in adult prisons**:

        (i) The requirements contained in Section 1412(a)(16)[207] of this title and paragraph 1414(d)(1)(A)(i)(VI) (relating to participation of children with disabilities in general assessments).

        (ii) The requirements of items (aa) and (bb) of paragraph 1414(d)(1)(A)(i)(VIII) (relating to transition planning and transition services), do not apply with respect to such children whose eligibility under this part will end, because of such children's age, before such children will be released from prison.

    (B) Additional Requirement. If a child with a disability is convicted as an adult under State law and incarcerated in an adult prison, the child's IEP Team may **modify the child's IEP** or placement notwithstanding the requirements of Section 1412(a)(5)(A)[208] of this title and paragraph (1)(A) if the State has demonstrated a bona fide security or compelling penological interest that cannot otherwise be accommodated.[209]

(e) Educational Placements.

Each local educational agency or State educational agency shall ensure that the **parents** of each child with a disability are **members of any group that makes decisions** on the educational placement of their child.[210]

(f) Alternative Means of Meeting Participation.[211]

When conducting **IEP Team meetings** and placement meetings pursuant to this section, Section 1415(e) of this title, and Section 1415(f)(1)(B) of this title, and carrying out administrative matters under Section 1415 of this title (such as scheduling, exchange of witness lists, and status conferences), the parent of a child with a disability and a local educational agency may agree to use alternative means of meeting participation, such as **video conferences and conference calls**.

---

204   Assume another agency was to provide vocational rehabilitation services, but failed to do so. The burden shifts back to the IEP team to develop alternative strategies.

205   An incarcerated "child with a disability" as defined in IDEA at 20 U.S.C. § 1401(3) should continue to receive services and an appropriate education unless if the state can demonstrate "a bona fide security or compelling penological interest" to avoid providing such services. However, as provided in this section, least restrictive environment, statewide assessments and transition planning is not required.

206   In other words, subsections i and ii.

207   Statewide assessments.

208   Least Restrictive Environment (LRE).

209   A child or an adult who is classified as a "child with a disability" is entitled to FAPE unless there is a compelling **reason** to deny it. *See* 20 U.S.C. § 1411(e)(2)(C)(ix) in regard to funding "for children with disabilities in correctional facilities."

210   An educational placement "refers to the provision of special education and related services **rather than a specific place,** such as a specific classroom or specific school." *See* Commentary in the *Federal Register,* page 46687. Decisions about the child's placement cannot be made until after the IEP Team, which includes the child's parent(s), meets and reaches consensus about the IEP goals. Although the law on this issue is clear, school personnel sometimes determine the child's placement before the IEP meeting.

211   There is no legal requirement that school meetings have to be face-to-face. IEP and placement meetings (Sections 1414(d) and (e)), mediation (Section 1415(e)), and due process (IEP) resolution sessions (Section 1415(f)(1)(B)) may be convened by conference calls or video conferences.

20 U.S.C. § 1415. Procedural Safeguards.[212]

(a) Establishment of Procedures.

Any State educational agency, State agency, or local educational agency that receives assistance under this part shall establish and maintain procedures in accordance with this section to ensure that children with disabilities and their parents are guaranteed procedural safeguards with respect to the provision of a free appropriate public education by such agencies.

(b) Types of Procedures.[213] The procedures required by this section shall include the following:

(1) An opportunity for the parents of a child with a disability **to examine all records** relating to such child and **to participate in meetings** with respect to the **identification, evaluation, and educational placement** of the child, and the provision of a free appropriate public education to such child, and **to obtain an independent educational evaluation**[214, 215] of the child.[216]

(2)

(A) Procedures to protect the rights of the child whenever the parents of the child are not known, the agency cannot, after reasonable efforts, locate the parents, or the child is a ward of the State, including

---

212   **Wrightslaw Overview:** Section 1415 describes the procedural safeguards designed to protect the rights of children with disabilities and their parents. These safeguards include the right to participate in all meetings, to examine all educational records, and to obtain an **independent educational evaluation (IEE)** of the child. Parents have the right to written notice when the school proposes to change or refuses to change the identification, evaluation or placement of the child as explained in Section 1415(c). Section 1415(d) describes requirements for the Procedural Safeguards Notice that must be provided to parents. This section provides for the appointment of a surrogate parent.

Section 1415(e) describes requirements for using **mediation** to resolve disputes, legally binding written mediation agreements, and confidentiality. Section 1415(f) describes the requirements for **due process hearings** and the Resolution Session that may allow the parties to resolve their dispute before a due process hearing. Section 1415(f) includes requirements for hearing officers and timelines, including a two-year statute of limitations. Section 1415(i) describes the **appeals process** and the 90-day deadline on appeals. Section 1415(j) is the **"stay-put"** statute that allows the child to remain in the "current educational placement" during litigation.

Section 1415(k) about discipline authorizes school personnel to place children in interim alternative educational settings. This section includes **manifestation determinations**, placement as determined by the IEP Team, appeals, authority of the hearing officer, and transfer of rights at the age of majority. The "exhaustion of administrative remedies" statute is the next one, 1415(l).

The regulations for the **procedural safeguards** begin at <34 CFR § 300.500>. Procedural safeguards in the Commentary are in the Federal Register beginning at 46688. (71 Fed. Reg. 46688 (August 14, 2006)).

213   Parents have the right to examine all educational records, including test data. The right to examine records may include personal notes, if these notes have been shared with other staff. **Parents should request, in writing,** a complete copy of all files, including test data (i.e., standard scores, percentile ranks, age equivalent scores, and grade equivalent scores). *See* the Wrightslaw YouTube video about the right to access test protocols located at: https://youtu.be/RxQoiMDpNuY.

214   **The comprehensive IEE regulation is <34 CFR § 300.502.>** Parents have the right to obtain an Independent Educational Evaluation (IEE) of their child at the school's expense. Many school districts attempt to restrict the parent's choice of evaluators to a list of approved evaluators selected by the school. The Office of Special Education Programs issued a policy letter clarifying that parents have the right to choose their independent evaluator. *See* OSEP, Letter to Parker, 2004 on the Wrightslaw website at: https://www.wrightslaw.com/info/test.eval.choice.osep.htm. *See also* https://www.wrightslaw.com/info/test.iee.steedman.htm and the Commentary in the *Federal Register,* 71 Fed. Reg. 46689, 46690 (August 14, 2006) regarding fees for an IEE.

215   At a minimum, the IEE should determine if the child has or continues to have a disability, and the child's educational needs. "There is an affirmative obligation on a public agency to consider the results of a parent initiated evaluation at private expense in any decision regarding the provision of FAPE to the child." However, if an evaluation issued by a private evaluator is rejected or not given proper consideration by the LEA, it is "appropriate for the agency to explain to the parent why it believes that the parent-initiated evaluation does not meet agency criteria." *See* Commentary in the *Federal Register,* 71 Fed. Reg. 46690 (August 14, 2006) and the *Rogich v. Clark County* case cited in the footnote to 20 U.S.C. § 1414(d)(3)(A)(iii) and the **"shall consider"** language in the statute and *Rogich* case.

216   The 2016 edition of *Wrightslaw Year in Review* includes the *Cobb County* case in which the school district was found to have "unreasonably protracted" the litigation in a "reverse due process" IEE case. The district was assessed approximately $300,000 in attorneys' fees to be paid to Jonathan Zimring, the parent's attorney in *Cobb County Sch. Dist. v. D.B.* (11th Cir. 2016, Case No. 16-11077). This is the same Zimring in the SCOTUS *Olmstead* case.

the assignment of an individual to act as a **surrogate**[217] **for the parents**, which surrogate shall not be an employee of the State educational agency, the local educational agency, or any other agency that is involved in the education or care of the child. In the case of–

> (i) a child who is a **ward of the State**, such surrogate may alternatively be appointed by the judge overseeing the child's care provided that the surrogate meets the requirements of this paragraph; and

> (ii) an **unaccompanied homeless youth** as defined in Section 11434a(6) of title 42, the local educational agency shall appoint a surrogate in accordance with this paragraph.

(B) The State shall make reasonable efforts to ensure the assignment of a surrogate **not more than 30 days after** there is a determination by the agency that the child needs a surrogate.

(3) Written prior notice[218] to the parents of the child, in accordance with subsection (c)(1), whenever the local educational agency–

> (A) **proposes to initiate or change**; or

> (B) **refuses to initiate or change**, the identification, evaluation, or educational placement of the child, or the provision of a free appropriate public education to the child.

(4) Procedures designed to ensure that the notice required by paragraph (3) is in the **native language** of the parents, unless it clearly is not feasible to do so.

(5) An opportunity for mediation, in accordance with subsection (e).

(6) An opportunity for any party to present a **complaint**

> (A) with respect to **any matter** relating to the identification, evaluation, or educational placement of the child, or the provision of a free appropriate public education to such child; and

> (B) which sets forth an alleged violation that occurred **not more than 2 years before** the date[219] the parent or public agency knew **or should have known** about the alleged action that forms the basis of the complaint, **or, if the State has an explicit time limitation**[220] for presenting such a complaint under this part, in such time as the State law allows, except that the exceptions to the timeline described in subsection (f)(3)(D) shall apply to the timeline described in this subparagraph.

(7)

> (A) Procedures that require either party, or the attorney representing a party, to provide **due process complaint notice** in accordance with subsection (c)(2) (which shall remain confidential)–

>> (i) to the other party, in the complaint filed under paragraph (6), and **forward a copy** of such notice to the State educational agency; and

>> (ii) that **shall** include–

>>> (I) the name of the child, the address of the residence of the child (or available contact information in the case of a homeless child), and the name of the school the child is attending;

---

217 *See also* the definition of a parent in 20 U.S.C. § 1401(23).

218 The school district must provide, in writing, the reasons for refusing to evaluate a child or change the educational program.

219 With this two year Statute of Limitations (SOL) rule, the Third Circuit held that the compensatory education remedy in *G.L. v. Ligonier Valley Sch. Dist.*, 802 F.3d 601 (3d Cir. 2015) was not limited to two years and that the court may go beyond two years and award compensatory education "to whatever extent necessary to make up for the child's lost progress." In 2016, the First Circuit held in *Ms. S v. Regional Sch. Unit 72*, 829 F.3d 95, (1st Cir. 2016) that "the two-year filing limitation [in the state regulations] was not promulgated in compliance with the Maine Administrative Procedure Act (Maine APA or MAPA) and is therefore void and of no legal effect." In 2017, in *Avila v. Spokane Sch. Dist.*, 852 F.3d 936 (9th Cir. 2017) the Ninth Circuit held that "Congress did not intend the IDEA's statute of limitations to be governed by a strict occurrence rule." **Note:** The preceding cases are in *Wrightslaw Year in Review* for each respective year.

220 Caution, your state may have a shorter statute of limitations period. Be sure to check your state's statutes and regulations.

(II) in the case of a homeless child or youth (within the meaning of Section 11434a(2) of title 42), available contact information for the child and the name of the school the child is attending;

(III) a **description of the nature of the problem** of the child relating to such proposed initiation or change, including facts relating to such problem; and

(IV) a **proposed resolution of the problem** to the extent known and available to the party at the time.[221]

(B) A requirement that a party **may not have a due process hearing until** the party, or the attorney representing the party, **files a notice** that meets the requirements of subparagraph (A)(ii).

(8) Procedures that require the State educational agency to develop a model form to assist parents in filing a complaint and due process complaint notice in accordance with paragraphs (6) and (7), respectively.

(c) Notification Requirements.

(1) Content of Prior Written Notice.[222] The notice required by subsection (b)(3) shall include–

(A) a description of the action **proposed or refused** by the agency;

(B) an **explanation** of why the agency proposes or refuses to take the action and a **description of each evaluation procedure, assessment, record, or report** the agency used as a basis for the proposed or refused action;

(C) a statement that the parents of a child with a disability have protection under the procedural safeguards of this part and, if this notice is not an initial referral for evaluation, the means by which a copy of a description of the procedural safeguards can be obtained;

(D) sources for parents to contact to obtain assistance in understanding the provisions of this part;

(E) a **description of other options** considered by the IEP Team and the reason why those options were rejected; and

(F) a **description of the factors** that are relevant to the agency's proposal or refusal.

(2) Due Process Complaint Notice.[223]

(A) Complaint. The **due process complaint notice** required under subsection (b)(7)(A) shall be deemed to be sufficient unless the party receiving the notice notifies the hearing officer and the other party in writing that the receiving party believes the notice has not met the requirements of subsection (b)(7)(A).

(B) Response to Complaint.

(i) Local Educational Agency Response.

---

221 A Due Process Complaint Notice can be a letter to request a due process hearing that includes the required components. To learn how to write persuasive letters that make a reader want to help, read Chapter 24, "Letter to the Stranger," in *Wrightslaw: From Emotions to Advocacy.* Your state is required to have a Model Form to request a due process hearing, however parents are not required to use that form. *See* 34 CFR § 300.509.

222 **Prior Written Notice (PWN)** is easier to understand if you **remove the word "prior" from your analysis.** Assume a parent requests that the school increase the child's speech language therapy from three 15-minute sessions per week (45 minutes per week) to three 30-minute sessions per week (90 minutes per week). If the school refuses, they must provide "written notice" about their refusal. This written notice must describe what they refused to do and their alternate proposal, if any.

The notice must explain their rationale and must describe each evaluation procedure, assessment, record, or report used as the basis of their refusal. The notice must also provide a description of all other options the IEP Team considered and the reasons why the team rejected these options. Finally, the notice must describe any other factors that are relevant to their proposal or refusal. Schools often fail to provide Prior Written Notice when parents request more services or different services.

When this happens, we advise parents that the **power is in the pen.** The parent should write a letter that describes their understanding about to what happened at the meeting and use the elements of PWN.

223 This contains critical requirements and timelines for the Due Process Complaint Notice and the Amended Complaint Notice. Failure to comply can be fatal to a case. If the school did not provide the parent with Prior Written Notice, the school must send this Notice within 10 days. The non-complaining party must respond to the complaint within 10 days. If the notice is insufficient, the receiving party must complain to the Hearing Officer within 15 days. The Hearing Officer has 5 days to determine whether the complaint is sufficient. If it is not sufficient, an amended complaint may be filed.

(I) In General. If the local educational agency **has not sent a prior written notice** to the parent regarding the subject matter contained in the parent's due process complaint notice, such local educational agency **shall**, within 10 days of receiving the complaint, send to the parent a response that **shall include**–

(aa) an explanation of why the agency proposed or refused to take the action raised in the complaint;

(bb) a description of other options that the IEP Team considered and the reasons why those options were rejected;

(cc) a description of each evaluation procedure, assessment, record, or report the agency used as the basis for the proposed or refused action; and

(dd) a description of the factors that are relevant to the agency's proposal or refusal.

(II) Sufficiency. A response filed by a local educational agency pursuant to subclause (I) shall not be construed to preclude such local educational agency from asserting that the parent's due process complaint notice was insufficient where appropriate.

(ii) Other Party Response. Except as provided in clause (i), the non-complaining party **shall, within 10 days** of receiving the complaint, **send to the complainant a response** that specifically addresses the issues raised in the complaint.

(C) Timing. The party providing a hearing officer notification under subparagraph (A) shall provide the notification within 15 days of receiving the complaint.

(D) Determination. **Within 5 days** of receipt of the notification provided under subparagraph (C), the hearing officer shall make a determination on the face of the notice of whether the notification meets the requirements of subsection (b)(7)(A), and shall immediately notify the parties in writing of such determination.

(E) Amended Complaint Notice.

(i) In General. A party **may amend** its due process complaint notice **only if**–

(I) the other party **consents in writing** to such amendment and is given the opportunity to resolve the complaint through a meeting held pursuant to subsection (f)(1)(B); or

(II) the **hearing officer grants permission**, except that the hearing officer may only grant such permission at any time not later than 5 days before a due process hearing occurs.

(ii) Applicable Timeline. The applicable timeline for a due process hearing under this part shall commence at the time the party files an amended notice, including the timeline under subsection (f)(1)(B).

(d) Procedural Safeguards Notice.[224]

(1) In General.

(A) Copy to Parents. A copy of the procedural safeguards available to the parents of a child with a disability **shall be given to the parents** only 1 time a year, **except** that a copy also shall be given to the parents–

(i) upon initial referral or parental request for evaluation;

(ii) upon the first occurrence of the filing of a complaint under subsection (b)(6); and

(iii) upon request by a parent.

(B) Internet Websites. A local educational agency may place a current copy of the procedural safeguards notice on its Internet website if such website exists.[225]

---

224 The purpose of the Procedural Safeguards Notice is to provide parents with information about their rights and protections under the law. Upon request for a due process hearing or at least once a year, parents must be provided with notice of the time period (statute of limitations) within which "to make a complaint." The Procedural Safeguards Notice also includes rights about mediation, "stay-put," discipline, reimbursement for private placements, and attorneys' fees.

225 Simply referring the parent to the Procedural Safeguard Notice on the school website is not sufficient.

(2) Contents. The procedural safeguards notice[226] shall include a **full explanation** of the procedural safeguards, written **in the native language of the parents** (unless it clearly is not feasible to do so) and **written in an easily understandable manner**, available under this section and under regulations promulgated by the Secretary relating to–

(A) **independent educational evaluation;**

(B) **prior written notice;**

(C) parental consent;

(D) access to educational records;

(E) the opportunity to present and resolve complaints, including–

(i) the time period in which to make a complaint;

(ii) the opportunity for the agency to resolve the complaint; and

(iii) the availability of mediation;

(F) **the child's placement during pendency of due process proceedings;**

(G) procedures for students who are subject to placement in an interim alternative educational setting;

(H) **requirements for unilateral placement by parents of children in private schools at public expense;**

(I) **due process hearings**, including requirements for disclosure of evaluation results and recommendations;

(J) State-level appeals (if applicable in that State);

(K) civil actions, including the time period in which to file such actions; and

(L) attorneys' fees.

(e) Mediation.[227]

(1) In General. Any State educational agency or local educational agency that receives assistance under this part shall ensure that procedures are established and implemented to allow parties to disputes involving any matter, including matters arising **prior to the filing of a complaint** pursuant to subsection (b)(6), to resolve such disputes through a mediation process.

(2) Requirements. Such procedures **shall** meet the following requirements:

(A) The procedures shall ensure that the mediation process–

(i) **is voluntary** on the part of the parties;

(ii) is **not used to deny or delay a parent's right to a due process hearing** under subsection (f), or to deny any other rights afforded under this part; and

(iii) is conducted by a **qualified and impartial** mediator who is trained in effective mediation techniques.[228]

(B) Opportunity to Meet with a Disinterested Party. A local educational agency or a State agency may establish procedures to offer to parents and schools that choose not to use the mediation process, an

---

226   Many states have their own forms for Procedural Safeguards Notice. USDOE published model IEP, Prior Written Notice and Notice of Procedural Safeguards forms. They are available on our website at: https://www.wrightslaw.com/idea/law.htm. Scroll to the bottom for the heading "Model Forms."

227   Mediation is a confidential process that allows parties to resolve disputes without litigation. The mediator helps the parties express their views and positions and understand the views and positions of the other party. To be successful, both parties must discuss their views and differences frankly. Before entering into mediation, you need to understand your rights and the law. You do not have to request a due process hearing prior to requesting mediation.

228   On the "Negotiation" page of The Advocate's Bookstore at: https://www.wrightslaw.com/bkstore/bks_negotiate.htm, we have a number of recommended books. Tops on the list and required reading by Pete's clients and our law students are Fisher and Ury's *Getting to Yes* and Gerry Spence's *How to Argue and Win Every Time.* The terms of a mediated agreement can be incorporated into an IEP so that the IEP reflects the agreement. The mediator can act as a facilitator for an IEP meeting. *See* Commentary in the *Federal Register,* 71 Fed. Reg. 46695 (August 14, 2006).

opportunity to meet, at a time and location convenient to the parents, with a disinterested party who is under contract with–

(i) a parent training and information center or community parent resource center in the State established under Section 1471 of this title or 1472 of this title; or

(ii) an appropriate alternative dispute resolution entity, to encourage the use, and explain the benefits, of the mediation process to the parents.

(C) List of Qualified Mediators.[229] The State shall maintain a list of individuals who are qualified mediators[230] and knowledgeable in laws and regulations relating to the provision of special education and related services.

(D) Costs. The State **shall bear the cost** of the mediation process, including the costs of meetings described in subparagraph (B).

(E) Scheduling and Location. Each session in the mediation process shall be scheduled in a timely manner and shall be held in a location that is convenient to the parties to the dispute.[231]

(F) Written Agreement.[232] In the case that a resolution is reached to resolve the complaint through the mediation process, the parties shall execute **a legally binding agreement** that sets forth such resolution and that–

(i) states that **all discussions** that occurred during the mediation process **shall be confidential** and may not be used as evidence in any subsequent due process hearing or civil proceeding;

(ii) is signed by both the parent and a representative of the agency who has the authority to bind such agency; and[233]

(iii) **is enforceable** in any State court of competent jurisdiction or in a district court of the United States.

(G) Mediation Discussions. Discussions that occur during the mediation process **shall be confidential**[234] and may not be used as evidence in any subsequent due process hearing or civil proceeding.

(f) Impartial Due Process Hearing.[235]

(1) In General.

(A) Hearing. Whenever a complaint has been received under subsection (b)(6) or (k), the parents or the local educational agency involved in such complaint shall have an opportunity for an impartial due process

---

229   The mediator's role is to facilitate the communication process. Mediators should not take positions or take sides. A good mediator does not have to be knowledgeable about special education law and practice but must know how to facilitate communication between parties. If mediators are not well trained in the process of mediation, their biases and opinions will have an adverse impact on the mediation process. Mediators are not arbitrators. Arbitrators issue rulings in favor of one party or the other.

230   Mediators are selected "on a random, rotational, or other impartial basis." *See* 34 CFR § 300.506(b)(3)(ii).

231   Mediation sessions and resolution sessions do not have to be face-to-face, and per 20 U.S.C. § 1414(f), may be may be convened by conference calls or video conferences.

232   Mediation agreements are legally binding and can be enforced in federal or state court.

233   For a sample settlement agreement and explanation about the terms, *see* the article by Steven Wyner and Marcy Tiffany *"Demystifying Settlement Agreements"* located at:

https://www.wrightslaw.com/law/art/settlement.agreement.htm

234   In mediation, discussions and **admissions against interests** by the parties are confidential. If the case is not settled, confidential disclosures may not be used in a subsequent trial. An attempt to use confidential disclosures from mediation or settlement discussions in court could cause the case to be dismissed or the judge to issue an adverse ruling.

235   In litigation, you must rigorously adhere to the pretrial procedures and timelines for due process hearings as described in Section 1415(f), in the Code of Federal Regulations <(34 CFR §§ 300.500 - 300.520)> and in your own state statutes and state regulations. Failure will often result in a case being dismissed.

hearing, which shall be conducted by the State educational agency or by the local educational agency, as determined by State law or by the State educational agency.[236]

(B) Resolution Session.[237]

> **(i) Preliminary Meeting.** Prior to the opportunity for an impartial due process hearing under subparagraph (A), the local educational agency **shall convene a meeting with the parents and the relevant member or members of the IEP Team who have specific knowledge of the facts identified in the complaint**
>
> > (I) **within 15 days** of receiving notice of the parents' complaint;[238]
> >
> > (II) which shall include a representative of the agency who has **decisionmaking authority** on behalf of such agency;
> >
> > (III) which **may not include an attorney** of the local educational agency **unless the parent is accompanied by an attorney**; and
> >
> > (IV) where the **parents of the child discuss their complaint, and the facts** that form the basis of the complaint, and the local educational agency is provided the opportunity to resolve the complaint, unless the parents and the local educational agency agree[239] in writing to waive such meeting, or agree to use the mediation process described in subsection (e)
>
> **(ii) Hearing.** If the local educational agency has not resolved the complaint to the satisfaction of the parents **within 30 days** of the receipt of the complaint, the due process hearing may occur, and all of the applicable timelines for a due process hearing under this part shall commence.[240]
>
> **(iii) Written Settlement Agreement.**[241] In the case that a resolution is reached to resolve the complaint at a meeting described in clause (i), the parties **shall** execute a **legally binding agreement** that is—
>
> > (I) signed by both the parent and a representative of the agency who has the authority to bind such agency; and
> >
> > (II) enforceable in any State court of competent jurisdiction or in a district court of the United States.
>
> **(iv) Review Period.** If the parties execute an agreement pursuant to clause (iii), a party **may void such agreement within 3 business days** of the agreement's execution.

---

236   States have "one-tier" or "two-tier" systems for due process hearings. In a one-tier system, the state department of education or state office of administrative hearings conducts the hearing and the losing party at the due process hearing can appeal to state or federal court. In a two-tier system, the losing party at the due process hearing must appeal to the review level for appointment of a review officer or review panel. After the review officer or panel issues a decision, the losing party can then appeal to state or federal court as with the single-tier system. In earlier years, many states used a two-tier approach but most found it was too costly and delayed the process, so most states now use a single-tier approach.

237   The resolution session provides the parties with an opportunity to resolve their complaint before the due process hearing. The school district is required to convene the resolution session within 15 days of receiving the parent's due process complaint notice. The school district must send "the relevant member or members of the IEP Team" who have knowledge of the facts in the parent's complaint and a district representative who has decision-making authority (settlement authority). A school board attorney may not attend the resolution session, unless the parent is accompanied by an attorney. The parents and district may agree to waive the resolution session or use the mediation process. If the school district initiates the due process hearing, a resolution session is not required. The meeting can be conducted by telephone or video conference call. *See* Commentary in the *Federal Register,* pages 46700-46701 and 34 CFR § 300.328.

238   The "resolution session should not be postponed" even if the parent's complaint is insufficient. *See* Commentary in the *Federal Register,* 71 Fed. Reg. 46698 (August 14, 2006).

239   Waiver of the resolution session must be a joint written agreement. *See* 34 CFR § 300.510.

240   The due process decision must be rendered within 45 days after the 30-day window. *See* 34 CFR § 300.515(a).

241   For a sample settlement agreement, *see* the earlier footnote for 20 U.S.C. § 1415(e)(2)(F). Federal or state courts can be used to ensure compliance with settlement agreements. Either party may void a settlement agreement within 3 business days. This three-day rule does not apply to settlement agreements created in mediation.

(2) Disclosure of Evaluations and Recommendations.[242]

(A) In General. Not less than **5 business days** prior to a hearing conducted pursuant to paragraph (1), each party **shall disclose** to all other parties all evaluations completed by that date, and recommendations based on the offering party's evaluations, that the party intends to use at the hearing.

(B) Failure to Disclose. A hearing officer **may bar any party** that fails to comply with subparagraph (A) from introducing the relevant evaluation or recommendation at the hearing without the consent of the other party.

(3) Limitations on Hearing.

(A) Person Conducting Hearing.[243] A hearing officer conducting a hearing pursuant to paragraph (1)(A) shall, at a minimum–[244]

(i) not be–

(I) an employee of the State educational agency or the local educational agency involved in the education or care of the child; or

(II) a person having a personal or professional interest that conflicts with the person's objectivity in the hearing;[245]

(ii) possess knowledge of, and the ability to understand, the provisions of this title, Federal and State regulations pertaining to this title, and legal interpretations of this title by Federal and State courts;

(iii) **possess the knowledge and ability to conduct hearings in accordance with appropriate, standard legal practice**; and

(iv) possess the knowledge and ability to **render and write decisions** in accordance with appropriate, standard legal practice.

(B) Subject Matter of Hearing. The party requesting the due process hearing **shall not be allowed** to raise issues at the due process hearing that were not raised in the notice filed under subsection (b)(7), unless the other party agrees otherwise.

(C) Timeline for Requesting Hearing.[246] A parent or agency shall request an impartial due process hearing within **2 years** of the date the parent or agency knew or should have known about the alleged action that forms the basis of the complaint, **or**, if the State has an explicit time limitation for requesting such a hearing under this part, in such time as the State law allows.

(D) Exceptions to the Timeline. The timeline described in subparagraph (C) shall not apply to a parent if the parent was prevented from requesting the hearing due to–

(i) specific misrepresentations by the local educational agency that it had resolved the problem forming the basis of the complaint; or

---

242 Evaluations and recommendations must be disclosed at least 5 business days before a due process hearing. Most state statutes and regulations, and standards of practice require that all exhibits (including evaluations and recommendations), exhibit lists, and witness lists, be disclosed at least 5 business days prior to a hearing. Failure to comply with requirements about disclosure often causes hearing officers to dismiss or postpone cases. For a sample document list that can be used as an exhibit list, *see* Chapter 9, "The File: Do It Right," in **Wrightslaw: From Emotions to Advocacy.** See also 34 CFR § 300.512.

243 Hearing officers must be knowledgeable about the law, federal and state regulations, and caselaw. Hearing officers must also have the knowledge and ability to "conduct hearings and write decisions in accordance with appropriate standard legal practice." Hearing Officers may not be employees of the state department of education or the school district that is involved in the child's education, nor may they have a "personal or professional conflict of interest" that may affect their ability to be objective.

244 In some states, the "Hearing Officer" is known as an "Administrative Law Judge" and in others as a "Fair Hearing Officer."

245 This author is personally familiar with two instances, in earlier years, in two states, where the spouse of a Hearing Officer and a State Review Officer were employed by an LEA and by a SEA. The respective states have removed those individuals.

246 If your state does not have a statute of limitations, you must request a due process hearing within two years. The two-year statute of limitations may not apply if the parent was prevented from requesting a hearing because of misrepresentations by the district or because the district withheld information it was required to provide.

(ii) the local educational agency's withholding of information from the parent that was required under this part to be provided to the parent.[247]

(E) Decision of Hearing Officer.[248]

(i) In General. Subject to clause (ii), a decision made by a hearing officer **shall be made on substantive grounds** based on a determination of whether the child received a free appropriate public education.[249]

(ii) Procedural Issues.[250] In matters alleging a procedural violation, a hearing officer may find that a child did not receive a free appropriate public education **only if** the procedural inadequacies–

(I) impeded the child's right to a free appropriate public education;

(II) significantly impeded the parents' opportunity to participate in the decisionmaking process regarding the provision of a free appropriate public education to the parents' child; or

(III) **caused a deprivation of educational benefits**.

(iii) Rule of Construction. Nothing in this subparagraph shall be construed to preclude a hearing officer from ordering a local educational agency to comply with procedural requirements under this section.

(F) Rule of Construction. Nothing in this paragraph shall be construed to affect the right of a parent[251] to file a complaint with the State educational agency.

(g) Appeal.[252]

(1) In General. If the hearing required by subsection (f) is conducted by a local educational agency, any party aggrieved by the findings and decision rendered in such a hearing may appeal such findings and decision **to the State educational agency.**

(2) Impartial Review and Independent Decision. The State educational agency shall conduct an impartial review of the findings and decision appealed under paragraph (1). The officer conducting such review shall make an independent decision upon completion of such review.

(h) Safeguards.[253]

Any party to a hearing conducted pursuant to subsection (f) or (k), or an appeal conducted pursuant to subsection (g), **shall be accorded** –

---

247   This is known as a "tolling of the statute of limitations."

248   Rulings by hearing officers should be based on substantive issues, not procedural issues, unless the procedural violation impeded the child's right to FAPE, significantly impeded the parents' opportunity to participate in the decision-making, process or deprived the child of educational benefit. This language incorporates existing caselaw about procedural and substantive issues.

249   Examples of substantive issues are whether the child has a disability that adversely affects educational performance (eligibility), whether a child has received FAPE (a free appropriate public education), or whether a child needs extended school year (ESY) services.

250   Procedural issues include delays in scheduling evaluations, determining eligibility, convening IEP meetings, or the failure to include appropriate personnel in IEP meetings. The facts of a case will determine whether the procedural breach rises to the level identified in this subsection.

251   **In lieu of filing a request for a due process hearing, parents can file complaints** with their state department of education. The state complaint procedure is detailed in 34 CFR §§ 300.151 - 300.153. Depending on the factual and legal issue, complaints can be filed with the Office for Civil Rights (OCR) and / or the U.S. Department of Justice (USDOJ).

For OCR - https://www2.ed.gov/about/offices/list/ocr/complaintprocess.html
For USDOJ - https://www.justice.gov/crt/how-file-complaint

252   **This is the appeal process in a two-tier state.** Only six states remain as two-tier. Most states have single-tier due process hearing systems. In a single-tier state, after the hearing, the losing party can appeal to state or federal court. In a two-tier state, after an adverse state level review decision, the losing party can appeal to court.

253   In a due process hearing, the parents or their attorney have the right to present evidence and cross-examine witnesses, and to issue subpoenas for witnesses. Parents have the right to a written verbatim record (transcript) of the hearing and to written findings of fact and decisions. In some states, parents may be represented by lay advocates.

(1) the right to be **accompanied and advised by counsel** and by individuals with special knowledge or training with respect to the problems of children with disabilities;

(2) the right to **present evidence and confront, cross-examine, and compel the attendance of witnesses**;

(3) the right to a written, or, at the option of the parents, electronic verbatim record of such hearing; and

(4) the right to written, or, at the option of the parents, electronic findings of fact and decisions, which findings and decisions–

> (A) shall be made available to the public consistent with the requirements of **Section 1417(b)** of this title (relating to the **confidentiality** of data, information, and records); and

> (B) shall be transmitted to the advisory panel established pursuant to Section 1412(a)(21) of this title.

(i) Administrative Procedures.

> **(1) In General**.

>> **(A) Decision Made in Hearing** – A decision made in a hearing conducted **pursuant to subsection (f) or (k) shall be final**, **except that** any party involved in such hearing **may appeal** such decision under the provisions of subsection (g) and paragraph (2).

>> **(B) Decision Made at Appeal**. A decision made under subsection (g) **shall be final**, except that **any party may bring an action** under paragraph (2).[254]

> **(2) Right to Bring Civil Action**.

>> **(A) In General**.[255] Any party aggrieved by the findings and decision made under subsection (f) or (k) who does not have the right to an appeal under subsection (g), and **any party** aggrieved by the findings and decision made under this subsection, **shall have the right to bring a civil action** with respect to the complaint presented pursuant to this section, which action may be brought in any State court of competent jurisdiction or in a district court of the United States,[256] without regard to the amount in controversy.[257]

>> **(B) Limitation**. The party bringing the action shall have **90 days** from the date of the decision of the hearing officer to bring such an action, **or**, if the State has an explicit time limitation for bringing such action under this part, in such time as the State law allows.[258]

>> **(C) Additional Requirements**. In any action brought under this paragraph, the court

>>> (i) shall receive the records of the administrative proceedings;

>>> (ii) shall hear additional evidence at the request of a party;[259] and

>>> (iii) basing its decision on the preponderance of the evidence, shall grant such relief as the court determines is appropriate.

---

254   In two-tier states (discussed in 20 U.S.C. § 1415(f)(1)(A)), the losing party must first appeal to the state department of education (SEA). If the party does not appeal, the due process decision is the final decision.

255   **This is the appeal procedure in a single-tier state after the due process hearing decision.** This is also the appeal procedure in a two-tier state, after the decision at the state level review proceeding. The SEA **must** resolve an LEA's failure to implement a special education due process decision. *See* 34 CFR § 300.152(c)(3).

256   Most special education due process hearings are related to a "Federal Question" such as whether the IEP is appropriate, as defined by IDEA. If a case is filed in state court and involves a "Federal Question," the defendant has the right to remove the case to the U.S. District Court in that jurisdiction. (*See* 28 U.S.C. § 1331 and § 1441 in Chapter 9.) Because of the right to seek removal, most special education due process appeals are filed in federal court and not state court.

257   In two-tier states, the losing party does not have a right to appeal to court until a decision is rendered by a Review Officer or Review Panel. After an adverse decision at the Review level, the losing party has a right to appeal to state or federal court.

258   The losing party has 90 days to appeal to state or federal court. This 90-day timeline was added to IDEA in 2004. States may provide different or shorter timelines. You need to know your state's statute of limitations for filing appeals in court. To be safe, if it is longer than 90 days, assume that the longer timeline does not apply and follow the shorter timeline.

259   Despite language in IDEA that the Court "shall hear additional evidence at the request of a party," Courts will rarely hear evidence that could have been offered at the due process hearing. Parties should put all their evidence into the record during the due process hearing.

(3) Jurisdiction of District Courts; Attorneys' Fees.

(A) In General. The district courts of the United States shall have jurisdiction of actions brought under this section without regard to the amount in controversy.

(B) Award of Attorneys' Fees.

(i) In General. In any action or proceeding brought under this section, the court, in its discretion, **may award reasonable attorneys' fees** as part of the costs–

(I) to a prevailing party who is the parent of a child with a disability;

(II) to a prevailing party who is a State educational agency or local educational agency against the attorney of a parent who files a complaint or subsequent cause of action that is **frivolous, unreasonable, or without foundation**, or against the attorney of a parent who continued to litigate after the litigation clearly became frivolous, unreasonable, or without foundation;[260] or

(III) to a prevailing State educational agency or local educational agency against the attorney of a parent, or against the parent, if the parent's complaint or subsequent cause of action was presented for any improper purpose, such as to **harass, to cause unnecessary delay, or to needlessly increase the cost of litigation**.[261]

(ii) Rule of Construction. Nothing in this subparagraph shall be construed to affect section 327 of the District of Columbia Appropriations Act, 2005.

(C) Determination of Amount of Attorneys' Fees. Fees awarded under this paragraph shall be based on rates prevailing in the community in which the action or proceeding arose for the kind and quality of services furnished. No bonus or multiplier may be used in calculating the fees awarded under this subsection.

(D) Prohibition of Attorneys' Fees and Related Costs for Certain Services.

(i) In General. Attorneys' fees **may not be awarded** and related costs may not be reimbursed in any action or proceeding under this section for services performed subsequent to the time of a written offer of settlement to a parent **if**–

(I) the offer is made **within the time prescribed by <Rule 68 of the Federal Rules of Civil Procedure>**[262] or, in the case of an administrative proceeding, at any time more than **10 days before** the proceeding begins;

(II) the offer is not accepted within 10 days; and

(III) the court or administrative hearing officer finds that the relief finally obtained by the parents is not more favorable to the parents than the offer of settlement.[263]

(ii) IEP Team Meetings. Attorneys' fees **may not be awarded** relating to any **meeting of the IEP Team** unless such meeting is convened as a result of an administrative proceeding or judicial action, **or**, at the discretion of the State, **for a mediation** described in subsection (e).

---

260 Parents who prevail can recover attorneys' fees from school districts. School districts may recover attorneys' fees from the parent or the parents' attorney under specific, limited circumstances. If the parent or the parent's attorney files a complaint that is frivolous, unreasonable, or for an improper purpose (i.e., to harass, cause unnecessary delay, or needlessly increase the cost of litigation), the court may award attorneys' fees to the school district.

261 Some parents, driven by anger and frustration, request due process hearings although they have not prepared their case. They may be focused on perceived wrongs by the school, not on obtaining a program that will meet their child's needs. Unfortunately, many hearing officers and judges view parents of children with disabilities as emotional "loose cannons." Parents who are driven by emotions, lose their cases and create ill will for other parents who use due process procedures to resolve disputes.

262 This <**FRCP 68**> **is known as an "Offer of Judgment."** It is included in Chapter 9 of this book and can also be viewed at: https://www.law.cornell.edu/rules/frcp/rule_68.

263 If the school district makes a written settlement offer 10 days before the due process hearing and the terms of the offer are the same or similar to the relief obtained through litigation, the parents may not be entitled to attorneys' fees. Attorneys' fees will not be awarded for IEP meetings. Some courts have held that only federal courts can award attorney's fees. Other courts have held that a state court or federal court can award attorneys' fees.

(iii) Opportunity to Resolve Complaints. A meeting conducted pursuant to subsection (f)(1)(B)(i)[264] shall not be considered–

(I) a meeting convened as a result of an administrative hearing or judicial action; or

(II) an administrative hearing or judicial action for purposes of this paragraph.

(E) Exception to Prohibition on Attorneys' Fees and Related Costs. Notwithstanding subparagraph (D), an award of attorneys' fees and related costs[265] may be made to a parent who is the prevailing party and who was substantially justified in rejecting the settlement offer.

(F) Reduction in Amount of Attorneys' Fees. Except as provided in subparagraph (G), whenever the court finds that

(i) the parent, or the parent's attorney, during the course of the action or proceeding, **unreasonably protracted** the final resolution of the controversy;

(ii) the amount of the attorneys' fees otherwise authorized to be awarded unreasonably exceeds the hourly rate prevailing in the community for similar services by attorneys of reasonably comparable skill, reputation, and experience;

(iii) the time spent and legal services furnished **were excessive** considering the nature of the action or proceeding; or

(iv) the attorney representing the parent did not provide to the local educational agency the appropriate information in the notice of the complaint described in subsection (b)(7)(A), the court shall reduce, accordingly, the amount of the attorneys' fees awarded under this section.

(G) Exception to Reduction in Amount of Attorneys' Fees. The provisions of subparagraph (F) shall not apply in any action or proceeding if the court finds that the State or **local educational agency unreasonably protracted**[266] the final resolution of the action or proceeding or there was a violation of this section.

(j) Maintenance of Current Educational Placement.[267]

Except as provided in **subsection (k)(4)**,[268] during the **pendency** of any proceedings conducted pursuant to this section, unless the State or local educational agency and the parents otherwise agree, the **child shall remain in the then-current educational placement** of the child, or, if applying for initial admission to a public school, shall, with the consent of the parents, be placed in the public school program until all such proceedings have been completed.[269]

---

264 This refers to a <Resolution Session> meeting, thus no attorneys fees. *See also Federal Register* Commentary at 71 Fed. Reg. 46708 (August 14, 2006) regarding 34 CFR § 300.517.

265 Pursuant to the SCOTUS decision in *Arlington Central School Dist. Bd. of Ed. v. Murphy* 548 U.S. 291 (2006), parents may not recover fees for expert witnesses even if the parents prevail.

266 *See Cobb County Sch. Dist. v. D.B.* (No. 16-11077), a decision in the U.S. Court of Appeals for the 11th Circuit, issued on November 14, 2016 in which Cobb County was found to have "unreasonably protracted" the litigation in an IEE case and was assessed approximately $300,000 in attorneys' fees. The case is in the 2016 edition of *Wrightslaw Year in Review*.

267 The "Stay-Put" statute, also known as the "**Pendency statute**," holds that during the due process hearing and appeal, the child will remain (stay-put) in the current educational placement. This does not apply to a child's transition from an early intervention program under Part C to a program under Part B. *See* 34 CFR § 300.518(c) and Commentary in the *Federal Register,* 71 Fed. Reg. 46709 (August 14, 2006). Also, it **does not apply to discipline proceedings** which are in the next section at 20 U.S.C. § 1415(k).

268 20 U.S.C. § 1415(k)(4) just below, is the discipline statute.

269 Pursuant to the U.S. Supreme Court decisions in *Burlington Sch. Comm. v. Massachusetts Dept. of Ed.,* 471 U.S. 359 (1985) and *Florence County Sch. Dist. IV v. Carter* 510 U.S. 7 (1993), the parent may remove a child from an inappropriate placement, place their child into a private program, and request reimbursement for the private placement, subject to the restrictions in 20 U.S.C. § 1412(a) (10). When the final decision awards reimbursement for a private placement, that private placement is the "current educational placement." If the school district appeals this decision, they must pay for the child's private placement while the case is appealed. *See* the regulation at 34 CFR § 300.518(d).

(k) Placement in Alternative Educational Setting.[270, 271]

(1) Authority of School Personnel.

(A) Case-by-Case Determination. School personnel may consider any unique circumstances on a **case-by-case** basis[272] when determining whether to order a change in placement for a child with a disability who violates a **code of student conduct**.

(B) Authority. School personnel under this subsection **may remove** a child with a disability who violates a code of student conduct[273] from their current placement to an appropriate interim alternative educational setting, another setting, or suspension, for **not more than 10 school days** (to the extent such alternatives are applied to children without disabilities).

(C) Additional Authority.[274] If school personnel seek to order a **change in placement that would exceed 10 school days** and the behavior that gave rise to the violation of the school code is **determined not to be a manifestation** of the child's disability pursuant to subparagraph (E), the relevant disciplinary procedures applicable to children without disabilities may be applied[275] to the child in the same manner and for the same duration in which the procedures would be applied to children without disabilities, except as provided in Section 1412(a)(1)[276] of this title although it may be provided in an interim alternative educational setting.

(D) Services. A child with a disability who is removed from the child's current placement under subparagraph (G) (irrespective of whether the behavior is determined to be a manifestation of the child's disability) or subparagraph (C) **shall** –

(i) **continue to receive educational services**, as provided in **<Section 1412(a)(1)>** of this title, so as to enable the child **to continue to participate in the general education curriculum**, although in another setting, **and to progress toward meeting the goals set out in the child's IEP**; and

(ii) receive, as appropriate, **a functional behavioral assessment, behavioral intervention services and modifications**, that are designed to address the behavior violation so that it does not recur.[277]

---

270 **This is the discipline statute.** Its regulations begin at <34 CFR § 300.530.> *See also* <Selected Topics: Discipline in Chapter 10.>

271 "A free appropriate public education is available to all children with disabilities residing in the State between the ages of 3 and 21, inclusive, including children with disabilities who have been suspended or expelled from school." 20 U.S.C. § 1412(a)(1)(A)

272 Many school administrators and school boards refuse to exercise discretion in disciplinary matters. They claim "the law" does not allow them to evaluate the circumstances of a particular child's case. Congress added language that school personnel may "consider any unique circumstances on a case-by-case basis" in determining whether to order a change of placement. This clarifies that school officials may use discretion and consider each individual situation carefully, and rebuts arguments by administrators who refuse to exercise discretion.

273 If a child with a disability violates a code of student conduct, school officials may suspend the child for up to 10 days. These codes of student conduct are written policies adopted by the School Board.

274 Look at subsections (b), (c), and (d) of <34 CFR § 300.530> for the distinctions between change of placement, a 10 day removal for one incident, a series of additional 10 day removals in one school year, and cumulative removals that exceed 10 days in one year. *See* Commentary in the *Federal Register*, 71 Fed. Reg. 46,714 - 46719 (August 14, 2006).

275 If the school suspends a child with a disability for more than 10 days and determines that the child's behavior was not a manifestation of the disability, they may use the same procedures as with non-disabled children, but they must continue to provide the child with a free appropriate public education (FAPE). *See* <20 U.S.C. § 1412(a)(1)(A).> However, as you will see in **Section 504**, if a change of placement is being considered for a Section 504 child, the **school district must provide the child with an evaluation prior** to a change of placement, such as suspension or expulsion, unlike the child with an IEP. Some legal pundits assert that the **Section 504 child has more rights** related to discipline and other matters, such as retaliation, than the child with an IEP under IDEA. <*See* 34 CFR § 104.35.>

276 The school is obligated to provide a free, appropriate public education to the child, **even if the child with an IEP has been suspended** or expelled. <*See* 20 U.S.C. § 1412(a)(1).>

277 If the school district suspends a child with a disability for more than 10 days, regardless of severity of the child's misconduct (i.e., violation of a code of conduct v. possession of a weapon), the school must continue to provide the child with FAPE <(*see* Section 1412(a)(1)(A))>, so the child can participate in the general education curriculum, make progress on the IEP goals, and receive a functional behavioral assessment, behavioral intervention services and modifications to prevent the behavior from reoccurring.

(E) Manifestation Determination.[278, 279, 280]

(i) In General. Except as provided in subparagraph (B), **within 10 school days of any decision to change the placement** of a child with a disability **because of a violation of a code of student conduct**, the local educational agency, the parent, and relevant members of the IEP Team (as determined by the parent and the local educational agency) **shall review all relevant information** in the student's file, including the child's IEP, any teacher observations, and any relevant information provided by the parents to determine–

(I) **if the conduct** in question **was caused by, or had a direct and substantial relationship to, the child's disability**; or[281]

(II) **if the conduct** in question **was the direct result of the local educational agency's failure to implement the IEP.**

(ii) Manifestation. If the local educational agency, the parent, and relevant members of the IEP Team determine that either subclause (I) or (II) of clause (i) is applicable for the child, the conduct **shall be determined to be a manifestation of the child's disability.**

(F) Determination That Behavior Was a Manifestation. If the local educational agency, the parent, and relevant members of the IEP Team make the determination that the conduct was a manifestation of the child's disability, **the IEP Team shall**–

(i) **conduct a functional behavioral assessment, and implement a behavioral intervention plan**[282] for such child, provided that the local educational agency had not conducted such assessment prior to such determination before the behavior that resulted in a change in placement described in subparagraph (C) or (G);

(ii) in the situation where a behavioral intervention plan has been developed, **review** the behavioral intervention plan if the child already has such a behavioral intervention plan, and **modify** it, as necessary, **to address the behavior**; and

(iii) except as provided in subparagraph (G), return the child to the placement from which the child was removed, unless the parent and the local educational agency agree to a change of placement as part of the modification of the behavioral intervention plan.

(G) Special Circumstances. School personnel may remove a student to an interim alternative educational setting for **not more than 45 school days** without regard to whether the behavior is determined to be a manifestation of the child's disability, in cases where a child–

(i) **carries or possesses a weapon**[283] to or at school, on school premises, or to or at a school function under the jurisdiction of a State or local educational agency;

---

278   The key to the outcome in most discipline cases is whether or not the violation of the code of student conduct was a manifestation of the child's disability.

279   The IEP Team must review all information about the child and determine if the negative behavior was caused by the child's disability, had a direct and substantial relationship to the disability, or was the result of the school's failure to implement the IEP.

280   If you are the parent of a child with special needs and are dealing with a discipline issue, you need to obtain a comprehensive neuropsychological or psycho-educational evaluation of the child by an evaluator in the private sector who has expertise in the disability (i.e., autism, attention deficit, bipolar disorder, Asperger's syndrome, auditory processing deficits, etc.). The evaluator must analyze the relationship between the child's disability and behavior. If there is a causal relationship, the evaluator should write a detailed report that describes the child's disability, the basis for determining that the behavior was a manifestation of the disability, and recommendations for an appropriate program. Your goal is to develop a win-win solution to the problem.

281   Often this is the main issue in discipline cases. As an attorney representing such children in this situation, I quickly obtained input from a psychologist or neuro-psychologist about the child's disability vis-à-vis the behavior.

282   If the child's behavior did not involve weapons, drugs, or serious bodily injury, the child should return to the prior placement. *See* 20 U.S.C. § 1415(k)(1)(G).

283   20 U.S.C. § 1415(k)(7)(C) clarifies that the term "weapon" means a "dangerous weapon" capable of causing death or serious bodily injury.

(ii) **knowingly possesses or uses illegal drugs**, or sells or solicits the sale of a controlled substance,[284] while at school, on school premises, or at a school function under the jurisdiction of a State or local educational agency; **or**

(iii) **has inflicted serious bodily injury** upon another person while at school, on school premises, or at a school function under the jurisdiction of a State or local educational agency.[285, 286]

(H) Notification. Not later than the date on which the decision to take disciplinary action is made, the local educational agency shall notify the parents of that decision, and of all procedural safeguards accorded under this section.

(2) Determination of Setting. The interim alternative educational setting in subparagraphs (C) and (G) of paragraph (1) **shall be determined by the IEP Team**.[287]

(3) Appeal.

(A) **In General**. The parent[288] of a child with a disability who disagrees with any decision regarding placement, or the manifestation determination under this subsection, or a local educational agency that believes that maintaining the current placement of the child is substantially likely to result in injury to the child or to others, may request a hearing.

(B) **Authority of Hearing Officer**.[289]

(i) **In General**. A hearing officer shall hear, and make a determination regarding, an appeal requested under subparagraph (A).

(ii) **Change of Placement Order**. In making the determination under clause (i), the hearing officer may order a change in placement of a child with a disability. In such situations, the **hearing officer may**

(I) **return a child** with a disability to the placement from which the child was removed; or

(II) **order a change in placement** of a child with a disability to an appropriate interim alternative educational setting for not more than 45 school days if the hearing officer determines that maintaining the current placement of such child is substantially likely to result in injury to the child or to others.

(4) Placement During Appeals. When an appeal under paragraph (3) has been requested by either the parent or the local educational agency–

(A) the **child shall remain in the interim alternative educational setting** pending the decision of the hearing officer or until the expiration of the time period provided for in paragraph (1)(C), whichever occurs first, unless the parent and the State or local educational agency agree otherwise; and

---

284   If a doctor prescribes a controlled substance for the child, and the child has possession of the medication at school, this is not illegal possession or illegal use. The school may not expel or suspend the child for possessing prescribed medication. If the child attempts to sell or solicit the sale of the controlled substance, this "special circumstance" warrants a suspension for 45 school days and possible criminal prosecution.

285   *See* 20 U.S.C. § 1415(k)(7) for the statutory differences between "controlled drugs," "illegal drugs," and definitions of "weapon" and "serious bodily injury."

286   If the child's behavior involves those in the above footnote, the child may be suspended for 45 school days even if the behavior was a manifestation of the disability. The child is still entitled to FAPE.

287   The decision to place a child into an interim alternative educational setting shall be made by the IEP Team, not by an administrator or school board member. **This is mandatory**. The educational setting is an interim placement, not a permanent placement. Remember: parents are full members of the IEP Team.

288   The parent can request a hearing to appeal the manifestation determination or the decision to place the child in an interim alternative educational setting. The school can request a hearing to maintain the current educational placement if they think changing the placement is "substantially likely to result in injury." Appeal of a manifestation determination may be futile in a case that involves a dangerous weapon, illegal drugs, or serious bodily injury. The school can suspend a student for 45 school days for these behaviors even if the behavior was a manifestation of the child's disability.

289   A hearing officer has the authority to return the child to the original placement. If the hearing officer concludes that the child is likely to injure himself or others, the hearing officer may order that the child be placed in an interim alternative educational setting for not more than 45 school days.

(B) the State or local educational agency shall arrange for an **expedited hearing**, which shall occur within **20 school days** of the date the hearing is requested and shall result in a determination within **10 school days** after the hearing.[290]

(5) Protections for Children Not Yet Eligible for Special Education and Related Services.

(A) In General. A child who has not been determined to be eligible for special education and related services under this part and who has engaged in behavior that violates a code of student conduct, **may assert any of the protections** provided for in this part **if the local educational agency had knowledge** (as determined in accordance with this paragraph) that the child was a child with a disability before the behavior that precipitated the disciplinary action occurred.

(B) Basis of Knowledge. A local educational agency shall be deemed to have **knowledge**[291] that a child is a child with a disability if, **before** the behavior that precipitated the disciplinary action occurred–

(i) the parent of the child has **expressed concern in writing** to supervisory or administrative personnel of the appropriate educational agency, or a teacher of the child, that the child is in need of special education and related services;

(ii) the parent of the child has **requested an evaluation** of the child pursuant to Section 1414(a)(1)(B) of this title; **or**

(iii) the teacher of the child, or other personnel of the local educational agency, **has expressed specific concerns** about a pattern of behavior demonstrated by the child, directly to the director of special education of such agency or to other supervisory personnel of the agency.[292]

(C) Exception. A local educational agency shall not be deemed to have knowledge that the child is a child with a disability if the **parent of the child has not allowed an evaluation** of the child pursuant to Section 1414 of this title **or has refused services**[293] under this part or the child has been evaluated and it was determined that the child was not a child with a disability under this part.

(D) Conditions that Apply if No Basis of Knowledge.

(i) In General. If a local educational agency does not have knowledge that a child is a child with a disability (in accordance with subparagraph (B) or (C)) prior to taking disciplinary measures against the child, the child may be subjected to disciplinary measures applied to children without disabilities who engaged in comparable behaviors consistent with clause (ii).

(ii) Limitations. If a request is made for an evaluation of a child during the time period in which the child is subjected to disciplinary measures under this subsection, the evaluation **shall be conducted in an expedited manner**. If the child is determined to be a child with a disability, taking into consideration information from the evaluation conducted by the agency and information provided by the parents,

---

290 Expedited hearings must be held within 20 school days and a decision rendered within 10 school days. While the decision is pending, the child shall remain in the alternative setting, unless the time limit for this placement expired.

291 If the school knew, or should have known, that the child is a child with a disability and entitled to an IEP, then the child is protected under IDEA. The factors affecting "knowledge" are listed.

292 If you are concerned that your child may have a disability, you must put your concerns in writing. You should document important conversations, meetings, and telephone calls with notes or letters that describe what happened, what you were told, and your concerns. To do less is unwise. Courts have little sympathy for individuals who know or should know they have rights, fail to safeguard their rights, then complain that their rights were violated. Courts believe that the party who complains that their rights were violated must prove that they took reasonable steps to protect themselves, yet their rights were still violated.

293 If the parent refused to permit an evaluation or consent to special education services, the child loses these protections.

the agency shall provide special education and related services[294] in accordance with this part, except that, pending the results of the evaluation, the child shall remain in the educational placement determined by school authorities.

(6) Referral to and Action by Law Enforcement and Judicial Authorities.[295]

(A) **Rule of Construction.** Nothing in this part shall be construed to prohibit an agency from reporting a crime committed by a child with a disability to appropriate authorities or to prevent State law enforcement and judicial authorities from exercising their responsibilities with regard to the application of Federal and State law to crimes committed by a child with a disability.

(B) **Transmittal of Records.** An agency reporting a crime committed by a child with a disability shall ensure that copies of the special education and disciplinary records of the child are transmitted for consideration by the appropriate authorities to whom the agency reports the crime.

(7) Definitions. In this subsection:

(A) **Controlled Substance.** The term '**controlled substance**' means a drug or other substance identified under schedule I, II, III, IV, or V in Section 812(c) of title 21, United States Code.[296]

(B) **Illegal Drug.** The term '**illegal drug**' means a controlled substance but does **not** include a controlled substance that is legally possessed or used under the supervision of a licensed health-care professional or that is legally possessed[297] or used under any other authority under that Act or under any other provision of Federal law.

(C) **Weapon.** The term '**weapon**'[298] has the meaning given the term 'dangerous weapon' under Section 930(g)(2) of title 18, United States Code.

(D) **Serious Bodily Injury.** The term 'serious bodily injury'[299] has the meaning given the term 'serious bodily injury' under paragraph (3) of subsection (h) of Section 1365 of title 18, United States Code.

---

294   If the school did not have knowledge that the child had a disability and was entitled to an IEP, the child may be treated like a nondisabled child. If an evaluation is requested, it shall be expedited. Once it is determined that the child is eligible for special education and is entitled to an IEP, the child will receive all rights and protections under IDEA, including the detailed procedures provided in 20 U.S.C. § 1415(k).

295   The school is not prohibited from or required to report crimes committed by children with disabilities. Discretion and common sense should prevail. The practice of reporting behavior caused by emotional disturbances as "crimes" puts law enforcement personnel into positions for which they have not been trained. Treating children who have emotional disabilities as criminals may inflict permanent damage on these children.

296   https://www.law.cornell.edu/uscode/text/21/812

297   It is not unusual for schools to suspend or expel students who bring over-the-counter medications (i.e., aspirin, ibuprofen, Tums) to school, claiming that the medications are "drugs." This subsection clarifies that **over-the-counter medications are not illegal drugs or controlled substances.** A child with a disability who receives services under IDEA is protected from such actions by school officials.

298   The "term 'dangerous weapon' means a weapon, device, instrument, material, or substance, animate or inanimate, that is used for, or is readily capable of, causing death or serious bodily injury, except that such term does not include a pocket knife with a blade of less than 2 1/2 inches in length." *See* 18 U.S.C. § 930(g)(2) at https://www.law.cornell.edu/uscode/text/18/930.

299   The term '**serious bodily injury**' means bodily injury which involves **(A) a substantial risk of death; (B) extreme physical pain;** (C) protracted and obvious **disfigurement**; or (D) protracted loss or impairment of the function of a bodily member, organ, or mental faculty." (18 U.S.C. § 1365(h)(3)) *See* https://www.law.cornell.edu/uscode/text/18/1365

(l) Rule of Construction.[300]

Nothing in this title shall be construed to restrict or limit the rights, procedures, and remedies available under the Constitution, the Americans with Disabilities Act of 1990, [42 U.S.C. § 12101 *et seq.*] title V of the Rehabilitation Act of 1973, [29 U.S.C. § 790 *et seq.*] or other Federal laws protecting the rights of children with disabilities, except that **before the filing of a civil action** under such laws seeking relief that is also available under this part, **the procedures under subsections (f) and (g) shall be exhausted** to the same extent as would be required had the action been brought under this part.

(m) Transfer of Parental Rights at Age of Majority.[301]

(1) In General. A State that receives amounts from a grant under this part may provide that, **when a child with a disability reaches the age of majority** under State law (except for a child with a disability who has been determined to be incompetent under State law)–

(A) the agency shall provide any notice required by this section to both the individual and the parents;

(B) all other **rights accorded to parents** under this part **transfer to the child**;

(C) the agency shall notify the individual and the parents of the transfer of rights; and

(D) all rights accorded to parents under this part transfer to children who are incarcerated in an adult or juvenile Federal, State, or local correctional institution.

(2) Special Rule.[302] If, under State law, a child with a disability who has reached the age of majority under State law, who has not been determined to be incompetent, but **who is determined not to have the ability to provide informed consent** with respect to the educational program of the child, the State shall establish procedures **for appointing the parent of the child,**[303] or if the parent is not available, another appropriate individual, to represent the educational interests of the child throughout the period of eligibility of the child under this part.

---

300 This explains that you must first exhaust the special due process procedures before filing suit in federal court. This is known as the "**Exhaustion of Administrative Remedies**" statute.

This is the subject of the SCOTUS ruling in *Fry v. Napoleon Comm. Sch. Dist.* and in *Perez v. Sturgis*. In a **unanimous 8-0** decision, SCOTUS reversed the Sixth Circuit Court of Appeals decision in *Fry* and ruled in favor of the parents. Justice Kagan explained that "We hold that exhaustion is not necessary when the **gravamen** of the plaintiff's suit is something **other than the denial** of the IDEA's core guarantee - what the Act calls a 'free appropriate public education.'" Gravamen has been defined by various courts as the essence, **the gist of the case.**

A parent or child with a disability, who has a case against a school district or school employee, if IDEA can provide a remedy, must comply with this statute by requesting and pursuing a special education due process hearing.

However, if IDEA provides no relief, such as in a discrimination or retaliation issue, the plaintiff may file suit under Section 504, ADA, or another legal remedy. Under Section 504 or another legal theory, they may proceed straight to federal court. However, some Court of Appeals since *Fry* have held that parents must still exhaust their administrative remedies, i.e., request a due process hearing, prior to suit in federal court if there was **any possible relief** under IDEA, even if IDEA relief was not sought as a remedy **and the child did not have an IEP.** There is a split between circuits on this issue. Another case about "exhaustion" **is pending** before SCOTUS. *See <**Perez v. Sturgis Public Schools**.>* https://www.wrightslaw.com/law/scotus/sturgis/

Caselaw continues to evolve in this area. Presumably exhaustion is not required in a lawsuit for dollar damages under Section 504 of the Rehabilitation Act for a harm not related to IDEA. To determine the effect of *Fry* in your state, you must read the most recent District Court and Court of Appeals decisions issued in your Circuit since February 22, 2017. The full decision and transcript of Justice Kagan's Announcement is in the 2017 edition of *Wrightslaw Year in Review* available on our website at:

https://www.wrightslaw.com/store/2017law.html

An **analysis of Fry** and *Sturgis* are on Wrightslaw at: https://www.wrightslaw.com/law/art/fry.napoleon.504.service.dog.htm and https://www.wrightslaw.com/law/art/2022.perez.sturgis.scotus.htm.

301 The district must provide notice to the parent and child that the parents' rights will transfer to the child when the child reaches the "age of majority," which, depending on state law, is usually age eighteen. With a "grant of authority" or "power of attorney," a parent can continue to represent the educational interests of the child.

302 If possible, have your child write a statement that says, "I [child's name], pursuant to 20 U.S.C. Section 1415(m) and [your state's special education regulation section], hereby appoint my parent, [your name], to represent my educational interests." If the child is able, have this statement written out longhand, signed and dated. Use the language in your state's special education regulation verbatim. If possible, do not add to it, subtract from it, or rephrase it. Some states have forms for this purpose.

303 *See also* 34 CFR § 300.520(b).

(n) Electronic Mail.

A parent of a child with a disability may elect to receive notices required under this section by an electronic mail (**e-mail**) communication, if the agency makes such option available.[304]

(o) Separate Complaint.

Nothing in this section shall be construed to preclude a parent from filing a separate due process complaint on an issue separate from a due process complaint already filed.[305]

20 U.S.C. § 1416. Monitoring, Technical Assistance, and Enforcement.[306]

(a) Federal and State Monitoring.

(1) In General. The Secretary shall–

(A) monitor implementation of this part through–

(i) oversight of the exercise of general supervision by the States, as required in Section 1412(a)(11) of this title; and

(ii) the State performance plans, described in subsection (b);

(B) enforce this part in accordance with subsection (e); and

(C) require States to–

(i) monitor implementation of this part by local educational agencies; and

(ii) enforce this part in accordance with paragraph (3) and subsection (e).

(2) Focused Monitoring.[307] The primary focus of Federal and State monitoring activities described in paragraph (1) shall be on–

(A) improving educational results[308] and functional outcomes for all children with disabilities; and

(B) ensuring that States meet the program requirements under this part, with a particular emphasis on those requirements that are most closely related to improving educational results for children with disabilities.

(3) Monitoring Priorities. The Secretary shall monitor the States, and **shall require each State to monitor the local educational agencies** located in the State (except the State exercise of general supervisory responsibility),

---

304   At the parent's option, the district can send notices by e-mail. Given the prevalence of problems with email, this option is not recommended as the primary means of providing or receiving notice. You may want to receive notice by email as a supplement to the usual notification procedures.

305   If a due process hearing is pending on one issue, and a new issue arises, the parent may file a separate due process complaint notice. *See also* 34 CFR § 300.513(c) In the alternative, if the hearing officer and the other party agrees, and the hearing has not been held, the parent may be able to file an Amended Complaint as described in 20 U.S.C. § 1415(c)(2)(E).

306   **Wrightslaw Overview**: Section 1416 is the enforcement section. Although USDOE is responsible for enforcing IDEA, the National Council on Disability found that the Department had never required a state to enforce the law. As a result, no state was in compliance with the law, leaving parents who requested due process hearings to act as the main enforcers of the law. Enforcement efforts have generally focused on procedural compliance. The Department of Education has a minimal focus on whether schools and districts were teaching children with disabilities to read, write, spell, do arithmetic, and prepare the children for further education, employment, independent living. Section 1416 includes language about accountability. If the Department of Education determines that a state department of education (SEA) "needs assistance" for two consecutive years, the Department shall take corrective action and impose special conditions. If the state remains in the "needs assistance" category for three consecutive years, the Department of Education may recover funds paid, withhold further funds, and refer the matter to the Department of Justice.

307   In IDEA, monitoring is to focus on educational results and functional outcomes. When the special education law was passed in 1975 (Public Law 94-142), many children with disabilities were denied services without due process of law. As a result, the law then focused on protecting the rights of children and their parents (20 U.S.C. § 1400(d)(1)(B)) and providing remedies for violations. During the early years, educational outcomes took a back seat to procedural compliance. Before the IDEA was reauthorized in 1997, the word "measurable" (or any variation of the word) was rarely used to describe outcomes, goals, or objectives. When the law was reauthorized in 1997, the word "measurable" (or a variation of the word) appeared 16 times. In IDEA 2004, the word "measurable" appears 30 times. This doubling in the frequency of the word "measurable" may bode well for the future.

308   However, attempting to measure educational results from year to year appears to be a moving target. Why not take a child's initial standardized test data from eligibility and use the same tests to compare results after one year, two years, and three years later?

using quantifiable indicators in each of the following priority areas, and using such qualitative indicators as are needed to adequately measure performance in the following priority areas:

(A) Provision of a free appropriate public education in the least restrictive environment.

(B) State exercise of general supervisory authority, including child find, effective monitoring, the use of resolution sessions, mediation, voluntary binding arbitration, and a system of transition services as defined in Sections 1401(34) and 1437(a)(9) of this title.

(C) Disproportionate representation of racial and ethnic groups in special education and related services, to the extent the representation is the result of inappropriate identification.

(4) Permissive Areas of Review. The Secretary shall consider other relevant information and data, including data provided by States under Section 1418 of this title.

(b) State Performance Plans.[309]

(1) Plan.

(A) **In General**. Not later than 1 year after the date of enactment of the Individuals with Disabilities Education Improvement Act of 2004, each State shall have in place a performance plan that evaluates that State's efforts to implement the requirements and purposes of this part and describes how the State will improve such implementation.

(B) **Submission for Approval**. Each State shall submit the State's performance plan to the Secretary for approval in accordance with the approval process described in subsection (c).

(C) **Review**. Each State shall review its State performance plan at least once every 6 years and submit any amendments to the Secretary.

(2) Targets.

(A) **In General**. As a part of the State performance plan described under paragraph (1), each State **shall establish measurable and rigorous targets** for the indicators established under the priority areas described in subsection (a)(3).

(B) **Data Collection**.

(i) **In General**. Each State shall collect valid and reliable information as needed to report annually to the Secretary on the priority areas described in subsection (a)(3).

(ii) **Rule of Construction**. Nothing in this title shall be construed to authorize the development of a nationwide database of personally identifiable information on individuals involved in studies or other collections of data under this part.

(C) **Public Reporting and Privacy**.

(i) **In General**. The State shall use the targets established in the plan and priority areas described in subsection (a)(3) to analyze the performance of each local educational agency in the State in implementing this part.

(ii) **Report**.

(I) **Public Report**. The State **shall report** annually **to the public** on **the performance of each local educational agency** located in the State on the targets in the State's performance plan. The State shall make the State's performance plan available through public means, including by posting on the website of the State educational agency, distribution to the media, and distribution through public agencies.

(II) **State Performance Report**. The State shall report annually to the Secretary on the performance of the State under the State's performance plan.

---

309   Information on Monitoring and Enforcement activities of the U.S. Department of Education is at: https://www2.ed.gov/policy/speced/guid/idea/monitor/index.html.

(iii) Privacy. The State shall not report to the public or the Secretary any information on performance that would result in the disclosure of personally identifiable information about individual children or where the available data is insufficient to yield statistically reliable information.

(c) Approval Process.

(1) Deemed Approval. The Secretary shall review (including the specific provisions described in subsection (b)) each performance plan submitted by a State pursuant to subsection (b)(1)(B) and the plan shall be deemed to be approved by the Secretary unless the Secretary makes a written determination, prior to the expiration of the 120-day period beginning on the date on which the Secretary received the plan, that the plan does not meet the requirements of this section, including the specific provisions described in subsection (b).

(2) Disapproval. The Secretary shall not finally disapprove a performance plan, except after giving the State notice and an opportunity for a hearing.

(3) Notification. If the Secretary finds that the plan does not meet the requirements, in whole or in part, of this section, the Secretary **shall** –

(A) give the State notice and an opportunity for a hearing; and

(B) notify the State of the finding, and in such notification shall–

(i) cite the specific provisions in the plan that do not meet the requirements; and

(ii) request additional information, only as to the provisions not meeting the requirements, needed for the plan to meet the requirements of this section.

(4) Response. If the State responds to the Secretary's notification described in paragraph (3)(B) during the 30-day period beginning on the date on which the State received the notification, and resubmits the plan with the requested information described in paragraph (3)(B)(ii), the Secretary shall approve or disapprove such plan prior to the later of –

(A) the expiration of the 30-day period beginning on the date on which the plan is resubmitted; or

(B) the expiration of the 120-day period described in paragraph (1).

(5) Failure to Respond. If the State does not respond to the Secretary's notification described in paragraph (3)(B) during the 30-day period beginning on the date on which the State received the notification, such plan shall be deemed to be disapproved.

(d) Secretary's Review and Determination.

(1) Review. The Secretary shall annually review the State performance report submitted pursuant to subsection (b)(2)(C)(ii)(II) in accordance with this section.

(2) Determination.

(A) In General. Based on the information provided by the State in the State performance report, information obtained through monitoring visits, and any other public information made available, the Secretary shall determine if the State–

(i) meets the requirements and purposes of this part;

(ii) needs assistance in implementing the requirements of this part;

(iii) needs intervention in implementing the requirements of this part; or

(iv) needs substantial intervention in implementing the requirements of this part.

(B) Notice and Opportunity for a Hearing. For determinations made under clause (iii) or (iv) of subparagraph (A), the Secretary shall provide reasonable notice and an opportunity for a hearing on such determination.

(e) Enforcement.

(1) Needs Assistance. If the Secretary determines, **for 2 consecutive years**, that a State needs assistance under subsection (d)(2)(A)(ii) in implementing the requirements of this part, the Secretary **shall take 1 or more of the following actions**:

(A) Advise the State of available sources of technical assistance that may help the State address the areas in which the State needs assistance, which may include assistance from the Office of Special Education Programs, other offices of the Department of Education, other Federal agencies, technical assistance providers approved by the Secretary, and other federally funded nonprofit agencies, and require the State to work with appropriate entities. Such technical assistance may include–

(i) the provision of advice by experts to address the areas in which the State needs assistance, including explicit plans for addressing the area for concern within a specified period of time;

(ii) assistance in identifying and implementing professional development, instructional strategies, and methods of instruction that are based on scientifically based research;

(iii) designating and using distinguished superintendents, principals, special education administrators, special education teachers, and other teachers to provide advice, technical assistance, and support; and

(iv) devising additional approaches to providing technical assistance, such as collaborating with institutions of higher education, educational service agencies, national centers of technical assistance supported under part D, and private providers of scientifically based technical assistance.

(B) Direct the use of State-level funds under Section 1411(e) of this title on the area or areas in which the State needs assistance.

(C) Identify the State as a high-risk grantee and **impose special conditions** on the State's grant under this part.

(2) Needs Intervention. If the Secretary determines, **for 3 or more consecutive years**, that a State needs intervention under subsection (d)(2)(A)(iii) in implementing the requirements of this part, the following shall apply:

(A) The Secretary may take any of the actions described in paragraph (1).

(B) The Secretary **shall take 1 or more of the following actions**:

(i) Require the State to prepare a corrective action plan or improvement plan if the Secretary determines that the State should be able to correct the problem within 1 year.

(ii) Require the State to enter into a compliance agreement under Section 1234f of this title, if the Secretary has reason to believe that the State cannot correct the problem within 1 year.

(iii) For each year of the determination, withhold not less than 20 percent and not more than 50 percent of the State's funds under Section 1411(e) of this title, until the Secretary determines the State has sufficiently addressed the areas in which the State needs intervention.

(iv) Seek to recover funds under Section 1234a this title.

(v) **Withhold**, in whole or in part, **any further payments** to the State under this part pursuant to paragraph (5).

(vi) Refer the matter for appropriate enforcement action, which may include referral to the Department of Justice.

(3) Needs Substantial Intervention. Notwithstanding paragraph (1) or (2), **at any time** that the Secretary determines that a State needs substantial intervention in implementing the requirements of this part or that there is a substantial failure to comply with any condition of a State educational agency's or local educational agency's eligibility under this part, the Secretary **shall take 1 or more of the following actions**:

(A) Recover funds under Section 1234a of this title.

(B) Withhold, in whole or in part, any further payments to the State under this part.

(C) Refer the case to the Office of the Inspector General at the Department of Education.

(D) Refer the matter for appropriate enforcement action, which may include **referral to the Department of Justice**.

(4) Opportunity for Hearing.[310]

    (A) Withholding Funds. Prior to withholding any funds under this section, the Secretary shall provide reasonable notice and an opportunity for a hearing to the State educational agency involved.

    (B) Suspension. Pending the outcome of any hearing to withhold payments under subsection (b), the Secretary may suspend payments to a recipient, suspend the authority of the recipient to obligate funds under this part, or both, after such recipient has been given reasonable notice and an opportunity to show cause why future payments or authority to obligate funds under this part should not be suspended.

(5) Report to Congress. The Secretary shall report to the **Committee on Education and the Workforce of the House of Representatives and the Committee on Health, Education, Labor, and Pensions of the Senate** within 30 days of taking enforcement action pursuant to paragraph (1), (2), or (3), on the specific action taken and the reasons why enforcement action was taken.

(6) Nature of Withholding.

    (A) Limitation. If the Secretary withholds further payments pursuant to paragraph (2) or (3), the Secretary may determine–

        (i) that such withholding will be limited to programs or projects, or portions of programs or projects, that affected the Secretary's determination under subsection (d)(2); or

        (ii) that the State educational agency shall not make further payments under this part to specified State agencies or local educational agencies that caused or were involved in the Secretary's determination under subsection (d)(2).

    (B) Withholding Until Rectified. Until the Secretary is satisfied that the condition that caused the initial withholding has been substantially rectified–

        (i) payments to the State under this part shall be withheld in whole or in part; and

        (ii) payments by the State educational agency under this part shall be limited to State agencies and local educational agencies whose actions did not cause or were not involved in the Secretary's determination under subsection (d)(2), as the case may be.

(7) Public Attention. Any State that has received notice under subsection (d)(2) shall, by means of a public notice, take such measures as may be necessary to bring the pendency of an action pursuant to this subsection to the attention of the public within the State.

(8) Judicial Review.

    (A) In General. If any State is dissatisfied with the Secretary's action with respect to the eligibility of the State under Section 1412 of this title, **such State may,** not later than 60 days after notice of such action, **file** with the United States court of appeals for the circuit in which such State is located **a petition for review** of that action. A copy of the petition shall be transmitted by the clerk of the court to the Secretary. The Secretary thereupon shall file in the court the record of the proceedings upon which the Secretary's action was based, as provided in Section 2112 of title 28, United States Code.

    (B) Jurisdiction; Review by United States Supreme Court. Upon the filing of such petition, the court shall have jurisdiction to affirm the action of the Secretary or to set it aside, in whole or in part. The judgment of the court **shall be subject to review by the Supreme Court of the United States upon certiorari** or certification as provided in Section 1254 of title 28, United States Code.

    (C) Standard of Review. The findings of fact by the Secretary, **if supported by substantial evidence, shall be conclusive,** but the court, for good cause shown, may remand the case to the Secretary to take further evidence, and the Secretary may thereupon make new or modified findings of fact and may modify the Secretary's previous action, and shall file in the court the record of the further proceedings. Such new or modified findings of fact shall be conclusive if supported by substantial evidence.

---

310   *See* the earlier reference in footnotes to 20 U.S.C. § 1412(a)(17) and the *Texas Education Agency v. USDOE* case. The USDOE withheld approximately Thirty-three million dollars from Texas. The decision was upheld on November 7, 2018 by the Fifth Circuit. The case is in the 2018 edition of ***Wrightslaw Year in Review***.

(f) State Enforcement.

If a State educational agency determines that **a local educational agency is not meeting the requirements** of this part, including the targets in the State's performance plan, the State educational agency **shall prohibit** the local educational agency from reducing the local educational agency's maintenance of effort under Section 1413(a)(2)(C) of this title for any fiscal year.

(g) Rule of Construction.

Nothing in this section shall be construed to restrict the Secretary from utilizing any authority under the General Education Provisions Act to monitor and enforce the requirements of this title.

(h) Divided State Agency Responsibility.

For purposes of this section, where responsibility for ensuring that the requirements of this part are met with respect to children with disabilities who are convicted as adults under State law and incarcerated in adult prisons is assigned to a public agency other than the State educational agency pursuant to Section 1412(a)(11)(C) of this title, the Secretary, in instances where the Secretary finds that the failure to comply substantially with the provisions of this part are related to a failure by the public agency, shall take appropriate corrective action to ensure compliance with this part, except that

(1) any reduction or withholding of payments to the State shall be proportionate to the total funds allotted under Section 1411 of this title to the State as the number of eligible children with disabilities in adult prisons under the supervision of the other public agency is proportionate to the number of eligible individuals with disabilities in the State under the supervision of the State educational agency; and

(2) any withholding of funds under paragraph (1) shall be limited to the specific agency responsible for the failure to comply with this part.

(i) Data Capacity and Technical Assistance Review. The Secretary shall–

(1) review the data collection and analysis capacity of States to ensure that data and information determined necessary for implementation of this section is collected, analyzed, and accurately reported to the Secretary; and

(2) provide technical assistance (from funds reserved under Section 1411(c) of this title), where needed, to improve the capacity of States to meet the data collection requirements.

20 U.S.C. § 1417. Administration.[311]

(a) Responsibilities of Secretary. The Secretary **shall–**

(1) cooperate with, and (directly or by grant or contract) furnish technical assistance necessary to, a State in matters relating to–

   (A) the education of children with disabilities; and

   (B) carrying out this part; and

(2) provide short-term training programs and institutes.

(b) Prohibition Against Federal Mandates, Direction, or Control.

Nothing in this title shall be construed to authorize an officer or employee of the Federal Government to mandate, direct, or **control a State, local educational agency, or school's specific instructional content**, academic achievement standards and assessments, curriculum, or program of instruction.

(c) Confidentiality.

The Secretary shall take appropriate action, in accordance with Section 1232g of this title, **to ensure the protection of the confidentiality of any personally identifiable data,** information, and records collected or maintained by the Secretary **and by** State educational agencies and local educational agencies pursuant to this part.

---

311 **Wrightslaw Overview:** Section 1417 describes requirements for administering the law. The Department of Education may not mandate, direct, or control specific instructional content, curriculum or programs of instruction. When the special education regulations were published, the Department of Education published a model Individualized Education Program (IEP) form, an Individualized Family Service Plan (IFSP) form, procedural safeguards notice form, and prior written notice form.

(d) Personnel.

The Secretary is authorized to hire qualified personnel necessary to carry out the Secretary's duties under subsection (a), under Section 1418 of this title, and under subpart 4 of part D, without regard to the provisions of title 5, United States Code, relating to appointments in the competitive service and without regard to chapter 51 and subchapter III of chapter 53 of such title relating to classification and general schedule pay rates, except that no more than 20 such personnel shall be employed at any time.

(e) Model Forms.[312]

Not later than the date that the Secretary publishes final regulations under this title, to implement amendments made by the Individuals with Disabilities Education Improvement Act of 2004, the Secretary shall publish and disseminate widely to States, local educational agencies, and parent and community training and information centers–

(1) a model **IEP form;**

(2) a model **individualized family service plan (IFSP) form;**

(3) a model form of the **notice of procedural safeguards** described in Section 1415(d) of this title; and

(4) a model form of the **prior written notice** described in subsections (b)(3) and (c)(1) of Section 1415 of this title that is consistent with the requirements of this part and is sufficient to meet such requirements.

20 U.S.C. § 1418. Program Information.[313]

(a) In General.

Each State that receives assistance under this part, and the Secretary of the Interior,[314] **shall provide data each year to** the Secretary of Education and **the public** on the following:

(1)

(A) The **number and percentage of children with disabilities, by race, ethnicity, limited English proficiency status, gender, and disability category,** who are in each of the following separate categories:

(i) Receiving a free appropriate public education.

(ii) Participating in regular education.

(iii) In separate classes, separate schools or facilities, or public or private residential facilities.

(iv) For each year of age from age 14 through 21, stopped receiving special education and related services because of program completion (including graduation with a regular secondary school diploma), or other reasons, and the **reasons why those children stopped receiving special education and related services.**

(v)

(I) Removed to an interim alternative educational setting under Section 1415(k)(1) of this title.

(II) The acts or items precipitating those removals.

(III) The number of children with disabilities who are subject to long-term **suspensions or expulsions.**

(B) The number and percentage of children with disabilities, by race, gender, and ethnicity, who are receiving **early intervention services.**

(C) The number and percentage of children with disabilities, by race, gender, and ethnicity, who, from birth through age 2, stopped receiving early intervention services because of program completion or for other reasons.

---

312   Download the model forms from https://www.wrightslaw.com/idea/law.htm .

313   **Wrightslaw Overview**: IDEA requires States to provide detailed reports about the number and percentage of children with disabilities by race, ethnicity, English proficiency, gender, and disability category, including children removed from school. The state must report Information about the number of due process complaints, hearings, changes in placement, mediations, and settlement agreements. To address issues of over-identification of minority children and the disproportionate number of minority children in special education, the Department of Education requires states to review and revise policies, procedures, and practices, and requires districts to publicly report on their revised policies, procedures and practices.

314   The Bureau of Indian Education implements federal Indian education programs for roughly 46,000 students at 183 schools across the United States.

(D) The incidence and duration of disciplinary actions by race, ethnicity, limited English proficiency status, gender, and disability category, of children with disabilities, including **suspensions** of 1 day or more.

(E) The number and percentage of children with disabilities who are **removed to alternative educational settings or expelled** as compared to children without disabilities who are removed to alternative educational settings or expelled.

(F) The **number of due process complaints** filed under Section 1415 of this title and the **number of hearings** conducted.

(G) The number of hearings requested under Section 1415(k) of this title and the **number of changes in placements** ordered as a result of those hearings.

(H) The number of **mediations** held and the number of **settlement agreements** reached through such mediations.

(2) The number and percentage of infants and toddlers, by race, and ethnicity, who are at risk of having substantial developmental delays (as defined in Section 1432 of this title), and who are receiving early intervention services under part C.

(3) Any other information that may be required by the Secretary.

(b) Data Reporting.

(1) Protection of Identifiable Data. The data described in subsection (a) shall be publicly reported by each State in a manner that does not result in the disclosure of data identifiable to individual children.

(2) Sampling. The Secretary may permit States and the Secretary of the Interior to obtain the data described in subsection (a) through sampling.

(c) Technical Assistance. The Secretary may provide technical assistance to States to ensure compliance with the data collection and reporting requirements under this title.

(d) Disproportionality.[315]

(1) In General. Each State that receives assistance under this part, and the Secretary of the Interior, shall provide for the collection and examination of data to determine if significant disproportionality based on race and ethnicity is occurring in the State and the local educational agencies of the State with respect to–

(A) the identification of children as children with disabilities, including the identification of children as children with disabilities in accordance with a particular impairment described in Section 1401(3) of this title;

(B) the placement in particular educational settings of such children; and

(C) the incidence, duration, and type of disciplinary actions, including suspensions and expulsions.

(2) Review and Revision of Policies, Practices, and Procedures. In the case of a determination of significant disproportionality with respect to the identification of children as children with disabilities, or the placement in particular educational settings of such children, in accordance with paragraph (1), the State or the Secretary of the Interior, as the case may be, shall–

(A) provide for the review and, if appropriate, revision of the policies, procedures, and practices used in such identification or placement to ensure that such policies, procedures, and practices comply with the requirements of this title;

(B) require any local educational agency identified under paragraph (1) to reserve the maximum amount of funds under Section 1413(f) of this title to provide comprehensive coordinated early intervening services to serve children in the local educational agency, particularly children in those groups that were significantly overidentified under paragraph (1); and

(C) require the local educational agency to publicly report on the revision of policies, practices, and procedures described under subparagraph (A).

---

315 *See* 20 U.S.C. § 1412(a)(24) about policies and practices about longstanding problems related to the over-identification and disproportionate representation by race and ethnicity.

20 U.S.C. § 1419. Preschool Grants.

(a) In General. The Secretary shall provide grants under this section to assist States to provide special education and related services, in accordance with this part

(1) to children with disabilities aged 3 through 5, inclusive; and

(2) at the State's discretion, to 2-year-old children with disabilities who will turn 3 during the school year.

(b) Eligibility. A State shall be eligible for a grant under this section if such State–

(1) is eligible under Section 1412 of this title to receive a grant under this part; and

(2) makes a free appropriate public education available to all children with disabilities, aged 3 through 5, residing in the State.

(c) Allocations to States.

(1) In General. The Secretary shall allocate the amount made available to carry out this section for a fiscal year among the States in accordance with paragraph (2) or (3), as the case may be.

(2) Increase in Funds. If the amount available for allocations to States under paragraph (1) for a fiscal year is equal to or greater than the amount allocated to the States under this section for the preceding fiscal year, those allocations shall be calculated as follows:

(A) Allocation.

(i) **In General.** Except as provided in subparagraph (B), the Secretary shall–

(I) allocate to each State the amount the State received under this section for fiscal year 1997;

(II) allocate 85 percent of any remaining funds to States on the basis of the States' relative populations of children aged 3 through 5; and

(III) allocate 15 percent of those remaining funds to States on the basis of the States' relative populations of all children aged 3 through 5 who are living in poverty.

(ii) **Data.** For the purpose of making grants under this paragraph, the Secretary shall use the most recent population data, including data on children living in poverty, that are available and satisfactory to the Secretary.

(B) **Limitations.** Notwithstanding subparagraph (A), allocations under this paragraph shall be subject to the following:

(i) **Preceding Years.** No State's allocation shall be less than its allocation under this section for the preceding fiscal year.

(ii) **Minimum.** No State's allocation shall be less than the greatest of–

(I) the sum of–

(aa) the amount the State received under this section for fiscal year 1997; and

(bb) 1/3 of 1 percent of the amount by which the amount appropriated under subsection (j) for the fiscal year exceeds the amount appropriated for this section for fiscal year 1997;

(II) the sum of–

(aa) the amount the State received under this section for the preceding fiscal year; and

(bb) that amount multiplied by the percentage by which the increase in the funds appropriated under this section from the preceding fiscal year exceeds 1.5 percent; or

(III) the sum of–

(aa) the amount the State received under this section for the preceding fiscal year; and

(bb) that amount multiplied by 90 percent of the percentage increase in the amount appropriated under this section from the preceding fiscal year.

(iii) **Maximum.** Notwithstanding clause (ii), no State's allocation under this paragraph shall exceed the sum of

(I) the amount the State received under this section for the preceding fiscal year; and

(II) that amount multiplied by the sum of 1.5 percent and the percentage increase in the amount appropriated under this section from the preceding fiscal year.

(C) Ratable Reductions. If the amount available for allocations under this paragraph is insufficient to pay those allocations in full, those allocations shall be ratably reduced, subject to subparagraph (B)(i).

(3) Decrease in Funds. If the amount available for allocations to States under paragraph (1) for a fiscal year is less than the amount allocated to the States under this section for the preceding fiscal year, those allocations shall be calculated as follows:

(A) Allocations. If the amount available for allocations is greater than the amount allocated to the States for fiscal year 1997, each State shall be allocated the sum of–

(i) the amount the State received under this section for fiscal year 1997; and

(ii) an amount that bears the same relation to any remaining funds as the increase the State received under this section for the preceding fiscal year over fiscal year 1997 bears to the total of all such increases for all States.

(B) Ratable Reductions. If the amount available for allocations is equal to or less than the amount allocated to the States for fiscal year 1997, each State shall be allocated the amount the State received for fiscal year 1997, ratably reduced, if necessary.

(d) Reservation for State Activities.

(1) In General. Each State may reserve not more than the amount described in paragraph (2) for administration and other State-level activities in accordance with subsections (e) and (f).

(2) Amount Described. For each fiscal year, the Secretary shall determine and report to the State educational agency an amount that is 25 percent of the amount the State received under this section for fiscal year 1997, cumulatively adjusted by the Secretary for each succeeding fiscal year by the lesser of –

(A) the percentage increase, if any, from the preceding fiscal year in the State's allocation under this section; or

(B) the percentage increase, if any, from the preceding fiscal year in the Consumer Price Index For All Urban Consumers published by the Bureau of Labor Statistics of the Department of Labor.

(e) State Administration.

(1) In General. For the purpose of administering this section (including the coordination of activities under this part with, and providing technical assistance to, other programs that provide services to children with disabilities) a State may use not more than 20 percent of the maximum amount the State may reserve under subsection (d) for any fiscal year.

(2) Administration of Part C. Funds described in paragraph (1) may be used for the administration of part C.

(f) Other State-Level Activities.

Each State shall use any funds the State reserves under subsection (d) and does not use for administration under subsection (e)–

(1) for support services (including establishing and implementing the mediation process required by Section 1415(e) of this title), which may benefit children with disabilities younger than 3 or older than 5 as long as those services also benefit children with disabilities aged 3 through 5;

(2) for direct services for children eligible for services under this section;

(3) for activities at the State and local levels to meet the performance goals established by the State under Section 1412(a)(15) of this title;

(4) to supplement other funds used to develop and implement a statewide coordinated services system designed to improve results for children and families, including children with disabilities and their families, but not more than 1 percent of the amount received by the State under this section for a fiscal year;

(5) to provide early intervention services (which shall include an educational component that promotes school readiness and incorporates preliteracy, language, and numeracy skills) in accordance with part C to children with disabilities who are eligible for services under this section and who previously received services under part C until such children enter, or are eligible under State law to enter, kindergarten; or

(6) at the State's discretion, to continue service coordination or case management for families who receive services under part C.

(g) Subgrants to Local Educational Agencies.

(1) Subgrants Required. Each State that receives a grant under this section for any fiscal year **shall distribute** all of the grant funds that the State does not reserve under subsection (d) to local educational agencies in the State that have established their eligibility under Section 1413 of this title, as follows:

(A) Base Payments. The State shall first award each local educational agency described in paragraph (1) the amount that agency would have received under this section for fiscal year 1997 if the State had distributed 75 percent of its grant for that year under Section 1419(c)(3) of this title, as such section was then in effect.

(B) Allocation of Remaining Funds. After making allocations under subparagraph (A), the State shall

(i) allocate 85 percent of any remaining funds to those local educational agencies on the basis of the relative numbers of children enrolled in public and private elementary schools and secondary schools within the local educational agency's jurisdiction; and

(ii) allocate 15 percent of those remaining funds to those local educational agencies in accordance with their relative numbers of children living in poverty, as determined by the State educational agency.

(2) Reallocation of Funds. If a State educational agency determines that a local educational agency is adequately providing a free appropriate public education to all children with disabilities aged 3 through 5 residing in the area served by the local educational agency with State and local funds, the State educational agency may reallocate any portion of the funds under this section that are not needed by that local educational agency to provide a free appropriate public education to other local educational agencies in the State that are not adequately providing special education and related services to all children with disabilities aged 3 through 5 residing in the areas the other local educational agencies serve.

End of Part B

HyperLinks to Specific Sections in IDEA

20 U.S.C. § 1400	Findings and Purposes	20 U.S.C. § 1415	Procedural Safeguards
20 U.S.C. § 1401	Definitions	20 U.S.C. § 1415(b)(1)	Indep. Educ. Eval. IEE
20 U.S.C. § 1412	State Responsibilities	20 U.S.C. § 1415(f)	Due Process Hearing
20 U.S.C. § 1414(a)	Evaluations	20 U.S.C. § 1415(j)	Stay-Put / Pendency
20 U.S.C. § 1414(d)	IEPs	20 U.S.C. § 1415(k)	Discipline

Part C - Infants and Toddlers with Disabilities[316]

20 U.S.C. § 1431. Findings and Policy
20 U.S.C. § 1432. Definitions
20 U.S.C. § 1433. General Authority
20 U.S.C. § 1434. Eligibility
20 U.S.C. § 1435. Requirements for Statewide System
<20 U.S.C. § 1436. Individualized Family Service Plans>
20 U.S.C. § 1437. State Application and Assurances
20 U.S.C. § 1438. Uses of Funds
20 U.S.C. § 1439. Procedural Safeguards
20 U.S.C. § 1440. Payor of Last Resort
20 U.S.C. § 1441. State Interagency Coordinating Council
20 U.S.C. § 1442. Federal Administration
20 U.S.C. § 1443. Allocation of Funds
20 U.S.C. § 1444. Authorization of Appropriations

20 U.S.C. § 1431. Findings and Policy.[317]

(a) Findings -

Congress finds that there is an urgent and substantial need –

(1) to enhance the development of infants and toddlers with disabilities, to **minimize their potential for developmental delay**, and to recognize the **significant brain development that occurs during a child's first 3 years of life**;

(2) to reduce the educational costs to our society, including our Nation's schools, **by minimizing the need for special education and related services** after infants and toddlers with disabilities reach school age;

(3) to **maximize the potential for individuals with disabilities to live independently in society**.

(4) to enhance the capacity of families to meet the special needs of their infants and toddlers with disabilities; and

(5) to enhance the capacity of State and local agencies and service providers to **identify, evaluate, and meet the needs of all children, particularly minority, low-income, inner city, and rural children,** and infants and toddlers in foster care.

(b) Policy -

It is the policy of the United States to provide financial assistance to States –

(1) to develop and implement a **statewide, comprehensive, coordinated, multidisciplinary, interagency system that provides early intervention services** for infants and toddlers with disabilities and their families;

(2) to facilitate the coordination of payment for early intervention services from Federal, State, local, and private sources (including public and private insurance coverage);

(3) to enhance State capacity to **provide quality early intervention services** and **expand and improve existing early intervention services** being provided to infants and toddlers with disabilities and their families; and

(4) to encourage States to **expand opportunities for children under 3 years of age who would be at risk of having substantial developmental delay** if they did not receive early intervention services.

---

316 **Wrightslaw Overview:** Part C of IDEA governs early intervention services for infants and toddlers under age 3 from Sections 1431 through Section 1444.

317 **Wrightslaw Overview:** Congress has stressed the need "to recognize the significant brain development that occurs during a child's first 3 years of life" and explains that there is a need "to **maximize the potential** for individuals with disabilities to live independently in society." In the 2017 SCOTUS *Endrew F.* case, Chief Justice Roberts focused on the word, "**potential**."

20 U.S.C. § 1432. Definitions.[318]

In this part:

(1) At-Risk Infant or Toddler - The term 'at-risk infant or toddler' means an individual under 3 years of age who would be at risk of experiencing a substantial developmental delay if early intervention services were not provided to the individual.

(2) Council - The term 'council' means a State interagency coordinating council established under Section 1441.

(3) Developmental Delay - The term 'developmental delay', when used with respect to an individual residing in a State, has the meaning given such term by the State under Section 1435(a)(1).

(4) Early Intervention Services - The term '**early intervention services**'[319] means developmental services that

(A) are provided under public supervision;

(B) are provided **at no cost** except where Federal or State law provides for a system of payments by families, including a schedule of sliding fees;

(C) are designed **to meet the developmental need**s of an infant or toddler with a disability, as identified by the individualized family service plan team, in any 1 or more of the following areas:

(i) physical development;

(ii) cognitive development;

(iii) communication development;

(iv) social or emotional development; or

(v) adaptive development;

(D) meet the standards of the State in which the services are provided, including the requirements of this part;

(E) include -

(i) family training, counseling, and home visits;

(ii) special instruction;

(iii) speech-language pathology and audiology services, and sign language and cued language services;

(iv) occupational therapy;

(v) physical therapy;

(vi) psychological services;

(vii) service coordination services;

(viii) medical services only for diagnostic or evaluation purposes;

(ix) early identification, screening, and assessment services;

(x) health services necessary to enable the infant or toddler to benefit from the other early intervention services;

(xi) social work services;

(xii) vision services;

(xiii) assistive technology devices and assistive technology services; and

(xiv) transportation and related costs that are necessary to enable an infant or toddler and the infant's or toddler's family to receive another service described in this paragraph;

---

318   **Wrightslaw Overview:** Section 1432 is similar to 20 U.S.C. § 1401 in Part A and. in alphabetical order, provides key definitions of early intervention services to infants and toddlers with disabilities in Part C of IDEA.

319   Early intervention services must be designed to meet the child's developmental needs, including needs in the physical, cognitive, communication, social and emotional, and adaptive areas. School districts are not empowered to offer one-size-fits-all school-based programs that are not "designed to meet the developmental needs" of a particular infant or toddler.

(F) are **provided by qualified personnel**, including–

    (i) special educators;

    (ii) speech-language pathologists and audiologists;

    (iii) occupational therapists;

    (iv) physical therapists;

    (v) psychologists;

    (vi) social workers;

    (vii) nurses;

    (viii) registered dietitians;

    (ix) family therapists;

    (x) vision specialists, including ophthalmologists and optometrists;

    (xi) orientation and mobility specialists; and

    (xii) pediatricians and other physicians;[320]

(G) to the maximum extent appropriate, are **provided in natural environments, including the home,** and community settings in which children without disabilities participate; and

(H) are provided in conformity with an individualized family service plan[321] adopted in accordance with Section 1436.

(5) Infant or Toddler with a Disability - The term '**infant or toddler with a disability**'-

(A) means an individual **under 3 years of age** who needs early intervention services because the individual

    (i) is experiencing **developmental delays**, as measured by appropriate diagnostic instruments and procedures in **one or more of the areas** of cognitive development, physical development, communication development, social or emotional development, and adaptive development; or

    (ii) has a **diagnosed physical or mental condition** that has a high probability of resulting in developmental delay; and

(B) **may** also include, at a State's discretion -

    (i) at-risk infants and toddlers; and

    (ii) children with disabilities who are eligible for services under Section 1419 and who previously received services under this part until such children enter, or are eligible under State law to enter, kindergarten or elementary school, as appropriate, provided that any programs under this part serving such children **shall include** -

        (I) an educational component that promotes school readiness and incorporates pre-literacy, language, and numeracy skills; and

        (II) a written notification to parents of their rights and responsibilities in determining whether their child will continue to receive services under this part or participate in preschool programs under Section 1419.

20 U.S.C. § 1433. General Authority.

The Secretary shall, in accordance with this part, make grants to States (from their allotments under Section 1443) to assist each State to maintain and implement a statewide, comprehensive, coordinated, multidisciplinary, interagency system to provide early intervention services for infants and toddlers with disabilities and their families.

---

320   IDEA authorizes early intervention services from professional providers. An issue may arise as to whether service providers are "qualified" or whether services are provided by inadequately trained staff, including aides and paraprofessionals. Children may receive services from physicians for diagnostic and evaluation purposes, if necessary.

321   For the legal requirements for Individualized Family Service Plans, *see* 20 U.S.C. § 1436.

20 U.S.C. § 1434. Eligibility.

In order to be eligible for a grant under Section 1433, a State shall provide assurances to the Secretary that the State –

(1) has adopted a policy that **appropriate early intervention services are available to all infants and toddlers with disabilities** in the State and their families, including Indian infants and toddlers with disabilities and their families residing on a reservation geographically located in the State, infants and toddlers with disabilities who are homeless children and their families, and infants and toddlers with disabilities who are wards of the State; and

(2) has in effect a statewide system that meets the requirements of Section 1435.

20 U.S.C. § 1435. Requirements for Statewide System.[322]

(a) In General - A statewide system described in Section 1433 shall include, at a minimum, the following components:

(1) A **rigorous definition of** the term **'developmental delay'** that will be used by the State in carrying out programs under this part in order to appropriately identify infants and toddlers with disabilities that are in need of services under this part.

(2) A State policy that is in effect and that ensures that appropriate **early intervention services based on scientifically based research**, to the extent practicable, are available to all infants and toddlers with disabilities and their families, including Indian infants and toddlers with disabilities and their families residing on a reservation geographically located in the State and infants and toddlers with disabilities who are homeless children and their families.

(3) A **timely, comprehensive, multidisciplinary evaluation** of the functioning of each infant or toddler with a disability in the State, and a **family-directed identification of the needs of each family** of such an infant or toddler, to assist appropriately in the development of the infant or toddler.

(4) For each infant or toddler with a disability in the State, an **individualized family service plan** in accordance with Section 1436, including service coordination services in accordance with such service plan.

(5) A **comprehensive child find system,** consistent with part B, including a system for making referrals to service providers that includes timelines and provides for participation by primary referral sources and that ensures **rigorous standards for appropriately identifying infants and toddlers with disabilities** for services under this part that will reduce the need for future services.

(6) A **public awareness program focusing on early identification** of infants and toddlers with disabilities, including the preparation and dissemination by the lead agency designated or established under paragraph (10) to all primary referral sources, especially hospitals and physicians, of information to be given to parents, especially to inform parents with premature infants, or infants with other physical risk factors associated with learning or developmental complications, on the availability of early intervention services under this part and of services under Section 1419, and procedures for assisting such sources in disseminating such information to parents of infants and toddlers with disabilities.

(7) A **central directory that includes information on early intervention services, resources, and experts** available in the State and research and demonstration projects being conducted in the State.

(8) A **comprehensive system of personnel development**, including the **training of paraprofessionals** and the **training of primary referral sources** with respect to the basic components of early intervention services available in the State that -

322 **Wrightslaw Overview:** This section describes the minimum requirements for early intervention programs. States must ensure that early intervention services are based on scientifically based research. (See 20 U.S.C. § 1463(f)(2) Evaluations must be timely, comprehensive, multidisciplinary and must include a "family-directed identification of the needs of each family." The state must have a comprehensive child find system and public awareness programs and must maintain a central directory of information about early intervention services and resources. States must have personnel development systems that include training for paraprofessionals and primary referral sources, and procedures to ensure that personnel are adequately trained. States must ensure that early intervention services are provided in natural environments.

(A) **shall include -**

(i) implementing innovative strategies and activities for the recruitment and retention of early education service providers;

(ii) promoting the preparation of early intervention providers who are fully and appropriately qualified to provide early intervention services under this part; and

(iii) training personnel to coordinate transition services for infants and toddlers served under this part from a program providing early intervention services under this part and under part B (other than Section 1419), to a preschool program receiving funds under Section 1419, or another appropriate program; and

(B) **may include -**

(i) training personnel to work in rural and inner-city areas; and

(ii) training personnel in the emotional and social development of young children.

(9) Policies and procedures relating to the establishment and maintenance of **qualifications to ensure that personnel** necessary to carry out this part **are appropriately and adequately prepared and trained**, including the establishment and maintenance of qualifications that are consistent with any State-approved or recognized certification, licensing, registration, or other comparable requirements that apply to the area in which such personnel are providing early intervention services, except that nothing in this part (including this paragraph) shall be construed to prohibit the use of paraprofessionals and assistants who are appropriately trained and supervised in accordance with State law, regulation, or written policy, to assist in the provision of early intervention services under this part to infants and toddlers with disabilities.

(10) A single line of responsibility in a lead agency designated or established by the Governor for carrying out

(A) the general administration and supervision of programs and activities receiving assistance under Section 1433, and the monitoring of programs and activities used by the State to carry out this part, whether or not such programs or activities are receiving assistance made available under Section 1433, to ensure that the State complies with this part;

(B) the identification and coordination of all available resources within the State from Federal, State, local, and private sources;

(C) the assignment of financial responsibility in accordance with Section 1437(a)(2) to the appropriate agencies;

(D) the development of procedures to ensure that services are provided to infants and toddlers with disabilities and their families under this part in a timely manner pending the resolution of any disputes among public agencies or service providers;

(E) the resolution of intra- and interagency disputes; and

(F) the entry into formal interagency agreements that define the financial responsibility of each agency for paying for early intervention services (consistent with State law) and procedures for resolving disputes and that include all additional components necessary to ensure meaningful cooperation and coordination.

(11) A policy pertaining to the contracting or making of other arrangements with service providers to provide early intervention services in the State, consistent with the provisions of this part, including the contents of the application used and the conditions of the contract or other arrangements.

(12) A procedure for securing timely reimbursements of funds used under this part in accordance with Section 1440(a).

(13) Procedural safeguards with respect to programs under this part, as required by Section 1439.

(14) A system for compiling data requested by the Secretary under Section 1418 that relates to this part.

(15) A State interagency coordinating council that meets the requirements of Section 1441.

(16) Policies and procedures to ensure that, consistent with Section 1436(d)(5) -

(A) to the maximum extent appropriate, early intervention services are **provided in natural environments**;

and

(B) the provision of early intervention services for any infant or toddler with a disability occurs in a setting **other than** a natural environment that is most appropriate, as determined by the parent and the individualized family service plan team, **only when** early intervention cannot be achieved satisfactorily for the infant or toddler in a natural environment.

(b) Policy -

In implementing subsection (a)(9), a State may adopt a policy that includes making ongoing good-faith efforts to recruit and hire appropriately and adequately trained personnel to provide early intervention services to infants and toddlers with disabilities, including, in a geographic area of the State where there is a shortage of such personnel, the most qualified individuals available who are making satisfactory progress toward completing applicable course work necessary to meet the standards described in subsection (a)(9).

(c) Flexibility To Serve Children 3 Years of Age Until Entrance Into Elementary School

(1) In General - A statewide system described in Section 1433 may include a State policy, developed and implemented jointly by the lead agency and the State educational agency, under which parents of children with disabilities who are eligible for services under Section 1419 and previously received services under this part, may choose the continuation of early intervention services (which shall include an educational component that promotes school readiness and incorporates preliteracy, language, and numeracy skills) for such children under this part until such children enter, or are eligible under State law to enter, kindergarten.

(2) Requirements - If a statewide system includes a State policy described in paragraph (1), the statewide system shall ensure that -

(A) parents of children with disabilities served pursuant to this subsection are provided annual notice that contains -

(i) a description of the rights of such parents to elect to receive services pursuant to this subsection or under part B; and

(ii) an explanation of the differences between services provided pursuant to this subsection and services provided under part B, including–

(I) types of services and the locations at which the services are provided;

(II) applicable procedural safeguards; and

(III) possible costs (including any fees to be charged to families as described in Section 1432(4)(B)), if any, to parents of infants or toddlers with disabilities;

(B) **services** provided pursuant to this subsection include an educational component that **promotes school readiness** and incorporates **preliteracy, language, and numeracy skills**;

(C) the State policy will not affect the right of any child served pursuant to this subsection to instead receive a free appropriate public education under part B;

(D) all early intervention services outlined in the child's individualized family service plan under Section 1436 are continued while any eligibility determination is being made for services under this subsection;

(E) the **parents** of infants or toddlers with disabilities (as defined in Section 1432(5)(A)) **provide informed written consent** to the State, before such infants or toddlers reach 3 years of age, as to **whether such parents intend to choose the continuation of early intervention services** pursuant to this subsection for such infants or toddlers;

(F) the requirements under Section 1437(a)(9) shall not apply with respect to a child who is receiving services in accordance with this subsection until not less than 90 days (and at the discretion of the parties to the conference, not more than 9 months) before the time the child will no longer receive those services; and

(G) there will be a **referral for evaluation** for early intervention services **of a child who experiences a substantiated case of trauma due to exposure to family violence** (as defined in Section 10402 of title 42).

(3) Reporting Requirement - If a statewide system includes a State policy described in paragraph (1), the State shall submit to the Secretary, in the State's report under Section 1437(b)(4)(A), a report on the number and percentage of children with disabilities who are eligible for services under Section 1419 but whose parents choose for such children to continue to receive early intervention services under this part.

(4) Available Funds - If a statewide system includes a State policy described in paragraph (1), the policy shall describe the funds (including an identification as Federal, State, or local funds) that will be used to ensure that the option described in paragraph (1) is available to eligible children and families who provide the consent described in paragraph (2)(E), including fees (if any) to be charged to families as described in Section 1432(4)(B).

(5) Rules of Construction -

(A) Services Under Part B - If a statewide system includes a State policy described in paragraph (1), a State that provides services in accordance with this subsection to a child with a disability who is eligible for services under Section 1419 shall not be required to provide the child with a free appropriate public education under part B for the period of time in which the child is receiving services under this part.

(B) Services Under This Part - Nothing in this subsection **shall be construed** to require a provider of services under this part to provide a child served under this part with a **free appropriate public education**.

20 U.S.C. § 1436. Individualized Family Service Plan.[323, 324]

(a) Assessment and Program Development -

A statewide system described in Section 1433 **shall provide, at a minimum**, for each infant or toddler with a disability, and the infant's or toddler's family, to receive -

(1) a **multidisciplinary assessment** of the **unique strengths and needs** of the infant or toddler and the identification of **services** appropriate to meet such needs;

(2) a **family-directed assessment** of the resources, priorities, and concerns of the family and the identification of the supports and services necessary to enhance the family's capacity to meet the developmental needs of the infant or toddler; and

(3) a **written individualized family service plan** developed by a multidisciplinary team, including the parents, as required by subsection (e), including a description of the appropriate transition services for the infant or toddler.

(b) Periodic Review -

The individualized family service plan shall be evaluated once a year and the family shall be provided a review of the plan at 6-month intervals (or more often where appropriate based on infant or toddler and family needs).

(c) Promptness After Assessment -

The individualized family service plan shall be developed within a reasonable time after the assessment required by subsection (a)(1) is completed. With the parents' consent, early intervention services may commence prior to the completion of the assessment.

(d) Content of Plan - The individualized family service plan[325] **shall be in writing and contain** -

(1) a statement of the infant's or toddler's **present levels of physical development, cognitive development, communication development, social or emotional development, and adaptive development, based on objective criteria**;

---

323   Note that the **IFSP** is a "**Plan**," unlike an **IEP**, which is characterized in the statute and regulations as a "**Program**."

324   **Wrightslaw Overview:** Section 1436 describes the legal requirements for Individualized Family Service Plans (IFSPs) which are similar to the requirements for Individualized Education Programs in Section 1414(d). Subsection (a) describes the assessment and program development process, including a "family-directed assessment" of the resources, priorities, and concerns of the family. Subsection (d) describes the required components of Individualized Family Service Plans and requires the "measurable results or outcomes expected to be achieved . . . including pre-literacy and language skills" and the "criteria, procedures, and timelines" that will be used to measure the child's progress. They are to be "based on peer-reviewed research" in subsection (d)(4).

325   As the child ages and moves from Part C services and from an IFSP to an IEP, the IEP team, if requested by the parent, must invite the "Part C service coordinator" and must consider this IFSP. *See* 20 U.S.C. § 1414(d)(1)(D) and § 1414(d)(2)(B). The IFSP may serve as the IEP.

(2) a statement of the **family's resources, priorities, and concerns** relating to enhancing the development of the family's infant or toddler with a disability;

(3) a statement of the **measurable results or outcomes** expected to be achieved for the infant or toddler and the family, including **pre-literacy and language skills**, as developmentally appropriate for the child, and the **criteria**, procedures, and timelines used **to determine** the degree to which **progress toward achieving the results or outcomes** is being made and whether modifications or revisions of the results or outcomes or services are necessary;

(4) a statement of specific **early intervention services based on peer-reviewed research**, to the extent practicable, necessary to meet the unique needs of the infant or toddler and the family, including the frequency, intensity, and method of delivering services;

(5) a statement of the **natural environments** in which early intervention services will appropriately be provided, including a justification of the extent, if any, to which the services will not be provided in a natural environment;

(6) the projected **dates for initiation of services** and the anticipated **length, duration, and frequency of the services**;

(7) the identification of the **service coordinator** from the profession most immediately relevant to the infant's or toddler's or family's needs (or who is otherwise qualified to carry out all applicable responsibilities under this part) who will be responsible for the implementation of the plan and coordination with other agencies and persons, including transition services; and

(8) the **steps to be taken to support the transition** of the toddler with a disability to preschool or other appropriate services.

(e) Parental Consent -

The contents of the individualized family service plan shall be fully explained to the parents and informed written consent from the parents shall be obtained prior to the provision of early intervention services described in such plan. If the parents do not provide consent with respect to a particular early intervention service, then only the early intervention services to which consent is obtained shall be provided.

20 U.S.C. § 1437. State Application and Assurances.[326]

(a) Application -

A State desiring to receive a grant under Section 1433 shall submit an application to the Secretary at such time and in such manner as the Secretary may reasonably require. The application shall contain-

(1) a designation of the lead agency in the State that will be responsible for the administration of funds provided under Section 1433;

(2) a certification to the Secretary that the arrangements to establish financial responsibility for services provided under this part pursuant to Section 1440(b) are current as of the date of submission of the certification;

(3) information demonstrating eligibility of the State under Section 1434, including -

(A) information demonstrating to the Secretary's satisfaction that the State has in effect the statewide system required by Section 1433; and

(B) **a description of services to be provided to infants and toddlers with disabilities** and their families through the system;

(4) if the State provides services to at-risk infants and toddlers through the statewide system, a description of such services;

(5) a description of the uses for which funds will be expended in accordance with this part;

---

326   **Wrightslaw Overview**: This section describes the state grant application process, policies and procedures that must be used to ensure a smooth transition from early intervention, and assurances that States must provide about early intervention services for infants and toddlers with disabilities and their families.

(6) a description of the State policies and procedures that require the referral for early intervention services under this part of a child under the age of 3 who -

(A) is involved in a substantiated case of child abuse or neglect; or

(B) is identified as affected by illegal substance abuse, or withdrawal symptoms resulting from prenatal drug exposure;

(7) a description of the procedure used to ensure that resources are made available under this part for all geographic areas within the State;

(8) a description of State policies and procedures that ensure that, prior to the adoption by the State of any other policy or procedure necessary to meet the requirements of this part, there are public hearings, adequate notice of the hearings, and an opportunity for comment available to the general public, including individuals with disabilities and parents of infants and toddlers with disabilities;

(9) a description of the **policies and procedures** to be used -

(A) to ensure a **smooth transition for toddlers receiving early intervention services** under this part (and children receiving those services under Section 1435(c)) **to preschool, school, other appropriate services, or exiting the program**, including a description of how -

(i) the families of such toddlers and children will be included in the transition plans required by subparagraph (c); and

(ii) the lead agency designated or established under Section 1435(a)(10) will -

(I) notify the local educational agency for the area in which such a child resides that the child will shortly reach the age of eligibility for preschool services under part B, as determined in accordance with State law;

(II) in the case of a child who may be eligible for such preschool services, with the approval of the family of the child, convene a conference among the lead agency, the family, and the local educational agency not less than 90 days (and at the discretion of all such parties, not more than 9 months) before the child is eligible for the preschool services, to discuss any such services that the child may receive; and

(III) in the case of a child who may not be eligible for such preschool services, with the approval of the family, make reasonable efforts to convene a conference among the lead agency, the family, and providers of other appropriate services for children who are not eligible for preschool services under part B, to discuss the appropriate services that the child may receive;

(B) to review the child's program options for the period from the child's third birthday through the remainder of the school year; and

(C) to establish a transition plan, including, as appropriate, steps to exit from the program;

(10) a description of State efforts to promote collaboration among Early Head Start programs under Section 1445A of the Head Start Act, early education and child care programs, and services under part C; and

(11) such other information and assurances as the Secretary may reasonably require.

(b) Assurances - The application described in subsection (a) -

(1) shall provide satisfactory assurance that Federal funds made available under Section 1443 to the State will be expended in accordance with this part;

(2) shall contain an assurance that the State will comply with the requirements of Section 1440;

(3) shall provide satisfactory assurance that the control of funds provided under Section 1443, and title to property derived from those funds, will be in a public agency for the uses and purposes provided in this part and that a public agency will administer such funds and property;

(4) shall provide for -

(A) making such reports in such form and containing such information as the Secretary may require to carry out the Secretary's functions under this part; and

(B) keeping such reports and affording such access to the reports as the Secretary may find necessary to ensure the correctness and verification of those reports and proper disbursement of Federal funds under this part;

(5) provide satisfactory assurance that Federal funds made available under Section 1443 to the State -

(A) will not be commingled with State funds; and

(B) will be used so as **to supplement** the level of **State and local funds** expended for infants and toddlers with disabilities and their families and **in no case to supplant those State and local funds**;

(6) shall provide satisfactory assurance that such fiscal control and fund accounting procedures will be adopted as may be necessary to ensure proper disbursement of, and accounting for, Federal funds paid under Section 1443 to the State;

(7) shall provide satisfactory **assurance that policies and procedures have been adopted to ensure meaningful involvement of underserved groups**, including minority, low-income, homeless, and rural families and children with disabilities who are wards of the State, in the planning and implementation of all the requirements of this part; and

(8) shall contain such other information and assurances as the Secretary may reasonably require by regulation.

(c) Standard for Disapproval of Application -

The Secretary may not disapprove such an application unless the Secretary determines, after notice and opportunity for a hearing, that the application fails to comply with the requirements of this section.

(d) Subsequent State Application -

If a State has on file with the Secretary a policy, procedure, or assurance that demonstrates that the State meets a requirement of this section, including any policy or procedure filed under this part (as in effect before the date of enactment of the Individuals with Disabilities Education Improvement Act of 2004), the Secretary shall consider the State to have met the requirement for purposes of receiving a grant under this part.

(e) Modification of Application -

An application submitted by a State in accordance with this section shall remain in effect until the State submits to the Secretary such modifications as the State determines necessary. This section shall apply to a modification of an application to the same extent and in the same manner as this section applies to the original application.

(f) Modifications Required by the Secretary -

The Secretary may require a State to modify its application under this section, but only to the extent necessary to ensure the State's compliance with this part, if–

(1) an amendment is made to this title, or a Federal regulation issued under this title;

(2) a new interpretation of this title is made by a Federal court or the State's highest court; or

(3) an official finding of noncompliance with Federal law or regulations is made with respect to the State.

20 U.S.C. § 1438. Uses of Funds.

In addition to using funds provided under Section 1433 to maintain and implement the statewide system required by such section, a State may use such funds–

(1) for **direct early intervention services** for infants and toddlers with disabilities, and their families, under this part that are not otherwise funded through other public or private sources;

(2) to **expand and improve on services** for infants and toddlers and their families under this part that are otherwise available;

(3) to provide a free appropriate public education, in accordance with Part B, to **children with disabilities from their third birthday to the beginning of the following school year**;

(4) with the written consent of the parents, to continue to **provide early intervention services** under this part **to children with disabilities from their 3rd birthday until such children enter**, or are eligible under State law to

enter, **kindergarten,** in lieu of a free appropriate public education provided in accordance with part B; and

(5) in any State that does not provide services for at-risk infants and toddlers under Section 1437(a)(4), to strengthen the statewide system by initiating, expanding, or improving collaborative efforts related to at-risk infants and toddlers, including establishing linkages with appropriate public or private community-based organizations, services, and personnel for the purposes of–

   (A) identifying and evaluating at-risk infants and toddlers;

   (B) making referrals of the infants and toddlers identified and evaluated under subparagraph (A); and

   (C) conducting periodic follow-up on each such referral to determine if the status of the infant or toddler involved has changed with respect to the eligibility of the infant or toddler for services under this part.

20 U.S.C. § 1439. Procedural Safeguards.[327]

(a) Minimum Procedures -

The procedural safeguards required to be included in a statewide system under Section 1435(a)(13) shall provide, at a minimum, the following:

   (1) The timely administrative resolution of complaints by parents. Any party aggrieved by the findings and decision regarding an administrative complaint shall have the right to bring a civil action with respect to the complaint in any State court of competent jurisdiction or in a district court of the United States without regard to the amount in controversy. In any action brought under this paragraph, the court shall receive the records of the administrative proceedings, shall hear additional evidence at the request of a party, and, basing its decision on the preponderance of the evidence, shall grant such relief as the court determines is appropriate.

   (2) The **right to confidentiality of personally identifiable information**, including the right of parents to written notice of and written consent to the exchange of such information among agencies consistent with Federal and State law.

   (3) The **right of the parents to** determine whether they, their infant or toddler, or other family members will **accept or decline any early intervention service** under this part in accordance with State law **without jeopardizing other early intervention services** under this part.

   (4) The opportunity for parents **to examine records** relating to assessment, screening, eligibility determinations, and the development and implementation of the individualized family service plan.

   (5) **Procedures to protect the rights of the infant or toddler whenever the parents** of the infant or toddler **are not known or cannot be found or** the infant or toddler is a ward of the State, including the assignment of an individual (who shall not be an employee of the State lead agency, or other State agency, and who shall not be any person, or any employee of a person, providing early intervention services to the infant or toddler or any family member of the infant or toddler) **to act as a surrogate for the parents.**

   (6) **Written prior notice** to the parents of the infant or toddler with a disability whenever the State agency or service provider **proposes to initiate or change, or refuses to initiate or change, the identification, evaluation, or placement** of the infant or toddler with a disability, **or the provision of appropriate early intervention services** to the infant or toddler.

   (7) Procedures designed to ensure that the notice required by paragraph (6) **fully informs the parents**, in the parents' native language, unless it clearly is not feasible to do so, of all procedures available pursuant to this section.

   (8) The right of parents to **use mediation** in accordance with Section 1415, except that–

   (A) any reference in the section to a State educational agency shall be considered to be a reference to a State's lead agency established or designated under Section 1435(a)(10);

---

327 **Wrightslaw Overview:** Section 1439 describes the protections and safeguards for young children with disabilities and their parents. The wording in Section 1439 is similar to Section 1415 in Part B. Unlike Part B, parents have a right to accept or decline any early intervention service without jeopardizing their right to other early intervention services. Subsection (a)(5) describes procedures to protect the rights of the child when the parents are not known or cannot be found. Caselaw referencing Section 1415 will be used to resolve disputes about appropriate early intervention services.

(B) any reference in the section to a local educational agency shall be considered to be a reference to a local service provider or the State's lead agency under this part, as the case may be; and

(C) any reference in the section to the provision of a free appropriate public education to children with disabilities shall be considered to be a reference to the provision of appropriate early intervention services to infants and toddlers with disabilities.

(b) Services During Pendency of Proceedings -

During the pendency of any proceeding or action involving a complaint by the parents of an infant or toddler with a disability, unless the State agency and the parents otherwise agree, the infant or toddler **shall continue to receive the appropriate early intervention services currently being provided or**, if applying for initial services, shall receive the **services not in dispute**.

20 U.S.C. § 1440. Payor of Last Resort.[328]

(a) Nonsubstitution -

Funds provided under Section 1443 may not be used to satisfy a financial commitment for services that would have been paid for from another public or private source, including any medical program administered by the Secretary of Defense, but for the enactment of this part, except that whenever considered necessary to prevent a delay in the receipt of appropriate early intervention services by an infant, toddler, or family in a timely fashion, funds provided under Section 1443 may be used to pay the provider of services pending reimbursement from the agency that has ultimate responsibility for the payment.

(b) Obligations Related to and Methods of Ensuring Services -

(1) Establishing Financial Responsibility for Services -

(A) In General - The Chief Executive Officer of a State or designee of the officer shall ensure that an interagency agreement or other mechanism for interagency coordination is in effect between each public agency and the designated lead agency, in order to ensure–

(i) the provision of, and financial responsibility for, services provided under this part; and

(ii) such services are consistent with the requirements of Section 1435 and the State's application pursuant to Section 1437, including the provision of such services during the pendency of any such dispute.

(B) Consistency Between Agreements or Mechanisms Under Part B - The Chief Executive Officer of a State or designee of the officer shall ensure that the terms and conditions of such agreement or mechanism are consistent with the terms and conditions of the State's agreement or mechanism under Section 1412(a)(12), where appropriate.

(2) Reimbursement for Services by Public Agency -

(A) In General - If a public agency other than an educational agency fails to provide or pay for the services pursuant to an agreement required under paragraph (1), the local educational agency or State agency (as determined by the Chief Executive Officer or designee) **shall provide or pa**y for the provision of such services to the child.

(B) Reimbursement - Such local educational agency or State agency is authorized to claim reimbursement for the services from the public agency that failed to provide or pay for such services and such public agency shall reimburse the local educational agency or State agency pursuant to the terms of the interagency agreement or other mechanism required under paragraph (1).

(3) Special Rule - The requirements of paragraph (1) may be met through–

(A) State statute or regulation;

(B) signed agreements between respective agency officials that clearly identify the responsibilities of each

---

328 **Wrightslaw Overview:** This section clarifies that schools cannot require parents to use the child's medical insurance benefits to pay for a free appropriate public education.

agency relating to the provision of services; or

(C) other appropriate written methods as determined by the Chief Executive Officer of the State or designee of the officer and approved by the Secretary through the review and approval of the State's application pursuant to Section 1437.

(c) Reduction of Other Benefits -

Nothing in this part shall be construed to permit the State to reduce medical or other assistance available or to alter eligibility under title V of the Social Security Act (relating to maternal and child health) or title XIX of the Social Security Act (relating to Medicaid for infants or toddlers with disabilities) within the State.

20 U.S.C. § 1441. State Interagency Coordinating Council.

(a) Establishment -

(1) In General - A State that desires to receive financial assistance under this part shall establish a State interagency coordinating council.

(2) Appointment - The council shall be appointed by the Governor. In making appointments to the council, the Governor shall ensure that the membership of the council reasonably represents the population of the State.

(3) Chairperson - The Governor shall designate a member of the council to serve as the chairperson of the council, or shall require the council to so designate such a member. Any member of the council who is a representative of the lead agency designated under Section 1435(a)(10) may not serve as the chairperson of the council.

(b) Composition -

(1) In General - The council shall be composed as follows:

(A) **Parents** - Not less than 20 percent of the members shall be parents of infants or toddlers with disabilities or children with disabilities aged 12 or younger, with knowledge of, or experience with, programs for infants and toddlers with disabilities. Not less than 1 such member shall be a parent of an infant or toddler with a disability or a child with a disability aged 6 or younger.

(B) **Service Providers** - Not less than 20 percent of the members shall be public or private providers of early intervention services.

(C) **State Legislature** - Not less than 1 member shall be from the State legislature.

(D) **Personnel Preparation** - Not less than 1 member shall be involved in personnel preparation.

(E) **Agency for Early Intervention Services** - Not less than 1 member shall be from each of the State agencies involved in the provision of, or payment for, early intervention services to infants and toddlers with disabilities and their families and shall have sufficient authority to engage in policy planning and implementation on behalf of such agencies.

(F) **Agency for Preschool Services** - Not less than 1 member shall be from the State educational agency responsible for preschool services to children with disabilities and shall have sufficient authority to engage in policy planning and implementation on behalf of such agency.

(G) **State Medicaid Agency** - Not less than 1 member shall be from the agency responsible for the State Medicaid program.

(H) **Head Start Agency** - Not less than 1 member shall be a representative from a Head Start agency or program in the State.

(I) **Child Care Agency** - Not less than 1 member shall be a representative from a State agency responsible for child care.

(J) **Agency for Health Insurance** - Not less than 1 member shall be from the agency responsible for the State regulation of health insurance.

(K) **Office of the Coordinator of Education of Homeless Children and Youth** - Not less than 1 member shall be a representative designated by the Office of Coordinator for Education of Homeless Children and Youths.

(L) State Foster Care Representative - Not less than 1 member shall be a representative from the State child welfare agency responsible for foster care.

(M) Mental Health Agency - Not less than 1 member shall be a representative from the State agency responsible for children's mental health.

(2) Other Members - The council may include other members selected by the Governor, including a representative from the Bureau of Indian Affairs (BIA), or where there is no BIA-operated or BIA-funded school, from the Indian Health Service or the tribe or tribal council.

(c) Meetings -

The council shall meet, at a minimum, on a quarterly basis, and in such places as the council determines necessary. The meetings shall be publicly announced, and, to the extent appropriate, open and accessible to the general public.

(d) Management Authority -

Subject to the approval of the Governor, the council may prepare and approve a budget using funds under this part to conduct hearings and forums, to reimburse members of the council for reasonable and necessary expenses for attending council meetings and performing council duties (including child care for parent representatives), to pay compensation to a member of the council if the member is not employed or must forfeit wages from other employment when performing official council business, to hire staff, and to obtain the services of such professional, technical, and clerical personnel as may be necessary to carry out its functions under this part.

(e) Functions of Council -

(1) Duties - The council shall -

(A) advise and assist the lead agency designated or established under Section 1435(a)(10) in the performance of the responsibilities set forth in such section, particularly the identification of the sources of fiscal and other support for services for early intervention programs, assignment of financial responsibility to the appropriate agency, and the promotion of the interagency agreements;

(B) advise and assist the lead agency in the preparation of applications and amendments thereto;

(C) advise and assist the State educational agency regarding the transition of toddlers with disabilities to preschool and other appropriate services; and

(D) prepare and submit an annual report to the Governor and to the Secretary on the status of early intervention programs for infants and toddlers with disabilities and their families operated within the State.

(2) Authorized Activity - The council may advise and assist the lead agency and the State educational agency regarding the provision of appropriate services for children from birth through age 5. The council may advise appropriate agencies in the State with respect to the integration of services for infants and toddlers with disabilities and at-risk infants and toddlers and their families, regardless of whether at-risk infants and toddlers are eligible for early intervention services in the State.

(f) Conflict of Interest -

No member of the council shall cast a vote on any matter that is likely to provide a direct financial benefit to that member or otherwise give the appearance of a conflict of interest under State law.

20 U.S.C. § 1442. Federal Administration.[329]

Sections 1416, 1417, and 1418 shall, to the extent not inconsistent with this part, apply to the program authorized by this part, except that -

(1) any reference in such sections to a State educational agency shall be considered to be a reference to a

---

329 **Wrightslaw Overview**: Much of the language in Part B applies to this section. This incorporates by reference the provisions contained in the earlier Part B. If the "lead agency" is not the State Education Agency (SEA), these requirements shall apply to the state and local mental health, social service, early intervention, health department, or other such agency that is appointed as the "lead agency."

State's lead agency established or designated under Section 1435(a)(10);

(2) any reference in such sections to a local educational agency, educational service agency, or a State agency shall be considered to be a reference to an early intervention service provider under this part; and

(3) any reference to the **education of children with disabilitie**s or the education of all children with disabilities shall be considered to be a reference to the provision of appropriate early intervention services to infants and toddlers with disabilities.

20 U.S.C. § 1443. Allocation of Funds.

(a) Reservation of Funds for Outlying Areas -

(1) In General - From the sums appropriated to carry out this part for any fiscal year, the Secretary may reserve not more than 1 percent for payments to Guam, American Samoa, the United States Virgin Islands, and the Commonwealth of the Northern Mariana Islands in accordance with their respective needs for assistance under this part.

(2) Consolidation of Funds - The provisions of Public Law 95-134, permitting the consolidation of grants to the outlying areas, shall not apply to funds those areas receive under this part.

(b) Payments to Indians -

(1) In General - The Secretary shall, subject to this subsection, make payments to the Secretary of the Interior to be distributed to tribes, tribal organizations (as defined under Section 4 of the Indian Self-Determination and Education Assistance Act), or consortia of the above entities for the coordination of assistance in the provision of early intervention services by the States to infants and toddlers with disabilities and their families on reservations served by elementary schools and secondary schools for Indian children operated or funded by the Department of the Interior. The amount of such payment for any fiscal year shall be 1.25 percent of the aggregate of the amount available to all States under this part for such fiscal year.

(2) Allocation - For each fiscal year, the Secretary of the Interior shall distribute the entire payment received under paragraph (1) by providing to each tribe, tribal organization, or consortium an amount based on the number of infants and toddlers residing on the reservation, as determined annually, divided by the total of such children served by all tribes, tribal organizations, or consortia.

(3) Information - To receive a payment under this subsection, the tribe, tribal organization, or consortium shall submit such information to the Secretary of the Interior as is needed to determine the amounts to be distributed under paragraph (2).

(4) Use of Funds - The funds received by a tribe, tribal organization, or consortium shall be used to assist States in child find, screening, and other procedures for the early identification of Indian children under 3 years of age and for parent training. Such funds may also be used to provide early intervention services in accordance with this part. Such activities may be carried out directly or through contracts or cooperative agreements with the Bureau of Indian Affairs, local educational agencies, and other public or private nonprofit organizations. The tribe, tribal organization, or consortium is encouraged to involve Indian parents in the development and implementation of these activities. The above entities shall, as appropriate, make referrals to local, State, or Federal entities for the provision of services or further diagnosis.

(5) Reports - To be eligible to receive a payment under paragraph (2), a tribe, tribal organization, or consortium shall make a biennial report to the Secretary of the Interior of activities undertaken under this subsection, including the number of contracts and cooperative agreements entered into, the number of infants and toddlers contacted and receiving services for each year, and the estimated number of infants and toddlers needing services during the 2 years following the year in which the report is made. The Secretary of the Interior shall include a summary of this information on a biennial basis to the Secretary of Education along with such other information as required under Section 1411(h)(3)(E). The Secretary of Education may require any additional information from the Secretary of the Interior.

(6) Prohibited Uses of Funds - None of the funds under this subsection may be used by the Secretary of the Interior for administrative purposes, including child count, and the provision of technical assistance.

(c) State Allotments -

(1) In General - Except as provided in paragraphs (2) and (3), from the funds remaining for each fiscal year after the reservation and payments under subsections (a), (b), and (e), the Secretary shall first allot to each State an amount that bears the same ratio to the amount of such remainder as the number of infants and toddlers in the State bears to the number of infants and toddlers in all States.

(2) Minimum Allotments - Except as provided in paragraph (3), no State shall receive an amount under this section for any fiscal year that is less than the greater of –

(A) 1/2 of 1 percent of the remaining amount described in paragraph (1); or

(B) $500,000.

(3) Ratable Reduction -

(A) In General - If the sums made available under this part for any fiscal year are insufficient to pay the full amounts that all States are eligible to receive under this subsection for such year, the Secretary shall ratably reduce the allotments to such States for such year.

(B) Additional Funds - If additional funds become available for making payments under this subsection for a fiscal year, allotments that were reduced under subparagraph (A) shall be increased on the same basis the allotments were reduced.

(4) Definitions - In this subsection–

(A) the terms '**infants and toddlers**' mean children under 3 years of age; and

(B) the term 'State' means each of the 50 States, the District of Columbia, and the Commonwealth of Puerto Rico.

(d) Reallotment of Funds -

If a State elects not to receive its allotment under subsection (c), the Secretary shall reallot, among the remaining States, amounts from such State in accordance with such subsection.

(e) Reservation for State Incentive Grants -

(1) In General - For any fiscal year for which the amount appropriated pursuant to the authorization of appropriations under Section 1444 exceeds $460,000,000, the Secretary shall reserve 15 percent of such appropriated amount to provide grants to States that are carrying out the policy described in Section 1435(c) in order to facilitate the implementation of such policy.

(2) Amount of Grant -

(A) In General - Notwithstanding paragraphs (2) and (3) of subsection (c), the Secretary shall provide a grant to each State under paragraph (1) in an amount that bears the same ratio to the amount reserved under such paragraph as the number of infants and toddlers in the State bears to the number of infants and toddlers in all States receiving grants under such paragraph.

(B) Maximum Amount - No State shall receive a grant under paragraph (1) for any fiscal year in an amount that is greater than 20 percent of the amount reserved under such paragraph for the fiscal year.

(3) Carryover of Amounts -

(A) First Succeeding Fiscal Year - Pursuant to Section 421(b) of the General Education Provisions Act, amounts under a grant provided under paragraph (1) that are not obligated and expended prior to the beginning of the first fiscal year succeeding the fiscal year for which such amounts were appropriated shall remain available for obligation and expenditure during such first succeeding fiscal year.

(B) Second Succeeding Fiscal Year - Amounts under a grant provided under paragraph (1) that are not obligated and expended prior to the beginning of the second fiscal year succeeding the fiscal year for which such amounts were appropriated shall be returned to the Secretary and used to make grants to States under Section 1433 (from their allotments under this section) during such second succeeding fiscal year.

20 U.S.C. § 1444. Authorization of Appropriations.

For the purpose of carrying out this part, there are authorized to be appropriated such sums as may be necessary for each of the fiscal years 2005 through 2010.

End of Part C

Part D — National Activities to Improve Education of Children with Disabilities[330]

20 U.S.C. § 1450. Findings.[331]

Congress finds the following:

(1) The Federal Government has an ongoing obligation to support activities that contribute to positive results for children with disabilities, enabling those children to lead productive and independent adult lives.

---

330 **Wrightslaw Overview**: Part D of IDEA, also known as Subsection IV, has four subparts: A, B, C, and D. This Part authorizes and provides funding for activities to improve the educational outcomes for children with disabilities. "Findings" is in Section 1450. Part A is "State Personnel Development Grants," and includes purpose, definition of personnel, eligibility, applications, and how funds may be used. Part B is "Personnel Preparation" and focuses on improving educational outcomes and results by improving teacher training and professional development. Part C describes requirements for Parent Training and Information Centers and Community Resource Centers. Part D is General Provisions.

331 **Wrightslaw Overview**: "Findings" in Section 1450 describes an effective educational system and the critical need adequately trained personnel with "high quality, comprehensive professional development programs" so individuals who teach children with disabilities have the necessary knowledge and skills. Congress also emphasized the needs of parents for information and training to deal with the "multiple pressures of parenting," to build constructive working relationships with school personnel, and to be involved in planning and decision-making about early intervention, educational, and transition services for their children.

(2) Systemic change benefiting all students, including children with disabilities, requires the involvement of States, local educational agencies, parents, individuals with disabilities and their families, teachers and other service providers, and other interested individuals and organizations to develop and implement comprehensive strategies that improve educational results for children with disabilities.

(3) State educational agencies, in partnership with local educational agencies, parents of children with disabilities, and other individuals and organizations, are in the best position to improve education for children with disabilities and to address their special needs.

(4) **An effective educational system serving students with disabilities should** -

(A) **maintain high academic achievement standards** and clear performance goals for children with disabilities, consistent with the standards and expectations for all students in the educational system, and provide for appropriate and effective strategies and methods to ensure that all children with disabilities have the opportunity to achieve those standards and goals;

(B) clearly **define, in objective, measurable terms, the school and post-school results** that children with disabilities are expected to achieve; and

(C) **promote transition services** and coordinate State and local education, social, health, mental health, and other services, in addressing the full range of student needs, particularly the needs of children with disabilities who need significant levels of support to participate and learn in school and the community.

(5) The availability of an adequate number of qualified personnel is critical -

(A) to serve effectively children with disabilities;

(B) to assume leadership positions in administration and direct services;

(C) to provide teacher training; and

(D) to conduct high quality research to improve special education.

(6) High quality, comprehensive professional development programs are essential to ensure that the persons responsible for the education or transition of children with disabilities possess the skills and knowledge necessary to address the educational and related needs of those children.

(7) **Models of professional development should be scientifically based** and reflect successful practices, including strategies for recruiting, preparing, and retaining personnel.

(8) Continued support is essential for the development and maintenance of a coordinated and high quality program of research to inform successful teaching practices and model curricula for educating children with disabilities.

(9) Training, technical assistance, support, and dissemination activities are necessary to ensure that Parts B and C are fully implemented and achieve high quality early intervention, educational, and transitional results for children with disabilities and their families.

(10) Parents, teachers, administrators, and related services personnel need technical assistance and information in a timely, coordinated, and accessible manner in order to improve early intervention, educational, and transitional services and results at the State and local levels for children with disabilities and their families.

(11) **Parent training and information activities** assist parents of a child with a disability in dealing with the **multiple pressures of parenting such a child** and are of particular importance in -

(A) playing a vital role in creating and preserving constructive relationships between parents of children with disabilities and schools **by facilitating open communication** between the parents and schools; **encouraging dispute resolution** at the earliest possible point in time; and **discouraging the escalation of an adversarial process** between the parents and schools;

(B) ensuring the involvement of parents in planning and decisionmaking with respect to early intervention, educational, and transitional services;

(C) achieving high quality early intervention, educational, and transitional results for children with disabilities;

(D) **providing such parents information on their rights, protections, and responsibilities** under this title to ensure improved early intervention, educational, and transitional results for children with disabilities;

(E) assisting such parents in the development of skills to participate effectively in the education and development of their children and in the transitions described in Section 1473(b)(6);

(F) supporting the roles of such parents as participants within partnerships seeking to improve early intervention, educational, and transitional services and results for children with disabilities and their families; and

(G) supporting such parents who may have limited access to services and supports, due to economic, cultural, or linguistic barriers.

(12) Support is needed to improve technological resources and integrate technology, including universally designed technologies, into the lives of children with disabilities, parents of children with disabilities, school personnel, and others through curricula, services, and assistive technologies.

Part A (of Part D) - State Personnel Development Grants

20 U.S.C. § 1451. Purpose; Definition of Personnel; Program Authority.[332]

(a) Purpose.

The purpose of this subpart is to assist State educational agencies in reforming and improving their systems for personnel preparation and professional development in early intervention, educational, and transition services in order to improve results for children with disabilities.

(b) Definition of Personnel.

In this subpart the term 'personnel' means special education teachers, regular education teachers, principals, administrators, related services personnel, paraprofessionals, and early intervention personnel serving infants, toddlers, preschoolers, or children with disabilities, except where a particular category of personnel, such as related services personnel, is identified.

(c) Competitive Grants.

(1) In General. Except as provided in subsection (d), for any fiscal year for which the amount appropriated under Section 1455, that remains after the Secretary reserves funds under subsection (e) for the fiscal year, is less than $100,000,000, the Secretary shall award grants, on a competitive basis, to State educational agencies to carry out the activities described in the State plan submitted under Section 1453.

(2) Priority. In awarding grants under paragraph (1), the Secretary may give priority to State educational agencies that -

(A) are in States with the greatest personnel shortages; or

(B) demonstrate the greatest difficulty meeting the requirements of Section 1412(a)(14).

(3) Minimum Amount. The Secretary shall make a grant to each State educational agency selected under paragraph (1) in an amount for each fiscal year that is -

(A) not less than $500,000, nor more than $4,000,000, in the case of the 50 States, the District of Columbia, and the Commonwealth of Puerto Rico; and

(B) not less than $80,000 in the case of an outlying area.

(4) Increase in Amount. The Secretary may increase the amounts of grants under paragraph (4) to account for inflation.

(5) Factors. The Secretary shall determine the amount of a grant under paragraph (1) after considering -

(A) the amount of funds available for making the grants;

---

332 **Wrightslaw Overview**: Section 1451(a) describes the need to reform and improve personnel preparation and professional development programs to improve results for children with disabilities. The definition of "personnel" is in Section 1451(b). This section includes information about competitive grants, formula grants and continuation awards.

(B) the relative population of the State or outlying area;

(C) the types of activities proposed by the State or outlying area;

(D) the alignment of proposed activities with Section 1412(a)(14);

(E) the alignment of proposed activities with the State plans and applications submitted under sections 6311 and 6611(d) [1] respectively, of this title; and

(F) the use, as appropriate, of scientifically based research activities.

(d) Formula Grants.

(1) In General. Except as provided in paragraphs (2) and (3), for the first fiscal year for which the amount appropriated under Section 1455, that remains after the Secretary reserves funds under subsection (e) for the fiscal year, is equal to or greater than $100,000,000, and for each fiscal year thereafter, the Secretary shall allot to each State educational agency, whose application meets the requirements of this subpart, an amount that bears the same relation to the amount remaining as the amount the State received under Section 1411(d) for that fiscal year bears to the amount of funds received by all States (whose applications meet the requirements of this subpart) under Section 1411(d) for that fiscal year.

(2) Minimum Allotments for States That Received Competitive Grants.

(A) In General. The amount allotted under this subsection to any State educational agency that received a competitive multi-year grant under subsection (c) for which the grant period has not expired shall be not less than the amount specified for that fiscal year in the State educational agency's grant award document under that subsection.

(B) Special Rule. Each such State educational agency shall use the minimum amount described in subparagraph (A) for the activities described in the State educational agency's competitive grant award document for that year, unless the Secretary approves a request from the State educational agency to spend the funds on other activities.

(3) Minimum Allotment. The amount of any State educational agency's allotment under this subsection for any fiscal year shall not be less than -

(A) the greater of $500,000 or 1/2 of 1 percent of the total amount available under this subsection for that year, in the case of each of the 50 States, the District of Columbia, and the Commonwealth of Puerto Rico; and

(B) $80,000, in the case of an outlying area.

(4) Direct Benefit. In using grant funds allotted under paragraph (1), a State educational agency shall, through grants, contracts, or cooperative agreements, undertake activities that significantly and directly benefit the local educational agencies in the State.

(e) Continuation Awards.

(1) In General. Notwithstanding any other provision of this subpart, from funds appropriated under Section 1455 for each fiscal year, the Secretary shall reserve the amount that is necessary to make a continuation award to any State educational agency (at the request of the State educational agency) that received a multi-year award under this part (as this part was in effect on the day before the date of enactment of the Individuals with Disabilities Education Improvement Act of 2004), to enable the State educational agency to carry out activities in accordance with the terms of the multi-year award.

(2) Prohibition. A State educational agency that receives a continuation award under paragraph (1) for any fiscal year may not receive any other award under this Subpart for that fiscal year.

20 U.S.C. § 1452. Eligibility and Collaborative Process.

(a) Eligible Applicants.

A State educational agency may apply for a grant under this subpart for a grant period of not less than 1 year and not more than 5 years.

(b) Partners.

(1) In General. In order to be considered for a grant under this subpart, a State educational agency shall establish a partnership with local educational agencies and other State agencies involved in, or concerned with, the education of children with disabilities, including -

(A) not less than 1 institution of higher education; and

(B) the State agencies responsible for administering Part C, early education, child care, and vocational rehabilitation programs.

(2) Other Partners. In **order to be considered for a grant** under this subpart, a State educational agency shall work **in partnership with other persons and organizations** involved in, and concerned with, the education of children with disabilities, which may include -

(A) the Governor;

(B) parents of children with disabilities ages birth through 26;

(C) parents of nondisabled children ages birth through 26;

(D) individuals with disabilities;

(E) parent training and information centers or community parent resource centers funded under Sections 1471 and 1472, respectively;

(F) **community based and other nonprofit organizations** involved in the education and employment of individuals with disabilities;

(G) personnel as defined in Section 1451(b);

(H) the State advisory panel established under Part B;

(I) the State interagency coordinating council established under Part C;

(J) individuals knowledgeable about vocational education;

(K) the State agency for higher education;

(L) public agencies with jurisdiction in the areas of health, mental health, social services, and juvenile justice;

(M) other providers of professional development that work with infants, toddlers, preschoolers, and children with disabilities; and

(N) other individuals.

(3) Required Partner. If State law assigns responsibility for teacher preparation and certification to an individual, entity, or agency other than the State educational agency, the State educational agency shall -

(A) include that individual, entity, or agency as a partner in the partnership under this subsection; and

(B) ensure that any activities the State educational agency will carry out under this subpart that are within that partner's jurisdiction (which may include activities described in Section 1454(b)) are carried out by that partner.

20 U.S.C. § 1453. Applications.[333]

(a) In General.

(1) Submission. A State educational agency that desires to receive a grant under this subpart shall submit to the Secretary an application at such time, in such manner, and including such information as the Secretary may require.

(2) State Plan. The application **shall include a plan** that identifies and addresses the State and local needs for the personnel preparation and professional development of personnel, as well as individuals who provide direct supplementary aids and services to children with disabilities, and that -

(A) is designed to enable the State to meet the requirements of Section 1412(a)(14) and Section 1435(a)(8) and (9);

(B) is based on an assessment of State and local needs that identifies critical aspects and areas in need of improvement related to the preparation, ongoing training, and professional development of personnel who serve infants, toddlers, preschoolers, and children with disabilities within the State, including -

(i) current and anticipated personnel vacancies and shortages; and

(ii) the number of preservice and inservice programs; and

(C) is integrated and aligned, to the maximum extent possible, with State plans and activities under the Elementary and Secondary Education Act of 1965, the Rehabilitation Act of 1973, and the Higher Education Act of 1965.

(3) Requirement. The State application shall contain an assurance that the State educational agency will carry out each of the strategies described in subsection (b)(4).

(b) Elements of State Personnel Development Plan.

Each State personnel development plan under subsection (a)(2) **shall**-

(1) describe a partnership agreement that is in effect for the period of the grant, which agreement shall specify-

(A) the nature and extent of the partnership described in Section 1452(b) and the respective roles of each member of the partnership, including the partner described in Section 1452(b)(3) if applicable; and

(B) how the State educational agency will work with other persons and organizations involved in, and concerned with, the education of children with disabilities, including the respective roles of each of the persons and organizations;

(2) describe how the strategies and activities described in paragraph (4) will be coordinated with activities supported with other public resources (including Part B and Part C funds retained for use at the State level for personnel and professional development purposes) and private resources;

(3) describe how the State educational agency will align its personnel development plan under this part with the plan and application submitted under Sections 1111 and 2101(d), respectively, of the Elementary and Secondary Education Act of 1965; [20 U.S.C. 6311, 6611(d)];

(4) describe those strategies the State educational agency will use to address the professional development and personnel needs identified under subsection (a)(2) and how such strategies will be implemented, including

(A) a description of the programs and activities to be supported under this subpart that will provide personnel with the knowledge and skills to meet the needs of, and improve the performance and achievement of, infants, toddlers, preschoolers, and children with disabilities; and

(B) how such strategies will be integrated, to the maximum extent possible, with other activities supported by grants funded under Section 1462;

333 **Wrightslaw Overview**: This describes the application process that state departments of education must complete before they can receive grants under Part D. The state applications shall include a plan that identifies and addresses state and local needs for personnel preparation and professional development. Section 1453(b) describes required elements of the state personnel development plan. Section 1453(c) describes requirements for using experts as peer reviewers of state plans.

(5) provide an assurance that the State educational agency will provide technical assistance to local educational agencies to improve the quality of professional development available to meet the needs of personnel who serve children with disabilities;

(6) provide an assurance that the State educational agency will provide technical assistance to entities that provide services to infants and toddlers with disabilities to improve the quality of professional development available to meet the needs of personnel serving such children;

(7) describe how the State educational agency will recruit and retain teachers who meet the qualifications described in section 1412(a)(14)(C) of this title and other qualified personnel in geographic areas of greatest need;

(8) describe the steps the State educational agency will take to ensure that poor and minority children are not taught at higher rates by teachers who do not meet the qualifications described in section 1412(a)(14)(C) of this title; and

(9) describe how the State educational agency will assess, on a regular basis, the extent to which the strategies implemented under this subpart have been effective in meeting the performance goals described in Section 1412(a)(15).

(c) Peer Review.

(1) In General. The Secretary shall use a **panel of experts** who are competent, by virtue of their training, expertise, or experience, to evaluate applications for grants under Section 1451(c)(1).

(2) Composition of Panel. A majority of a panel described in paragraph (1) shall be composed of individuals who are not employees of the Federal Government.

(3) Payment of Fees and Expenses of Certain Members. The Secretary may use available funds appropriated to carry out this subpart to pay the expenses and fees of panel members who are not employees of the Federal Government.

(d) Reporting Procedures.

Each State educational agency that receives a grant under this subpart shall submit annual performance reports to the Secretary. The reports shall -

(1) describe the progress of the State educational agency in implementing its plan;

(2) analyze the effectiveness of the State educational agency's activities under this subpart and of the State educational agency's strategies for meeting its goals under Section 1412(a)(15); and

(3) identify changes in the strategies used by the State educational agency and described in subsection (b)(4), if any, to improve the State educational agency's performance.

20 U.S.C. § 1454. Use of Funds.[334]

(a) Professional Development Activities.

A State educational agency that receives a grant under this subpart **shall** use the grant funds to support activities in accordance with the State's plan described in Section 1453, **including 1 or more of the following**:

(1) Carrying out programs that provide support to both special education and regular education teachers of children with disabilities and principals, such as programs that -

(A) provide teacher mentoring, team teaching, reduced class schedules and case loads, and intensive professional development;

(B) use standards or assessments for guiding beginning teachers that are consistent with challenging State

---

334 **Wrightslaw Overview**: Section 1454 describes how states may use funds under Part D. Funds may be used for professional development to improve teaching practices by using effective instructional strategies, methods of positive behavioral interventions, and scientifically based reading instruction, etc. Funds may be used to train administrators and other school personnel to conduct effective IEP and IFSP meetings. Funds may be used to recruit and retain highly qualified special education teachers, reform tenure systems, test the subject matter knowledge of teachers, and reform certification and licensing requirements so teachers have subject matter knowledge and teaching skills.

academic achievement standards and with the requirements for professional development, as defined in Section 7801 of this title; and

(C) encourage collaborative and consultative models of providing early intervention, special education, and related services.

(2) Encouraging and supporting the training of special education and regular education teachers and administrators to effectively use and integrate technology -

(A) into curricula and instruction, including training to improve the ability to collect, manage, and analyze data to improve teaching, decision-making, school improvement efforts, and accountability;

(B) to enhance learning by children with disabilities; and

(C) to effectively communicate with parents.

(3) Providing professional development activities that -

(A) improve the knowledge of special education and regular education teachers concerning -

(i) the academic and developmental or functional needs of students with disabilities; or

(ii) effective instructional strategies, methods, and skills, and the use of State academic content standards and student academic achievement and functional standards, and State assessments, to improve teaching practices and student academic achievement;

(B) improve the **knowledge of special education and regular education teachers and principals** and, in appropriate cases, **paraprofessionals, concerning effective instructional practices**, and that -

(i) provide training in how to teach and address the needs of children with different learning styles and children who are limited English proficient;

(ii) involve collaborative groups of teachers, administrators, and, in appropriate cases, related services personnel;

(iii) provide **training in methods of** -

(I) **positive behavioral interventions** and supports to improve student behavior in the classroom;

(II) **scientifically based reading instruction**, including early literacy instruction;

(III) **early and appropriate interventions** to identify and help children with disabilities;

(IV) effective instruction for children with **low incidence disabilities**;

(V) successful transitioning to postsecondary opportunities; and

(VI) using classroom-based techniques to assist children prior to referral for special education;

(iv) provide training to enable personnel to work with and involve parents in their child's education, including parents of low income and limited English proficient children with disabilities;

(v) provide training for **special education personnel and regular education personnel** in planning, developing, and implementing effective and appropriate IEPs; and

(vi) provide training to meet the needs of students with significant health, mobility, or behavioral needs prior to serving such students;

(C) train administrators, principals, and other relevant school personnel in conducting effective IEP meetings; and

(D) train early intervention, preschool, and related services providers, and other relevant school personnel, in conducting effective individualized family service plan (IFSP) meetings.

(4) Developing and implementing initiatives to promote the recruitment and retention of special education teachers, who meet the qualifications described in section 1412(a)(14)(C) of this title, particularly initiatives

that have been proven effective in recruiting and retaining highly qualified teachers, including programs that provide-

(A) teacher mentoring from exemplary special education teachers, principals, or superintendents;

(B) induction and support for special education teachers during their first 3 years of employment as teachers; or

(C) incentives, including financial incentives, to retain special education teachers who have a record of success in helping students with disabilities.

(5) Carrying out programs and activities that are designed to improve the quality of personnel who serve children with disabilities, such as -

(A) innovative professional development programs (which may be provided through partnerships that include institutions of higher education), including programs that train teachers and principals to integrate technology into curricula and instruction to improve teaching, learning, and technology literacy, which professional development shall be consistent with the definition of professional development in Section 7801 of this title; and

(B) the development and use of proven, cost effective strategies for the implementation of professional development activities, such as through the use of technology and distance learning.

(6) Carrying out programs and activities that are designed to improve the quality of early intervention personnel, including paraprofessionals and primary referral sources, such as -

(A) professional development programs to improve the delivery of early intervention services;

(B) initiatives to promote the recruitment and retention of early intervention personnel; and

(C) interagency activities to ensure that early intervention personnel are adequately prepared and trained.

(b) Other Activities.

A State educational agency that receives a grant under this subpart shall use the grant funds to support activities in accordance with the State's plan described in Section 1453, including 1 or more of the following

(1) **Reforming special education and regular education teacher certification** (including recertification) or licensing requirements **to ensure that** -

(A) **special education and regular education teachers** have -

(i) the training and information necessary to address the full range of needs of children with disabilities across disability categories; and

(ii) the necessary subject matter knowledge and teaching skills in the academic subjects that the teachers teach;

(B) special education and regular education teacher certification (including recertification) or licensing requirements are aligned with challenging State academic content standards; and

(C) special education and regular education teachers have the **subject matter knowledge and teaching skills**, including technology literacy, necessary to help students with disabilities meet challenging State student academic achievement and functional standards.

(2) Programs that establish, expand, or improve alternative routes for State certification of special education teachers for individuals with a baccalaureate or master's degree who meet the qualifications described in section 1412(a)(14)(C) of this title, **including mid-career professionals from other occupations,** paraprofessionals, and recent college or university graduates with records of academic distinction who demonstrate the potential to become highly effective special education teachers.

(3) Teacher advancement initiatives for special education teachers that promote professional growth and emphasize multiple career paths (such as paths to becoming a career teacher, mentor teacher, or exemplary teacher) and pay differentiation.

(4) Developing and implementing mechanisms to assist local educational agencies and schools in effectively

recruiting and retaining special education teachers who meet the qualifications described in section 1412(a)(14)(C) of this title.

(5) Reforming tenure systems, **implementing teacher testing for subject matter knowledge**, and implementing teacher testing for State certification or licensing, consistent with title II of the Higher Education Act of 1965.

(6) Funding projects to promote **reciprocity of teacher certification or licensing** between or among States for special education teachers, except that no reciprocity agreement developed under this paragraph or developed using funds provided under this subpart may lead to the weakening of any State teaching certification or licensing requirement.

(7) Assisting local educational agencies to serve children with disabilities through the development and use of proven, innovative strategies to deliver intensive professional development programs that are both cost effective and easily accessible, such as strategies that involve delivery through the use of technology, peer networks, and distance learning.

(8) Developing, or assisting local educational agencies in developing, merit based performance systems, and strategies that provide differential and bonus pay for special education teachers.

(9) Supporting activities that ensure that teachers are able to use challenging State academic content standards and student academic achievement and functional standards, and State assessments for all children with disabilities, to improve instructional practices and improve the academic achievement of children with disabilities.

(10) When applicable, coordinating with, and expanding centers established under, section 6613(c)(18) of this title (as such section was in effect on the day before December 10, 2015) to benefit special education teachers.

(c) Contracts and Subgrants.

A State educational agency that receives a grant under this subpart -

(1) shall award contracts or subgrants to local educational agencies, institutions of higher education, parent training and information centers, or community parent resource centers, as appropriate, to carry out its State plan under this subpart; and

(2) may award contracts and subgrants to other public and private entities, including the lead agency under Part C, to carry out the State plan.

(d) Use of Funds for Professional Development.

A State educational agency that receives a grant under this subpart shall use -

(1) not less than 90 percent of the funds the State educational agency receives under the grant for any fiscal year for activities under subsection (a); and

(2) not more than 10 percent of the funds the State educational agency receives under the grant for any fiscal year for activities under subsection (b).

(e) Grants to Outlying Areas.

Public Law 95-134, permitting the consolidation of grants to the outlying areas, shall not apply to funds received under this subpart.

20 U.S.C. § 1455. Authorization of Appropriations.

There are authorized to be appropriated to carry out this subpart such sums as may be necessary for each of the fiscal years 2005 through 2010.

Part B (of Part D) – Personnel Preparation, Technical Assistance, Model Demonstration Projects, and Dissemination of Information

20 U.S.C. § 1461. Purpose; Definition of Eligible Entity.[335]

(a) Purpose. The purpose of this subpart is -

(1) to provide Federal funding for personnel preparation, technical assistance, model demonstration projects, information dissemination, and studies and evaluations, in order to improve early intervention, educational, and transitional results for children with disabilities; and

(2) to assist State educational agencies and local educational agencies in improving their education systems for children with disabilities.

(b) Definition of Eligible Entity.

(1) In General. In this subpart, the term '**eligible entity**' means -

(A) a State educational agency;

(B) a local educational agency;

(C) a public charter school that is a local educational agency under State law;

(D) an institution of higher education;

(E) a public agency not described in subparagraphs (A) through (D);

(F) a **private nonprofit organization**;

(G) an outlying area;

(H) an Indian tribe or a tribal organization (as defined under Section 4 of the Indian Self-Determination and Education Assistance Act); or

(I) a **for-profit organization**, if the Secretary finds it appropriate in light of the purposes of a particular competition for a grant, contract, or cooperative agreement under this subpart.

(2) Special Rule. The Secretary may limit which eligible entities described in paragraph (1) are eligible for a grant, contract, or cooperative agreement under this subpart to 1 or more of the categories of eligible entities described in paragraph (1).

20 U.S.C. § 1462. Personnel Development to Improve Services and Results for Children with Disabilities.[336]

(a) In General.

The Secretary, on a competitive basis, shall award grants to, or enter into contracts or cooperative agreements with, eligible entities to carry out 1 or more of the following objectives:

(1) To help address the needs identified in the State plan described in Section 1453(a)(2) for personnel, as defined in Section 1451(b) of this title who meet the qualifications described in section 1412(a)(14)(C) of this title, to work with infants or toddlers with disabilities, or children with disabilities, consistent with the qualifications described in Section 1412(a)(14) of this title.

(2) To ensure that those personnel have the necessary skills and knowledge, derived from practices that have been determined, through scientifically based research, to be successful in serving those children.

---

335 **Wrightslaw Overview:** This describes the purpose to improve early intervention, educational and transitional results for children with disabilities by helping states improve their educational systems.

336 **Wrightslaw Overview:** Section 1462 addresses the need to ensure that all teachers have the necessary skills and knowledge of educational practices that have been determined, through scientifically based research. States need to shift the focus to academics in special education teacher preparation programs. Section 1462(a)(7) describes professional development for administrators in instructional leadership, behavior support, assessment, accountability, and positive relationships with parents. Section 1462(b) describes personnel development and support for beginning special educators, including an extended clinical learning opportunity or supervised practicum. Section 1462(c) describes preparation of individuals to work with students with low incidence disabilities. Section 1462(g) and (h) describe scholarships and service obligations.

(3) To encourage **increased focus on academics and core content areas** in special education personnel preparation programs.

(4) To ensure that regular education teachers have the necessary skills and knowledge to provide instruction to students with disabilities in the regular education classroom.

(5) To ensure that all special education teachers meet the qualifications described in section 1412(a)(14)(C) of this title.

(6) To ensure that preservice and in-service personnel preparation programs include training in -

    (A) the use of new technologies;

    (B) the area of early intervention, educational, and transition services;

    (C) effectively involving parents; and

    (D) positive behavioral supports.

(7) To provide high-quality professional development for principals, superintendents, and other administrators, including training in -

    (A) instructional leadership;

    (B) behavioral supports in the school and classroom;

    (C) paperwork reduction;

    (D) promoting improved collaboration between special education and general education teachers;

    (E) assessment and accountability;

    (F) ensuring effective learning environments; and

    (G) fostering positive relationships with parents.

(b) Personnel Development; Enhanced Support for Beginning Special Educators.

    (1) In General. In carrying out this section, the Secretary shall support activities -

    (A) for personnel development, including activities for the preparation of personnel who will serve children with high incidence and low incidence disabilities, to prepare special education and general education teachers, principals, administrators, and related services personnel (and school board members, when appropriate) to meet the diverse and individualized instructional needs of children with disabilities and improve early intervention, educational, and transitional services and results for children with disabilities, consistent with the objectives described in subsection (a); and

    (B) for enhanced support for beginning special educators, consistent with the objectives described in subsection (a).

    (2) Personnel Development. In carrying out paragraph (1)(A), the Secretary shall support not less than 1 of the following activities:

    (A) Assisting effective existing, improving existing, or developing new, collaborative personnel preparation activities undertaken by institutions of higher education, local educational agencies, and other local entities that incorporate best practices and scientifically based research, where applicable, in providing special education and general education teachers, principals, administrators, and related services personnel with the knowledge and skills to effectively support students with disabilities, including -

        (i) working collaboratively in regular classroom settings;

        (ii) using appropriate supports, accommodations, and curriculum modifications;

        (iii) implementing effective teaching strategies, classroom-based techniques, and interventions to ensure appropriate identification of students who may be eligible for special education services, and to prevent the misidentification, inappropriate overidentification, or under-identification of children as having a disability, especially minority and limited English proficient children;

        (iv) effectively working with and involving parents in the education of their children;

        (v) utilizing strategies, including positive behavioral interventions, for addressing the conduct of children with disabilities that impedes their learning and that of others in the classroom;

(vi) effectively constructing IEPs, participating in IEP meetings, and implementing IEPs;

(vii) preparing children with disabilities to participate in statewide assessments (with or without accommodations) and alternate assessments, as appropriate, and to ensure that all children with disabilities are a part of all accountability systems under the Elementary and Secondary Education Act of 1965; and

(viii) working in high need elementary schools and secondary schools, including urban schools, rural schools, and schools operated by an entity described in Section 6113(d)(1)(A)(ii) of the Elementary and Secondary Education Act of 1965 [20 U.S.C. 7423(d)(1)(A)(ii)], and schools that serve high numbers or percentages of limited English proficient children.

(B) Developing, evaluating, and disseminating innovative models for the recruitment, induction, retention, and assessment of new, special education teachers who meet the qualifications described in section 1412(a)(14)(C) of this title to reduce teacher shortages, especially from groups that are underrepresented in the teaching profession, including individuals with disabilities.

(C) Providing continuous personnel preparation, training, and professional development designed to provide support and ensure retention of special education and general education teachers and personnel who teach and provide related services to children with disabilities.

(D) Developing and improving programs for paraprofessionals to become special education teachers, related services personnel, and early intervention personnel, including interdisciplinary training to enable the paraprofessionals to improve early intervention, educational, and transitional results for children with disabilities.

(E) In the case of principals and superintendents, providing activities to promote instructional leadership and improved collaboration between general educators, special education teachers, and related services personnel.

(F) Supporting institutions of higher education with minority enrollments of not less than 25 percent for the purpose of preparing personnel to work with children with disabilities.

(G) Developing and improving programs to train special education teachers to develop an expertise in autism spectrum disorders.

(H) Providing continuous personnel preparation, training, and professional development designed to provide support and improve the qualifications of personnel who provide related services to children with disabilities, including to enable such personnel to obtain advanced degrees.

(3) Enhanced Support for Beginning Special Educators. In carrying out paragraph (1)(B), the Secretary shall support not less than 1 of the following activities:

(A) Enhancing and restructuring existing programs or developing preservice teacher education programs to prepare special education teachers, at colleges or departments of education within institutions of higher education, by incorporating an extended (such as an additional 5th year) clinical learning opportunity, field experience, or supervised practicum into such programs.

(B) Creating or supporting teacher-faculty partnerships (such as professional development schools) that

(i) consist of not less than -

(I) 1 or more institutions of higher education with special education personnel preparation programs;

(II) 1 or more local educational agencies that serve high numbers or percentages of low-income students; or

(III) 1 or more elementary schools or secondary schools, particularly schools that have failed to make adequate yearly progress on the basis, in whole and in part, of the assessment results of the disaggregated subgroup of students with disabilities;

(ii) may include other entities eligible for assistance under this part; and

(iii) provide -

(I) high-quality mentoring and induction opportunities with ongoing support for beginning special education teachers; or

(II) inservice professional development to beginning and veteran special education teachers through the ongoing exchange of information and instructional strategies with faculty.

(c) Low Incidence Disabilities; Authorized Activities.

(1) In General. In carrying out this section, the Secretary shall support activities, consistent with the objectives described in subsection (a) that benefit children with low incidence disabilities.

(2) Authorized Activities. Activities that may be carried out under this subsection include activities such as the following:

(A) Preparing persons who -

(i) have prior training in educational and other related service fields; and

(ii) are studying to obtain degrees, certificates, or licensure that will enable the persons to assist children with low incidence disabilities to achieve the objectives set out in their individualized education programs described in Section 1414(d), or to assist infants and toddlers with low incidence disabilities to achieve the outcomes described in their individualized family service plans described in Section 1436.

(B) Providing personnel from various disciplines with interdisciplinary training that will contribute to improvement in early intervention, educational, and transitional results for children with low incidence disabilities.

(C) Preparing personnel in the innovative uses and application of technology, including universally designed technologies, assistive technology devices, and assistive technology services -

(i) to enhance learning by children with low incidence disabilities through early intervention, educational, and transitional services; and

(ii) to improve communication with parents.

(D) Preparing personnel who provide services to visually impaired or blind children to teach and use Braille in the provision of services to such children.

(E) Preparing personnel to be qualified educational interpreters, to assist children with low incidence disabilities, particularly deaf and hard of hearing children in school and school related activities, and deaf and hard of hearing infants and toddlers and preschool children in early intervention and preschool programs.

(F) Preparing personnel who provide services to children with significant cognitive disabilities and children with multiple disabilities.

(G) Preparing personnel who provide services to children with low incidence disabilities and limited English proficient children.

(3) Definition. In this section, the term '**low incidence**' means -

(A) a visual or hearing impairment, or simultaneous visual and hearing impairments;

(B) a significant cognitive impairment; or

(C) any impairment for which a small number of personnel with highly specialized skills and knowledge are needed in order for children with that impairment to receive early intervention services or a free appropriate public education.

(4) Selection of Recipients. In selecting eligible entities for assistance under this subsection, the Secretary may give preference to eligible entities submitting applications that include 1 or more of the following:

(A) A proposal to prepare personnel in more than 1 low incidence disability, such as deafness and blindness.

(B) A demonstration of an effective collaboration between an eligible entity and a local educational agency that promotes recruitment and subsequent retention of personnel who meet the qualifications described in section 1412(a)(14)(C) of this title to serve children with low incidence disabilities.

(5) Preparation in Use of Braille. The Secretary shall ensure that all recipients of awards under this subsection who will use that assistance to prepare personnel to provide services to visually impaired or blind children that can appropriately be provided in Braille, will prepare those individuals to provide those services in Braille.

(d) Leadership Preparation; Authorized Activities.

(1) In General. In carrying out this section, the Secretary shall support leadership preparation activities that are consistent with the objectives described in subsection (a).

(2) Authorized Activities. Activities that may be carried out under this subsection include activities such as the following:

(A) Preparing personnel at the graduate, doctoral, and postdoctoral levels of training to administer, enhance, or provide services to improve results for children with disabilities.

(B) Providing interdisciplinary training for various types of leadership personnel, including teacher preparation faculty, related services faculty, administrators, researchers, supervisors, principals, and other persons whose work affects early intervention, educational, and transitional services for children with disabilities, including children with disabilities who are limited English proficient children.

(e) Applications.

(1) In General. An eligible entity that wishes to receive a grant, or enter into a contract or cooperative agreement, under this section shall submit an application to the Secretary at such time, in such manner, and containing such information as the Secretary may require.

(2) Identified State Needs.

(A) Requirement to Address Identified Needs. An application for assistance under subsection (b), (c), or (d) shall include information demonstrating to the satisfaction of the Secretary that the activities described in the application will address needs identified by the State or States the eligible entity proposes to serve.

(B) Cooperation with State Educational Agencies. An eligible entity that is not a local educational agency or a State educational agency shall include in the eligible entity's application information demonstrating to the satisfaction of the Secretary that the eligible entity and 1 or more State educational agencies or local educational agencies will cooperate in carrying out and monitoring the proposed project.

(3) Acceptance by States of Personnel Preparation Requirements. The Secretary may require eligible entities to provide in the eligible entities' applications assurances from 1 or more States that such States intend to accept successful completion of the proposed personnel preparation program as meeting State personnel standards or other requirements in State law or regulation for serving children with disabilities or serving infants and toddlers with disabilities.

(f) Selection of Recipients.

(1) Impact of Project. In selecting eligible entities for assistance under this section, the Secretary shall consider the impact of the proposed project described in the application in meeting the need for personnel identified by the States.

(2) Requirement for Eligible Entities to Meet State and Professional Qualifications. The Secretary shall make grants and enter into contracts and cooperative agreements under this section only to eligible entities that meet State and professionally recognized qualifications for the preparation of special education and related services personnel, if the purpose of the project is to assist personnel in obtaining degrees.

(3) Preferences. In selecting eligible entities for assistance under this section, the Secretary may give preference to eligible entities that are institutions of higher education that are -

(A) educating regular education personnel to meet the needs of children with disabilities in integrated settings;

(B) educating special education personnel to work in collaboration with regular educators in integrated settings; and

(C) successfully recruiting and preparing individuals with disabilities and individuals from groups that are underrepresented in the profession for which the institution of higher education is preparing individuals.

(g) Scholarships.

The Secretary may include funds for scholarships, with necessary stipends and allowances, in awards under subsections (b), (c), and (d).

(h) Service Obligation.

(1) In General. Each application for assistance under subsections (b), (c), and (d) shall include an assurance that the eligible entity will ensure that individuals who receive a scholarship under the proposed project agree to subsequently provide special education and related services to children with disabilities, or in the case of leadership personnel to subsequently work in the appropriate field, for a period of **2 years for every year** for which the scholarship was received or repay all or part of the amount of the scholarship, in accordance with regulations issued by the Secretary.

(2) Special Rule. Notwithstanding paragraph (1), the Secretary may reduce or waive the service obligation requirement under paragraph (1) if the Secretary determines that the service obligation is acting as a deterrent to the recruitment of students into special education or a related field.

(3) Secretary's Responsibility. The Secretary -

(A) shall ensure that individuals described in paragraph (1) comply with the requirements of that paragraph; and

(B) may use not more than 0.5 percent of the funds appropriated under subsection (i) for each fiscal year, to carry out subparagraph (A), in addition to any other funds that are available for that purpose.

(i) Authorization of Appropriations.

There are authorized to be appropriated to carry out this section such sums as may be necessary for each of the fiscal years 2005 through 2010.

20 U.S.C. § 1463. Technical Assistance, Demonstration Projects, Dissemination of Information, and Implementation of Scientifically Based Research.[337]

(a) In General.

The Secretary shall make competitive grants to, or enter into contracts or cooperative agreements with, eligible entities to provide technical assistance, support model demonstration projects, disseminate useful information, and implement activities that are supported by scientifically based research.

(b) Required Activities.

Funds received under this section shall be used to support activities to improve services provided under this title, including the practices of professionals and others involved in providing such services to children with disabilities, that promote academic achievement and improve results for children with disabilities through -

(1) implementing effective strategies for addressing inappropriate behavior of students with disabilities in schools, including strategies to prevent children with emotional and behavioral problems from developing emotional disturbances that require the provision of special education and related services;

(2) improving the alignment, compatibility, and development of valid and reliable assessments and alternate assessments for assessing student academic achievement, as described under Section 6311(b)(2)(B) of this title;

(3) providing training for both regular education teachers and special education teachers to address the needs of students with different learning styles;

(4) disseminating information about innovative, effective, and efficient curricula designs, instructional approaches, and strategies, and identifying positive academic and social learning opportunities, that -

(A) provide effective transitions between educational settings or from school to post school settings; and

(B) improve educational and transitional results at all levels of the educational system in which the activities

---

337 **Wrightslaw Overview**: The federal government shall award grants and enter into contracts with entities to produce and disseminate information that is supported by scientifically based research to promote academic achievement and improve results for children with disabilities.

are carried out and, in particular, that improve the progress of children with disabilities, as measured by assessments within the general education curriculum involved; and

(5) applying scientifically based findings to facilitate systemic changes, related to the provision of services to children with disabilities, in policy, procedure, practice, and the training and use of personnel.

(c) Authorized Activities.

Activities that may be carried out under this section include activities to improve services provided under this title, including the practices of professionals and others involved in providing such services to children with disabilities, that promote academic achievement and improve results for children with disabilities through -

(1) applying and testing research findings in typical settings where children with disabilities receive services to determine the usefulness, effectiveness, and general applicability of such research findings in such areas as improving instructional methods, curricula, and tools, such as textbooks and media;

(2) supporting and promoting the coordination of early intervention and educational services for children with disabilities with services provided by health, rehabilitation, and social service agencies;

(3) promoting improved alignment and compatibility of general and special education reforms concerned with curricular and instructional reform, and evaluation of such reforms;

(4) enabling professionals, parents of children with disabilities, and other persons to learn about, and implement, the findings of scientifically based research, and successful practices developed in model demonstration projects, relating to the provision of services to children with disabilities;

(5) conducting outreach, and disseminating information, relating to successful approaches to overcoming systemic barriers to the effective and efficient delivery of early intervention, educational, and transitional services to personnel who provide services to children with disabilities;

(6) assisting States and local educational agencies with the process of planning systemic changes that will promote improved early intervention, educational, and transitional results for children with disabilities;

(7) promoting change through a multistate or regional framework that benefits States, local educational agencies, and other participants in partnerships that are in the process of achieving systemic-change outcomes;

(8) focusing on the needs and issues that are specific to a population of children with disabilities, such as providing single-State and multi-State technical assistance and in-service training -

   (A) to schools and agencies serving deaf-blind children and their families;

   (B) to programs and agencies serving other groups of children with low incidence disabilities and their families;

   (C) addressing the postsecondary education needs of individuals who are deaf or hard-of-hearing; and

   (D) to schools and personnel providing special education and related services for children with autism spectrum disorders;

(9) demonstrating models of personnel preparation to ensure appropriate placements and services for all students and to reduce disproportionality in eligibility, placement, and disciplinary actions for minority and limited English proficient children; and

(10) disseminating information on how to reduce inappropriate racial and ethnic disproportionalities identified under Section 1418.

(d) Balance Among Activities and Age Ranges.

In carrying out this section, the Secretary shall ensure that there is an appropriate balance across all age ranges of children with disabilities.

(e) Linking States to Information Sources.

In carrying out this section, the Secretary shall support projects that link States to technical assistance resources, including special education and general education resources, and shall make research and related products available through libraries, electronic networks, parent training projects, and other information sources, including through the activities of the National Center for Education Evaluation and Regional Assistance established under part D of the Education Sciences Reform Act of 2002.

(f) Applications.

(1) In General. An eligible entity that wishes to receive a grant, or enter into a contract or cooperative agreement, under this section shall submit an application to the Secretary at such time, in such manner, and containing such information as the Secretary may require.

(2) Standards. To the maximum extent feasible, each eligible entity shall demonstrate that the project described in the eligible entity's application **is supported by scientifically valid research** that has been carried out in accordance with the standards for the conduct and evaluation of all relevant research and development **established by the National Center for Education Research**.[338]

(3) Priority. As appropriate, the Secretary shall give priority to applications that propose to serve teachers and school personnel directly in the school environment.

20 U.S.C. § 1464. Studies and Evaluations.[339]

(a) Studies and Evaluations.

(1) Delegation. The Secretary shall delegate to the Director of the Institute of Education Sciences responsibility to carry out this section, other than subsections (d) and (f).

(2) Assessment. The Secretary shall, directly or through grants, contracts, or cooperative agreements awarded to eligible entities on a competitive basis, assess the progress in the implementation of this title, including the effectiveness of State and local efforts to provide -

(A) a free appropriate public education to children with disabilities; and

(B) early intervention services to infants and toddlers with disabilities, and infants and toddlers who would be at risk of having substantial developmental delays if early intervention services were not provided to the infants and toddlers.

(b) Assessment of National Activities.

(1) In General. The Secretary shall carry out a national assessment of activities carried out with Federal funds under this title in order -

(A) to determine the effectiveness of this title in achieving the purposes of this title;

(B) to provide timely information to the President, Congress, the States, local educational agencies, and the public on how to implement this title more effectively; and

(C) to provide the President and Congress with information that will be useful in developing legislation to achieve the purposes of this title more effectively.

(2) Scope of Assessment. The national assessment shall assess activities supported under this title, including

(A) the implementation of programs assisted under this title and the impact of such programs on addressing the developmental needs of, and improving the academic achievement of, children with disabilities to enable the children to reach challenging developmental goals and challenging State academic content standards based on State academic assessments;

(B) the types of programs and services that have demonstrated the greatest likelihood of helping students reach the challenging State academic content standards and developmental goals;

(C) the implementation of the professional development activities assisted under this title and the impact on instruction, student academic achievement, and teacher qualifications to enhance the ability of special education teachers and regular education teachers to improve results for children with disabilities; and

(D) the effectiveness of schools, local educational agencies, States, other recipients of assistance under this

---

338   https://ies.ed.gov/ncer/

339   **Wrightslaw Overview**: Section 1464 authorizes assessments, longitudinal studies, and a national assessment to determine if children with disabilities are benefiting from special education.

title, and the Secretary in achieving the purposes of this title by -

(i) improving the academic achievement of children with disabilities and their performance on regular statewide assessments as compared to nondisabled children, and the performance of children with disabilities on alternate assessments;

(ii) improving the participation of children with disabilities in the general education curriculum;

(iii) improving the transitions of children with disabilities at natural transition points;

(iv) placing and serving children with disabilities, including minority children, in the least restrictive environment appropriate;

(v) preventing children with disabilities, especially children with emotional disturbances and specific learning disabilities, from dropping out of school;

(vi) addressing the reading and literacy needs of children with disabilities;

(vii) reducing the inappropriate overidentification of children, especially minority and limited English proficient children, as having a disability;

(viii) improving the participation of parents of children with disabilities in the education of their children; and

(ix) resolving disagreements between education personnel and parents through alternate dispute resolution activities, including mediation.

(3) Interim and Final Reports. The Secretary shall submit to the President and Congress -

(A) an interim report that summarizes the preliminary findings of the assessment not later than 3 years after the date of enactment of the Individuals with Disabilities Education Improvement Act of 2004; and

(B) a final report of the findings of the assessment not later than 5 years after the date of enactment of such Act.

(c) Study on Ensuring Accountability for Students Who Are Held to Alternative Achievement Standards.

The Secretary shall carry out a national study or studies to examine -

(1) the criteria that States use to determine -

(A) eligibility for alternate assessments; and

(B) the number and type of children who take those assessments and are held accountable to alternative achievement standards;

(2) the validity and reliability of alternate assessment instruments and procedures;

(3) the alignment of alternate assessments and alternative achievement standards to State academic content standards in reading, mathematics, and science; and

(4) the use and effectiveness of alternate assessments in appropriately measuring student progress and outcomes specific to individualized instructional need.

(d) Annual Report.

The Secretary shall provide an annual report to Congress that -

(1) summarizes the research conducted under Part E of the Education Sciences Reform Act of 2002;

(2) analyzes and summarizes the data reported by the States and the Secretary of the Interior under Section 1418;

(3) summarizes the studies and evaluations conducted under this section and the timeline for their completion;

(4) describes the extent and progress of the assessment of national activities; and

(5) describes the findings and determinations resulting from reviews of State implementation of this title.

(e) Authorized Activities.

In carrying out this section, the Secretary may support objective studies, evaluations, and assessments, including studies that -

(1) analyze measurable impact, outcomes, and results achieved by State educational agencies and local

educational agencies through their activities to reform policies, procedures, and practices designed to improve educational and transitional services and results for children with disabilities;

(2) analyze State and local needs for professional development, parent training, and other appropriate activities that can reduce the need for disciplinary actions involving children with disabilities;

(3) assess educational and transitional services and results for children with disabilities from minority backgrounds, including -

(A) data on -

(i) the number of minority children who are referred for special education evaluation;

(ii) the number of minority children who are receiving special education and related services and their educational or other service placement;

(iii) the number of minority children who graduated from secondary programs with a regular diploma in the standard number of years; and

(iv) the number of minority children who drop out of the educational system; and

(B) the performance of children with disabilities from minority backgrounds on State assessments and other performance indicators established for all students;

(4) measure educational and transitional services and results for children with disabilities served under this title, including longitudinal studies that -

(A) examine educational and transitional services and results for children with disabilities who are 3 through 17 years of age and are receiving special education and related services under this title, using a national, representative sample of distinct age cohorts and disability categories; and

(B) examine educational results, transition services, postsecondary placement, and employment status for individuals with disabilities, 18 through 21 years of age, who are receiving or have received special education and related services under this title; and

(5) identify and report on the placement of children with disabilities by disability category.

(f) Study.

The Secretary shall study, and report to Congress regarding, the extent to which States adopt policies described in Section 1435(c)(1) and on the effects of those policies.

20 U.S.C. § 1465. Interim Alternative Educational Settings, Behavioral Supports, and Systematic School Interventions.[340]

(a) Program Authorized.

The Secretary may award grants, and enter into contracts and cooperative agreements, to support safe learning environments that support academic achievement for all students by -

(1) improving the quality of interim alternative educational settings; and

(2) providing increased behavioral supports and research-based, systemic interventions in schools.

(b) Authorized Activities.

In carrying out this section, the Secretary may support activities to -

(1) establish, expand, or increase the scope of **behavioral supports and systemic interventions** by providing for **effective, research-based practices**, including -

(A) **training for school staff** on early identification, prereferral, and referral procedures;

(B) **training for** administrators, teachers, related services personnel, behavioral specialists, and other **school staff in positive behavioral interventions** and supports, **behavioral intervention planning**, and **classroom and student management techniques**;

---

340 **Wrightslaw Overview:** This lengthy Section 1465 focuses on the use of effective, research-based practices to improve the quality of behavioral supports and interim alternative educational settings. Strategies include better training in behavioral supports and interventions, using research-based interventions, curriculum, ensuring that services are consistent with the IEP goals, and providing behavior specialists.

(C) **joint training** for administrators, parents, teachers, related services personnel, behavioral specialists, and other school staff on effective strategies for positive behavioral interventions and behavior management strategies that focus on the **prevention of behavior problems**;

(D) developing or implementing specific curricula, programs, or interventions aimed at addressing behavioral problems;

(E) stronger linkages between school-based services and community-based resources, such as community mental health and primary care providers; or

(F) using behavioral specialists, related services personnel, and other staff necessary to implement behavioral supports; or

(2) **improve interim alternative educational settings** by -

(A) improving the training of administrators, teachers, related services personnel, behavioral specialists, and other school staff (including ongoing mentoring of new teachers) in behavioral supports and interventions;

(B) attracting and retaining a high quality, diverse staff;

(C) providing for referral to counseling services;

(D) utilizing research-based interventions, curriculum, and practices;

(E) allowing students to use instructional technology that provides individualized instruction;

(F) ensuring that the services are fully consistent with the goals of the individual student's IEP;

(G) promoting effective case management and collaboration among parents, teachers, physicians, related services personnel, behavioral specialists, principals, administrators, and other school staff;

(H) promoting interagency coordination and coordinated service delivery among schools, juvenile courts, child welfare agencies, community mental health providers, primary care providers, public recreation agencies, and community-based organizations; or

(I) providing for behavioral specialists to help students transitioning from interim alternative educational settings reintegrate into their regular classrooms.

(c) Definition of Eligible Entity.

In this section, the term '**eligible entity**' means -

(1) a local educational agency; or

(2) a consortium consisting of a local educational agency and 1 or more of the following entities:

(A) Another local educational agency.

(B) A **community-based organization** with a demonstrated record of effectiveness in helping children with disabilities who have behavioral challenges succeed.

(C) An institution of higher education.

(D) A **community mental health provider**.

(E) An educational service agency.

(d) Applications.

Any eligible entity that wishes to receive a grant, or enter into a contract or cooperative agreement, under this section shall -

(1) submit an application to the Secretary at such time, in such manner, and containing such information as the Secretary may require; and

(2) **involve parents of participating students** in the design and implementation of the activities funded under this section.

(e) Report and Evaluation.

Each eligible entity receiving a grant under this section shall prepare and submit annually to the Secretary a report on the outcomes of the activities assisted under the grant.

20 U.S.C. § 1466. Authorization of Appropriations.

(a) In General.

There are authorized to be appropriated to carry out this subpart (other than Section 1462) such sums as may be necessary for each of the fiscal years 2005 through 2010.

(b) Reservation.

From amounts appropriated under subsection (a) for fiscal year 2005, the Secretary shall reserve $1,000,000 to carry out the study authorized in Section 1464(c). From amounts appropriated under subsection (a) for a succeeding fiscal year, the Secretary may reserve an additional amount to carry out such study if the Secretary determines the additional amount is necessary.

Part C (of Part D) — Supports To Improve Results for Children with Disabilities[341]

20 U.S.C. § 1470. Purposes.

The **purposes** of this subpart are to ensure that -

(1) children with disabilities and their **parents receive training and information** designed to assist the children in meeting **developmental and functional goals** and challenging **academic achievement goals**, and in preparing to **lead productive independent adult lives**;

(2) children with disabilities and their parents receive **training and information on their rights, responsibilities, and protections** under this title, in order to **develop the skills necessary to cooperatively and effectively participate in planning and decision making** relating to early intervention, educational, and transitional services;

(3) parents, teachers, administrators, early intervention personnel, related services personnel, and transition personnel receive coordinated and accessible technical assistance and information to assist such personnel in **improving early intervention, educational, and transitional services and results** for children with disabilities and their families; and

(4) appropriate technology and media are researched, developed, and demonstrated, to improve and implement early intervention, educational, and transitional services and results for children with disabilities and their families.

20 U.S.C. § 1471. Parent Training and Information Centers.[342]

(a) Program Authorized.

(1) In General. The Secretary may award grants to, and enter into contracts and cooperative agreements with, parent organizations to support **parent training and information centers** to carry out activities under this section.

(2) Definition of Parent Organization. In this section, the term **'parent organization' means a private nonprofit organization** (other than an institution of higher education) that -

    (A) has a board of directors -

        (i) the majority of whom are parents of children with disabilities ages birth through 26;

        (ii) that includes -

            (I) individuals working in the fields of special education, related services, and early intervention; and

            (II) individuals with disabilities; and

---

341 **Wrightslaw Overview:** Part C focuses on the need to ensure that children with disabilities and their parents receive information and training. Section 1471 describes Parent Training and Information Centers; Section 1472 describes Community Parent Resource Centers. Section 1474 describes educational media services and the National Instructional Materials Access Center.

342 **Wrightslaw Overview:** The Department of Education shall award grants to at least one parent organization in each state for a parent training and information center. Parent Training and Information Centers help parents learn about their children's disabilities, educational needs, how to communicate effectively with school personnel, how to participate in education decision-making and about their rights and how to use their rights.

(iii) the parent and professional members of which are broadly representative of the population to be served, including low-income parents and parents of limited English proficient children; and

(B) has as its mission serving families of children with disabilities who -

(i) are ages birth through 26; and

(ii) have the full range of disabilities described in Section 1402(3).

(b) Required Activities.

Each **parent training and information center** that receives assistance under this section **shall** -

(1) **provide training and information that meets the needs of parents** of children with disabilities living in the area served by the center, particularly underserved parents and parents of children who may be inappropriately identified, to enable their children with disabilities to -

(A) meet developmental and functional goals, and challenging academic achievement goals that have been established for all children; and

(B) be prepared to lead productive independent adult lives, to the maximum extent possible;

(2) serve the parents of infants, toddlers, and children with the full range of disabilities described in Section 1402(3);

(3) ensure that the training and information provided meets the needs of low-income parents and parents of limited English proficient children;

(4) assist parents to -

(A) better understand the nature of their children's disabilities and their educational, developmental, and transitional needs;

(B) communicate effectively and work collaboratively with personnel responsible for providing special education, early intervention services, transition services, and related services;

(C) participate in decision-making processes and the development of individualized education programs under part B and individualized family service plans under part C;

(D) obtain appropriate information about the range, type, and quality of -

(i) options, programs, services, technologies, practices and interventions based on scientifically based research, to the extent practicable; and

(ii) resources available to assist children with disabilities and their families in school and at home;

(E) understand the provisions of this title for the education of, and the provision of early intervention services to, children with disabilities;

(F) participate in activities at the school level that benefit their children; and

(G) participate in school reform activities;

(5) in States where the State elects to contract with the parent training and information center, contract with State educational agencies to provide, consistent with subparagraphs (B) and (D) of Section 1415(e)(2), individuals who meet with parents to explain the mediation process to the parents;

(6) assist parents in resolving disputes in the most expeditious and effective way possible, including encouraging the use, and explaining the benefits, of alternative methods of dispute resolution, such as the mediation process described in Section 1415(e);

(7) assist parents and students with disabilities to **understand their rights and responsibilities** under this title, including those under Section 1415(m) upon the student's reaching the age of majority (as appropriate under State law);

(8) assist parents to understand the availability of, and how to effectively use, procedural safeguards under this title, including the resolution session described in Section 1415(e);

(9) assist parents in understanding, preparing for, and participating in, the process described in Section 1415(f)(1)(B);

(10) establish cooperative partnerships with community parent resource centers funded under Section 1472;

(11) network with appropriate clearinghouses, including organizations conducting national dissemination activities under Section 1463 and the Institute of Education Sciences, and with other national, State, and local organizations and agencies, such as protection and advocacy agencies, that serve parents and families of children with the full range of disabilities described in Section 1402(3); and

(12) annually report to the Secretary on -

(A) the number and demographics of parents to whom the center provided information and training in the most recently concluded fiscal year;

(B) the effectiveness of strategies used to reach and serve parents, including underserved parents of children with disabilities; and

(C) the number of parents served who have resolved disputes through alternative methods of dispute resolution.

(c) Optional Activities.

A parent training and information center that receives assistance under this section may provide information to teachers and other professionals to assist the teachers and professionals in improving results for children with disabilities.

(d) Application Requirements.

Each application for assistance under this section shall identify with specificity the special efforts that the parent organization will undertake -

(1) to ensure that the needs for training and information of underserved parents of children with disabilities in the area to be served are effectively met; and

(2) to work with community based organizations, including community based organizations that work with low-income parents and parents of limited English proficient children.

(e) Distribution of Funds.

(1) In General. The Secretary shall -

(A) make not less than 1 award to a parent organization in each State for a parent training and information center that is designated as the statewide parent training and information center; or

(B) in the case of a large State, make awards to multiple parent training and information centers, but only if the centers demonstrate that coordinated services and supports will occur among the multiple centers.

(2) Selection Requirement. The Secretary shall select among applications submitted by parent organizations in a State in a manner that ensures the most effective assistance to parents, including parents in urban and rural areas, in the State.

(f) Quarterly Review.

(1) Meetings. The board of directors of each parent organization that receives an award under this section shall meet not less than once in each calendar quarter to review the activities for which the award was made.

(2) Continuation Award. When a parent organization requests a continuation award under this section, the board of directors shall submit to the Secretary a written review of the parent training and information program conducted by the parent organization during the preceding fiscal year.

20 U.S.C. § 1472. Community Parent Resource Centers.[343]

(a) Program Authorized.

(1) In General. The Secretary may award grants to, and enter into contracts and cooperative agreements with, local parent organizations to support **community parent resource centers** that will help ensure that

---

343   **Wrightslaw Overview**: The Department of Education may award grants to parent organizations that do not meet the criteria for a Parent Training and Information Center but focus on helping under-served parents. For example, centers may focus on helping low-income parents, parents of children with limited English proficiency, and parents of children with disabilities.

underserved parents of children with disabilities, including low income parents, parents of limited English proficient children, and parents with disabilities, have the training and information the parents need to enable the parents to participate effectively in helping their children with disabilities -

(A) to meet developmental and functional goals, and challenging academic achievement goals that have been established for all children; and

(B) to be prepared to lead productive independent adult lives, to the maximum extent possible.

(2) Definition of Local Parent Organization. In this section, the term 'local parent organization' means a parent organization, as defined in Section 1471(a)(2), that -

(A) has a board of directors the majority of whom are parents of children with disabilities ages birth through 26 from the community to be served; and

(B) has as its mission serving parents of children with disabilities who -

(i) are ages birth through 26; and

(ii) have the full range of disabilities described in Section 1402(3).

(b) Required Activities.

Each **community parent resource center** assisted under this section **shall** -

(1) **provide training and information that meets the training and information needs of parents** of children with disabilities proposed to be served by the grant, contract, or cooperative agreement;

(2) carry out the activities required of parent training and information centers under paragraphs (2) through (9) of Section 1471(b);

(3) establish cooperative partnerships with the parent training and information centers funded under Section 1471; and

(4) be designed to meet the specific needs of families who experience significant isolation from available sources of information and support.

20 U.S.C. § 1473. Technical Assistance for Parent Training and Information Centers.[344]

(a) Program Authorized.

(1) In General. The Secretary may, directly or through awards to eligible entities, provide technical assistance for developing, assisting, and coordinating parent training and information programs carried out by parent training and information centers receiving assistance under Section 1471 and community parent resource centers receiving assistance under Section 1472.

(2) Definition of Eligible Entity. In this section, the term 'eligible entity' has the meaning given the term in Section 1461(b).

(b) Authorized Activities.

The Secretary may provide technical assistance to a parent training and information center or a community parent resource center under this section in areas such as -

(1) effective coordination of parent training efforts;

(2) dissemination of scientifically based research and information;

(3) promotion of the use of technology, including assistive technology devices and assistive technology services;

(4) reaching underserved populations, including parents of low-income and limited English proficient children with disabilities;

(5) including children with disabilities in general education programs;

(6) facilitation of transitions from -

(A) early intervention services to preschool;

---

344 **Wrightslaw Overview**: The Department of Education may provide technical assistance to Parent Training and Information Centers and Community Parent Resource Centers.

(B) preschool to elementary school;

(C) elementary school to secondary school; and

(D) secondary school to postsecondary environments; and

(7) promotion of alternative methods of dispute resolution, including mediation.

(c) Collaboration with Resource Centers.

Each eligible entity receiving an award under subsection (a) **shall develop collaborative agreements** with the geographically appropriate regional resource center and, as appropriate, the regional educational laboratory supported under Section 174 of the Education Sciences Reform Act of 2002, to further parent and professional collaboration.

20 U.S.C. § 1474. Technology Development, Demonstration and Utilization; Media Services; and Instructional Materials.[345]

(a) Program Authorized.

(1) In General. The Secretary, on a competitive basis, shall award grants to, and enter into contracts and cooperative agreements with, eligible entities to support activities described in subsections (b) and (c).

(2) Definition of Eligible Entity. In this section, the term 'eligible entity' has the meaning given the term in Section 1461(b).

(b) Technology Development, Demonstration, and Use.

(1) In General. In carrying out this section, the Secretary shall support activities to promote the development, demonstration, and use of technology.

(2) Authorized Activities. The following activities may be carried out under this subsection:

(A) Conducting research on and promoting the demonstration and use of innovative, emerging, and universally designed technologies for children with disabilities, by improving the transfer of technology from research and development to practice.

(B) Supporting research, development, and dissemination of technology with universal design features, so that the technology is accessible to the broadest range of individuals with disabilities without further modification or adaptation.

(C) Demonstrating the use of systems to provide parents and teachers with information and training concerning **early diagnosis of, intervention for, and effective teaching strategies for, young children with reading disabilities**.

(D) Supporting the use of **Internet-based communications** for students with cognitive disabilities in order to **maximize their academic and functional skills**.

(c) Educational Media Services.

(1) In General. In carrying out this section, the Secretary shall support -

(A) **educational media activities** that are designed to be of educational value in the classroom setting to children with disabilities;

(B) providing video description, open captioning, or closed captioning, that is appropriate for use in the classroom setting, of -

(i) television programs;

(ii) videos;

(iii) other materials, including programs and materials associated with new and emerging technologies, such as CDs, DVDs, video streaming, and other forms of multimedia; or

(iv) news (but only until September 30, 2006);

---

345 **Wrightslaw Overview**: Federal grants are available to promote the development of technology and educational media services. Section 1474(e) authorizes the National Instructional Materials Access Center that provides instructional materials to individuals who are blind or who have print disabilities.

(C) distributing materials described in subparagraphs (A) and (B) through such mechanisms as a loan service; and

(D) providing free educational materials, including textbooks, in accessible media for visually impaired and print disabled students in elementary schools and secondary schools, postsecondary schools, and graduate schools.

(2) Limitation. The video description, open captioning, or closed captioning described in paragraph (1)(B) shall be provided only when the description or captioning has not been previously provided by the producer or distributor, or has not been fully funded by other sources.

(d) Applications.

(1) In General. Any eligible entity that wishes to receive a grant, or enter into a contract or cooperative agreement, under subsection (b) or (c) shall submit an application to the Secretary at such time, in such manner, and containing such information as the Secretary may require.

(2) Special Rule. For the purpose of an application for an award to carry out activities described in subsection (c)(1)(D), such eligible entity shall -

(A) be a national, nonprofit entity with a proven track record of meeting the needs of students with print disabilities through services described in subsection (c)(1)(D);

(B) have the capacity to produce, maintain, and distribute in a timely fashion, up-to-date textbooks in digital audio formats to qualified students; and

(C) have a demonstrated ability to significantly leverage Federal funds through other public and private contributions, as well as through the expansive use of volunteers.

(e) National Instructional Materials Access Center.

(1) In General. The Secretary shall establish and support, through the American Printing House for the Blind, a center to be known as the **National Instructional Materials Access Center** not later than 1 year after the date of enactment of the Individuals with Disabilities Education Improvement Act of 2004.

(2) Duties. The **duties of the National Instructional Materials Access Center** are the following:

(A) To receive and **maintain a catalog of print instructional materials** prepared in the National Instructional Materials Accessibility Standard, as established by the Secretary, made available to such center by the textbook publishing industry, State educational agencies, and local educational agencies.

(B) To provide **access to print instructional materials**, including textbooks, in accessible media, free of charge, **to blind or other persons with print disabilities in elementary schools and secondary schools**, in accordance with such terms and procedures as the National Instructional Materials Access Center may prescribe.

(C) To develop, adopt and publish procedures to protect against copyright infringement, with respect to the print instructional materials provided under Sections 1412(a)(23) and 1413(a)(6).

(3) Definitions. In this subsection:

(A) **Blind or Other Persons with Print Disabilities**. The term 'blind or other persons with print disabilities' means children served under this Act and who may qualify in accordance with the Act entitled 'An Act to provide books for the adult blind', approved March 3, 1931 (2 U.S.C. 135a; 46 Stat. 1487) to receive books and other publications produced in specialized formats.

(B) **National Instructional Materials Accessibility Standard**. The term 'National Instructional Materials Accessibility Standard' means the standard established by the Secretary to be used in the preparation of electronic files suitable and used solely for efficient conversion into specialized formats.[346]

---

346   The National Instructional Materials Accessibility Standard (NIMAS) provides a system to produce and distribute digital versions of textbooks and other instructional materials that can be converted to accessible formats. The American Printing House for the Blind is the coordinating agency and the Center for Applied Special Technology (CAST) is providing technical support. *See also* 20 U.S.C. § 1412(a)(23) Websites: https://aem.cast.org/nimas-nimac/nimas-nimac   and   https://www.cast.org/

(C) **Print Instructional Materials**. The term '**print instructional materials**' means printed textbooks and related printed core materials that are written and published primarily for use in elementary school and secondary school instruction and are required by a State educational agency or local educational agency for use by students in the classroom.

(D) **Specialized Formats**. The term '**specialized formats**' has the meaning given the term in Section 121(d)(3) of Title 17, United States Code.

(4) **Applicability**. This subsection shall apply to print instructional materials published after the date on which the final rule establishing the National Instructional Materials Accessibility Standard was published in the Federal Register.

(5) **Liability of the Secretary**. Nothing in this subsection shall be construed to establish a private right of action against the Secretary for failure to provide instructional materials directly, or for failure by the National Instructional Materials Access Center to perform the duties of such center, or to otherwise authorize a private right of action related to the performance by such center, including through the application of the rights of children and parents established under this Act.

(6) **Inapplicability**. Subsections (a) through (d) shall not apply to this subsection.

20 U.S.C. § 1475. Authorization of Appropriations.

There are authorized to be appropriated to carry out this subpart such sums as may be necessary for each of the fiscal years 2005 through 2010.

Part D (of Part D) — General Provisions

20 U.S.C. § 1481. Comprehensive Plan for Parts B and C.

(a) Comprehensive Plan.

(1) **In General**. After receiving input from interested individuals with relevant expertise, the Secretary shall develop and implement a comprehensive plan for activities carried out under Subparts 2 and 3 in order to enhance the provision of early intervention services, educational services, related services, and transitional services to children with disabilities under Parts B and C. To the extent practicable, the plan shall be coordinated with the plan developed pursuant to Section 178(c) of the Education Sciences Reform Act of 2002 and shall include mechanisms to address early intervention, educational, related service and transitional needs identified by State educational agencies in applications submitted for State personnel development grants under Subpart 1 and for grants under parts B and C

(2) **Public Comment**. The Secretary shall provide a public comment period of not less than 45 days on the plan.

(3) **Distribution of Funds**. In implementing the plan, the Secretary shall, to the extent appropriate, ensure that funds awarded under subparts 2 and 3 are used to carry out activities that benefit, directly or indirectly, children with the full range of disabilities and of all ages.

(4) **Reports to Congress**. The Secretary shall annually report to Congress on the Secretary's activities under Subparts 2 and 3, including an initial report not later than 12 months after the date of enactment of the Individuals with Disabilities Education Improvement Act of 2004.

(b) Assistance Authorized.

The Secretary is authorized to award grants to, or enter into contracts or cooperative agreements with, eligible entities to enable the eligible entities to carry out the purposes of such subparts in accordance with the comprehensive plan described in subsection (a).

(c) Special Populations.

(1) **Application Requirement**. In making an award of a grant, contract, or cooperative agreement under Subpart 2 or 3, the Secretary shall, as appropriate, require an eligible entity to demonstrate how the eligible entity will address the needs of children with disabilities from minority backgrounds.

(2) Required Outreach and Technical Assistance. Notwithstanding any other provision of this title, the Secretary shall reserve not less than 2 percent of the total amount of funds appropriated to carry out Subparts 2 and 3 for either or both of the following activities:

(A) Providing outreach and technical assistance to historically Black colleges and universities, and to institutions of higher education with minority enrollments of not less than 25 percent, to promote the participation of such colleges, universities, and institutions in activities under this Subpart.

(B) Enabling historically Black colleges and universities, and the institutions described in subparagraph (A), to assist other colleges, universities, institutions, and agencies in improving educational and transitional results for children with disabilities, if the historically Black colleges and universities and the institutions of higher education described in subparagraph (A) meet the criteria established by the Secretary under this subpart.

(d) Priorities.

The Secretary, in making an award of a grant, contract, or cooperative agreement under Subpart 2 or 3, may, without regard to the rulemaking procedures under Section 553 of Title 5, United States Code, limit competitions to, or otherwise **give priority to** -

(1) projects that address 1 or more -

(A) age ranges;

(B) disabilities;

(C) school grades;

(D) types of educational placements or early intervention environments;

(E) types of services;

(F) content areas, such as reading; or

(G) effective strategies for helping children with disabilities learn appropriate behavior in the school and other community based educational settings;

(2) projects that address the needs of children based on the **severity or incidence of their disability;**

(3) projects that address the needs of -

(A) low achieving students;

(B) underserved populations;

(C) children from low income families;

(D) limited English proficient children;

(E) unserved and underserved areas;

(F) rural or urban areas;

(G) children whose behavior interferes with their learning and socialization;

(H) children with reading difficulties;

(I) children in public charter schools;

(J) children who are gifted and talented; or

(K) children with disabilities served by local educational agencies that receive payments under Title VII of the Elementary and Secondary Education Act of 1965;

(4) projects to reduce inappropriate identification of children as children with disabilities, particularly among minority children;

(5) projects that are carried out in particular areas of the country, to ensure broad geographic coverage;

(6) projects that promote the development and use of technologies with universal design, assistive technology devices, and assistive technology services to maximize children with disabilities' access to and participation in the general education curriculum; and

(7) any activity that is authorized in Subpart 2 or 3.

(e) Eligibility for Financial Assistance.

No State or local educational agency, or other public institution or agency, may receive a grant or enter into a contract or cooperative agreement under Subpart 2 or 3 that relates exclusively to programs, projects, and activities pertaining to children aged 3 through 5, inclusive, unless the State is eligible to receive a grant under Section 1419(b).

20 U.S.C. § 1482. Administrative Provisions.

(a) Applicant and Recipient Responsibilities.

(1) Development and Assessment of Projects. The Secretary shall require that an applicant for, and a recipient of, a grant, contract, or cooperative agreement for a project under Subpart 2 or 3 -

(A) involve individuals with disabilities or parents of individuals with disabilities ages birth through 26 in planning, implementing, and evaluating the project; and

(B) where appropriate, determine whether the project has any potential for replication and adoption by other entities.

(2) Additional Responsibilities. The Secretary may require a recipient of a grant, contract, or cooperative agreement under Subpart 2 or 3 to -

(A) share in the cost of the project;

(B) prepare any findings and products from the project in formats that are useful for specific audiences, including parents, administrators, teachers, early intervention personnel, related services personnel, and individuals with disabilities;

(C) disseminate such findings and products; and

(D) collaborate with other such recipients in carrying out subparagraphs (B) and (C).

(b) Application Management.

(1) Standing Panel.

(A) **In General**. The Secretary shall establish and use a **standing panel of experts** who are qualified, by virtue of their training, expertise, or experience, to evaluate each application under Subpart 2 or 3 that requests more than $75,000 per year in Federal financial assistance.

(B) **Membership**. The standing panel shall include, at a minimum -

(i) individuals who are representatives of institutions of higher education that plan, develop, and carry out high quality programs of personnel preparation;

(ii) individuals who design and carry out scientifically based research targeted to the improvement of special education programs and services;

(iii) individuals who have recognized experience and knowledge necessary to integrate and apply scientifically based research findings to improve educational and transitional results for children with disabilities;

(iv) individuals who administer programs at the State or local level in which children with disabilities participate;

(v) individuals who prepare parents of children with disabilities to participate in making decisions about the education of their children;

(vi) individuals who establish policies that affect the delivery of services to children with disabilities;

(vii) individuals who are parents of children with disabilities ages birth through 26 who are benefiting, or have benefited, from coordinated research, personnel preparation, and technical assistance; and

(viii) individuals with disabilities.

(C) **Term**. No individual shall serve on the standing panel for more than 3 consecutive years.

(2) Peer-Review Panels for Particular Competitions.

(A) **Composition**. The Secretary shall ensure that **each subpanel selected** from the standing panel that reviews an application under Subpart 2 or 3 includes -

(i) individuals with knowledge and expertise on the issues addressed by the activities described in the application; and

(ii) to the extent practicable, parents of children with disabilities ages birth through 26, individuals with disabilities, and persons from diverse backgrounds.

(B) Federal Employment Limitation. A majority of the individuals on each subpanel that reviews an application under Subpart 2 or 3 shall be individuals who are not employees of the Federal Government.

(3) Use of Discretionary Funds for Administrative Purposes.

(A) Expenses and Fees of Non-Federal Panel Members. The Secretary may use funds available under subpart 2 or 3 to pay the expenses and fees of the panel members who are not officers or employees of the Federal Government.

(B) Administrative Support. The Secretary may use not more than 1 percent of the funds appropriated to carry out Subpart 2 or 3 to pay non-Federal entities for administrative support related to management of applications submitted under Subpart 2 or 3, respectively.

(c) Program Evaluation.

The Secretary may use funds made available to carry out Subpart 2 or 3 to evaluate activities carried out under Subpart 2 or 3, respectively.

(d) Minimum Funding Required.

(1) In General. Subject to paragraph (2), the Secretary shall ensure that, for each fiscal year, not less than the following amounts are provided under subparts 2 and 3 to address the following needs:

(A) $12,832,000 to address the educational, related services, transitional, and early intervention needs of children with deaf-blindness.

(B) $4,000,000 to address the postsecondary, vocational, technical, continuing, and adult education needs of individuals with deafness.

(C) $4,000,000 to address the educational, related services, and transitional needs of children with an emotional disturbance and those who are at risk of developing an emotional disturbance.

(2) Ratable Reduction. If the sum of the amount appropriated to carry out Subparts 2 and 3, and Part E of the Education Sciences Reform Act of 2002 for any fiscal year is less than $130,000,000, the amounts listed in paragraph (1) shall be ratably reduced for the fiscal year.

End of IDEA, Part D

In Summation

Chapter 5 includes the full text of IDEA 2004 beginning with Title 20 at Section 1400 (20 U.S.C. § 1400) with comments and footnotes.

Chapter 6, next, includes the complete IDEA regulations in the Code of Federal Regulations, beginning at Title 34, Part 300, the first regulation being 34 CFR § 300.1.

End of Chapter 5 - IDEA statute

Hyperlinks to Chapters

Ch. 01 Introduction	Ch. 06 IDEA Regulations	
Ch. 02 History	Ch. 07 Section 504	
Ch. 03 Overview of Law, Courts, Research	Ch. 08 ADA	
Ch. 04 Overview of IDEA, Section 504, ADA	Ch. 09 Other laws	
Ch. 05 IDEA (US Code)	Ch. 10 Selected Topics	

CHAPTER 6

IDEA 2004 Regulations
34 CFR Part 300

Wrightslaw Overview: After IDEA 2004 was enacted, the USDOE issued regulations to implement the statute. These regulations are published in Title 34 of the Code of Federal Regulations (CFR). At the end of each regulation is the legal authority for the regulation, i.e., the citation in the U.S. Code. Regulations have the "force of law."[1]

Chapter 6 includes the IDEA regulations as published in Part 300 of the Code of Federal Regulations, beginning at 34 CFR § 300.1 and continuing to 311.818. The Early Intervention regulations in Part 303 would have added another 100 pages to this book and are not included.[2] The regulations also include Appendices A through F, also not included.[3]

A Table of the Part 300 Regulations begins on the next page. Per the information provided in Chapter 1, regulations marked with arrows to the <left and to the right> are embedded hyperlinks that allow you to go directly to that regulation.

We recommend that you obtain your own state's regulations from your state, print out critical portions such as the evaluations, eligibility, and IEPs and cross-reference, in this book, the statute with the federal regulation and with your state's regulation. For any legal issue, always start with the federal statute, i.e., IDEA in the United States Code, then read the federal regulation, then your own state's statute on an issue, followed by your state's regulation. Pursuant to the <Supremacy Clause> in Chapter 9 of this book, the federal law is always supreme, thus that is the reason to start with the federal law. Once you have reviewed the statutes and regulations, you may want to <continue your legal research and search caselaw> on an issue.

---

1 The Congressional Research Service explains that "By delegating authority to administrative agencies to write and enforce regulations that have the **force and effect of law,** Congress provides federal agencies with considerable power." https://sgp.fas.org/crs/misc/IF10003.pdf

2 The Early Interventions regulations are available at: https://www.law.cornell.edu/cfr/text/34/part-303

3 https://www.law.cornell.edu/cfr/text/34/appendix-A_to_part_300

Table of Regulations

---

4 **Wrightslaw Note:** Per the information provided in Chapter 1, we have **embedded hyperlinks** so that those who have the **E-book (adobe.pdf) edition** of this book, can click on the link and go directly to that webpage or to a specific location in this book. They are marked with **arrows**, at the beginning and end of the link. The arrows point to the <left and to the right>, as in this example.

Acquisition of Equipment and Construction or Alteration of Facilities

34 CFR § 300.718 Acquisition of equipment and construction or alteration of facilities.

Subpart H - Preschool Grants for Children With Disabilities

Appendices[5]

---

5   Not included, but available at: https://www.law.cornell.edu/cfr/text/34/part-300

Assistance to States for the Education of Children with Disabilities 34 CFR Part 300

Subpart A—General
Purposes and Applicability

34 CFR § 300.1 Purposes. The purposes of this part are—

(a) To ensure that all children with disabilities have available to them a free appropriate public education that emphasizes special education and related services designed to meet their unique needs and prepare them for further education, employment, and independent living;

(b) To ensure that the rights of children with disabilities and their parents are protected;

(c) To assist States, localities, educational service agencies, and Federal agencies to provide for the education of all children with disabilities; and

(d) To assess and ensure the effectiveness of efforts to educate children with disabilities. (Authority: 20 U.S.C. 1400(d))

34 CFR § 300.2 Applicability of this part to State and local agencies.

(a) States. This part applies to each State that receives payments under Part B of the Act, as defined in 34 CFR § 300.4.

(b) Public agencies within the State. The provisions of this part—

(1) Apply to all political subdivisions of the State that are involved in the education of children with disabilities, including:

(i) The State educational agency (SEA).

(ii) Local educational agencies (LEAs), educational service agencies (ESAs), and public charter schools that are not otherwise included as LEAs or ESAs and are not a school of an LEA or ESA.

(iii) Other State agencies and schools (such as Departments of Mental Health and Welfare and State schools for children with deafness or children with blindness).

(iv) State and local juvenile and adult correctional facilities; and

(2) Are binding on each public agency in the State that provides special education and related services to children with disabilities, regardless of whether that agency is receiving funds under Part B of the Act.

(c) Private schools and facilities. Each public agency in the State is responsible for ensuring that the rights and protections under Part B of the Act are given to children with disabilities—

(1) Referred to or placed in private schools and facilities by that public agency; or

(2) Placed in private schools by their parents under the provisions of 34 CFR § 300.148. (Authority: 20 U.S.C. 1412)

Definitions Used in This Part

34 CFR § 300.4 Act.

Act means the **Individuals with Disabilities Education Act,** as amended. (Authority: 20 U.S.C. 1400(a))

34 CFR § 300.5 Assistive technology device.

Assistive technology device means any item, piece of equipment, or product system, whether acquired commercially off the shelf, modified, or customized, that is used to increase, maintain, or improve the functional capabilities of a child with a disability. The term does not include a medical device that is surgically implanted, or the replacement of such device. (Authority: 20 U.S.C. 1401(1))

34 CFR § 300.6 Assistive technology service.

Assistive technology service means any service that directly assists a child with a disability in the selection, acquisition, or use of an assistive technology device. The **term includes—**

(a) The evaluation of the needs of a child with a disability, including a functional evaluation of the child in the child's customary environment;

(b) Purchasing, leasing, or otherwise providing for the acquisition of assistive technology devices by children with disabilities;

(c) Selecting, designing, fitting, customizing, adapting, applying, maintaining, repairing, or replacing assistive technology devices;

(d) Coordinating and using other therapies, interventions, or services with assistive technology devices, such as those associated with existing education and rehabilitation plans and programs;

(e) Training or technical assistance for a child with a disability or, if appropriate, that child's family; and

(f) Training or technical assistance for professionals (including individuals providing education or rehabilitation services), employers, or other individuals who provide services to, employ, or are otherwise substantially involved in the major life functions of that child. (Authority: 20 U.S.C. 1401(2))

34 CFR § 300.7 Charter school.

Charter school has the meaning given the term in section 5210(1) of the Elementary and Secondary Education Act of 1965, as amended, 20 U.S.C. 6301 *et seq.* (ESEA). (Authority: 20 U.S.C. 7221i(1))

34 CFR § 300.8 Child with a disability.

(a) General.

(1) Child with a disability means a child evaluated in accordance with 34 CFR § 300.304 through 300.311 as having an intellectual disability, a hearing impairment (including deafness), a speech or language impairment, a visual impairment (including blindness), a serious emotional disturbance (referred to in this part as "emotional disturbance"), an orthopedic impairment, autism, traumatic brain injury, an other health impairment, a specific learning disability, deaf-blindness, or multiple disabilities, and **who, by reason thereof**, needs special education and related services.

(2)

(i) Subject to paragraph (a)(2)(ii) of this section, if it is determined, through an appropriate evaluation under 34 CFR § 300.304 through 300.311, that a child has one of the disabilities identified in paragraph (a)(1) of this section, **but only needs a related service and not special education, the child is not a child with a disability under this part**.

(ii) If, consistent with 34 CFR § 300.39(a)(2), the related service required by the child is considered special education rather than a related service under **State standards**, the child would be determined to be a child with a disability under paragraph (a)(1) of this section.

(b) Children aged three through nine experiencing developmental delays. Child with a disability for children aged three through nine (or any subset of that age range, including ages three through five), may, subject to the conditions described in 34 CFR § 300.111(b), include a child—

(1) Who is experiencing developmental delays, as defined by the State and as measured by appropriate diagnostic instruments and procedures, in one or more of the following areas: physical development, cognitive development, communication development, social or emotional development, or adaptive development; and

(2) Who, by reason thereof, needs special education and related services.

(c) Definitions of disability terms. The terms used in this definition of a child with a disability are defined as follows:

(1)

(i) Autism means a developmental disability significantly affecting verbal and nonverbal communication and social interaction, generally evident before age three, that adversely affects a child's educational performance. Other characteristics often associated with autism are engagement in repetitive activities and stereotyped movements, resistance to environmental change or change in daily routines, and unusual responses to sensory experiences.

(ii) Autism **does not apply** if a child's educational performance is adversely affected primarily because the child has an emotional disturbance, as defined in paragraph (c)(4) of this section.

(iii) A child who manifests the characteristics of autism after age three could be identified as having autism if the criteria in paragraph (c)(1)(i) of this section are satisfied.

(2) Deaf-blindness means concomitant hearing and visual impairments, the combination of which causes such severe communication and other developmental and educational needs that they cannot be accommodated in special education programs solely for children with deafness or children with blindness.

(3) Deafness means a hearing impairment that is so severe that the child is impaired in processing linguistic information through hearing, with or without amplification, that adversely affects a child's educational performance.

(4)

(i) Emotional disturbance means a condition exhibiting one or more of the following characteristics over a long period of time and to a marked degree that **adversely affects a child's educational performance**:

   (A) An inability to learn that cannot be explained by intellectual, sensory, or health factors.

   (B) An inability to build or maintain satisfactory interpersonal relationships with peers and teachers.

   (C) Inappropriate types of behavior or feelings under normal circumstances.

   (D) A general pervasive mood of unhappiness or depression.

   (E) A tendency to develop physical symptoms or fears associated with personal or school problems.

(ii) Emotional disturbance includes schizophrenia. The term does not apply to children who are socially maladjusted, unless it is determined that they have an emotional disturbance under paragraph (c)(4)(i) of this section.

(5) Hearing impairment means an impairment in hearing, whether permanent or fluctuating, that adversely affects a child's educational performance but that is not included under the definition of deafness in this section.

(6) Intellectual disability means significantly subaverage general intellectual functioning, existing concurrently with deficits in adaptive behavior and manifested during the developmental period, that adversely affects a child's educational performance. The term "intellectual disability" was formerly termed "mental retardation."

(7) Multiple disabilities means concomitant impairments (such as intellectual disability-blindness or intellectual disability-orthopedic impairment), the combination of which causes such severe educational needs that they cannot be accommodated in special education programs solely for one of the impairments. Multiple disabilities does not include deaf-blindness.

(8) Orthopedic impairment means a severe orthopedic impairment that adversely affects a child's educational performance. The term includes impairments caused by a congenital anomaly, impairments caused by disease (e.g., poliomyelitis, bone tuberculosis), and impairments from other causes (e.g., cerebral palsy, amputations, and fractures or burns that cause contractures).

(9) Other health impairment means having limited strength, vitality, or alertness, including a heightened alertness to environmental stimuli, that results in limited alertness with respect to the educational environment, that—

   (i) Is due to chronic or acute health problems such as **asthma, attention deficit disorder or attention deficit hyperactivity disorder, diabetes, epilepsy, a heart condition, hemophilia, lead poisoning, leukemia, nephritis, rheumatic fever, sickle cell anemia, and Tourette syndrome**; and

   (ii) **Adversely affects a child's educational performance.**

(10) Specific learning disability.

   (i) General. Specific learning disability means a disorder in one or more of the basic psychological processes involved in understanding or in using language, spoken or written, that may manifest itself in the imperfect ability to listen, think, speak, read, write, spell, or to do mathematical calculations, including conditions such as **perceptual disabilities**, brain injury, minimal brain dysfunction, **dyslexia**, and developmental aphasia.

   (ii) Disorders not included. Specific learning disability does not include learning problems that are primarily the result of visual, hearing, or motor disabilities, of intellectual disability, of emotional disturbance, or of environmental, cultural, or economic disadvantage.

(11) Speech or language impairment means a communication disorder, such as stuttering, impaired articulation, a language impairment, or a voice impairment, that **adversely affects** a child's educational performance.

(12) Traumatic brain injury means **an acquired injury** to the brain caused by an external physical force, resulting in total or partial functional disability or psychosocial impairment, or both, that adversely affects a child's educational performance. Traumatic brain injury applies to **open or closed head injuries** resulting in impairments in one or more areas, such as cognition; language; memory; attention; reasoning; abstract thinking; judgment; problem-solving; sensory, perceptual, and motor abilities; psychosocial behavior; physical functions; information processing; and speech. Traumatic brain injury **does not apply** to brain injuries that are congenital or degenerative, or to brain injuries induced by birth trauma.

(13) Visual impairment including blindness means an impairment in vision that, **even with correction**, adversely affects a child's educational performance. The term includes both **partial sight and blindness**. (Authority: <20 U.S.C. 1401(3); 1401(30))>

34 CFR § 300.9 Consent. Consent means that—

(a) The parent has been **fully informed of all information** relevant to the activity for which consent is sought, **in his or her native language**, or through another mode of communication;

(b) The parent **understands and agrees in writing** to the carrying out of the activity for which his or her consent is sought, and the consent describes that activity and lists the records (if any) that will be released and to whom; and

(c)

(1) The parent understands that the granting of consent is voluntary on the part of the parent and may be revoked at any time.

(2) If a parent revokes consent, that revocation is not retroactive (i.e., it does not negate an action that has occurred after the consent was given and before the consent was revoked). (Authority: 20 U.S.C. 1414(a)(1)(D))

34 CFR § 300.10 ~~Core academic subjects~~. [Reserved]

[This regulation was removed after ESSA replaced NCLB in 2015.]

34 CFR § 300.11 Day; business day; school day.

(a) Day means calendar day unless otherwise indicated as business day or school day.

(b) Business day means **Monday through Friday**, except for Federal and State holidays (unless holidays are specifically included in the designation of business day, as in 34 CFR § 300.148(d)(1)(ii)).

(c)

(1) School day means any day, including a partial day that **children are in attendance at school** for instructional purposes.

(2) School day has the same meaning for all children in school, including children with and without disabilities. (Authority: 20 U.S.C. 1221e-3)

34 CFR § 300.12 Educational service agency. Educational service agency means—

(a) A regional public multiservice agency—

(1) Authorized by State law to develop, manage, and provide services or programs to LEAs;

(2) Recognized as an administrative agency for purposes of the provision of special education and related services provided within public elementary schools and secondary schools of the State;

(b) Includes any other public institution or agency having administrative control and direction over a public elementary school or secondary school; and

(c) Includes entities that meet the definition of intermediate educational unit in **section 602(23)** of the Act as in effect prior to June 4, 1997. (Authority: 20 U.S.C. 1401(5))

34 CFR § 300.13 Elementary school.

Elementary school means a nonprofit institutional day or residential school, including a public elementary charter school, that provides elementary education, as determined under State law. (Authority: 20 U.S.C. 1401(6))

34 CFR § 300.14 Equipment. Equipment means —

(a) Machinery, utilities, and built-in equipment, and any necessary enclosures or structures to house the machinery, utilities, or equipment; and

(b) All other items necessary for the functioning of a particular facility as a facility for the provision of educational services, including items such as instructional equipment and necessary furniture; printed, published and audio-visual instructional materials; telecommunications, sensory, and other technological aids and devices; and books, periodicals, documents, and other related materials. (Authority: 20 U.S.C. 1401(7))

34 CFR § 300.15 Evaluation.

Evaluation means procedures used in accordance with 34 CFR § 300.304 through 300.311 to determine whether a child has a disability and the nature and extent of the special education and related services that the child needs. (Authority: 20 U.S.C. 1414(a)-(c))

34 CFR § 300.16 Excess costs.

Excess costs means those costs that are in excess of the average annual per-student expenditure in an LEA during the preceding school year for an elementary school or secondary school student, as may be appropriate, and that must be computed after deducting—

(a) Amounts received—

(1) Under Part B of the Act;

(2) Under Part A of title I of the ESEA; and

(3) Under Parts A and B of title III of the ESEA and;

(b) Any State or local funds expended for programs that would qualify for assistance under any of the parts described in paragraph (a) of this section, but excluding any amounts for capital outlay or debt service. (See Appendix A to part 300 for an example of how excess costs must be calculated.) (Authority: 20 U.S.C. 1401(8))

34 CFR § 300.17 Free appropriate public education.

Free appropriate public education or FAPE **means special education and related services that—**

(a) Are provided at public expense, under public supervision and direction, and without charge;

(b) Meet the standards of the SEA, including the requirements of this part;

(c) Include an appropriate preschool, elementary school, or secondary school education in the State involved; and

(d) Are provided in conformity with an individualized education program (IEP) that meets the requirements of 34 CFR § 300.320 through 300.324. (Authority: 20 U.S.C. 1401(9))

34 CFR § 300.18 Highly qualified special education teachers. [Reserved]

[This regulation was removed after ESSA replaced NCLB in 2015.]

34 CFR § 300.19 Homeless children.

Homeless children has the meaning given the term homeless children and youths in section 725 (42 U.S.C. 11434a) of the McKinney-Vento Homeless Assistance Act, as amended, 42 U.S.C. 11431 *et seq.* (Authority: 20 U.S.C. 1401(11))

34 CFR § 300.20 Include. Include means that the items named are not all of the possible items that are covered, whether like or unlike the ones named. (Authority: 20 U.S.C. 1221e-3)

34 CFR § 300.21 Indian and Indian tribe.

(a) **Indian** means an individual who is a member of an Indian tribe.

(b) **Indian tribe** means any Federal or State Indian tribe, band, rancheria, pueblo, colony, or community, including any Alaska Native village or regional village corporation (as defined in or established under the Alaska Native Claims Settlement Act, 43 U.S.C. 1601 *et seq.*).

(c) Nothing in this definition is intended to indicate that the Secretary of the Interior is required to provide services or funding to a State Indian tribe that is not listed in the *Federal Register* list of Indian entities recognized as eligible to receive services from the United States, published pursuant to Section 104 of the Federally Recognized Indian Tribe List Act of 1994, 25 U.S.C. 479a-1. (Authority: 20 U.S.C. 1401(12) and (13))

34 CFR § 300.22 Individualized education program.

Individualized education program or IEP means a written statement for a child with a disability that is developed, reviewed, and revised in accordance with 34 CFR § 300.320 through 300.324. (Authority: 20 U.S.C. 1401(14))

34 CFR § 300.23 Individualized education program team.

Individualized education program team or IEP Team means a group of individuals described in 34 CFR § 300.321 that is responsible for developing, reviewing, or revising an IEP for a child with a disability. (Authority: 20 U.S.C. 1414(d)(1)(B))

34 CFR § 300.24 Individualized family service plan.

Individualized family service plan or IFSP has the meaning given the term in section 636 of the Act. (Authority: 20 U.S.C. 1401(15))

34 CFR § 300.25 Infant or toddler with a disability. Infant or toddler with a disability—

(a) Means an individual **under three years of age who needs early intervention services** because the individual—

(1) Is experiencing developmental delays, as measured by appropriate diagnostic instruments and procedures in one or more of the areas of cognitive development, physical development, communication development, social or emotional development, and adaptive development; or

(2) Has a diagnosed physical or mental condition that has a high probability of resulting in developmental delay; and

(b) May also include, at a State's discretion—

(1) At-risk infants and toddlers; and

(2) Children with disabilities who are eligible for services under section 619 and who previously received services under

Part C of the Act until such children enter, or are eligible under State law to enter, kindergarten or elementary school, as appropriate, provided that any programs under Part C of the Act serving such children shall include—

(i) An educational component that promotes school readiness and incorporates pre-literacy, language, and numeracy skills; and

(ii) A written notification to parents of their rights and responsibilities in determining whether their child will continue to receive services under Part C of the Act or participate in preschool programs under section 619. (Authority: 20 U.S.C. 1401(16) and 1432(5))

34 CFR § 300.26 Institution of higher education. Institution of higher education—

(a) Has the meaning given the term in section 101 of the Higher Education Act of 1965, as amended, 20 U.S.C. 1021 *et seq.* (HEA); and

(b) Also includes any community college receiving funds from the Secretary of the Interior under the Tribally Controlled Community College or University Assistance Act of 1978, 25 U.S.C. 1801, *et seq.* (Authority: 20 U.S.C. 1401(17))

34 CFR § 300.27 Limited English proficient.

Limited English proficient has the meaning given the term in section 9101(25) of the ESEA. (Authority: 20 U.S.C. 1401(18))

34 CFR § 300.28 Local educational agency.

(a) General. Local educational agency or LEA means a public board of education or other public authority legally constituted within a State for either administrative control or direction of, or to perform a service function for, public elementary or secondary schools in a city, county, township, school district, or other political subdivision of a State, or for a combination of school districts or counties as are recognized in a State as an administrative agency for its public elementary schools or secondary schools.

(b) Educational service agencies and other public institutions or agencies. The term includes—

(1) An educational service agency, as defined in 34 CFR § 300.12; and

(2) Any other public institution or agency having administrative control and direction of a public elementary school or secondary school, including a public nonprofit charter school that is established as an LEA under State law.

(c) BIA funded schools. The term includes an elementary school or secondary school funded by the Bureau of Indian Affairs, and not subject to the jurisdiction of any SEA other than the Bureau of Indian Affairs, but only to the extent that the inclusion makes the school eligible for programs for which specific eligibility is not provided to the school in another provision of law and the school does not have a student population that is smaller than the student population of the LEA receiving assistance under the Act with the smallest student population. (Authority: 20 U.S.C. 1401(19))

34 CFR § 300.29 Native language.

(a) Native language, when used **with respect to an individual who is limited English proficient**, means the following:

(1) **The language normally used by that individual**, or, in the case of a child, the language normally used by the parents of the child, except as provided in paragraph (a)(2) of this section.

(2) In all direct contact with a child (including evaluation of the child), the language normally used by the child in the home or learning environment.

(b) For an individual with deafness or blindness, or for an individual with no written language, **the mode of communication is that normally used** by the individual (such as sign language, Braille, or oral communication). (Authority: 20 U.S.C. 1401(20))

34 CFR § 300.30 Parent.

(a) Parent means—

(1) A **biological or adoptive parent** of a child;

(2) A **foster parent**, unless State law, regulations, or contractual obligations with a State or local entity prohibit a foster parent from acting as a parent;

(3) A **guardian** generally authorized to act as the child's parent, or authorized to make educational decisions for the child (but not the State if the child is a ward of the State);

(4) An individual acting in the place of a biological or adoptive parent (including a **grandparent, stepparent, or other relative**) with whom the child lives, or an individual who is legally responsible for the child's welfare; or

(5) A **surrogate parent** who has been appointed in accordance with 34 CFR § 300.519 or section 639(a)(5) of the Act.

(b)

(1) Except as provided in paragraph (b)(2) of this section, the biological or adoptive parent, when attempting to act as the parent under this part and when more than one party is qualified under paragraph (a) of this section to act as a parent, **must be presumed** to be the parent for purposes of this section **unless the biological or adoptive parent does not have legal authority** to make educational decisions for the child.

(2) If a judicial decree or order identifies a specific person or persons under paragraphs (a)(1) through (4) of this section to act as the "parent" of a child or to make educational decisions on behalf of a child, then such person or persons **shall** be determined to be the "parent" for purposes of this section. (Authority: 20 U.S.C. 1401(23))

34 CFR § 300.31 Parent training and information center.

Parent training and information center means a center assisted under sections 671 or 672 of the Act. (Authority: 20 U.S.C. 1401(25))

34 CFR § 300.32 Personally identifiable.

Personally identifiable means information that contains—

(a) The name of the child, the child's parent, or other family member;

(b) The address of the child;

(c) A personal identifier, such as the child's social security number or student number; or

(d) A list of personal characteristics or other information that would make it possible to identify the child with reasonable certainty. (Authority: 20 U.S.C. 1415(a))

34 CFR § 300.33 Public agency.

Public agency includes the **SEA, LEAs, ESAs, nonprofit public charter schools** that are not otherwise included as LEAs or ESAs and are not a school of an LEA or ESA, and any other political subdivisions of the State that are responsible for providing education to children with disabilities. (Authority: 20 U.S.C. 1412(a)(11))

34 CFR § 300.34 Related services.

(a) General. Related services means **transportation** and such developmental, corrective, and **other supportive services** as are required **to assist a child with a disability to benefit from special education**, and includes **speech-language pathology and audiology services**, interpreting services, psychological services, **physical and occupational therapy**, recreation, including therapeutic recreation, early identification and assessment of disabilities in children, counseling services, including rehabilitation counseling, orientation and mobility services, and medical services for diagnostic or evaluation purposes. Related services also include school health services and school nurse services, social work services in schools, and parent counseling and training.

(b) Exception; services that apply to children with surgically implanted devices, including cochlear implants.

(1) Related services **do not include a medical device that is surgically implanted**, the optimization of that device's functioning (e.g., mapping), maintenance of that device, or the replacement of that device.

(2) **Nothing** in paragraph (b)(1) of this section—

(i) **Limits** the right of a child with a surgically implanted device (e.g., cochlear implant) to receive related services (as listed in paragraph (a) of this section) that are determined by the IEP Team to be necessary for the child to receive FAPE.

(ii) **Limits** the responsibility of a public agency to appropriately monitor and maintain medical devices that are needed to maintain the health and safety of the child, including breathing, nutrition, or operation of other bodily functions, while the child is transported to and from school or is at school; **or**

(iii) **Prevents the routine checking** of an external component of a surgically-implanted device to make sure it is functioning properly, as required in 34 CFR § 300.113(b).

(c) Individual related services terms defined.

The terms used in this definition are defined as follows:

(1) **Audiology** includes—

(i) Identification of children with hearing loss;

(ii) Determination of the range, nature, and degree of hearing loss, including referral for medical or other professional attention for the habilitation of hearing;

(iii) Provision of habilitative activities, such as language habilitation, auditory training, speech reading (lip-reading), hearing evaluation, and speech conservation;

(iv) Creation and administration of programs for prevention of hearing loss;

(v) Counseling and guidance of children, parents, and teachers regarding hearing loss; and

(vi) Determination of children's needs for group and individual amplification, selecting and fitting an appropriate aid, and evaluating the effectiveness of amplification.

(2) **Counseling services** means services provided by qualified social workers, psychologists, guidance counselors, or other qualified personnel.

(3) **Early identification and assessment of disabilities in children** means the implementation of a formal plan for identifying a disability as early as possible in a child's life.

(4) **Interpreting services** includes—

(i) The following, when used with respect to children who are deaf or hard of hearing: Oral transliteration services, cued language transliteration services, sign language transliteration and interpreting services, and transcription services, such as communication access real-time translation (CART), C-Print, and TypeWell; and

(ii) Special interpreting services for children who are deaf-blind.

(5) **Medical services** means services provided by a licensed physician to determine a child's medically related disability that results in the child's need for special education and related services.

(6) **Occupational therapy** —

(i) Means services provided by a qualified occupational therapist; and

(ii) Includes—

(A) Improving, developing, or restoring functions impaired or lost through illness, injury, or deprivation;

(B) Improving ability to perform tasks for independent functioning if functions are impaired or lost; and

(C) Preventing, through early intervention, initial or further impairment or loss of function.

(7) **Orientation and mobility services**—

(i) Means **services provided to blind or visually impaired children by qualified personnel** to enable those students to attain systematic orientation to and safe movement within their environments in school, home, and community; and

(ii) Includes **teaching children the following**, as appropriate:

(A) Spatial and environmental concepts and use of information received by the senses (such as sound, temperature and vibrations) to establish, maintain, or regain orientation and line of travel (e.g., using sound at a traffic light to cross the street);

(B) To use the long cane or a service animal to supplement visual travel skills or as a tool for safely negotiating the environment for children with no available travel vision;

(C) To understand and use remaining vision and distance low vision aids; and

(D) Other concepts, techniques, and tools.

(8)

(i) **Parent counseling and training** means assisting parents in understanding the special needs of their child;

(ii) Providing parents with information about child development; and

(iii) Helping parents to acquire the necessary skills that will allow them to support the implementation of their child's IEP or IFSP.

(9) **Physical therapy** means services provided by a qualified physical therapist.

(10) **Psychological services** includes—

(i) Administering psychological and educational tests, and other assessment procedures;

(ii) Interpreting assessment results;

(iii) Obtaining, integrating, and interpreting information about child behavior and conditions relating to learning;

(iv) Consulting with other staff members in planning school programs to meet the special educational needs of children as indicated by psychological tests, interviews, direct observation, and behavioral evaluations;

(v) Planning and managing a program of psychological services, including psychological counseling for children and parents; and

(vi) Assisting in developing **positive behavioral intervention** strategies.

(11) **Recreation** includes—

(i) Assessment of leisure function;

(ii) Therapeutic recreation services;

(iii) Recreation programs in schools and community agencies; and

(iv) Leisure education.

(12) **Rehabilitation counseling services** means services provided by qualified personnel in individual or group sessions that focus specifically on career development, employment preparation, achieving independence, and integration in the workplace and community of a student with a disability. The term also includes vocational rehabilitation services provided to a student with a disability by vocational rehabilitation programs funded under the Rehabilitation Act of 1973, as amended, 29 U.S.C. 701 *et seq.*

(13) **School health services and school nurse services** means health services that are designed to enable a child with a disability to receive FAPE as described in the child's IEP. School nurse services are services provided by a qualified school nurse. School health services are services that may be provided by either a qualified school nurse or other qualified person.

(14) **Social work services in schools** includes—

(i) Preparing a social or developmental history on a child with a disability;

(ii) Group and individual counseling with the child and family;

(iii) Working in partnership with parents and others on those problems in a child's living situation (home, school, and community) that affect the child's adjustment in school;

(iv) Mobilizing school and community resources to enable the child to learn as effectively as possible in his or her educational program; and

(v) Assisting in developing positive behavioral intervention strategies.

(15) **Speech-language pathology services** includes—

(i) Identification of children with speech or language impairments;

(ii) Diagnosis and appraisal of specific speech or language impairments;

(iii) Referral for medical or other professional attention necessary for the habilitation of speech or language impairments;

(iv) Provision of speech and language services for the habilitation or prevention of communicative impairments; and

(v) Counseling and guidance of parents, children, and teachers regarding speech and language impairments.

(16) **Transportation** includes—

(i) Travel to and from school and between schools;

(ii) Travel in and around school buildings; and

(iii) **Specialized equipment (such as special or adapted buses, lifts, and ramps)**, if required to provide special transportation for a child with a disability. (Authority: 20 U.S.C. 1401(26))

34 CFR § 300.35 Scientifically based research. [Reserved]

[This regulation was removed after ESSA replaced NCLB in 2015.]

34 CFR § 300.36 Secondary school.

Secondary school means a nonprofit institutional day or residential school, including a public secondary charter school that provides secondary education, as determined under State law, except that it does not include any education beyond grade 12. (Authority: 20 U.S.C. 1401(27))

34 CFR § 300.37 Services plan.

Services plan means a written statement that describes the special education and related services the LEA will provide to a parentally-placed child with a disability enrolled in a private school who has been designated to receive services, including the location of the services and any transportation necessary, consistent with 34 CFR § 300.132, and is developed and implemented in accordance with 34 CFR § 300.137 through 300.139. (Authority: 20 U.S.C. 1412(a)(10)(A))

34 CFR § 300.38 Secretary. Secretary means the Secretary of Education. (Authority: 20 U.S.C. 1401(28))

34 CFR § 300.39 Special education.

(a) General.

(1) Special education means **specially designed instruction**, at no cost to the parents, **to meet the unique needs of a child** with a disability, including—

(i) Instruction conducted in the classroom, in the home, in hospitals and institutions, and in other settings; and

(ii) Instruction in physical education.

(2) Special education **includes** each of the following, **if the services** otherwise meet the requirements of paragraph (a) (1) of this section—

(i) Speech-language pathology services, or any other related service, **if the service** is considered special education rather than a related service under State standards;

(ii) Travel training; and

(iii) Vocational education.

(b) Individual special education terms defined. The terms in this definition are defined as follows:

(1) At no cost means that all specially-designed instruction is provided without charge, **but does not preclude incidental fees that are normally charged to nondisabled students** or their parents as a part of the regular education program.

(2) Physical education means—

(i) The development of—

(A) Physical and motor fitness;

(B) Fundamental motor skills and patterns; and

(C) Skills in aquatics, dance, and individual and group games and sports (including intramural and lifetime sports); and

(ii) Includes special physical education, adapted physical education, movement education, and motor development.

(3) Specially designed instruction means **adapting, as appropriate to the needs of an eligible child** under this part, **the content, methodology, or delivery of instruction—**

(i) **To address the unique needs of the child** that result from the child's disability; and

(ii) **To ensure access of the child to the general curriculum**, so that the child can meet the educational standards within the jurisdiction of the public agency that apply to all children.

(4) Travel training means providing instruction, as appropriate, to children with **significant cognitive disabilities**, and any other children with disabilities who require this instruction, to enable them to—

(i) Develop **an awareness of the environment** in which they live; and

(ii) Learn the **skills necessary to move effectively and safely** from place to place within that environment (e.g., in school, in the home, at work, and in the community).

(5) Vocational education means organized educational programs that are directly related to the preparation of individuals for paid or unpaid employment, or for additional preparation for a career not requiring a baccalaureate or advanced degree. (Authority: 20 U.S.C. 1401(29))

34 CFR § 300.40 State.

State means each of the 50 States, the District of Columbia, the Commonwealth of Puerto Rico, and each of the outlying areas. (Authority: 20 U.S.C. 1401(31))

34 CFR § 300.41 State educational agency.

State educational agency or SEA means the State board of education or other agency or officer primarily responsible for the State supervision of public elementary schools and secondary schools, or, if there is no such officer or agency, an officer or agency designated by the Governor or by State law. (Authority: 20 U.S.C. 1401(32))

34 CFR § 300.42 Supplementary aids and services.

Supplementary aids and services means aids, services, and other supports **that are provided in regular education classes,** other education-related settings, and in extracurricular and nonacademic settings, to enable children with disabilities to be educated with nondisabled children to the maximum extent appropriate in accordance with 34 CFR § 300.114 through 300.116. (Authority: 20 U.S.C. 1401(33))

34 CFR § 300.43 Transition services.

(a) Transition services means a **coordinated set of activities** for a child with a disability that—

(1) Is designed to be within a **results-oriented process**, that is focused on improving the academic and functional achievement of the child with a disability to facilitate the child's movement from **school to post school activities, including postsecondary education**, vocational education, integrated employment (including supported employment), continuing and adult education, adult services, independent living, or community participation;

(2) Is based on the individual child's needs, taking into account the child's strengths, preferences, and interests; and includes—

(i) Instruction;

(ii) Related services;

(iii) Community experiences;

(iv) The development of employment and other post-school adult living objectives; and

(v) If appropriate, acquisition of daily living skills and provision of a functional vocational evaluation.

(b) Transition services for children with disabilities may be special education, if provided as specially designed instruction, or a related service, if required to assist a child with a disability to benefit from special education. (Authority: 20 U.S.C. 1401(34))

34 CFR § 300.44 Universal design.

Universal design has the meaning given the term in section 3 of the Assistive Technology Act of 1998, as amended, 29 U.S.C. 3002. (Authority: 20 U.S.C. 1401(35))

34 CFR § 300.45 Ward of the State.

(a) General. Subject to paragraph (b) of this section, **ward of the State** means a child who, as determined by the State where the child resides, is—

(1) A foster child;

(2) A ward of the State; or

(3) In the custody of a public child welfare agency.

(b) Exception. Ward of the State **does not** include a foster child who has a foster parent who meets the definition of a parent in 34 CFR § 300.30. (Authority: 20 U.S.C. 1401(36))

Subpart B—State Eligibility

General

34 CFR § 300.100 Eligibility for assistance.

A State is eligible for assistance under Part B of the Act for a fiscal year if the State submits a plan that provides assurances to the Secretary that the State has in effect policies and procedures to ensure that the State meets the conditions in 34 CFR § 300.101 through 300.176. (Authority: 20 U.S.C. 1412(a))

FAPE Requirements

34 CFR § 300.101 Free appropriate public education (FAPE).

(a) General. A **free appropriate public education** must be available to all children residing in the State between the ages of **3 and 21**, inclusive, including children with disabilities who have been suspended or expelled from school, as provided for in 34 CFR § 300.530(d).

(b) FAPE for children beginning at age 3.

(1) Each State must ensure that—

(i) The obligation to make **FAPE** available to each eligible child residing in the State begins **no later than the child's third birthday**; and

(ii) **An IEP or an IFSP is in effect for the child by that date**, in accordance with 34 CFR § 300.323(b).

(2) If a child's third birthday occurs during the summer, the child's IEP Team shall determine the date when services under the IEP or IFSP will begin.

(c) Children advancing from grade to grade.

(1) Each State must ensure that FAPE is available to any individual child with a disability who needs special education and related services, **even though the child has not failed or been retained in a course or grade, and is advancing from grade to grade**.

(2) The determination that a child described in paragraph (a) of this section is eligible under this part, must be made on an individual basis by the group responsible within the child's LEA for making eligibility determinations. (Authority: 20 U.S.C. 1412(a)(1)(A))

34 CFR § 300.102 Limitation—exception to FAPE for certain ages.

(a) General. The obligation to make FAPE available to all children with disabilities does not apply with respect to the following:

(1) Children aged 3, 4, 5, 18, 19, 20, or 21 in a State to the extent that its application to those children would be inconsistent with State law or practice, or the order of any court, respecting the provision of public education to children of those ages.

(2)

(i) Children aged 18 through 21 to the extent that State law does not require that special education and related services under Part B of the Act be provided to students with disabilities who, in the last educational placement prior to their incarceration in an adult correctional facility—

(A) Were not actually identified as being a child with a disability under 34 CFR § 300.8; and

(B) Did not have an IEP under Part B of the Act.

(ii) The exception in paragraph (a)(2)(i) of this section **does not apply to children with disabilities**, aged 18 through 21, who—

(A) Had been identified as a child with a disability under 34 CFR § 300.8 and had received services in accordance with an IEP, but who left school prior to their incarceration; or

(B) Did not have an IEP in their last educational setting, but who had actually been identified as a child with a disability under 34 CFR § 300.8.

(3)

(i) Children with disabilities who have **graduated** from high school with a **regular high school diploma**.

(ii) The exception in paragraph (a)(3)(i) of this section does not apply to children who have graduated from high school but have not been awarded a regular high school diploma.

(iii) Graduation from high school with a regular high school diploma constitutes a change in placement, requiring written prior notice in accordance with 34 CFR § 300.503.

(iv) As used in paragraphs (a)(3)(i) through (iii) of this section, the term **regular high school diploma means** the standard high school diploma awarded to the preponderance of students in the State that is fully aligned with State standards, or a higher diploma, except that a regular high school diploma **shall not be aligned** to the alternate academic achievement standards described in section 1111(b)(1)(E) of the ESEA. A regular high school diploma does not include a recognized equivalent of a diploma, such as a general equivalency diploma, certificate of completion, certificate of attendance, or similar lesser credential.

(4) Children with disabilities who are eligible under subpart H of this part, but who receive early intervention services under Part C of the Act.

(b) Documents relating to exceptions. The State must assure that the information it has provided to the Secretary regarding the exceptions in paragraph (a) of this section, as required by 34 CFR § 300.700 (for purposes of making grants to States under this part), is current and accurate. (Authority: 20 U.S.C. 1412(a)(1)(B)-(C))

Other FAPE Requirements

34 CFR § 300.103 FAPE—methods and payments.

(a) Each State may use whatever State, local, Federal, and private sources of support that are available in the State to meet the requirements of this part. For example, if it is necessary to place a child with a disability in a residential facility, a State could use joint agreements between the agencies involved for sharing the cost of that placement.

(b) Nothing in this part relieves an insurer or similar third party from an otherwise valid obligation to provide or to pay for services provided to a child with a disability.

(c) Consistent with 34 CFR § 300.323(c), **the State must ensure that there is no delay in implementing a child's IEP,** including any case in which the payment source for providing or paying for special education and related services to the child is being determined. (Authority: 20 U.S.C. 1401(8), 1412(a)(1))

34 CFR § 300.104 Residential placement.

If placement in a public or private residential program is necessary to provide special education and related services to a child with a disability, **the program,** including non-medical care and room and board, **must be at no cost to the parents of the child**. (Authority: 20 U.S.C. 1412(a)(1), 1412(a)(10)(B))

34 CFR § 300.105 Assistive technology.

(a) Each public agency **must ensure that assistive technology devices** or **assistive technology services,** or both, as those terms are defined in 34 CFR § 300.5 and 300.6, respectively, **are made available** to a child with a disability if required as a part of the child's—

(1) Special education under 34 CFR § 300.36;

(2) Related services under 34 CFR § 300.34; or

(3) Supplementary aids and services under 34 CFR § 300.38 and 300.114(a)(2)(ii).

(b) On a case-by-case basis, the use of **school-purchased assistive technology devices in a child's home or in other settings is required** if the child's IEP Team determines that the child needs access to those devices in order to receive FAPE. (Authority: 20 U.S.C. 1412(a)(1), 1412(a)(12)(B)(i))

34 CFR § 300.106 Extended school year services.

(a) General.

(1) Each public agency must ensure that **extended school year services** are available as necessary to provide FAPE, consistent with paragraph (a)(2) of this section.

(2) Extended school year services must be provided only if a child's IEP Team determines, on an individual basis, in accordance with 34 CFR § 300.320 through 300.324, that the services are necessary for the provision of FAPE to the child.

(3) In implementing the requirements of this section, a public agency may not—

(i) Limit extended school year services to particular categories of disability; or

(ii) Unilaterally limit the type, amount, or duration of those services.

(b) Definition. As used in this section, the term **extended school year services** means special education and related services that—

(1) Are provided to a child with a disability—

(i) Beyond the normal school year of the public agency;

(ii) In accordance with the child's IEP; and

(iii) At no cost to the parents of the child; and

(2) Meet the standards of the SEA. (Authority: 20 U.S.C. 1412(a)(1))

34 CFR § 300.107 Nonacademic services. The State must ensure the following:

(a) Each public agency **must take steps**, including the provision of **supplementary aids and services** determined appropriate and necessary by the child's IEP Team, **to provide nonacademic and extracurricular services** and activities in the manner necessary to afford children with disabilities **an equal opportunity** for participation in those services and activities.

(b) **Nonacademic and extracurricular services and activities may include counseling services, athletics, transportation, health services, recreational activities, special interest groups or clubs** sponsored by the public agency, referrals to agencies that provide assistance to individuals with disabilities, and employment of students, including both employment by the public agency and assistance in making outside employment available. (Authority: 20 U.S.C. 1412(a) (1))

34 CFR § 300.108 Physical education.

The State must ensure that public agencies in the State comply with the following:

(a) General. Physical education services, specially designed if necessary, **must be made available to every child** with a disability receiving FAPE, **unless** the public agency enrolls children without disabilities **and does not provide** physical education to children without disabilities in the same grades.

(b) Regular physical education. Each child with a disability must be afforded the opportunity to participate in the regular physical education program available to nondisabled children **unless**—

(1) The child is enrolled full time in a separate facility; or

(2) The child **needs specially designed physical education**, as prescribed in the child's IEP.

(c) Special physical education. If specially designed physical education is prescribed in a child's IEP, the public agency responsible for the education of that child **must provide the services directly or make arrangement**s for those services to be provided through other public or private programs.

(d) Education in separate facilities. The public agency responsible for the education of a child with a disability who is enrolled in a separate facility must ensure that the child receives appropriate physical education services in compliance with this section. (Authority: 20 U.S.C. 1412(a)(5)(A))

34 CFR § 300.109 Full educational opportunity goal (FEOG).

The State must have in effect policies and procedures to demonstrate that the State has established a goal of providing **full educational opportunity to all children with disabilities**, aged birth through 21, and a detailed timetable for accomplishing that goal. (Authority: 20 U.S.C. 1412(a)(2))

34 CFR § 300.110 Program options.

The State must ensure that each public agency takes steps to ensure that **its children with disabilities have available** to them **the variety of educational programs and services available to nondisabled children** in the area served by the agency, including **art, music,** industrial arts, consumer and homemaking education, and vocational education. (Authority: 20 U.S.C. 1412(a)(2), 1413(a)(1))

34 CFR § 300.111 Child find.

(a) General.

(1) The State must have in effect policies and procedures to ensure that—

(i) **All children with disabilities residing in the State, including children with disabilities who are homeless children or are wards of the State, and children with disabilities attending private schools**, regardless of the severity of their disability, and who are in need of special education and related services, **are identified, located, and evaluated**; and

(ii) A practical method is developed and implemented to determine which children are currently receiving needed special education and related services.

(b) Use of term developmental delay. The following provisions apply with respect to implementing the child find requirements of this section:

(1) A State that adopts a definition of developmental delay under 34 CFR § 300.8(b) determines whether the term applies to children aged three through nine, or to a subset of that age range (e.g., ages three through five).

(2) A State may not require an LEA to adopt and use the term developmental delay for any children within its jurisdiction.

(3) **If an LEA uses the term developmental delay** for children described in 34 CFR § 300.8(b), the LEA must conform to both the State's definition of that term and to the age range that has been adopted by the State.

(4) If a State does not adopt the term developmental delay, an LEA may not independently use that term as a basis for establishing a child's eligibility under this part.

(c) Other children in child find. Child find **also must include**—

(1) Children **who are suspected of being a child** with a disability under 34 CFR § 300.8 and in need of special education, **even though they are advancing from grade to grade;** and

(2) Highly mobile children, including **migrant children.**

(d) Construction. Nothing in the Act requires that children be classified by their disability so long as each child who has a disability that is listed in 34 CFR § 300.8 and who, by reason of that disability, needs special education and related services is regarded as a child with a disability under Part B of the Act. (Authority: 20 U.S.C. 1401(3)); 1412(a)(3))

34 CFR § 300.112 Individualized education programs (IEP).

The State must ensure that an IEP, or an IFSP that meets the requirements of section 636(d) of the Act, is developed, reviewed, and revised for each child with a disability in accordance with 34 CFR § 300.320 through 300.324, except as provided in 34 CFR § 300.300(b)(3)(ii). (Authority: 20 U.S.C. 1412(a)(4))

34 CFR § 300.113 Routine checking of hearing aids and external components of surgically implanted medical devices.

(a) Hearing aids. Each public agency **must ensure that** hearing aids worn in school by children with hearing impairments, including deafness, are functioning properly.

(b) External components of surgically implanted medical devices.

(1) Subject to paragraph (b)(2) of this section, each public agency **must ensure** that the external components of surgically implanted medical devices **are functioning properly**.

(2) For a child with a surgically implanted medical device who is receiving special education and related services under this part, a public agency is not responsible for the **post-surgical maintenance, programming, or replacement** of the medical device that has been surgically implanted (or of an external component of the surgically implanted medical device). (Authority: 20 U.S.C. 1401(1), 1401(26)(B))

Least Restrictive Environment (LRE)

34 CFR § 300.114 LRE requirements.

(a) General.

(1) Except as provided in 34 CFR § 300.324(d)(2) (regarding children with disabilities in adult prisons), the State must have in effect policies and procedures to ensure that public agencies in the State meet the LRE requirements of this section and 34 CFR § 300.115 through 300.120.

(2) Each public agency **must ensure that**—

(i) To the maximum extent appropriate, **children with disabilities**, including children in public or private institutions or other care facilities, **are educated with children who are nondisabled**; and

(ii) **Special classes, separate schooling, or other removal** of children with disabilities from the regular educational environment **occurs only if** the nature or severity of the disability is such that education in regular classes with the use of **supplementary aids and services** cannot be achieved satisfactorily.

(b) Additional requirement—State funding mechanism.

(1) **General.**

(i) A State funding mechanism must not result in placements that violate the requirements of paragraph (a) of this section; and

(ii) A State must not use a funding mechanism by which the State distributes funds on the basis of the type of setting in which a child is served that will result in the failure to provide a child with a disability FAPE according to the unique needs of the child, as described in the child's IEP.

(2) **Assurance.** If the State does not have policies and procedures to ensure compliance with paragraph (b)(1) of this section, the State must provide the Secretary an assurance that the State will revise the funding mechanism as soon as feasible to ensure that the mechanism does not result in placements that violate that paragraph. (Authority: 20 U.S.C. 1412(a)(5))

34 CFR § 300.115 Continuum of alternative placements.

(a) Each public agency must ensure that **a continuum of alternative placements** is available to meet the needs of children with disabilities for special education and related services.

(b) The continuum required in paragraph (a) of this section must—

(1) Include the alternative placements listed in the definition of special education under 34 CFR § 300.39 (instruction in regular classes, special classes, special schools, home instruction, and instruction in hospitals and institutions); and

(2) Make provision for **supplementary services** (such as resource room or itinerant instruction) to be provided in conjunction with regular class placement. (Authority: 20 U.S.C. 1412(a)(5))

34 CFR § 300.116 Placements.

In determining the educational placement of a child with a disability, including a preschool child with a disability, **each public agency must ensure that**—

(a) The placement decision—

(1) Is made by a group of persons, **including the parents**, and other persons knowledgeable about the child, the meaning of the evaluation data, and the placement options; and

(2) Is made in conformity with the LRE provisions of this subpart, including 34 CFR § 300.114 through 300.118;

(b) The child's **placement**—

(1) Is determined at least annually;

(2) Is based on the child's IEP; and

(3) Is **as close as possible to the child's home**;

(c) **Unless** the IEP of a child with a disability **requires some other arrangement, the child is educated in the school that he or she would attend if nondisabled**;

(d) In selecting the LRE, consideration is given to any **potential harmful effect on the child or on the quality of services** that he or she needs; and

(e) A child with a disability is **not removed from education in age-appropriate regular classrooms solely because of needed modifications** in the general education curriculum. (Authority: 20 U.S.C. 1412(a)(5))

34 CFR § 300.117 Nonacademic settings.

In providing or arranging for the provision of **nonacademic and extracurricular services** and activities, including **meals, recess periods**, and the services and activities set forth in 34 CFR § 300.107, each public agency must ensure that each child with a disability **participates** with nondisabled children in the extracurricular services and activities **to the maximum extent appropriate** to the needs of that child. **The public agency must ensure that each child with a disability has the supplementary aids and services** determined by the child's IEP Team to be appropriate and necessary for the child **to participate** in nonacademic settings. (Authority: 20 U.S.C. 1412(a)(5))

34 CFR § 300.118 Children in public or private institutions.

Except as provided in 34 CFR § 300.149(d) (regarding agency responsibility for general supervision of some individuals in adult prisons), an SEA must ensure that 34 CFR § 300.114 is effectively implemented, including, if necessary, making arrangements with public and private institutions (such as a memorandum of agreement or special implementation procedures). (Authority: 20 U.S.C. 1412(a)(5))

34 CFR § 300.119 Technical assistance and training activities.

Each SEA must carry out activities to ensure that teachers and administrators in all public agencies—

(a) Are fully informed about their responsibilities for implementing 34 CFR § 300.114; and

(b) Are provided with technical assistance and training necessary to assist them in this effort. (Authority: 20 U.S.C. 1412(a)(5))

34 CFR § 300.120 Monitoring activities.

(a) The SEA must carry out activities to **ensure that 34 CFR § 300.114 is implemented** by each public agency.

(b) If there is evidence that a public agency makes placements that are inconsistent with 34 CFR § 300.114, the SEA must—

    (1) Review the public agency's justification for its actions; and

    (2) Assist in planning and implementing any necessary corrective action. (Authority: 20 U.S.C. 1412(a)(5))

Additional Eligibility Requirements

34 CFR § 300.121 Procedural safeguards.

(a) General. The State must have procedural safeguards in effect to ensure that each public agency in the State meets the requirements of 34 CFR § 300.500 through 300.536.

(b) Procedural safeguards identified. Children with disabilities and their parents must be afforded the procedural safeguards identified in paragraph (a) of this section. (Authority: 20 U.S.C. 1412(a)(6)(A))

34 CFR § 300.122 Evaluation.

Children with disabilities must be evaluated in accordance with 34 CFR § 300.300 through 300.311 of subpart D of this part. (Authority: 20 U.S.C. 1412(a)(7))

34 CFR § 300.123 Confidentiality of personally identifiable information.

The State must have policies and procedures in effect to ensure that public agencies in the State comply with 34 CFR § 300.610 through 300.626 related to protecting the confidentiality of any personally identifiable information collected, used, or maintained under Part B of the Act. (Authority: 20 U.S.C. 1412(a)(8); 1417(c))

34 CFR § 300.124 Transition of children from the Part C program to preschool programs.

The State must have in effect policies and procedures to ensure that—

(a) Children participating in **early intervention programs assisted under Part C of the Act, and who will participate in** preschool programs assisted under **Part B** of the Act, **experience a smooth and effective transition** to those preschool programs in a manner consistent with section 637(a)(9) of the Act;

(b) By the **third birthday** of a child described in paragraph (a) of this section, **an IEP** or, if consistent with 34 CFR § 300.323(b) and section 636(d) of the Act, an **IFSP, has been developed** and is being implemented for the child consistent with 34 CFR § 300.101(b); and

(c) **Each affected LEA will participate in transition planning conferences arranged by the designated lead agency** under section 635(a)(10) of the Act. (Authority: 20 U.S.C. 1412(a)(9))

34 CFR § 300.125-300.128 [Reserved]

Children in Private Schools

34 CFR § 300.129 State responsibility regarding children in private schools.

The State must have in effect policies and procedures that ensure that LEAs, and, if applicable, the SEA, meet the private school requirements in 34 CFR § 300.130 through 300.148. (Authority: 20 U.S.C. 1412(a)(10))

Children With Disabilities Enrolled by Their Parents in Private Schools

34 CFR § 300.130 Definition of parentally-placed private school children with disabilities.

Parentally-placed private school children with disabilities means children with disabilities enrolled by their parents in private, including religious, schools or facilities that meet the definition of elementary school in 34 CFR § 300.13 or secondary school in 34 CFR § 300.36, other than children with disabilities covered under 34 CFR § 300.145 through 300.147. (Authority: 20 U.S.C. 1412(a)(10)(A))

34 CFR § 300.131 Child find for parentally-placed private school children with disabilities.

(a) General. Each LEA must locate, identify, and evaluate all children with disabilities who are enrolled by their parents in private, including religious, elementary schools and secondary schools located in the school district served by the LEA, in accordance with paragraphs (b) through (e) of this section, and 34 CFR § 300.111 and 300.201.

(b) Child find design. The child find process must be designed to ensure—

(1) The **equitable participation** of parentally-placed private school children; and

(2) An accurate count of those children.

(c) Activities. In carrying out the requirements of this section, the LEA, or, if applicable, the SEA, **must undertake activities similar to the activities undertaken for the agency's public school children**.

(d) Cost. The cost of carrying out the child find requirements in this section, including individual evaluations, may not be considered in determining if an LEA has met its obligation under 34 CFR § 300.133.

(e) Completion period. The child find process must be completed in a time period comparable to that for students attending public schools in the LEA consistent with 34 CFR § 300.301.

(f) Out-of-State children. Each LEA in which private, including religious, elementary schools and secondary schools are located must, in carrying out the child find requirements in this section, **include parentally-placed private school children who reside in a State other than the State** in which the private schools that they attend are located. (Authority: 20 U.S.C. 1412(a)(10)(A)(ii))

34 CFR § 300.132 Provision of services for parentally-placed private school children with disabilities—basic requirement.

(a) General. To the extent consistent with the number and location of children with disabilities who are enrolled by their parents in private, including religious, elementary schools and secondary schools located in the school district served by the LEA, provision is made for the participation of those children in the program assisted or carried out under Part B of the Act by providing them with special education and related services, including direct services determined in accordance with 34 CFR § 300.137, unless the Secretary has arranged for services to those children under the by-pass provisions in 34 CFR § 300.190 through 300.198.

(b) Services plan for parentally-placed private school children with disabilities. In accordance with paragraph (a) of this section and 34 CFR § 300.137 through 300.139, a services plan must be developed and implemented for each private school child with a disability who has been designated by the LEA in which the private school is located to receive special education and related services under this part.

(c) Record keeping. Each LEA must maintain in its records, and provide to the SEA, the following information related to parentally-placed private school children covered under 34 CFR § 300.130 through 300.144:

(1) The number of children evaluated;

(2) The number of children determined to be children with disabilities; and

(3) The number of children served. (Authority: 20 U.S.C. 1412(a)(10)(A)(i))

34 CFR § 300.133 Expenditures.

(a) Formula. To meet the requirement of 34 CFR § 300.132(a), each LEA **must spend the following** on providing special education and related services (including direct services) **to parentally-placed private school children** with disabilities:

(1) For children **aged 3 through 21**, an amount that is the same proportion of the LEA's total subgrant under section 611(f) of the Act as the number of private school children with disabilities aged 3 through 21 who are enrolled by their parents in private, including religious, elementary schools and secondary schools located in the school district served

by the LEA, is to the total number of children with disabilities in its jurisdiction aged 3 through 21.

(2)

(i) For children aged **three through five**, an amount that is the same proportion of the LEA's total subgrant under section 619(g) of the Act as the number of parentally-placed private school children with disabilities aged three through five who are enrolled by their parents in a private, including religious, elementary school located in the school district served by the LEA, is to the total number of children with disabilities in its jurisdiction aged three through five.

(ii) As described in paragraph (a)(2)(i) of this section, children aged three through five are considered to be parentally-placed private school children with disabilities enrolled by their parents in private, including religious, elementary schools, if they are enrolled in a private school that meets the definition of elementary school in 34 CFR § 300.13.

(3) If an LEA has not expended for equitable services all of the funds described in paragraphs (a)(1) and (a)(2) of this section by the end of the fiscal year for which Congress appropriated the funds, the LEA must obligate the remaining funds for special education and related services (including direct services) to parentally-placed private school children with disabilities during a carry-over period of one additional year.

(b) Calculating proportionate amount. In calculating the proportionate amount of Federal funds to be provided for parentally-placed private school children with disabilities, the LEA, after timely and meaningful consultation with representatives of private schools under 34 CFR § 300.134, must conduct a thorough and complete child find process to determine the number of parentally-placed children with disabilities attending private schools located in the LEA. (See Appendix B for an example of how proportionate share is calculated).

(c) Annual count of the number of parentally-placed private school children with disabilities.

(1) Each LEA must—

(i) After timely and meaningful consultation with representatives of parentally-placed private school children with disabilities (consistent with 34 CFR § 300.134), determine the number of parentally-placed private school children with disabilities attending private schools located in the LEA; and

(ii) Ensure that the count is conducted on any date between October 1 and December 1, inclusive, of each year.

(2) The count must be used to determine the amount that the LEA must spend on providing special education and related services to parentally-placed private school children with disabilities in the next subsequent fiscal year.

(d) Supplement, not supplant. State and local funds may supplement and in no case supplant the proportionate amount of Federal funds required to be expended for parentally-placed private school children with disabilities under this part. (Authority: 20 U.S.C. 1412(a)(10)(A))

34 CFR § 300.134 Consultation.

To ensure timely and meaningful consultation, **an LEA**, or, if appropriate, an SEA, **must consult with private school representatives** and representatives of parents of parentally-placed private school children with disabilities during the design and development of special education and related services for the children regarding the following:

(a) Child find. The child find process, including—

(1) How parentally-placed private school children suspected of having a disability can participate equitably; and

(2) How parents, teachers, and private school officials will be informed of the process.

(b) Proportionate share of funds. The determination of the proportionate share of Federal funds available to serve parentally-placed private school children with disabilities under 34 CFR § 300.133(b), including the determination of how the proportionate share of those funds was calculated.

(c) Consultation process. The consultation process among the LEA, private school officials, and representatives of parents of parentally-placed private school children with disabilities, including how the process will operate throughout the school year to ensure that parentally-placed children with disabilities identified through the child find process can meaningfully participate in special education and related services.

(d) Provision of special education and related services. How, where, and by whom special education and related services will be provided for parentally-placed private school children with disabilities, including a discussion of—

(1) The types of services, including direct services and alternate service delivery mechanisms; and

(2) How special education and related services will be apportioned if funds are insufficient to serve all parentally-placed private school children; and

(3) How and when those decisions will be made;

(e) Written explanation by LEA regarding services. How, if the LEA disagrees with the views of the private school officials on the provision of services or the types of services (whether provided directly or through a contract), the LEA will provide to the private school officials a written explanation of the reasons why the LEA chose not to provide services directly or through a contract. (Authority: 20 U.S.C. 1412(a)(10)(A)(iii))

34 CFR § 300.135 Written affirmation.

(a) When timely and meaningful consultation, as required by 34 CFR § 300.134, has occurred, the LEA must obtain a written affirmation signed by the representatives of participating private schools.

(b) If the representatives do not provide the affirmation within a reasonable period of time, the LEA must forward the documentation of the consultation process to the SEA. (Authority: 20 U.S.C. 1412(a)(10)(A)(iv))

34 CFR § 300.136 Compliance.

(a) General. A private school official has **the right to submit a complaint to the SEA** that the LEA—

(1) Did not engage in consultation that was meaningful and timely; or

(2) Did not give due consideration to the views of the private school official.

(b) Procedure.

(1) If the private school official wishes to submit a complaint, the official must provide to the SEA the basis of the noncompliance by the LEA with the applicable private school provisions in this part; and

(2) The LEA must forward the appropriate documentation to the SEA.

(3)

(i) If the private school official is dissatisfied with the decision of the SEA, the official may submit a complaint to the Secretary by providing the information on noncompliance described in paragraph (b)(1) of this section; and

(ii) The SEA must forward the appropriate documentation to the Secretary. (Authority: 20 U.S.C. 1412(a)(10)(A)(v))

34 CFR § 300.137 Equitable services determined.

(a) No individual right to special education and related services. No parentally-placed private school child with a disability **has an individual right to receive some or all of the special education and related services** that the child would receive if enrolled in a public school.

(b) Decisions.

(1) **Decisions** about the services that will be provided to parentally-placed private school children with disabilities under 34 CFR § 300.130 through 300.144 **must be made in accordance with paragraph (c) of this section** and 34 CFR § 300.134(d).

(2) The LEA must make the final decisions with respect to the services to be provided to eligible parentally-placed private school children with disabilities.

(c) Services plan for each child served under 34 CFR § 300.130 through 300.144. If a child with a disability is enrolled in a religious or other private school by the child's parents and will receive special education or related services from an LEA, the LEA must—

(1) Initiate and conduct meetings to develop, review, and revise a services plan for the child, in accordance with 34 CFR § 300.138(b); and

(2) Ensure that a representative of the religious or other private school attends each meeting. If the representative cannot attend, the LEA shall use other methods to ensure participation by the religious or other private school, including individual or conference telephone calls. (Authority: 20 U.S.C. 1412(a)(10)(A))

34 CFR § 300.138 Equitable services provided.

(a) General.

(1) The services provided to parentally-placed private school children with disabilities must be provided by personnel meeting the same standards as personnel providing services in the public schools, **except** that private elementary school and secondary school teachers who are providing equitable services to parentally-placed private school children with disabilities do not have to meet the special education teacher requirements of 34 CFR § 300.156(c).

(2) Parentally-placed private school children with disabilities **may receive a different amount of services** than children with disabilities in public schools.

(b) Services provided in accordance with a services plan.

(1) Each parentally-placed private school child with a disability who has been designated to receive services under 34 CFR § 300.132 must have a **services plan** that describes the specific special education and related services that the LEA will provide to the child in light of the services that the LEA has determined, through the process described in 34 CFR § 300.134 and 300.137, it will make available to parentally-placed private school children with disabilities.

(2) The **services plan** must, to the extent appropriate—

(i) Meet the requirements of 34 CFR § 300.320, or for a child ages three through five, meet the requirements of 34 CFR § 300.323(b) with respect to the services provided; and

(ii) Be developed, reviewed, and revised consistent with 34 CFR § 300.321 through 300.324.

(c) Provision of equitable services.

(1) The provision of services pursuant to this section and 34 CFR § 300.139 through 300.143 must be provided:

(i) By employees of a public agency; or

(ii) Through contract by the public agency with an individual, association, agency, organization, or other entity.

(2) Special education and related services provided to parentally-placed private school children with disabilities, including materials and equipment, must be secular, neutral, and nonideological. (Authority: 20 U.S.C. 1412(a)(10)(A)(vi))

34 CFR § 300.139 Location of services and transportation.

(a) Services on private school premises. Services to parentally-placed private school children with disabilities **may be provided** on the premises of private, including religious, schools, to the extent consistent with law.

(b) Transportation.

(1) General.

(i) If necessary for the child to benefit from or participate in the services provided under this part, a parentally-placed private school child with a disability **must** be provided transportation—

(A) **From the child's school or the child's home** to a site other than the private school; and

(B) **From the service site to the private school, or to the child's home**, depending on the timing of the services.

(ii) LEAs are **not required to provide transportation** from the child's home to the private school.

(2) Cost of transportation. The cost of the transportation described in paragraph (b)(1)(i) of this section may be included in calculating whether the LEA has met the requirement of 34 CFR § 300.133. (Authority: 20 U.S.C. 1412(a)(10)(A))

34 CFR § 300.140 Due process complaints and State complaints.

(a) Due process not applicable, except for child find.

(1) Except as provided in paragraph (b) of this section, the procedures in 34 CFR § 300.504 through 300.519 do not apply to complaints that an LEA has failed to meet the requirements of 34 CFR § 300.132 through 300.139, including the provision of services indicated on the child's services plan.

(b) Child find complaints - to be filed with the LEA in which the private school is located.

(1) The procedures in 34 CFR § 300.504 through 300.519 apply to complaints that an LEA has failed to meet the child find requirements in 34 CFR § 300.131, including the requirements in 34 CFR § 300.300 through 300.311.

(2) Any due process complaint regarding the child find requirements (as described in paragraph (b)(1) of this section) **must be filed with the LEA in which the private school is located** and a copy must be forwarded to the SEA.

(c) State complaints.

(1) Any complaint that an SEA or LEA has failed to meet the requirements in 34 CFR § 300.132 through 300.135 and 300.137 through 300.144 **must be filed in accordance with the procedures** described in 34 CFR § 300.151 through 300.153.

(2) **A complaint filed by a private school official** under 34 CFR § 300.136(a) must be filed with the SEA in accordance with the procedures in 34 CFR § 300.136(b). (Authority: 20 U.S.C. 1412(a)(10)(A))

34 CFR § 300.141 Requirement that funds not benefit a private school.

(a) An LEA **may not** use funds provided under section 611 or 619 of the Act **to finance the existing level of instruction in a private school** or to otherwise benefit the private school.

(b) The LEA **must use funds** provided under Part B of the Act to meet the special education and related services needs of parentally-placed private school children with disabilities, **but not for meeting—**

(1) The needs of a private school; or

(2) The general needs of the students enrolled in the private school. (Authority: 20 U.S.C. 1412(a)(10)(A))

34 CFR § 300.142 Use of personnel.

(a) Use of public school personnel. An LEA **may use funds** available under sections 611 and 619 of the Act **to make public school personnel available** in other than public facilities—

(1) To the extent necessary to provide services under 34 CFR § 300.130 through 300.144 for parentally-placed private school children with disabilities; and

(2) If those services are not normally provided by the private school.

(b) Use of private school personnel. An LEA may use funds available under sections 611 and 619 of the Act **to pay for the services of an employee of a private school** to provide services under 34 CFR § 300.130 through 300.144 if—

(1) The employee performs the services outside of his or her regular hours of duty; and

(2) The employee performs the services under public supervision and control. (Authority: 20 U.S.C. 1412(a)(10)(A))

34 CFR § 300.143 Separate classes prohibited.

An LEA may not use funds available under section 611 or 619 of the Act for classes that are organized **separately on the basis of school enrollment or religion** of the children if —

(a) The classes are at the same site; and

(b) The classes include children enrolled in public schools and children enrolled in private schools. (Authority: 20 U.S.C. 1412(a)(10)(A))

34 CFR § 300.144 Property, equipment, and supplies.

(a) A public agency must control and administer the funds used to provide special education and related services under 34 CFR § 300.137 through 300.139, and hold title to and administer materials, equipment, and property purchased with those funds for the uses and purposes provided in the Act.

(b) The public agency **may place equipment and supplies in a private school** for the period of time needed for the Part B program.

(c) The public agency must ensure that the equipment and supplies placed in a private school—

(1) Are used only for Part B purposes; and

(2) Can be removed from the private school without remodeling the private school facility.

(d) The public agency must remove equipment and supplies from a private school if—

(1) The equipment and supplies are no longer needed for Part B purposes; or

(2) Removal is necessary to avoid unauthorized use of the equipment and supplies for other than Part B purposes.

(e) **No funds under Part B of the Act may be used** for repairs, minor remodeling, or construction of private school facilities. (Authority: 20 U.S.C. 1412(a)(10)(A)(vii))

Children With Disabilities in Private Schools Placed or Referred by Public Agencies

34 CFR § 300.145 Applicability of 34 CFR § 300.146 through 300.147.

Sections 300.146 through 300.147 apply only to children with disabilities **who are or have been placed** in or referred to a private school or facility **by a public agency** as a means of providing special education and related services. (Authority: 20 U.S.C. 1412(a)(10)(B))

34 CFR § 300.146 Responsibility of SEA.

Each **SEA** must ensure that a child with a disability who is **placed in or referred** to a private school or facility **by a public agency** -

(a) Is provided special education and related services—

(1) In conformance with an IEP that meets the requirements of 34 CFR § 300.320 through 300.325; and

(2) At no cost to the parents;

(b) Is provided an education that meets the standards that apply to education provided by the SEA and LEAs including the requirements of this part, except for 34 CFR § 300.18 and 34 CFR § 300.156(c); and

(c) **Has all of the rights of a child with a disability who is served by a public agency.** (Authority: 20 U.S.C. 1412(a)(10)(B))

34 CFR § 300.147 Implementation by SEA.

In implementing 34 CFR § 300.146, the SEA must—

(a) Monitor compliance through procedures such as written reports, on-site visits, and parent questionnaires;

(b) Disseminate copies of applicable standards to each private school and facility to which a public agency has referred or placed a child with a disability; and

(c) Provide an opportunity for those private schools and facilities to participate in the development and revision of State standards that apply to them. (Authority: 20 U.S.C. 1412(a)(10)(B))

Children With Disabilities Enrolled by Their Parents in Private Schools When FAPE is at Issue

34 CFR § 300.148 Placement of children by parents when FAPE is at issue.

(a) General. This part **does not require an LEA to pay for the cost of education**, including special education and related services, of a child with a disability **at a private school** or facility **if that agency made FAPE available** to the child and the parents elected to place the child in a private school or facility. However, the public agency must include that child in the population whose needs are addressed consistent with 34 CFR § 300.131 through 300.144.

(b) Disagreements about FAPE. Disagreements between the parents and a public agency regarding the availability of a program appropriate for the child, and the question of financial reimbursement, **are subject to the due process procedures** in 34 CFR § 300.504 through 300.520.

(c) Reimbursement for private school placement. If the parents of a child with a disability, **who previously received special education and related services** under the authority of a public agency, enroll the child in a private preschool, elementary school, or secondary school without the consent of or referral by the public agency, a court or a hearing officer may require the agency to reimburse the parents for the cost of that enrollment if the court or hearing officer finds that the agency had not made FAPE available to the child in a timely manner prior to that enrollment and that the private placement is appropriate. A parental placement may be found to be appropriate by a hearing officer or a court even if it does not meet the State standards that apply to education provided by the SEA and LEAs.

(d) Limitation on reimbursement. The cost of reimbursement described in paragraph (c) of this section may be **reduced or denied**—

(1) If—

(i) At the most recent IEP Team meeting that the parents attended prior to removal of the child from the public school, the parents **did not inform the IEP Team that they were rejecting the placement** proposed by the public agency to provide FAPE to their child, including stating their concerns and their intent to enroll their child in a private school at public expense; or

(ii) At **least ten (10) business** days (including any holidays that occur on a business day) **prior to the removal** of the child from the public school, the parents **did not give written notice** to the public agency of the information described in paragraph (d)(1)(i) of this section;

(2) If, prior to the parents' removal of the child from the public school, the public agency informed the parents, through the notice requirements described in 34 CFR § 300.503(a)(1), **of its intent to evaluate the child** (including a statement of the purpose of the evaluation that was appropriate and reasonable), but the **parents did not make the child available** for the evaluation; or

(3) Upon a judicial finding of unreasonableness with respect to actions taken by the parents.

(e) Exception. Notwithstanding the notice requirement in paragraph (d)(1) of this section, the cost of reimbursement—

(1) Must not be reduced or denied for failure to provide the notice if—

(i) The school prevented the parents from providing the notice;

(ii) The parents had not received notice, pursuant to 34 CFR § 300.504, of the notice requirement in paragraph (d)(1) of this section; or

(iii) Compliance with paragraph (d)(1) of this section would likely result in physical harm to the child; and

(2) May, in the discretion of the court or a hearing officer, not be reduced or denied for failure to provide this notice if

(i) The parents are not literate or cannot write in English; or

(ii) Compliance with paragraph (d)(1) of this section would likely result in serious emotional harm to the child. (Authority: 20 U.S.C. 1412(a)(10)(C))

SEA Responsibility for General Supervision and Implementation of Procedural Safeguards

34 CFR § 300.149 SEA responsibility for general supervision.

(a) The SEA is responsible for ensuring—

(1) That the requirements of this part are carried out; and

(2) That each educational program for children with disabilities administered within the State, including each program administered by any other State or local agency (but not including elementary schools and secondary schools for Indian children operated or funded by the Secretary of the Interior)—

(i) Is under the general supervision of the persons responsible for educational programs for children with disabilities in the SEA; and

(ii) Meets the educational standards of the SEA (including the requirements of this part).

(3) In carrying out this part with respect to homeless children, the requirements of subtitle B of title VII of the McKinney-Vento Homeless Assistance Act (42 U.S.C. 11431 *et seq.*) are met.

(b) The State must have in effect policies and procedures to ensure that it complies with the monitoring and enforcement requirements in 34 CFR § 300.600 through 300.602 and 34 CFR § 300.606 through 300.608.

(c) Part B of the Act does not limit the responsibility of agencies other than educational agencies for providing or paying some or all of the costs of FAPE to children with disabilities in the State.

(d) Notwithstanding paragraph (a) of this section, the Governor (or another individual pursuant to State law) may assign to any public agency in the State the responsibility of ensuring that the requirements of Part B of the Act are met **with respect to students with disabilities who are convicted as adults under State law and incarcerated in adult prisons**. (Authority: 20 U.S.C. 1412(a)(11); 1416)

34 CFR § 300.150 SEA implementation of procedural safeguards.

The SEA (and any agency assigned responsibility pursuant to 34 CFR § 300.149(d)) must have in effect procedures to inform each public agency of its responsibility for ensuring effective implementation of procedural safeguards for the children with disabilities served by that public agency. (Authority: 20 U.S.C. 1412(a)(11); 1415(a))

State Complaint Procedures

34 CFR § 300.151 Adoption of State complaint procedures.

(a) **General.** Each SEA must adopt written procedures for—

(1) Resolving any complaint, including a complaint filed by an organization or individual from another State, that meets the requirements of 34 CFR § 300.153 by—

(i) Providing for the filing of a complaint with the SEA; and

(ii) At the SEA's discretion, providing for the filing of a complaint with a public agency and the right to have the SEA review the public agency's decision on the complaint; and

(2) Widely disseminating to parents and other interested individuals, including parent training and information centers, protection and advocacy agencies, independent living centers, and other appropriate entities, the State procedures under 34 CFR § 300.151 through 300.153.

(b) **Remedies for denial of appropriate services.** In resolving a complaint in which the SEA has found a failure to provide appropriate services, an SEA, pursuant to its general supervisory authority under Part B of the Act, must address—

(1) The failure to provide appropriate services, including corrective action appropriate to address the needs of the child (such as **compensatory services or monetary reimbursement**); and

(2) Appropriate future provision of services for all children with disabilities.(Authority: 20 U.S.C. 1221e-3)

34 CFR § 300.152 Minimum State complaint procedures.

(a) **Time limit; minimum procedures.** Each SEA must include in its complaint procedures a **time limit of 60 days** after a complaint is filed under 34 CFR § 300.153 to—

(1) Carry out an independent on-site investigation, if the SEA determines that an investigation is necessary;

(2) Give the complainant the opportunity to submit additional information, either orally or in writing, about the allegations in the complaint;

(3) Provide the public agency with the opportunity to respond to the complaint, including, at a minimum—

(i) At the discretion of the public agency, a proposal to resolve the complaint; and

(ii) **An opportunity for a parent** who has filed a complaint and the public agency **to voluntarily engage in mediation** consistent with 34 CFR § 300.506;

(4) Review all relevant information and make an independent determination as to whether the public agency is violating a requirement of Part B of the Act or of this part; and

(5) **Issue a written decision** to the complainant that addresses each allegation in the complaint and contains—

(i) **Findings of fact and conclusions**; and

(ii) The reasons for the SEA's final decision.

(b) Time extension; final decision; implementation. The SEA's procedures described in paragraph (a) of this section also must—

(1) Permit an extension of the time limit under paragraph (a) of this section only if—

(i) Exceptional circumstances exist with respect to a particular complaint; or

(ii) The parent (or individual or organization, if mediation or other alternative means of dispute resolution is available to the individual or organization under State procedures) and the public agency involved agree to extend the time to engage in mediation pursuant to paragraph (a)(3)(ii) of this section, or to engage in other alternative means of dispute resolution, if available in the State; and

(2) Include procedures for effective implementation of the SEA's final decision, if needed, including—

(i) Technical assistance activities;

(ii) Negotiations; and

(iii) Corrective actions to achieve compliance.

(c) Complaints filed under this section and due process hearings under 34 CFR § 300.507 and 34 CFR § 300.530 through 300.532.

(1) If a **written complaint is received that is also the subject of a due process hearing** under 34 CFR § 300.507 or 34 CFR § 300.530 through 300.532, or contains multiple issues of which one or more are part of that hearing, the State **must set aside** any part of the complaint that is being addressed in the due process hearing until the conclusion of the hearing. However, any issue in the complaint that is not a part of the due process action must be resolved using the time limit and procedures described in paragraphs (a) and (b) of this section.

(2) If an issue raised in a complaint filed under this section **has previously been decided in a due process hearing involving the same parties**—

(i) The due process hearing decision is binding on that issue; and

(ii) The SEA must inform the complainant to that effect.

(3) A complaint alleging a public agency's failure to implement a due process hearing decision **must be resolved by the SEA.** (Authority: 20 U.S.C. 1221e-3)

34 CFR § 300.153 Filing a complaint.

(a) An organization or individual may file a signed written complaint under the procedures described in 34 CFR § 300.151 through 300.152.

(b) The complaint **must include**—

(1) A statement that a public agency has violated a requirement of Part B of the Act or of this part;

(2) The facts on which the statement is based;

(3) The signature and contact information for the complainant; and

(4) If alleging violations with respect to a specific child—

(i) The name and address of the residence of the child;

(ii) The name of the school the child is attending;

(iii) In the case of a **homeless child or youth** (within the meaning of section 725(2) of the McKinney-Vento Homeless Assistance Act (42 U.S.C. 11434a(2)), available contact information for the child, and the name of the school the child is attending;

(iv) A **description of the nature of the problem** of the child, including facts relating to the problem; and

(v) A **proposed resolution of the problem** to the extent known and available to the party at the time the complaint is filed.

(c) The complaint must allege a violation that occurred not more **than one year prior** to the date that the complaint is received in accordance with 34 CFR § 300.151.

(d) The party filing the complaint **must forward a copy of the complaint to the LEA** or public agency serving the child at the same time the party files the complaint with the SEA. (Authority: 20 U.S.C. 1221e-3)

Methods of Ensuring Services

34 CFR § 300.154 Methods of ensuring services.

(a) **Establishing responsibility for services.** The Chief Executive Officer of a State or designee of that officer must ensure that an interagency agreement or other mechanism for interagency coordination is in effect between each noneducational public agency described in paragraph (b) of this section and the SEA, in order to ensure that all services described in paragraph (b)(1) of this section that are needed to ensure FAPE are provided, including the provision of these services during the pendency of any dispute under paragraph (a)(3) of this section. The agreement or mechanism must include the following:

(1) An identification of, or a method for defining, the financial responsibility of each agency for providing services described in paragraph (b)(1) of this section to ensure FAPE to children with disabilities. The financial responsibility of each noneducational public agency described in paragraph (b) of this section, including the State Medicaid agency and other public insurers of children with disabilities, must precede the financial responsibility of the LEA (or the State agency responsible for developing the child's IEP).

(2) The conditions, terms, and procedures under which an LEA must be reimbursed by other agencies.

(3) Procedures for resolving interagency disputes (including procedures under which LEAs may initiate proceedings) under the agreement or other mechanism to secure reimbursement from other agencies or otherwise implement the provisions of the agreement or mechanism.

(4) Policies and procedures for agencies to determine and identify the interagency coordination responsibilities of each agency to promote the coordination and timely and appropriate delivery of services described in paragraph (b)(1) of this section.

(b) **Obligation of noneducational public agencies.**

(1)

(i) If any public agency other than an educational agency is otherwise obligated under Federal or State law, or assigned responsibility under State policy or pursuant to paragraph (a) of this section, to provide or pay for any services **that are also considered special education or related services** (such as, but not limited to, services described in 34 CFR § 300.5 relating to assistive technology devices, 34 CFR § 300.6 relating to assistive technology services, 34 CFR § 300.34 relating to related services, 34 CFR § 300.41 relating to supplementary aids and services, and 34 CFR § 300.42 relating to transition services) that are necessary for ensuring FAPE to children with disabilities within the State, **the public agency must fulfill that obligation** or responsibility, either directly or through contract or other arrangement pursuant to paragraph (a) of this section or an agreement pursuant to paragraph (c) of this section.

(ii) A noneducational public agency described in paragraph (b)(1)(i) of this section **may not disqualify an eligible service for Medicaid reimbursement because that service is provided in a school context.**

(2) If a public agency other than an educational agency fails to provide or pay for the special education and related services described in paragraph (b)(1) of this section, the LEA (or State agency responsible for developing the child's IEP) must provide or pay for these services to the child in a timely manner. The LEA or State agency is authorized to claim reimbursement for the services from the noneducational public agency that failed to provide or pay for these services and that agency must reimburse the LEA or State agency in accordance with the terms of the interagency agreement or other mechanism described in paragraph (a) of this section.

(c) **Special rule.** The requirements of paragraph (a) of this section may be met through—

(1) State statute or regulation;

(2) Signed agreements between respective agency officials that clearly identify the responsibilities of each agency relating to the provision of services; or

(3) Other appropriate written methods as determined by the Chief Executive Officer of the State or designee of that officer and approved by the Secretary.

(d) **Children with disabilities who are covered by public benefits or insurance.**

(1) A public agency **may use the Medicaid or other public benefits** or insurance programs in which a child participates to provide or pay for services required under this part, as permitted under the public benefits or insurance program, except as provided in paragraph (d)(2) of this section.

(2) With regard to services required to provide FAPE to an eligible child under this part, the public agency—

(i) **May not require parents to sign up for or enroll in public benefits or insurance programs in order for their child to receive FAPE under Part B of the Act**;

(ii) **May not require parents to incur an out-of-pocket expense such as the payment of a deductible or co-pay** amount incurred in filing a claim for services provided pursuant to this part, but pursuant to paragraph (g)(2) of this section, may pay the cost that the parents otherwise would be required to pay;

(iii) **May not use** a child's benefits under a public benefits or insurance program if that use would—

(A) **Decrease available lifetime coverage** or any other insured benefit;

(B) Result in the family paying for services that would otherwise be covered by the public benefits or insurance program and that are required for the child outside of the time the child is in school;

(C) **Increase premiums** or lead to the discontinuation of benefits or insurance; or

(D) **Risk loss of eligibility** for home and community-based waivers, based on aggregate health-related expenditures; and

(iv) Prior to accessing a child's or parent's public benefits or insurance **for the first time, and after providing notification to the child's parents** consistent with paragraph (d)(2)(v) of this section, must obtain written, parental consent that

(A) Meets the requirements of 34 CFR § 99.30 of this title and 34 CFR § 300.622, which consent must specify the personally identifiable information that may be disclosed (e.g., records or information about the services that may be provided to a particular child), the purpose of the disclosure (e.g., billing for services under part 300), and the agency to which the disclosure may be made (e.g., the State's public benefits or insurance program (e.g., Medicaid)); and

(B) Specifies that the parent understands and agrees that the public agency may access the parent's or child's public benefits or insurance to pay for services under part 300.

(v) Prior to accessing a child's or parent's public benefits or insurance **for the first time, and annually thereafter**, must provide written notification, consistent with 34 CFR § 300.503(c), to the child's parents, **that includes** -

(A) A statement of the parental consent provisions in paragraphs (d)(2)(iv)(A) and (B) of this section;

(B) A statement of the "**no cost**" provisions in paragraphs (d)(2)(i) through (iii) of this section;

(C) A statement that the parents have **the right** under 34 CFR part 99 and part 300 **to withdraw their consent** to disclosure of their child's personally identifiable information to the agency responsible for the administration of the State's public benefits or insurance program (e.g., Medicaid) **at any time**; and

(D) A statement that the **withdrawal of consent or refusal to provide consent** under 34 CFR part 99 and part 300 to disclose personally identifiable information to the agency responsible for the administration of the State's public benefits or insurance program (e.g., Medicaid) **does not relieve the public agency of its responsibility to ensure that all required services are provided at no cost to the parents.**

(e) **Children with disabilities who are covered by private insurance.**

(1) With regard to services required to provide FAPE to an eligible child under this part, a public agency **may access the parents' private insurance proceeds only if** the parents provide consent consistent with 34 CFR § 300.9.

(2) **Each time** the public agency proposes to access the parents' private insurance proceeds, the agency must—

(i) Obtain parental consent in accordance with paragraph (e)(1) of this section; and

(ii) Inform the parents that their refusal to permit the public agency to access their private insurance does not relieve the public agency of its responsibility to ensure that all required services are provided at no cost to the parents.

(f) **Use of Part B funds.**

(1) If a public agency is unable to obtain parental consent to use the parents' private insurance, or public benefits or insurance when the parents would incur a cost for a specified service required under this part, to ensure FAPE the public agency may use its Part B funds to pay for the service.

(2) To avoid financial cost to parents who otherwise would consent to use private insurance, or public benefits or insurance if the parents would incur a cost, the public agency may use its Part B funds to pay the cost that the parents otherwise would have to pay to use the parents' benefits or insurance (e.g., the deductible or co-pay amounts).

(g) **Proceeds from public benefits or insurance or private insurance.**

(1) Proceeds from public benefits or insurance or private insurance will not be treated as program income for purposes

of 34 CFR 80.25.

(2) If a public agency spends reimbursements from Federal funds (e.g., Medicaid) for services under this part, those funds will not be considered "State or local" funds for purposes of the maintenance of effort provisions in 34 CFR § 300.163 and 300.203.

(h) Construction.

Nothing in this part should be construed to alter the requirements imposed on a State Medicaid agency, or any other agency administering a public benefits or insurance program by Federal statute, regulations or policy under title XIX, or title XXI of the Social Security Act, 42 U.S.C. 1396 through 1396v and 42 U.S.C. 1397aa through 1397jj, or any other public benefits or insurance program. (Authority: 20 U.S.C. 1412(a)(12) and (e))

Additional Eligibility Requirements

34 CFR § 300.155 Hearings relating to LEA eligibility.

The SEA must not make any final determination that an LEA is not eligible for assistance under Part B of the Act without first giving the LEA reasonable notice and an opportunity for a hearing under 34 CFR 76.401(d). (Authority: 20 U.S.C. 1412(a)(13))

34 CFR § 300.156 Personnel qualifications.

(a) General. The SEA must establish and **maintain qualifications** to ensure that personnel necessary to carry out the purposes of this part are appropriately and adequately prepared and trained, including that those personnel have the content knowledge and skills to serve children with disabilities.

(b) Related services personnel and paraprofessionals. The qualifications under paragraph (a) of this section must include **qualifications** for **related services personnel** and **paraprofessionals** that—

(1) Are consistent with any State-approved or State-recognized certification, licensing, registration, or other comparable requirements that apply to the professional discipline in which those personnel are providing special education or related services; and

(2) Ensure that related services personnel who deliver services in their discipline or profession—

(i) Meet the requirements of paragraph (b)(1) of this section; and

(ii) Have not had certification or licensure requirements waived on an emergency, temporary, or provisional basis; and

(iii) Allow paraprofessionals and assistants who are appropriately trained and supervised, in accordance with State law, regulation, or written policy, in meeting the requirements of this part to be used to assist in the provision of special education and related services under this part to children with disabilities.

(c) Qualifications for special education teachers.

(1) The qualifications described in paragraph (a) of this section must ensure that each person employed as a public school special education teacher in the State who teaches in an elementary school, middle school, or secondary school -

(i) Has obtained full State certification as a special education teacher (including certification obtained through an alternate route to certification as a special educator, if such alternate route meets minimum requirements described in 34 CFR 200.56(a)(2)(ii) as such section was in effect on November 28, 2008), or passed the State special education teacher licensing examination, and holds a license to teach in the State as a special education teacher, except that when used with respect to any teacher teaching in a public charter school, the teacher must meet the certification or licensing requirements, if any, set forth in the State's public charter school law;

(ii) Has not had special education certification or licensure requirements waived on an emergency, temporary, or provisional basis; and

(iii) Holds at least a bachelor's degree.

(2) A teacher will be considered to meet the standard in paragraph (c)(1)(i) of this section if that teacher is participating in an alternate route to special education certification program under which -

(i) The teacher -

(A) Receives high-quality professional development that is sustained, intensive, and classroom-focused in order to have a positive and lasting impact on classroom instruction, before and while teaching;

(B) Participates in a program of intensive supervision that consists of structured guidance and regular ongoing support for teachers or a teacher mentoring program;

(C) Assumes functions as a teacher only for a specified period of time not to exceed three years; and

(D) Demonstrates satisfactory progress toward full certification as prescribed by the State; and

(ii) The State ensures, through its certification and licensure process, that the provisions in paragraph (c)(2)(i) of this section are met.

(d) Policy. In implementing this section, a State must adopt a policy that includes a requirement that LEAs in the State take measurable steps to recruit, hire, train, and retain personnel who meet the applicable requirements described in paragraph (c) of this section to provide special education and related services under this part to children with disabilities.

(e) Rule of construction. Notwithstanding any other individual right of action that a parent or student may maintain under this part, **nothing in this part shall be construed to create a right of action on behalf of an individual** student or a class of students for the failure of a particular SEA or LEA employee to meet the applicable requirements described in paragraph (c) of this section, or to prevent a parent from filing a complaint about staff qualifications with the SEA as provided for under this part. (Authority: 20 U.S.C. 1412(a)(14))

34 CFR § 300.157 Performance goals and indicators. The State must—

(a) Have in effect established goals for the performance of children with disabilities in the State that—

(1) Promote the purposes of this part, as stated in 34 CFR § 300.1;

(2) Are the same as the State's objectives for progress by children in its definition of adequate yearly progress, including the State's objectives for progress by children with disabilities, under section 1111(b)(2)(C) of the ESEA, 20 U.S.C. 6311;

(3) Address graduation rates and dropout rates, as well as such other factors as the State may determine; and

(4) Are consistent, to the extent appropriate, with any other goals and academic standards for children established by the State;

(b) Have in effect established performance indicators the State will use to assess progress toward achieving the goals described in paragraph (a) of this section, including measurable annual objectives for progress by children with disabilities under section 1111(b)(2)(C)(v)(II)(cc) of the ESEA, 20 U.S.C. 6311; and

(c) Annually report to the Secretary and the public on the progress of the State, and of children with disabilities in the State, toward meeting the goals established under paragraph (a) of this section, which may include elements of the reports required under section 1111(h) of the ESEA. (Authority: 20 U.S.C. 1412(a)(15))

34 CFR § 300.158-300.159, 300.161 [Reserved]

34 CFR § 300.160 Participation in assessments.

(a) General. A State must ensure that all children with disabilities are included in all general State and district-wide assessment programs, including assessments described under section 1111 of the ESEA, 20 U.S.C. 6311, with appropriate accommodations and alternate assessments, if necessary, as indicated in their respective IEPs.

(b) Accommodation guidelines.

(1) A State (or, in the case of a district-wide assessment, an LEA) **must develop guidelines for the provision of appropriate accommodations**.

(2) The State's (or, in the case of a district-wide assessment, the LEA's) guidelines must -

(i) Identify only those accommodations for each assessment that do not invalidate the score; and

(ii) **Instruct IEP Teams to select, for each assessment, only those accommodations that do not invalidate the score**.

(c) Alternate assessments aligned with alternate academic achievement standards for students with the most significant cognitive disabilities.

(1) If a State has adopted alternate academic achievement standards for children with disabilities who are students with the most significant cognitive disabilities as permitted in section 1111(b)(1)(E) of the ESEA, the State (or, in the case of a district-wide assessment, an LEA) must develop and implement alternate assessments and guidelines for the participation in alternate assessments of those children with disabilities who cannot participate in regular assessments, even with accommodations, as indicated in their respective IEPs, as provided in paragraph (a) of this section.

(2) For assessing the academic progress of children with disabilities who are students with the most significant cognitive disabilities under title I of the ESEA, the alternate assessments and guidelines in paragraph (c)(1) of this section must -

(i) Be aligned with the challenging State academic content standards under section 1111(b)(1) of the ESEA and alternate academic achievement standards under section 1111(b)(1)(E) of the ESEA; and

(ii) Measure the achievement of children with disabilities who are students with the most significant cognitive disabilities against those standards.

(3) Consistent with section 1111(b)(1)(E)(ii) of the ESEA and 34 CFR 200.6(c)(6), a State may not adopt modified academic achievement standards or any other alternate academic achievement standards that do not meet the requirements in section 1111(b)(1)(E) of the ESEA for any children with disabilities under section 602(3) of the IDEA.

(d) Explanation to IEP Teams. A State (or in the case of a district-wide assessment, an LEA) must -

(1) Provide to IEP teams a clear explanation of the differences between assessments based on grade-level academic achievement standards and those based on alternate academic achievement standards, including any effects of State and local policies on a student's education resulting from taking an alternate assessment aligned with alternate academic achievement standards, such as how participation in such assessments may delay or otherwise affect the student from completing the requirements for a regular high school diploma; and

(2) Not preclude a student with the most significant cognitive disabilities who takes an alternate assessment aligned with alternate academic achievement standards from attempting to complete the requirements for a regular high school diploma.

(e) Inform parents. A State (or in the case of a district-wide assessment, an LEA) must ensure that parents of students selected to be assessed using an alternate assessment aligned with alternate academic achievement standards under the State's guidelines in paragraph (c)(1) of this section are informed, consistent with 34 CFR 200.2(e), that their child's achievement will be measured based on alternate academic achievement standards, and of **how participation in such assessments** may delay or otherwise **affect the student from completing the requirements for a regular high school diploma**.

(f) Reports. An SEA (or, in the case of a district-wide assessment, an LEA) must make available to the public, and report to the public with the same frequency and in the same detail as it reports on the assessment of nondisabled children, the following:

(1) The number of children with disabilities participating in regular assessments, and the number of those children who were provided accommodations (that did not result in an invalid score) in order to participate in those assessments.

(2) The number of children with disabilities, if any, participating in alternate assessments based on grade-level academic achievement standards in school years prior to 2017-2018.

(3) The number of children with disabilities, if any, participating in alternate assessments aligned with modified academic achievement standards in school years prior to 2016-2017.

(4) The number of children with disabilities who are students with the most significant cognitive disabilities participating in alternate assessments aligned with alternate academic achievement standards.

(5) Compared with the achievement of all children, including children with disabilities, the performance results of children with disabilities on regular assessments, alternate assessments based on grade-level academic achievement standards (prior to 2017-2018), alternate assessments based on modified academic achievement standards (prior to 2016-2017), and alternate assessments aligned with alternate academic achievement standards if -

(i) The number of children participating in those assessments is sufficient to yield statistically reliable information; and

(ii) Reporting that information will not reveal personally identifiable information about an individual student on those assessments.

(g) Universal design. An SEA (or, in the case of a district-wide assessment, an LEA) must, to the extent possible, use universal design principles in developing and administering any assessments under this section. (Authority: 20 U.S.C. 1412(a)(16))[72 FR 17781, Apr. 9, 2007, as amended at 80 FR 50785, Aug. 21, 2015; 82 FR 29760, June 30, 2017]

34 CFR § 300.162 Supplementation of State, local, and other Federal funds.

(a) Expenditures. Funds paid to a State under this part must be expended in accordance with all the provisions of this part.

(b) Prohibition against commingling.

(1) Funds paid to a State under this part must not be commingled with State funds.

(2) The requirement in paragraph (b)(1) of this section is satisfied by the use of a separate accounting system that includes an audit trail of the expenditure of funds paid to a State under this part. Separate bank accounts are not required. (See 34 CFR 76.702 (Fiscal control and fund accounting procedures).)

(c) State-level nonsupplanting.

(1) Except as provided in 34 CFR § 300.203, funds paid to a State under Part B of the Act must be used to supplement

the level of Federal, State, and local funds (including funds that are not under the direct control of the SEA or LEAs) expended for special education and related services provided to children with disabilities under Part B of the Act, and in no case to supplant those Federal, State, and local funds.

(2) If the State provides clear and convincing evidence that all children with disabilities have available to them FAPE, the Secretary may waive, in whole or in part, the requirements of paragraph (c)(1) of this section if the Secretary concurs with the evidence provided by the State under 34 CFR § 300.164.

34 CFR § 300.163 Maintenance of State financial support.

(a) General. A State must not reduce the amount of State financial support for special education and related services for children with disabilities, or otherwise made available because of the excess costs of educating those children, below the amount of that support for the preceding fiscal year.

(b) Reduction of funds for failure to maintain support. The Secretary reduces the allocation of funds under section 611 of the Act for any fiscal year following the fiscal year in which the State fails to comply with the requirement of paragraph (a) of this section by the same amount by which the State fails to meet the requirement.

(c) Waivers for exceptional or uncontrollable circumstances. The Secretary may waive the requirement of paragraph (a) of this section for a State, for one fiscal year at a time, if the Secretary determines that—

(1) Granting a waiver would be equitable due to exceptional or uncontrollable circumstances such as a natural disaster or a precipitous and unforeseen decline in the financial resources of the State; or

(2) The State meets the standard in 34 CFR § 300.164 for a waiver of the requirement to supplement, and not to supplant, funds received under Part B of the Act.

(d) Subsequent years. If, for any fiscal year, a State fails to meet the requirement of paragraph (a) of this section, including any year for which the State is granted a waiver under paragraph (c) of this section, the financial support required of the State in future years under paragraph (a) of this section shall be the amount that would have been required in the absence of that failure and not the reduced level of the State's support. (Authority: 20 U.S.C. 1412(a)(18))

34 CFR § 300.164 Waiver of requirement regarding supplementing and not supplanting with Part B funds.

(a) Except as provided under 34 CFR § 300.202 through 300.205, **funds paid to a State under Part B of the Act must be used to supplement and increase the level of Federal, State, and local funds** (including funds that are not under the direct control of SEAs or LEAs) expended for special education and related services provided to children with disabilities under Part B of the Act and in no case to supplant those Federal, State, and local funds. A State may use funds it retains under 34 CFR § 300.704(a) and (b) without regard to the prohibition on supplanting other funds.

(b) If a State provides clear and convincing evidence that all eligible children with disabilities throughout the State have FAPE available to them, the Secretary may waive for a period of one year in whole or in part the requirement under 34 CFR § 300.162 (regarding State-level nonsupplanting) if the Secretary concurs with the evidence provided by the State.

(c) If a State wishes to request a waiver under this section, it must submit to the Secretary a written request that includes—

(1) An assurance that FAPE is currently available, and will remain available throughout the period that a waiver would be in effect, to all eligible children with disabilities throughout the State, regardless of the public agency that is responsible for providing FAPE to them. The assurance must be signed by an official who has the authority to provide that assurance as it applies to all eligible children with disabilities in the State;

(2) All evidence that the State wishes the Secretary to consider in determining whether all eligible children with disabilities have FAPE available to them, setting forth in detail—

(i) The basis on which the State has concluded that FAPE is available to all eligible children in the State; and

(ii) The procedures that the State will implement to ensure that FAPE remains available to all eligible children in the State, which must include—

(A) The State's procedures under 34 CFR § 300.111 for ensuring that all eligible children are identified, located and evaluated;

(B) The State's procedures for monitoring public agencies to ensure that they comply with all requirements of this part;

(C) The State's complaint procedures under 34 CFR § 300.151 through 300.153; and

(D) The State's hearing procedures under 34 CFR § 300.511 through 300.516 and 34 CFR § 300.530 through 300.536;

(3) A summary of all State and Federal monitoring reports, and State complaint decisions (see 34 CFR § 300.151 through 300.153) and hearing decisions (see 34 CFR § 300.511 through 300.516 and 34 CFR § 300.530 through

300.536), issued within three years prior to the date of the State's request for a waiver under this section, that includes any finding that FAPE has not been available to one or more eligible children, and evidence that FAPE is now available to all children addressed in those reports or decisions; and

(4) Evidence that the State, in determining that FAPE is currently available to all eligible children with disabilities in the State, has consulted with the State advisory panel under 34 CFR § 300.167.

(d) If the Secretary determines that the request and supporting evidence submitted by the State makes a prima facie showing that FAPE is, and will remain, available to all eligible children with disabilities in the State, the Secretary, after notice to the public throughout the State, conducts a public hearing at which all interested persons and organizations may present evidence regarding the following issues:

(1) Whether FAPE is currently available to all eligible children with disabilities in the State.

(2) Whether the State will be able to ensure that FAPE remains available to all eligible children with disabilities in the State if the Secretary provides the requested waiver.

(e) Following the hearing, the Secretary, based on all submitted evidence, will provide a waiver, in whole or in part, for a period of one year if the Secretary finds that the State has provided clear and convincing evidence that FAPE is currently available to all eligible children with disabilities in the State, and the State will be able to ensure that FAPE remains available to all eligible children with disabilities in the State if the Secretary provides the requested waiver.

(f) A State may receive a waiver of the requirement of section 612(a)(18)(A) of the Act and 34 CFR § 300.164 if it satisfies the requirements of paragraphs (b) through (e) of this section.

(g) The Secretary may grant subsequent waivers for a period of one year each, if the Secretary determines that the State has provided clear and convincing evidence that all eligible children with disabilities throughout the State have, and will continue to have throughout the one-year period of the waiver, FAPE available to them. (Authority: 20 U.S.C. 1412(a)(17)(C), (18)(C)(ii))

34 CFR § 300.165 Public participation.

(a) Prior to the adoption of any policies and procedures needed to comply with Part B of the Act (including any amendments to those policies and procedures), the State must ensure that there are public hearings, adequate notice of the hearings, and an opportunity for comment available to the general public, including individuals with disabilities and parents of children with disabilities.

(b) Before submitting a State plan under this part, a State must comply with the public participation requirements in paragraph (a) of this section and those in 20 U.S.C. 1232d(b)(7). (Authority: 20 U.S.C. 1412(a)(19); 20 U.S.C. 1232d(b)(7))

34 CFR § 300.166 Rule of construction.

In complying with 34 CFR § 300.162 and 300.163, a State may not use funds paid to it under this part to satisfy State-law mandated funding obligations to LEAs, including funding based on student attendance or enrollment, or inflation. (Authority: 20 U.S.C. 1412(a)(20))

State Advisory Panel

34 CFR § 300.167 State advisory panel.

The State must establish and maintain an advisory panel for the purpose of providing policy guidance with respect to special education and related services for children with disabilities in the State. (Authority: 20 U.S.C. 1412(a)(21)(A))

34 CFR § 300.168 Membership.

(a) General. The advisory panel must consist of members appointed by the Governor, or any other official authorized under State law to make such appointments, be representative of the State population and be composed of individuals involved in, or concerned with the education of children with disabilities, including—

(1) **Parents of children with disabilities** (ages birth through 26);

(2) **Individuals with disabilities**;

(3) **Teachers**;

(4) Representatives of institutions of higher education that prepare special education and related services personnel;

(5) State and local education officials, including officials who carry out activities under subtitle B of title VII of the McKinney-Vento Homeless Assistance Act, (42 U.S.C. 11431 et seq.);

(6) Administrators of programs for children with disabilities;

(7) Representatives of other State agencies involved in the financing or delivery of related services to children with disabilities;

(8) Representatives of private schools and public charter schools;

(9) Not less than one representative of a vocational, community, or business organization concerned with the provision of transition services to children with disabilities;

(10) A representative from the State child welfare agency responsible for foster care; and

(11) Representatives from the State juvenile and adult corrections agencies.

(b) Special rule. A **majority** of the members of the panel **must be individuals with disabilities or parents** of children with disabilities (ages birth through 26). (Authority: 20 U.S.C. 1412(a)(21)(B) and (C))

34 CFR § 300.169 Duties. The advisory panel must—

(a) Advise the SEA of unmet needs within the State in the education of children with disabilities;

(b) Comment publicly on any rules or regulations proposed by the State regarding the education of children with disabilities;

(c) Advise the SEA in developing evaluations and reporting on data to the Secretary under section 618 of the Act;

(d) Advise the SEA in developing corrective action plans to address findings identified in Federal monitoring reports under Part B of the Act; and

(e) Advise the SEA in developing and implementing policies relating to the coordination of services for children with disabilities. (Authority: 20 U.S.C. 1412(a)(21)(D))

Other Provisions Required for State Eligibility

34 CFR § 300.170 Suspension and expulsion rates.

(a) General. The SEA **must examine data**, including data disaggregated by race and ethnicity, to determine if significant discrepancies are occurring in the rate of long-term suspensions and expulsions of children with disabilities—

(1) Among LEAs in the State; or

(2) Compared to the rates for nondisabled children within those agencies.

(b) Review and revision of policies. If the discrepancies described in paragraph (a) of this section are occurring, the SEA must review and, if appropriate, revise (or require the affected State agency or LEA to revise) its policies, procedures, and practices relating to the development and implementation of IEPs, the use of positive behavioral interventions and supports, and procedural safeguards, to ensure that these policies, procedures, and practices comply with the Act. (Authority: 20 U.S.C. 1412(a)(22))

34 CFR § 300.171 Annual description of use of Part B funds.

(a) In order to receive a grant in any fiscal year a State must annually describe—

(1) How amounts retained for State administration and State-level activities under 34 CFR § 300.704 will be used to meet the requirements of this part; and

(2) How those amounts will be allocated among the activities described in 34 CFR § 300.704 to meet State priorities based on input from LEAs.

(b) If a State's plans for use of its funds under 34 CFR § 300.704 for the forthcoming year do not change from the prior year, the State may submit a letter to that effect to meet the requirement in paragraph (a) of this section.

(c) The provisions of this section do not apply to the Virgin Islands, Guam, American Samoa, the Commonwealth of the Northern Mariana Islands, and the freely associated States. (Authority: 20 U.S.C. 1411(e)(5))

34 CFR § 300.172 Access to instructional materials.

(a) General. The State **must**—

(1) **Adopt the National Instructional Materials Accessibility Standard** (NIMAS), published as appendix C to part 300, **for the purposes of providing instructional materials to)blind persons** or other persons with print disabilities, in a timely manner after publication of the NIMAS in the Federal Register on July 19,2006 (71 FR 41084); and

(2) Establish a State definition of "timely manner" for purposes of paragraphs (b)(2) and (b)(3) of this section if the State is not coordinating with the National Instructional Materials Access Center (NIMAC) or (b)(3) and (c)(2) of this section if the State is coordinating with the NIMAC.

(b) Rights and responsibilities of SEA.

(1) Nothing in this section shall be construed to require any SEA to coordinate with the NIMAC.

(2) If an SEA chooses not to coordinate with the NIMAC, the SEA must provide an assurance to the Secretary that it will provide instructional materials to blind persons or other persons with print disabilities in a timely manner.

(3) Nothing in this section relieves an SEA of its responsibility to ensure that children with disabilities who need instructional materials in accessible formats, but are not included under the definition of blind or other persons with print disabilities in 34 CFR § 300.172(e)(1)(i) or who need materials that cannot be produced from NIMAS files, receive those instructional materials in a timely manner.

(4) In order to meet its responsibility under paragraphs (b)(2), (b)(3), and (c) of this section to ensure that children with disabilities who need instructional materials in accessible formats are provided those materials in a timely manner, the SEA must ensure that all public agencies take all reasonable steps to provide instructional materials in accessible formats to children with disabilities who need those instructional materials at the same time as other children receive instructional materials.

(c) Preparation and delivery of files. If an SEA chooses to coordinate with the NIMAC, as of December 3, 2006, the SEA must—

(1) As part of any print instructional materials adoption process, procurement contract, or other practice or instrument used for purchase of print instructional materials, enter into a written contract with the publisher of the print instructional materials to—

(i) Require the publisher to prepare and, on or before delivery of the print instructional materials, provide to NIMAC electronic files containing the contents of the print instructional materials using the NIMAS; or

(ii) Purchase instructional materials from the publisher that are produced in, or may be rendered in, specialized formats.

(2) Provide instructional materials to blind persons or other persons with print disabilities in a timely manner.

(d) Assistive technology. In carrying out this section, the SEA, to the maximum extent possible, must work collaboratively with the State agency responsible for assistive technology programs.

(e) Definitions.

(1) In this section and 34 CFR § 300.210—

(i) **Blind persons or other persons with print disabilities** means children served under this part who may qualify to receive books and other publications produced in specialized formats in accordance with the Act entitled "An Act to provide books for adult blind," approved March 3, 1931, 2 U.S.C. 135a;

(ii) **National Instructional Materials Access Center or NIMAC** means the center established pursuant to section 674(e) of the Act;

(iii) **National Instructional Materials Accessibility Standard or NIMAS** has the meaning given the term in section 674(e)(3)(B) of the Act;

(iv) Specialized formats has the meaning given the term in section 674(e)(3)(D) of the Act.

(2) The definitions in paragraph (e)(1) of this section apply to each State and LEA, whether or not the State or LEA chooses to coordinate with the NIMAC. (Authority: 20 U.S.C. 1412(a)(23), 1474(e))

34 CFR § 300.173 Overidentification and disproportionality.

The State must have in effect, consistent with the purposes of this part and with section 618(d) of the Act, policies and procedures designed to prevent the inappropriate overidentification or disproportionate representation by race and ethnicity of children as children with disabilities, including children with disabilities with a particular impairment described in 34 CFR § 300.8. (Authority: 20 U.S.C. 1412(a)(24))

34 CFR § 300.174 Prohibition on mandatory medication.

(a) General. The SEA must **prohibit State and LEA personnel from requiring parents** to obtain a prescription for substances identified under schedules I, II, III, IV, or V in section 202(c) of the Controlled Substances Act (21 U.S.C. § 812(c)) for a child as a condition of attending school, receiving an evaluation under 34 CFR § 300.300 through 300.311, or receiving services under this part.

(b) Rule of construction. Nothing in paragraph (a) of this section shall be construed to create a Federal prohibition against teachers and other school personnel consulting or sharing classroom-based observations with parents or guardians regarding a student's academic and functional performance, or behavior in the classroom or school, or regarding the need for evaluation for special education or related services under 34 CFR § 300.111 (related to child find). (Authority: 20 U.S.C. 1412(a)(25))

34 CFR § 300.175 SEA as provider of FAPE or direct services.

If the SEA provides FAPE to children with disabilities, or provides direct services to these children, the agency—

(a) Must comply with any additional requirements of 34 CFR § 300.201 and 300.202 and 34 CFR § 300.206 through 300.226 as if the agency were an LEA; and

(b) May use amounts that are otherwise available to the agency under Part B of the Act to serve those children without regard to 34 CFR § 300.202(b) (relating to excess costs). (Authority: 20 U.S.C. 1412(b))

34 CFR § 300.176 Exception for prior State plans.

(a) General. If a State has on file with the Secretary policies and procedures approved by the Secretary that demonstrate that the State meets any requirement of 34 CFR § 300.100, including any policies and procedures filed under Part B of the Act as in effect before, December 3, 2004, the Secretary considers the State to have met the requirement for purposes of receiving a grant under Part B of the Act.

(b) Modifications made by a State.

(1) Subject to paragraph (b)(2) of this section, policies and procedures submitted by a State in accordance with this subpart remain in effect until the State submits to the Secretary the modifications that the State determines necessary.

(2) The provisions of this subpart apply to a modification to an application to the same extent and in the same manner that they apply to the original plan.

(c) Modifications required by the Secretary. The Secretary may require a State to modify its policies and procedures, but only to the extent necessary to ensure the State's compliance with this part, if—

(1) After December 3, 2004, the provisions of the Act or the regulations in this part are amended;

(2) There is a new interpretation of this Act by a Federal court or a State's highest court; or

(3) There is an official finding of noncompliance with Federal law or regulations. (Authority: 20 U.S.C. 1412(c)(2) and (3))

34 CFR § 300.177 States' sovereign immunity.

(a) General. A State that accepts funds under this part waives its immunity under the 11th amendment to the Constitution of the United States from suit in Federal court for a violation of this part.

(b) Remedies. In a suit against a State for a violation of this part, remedies (including remedies both at law and in equity) are available for such a violation in the suit against a public entity other than a State.

(c) Effective date. Paragraphs (a) and (b) of this section apply with respect to violations that occur in whole or part after the date of enactment of the Education of the Handicapped Act Amendments of 1990. (Authority: 20 U.S.C. 1404)

Department Procedures

34 CFR § 300.178 Determination by the Secretary that a State is eligible to receive a grant.

If the Secretary determines that a State is eligible to receive a grant under Part B of the Act, the Secretary notifies the State of that determination. (Authority: 20 U.S.C. 1412(d)(1))

34 CFR § 300.179 Notice and hearing before determining that a State is not eligible to receive a grant.

(a) General.

(1) The Secretary does not make a final determination that a State is not eligible to receive a grant under Part B of the Act until providing the State—

(i) With reasonable notice; and

(ii) With an opportunity for a hearing.

(2) In implementing paragraph (a)(1)(i) of this section, the Secretary sends a written notice to the SEA by certified mail with return receipt requested.

(b) Content of notice. In the written notice described in paragraph (a)(2) of this section, the Secretary—

(1) States the basis on which the Secretary proposes to make a final determination that the State is not eligible;

(2) May describe possible options for resolving the issues;

(3) Advises the SEA that it may request a hearing and that the request for a hearing must be made not later than 30 days after it receives the notice of the proposed final determination that the State is not eligible; and

(4) Provides the SEA with information about the hearing procedures that will be followed. (Authority: 20 U.S.C. 1412(d)(2))

34 CFR § 300.180 Hearing official or panel.

(a) If the SEA requests a hearing, the Secretary designates one or more individuals, either from the Department or elsewhere, not responsible for or connected with the administration of this program, to conduct a hearing.

(b) If more than one individual is designated, the Secretary designates one of those individuals as the Chief Hearing Official of the Hearing Panel. If one individual is designated, that individual is the Hearing Official. (Authority: 20 U.S.C. 1412(d)(2))

34 CFR § 300.181 Hearing procedures.

(a) As used in 34 CFR § 300.179 through 300.184 the term party or parties means the following:

(1) An SEA that requests a hearing regarding the proposed disapproval of the State's eligibility under this part.

(2) The Department official who administers the program of financial assistance under this part.

(3) A person, group or agency with an interest in and having relevant information about the case that has applied for and been granted leave to intervene by the Hearing Official or Hearing Panel.

(b) Within 15 days after receiving a request for a hearing, the Secretary designates a Hearing Official or Hearing Panel and notifies the parties.

(c) The Hearing Official or Hearing Panel may regulate the course of proceedings and the conduct of the parties during the proceedings. The Hearing Official or Hearing Panel takes all steps necessary to conduct a fair and impartial proceeding, to avoid delay, and to maintain order, including the following:

(1) The Hearing Official or Hearing Panel may hold conferences or other types of appropriate proceedings to clarify, simplify, or define the issues or to consider other matters that may aid in the disposition of the case.

(2) The Hearing Official or Hearing Panel may schedule a prehearing conference with the Hearing Official or Hearing Panel and the parties.

(3) Any party may request the Hearing Official or Hearing Panel to schedule a prehearing or other conference. The Hearing Official or Hearing Panel decides whether a conference is necessary and notifies all parties.

(4) At a prehearing or other conference, the Hearing Official or Hearing Panel and the parties may consider subjects such as—

(i) Narrowing and clarifying issues;

(ii) Assisting the parties in reaching agreements and stipulations;

(iii) Clarifying the positions of the parties;

(iv) Determining whether an evidentiary hearing or oral argument should be held; and

(v) Setting dates for—

(A) The exchange of written documents;

(B) The receipt of comments from the parties on the need for oral argument or evidentiary hearing;

(C) Further proceedings before the Hearing Official or Hearing Panel (including an evidentiary hearing or oral argument, if either is scheduled);

(D) Requesting the names of witnesses each party wishes to present at an evidentiary hearing and estimation of time for each presentation; or

(E) Completion of the review and the initial decision of the Hearing Official or Hearing Panel.

(5) A prehearing or other conference held under paragraph (c)(4) of this section may be conducted by telephone conference call.

(6) At a prehearing or other conference, the parties must be prepared to discuss the subjects listed in paragraph (b)(4) of this section.

(7) Following a prehearing or other conference the Hearing Official or Hearing Panel may issue a written statement describing the issues raised, the action taken, and the stipulations and agreements reached by the parties.

(d) The Hearing Official or Hearing Panel may require parties to state their positions and to provide all or part of the evidence in writing.

(e) The Hearing Official or Hearing Panel may require parties to present testimony through affidavits and to conduct cross-examination through interrogatories.

(f) The Hearing Official or Hearing Panel may direct the parties to exchange relevant documents or information and lists of witnesses, and to send copies to the Hearing Official or Panel.

(g) The Hearing Official or Hearing Panel may receive, rule on, exclude, or limit evidence at any stage of the proceedings.

(h) The Hearing Official or Hearing Panel may rule on motions and other issues at any stage of the proceedings.

(i) The Hearing Official or Hearing Panel may examine witnesses.

(j) The Hearing Official or Hearing Panel may set reasonable time limits for submission of written documents.

(k) The Hearing Official or Hearing Panel may refuse to consider documents or other submissions if they are not submitted in a timely manner unless good cause is shown.

(l) The Hearing Official or Hearing Panel may interpret applicable statutes and regulations but may not waive them or rule on their validity.

(m)

(1) The parties must present their positions through briefs and the submission of other documents and may request an oral argument or evidentiary hearing. The Hearing Official or Hearing Panel shall determine whether an oral argument or an evidentiary hearing is needed to clarify the positions of the parties.

(2) The Hearing Official or Hearing Panel gives each party an opportunity to be represented by counsel.

(n) If the Hearing Official or Hearing Panel determines that an evidentiary hearing would materially assist the resolution of the matter, the Hearing Official or Hearing Panel gives each party, in addition to the opportunity to be represented by counsel—

(1) An opportunity to present witnesses on the party's behalf; and

(2) An opportunity to cross-examine witnesses either orally or with written questions.

(o) The Hearing Official or Hearing Panel accepts any evidence that it finds is relevant and material to the proceedings and is not unduly repetitious.

(p)

(1) The Hearing Official or Hearing Panel—

(i) Arranges for the preparation of a transcript of each hearing;

(ii) Retains the original transcript as part of the record of the hearing; and

(iii) Provides one copy of the transcript to each party.

(2) Additional copies of the transcript are available on request and with payment of the reproduction fee.

(q) Each party must file with the Hearing Official or Hearing Panel all written motions, briefs, and other documents and must at the same time provide a copy to the other parties to the proceedings. (Authority: 20 U.S.C. 1412(d)(2))

34 CFR § 300.182 Initial decision; final decision.

(a) The Hearing Official or Hearing Panel prepares an initial written decision that addresses each of the points in the notice sent by the Secretary to the SEA under 34 CFR § 300.179 including any amendments to or further clarifications of the issues, under 34 CFR § 300.181(c)(7).

(b) The initial decision of a Hearing Panel is made by a majority of Panel members.

(c) The Hearing Official or Hearing Panel mails, by certified mail with return receipt requested, a copy of the initial decision to each party (or to the party's counsel) and to the Secretary, with a notice stating that each party has an opportunity to submit written comments regarding the decision to the Secretary.

(d) Each party may file comments and recommendations on the initial decision with the Hearing Official or Hearing Panel within 15 days of the date the party receives the Panel's decision.

(e) The Hearing Official or Hearing Panel sends a copy of a party's initial comments and recommendations to the other parties by certified mail with return receipt requested. Each party may file responsive comments and recommendations with the Hearing Official or Hearing Panel within seven days of the date the party receives the initial comments and recommendations.

(f) The Hearing Official or Hearing Panel forwards the parties' initial and responsive comments on the initial decision to the Secretary who reviews the initial decision and issues a final decision.

(g) The initial decision of the Hearing Official or Hearing Panel becomes the final decision of the Secretary unless, within 25 days after the end of the time for receipt of written comments and recommendations, the Secretary informs the Hearing Official or Hearing Panel and the parties to a hearing in writing that the decision is being further reviewed for possible modification.

(h) The Secretary rejects or modifies the initial decision of the Hearing Official or Hearing Panel if the Secretary finds that it is clearly erroneous.

(i) The Secretary conducts the review based on the initial decision, the written record, the transcript of the Hearing Official's or Hearing Panel's proceedings, and written comments.

(j) The Secretary may remand the matter to the Hearing Official or Hearing Panel for further proceedings.

(k) Unless the Secretary remands the matter as provided in paragraph (j) of this section, the Secretary issues the final decision, with any necessary modifications, within 30 days after notifying the Hearing Official or Hearing Panel that the initial decision is being further reviewed. (Authority: 20 U.S.C. 1412(d)(2))

34 CFR § 300.183 Filing requirements.

(a) Any written submission by a party under 34 CFR § 300.179 through 300.184 must be filed by hand delivery, by mail, or by facsimile transmission. The Secretary discourages the use of facsimile transmission for documents longer than five pages.

(b) The filing date under paragraph (a) of this section is the date the document is—

    (1) Hand-delivered;

    (2) Mailed; or

    (3) Sent by facsimile transmission.

(c) A party filing by facsimile transmission is responsible for confirming that a complete and legible copy of the document was received by the Department.

(d) If a document is filed by facsimile transmission, the Secretary, the Hearing Official, or the Hearing Panel, as applicable, may require the filing of a follow-up hard copy by hand delivery or by mail within a reasonable period of time.

(e) If agreed upon by the parties, service of a document may be made upon the other party by facsimile transmission. (Authority: 20 U.S.C. 1412(d))

34 CFR § 300.184 Judicial review.

If a State is dissatisfied with the Secretary's final decision with respect to the eligibility of the State under section 612 of the Act, the State may, not later than 60 days after notice of that decision, **file with the United States Court of Appeals for the circuit in which that State is located a petition for review of that decision.** A copy of the petition must be transmitted by the clerk of the court to the Secretary. The Secretary then files in the court the record of the proceedings upon which the Secretary's decision was based, as provided in 28 U.S.C. 2112. (Authority: 20 U.S.C. 1416(e)(8))

34 CFR § 300.185 [Reserved]

34 CFR § 300.186 Assistance under other Federal programs.

Part B of the Act may not be construed to permit a State to reduce medical and other assistance available, or to alter eligibility, under titles V and XIX of the Social Security Act with respect to the provision of FAPE for children with disabilities in the State. (Authority: 20 U.S.C. 1412(e))

By-pass for Children in Private Schools

34 CFR § 300.190 By-pass—general.

(a) If, on December 2, 1983, the date of enactment of the Education of the Handicapped Act Amendments of 1983, an SEA was prohibited by law from providing for the equitable participation in special programs of children with disabilities enrolled in private elementary schools and secondary schools as required by section 612(a)(10)(A) of the Act, or if the Secretary determines that an SEA, LEA, or other public agency has substantially failed or is unwilling to provide for such equitable participation then the Secretary shall, notwithstanding such provision of law, arrange for the provision of services to these children through arrangements which shall be subject to the requirements of section 612(a)(10)(A) of the Act.

(b) The Secretary waives the requirement of section 612(a)(10)(A) of the Act and of 34 CFR § 300.131 through 300.144 if the Secretary implements a by-pass. (Authority: 20 U.S.C. 1412(f)(1))

34 CFR § 300.191 Provisions for services under a by-pass.

(a) Before implementing a by-pass, the Secretary consults with appropriate public and private school officials, including SEA officials, in the affected State, and as appropriate, LEA or other public agency officials to consider matters such as—

    (1) Any prohibition imposed by State law that results in the need for a by-pass; and

    (2) The scope and nature of the services required by private school children with disabilities in the State, and the number of children to be served under the by-pass.

(b) After determining that a by-pass is required, the Secretary arranges for the provision of services to private school children with disabilities in the State, LEA or other public agency in a manner consistent with the requirements of section

612(a)(10)(A) of the Act and 34 CFR § 300.131 through 300.144 by providing services through one or more agreements with appropriate parties.

(c) For any fiscal year that a by-pass is implemented, the Secretary determines the maximum amount to be paid to the providers of services by multiplying—

(1) A per child amount determined by dividing the total amount received by the State under Part B of the Act for the fiscal year by the number of children with disabilities served in the prior year as reported to the Secretary under section 618 of the Act; by

(2) The number of private school children with disabilities (as defined in 34 CFR § 300.8(a) and 300.130) in the State, LEA or other public agency, as determined by the Secretary on the basis of the most recent satisfactory data available, which may include an estimate of the number of those children with disabilities.

(d) The Secretary deducts from the State's allocation under Part B of the Act the amount the Secretary determines is necessary to implement a by-pass and pays that amount to the provider of services. The Secretary may withhold this amount from the State's allocation pending final resolution of any investigation or complaint that could result in a determination that a by-pass must be implemented. (Authority: 20 U.S.C. 1412(f)(2))

34 CFR § 300.192 Notice of intent to implement a by-pass.

(a) Before taking any final action to implement a by-pass, the Secretary provides the SEA and, as appropriate, LEA or other public agency with written notice.

(b) In the written notice, the Secretary—

(1) States the reasons for the proposed by-pass in sufficient detail to allow the SEA and, as appropriate, LEA or other public agency to respond; and

(2) Advises the SEA and, as appropriate, LEA or other public agency that it has a specific period of time (at least 45 days) from receipt of the written notice to submit written objections to the proposed by-pass and that it may request in writing the opportunity for a hearing to show cause why a by-pass should not be implemented.

(c) The Secretary sends the notice to the SEA and, as appropriate, LEA or other public agency by certified mail with return receipt requested. (Authority: 20 U.S.C. 1412(f)(3)(A))

34 CFR § 300.193 Request to show cause.

An SEA, LEA or other public agency in receipt of a notice under 34 CFR § 300.192 that seeks an opportunity to show cause why a by-pass should not be implemented must submit a written request for a show cause hearing to the Secretary, within the specified time period in the written notice in 34 CFR § 300.192(b)(2). (Authority: 20 U.S.C. 1412(f)(3))

34 CFR § 300.194 Show cause hearing.

(a) If a show cause hearing is requested, the Secretary—

(1) Notifies the SEA and affected LEA or other public agency, and other appropriate public and private school officials of the time and place for the hearing;

(2) Designates a person to conduct the show cause hearing. The designee must not have had any responsibility for the matter brought for a hearing; and

(3) Notifies the SEA, LEA or other public agency, and representatives of private schools that they may be represented by legal counsel and submit oral or written evidence and arguments at the hearing.

(b) At the show cause hearing, the designee considers matters such as—

(1) The necessity for implementing a by-pass;

(2) Possible factual errors in the written notice of intent to implement a by-pass; and

(3) The objections raised by public and private school representatives.

(c) The designee may regulate the course of the proceedings and the conduct of parties during the pendency of the proceedings. The designee takes all steps necessary to conduct a fair and impartial proceeding, to avoid delay, and to maintain order.

(d) The designee has no authority to require or conduct discovery.

(e) The designee may interpret applicable statutes and regulations, but may not waive them or rule on their validity.

(f) The designee arranges for the preparation, retention, and, if appropriate, dissemination of the record of the hearing.

(g) Within 10 days after the hearing, the designee—

(1) Indicates that a decision will be issued on the basis of the existing record; or

(2) Requests further information from the SEA, LEA, other public agency, representatives of private schools or Department officials. (Authority: 20 U.S.C. 1412(f)(3))

34 CFR § 300.195 Decision.

(a) The designee who conducts the show cause hearing—

(1) Within 120 days after the record of a show cause hearing is closed, issues a written decision that includes a statement of findings; and

(2) Submits a copy of the decision to the Secretary and sends a copy to each party by certified mail with return receipt requested.

(b) Each party may submit comments and recommendations on the designee's decision to the Secretary within 30 days of the date the party receives the designee's decision.

(c) The Secretary adopts, reverses, or modifies the designee's decision and notifies all parties to the show cause hearing of the Secretary's final action. That notice is sent by certified mail with return receipt requested. (Authority: 20 U.S.C. 1412(f)(3))

34 CFR § 300.196 Filing requirements.

(a) Any written submission under 34 CFR § 300.194 must be filed by hand-delivery, by mail, or by facsimile transmission. The Secretary discourages the use of facsimile transmission for documents longer than five pages.

(b) The filing date under paragraph (a) of this section is the date the document is—

(1) Hand-delivered;

(2) Mailed; or

(3) Sent by facsimile transmission.

(c) A party filing by facsimile transmission is responsible for confirming that a complete and legible copy of the document was received by the Department.

(d) If a document is filed by facsimile transmission, the Secretary or the hearing officer, as applicable, may require the filing of a follow-up hard copy by hand-delivery or by mail within a reasonable period of time.

(e) If agreed upon by the parties, service of a document may be made upon the other party by facsimile transmission.

(f) A party must show a proof of mailing to establish the filing date under paragraph (b)(2) of this section as provided in 34 CFR 75.102(d). (Authority: 20 U.S.C. 1412(f)(3))

34 CFR § 300.197 Judicial review.

If dissatisfied with the Secretary's final action, the SEA may, within 60 days after notice of that action, file a petition for review with the United States Court of Appeals for the circuit in which the State is located. The procedures for judicial review are described in section 612(f)(3)(B) through (D) of the Act. (Authority: 20 U.S.C. 1412(f)(3)(B)-(D))

34 CFR § 300.198 Continuation of a by-pass.

The Secretary continues a by-pass until the Secretary determines that the SEA, LEA or other public agency will meet the requirements for providing services to private school children. (Authority: 20 U.S.C. 1412(f)(2)(C))

State Administration

34 CFR § 300.199 State administration.

(a) **Rulemaking.** Each State that receives funds under Part B of the Act must—

(1) Ensure that any State rules, regulations, and policies relating to this part conform to the purposes of this part;

(2) Identify in writing to LEAs located in the State and the Secretary any such rule, regulation, or policy as a State-imposed requirement that is not required by Part B of the Act and Federal regulations; and

(3) Minimize the number of rules, regulations, and policies to which the LEAs and schools located in the State are subject under Part B of the Act.

(b) **Support and facilitation.** State rules, regulations, and policies under Part B of the Act must support and facilitate LEA and school-level system improvement designed to enable children with disabilities to meet the challenging State student academic achievement standards. (Authority: 20 U.S.C. 1407)

Subpart C—Local Educational Agency Eligibility

34 CFR § 300.200 Condition of assistance.

An LEA is eligible for assistance under Part B of the Act for a fiscal year if the agency submits a plan that provides assurances to the SEA that the LEA meets each of the conditions in 34 CFR § 300.201 through 300.213. (Authority: 20 U.S.C. 1413(a))

34 CFR § 300.201 Consistency with State policies.

The LEA, in providing for the education of children with disabilities within its jurisdiction, must have in effect policies, procedures, and programs that are consistent with the State policies and procedures established under 34 CFR § 300.101 through 300.163, and 34 CFR § 300.165 through 300.174. (Authority: 20 U.S.C. 1413(a)(1))

34 CFR § 300.202 Use of amounts.

(a) General. Amounts provided to the LEA under Part B of the Act—

(1) Must be expended in accordance with the applicable provisions of this part;

(2) Must be used only to pay the excess costs of providing special education and related services to children with disabilities, consistent with paragraph (b) of this section; and

(3) Must be used to supplement State, local, and other Federal funds and not to supplant those funds.

(b) Excess cost requirement.

(1) General.

(i) The excess cost requirement prevents an LEA from using funds provided under Part B of the Act to pay for all of the costs directly attributable to the education of a child with a disability, subject to paragraph (b)(1)(ii) of this section.

(ii) The excess cost requirement does not prevent an LEA from using Part B funds to pay for all of the costs directly attributable to the education of a child with a disability in any of the ages 3, 4, 5, 18, 19, 20, or 21, if no local or State funds are available for nondisabled children of these ages. However, the LEA must comply with the nonsupplanting and other requirements of this part in providing the education and services for these children

(2)

(i) An LEA meets the excess cost requirement if it has spent at least a minimum average amount for the education of its children with disabilities before funds under Part B of the Act are used.

(ii) The amount described in paragraph (b)(2)(i) of this section is determined in accordance with the definition of excess costs in 34 CFR § 300.16. That amount may not include capital outlay or debt service.

(3) If two or more LEAs jointly establish eligibility in accordance with 34 CFR § 300.223, the minimum average amount is the average of the combined minimum average amounts determined in accordance with the definition of excess costs in 34 CFR § 300.16 in those agencies for elementary or secondary school students, as the case may be. (Authority: 20 U.S.C. 1413(a)(2)(A))

34 CFR § 300.203 Maintenance of effort.

(a) General. Except as provided in 34 CFR § 300.204 and 300.205, funds provided to an LEA under Part B of the Act must not be used to reduce the level of expenditures for the education of children with disabilities made by the LEA from local funds below the level of those expenditures for the preceding fiscal year.**(b) Standard.**

(1) Except as provided in paragraph (b)(2) of this section, the SEA must determine that an LEA complies with paragraph (a) of this section for purposes of establishing the LEA's eligibility for an award for a fiscal year if the LEA budgets, for the education of children with disabilities, at least the same total or per capita amount from either of the following sources as the LEA spent for that purpose from the same source for the most recent prior year for which information is available:

(i) Local funds only.

(ii) The combination of State and local funds.

(2) An LEA that relies on paragraph (b)(1)(i) of this section for any fiscal year must ensure that the amount of local funds it budgets for the education of children with disabilities in that year is at least the same, either in total or per capita, as the amount it spent for that purpose in the most recent fiscal year for which information is available and the standard in paragraph (b)(1)(i) of this section was used to establish its compliance with this section.

(3) The SEA may not consider any expenditures made from funds provided by the Federal Government for which the SEA is required to account to the Federal Government or for which the LEA is required to account to the Federal Government directly or through the SEA in determining an LEA's compliance with the requirement in paragraph (a) of this section. (Authority: 20 U.S.C. 1413(a)(2)(A))

34 CFR § 300.204 Exception to maintenance of effort.

Notwithstanding the restriction in 34 CFR § 300.203(a), an LEA may reduce the level of expenditures by the LEA under Part B of the Act below the level of those expenditures for the preceding fiscal year if the reduction is attributable to any of the following:

(a) The voluntary departure, by retirement or otherwise, or departure for just cause, of special education or related services personnel.

(b) A decrease in the enrollment of children with disabilities.

(c) The termination of the obligation of the agency, consistent with this part, to provide a program of special education to a particular child with a disability that is an exceptionally costly program, as determined by the SEA, because the child—

(1) Has left the jurisdiction of the agency;

(2) Has reached the age at which the obligation of the agency to provide FAPE to the child has terminated; or

(3) No longer needs the program of special education.

(d) The termination of costly expenditures for long-term purchases, such as the acquisition of equipment or the construction of school facilities.

(e) The assumption of cost by the high cost fund operated by the SEA under 34 CFR § 300.704(c). (Authority: 20 U.S.C. 1413(a)(2)(B))

34 CFR § 300.205 Adjustment to local fiscal efforts in certain fiscal years.

(a) Amounts in excess. Notwithstanding 34 CFR § 300.202(a)(2) and (b) and 34 CFR § 300.203(a), and except as provided in paragraph (d) of this section and 34 CFR § 300.230(e)(2), for any fiscal year for which the allocation received by an LEA under 34 CFR § 300.705 exceeds the amount the LEA received for the previous fiscal year, the LEA may reduce the level of expenditures otherwise required by 34 CFR § 300.203(a) by not more than 50 percent of the amount of that excess.

(b) Use of amounts to carry out activities under ESEA. If an LEA exercises the authority under paragraph (a) of this section, the LEA must use an amount of local funds equal to the reduction in expenditures under paragraph (a) of this section to carry out activities that could be supported with funds under the ESEA regardless of whether the LEA is using funds under the ESEA for those activities.

(c) State prohibition. Notwithstanding paragraph (a) of this section, if an SEA determines that an LEA is unable to establish and maintain programs of FAPE that meet the requirements of section 613(a) of the Act and this part or the SEA has taken action against the LEA under section 616 of the Act and subpart F of these regulations, the SEA must prohibit the LEA from reducing the level of expenditures under paragraph (a) of this section for that fiscal year.

(d) Special rule. The amount of funds expended by an LEA for early intervening services under 34 CFR § 300.226 shall count toward the maximum amount of expenditures that the LEA may reduce under paragraph (a) of this section. (Authority: 20 U.S.C. 1413(a)(2)(C))

34 CFR § 300.206 Schoolwide programs under Title I of the ESEA.

(a) General. Notwithstanding the provisions of 34 CFR § 300.202 and 300.203 or any other provision of Part B of the Act, an LEA may use funds received under Part B of the Act for any fiscal year to carry out a schoolwide program under section 1114 of the ESEA, except that the amount used in any schoolwide program may not exceed—

(1)

(i) The amount received by the LEA under Part B of the Act for that fiscal year; divided by

(ii) The number of children with disabilities in the jurisdiction of the LEA; and multiplied by

(2) The number of children with disabilities participating in the schoolwide program.

(b) Funding conditions. The funds described in paragraph (a) of this section are subject to the following conditions:

(1) The funds must be considered as Federal Part B funds for purposes of the calculations required by 34 CFR § 300.202(a)(2) and (a)(3).

(2) The funds may be used without regard to the requirements of 34 CFR § 300.202(a)(1).

(c) Meeting other Part B requirements. Except as provided in paragraph (b) of this section, all other requirements of Part B of the Act must be met by an LEA using Part B funds in accordance with paragraph (a) of this section, including ensuring that children with disabilities in schoolwide program schools—

(1) Receive services in accordance with a properly developed IEP; and

(2) Are afforded all of the rights and services guaranteed to children with disabilities under the Act. (Authority: 20 U.S.C. 1413(a)(2)(D))

34 CFR § 300.207 Personnel development.

The LEA must ensure that all personnel necessary to carry out Part B of the Act are appropriately and adequately prepared, subject to the requirements of 34 CFR § 300.156 (related to personnel qualifications) and section 2122 of the ESEA. (Authority: 20 U.S.C. 1413(a)(3))

34 CFR § 300.208 Permissive use of funds.

(a) Uses. Notwithstanding 34 CFR § 300.202, 300.203(a), and 300.162(b), funds provided to an LEA under Part B of the Act **may be used for the following activities**:

(1) **Services and aids that also benefit nondisabled children.** For the costs of special education and related services, and supplementary aids and services, provided in a regular class or other education-related setting to a child with a disability in accordance with the IEP of the child, even if one or more nondisabled children benefit from these services.

(2) **Early intervening services.** To develop and implement coordinated, early intervening educational services in accordance with 34 CFR § 300.226.

(3) **High cost special education and related services.** To establish and implement cost or risk sharing funds, consortia, or cooperatives for the LEA itself, or for LEAs working in a consortium of which the LEA is a part, to pay for high cost special education and related services.

(b) Administrative case management. An LEA may use funds received under Part B of the Act to purchase appropriate technology for recordkeeping, data collection, and related case management activities of teachers and related services personnel providing services described in the IEP of children with disabilities, that is needed for the implementation of those case management activities. (Authority: 20 U.S.C. 1413(a)(4))

34 CFR § 300.209 Treatment of charter schools and their students.

(a) Rights of children with disabilities. Children with disabilities who attend public charter schools and their parents retain all rights under this part.

(b) Charter schools that are public schools of the LEA.

(1) In carrying out Part B of the Act and these regulations with respect to charter schools that are public schools of the LEA, the **LEA must--**

(i) **Serve children with disabilities attending those charter schools in the same manner as the LEA serves children with disabilities in its other schools,** including providing **supplementary and related services on site at the charter school** to the same extent to which the LEA has a policy or practice of providing such services on the site to its other public schools; and

(ii) **Provide funds under Part B of the Act to those charter schools—**

(A) **On the same basis as the LEA provides funds to the LEA's other public schools,** including proportional distribution based on relative enrollment of children with disabilities; and

(B) At the same time as the LEA distributes other Federal funds to the LEA's other public schools, consistent with the State's charter school law.

(2) If the public charter school is a school of an LEA that receives funding under 34 CFR § 300.705 and includes other public schools—

(i) **The LEA is responsible for ensuring that the requirements of this part are met,** unless State law assigns that responsibility to some other entity; and

(ii) The LEA must meet the requirements of paragraph (b)(1) of this section.

(c) Public charter schools that are LEAs. If the public charter school is an LEA, consistent with 34 CFR § 300.28, that receives funding under 34 CFR § 300.705, that charter **school is responsible for ensuring that the requirements of this part are met, unless** State law assigns that responsibility to some other entity.

(d) Public charter schools that are not an LEA or a school that is part of an LEA.

(1) If the public charter school is not an LEA receiving funding under 34 CFR § 300.705, or a school that is part of an LEA receiving funding under 34 CFR § 300.705, **the SEA is responsible for ensuring that the requirements of this part are met**.

(2) Paragraph (d)(1) of this section does not preclude a State from assigning initial responsibility for ensuring the requirements of this part are met to another entity. However, the SEA must maintain the ultimate responsibility for ensuring compliance with this part, consistent with 34 CFR § 300.149. (Authority: 20 U.S.C. 1413(a)(5))

34 CFR § 300.210 Purchase of instructional materials.

(a) General. Not later than December 3, 2006, an LEA that chooses to coordinate with the National Instructional Materials Access Center (NIMAC), when purchasing print instructional materials, must acquire those instructional materials in the same manner, and subject to the same conditions as an SEA under 34 CFR § 300.172.

(b) Rights of LEA.

(1) Nothing in this section shall be construed to require an LEA to coordinate with the NIMAC.

(2) If an LEA chooses not to coordinate with the NIMAC, the LEA must provide an assurance to the SEA that the LEA will provide instructional materials to blind persons or other persons with print disabilities in a timely manner.

(3) Nothing in this section relieves an LEA of its responsibility to ensure that children with disabilities who need instructional materials in accessible formats but are not included under the definition of blind or other persons with print disabilities in 34 CFR § 300.172(e)(1)(i) or who need materials that cannot be produced from NIMAS files, receive those instructional materials in a timely manner. (Authority: 20 U.S.C. 1413(a)(6))

34 CFR § 300.211 Information for SEA.

The LEA must provide the SEA with information necessary to enable the SEA to carry out its duties under Part B of the Act, including, with respect to 34 CFR § 300.157 and 300.160, information relating to the performance of children with disabilities participating in programs carried out under Part B of the Act. (Authority: 20 U.S.C. 1413(a)(7))

34 CFR § 300.212 Public information.

The LEA must make available to parents of children with disabilities and to the general public all documents relating to the eligibility of the agency under Part B of the Act. (Authority: 20 U.S.C. 1413(a)(8))

34 CFR § 300.213 Records regarding migratory children with disabilities.

The LEA must cooperate in the Secretary's efforts under section 1308 of the ESEA to ensure the linkage of records pertaining to migratory children with disabilities for the purpose of electronically exchanging, among the States, health and educational information regarding those children. (Authority: 20 U.S.C. 1413(a)(9))

34 CFR § 300.214-300.219 [Reserved]

34 CFR § 300.220 Exception for prior local plans.

(a) General. If an LEA or a State agency described in 34 CFR § 300.228 has on file with the SEA policies and procedures that demonstrate that the LEA or State agency meets any requirement of 34 CFR § 300.200, including any policies and procedures filed under Part B of the Act as in effect before December 3, 2004, the SEA must consider the LEA or State agency to have met that requirement for purposes of receiving assistance under Part B of the Act.

(b) Modification made by an LEA or State agency. Subject to paragraph (c) of this section, policies and procedures submitted by an LEA or a State agency in accordance with this subpart remain in effect until the LEA or State agency submits to the SEA the modifications that the LEA or State agency determines are necessary.

(c) Modifications required by the SEA. The SEA may require an LEA or a State agency to modify its policies and procedures, but only to the extent necessary to ensure the LEA's or State agency's compliance with Part B of the Act or State law, if—

(1) After December 3, 2004, the effective date of the Individuals with Disabilities Education Improvement Act of 2004, the applicable provisions of the Act (or the regulations developed to carry out the Act) are amended;

(2) There is a new interpretation of an applicable provision of the Act by Federal or State courts; or

(3) There is an official finding of noncompliance with Federal or State law or regulations. (Authority: 20 U.S.C. 1413(b))

34 CFR § 300.221 Notification of LEA or State agency in case of ineligibility.

If the SEA determines that an LEA or State agency is not eligible under Part B of the Act, then the SEA must—

(a) Notify the LEA or State agency of that determination; and

(b) Provide the LEA or State agency **with reasonable notice and an opportunity for a hearing.** (Authority: 20 U.S.C. 1413(c))

34 CFR § 300.222 LEA and State agency compliance.

(a) General. If the SEA, after reasonable notice and an opportunity for a hearing, **finds that an LEA or State agency that** has been determined to be eligible under this subpart **is failing to comply with any requirement** described in 34 CFR § 300.201 through 300.213, **the SEA must reduce or must not provide any further payments to the LEA or State agency** until the SEA is satisfied that the LEA or State agency is complying with that requirement.

(b) Notice requirement. Any State agency or LEA in receipt of a notice described in paragraph (a) of this section must, by means of public notice, take the measures necessary to bring the pendency of an action pursuant to this section to the attention of the public within the jurisdiction of the agency.

(c) Consideration. In carrying out its responsibilities under this section, each SEA must consider any decision resulting from a hearing held under 34 CFR § 300.511 through 300.533 that is adverse to the LEA or State agency involved in the decision. (Authority: 20 U.S.C. 1413(d))

34 CFR § 300.223 Joint establishment of eligibility.

(a) General. An SEA may require an LEA to establish its eligibility jointly with another LEA if the SEA determines that the LEA will be ineligible under this subpart because the agency will not be able to establish and maintain programs of sufficient size and scope to effectively meet the needs of children with disabilities.

(b) Charter school exception. An SEA may not require a charter school that is an LEA to jointly establish its eligibility under paragraph (a) of this section unless the charter school is explicitly permitted to do so under the State's charter school statute.

(c) Amount of payments. If an SEA requires the joint establishment of eligibility under paragraph (a) of this section, the total amount of funds made available to the affected LEAs must be equal to the sum of the payments that each LEA would have received under 34 CFR § 300.705 if the agencies were eligible for those payments.

34 CFR § 300.224 Requirements for establishing eligibility.

(a) Requirements for LEAs in general. LEAs that establish joint eligibility under this section must—

(1) Adopt policies and procedures that are consistent with the State's policies and procedures under 34 CFR § 300.101 through 300.163, and 34 CFR § 300.165 through 300.174; and

(2) Be jointly responsible for implementing programs that receive assistance under Part B of the Act.

(b) Requirements for educational service agencies in general. If an educational service agency is required by State law to carry out programs under Part B of the Act, the joint responsibilities given to LEAs under Part B of the Act—

(1) Do not apply to the administration and disbursement of any payments received by that educational service agency; and

(2) Must be carried out only by that educational service agency.

(c) Additional requirement. Notwithstanding any other provision of 34 CFR § 300.223 through 300.224, an educational service agency must provide for the education of children with disabilities in the least restrictive environment, as required by 34 CFR § 300.112. (Authority: 20 U.S.C. 1413(e)(3) and (4))

34 CFR § 300.225 [Reserved]

34 CFR § 300.226 Early intervening services.

(a) General. An LEA **may not use more than 15 percent** of the amount the LEA receives under Part B of the Act for any fiscal year, less any amount reduced by the LEA pursuant to 34 CFR § 300.205, if any, in combination with other amounts (which may include amounts other than education funds), to develop and implement coordinated, early intervening services, which may include interagency financing structures, **for students in kindergarten through grade 12** (with a particular emphasis on students in kindergarten through grade three) who are not currently identified as needing special education or related services, but **who need additional academic and behavioral support** to succeed in a general education environment. (See Appendix D for examples of how 34 CFR § 300.205(d), regarding local maintenance of effort, and 34 CFR § 300.226(a) affect one another.)

(b) Activities. In implementing coordinated, early intervening services under this section, an LEA may carry out activities that include—

(1) **Professional development** (which may be provided by entities other than LEAs) for teachers and other school staff to enable such personnel to deliver scientifically based academic and behavioral interventions, including scientifically based literacy instruction, and, where appropriate, instruction on the use of adaptive and instructional software; and

(2) **Providing educational and behavioral evaluations, services, and supports, including scientifically based literacy instruction.**

(c) Construction. Nothing in this section shall be construed to either limit or create a right to FAPE under Part B of the Act or to delay appropriate evaluation of a child suspected of having a disability.

(d) Reporting. Each LEA that develops and maintains coordinated, early intervening services under this section must annually report to the SEA on—

(1) The number of children served under this section who received early intervening services; and

(2) The number of children served under this section who received early intervening services and subsequently receive special education and related services under Part B of the Act during the preceding two year period.

(e) Coordination with ESEA. Funds made available to carry out this section may be used to carry out coordinated, early intervening services aligned with activities funded by, and carried out under the ESEA if those funds are used to supplement, and not supplant, funds made available under the ESEA for the activities and services assisted under this section. (Authority: 20 U.S.C. 1413(f))

34 CFR § 300.227 Direct services by the SEA.

(a) General.

(1) An SEA must use the payments that would otherwise have been available to an LEA or to a State agency to provide special education and related services directly to children with disabilities residing in the area served by that LEA, or for whom that State agency is responsible, if the SEA determines that the LEA or State agency—

(i) Has not provided the information needed to establish the eligibility of the LEA or State agency, or elected not to apply for its Part B allotment, under Part B of the Act;

(ii) Is unable to establish and maintain programs of FAPE that meet the requirements of this part;

(iii) Is unable or unwilling to be consolidated with one or more LEAs in order to establish and maintain the programs; or

(iv) Has one or more children with disabilities who can best be served by a regional or State program or service delivery system designed to meet the needs of these children.

(2) SEA administrative procedures.

(i) In meeting the requirements in paragraph (a)(1) of this section, the SEA may provide special education and related services directly, by contract, or through other arrangements.

(ii) The excess cost requirements of 34 CFR § 300.202(b) do not apply to the SEA.

(b) Manner and location of education and services. The SEA may provide special education and related services under paragraph (a) of this section in the manner and at the locations (including regional or State centers) as the SEA considers appropriate. The education and services must be provided in accordance with this part. (Authority: 20 U.S.C. 1413(g))

34 CFR § 300.228 State agency eligibility.

Any State agency that desires to receive a subgrant for any fiscal year under 34 CFR § 300.705 must demonstrate to the satisfaction of the SEA that—

(a) All children with disabilities who are participating in programs and projects funded under Part B of the Act receive FAPE, and that those children and their parents are provided all the rights and procedural safeguards described in this part; and

(b) The agency meets the other conditions of this subpart that apply to LEAs. (Authority: 20 U.S.C. 1413(h))

34 CFR § 300.229 Disciplinary information.

(a) The State may require that a public agency include in the records of a child with a disability a statement of any current or previous disciplinary action that has been taken against the child and transmit the statement to the same extent that the disciplinary information is included in, and transmitted with, the student records of nondisabled children.

(b) The statement may include a description of any behavior engaged in by the child that required disciplinary action, a description of the disciplinary action taken, and any other information that is relevant to the safety of the child and other individuals involved with the child.

(c) If the State adopts such a policy, and the child transfers from one school to another, the transmission of any of the child's records must include both the child's current IEP and any statement of current or previous disciplinary action that has been taken against the child. (Authority: 20 U.S.C. 1413(i))

34 CFR § 300.230 SEA flexibility.

(a) Adjustment to State fiscal effort in certain fiscal years. For any fiscal year for which the allotment received by a State under 34 CFR § 300.703 exceeds the amount the State received for the previous fiscal year and if the State in school year 2003-2004 or any subsequent school year pays or reimburses all LEAs within the State from State revenue 100 percent of the non-Federal share of the costs of special education and related services, the SEA, notwithstanding 34 CFR § 300.162 through 300.163 (related to State-level nonsupplanting and maintenance of effort), and 34 CFR § 300.175 (related to direct services by the SEA) may reduce the level of expenditures from State sources for the education of children with disabilities by not more than 50 percent of the amount of such excess.

(b) Prohibition. Notwithstanding paragraph (a) of this section, if the Secretary determines that an SEA is unable to establish, maintain, or oversee programs of FAPE that meet the requirements of this part, or that the State needs assistance, intervention, or substantial intervention under 34 CFR § 300.603, the Secretary prohibits the SEA from exercising the authority in paragraph (a) of this section.

(c) Education activities. If an SEA exercises the authority under paragraph (a) of this section, the agency must use funds from State sources, in an amount equal to the amount of the reduction under paragraph (a) of this section, to support activities authorized under the ESEA, or to support need-based student or teacher higher education programs.

(d) Report. For each fiscal year for which an SEA exercises the authority under paragraph (a) of this section, the SEA must report to the Secretary—

(1) The amount of expenditures reduced pursuant to that paragraph; and

(2) The activities that were funded pursuant to paragraph (c) of this section.

(e) Limitation.

(1) Notwithstanding paragraph (a) of this section, an SEA may not reduce the level of expenditures described in paragraph (a) of this section if any LEA in the State would, as a result of such reduction, receive less than 100 percent of the amount necessary to ensure that all children with disabilities served by the LEA receive FAPE from the combination of Federal funds received under Part B of the Act and State funds received from the SEA.

(2) If an SEA exercises the authority under paragraph (a) of this section, LEAs in the State may not reduce local effort under 34 CFR § 300.205 by more than the reduction in the State funds they receive. (Authority: 20 U.S.C. 1413(j)

Subpart D—Evaluations, Eligibility Determinations, Individualized Education Programs, and Educational Placements
Parental Consent

34 CFR § 300.300 Parental consent.

(a) Parental consent for initial evaluation.

(1)

(i) The public agency proposing to conduct an **initial evaluation** to determine if a child qualifies as a child with a disability under 34 CFR § 300.8 **must**, after providing notice consistent with 34 CFR § 300.503 and 300.504, **obtain informed consent**, consistent with 34 CFR § 300.9, from the parent of the child before conducting the evaluation.

(ii) Parental consent for initial evaluation **must not be construed as consent for** initial provision of special education and related **services**.

(iii) The public agency must make reasonable efforts to obtain the informed consent from the parent for an initial evaluation to determine whether the child is a child with a disability.

(2) For initial evaluations only, if the child is a ward of the State and is not residing with the child's parent, the public agency is not required to obtain informed consent from the parent for an initial evaluation to determine whether the child is a child with a disability if—

(i) Despite reasonable efforts to do so, the public agency cannot discover the whereabouts of the parent of the child;

(ii) The rights of the parents of the child have been terminated in accordance with State law; or

(iii) The rights of the parent to make educational decisions have been subrogated by a judge in accordance with State law and consent for an initial evaluation has been given by an individual appointed by the judge to represent the child.

(3)

(i) If the parent of a child **enrolled in public school** or seeking to be enrolled in public school **does not provide consent for initial evaluation** under paragraph (a)(1) of this section, or the parent fails to respond to a request to provide consent, the public agency **may**, but is not required to, pursue the initial evaluation of the child by utilizing the **procedural safeguards** in subpart E of this part (including the mediation procedures under 34 CFR § 300.506 or the **due process procedures** under 34 CFR § 300.507 through 300.516), if appropriate, except to the extent inconsistent with State law relating to such parental consent.

(ii) The public agency does not violate its obligation under 34 CFR § 300.111 and 34 CFR § 300.301 through 300.311 if it declines to pursue the evaluation.

(b) Parental consent for services.

(1) A public agency that is responsible for making FAPE available to a child with a disability **must obtain informed**

consent from the parent of the child before the initial provision of special education and related services to the child.

(2) The public agency must make reasonable efforts to obtain informed consent from the parent for the initial provision of special education and related services to the child.

(3) If the parent of a child **fails to respond or refuses to consent to services** under paragraph (b)(1) of this section, the public agency **may not** use the procedures in subpart E of this part (including the mediation procedures under 34 CFR § 300.506 or the **due process procedures** under 34 CFR § 300.507 through 300.516) in order to obtain agreement or a ruling that the services may be provided to the child.

(4) If the parent of the child refuses to consent to the initial provision of special education and related services, or the parent fails to respond to a request to provide consent for the initial provision of special education and related services, the public agency—

(i) Will not be considered to be in violation of the requirement to make available FAPE to the child for the failure to provide the child with the special education and related services for which the public agency requests consent; and

(ii) **Is not required to convene an IEP Team** meeting or develop an IEP under 34 CFR § 300.320 and 300.324 for the child for the special education and related services for which the public agency requests such consent.

(c) Parental consent for reevaluations.

(1) Subject to paragraph (c)(2) of this section, each public agency—

(i) **Must obtain informed parental consent**, in accordance with 34 CFR § 300.300(a)(1), **prior to conducting any reevaluation** of a child with a disability.

(ii) If the parent refuses to consent to the reevaluation, the public agency may, but is not required to, pursue the reevaluation by using the consent override procedures described in paragraph (a)(3) of this section.

(iii) The public agency does not violate its obligation under 34 CFR § 300.111 and 34 CFR § 300.301 through 300.311 if it declines to pursue the evaluation or reevaluation.

(2) The informed parental consent described in paragraph (c)(1) of this section need not be obtained if the public agency can demonstrate that—

(i) It made reasonable efforts to obtain such consent; and

(ii) The child's parent has failed to respond.

(d) Other consent requirements.

(1) Parental consent **is not required before**—-

(i) Reviewing existing data as part of an evaluation or a reevaluation; or

(ii) Administering a test or other evaluation that is administered to all children unless, before administration of that test or evaluation, consent is required of parents of all children.

(2) In addition to the parental consent requirements described in paragraph (a) of this section, a State may require parental consent for other services and activities under this part if it ensures that each public agency in the State establishes and implements effective procedures to ensure that a parent's refusal to consent does not result in a failure to provide the child with FAPE.

(3) A public agency **may not use a parent's refusal** to consent to one service or activity under paragraphs (a) or (d)(2) of this section **to deny** the parent or child any other service, benefit, or activity of the public agency, except as required by this part.[6]

(4)

(i) If a parent of a child who is home schooled or placed in a private school by the parents at their own expense does not provide consent for the initial evaluation or the reevaluation, or the parent fails to respond to a request to provide consent, the public agency **may not** use the consent override procedures (described in paragraphs (a)(3) and (c)(1) of this section); and

(ii) The public agency is not required to consider the child as eligible for services under 34 CFR § 300.132 through 300.144.

---

6 See Chapter 3 of our *Wrightslaw: All About IEPs* book where a parent wrote that "I don't agree that the proposed IEP is sufficient, but it's better than nothing. The team says I have to 'take it or leave it!' Can I allow the school to implement parts of the IEP while we continue to negotiate the issues where we don't agree?" Our reply included a discussion about this specific regulation. Book URL is; https://www.wrightslaw.com/bks/aaiep/index.htm

(5) To meet the reasonable efforts requirement in paragraphs (a)(1)(iii), (a)(2)(i), (b)(2), and (c)(2)(i) of this section, **the public agency must document its attempts to obtain parental consent** using the procedures in 34 CFR § 300.322(d) (Authority: 20 U.S.C. 1414(a)(1)(D) and 1414(c))

Evaluations and Reevaluations

34 CFR § 300.301 Initial evaluations.

(a) General. Each public agency must conduct a full and individual initial evaluation, in accordance with 34 CFR § 300.304 through 300.306, before the initial provision of special education and related services to a child with a disability under this part.

(b) Request for initial evaluation. Consistent with the consent requirements in 34 CFR § 300.300, either a parent of a child or a public agency may initiate a request for an initial evaluation to determine if the child is a child with a disability.

(c) Procedures for initial evaluation. The initial evaluation—

(1)

(i) Must be conducted **within 60 days of receiving parental consent** for the evaluation; **or**

(ii) **If the State establishes a timeframe within which the evaluation must be conducted, within that timeframe**; and

(2) Must consist of procedures—

(i) To determine if the child is **a child with a disability** under 34 CFR § 300.8; and

(ii) To determine the **educational needs** of the child.

(d) Exception. The timeframe described in paragraph (c)(1) of this section **does not apply** to a public agency if—

(1) The parent of a child repeatedly fails or refuses to produce the child for the evaluation; or

(2) A child enrolls in a school of another public agency after the relevant timeframe in paragraph (c)(1) of this section has begun, and prior to a determination by the child's previous public agency as to whether the child is a child with a disability under 34 CFR § 300.8.

(e) The exception in paragraph (d)(2) of this section applies only if the subsequent public agency is making sufficient progress to ensure a prompt completion of the evaluation, and the parent and subsequent public agency agree to a specific time when the evaluation will be completed. (Authority: 20 U.S.C. 1414(a))

34 CFR § 300.302 Screening for instructional purposes is not evaluation.

The screening of a student by a teacher or specialist to determine appropriate instructional strategies for curriculum implementation shall not be considered to be an evaluation for eligibility for special education and related services. (Authority: 20 U.S.C. 1414(a)(1)(E))

34 CFR § 300.303 Reevaluations.

(a) General. A public agency must ensure that a reevaluation of each child with a disability is conducted in accordance with 34 CFR § 300.304 through 300.311—

(1) If the public agency determines that the **educational or related services needs, including improved academic achievement and functional performance**, of the child warrant a reevaluation; or

(2) If the child's parent or teacher requests a reevaluation.

(b) Limitation. A reevaluation conducted under paragraph (a) of this section—

(1) May occur not more than once a year, unless the parent and the public agency agree otherwise; and

(2) Must occur at least once every 3 years, unless the parent and the public agency agree that a reevaluation is unnecessary. (Authority: 20 U.S.C. 1414(a)(2))

34 CFR § 300.304 Evaluation procedures.

(a) Notice. The public agency must provide notice to the parents of a child with a disability, in accordance with 34 CFR § 300.503, that describes any evaluation procedures the agency proposes to conduct.

(b) Conduct of evaluation. In conducting the evaluation, the public agency must—

(1) Use a variety of assessment tools and strategies to gather relevant functional, developmental, and academic information about the child, including information provided by the parent, that may assist in determining—

(i) Whether the child is a child with a disability under 34 CFR § 300.8; and

(ii) **The content of the child's IEP**, including information related to enabling the child to be involved in and progress in the general education curriculum (or for a preschool child, to participate in appropriate activities);

(2) **Not use any single measure or assessment** as the sole criterion for determining whether a child is a child with a disability and for determining an appropriate educational program for the child; and

(3) Use technically sound instruments that may assess the relative contribution of cognitive and behavioral factors, in addition to physical or developmental factors.

(c) Other evaluation procedures. Each public agency must ensure that—

(1) Assessments and other evaluation materials used to assess a child under this part—

(i) Are selected and administered so as **not to be discriminatory** on a racial or cultural basis;

(ii) **Are provided and administered in the child's native language** or other mode of communication and in the form most likely to yield accurate information on what the child knows and can do academically, developmentally, and functionally, unless it is clearly not feasible to so provide or administer;

(iii) Are used for the purposes for which the assessments or measures are valid and reliable;

(iv) Are administered by trained and knowledgeable personnel; and

(v) **Are administered in accordance with any instructions provided by the producer of the assessments**.

(2) Assessments and other evaluation materials include those tailored **to assess specific areas of educational need and not merely those that are designed to provide a single general intelligence quotient**.

(3) Assessments are selected and administered so as best to ensure that if an assessment is administered to a child with impaired sensory, manual, or speaking skills, **the assessment results accurately reflect the child's aptitude or achievement level** or whatever other factors the test purports to measure, **rather than reflecting the child's impaired sensory, manual, or speaking skills** (unless those skills are the factors that the test purports to measure).

(4) The child is **assessed in all areas related to the suspected disability**, including, if appropriate, health, vision, hearing, social and emotional status, general intelligence, academic performance, communicative status, and motor abilities;

(5) Assessments of children with disabilities who transfer from one public agency to another public agency in the same school year are coordinated with those children's prior and subsequent schools, as necessary and as expeditiously as possible, consistent with 34 CFR § 300.301(d)(2) and (e), to ensure prompt completion of full evaluations.

(6) In evaluating each child with a disability under 34 CFR § 300.304 through 300.306, the **evaluation is sufficiently comprehensive to identify all of the child's special education and related services needs**, whether or not commonly linked to the disability category in which the child has been classified.

(7) Assessment tools and strategies that provide relevant information that directly assists persons in determining the **educational needs** of the child are provided. (Authority: 20 U.S.C. 1414(b)(1)-(3), 1412(a)(6)(B))

34 CFR § 300.305 Additional requirements for evaluations and reevaluations.

(a) Review of existing evaluation data. As part of an initial evaluation (if appropriate) and as part of any reevaluation under this part, the IEP Team and other qualified professionals, as appropriate, must—

(1) Review existing evaluation data on the child, including—

(i) **Evaluations and information provided by the parents of the child;**

(ii) Current classroom-based, local, or State assessments, and classroom-based observations; and

(iii) **Observations** by teachers and related services providers; and

(2) On the basis of that review, and input from the child's parents, identify what additional data, if any, are needed **to determine—**

(i)

(A) **Whether the child is a child with a disability, as defined in 34 CFR § 300.8, and the educational needs of the child**; or

(B) In case of a reevaluation of a child, whether the child continues to have such a disability, and the educational needs of the child;

(ii) The present levels of **academic achievement and related developmental needs of the child;**

(iii)

(A) **Whether the child needs special education and related services**; or

(B) In the case of a reevaluation of a child, whether the child **continues to need** special education and related services; and

(iv) Whether any additions or modifications to the special education and related services are needed to enable the child to meet **the measurable annual goals set out in the IEP** of the child and to participate, as appropriate, in the general education curriculum.

(b) Conduct of review. The group described in paragraph (a) of this section **may conduct its review without a meeting**.

(c) Source of data. The public agency must administer such assessments and other evaluation measures as may be needed to produce the data identified under paragraph (a) of this section.

(d) Requirements if additional data are not needed.

(1) If the IEP Team and other qualified professionals, as appropriate, determine that no additional data are needed to determine whether the child continues to be a child with a disability, and to determine the child's educational needs, the public agency must notify the child's parents of—-

(i) That determination and the reasons for the determination; and

(ii) The right of the parents to request an assessment to determine whether the child continues to be a child with a disability, and to determine the child's educational needs.

(2) The public agency is not required to conduct the assessment described in paragraph (d)(1)(ii) of this section unless requested to do so by the child's parents.

(e) Evaluations before change in eligibility.

(1) Except as provided in paragraph (e)(2) of this section, a public agency **must evaluate a child with a disability** in accordance with 34 CFR § 300.304 through 300.311 **before determining that the child is no longer a child with a disability**.

(2) The evaluation described in paragraph (e)(1) of this section is not required before the termination of a child's eligibility under this part due to **graduation** from secondary school **with a regular diplom**a, or due to **exceeding the age eligibility** for FAPE under State law.

(3) For a child whose eligibility terminates under circumstances described in paragraph (e)(2) of this section, a public agency **must provide the child with a summary of the child's academic achievement and functional performance**, which shall include recommendations on how to assist the child in meeting the child's postsecondary goals. (Authority: 20 U.S.C. 1414(c))

34 CFR § 300.306 Determination of eligibility.

(a) General. Upon completion of the administration of assessments and other evaluation measures—

(1) A group of qualified professionals and the parent of the child determines whether the child **is a child with a disability**, as defined in 34 CFR § 300.8, in accordance with paragraph (c) of this section **and the educational needs of the child**; and

(2) The public agency **provides a copy of the evaluation report** and the documentation of determination of eligibility at no cost **to the parent**.

(b) Special rule for eligibility determination. A child **must not be determined to be a child with a disability** under this part—

(1) **If** the determinant factor for that determination is—

(i) **Lack of appropriate instruction** in reading, including the **essential components of reading instruction** (as defined in section 1208(3) of the ESEA);

(ii) Lack of **appropriate instruction in math**; or

(iii) Limited English proficiency; and

(2) If the child does not otherwise meet the eligibility criteria under 34 CFR § 300.8(a).

(c) Procedures for determining eligibility and educational need.

(1) In interpreting evaluation data for the purpose of determining if a child is a child with a disability under 34 CFR § 300.8, and the **educational needs** of the child, each public agency must—

(i) Draw upon information from a variety of sources, including aptitude and achievement tests, parent input, and teacher recommendations, as well as information about the child's physical condition, social or cultural background, and adaptive behavior; and

(ii) Ensure that information obtained from all of these sources is documented and carefully considered.

(2) **If a determination is made that a child has a disability** and needs special education and related services, **an IEP must be developed for the child** in accordance with 34 CFR § 300.320 through 300.324. (Authority: 20 U.S.C. 1414(b)(4) and (5))

Additional Procedures for Identifying Children With Specific Learning Disabilities

34 CFR § 300.307 Specific learning disabilities.

(a) General. A State must adopt, consistent with 34 CFR § 300.309, criteria for determining whether a child has a **specific learning disability** as defined in 34 CFR § 300.8(c)(10). In addition, **the criteria adopted by the State**—

(1) Must **not require the use of a severe discrepancy** between intellectual ability and achievement for determining whether a child has a specific learning disability, as defined in 34 CFR § 300.8(c)(10);

(2) Must permit the use of a process based on the child's response to scientific, research-based intervention; and

(3) May permit the use of other alternative research-based procedures for determining whether a child has a specific learning disability, as defined in 34 CFR § 300.8(c)(10).

(b) Consistency with State criteria. A public agency must use the State criteria adopted pursuant to paragraph (a) of this section in determining whether a child has a specific learning disability. (Authority: 20 U.S.C. 1221e-3; 1401(30); 1414(b)(6))

34 CFR § 300.308 Additional group members.

The determination of whether a child suspected of having a **specific learning disability** is a child with a disability as defined in **34 CFR § 300.8**, must be made by the child's parents and a team of qualified professionals, **which must include**—

(a)

(1) The child's regular teacher; or

(2) If the child does not have a regular teacher, a regular classroom teacher qualified to teach a child of his or her age; or

(3) For a child of less than school age, an individual qualified by the SEA to teach a child of his or her age; and

(b) **At least one person qualified to conduct individual diagnostic examinations of children**, such as a school psychologist, speech-language pathologist, or remedial reading teacher. (Authority: 20 U.S.C. 1221e-3; 1401(30); 1414(b)(6))

34 CFR § 300.309 Determining the existence of a specific learning disability.

(a) The group described in 34 CFR § 300.306 may determine that a child has a specific learning disability, as defined in 34 CFR § 300.8(c)(10), **if**—

(1) The child does not achieve **adequately for the child's age or to meet State-approved grade-level standards in one or more** of the following areas, when provided with learning experiences and instruction appropriate for the child's age or State-approved grade–level standards:

(i) Oral expression.

(ii) Listening comprehension.

(iii) Written expression.

(iv) Basic reading skill.

(v) Reading fluency skills.

(vi) Reading comprehension.

(vii) Mathematics calculation.

(viii) Mathematics problem solving.

(2)

(i) The child does not make **sufficient progress to meet age or State-approved grade-level standards in one or more of the areas** identified in paragraph (a)(1) of this section when using a process based on the child's **response to scientific, research-based intervention**; or

(ii) The child exhibits a **pattern of strengths and weaknesses** in performance, achievement, or both, relative to age, State-approved grade-level standards, or intellectual development, that is determined by the group to be relevant to the identification of a specific learning disability, using appropriate assessments, consistent with 34 CFR § 300.304 and 300.305; and

(3) The group determines that its findings under paragraphs (a)(1) and (2) of this section are not primarily the result of—

(i) A visual, hearing, or motor disability;

(ii) Mental retardation;

(iii) Emotional disturbance;

(iv) Cultural factors;

(v) Environmental or economic disadvantage; or

(vi) Limited English proficiency.

(b) To ensure that underachievement in a child suspected of having a specific learning disability **is not due to lack of appropriate instruction** in reading or math, the group **must consider**, as part of the evaluation described in 34 CFR § 300.304 through 300.306—

(1) Data that demonstrate that prior to, or as a part of, the referral process, the child was provided appropriate instruction in regular education settings, delivered by qualified personnel; and

(2) Data-based documentation of **repeated assessments of achievement at reasonable intervals, reflecting formal assessment** of student progress during instruction, which was provided to the child's parents.

(c) The public agency must promptly request parental consent to evaluate the child to determine if the child needs special education and related services, and **must adhere to the timeframes** described in 34 CFR § 300.301 and 300.303, **unless extended by mutual written agreement** of the child's parents and a group of qualified professionals, as described in 34 CFR § 300.306(a)(1)—

(1) If, prior to a referral, a child has not made adequate progress after an appropriate period of time when provided instruction, as described in paragraphs (b)(1) and (b)(2) of this section; and

(2) Whenever a child is referred for an evaluation. (Authority: 20 U.S.C. 1221e-3; 1401(30); 1414(b)(6))

34 CFR § 300.310 Observation.

(a) The public agency must ensure that the **child is observed in the child's learning environment** (including the regular classroom setting) to document the child's academic performance and behavior in the areas of difficulty.

(b) The group described in 34 CFR § 300.306(a)(1), in determining whether a child has a specific learning disability, must decide to—

(1) Use information from an observation in routine classroom instruction and monitoring of the child's performance that was done before the child was referred for an evaluation; or

(2) Have at least one member of the group described in 34 CFR § 300.306(a)(1) conduct an **observation** of the child's academic performance **in the regular classroom** after the child has been referred for an evaluation and parental consent, consistent with 34 CFR § 300.300(a), is obtained.

(c) In the case of a child of less than school age or out of school, a group member must observe the child in an environment appropriate for a child of that age. (Authority: 20 U.S.C. 1221e-3; 1401(30); 1414(b)(6))

34 CFR § 300.311 Specific documentation for the eligibility determination.

(a) For a child suspected of having a specific learning disability, the documentation of the determination of eligibility, as required in 34 CFR § 300.306(a)(2), **must contain a statement** of—

(1) Whether the child has a specific learning disability;

(2) The basis for making the determination, including an assurance that the determination has been made in accordance with 34 CFR § 300.306(c)(1);

(3) The relevant behavior, if any, noted during the observation of the child and the relationship of that behavior to the child's academic functioning;

(4) The educationally relevant medical findings, if any;

(5) Whether—

(i) The child does not achieve adequately for the child's age or to meet State-approved grade-level standards consistent with 34 CFR § 300.309(a)(1); and

(ii)

(A) The child **does not make sufficient progress to meet age or State-approved grade-level standards** consistent with 34 CFR § 300.309(a)(2)(i); or

(B) The child exhibits a **pattern of strengths and weaknesses in performance, achievement, or both**, relative to age, State-approved grade level standards or intellectual development consistent with 34 CFR § 300.309(a)(2)(ii);

(6) The determination of the group concerning the effects of a visual, hearing, or motor disability; mental retardation; emotional disturbance; cultural factors; environmental or economic disadvantage; or limited English proficiency on the

child's achievement level; and

(7) If the child has participated in a process that assesses the child's **response to scientific, research-based intervention**--

(i) The instructional strategies used and **the student-centered data collected**; and

(ii) The documentation that the child's parents were notified about—

(A) The State's policies regarding the amount and nature of student performance data that would be collected and the general education services that would be provided;

(B) Strategies for increasing the child's rate of learning; and

(C) The parents' right to request an evaluation.

(b) Each group member **must certify in writing** whether the report reflects the member's conclusion. If it does not reflect the member's conclusion, the group member must submit a separate statement presenting the member's conclusions. (Authority: 20 U.S.C. 1221e-3; 1401(30); 1414(b)(6))

Individualized Education Programs[7]

34 CFR § 300.320 Definition of individualized education program.

(a) General. As used in this part, the term individualized education program or IEP means a written statement for each child with a disability that is developed, reviewed, and revised in a meeting in accordance with 34 CFR § 300.320 through 300.324, and that must include—

(1) A statement of the child's **present levels of academic achievement and functional performance**, including—

(i) How the child's disability affects the child's involvement and progress in the general education curriculum (i.e., the same curriculum as for nondisabled children); or

(ii) For preschool children, as appropriate, how the disability affects the child's participation in appropriate activities;

(2)

(i) A statement of **measurable annual goals**, including academic and functional goals designed to—

(A) Meet the child's needs that result from the child's disability to enable the child to be involved in and make progress in the general education curriculum; and

(B) Meet each of the child's other educational needs that result from the child's disability;

(ii) For children with disabilities who take **alternate assessments** aligned to alternate academic achievement standards, **a description of benchmarks or short-term objectives**;

(3) A description of—

(i) How the child's progress toward meeting the annual goals described in paragraph (2) of this section will be measured; and

(ii) When periodic reports on the progress the child is making toward meeting the annual goals (such as through the use of quarterly or other periodic reports, concurrent with the issuance of report cards) will be provided;

(4) A **statement of the special education and related services and supplementary aids and services, based on peer-reviewed research** to the extent practicable, to be provided to the child, or on behalf of the child, and a statement of the program **modifications or supports for school personnel** that will be provided to enable the child—

(i) To advance appropriately toward attaining the annual goals;

(ii) To be involved in and make progress in the general education curriculum in accordance with paragraph (a)(1) of this section, and to participate in extracurricular and other nonacademic activities; and

(iii) To be educated and participate with other children with disabilities and nondisabled children in the activities described in this section;

(5) An explanation of the extent, if any, to which the child will not participate with nondisabled children in the regular class and in the activities described in paragraph (a)(4) of this section;

(6)

(i) A statement of **any individual appropriate accommodations** that are necessary to measure the academic

---

7   <20 U.S.C. § 1414(d)>

achievement and functional performance of the child **on State and districtwide assessments** consistent with section 612(a)(16) of the Act; and

(ii) If the IEP Team determines that the child must take an alternate assessment instead of a particular regular State or districtwide assessment of student achievement, a statement of **why**—

(A) The child cannot participate in the regular assessment; and

(B) The particular alternate assessment selected is appropriate for the child; and

(7) The **projected date for the beginning of the services** and modifications described in paragraph (a)(4) of this section, and the anticipated **frequency, location, and duration** of those services and modifications.

(b) Transition services. Beginning **not later than the first IEP to be in effect when the child turns 16**, or younger if determined appropriate by the IEP Team, and updated annually, thereafter, the **IEP must include**—

(1) Appropriate measurable postsecondary goals based upon age appropriate transition assessments related to training, education, employment, and, where appropriate, independent living skills; and

(2) The **transition services (including courses of study)** needed to assist the child in reaching those goals.

(c) Transfer of rights at age of majority. Beginning not later than one year before the child reaches the age of majority under State law, the IEP must include a statement that the child has been informed of the child's rights under Part B of the Act, if any, that will transfer to the child on reaching the age of majority under 34 CFR § 300.520.

(d) Construction. Nothing in this section shall be construed to require—

(1) That additional information be included in a child's IEP beyond what is explicitly required in section 614 of the Act; or

(2) The IEP Team to **include information under one component** of a child's IEP **that is already contained** under another component of the child's IEP. (Authority: 20 U.S.C. 1414(d)(1)(A) and (d)(6))

34 CFR § 300.321 IEP Team.

(a) General. The public agency must ensure that the IEP Team for each child with a disability includes—

(1) The **parents** of the child;

(2) Not less than one **regular education teacher** of the child (if the child is, or may be, participating in the regular education environment);

(3) Not less than **one special education teacher** of the child, or where appropriate, not less than one special education provider of the child;

(4) A **representative** of the public agency who—

(i) Is qualified to provide, or supervise the provision of, specially designed instruction to meet the unique needs of children with disabilities;

(ii) Is knowledgeable about the general education curriculum; and

(iii) Is knowledgeable about the availability of resources of the public agency.

(5) An individual who can interpret **the instructional implications** of evaluation results, who may be a member of the team described in paragraphs (a)(2) through (a)(6) of this section;

(6) At the discretion of the parent or the agency, **other individuals** who have knowledge or special expertise regarding the child, including related services personnel as appropriate; and

(7) Whenever appropriate, **the child with a disability**.

(b) Transition services participants.

(1) In accordance with paragraph (a)(7) of this section, the public agency **must invite a child with a disability** to attend the child's IEP Team meeting **if a purpose of the meeting will be the consideration of the postsecondary goals for the child and the transition services** needed to assist the child in reaching those goals under 34 CFR § 300.320(b).

(2) If the child does not attend the IEP Team meeting, the public agency must take other steps to ensure that the child's preferences and interests are considered.

(3) To the extent appropriate, with the consent of the parents or a child who has reached the age of majority, in implementing the requirements of paragraph (b)(1) of this section, the public agency must invite a representative of any participating agency that is likely to be responsible for providing or paying for transition services.

(c) Determination of knowledge and special expertise. The determination of the knowledge or special expertise of any individual described in paragraph (a)(6) of this section **must be made by the party** (parents or public agency) **who invited the individual** to be a member of the IEP Team.

(d) Designating a public agency representative. A public agency may designate a public agency member of the IEP Team to also serve as the agency representative, if the criteria in paragraph (a)(4) of this section are satisfied.

(e) IEP Team attendance.

(1) A member of the IEP Team described in paragraphs (a)(2) through (a)(5) of this section **is not required to attend** an IEP Team meeting, in whole or in part, **if** the parent of a child with a disability and the public agency agree, in writing, that the attendance of the member is not necessary because the member's area of the curriculum or related services is not being modified or discussed in the meeting.

(2) A member of the IEP Team described in paragraph (e)(1) of this section **may be excused** from attending an IEP Team meeting, in whole or in part, when the meeting involves a modification to or discussion of the member's area of the curriculum or related services, if—

(i) The parent, in writing, and the public agency consent to the excusal; and

(ii) The member **submits, in writing** to the parent and the IEP Team, **input** into the development of the IEP prior to the meeting.

(f) Initial IEP Team meeting for child under Part C. In the case of a child who was previously served under Part C of the Act, **an invitation** to the initial IEP Team meeting **must, at the request of the parent, be sent** to the Part C service coordinator or other representatives of the Part C system to assist with the smooth transition of services. (Authority: 20 U.S.C. 1414(d)(1)(B)-(d)(1)(D))

34 CFR § 300.322 Parent participation.

(a) Public agency responsibility - general. Each public agency must take steps to **ensure** that one or both of the **parents** of a child with a disability **are present at each IEP Team** meeting or are afforded the opportunity to participate, including-

(1) Notifying parents of the meeting early enough to ensure that they will have an opportunity to attend; and

(2) Scheduling the meeting at a **mutually agreed on** time and place.

(b) Information provided to parents.

(1) The **notice** required under paragraph (a)(1) of this section must—

(i) Indicate the **purpose, time, and location of the meeting and who will be in attendance**; and

(ii) Inform the parents of the provisions in 34 CFR § 300.321(a)(6) and (c) (relating to the participation of other individuals on the IEP Team who have knowledge or special expertise about the child), and 34 CFR § 300.321(f) (relating to the participation of the Part C service coordinator or other representatives of the Part C system at the initial IEP Team meeting for a child previously served under Part C of the Act).

(2) For a child with a disability beginning not later than **the first IEP to be in effect when the child turns 16**, or younger if determined appropriate by the IEP Team, the **notice also must**—

(i) Indicate—

(A) That a **purpose** of the meeting will be **the consideration of the postsecondary goals and transition services** for the child, in accordance with 34 CFR § 300.320(b); and

(B) **That the agency will invite the student**; and

(ii) Identify any other agency that will be invited to send a representative.

(c) Other methods to ensure parent participation. If neither parent can attend an IEP Team meeting, the public agency must use other methods to ensure **parent participation**, including **individual or conference telephone calls**, consistent with 34 CFR § 300.328 (related to alternative means of meeting participation).

(d) Conducting an IEP Team meeting without a parent in attendance. A meeting may be conducted without a parent in attendance if the public agency is unable to convince the parents that they should attend. In this case, the public agency must keep a record of its attempts to arrange a mutually agreed on time and place, such as—

(1) Detailed records of telephone calls made or attempted and the results of those calls;

(2) Copies of correspondence sent to the parents and any responses received; and

(3) Detailed **records of visits** made to the parent's home or place of employment and the results of those visits.

(e) Use of interpreters or other action, as appropriate. The public agency **must take whatever action is necessary** to ensure that the parent understands the proceedings of the IEP Team meeting, including arranging for an **interpreter** for parents with deafness or whose native language is other than English.

(f) Parent copy of child's IEP. The public agency must give the parent a copy of the child's IEP at no cost to the parent. (Authority: 20 U.S.C. 1414(d)(1)(B)(i))

34 CFR § 300.323 When IEPs must be in effect.

(a) **General**. At the **beginning of each school year**, each public agency **must have in effect**, for each child with a disability within its jurisdiction, an IEP, as defined in 34 CFR § 300.320.

(b) **IEP or IFSP for children aged three through five**.

(1) In the case of **a child with a disability aged three through five** (**or**, at the discretion of the SEA, **a two-year-old** child with a disability **who will turn age three** during the school year), the **IEP Team must consider an IFSP** that contains the **IFSP content** (including the natural environments statement) described in section 636(d) of the Act and its implementing regulations (including an educational component that promotes school readiness and incorporates pre-literacy, language, and numeracy skills for children with IFSPs under this section who are at least three years of age), and that is developed in accordance with the IEP procedures under this part. The IFSP may serve as the IEP of the child, if using the IFSP as the IEP is—

(i) Consistent with State policy; and

(ii) Agreed to by the agency and the child's parents.

(2) In implementing the requirements of paragraph (b)(1) of this section, the public agency must—

(i) Provide to the child's parents a detailed explanation of the differences between an IFSP and an IEP; and

(ii) If the parents choose an IFSP, obtain written informed consent from the parents.

(c) **Initial IEPs; provision of services**. Each public agency must ensure that—

(1) A meeting to develop an IEP for a child is conducted **within 30 days** of a determination that the child needs special education and related services; **and**

(2) **As soon as possible** following development of the IEP, special education and related services are made available to the child in accordance with the child's IEP.

(d) **Accessibility of child's IEP to teachers and others**. Each public agency must ensure that—

(1) The child's **IEP is accessible to each regular education teacher**, special education teacher, related services provider, and any other service provider who is responsible for its implementation; **and**

(2) Each teacher and provider described in paragraph (d)(1) of this section is **informed of**—

(i) His or her **specific responsibilities** related to implementing the child's IEP; **and**

(ii) **The specific accommodations, modifications**, and supports that must be provided for the child in accordance with the IEP.

(e) **IEPs for children who transfer public agencies in the same State**.

If a child with a disability (who had an IEP that was in effect in a previous public agency in the same State) **transfers to a new public agency in the same State**, and enrolls in a new school within the same school year, the new public agency (in consultation with the parents) must provide FAPE to the child (**including services comparable to** those described in the child's IEP from the previous public agency), **until** the new public agency **either**—

(1) **Adopts the child's IEP** from the previous public agency; **or**

(2) **Develops, adopts, and implements a new IEP** that meets the applicable requirements in 34 CFR § 300.320 through 300.324.

(f) **IEPs for children who transfer from another State**.

If a child with a disability (who had an IEP that was in effect in a previous public agency in another State) **transfers to a public agency in a new State**, and enrolls in a new school within the same school year, the new public agency (in consultation with the parents) must provide the child with FAPE (**including services comparable to** those described in the child's IEP from the previous public agency), **until** the new public agency—

(1) **Conducts an evaluation** pursuant to 34 CFR § 300.304 through 300.306 (if determined to be necessary by the new public agency); **and**

(2) **Develops, adopts, and implements a new IEP**, if appropriate, that meets the applicable requirements in 34 CFR § 300.320 through 300.324.

(g) **Transmittal of records**. To facilitate the transition for a child described in paragraphs (e) and (f) of this section—

(1) The **new public agency** in which the child enrolls **must take reasonable steps to promptly obtain the child's records**, including the IEP and supporting documents and any other records relating to the provision of special education or related services to the child, from the previous public agency in which the child was enrolled, pursuant to 34 CFR 99.31(a)(2); and

(2) The previous public agency in which the child was enrolled must take **reasonable steps to promptly respond** to the request from the new public agency. (Authority: 20 U.S.C. 1414(d)(2)(A)-(C))

Development of IEP

34 CFR § 300.324 Development, review, and revision of IEP.

(a) Development of IEP.

(1) General. In developing each child's IEP, **the IEP Team must consider—**

(i) The **strengths** of the child;

(ii) The **concerns of the parents** for enhancing the education of their child;

(iii) The **results of the initial or most recent evaluation** of the child; and

(iv) The **academic, developmental, and functional needs** of the child.

(2) Consideration of special factors. The IEP Team must—

(i) In the case of a child whose behavior impedes the child's learning or that of others, consider the use of **positive behavioral interventions** and supports, and other strategies, to address that behavior;

(ii) In the case of a child with **limited English proficiency**, consider the language needs of the child as those needs relate to the child's IEP;

(iii) In the case of a child who is **blind or visually impaired**, provide for instruction in **Braille** and the use of Braille unless the IEP Team determines, after an evaluation of the child's reading and writing skills, needs, and appropriate reading and writing media (including an evaluation of the child's future needs for instruction in Braille or the use of Braille), that instruction in Braille or the use of Braille is not appropriate for the child;

(iv) Consider the **communication needs** of the child, and in the case of a child who is deaf or hard of hearing, consider the child's language and communication needs, opportunities for direct communications with peers and professional personnel in the child's language and communication mode, academic level, and full range of needs, including opportunities for direct instruction in the child's language and communication mode; and

(v) Consider whether the child needs assistive technology devices and services.

(3) Requirement with respect to regular education teacher. A regular education teacher of a child with a disability, as a member of the IEP Team, **must**, to the extent appropriate, **participate** in the development of the IEP of the child, including the determination of—

(i) Appropriate positive behavioral interventions and supports and other strategies for the child; and

(ii) Supplementary aids and services, program modifications, and support for school personnel consistent with 34 CFR § 300.320(a)(4).

(4) Agreement.

(i) In **making changes to a child's IEP** after the annual IEP Team meeting for a school year, the parent of a child with a disability and the public agency **may agree not to convene an IEP Team** meeting for the purposes of making those changes, and instead may develop a **written document to amend or modify** the child's current IEP.

(ii) If changes are made to the child's IEP in accordance with paragraph (a)(4)(i) of this section, the public agency must ensure that the child's IEP Team is informed of those changes.

(5) Consolidation of IEP Team meetings. To the extent possible, the public agency **must encourage the consolidation of reevaluation meetings for the child and other IEP Team meetings** for the child.

(6) Amendments. Changes to the IEP may be made either by the entire IEP Team at an IEP Team meeting, or as provided in paragraph (a)(4) of this section, **by amending the IEP** rather than by redrafting the entire IEP. Upon request, a parent must be provided with a revised copy of the IEP with the amendments incorporated.

(b) Review and revision of IEPs.

(1) General. Each public agency **must** ensure that, subject to paragraphs (b)(2) and (b)(3) of this section, the IEP Team—

(i) **Reviews the child's IEP periodically, but not less than annually**, to determine whether the annual goals for the child are being achieved; and

(ii) **Revises the IEP, as appropriate**, to address—

(A) Any lack of expected progress toward the annual goals described in 34 CFR § 300.320(a)(2), and in the general education curriculum, if appropriate;

(B) **The results of any reevaluation** conducted under 34 CFR § 300.303;

(C) **Information about the child provided** to, or **by, the parents**, as described under 34 CFR § 300.305(a)(2);

(D) The child's anticipated needs; or

(E) Other matters.

(2) Consideration of special factors. In conducting a review of the child's IEP, the IEP Team must consider the special factors described in paragraph (a)(2) of this section.

(3) Requirement with respect to regular education teacher. A regular education teacher of the child, as a member of the IEP Team, must, consistent with paragraph (a)(3) of this section, participate in the review and revision of the IEP of the child.

(c) Failure to meet transition objectives.

(1) Participating agency failure. If a participating agency, other than the public agency, fails to provide the transition services described in the IEP in accordance with 34 CFR § 300.320(b), the public agency must reconvene the IEP Team to identify alternative strategies to meet the transition objectives for the child set out in the IEP.

(2) Construction. Nothing in this part relieves any participating agency, including a State vocational rehabilitation agency, of the responsibility to provide or pay for any transition service that the agency would otherwise provide to children with disabilities who meet the eligibility criteria of that agency.

(d) Children with disabilities in adult prisons.

(1) Requirements that do not apply. The following requirements do not apply to children with disabilities who are **convicted as adults under State law and incarcerated in adult prisons**:

(i) The requirements contained in section 612(a)(16) of the Act and 34 CFR § 300.320(a)(6) (relating to participation of children with disabilities in **general assessments**).

(ii) The requirements in 34 CFR § 300.320(b) (relating to **transition planning and transition services**) do not apply with respect to the children whose eligibility under Part B of the Act will end, because of their age, before they will be eligible to be released from prison based on consideration of their sentence and eligibility for early release.

(2) Modifications of IEP or placement.

(i) Subject to paragraph (d)(2)(ii) of this section, the IEP Team of a child with a disability who is **convicted as an adult under State law and incarcerated in an adult prison** may modify the child's IEP or placement if the State has demonstrated **a bona fide security or compelling penological interest** that cannot otherwise be accommodated.

(ii) The requirements of 34 CFR § 300.320 (relating to IEPs), and 300.112 (relating to LRE), do not apply with respect to the modifications described in paragraph (d)(2)(i) of this section. (Authority: 20 U.S.C. 1412(a)(1), 1412(a)(12)(A)(i), 1414(d)(3), (4)(B), and (7); and 1414(e))

34 CFR § 300.325 Private school placements by public agencies.

(a) Developing IEPs.

(1) Before a public agency places a child with a disability **in**, or refers a child to, **a private school** or facility, the agency must initiate and conduct a meeting to develop an IEP for the child in accordance with 34 CFR § 300.320 and 300.324.

(2) The agency must ensure that **a representative of the private school or facility attends the meeting**. If the representative cannot attend, the agency must use other methods to ensure participation by the private school or facility, including individual or conference telephone calls.

(b) Reviewing and revising IEPs.

(1) After a child with a disability enters a private school or facility, **any meetings** to review and revise the child's IEP **may be** initiated and **conducted by the private school** or facility at the discretion of the public agency.

(2) If the private school or facility initiates and conducts these meetings, the public agency must ensure that the parents and an agency representative—

(i) Are involved in any decision about the child's IEP; and

(ii) Agree to any proposed changes in the IEP before those changes are implemented.

(c) Responsibility. Even if a private school or facility implements a child's IEP, responsibility for compliance with this part remains with the public agency and the SEA. (Authority: 20 U.S.C. 1412(a)(10)(B))

34 CFR § 300.326 [Reserved]

34 CFR § 300.327 Educational placements.

Consistent with 34 CFR § 300.501(c), each public agency must ensure that the **parents** of each child with a disability **are members of any group** that makes decisions on the educational placement of their child. (Authority: 20 U.S.C. 1414(e))

34 CFR § 300.328 Alternative means of meeting participation.

When conducting IEP Team meetings and placement meetings pursuant to this subpart, and subpart E of this part, and carrying out administrative matters under section 615 of the Act (such as scheduling, exchange of witness lists, and status conferences), the parent of a child with a disability and a public agency may agree to use alternative means of meeting participation, such as **video conferences and conference calls**. (Authority: 20 U.S.C. 1414(f))

Subpart E—Procedural Safeguards
Due Process Procedures for Parents and Children

34 CFR § 300.500 Responsibility of SEA and other public agencies.

Each SEA must ensure that each public agency establishes, maintains, and implements procedural safeguards that meet the requirements of 34 CFR § 300.500 through 300.536. (Authority: 20 U.S.C. 1415(a))

34 CFR § 300.501 Opportunity to examine records; parent participation in meetings.

(a) Opportunity to examine records.

The parents of a child with a disability must be afforded, in accordance with the procedures of 34 CFR § 300.613 through 300.621, an opportunity to inspect and review all education records with respect to—

(1) The identification, evaluation, and educational placement of the child; and

(2) The provision of FAPE to the child.

(b) Parent participation in meetings.

(1) The parents of a child with a disability must be afforded an opportunity **to participate in meetings with respect to—**

(i) The **identification, evaluation, and educational placement** of the child; and

(ii) The provision of FAPE to the child.

(2) Each public agency must provide notice consistent with 34 CFR § 300.322(a)(1) and (b)(1) to ensure that parents of children with disabilities have the opportunity to participate in meetings described in paragraph (b)(1) of this section.

(3) A **meeting does not include** informal or unscheduled conversations involving public agency personnel and conversations on issues such as teaching methodology, lesson plans, or coordination of service provision. A meeting also does not include preparatory activities that public agency personnel engage in to develop a proposal or response to a parent proposal that will be discussed at a later meeting.

(c) Parent involvement in placement decisions.

(1) Each public agency must ensure that a parent of **each child with a disability is a member of any group that makes decisions on the educational placement** of the parent's child.

(2) In implementing the requirements of paragraph (c)(1) of this section, the public agency must use procedures consistent with the procedures described in 34 CFR § 300.322(a) through (b)(1).

(3) If neither parent can participate in a meeting in which a decision is to be made relating to the educational placement of their child, the public agency must use other methods to ensure their participation, including individual or conference telephone calls, or video conferencing.

(4) A placement decision may be made by a group without the involvement of a parent, if the public agency is unable to obtain the parent's participation in the decision. In this case, the public agency must have a record of its attempt to ensure their involvement. (Authority: 20 U.S.C. 1414(e), 1415(b)(1))

34 CFR § 300.502 Independent educational evaluation.

(a) General.

(1) The parents of a child with a disability **have the right under this part to obtain an independent educational evaluation** of the child, subject to paragraphs (b) through (e) of this section.

(2) Each public agency must provide to parents, upon request for an independent educational evaluation, information about where an independent educational evaluation may be obtained, and the agency criteria applicable for independent educational evaluations as set forth in paragraph (e) of this section.

(3) For the purposes of this subpart—

(i) **Independent educational evaluation** means an evaluation conducted by a qualified examiner who is not employed by the public agency responsible for the education of the child in question; and

(ii) Public expense means that the public agency either pays for the full cost of the evaluation or ensures that the evaluation is otherwise provided at no cost to the parent, consistent with 34 CFR § 300.103.

(b) Parent right to evaluation at public expense.

(1) A parent has the **right to an independent educational evaluation** at public expense if the parent disagrees with an evaluation obtained by the public agency, subject to the conditions in paragraphs (b)(2) through (4) of this section.

(2) If a parent requests an independent educational evaluation at public expense, **the public agency must**, without unnecessary delay, **either—**

(i) **File a due process complaint** to request a hearing to show that its evaluation is appropriate; **or**

(ii) **Ensure that an independent educational evaluation is provided at public expense**, unless the agency demonstrates in a hearing pursuant to 34 CFR § 300.507 through 300.513 that the evaluation obtained by the parent did not meet agency criteria.

(3) If the public agency files a **due process complaint notice** to request a hearing and the final decision is that the agency's evaluation is appropriate, the parent still has the right to an independent educational evaluation, but not at public expense.

(4) If a parent requests an independent educational evaluation, the public agency may ask for the parent's reason why he or she objects to the public evaluation. However, the public agency **may not require the parent to provide an explanation and may not unreasonably delay** either providing the independent educational evaluation at public expense or filing a due process complaint to request a due process hearing to defend the public evaluation.

(5) A parent is entitled to only one independent educational evaluation at public expense each time the public agency conducts an evaluation with which the parent disagrees.

(c) Parent-initiated evaluations.

If the parent obtains an independent educational evaluation at public expense **or shares with the public agency an evaluation obtained at private expense**, the results of the evaluation—

(1) **Must be considered by the public agency**, if it meets agency criteria, in any decision made with respect to the provision of FAPE to the child; and

(2) May be presented by any party as evidence at a hearing on a due process complaint under subpart E of this part regarding that child.

(d) Requests for evaluations by hearing officers.

If a hearing officer requests an independent educational evaluation as part of a hearing on a due process complaint, the cost of the evaluation must be at public expense.

(e) Agency criteria.

(1) If an independent educational evaluation is at public expense, the criteria under which the evaluation is obtained, including the location of the evaluation and the qualifications of the examiner, must be the same as the criteria that the public agency uses when it initiates an evaluation, to the extent those criteria are consistent with the parent's right to an independent educational evaluation.

(2) **Except** for the criteria described in paragraph (e)(1) of this section, **a public agency may not impose conditions or timelines** related to obtaining an independent educational evaluation at public expense. (Authority: 20 U.S.C. 1415(b) (1) and (d)(2)(A))

34 CFR § 300.503 Prior notice by the public agency; content of notice.

(a) Notice.

Written notice that meets the requirements of paragraph (b) of this section must be given to the parents of a child with a disability a reasonable time before the public agency—

(1) Proposes to initiate or change the identification, evaluation, or educational placement of the child or the provision of FAPE to the child; or

(2) Refuses to initiate or change the identification, evaluation, or educational placement of the child or the provision of FAPE to the child.

(b) Content of notice. The notice required under paragraph (a) of this section must include—

(1) A **description of the action proposed or refused** by the agency;

(2) An **explanation of why** the agency proposes or refuses to take the action;

(3) A **description of each evaluation procedure, assessment, record, or report** the agency used as a basis for the proposed or refused action;

(4) A statement that the parents of a child with a disability have protection under the procedural safeguards of this part and, if this notice is not an initial referral for evaluation, the means by which a copy of a description of the procedural safeguards can be obtained;

(5) Sources for parents to contact to obtain assistance in understanding the provisions of this part;

(6) A **description of other options** that the IEP Team considered and the reasons why those options were rejected; and

(7) A **description of other factors** that are relevant to the agency's proposal or refusal.

(c) Notice in understandable language.

(1) The notice required under paragraph (a) of this section must be—

(i) Written in **language understandable** to the general public; and

(ii) Provided in the **native language of the parent** or other mode of communication used by the parent, unless it is clearly not feasible to do so.

(2) If the native language or other mode of communication of the parent is not a written language, the public agency must take steps to ensure—

(i) That the notice is **translated orally or by other means** to the parent in his or her native language or other mode of communication;

(ii) That **the parent understands the content** of the notice; and

(iii) That there is **written evidence that the requirements** in paragraphs (c)(2)(i) and (ii) of this section **have been met**. (Authority: 20 U.S.C. 1415(b)(3) and (4), 1415(c)(1), 1414(b)(1))

34 CFR § 300.504 Procedural safeguards notice.

(a) General. A copy of the procedural safeguards available to the parents of a child with a disability must be given to the parents only **one time a school year, except** that a copy also must be given to the parents—

(1) **Upon initial referral or parent request for evaluation**;

(2) Upon receipt of the first State complaint under 34 CFR § 300.151 through 300.153 and upon receipt of the first due process complaint under 34 CFR § 300.507 in a school year;

(3) In accordance with the **discipline procedures** in 34 CFR § 300.530(h); and

(4) **Upon request** by a parent.

(b) Internet Web site. A public agency may place a current copy of the procedural safeguards notice on its Internet Web site if a Web site exists.

(c) Contents.

The procedural safeguards notice **must include a full explanation of all of the procedural safeguards** available under 34 CFR § 300.148, 34 CFR § 300.151 through 300.153, 34 CFR § 300.300, 34 CFR § 300.502 through 300.503, 34 CFR § 300.505 through 300.518, 34 CFR § 300.530 through 300.536 and 34 CFR § 300.610 through 300.625 relating to—

(1) **Independent educational evaluations**;

(2) **Prior written notice**;

(3) **Parental consent**;

(4) **Access to education records**;

(5) Opportunity to present and resolve complaints through the **due process complaint** and **State complaint** procedures, including—

(i) The **time period in which to file a complaint**;

(ii) The opportunity for the agency to resolve the complaint; and

(iii) The **difference between the due process complaint and the State complaint procedures**, including the jurisdiction of each procedure, what issues may be raised, filing and decisional timelines, and relevant procedures;

(6) The availability of mediation;

(7) **The child's placement during the pendency of any due process complaint;**

(8) Procedures for students who are subject to placement in an interim alternative educational setting;

(9) Requirements for **unilateral placement by parents** of children in private schools at public expense;

(10) Hearings on due process complaints, including requirements for disclosure of evaluation results and recommendations;

(11) State-level appeals (if applicable in the State);

(12) Civil actions, including the time period in which to file those actions; and

(13) Attorneys' fees.

(d) Notice in understandable language. The notice required under paragraph (a) of this section must meet the requirements of 34 CFR § 300.503(c). (Authority: 20 U.S.C. 1415(d))

34 CFR § 300.505 Electronic mail.

A parent of a child with a disability may elect to receive notices required by 34 CFR § 300.503, 300.504, and 300.508 by an electronic mail communication, if the public agency makes that option available. (Authority: 20 U.S.C. 1415(n))

34 CFR § 300.506 Mediation.

(a) General.

Each public agency must ensure that procedures are established and implemented to allow parties to disputes involving any matter under this part, including matters arising prior to the filing of a due process complaint, **to resolve disputes through a mediation** process.

(b) Requirements. The procedures **must meet the following requirements**:

(1) The procedures must ensure that the mediation process—

(i) Is **voluntary** on the part of the parties;

(ii) Is **not used to deny or delay a parent's right** to a hearing on the parent's due process complaint, or to deny any other rights afforded under Part B of the Act; and

(iii) Is conducted by a **qualified and impartial mediator** who is trained in effective mediation techniques.

(2) A public agency may establish procedures to offer to parents and schools that choose not to use the mediation process, an opportunity to meet, at a time and location convenient to the parents, with a disinterested party—

(i) Who is under contract with an appropriate alternative dispute resolution entity, or a parent training and information center or community parent resource center in the State established under section 671 or 672 of the Act; and

(ii) Who would explain the benefits of, and encourage the use of, the mediation process to the parents.

(3)

(i) The State must maintain a **list of individuals** who are qualified mediators and knowledgeable in laws and regulations relating to the provision of special education and related services.

(ii) The SEA must select mediators on a **random, rotational, or other impartial** basis.

(4) The **State must bear the cost of the mediation process**, including the costs of meetings described in paragraph (b)(2) of this section.

(5) Each session in the mediation process must be scheduled in a timely manner and must be held in a **location that is convenient** to the parties to the dispute.

(6) If the parties resolve a dispute through the mediation process, the parties must execute a **legally binding agreement** that sets forth that resolution and that—

(i) States that all discussions that occurred during the mediation process will remain **confidential and may not be used as evidence** in any subsequent due process hearing or civil proceeding; and

(ii) Is signed by both the **parent** and a **representative of the agency who has the authority to bind** such agency.

(7) A written, signed mediation agreement under this paragraph is **enforceable in any State court** of competent jurisdiction **or in a district court of the United States**.

(8) Discussions that occur during the mediation process must be **confidential** and may not be used as evidence in any subsequent due process hearing or civil proceeding of any Federal court or State court of a State receiving assistance under this part.

(c) Impartiality of mediator.

(1) An individual who serves as a mediator under this part—

(i) **May not be an employee of the SEA or the LEA** that is involved in the education or care of the child; and

(ii) **Must not have a personal or professional interest that conflicts with the person's objectivity**.

(2) A person who otherwise qualifies as a mediator is not an employee of an LEA or State agency described under 34 CFR § 300.228 solely because he or she is paid by the agency to serve as a mediator.

34 CFR § 300.507 Filing a due process complaint.

(a) **General**.

(1) A **parent or a public agency may file a due process complaint** on **any of the matters** described in 34 CFR § 300.503(a)(1) and (2) (relating to the identification, evaluation or educational placement of a child with a disability, or the provision of FAPE to the child).

(2) The **due process complaint must allege a violation that occurred not more than two years** before the date the parent or public agency knew or should have known about the alleged action that forms the basis of the due process complaint, **or, if the State has an explicit time limitation** for filing a due process complaint under this part, in the time allowed by that State law, except that the exceptions to the timeline described in 34 CFR § 300.511(f) apply to the timeline in this section.

(b) **Information for parents**. The public agency must inform the parent of any free or low-cost legal and other relevant services available in the area if—

(1) The parent requests the information; or

(2) The parent or the agency files a due process complaint under this section. (Authority: 20 U.S.C. 1415(b)(6))

34 CFR § 300.508 Due process complaint.

(a) **General**.

(1) The public agency must have procedures that require either party, or the attorney representing a party, to provide to the other party a **due process complaint** (which must remain **confidential**).

(2) The party filing a due process complaint **must forward a copy of the due process complaint to the SEA**.

(b) **Content of complaint**. The due process complaint required in paragraph (a)(1) of this section **must include**—

(1) The name of the child;

(2) The address of the residence of the child;

(3) The name of the school the child is attending;

(4) In the case of a homeless child or youth (within the meaning of section 725(2) of the McKinney-Vento Homeless Assistance Act (42 U.S.C. 11434a(2)), available contact information for the child, and the name of the school the child is attending;

(5) A **description of the nature of the problem** of the child relating to the proposed or refused initiation or change, including **facts relating to the problem**; and

(6) A **proposed resolution** of the problem to the extent known and available to the party at the time.

(c) **Notice required before a hearing on a due process complaint**.

A party **may not have a hearing** on a due process complaint **until the party, or the attorney** representing the party, **files a due process complaint that meets the requirements** of paragraph (b) of this section.

(d) **Sufficiency of complaint.**

(1) The due process complaint required by this section **must be deemed sufficient unless** the party receiving the due process complaint notifies the hearing officer and the other party in writing, within 15 days of receipt of the due process complaint, that the receiving party believes the due process complaint does not meet the requirements in paragraph (b) of this section.

(2) **Within five days** of receipt of notification under paragraph (d)(1) of this section, the hearing officer must make a determination on the face of the due process complaint of whether the due process complaint meets the requirements of paragraph (b) of this section, and must immediately notify the parties in writing of that determination.

(3) A party may **amend** its due process complaint **only if**—

(i) The other party **consents** in writing to the amendment and **is given the opportunity to resolve** the due process complaint through a meeting held pursuant to 34 CFR § 300.510; **or**

(ii) The **hearing officer grants permission**, except that the hearing officer may only grant permission to amend at any time not later than five days before the due process hearing begins.

(4) If a party files an **amended due process complaint, the timelines** for the resolution meeting in 34 CFR § 300.510(a) and the time period to resolve in 34 CFR § 300.510(b) **begin again** with the filing of the amended due process complaint.

(e) **LEA response to a due process complaint**.

(1) If the LEA has not sent a **prior written notice** under 34 CFR § 300.503 to the parent regarding the subject matter contained in the parent's due process complaint, the LEA must, within 10 days of receiving the due process complaint,

send to the parent a response that includes—

(i) An explanation of why the agency proposed or refused to take the action raised in the due process complaint;

(ii) A description of other options that the IEP Team considered and the reasons why those options were rejected;

(iii) A description of each evaluation procedure, assessment, record, or report the agency used as the basis for the proposed or refused action; and

(iv) A description of the other factors that are relevant to the agency's proposed or refused action.

(2) A response by an LEA under paragraph (e)(1) of this section shall not be construed to preclude the LEA from asserting that the parent's due process complaint was insufficient, where appropriate.

(f) Other party response to a due process complaint.

Except as provided in paragraph (e) of this section, the party receiving a due process complaint **must, within 10 days** of receiving the due process complaint, **send to the other party a response** that specifically addresses the issues raised in the due process complaint. (Authority: 20 U.S.C. 1415(b)(7), 1415(c)(2))

34 CFR § 300.509 Model forms.

(a) **Each SEA must develop model for**ms to assist parents and public agencies in filing a due process complaint in accordance with 34 CFR § 300.507(a) and 300.508(a) through (c) and to assist parents and other parties in filing a State complaint under 34 CFR § 300.151 through 300.153. However, the SEA or LEA **may not require the use of the model forms**.

(b) Parents, public agencies, and other parties **may use** the appropriate model form described in paragraph (a) of this section, **or another form or other document, so long** as the form or document that is used meets, as appropriate, the content requirements in 34 CFR § 300.508(b) for filing a due process complaint, or the requirements in 34 CFR § 300.153(b) for filing a State complaint. (Authority: 20 U.S.C. 1415(b)(8))

\34 CFR § 300.510 Resolution process.

(a) **Resolution meeting**.

(1) **Within 15 days** of receiving notice of the parent's due process complaint, and prior to the initiation of a due process hearing under 34 CFR § 300.511, **the LEA must convene a meeting** with the parent and the **relevant member** or members **of the IEP** Team who have specific knowledge of the facts identified in the due process complaint that—

(i) Includes a representative of the public agency who has **decision-making authority** on behalf of that agency; and

(ii) **May not include an attorney of the LEA unless** the parent is accompanied by an attorney.

(2) The **purpose of the meeting is for the parent of the child to discuss the due process complaint, and the facts** that form the basis of the due process complaint, so that the LEA has the opportunity to resolve the dispute that is the basis for the due process complaint.

(3) The meeting described in paragraph (a)(1) and (2) of this section **need not be held if**—

(i) The **parent and the LEA agree in writing to waive** the meeting; or

(ii) The **parent and the LEA agree to use the mediation** process described in 34 CFR § 300.506.

(4) The parent and the LEA determine the relevant members of the IEP Team to attend the meeting.

(b) Resolution period.

(1) If the LEA has not resolved the due process complaint to the satisfaction of the parent **within 30 days** of the receipt of the due process complaint, the due process hearing may occur.

(2) Except as provided in paragraph (c) of this section, the timeline for issuing a final decision under 34 CFR § 300.515 begins at the expiration of this 30-day period.

(3) **Except where the parties have jointly agreed to waive the resolution process or to use mediation**, notwithstanding paragraphs (b)(1) and (2) of this section, the **failure of the parent** filing a due process complaint **to participate in the resolution meeting will delay** the timelines for the resolution process and due process hearing **until the meeting is held**.

(4) If the LEA is **unable to obtain the participation of the parent** in the resolution meeting after reasonable efforts have been made (and documented using the procedures in 34 CFR § 300.322(d)), the LEA may, at the conclusion of the 30-day period, request that a hearing officer **dismiss the parent's due process complaint**.

(5) If the **LEA fails to hold the resolution meeting** specified in paragraph (a) of this section **within 15 days** of receiving notice of a parent's due process complaint or fails to participate in the resolution meeting, the parent may seek the intervention of a hearing officer to **begin the due process hearing timeline**.

(c) Adjustments to 30-day resolution period. The **45-day timeline** for the due process hearing in 34 CFR § 300.515(a) starts the day **after one** of the following events:

(1) Both parties agree in writing to **waive** the resolution meeting;

(2) After either the mediation or resolution meeting starts but before the end of the 30-day period, the parties **agree** in writing that **no agreement is possible;**

(3) If both parties agree in writing to continue the mediation at the end of the 30-day resolution period, but later, the parent or public agency **withdraws** from the mediation process.

(d) Written settlement agreement. If a resolution to the dispute is reached at the meeting described in paragraphs (a)(1) and (2) of this section, **the parties must execute a legally binding agreeme**nt that is—

(1) Signed by both the parent and a representative of the agency who has the authority to bind the agency; and

(2) **Enforceable in any State court of competent jurisdiction or in a district court of the United States**, or, by the SEA, if the State has other mechanisms or procedures that permit parties to seek enforcement of resolution agreements, pursuant to 34 CFR § 300.537.

(e) Agreement review period. If the parties execute an agreement pursuant to paragraph (d) of this section, a **party may void the agreement within 3 business day**s of the agreement's execution. (Authority: 20 U.S.C. 1415(f)(1)(B))

34 CFR § 300.511 Impartial due process hearing.

(a) General. Whenever a due process complaint is received under 34 CFR § 300.507 or 34 CFR § 300.532, the parents or the LEA involved in the dispute must have an opportunity for an impartial due process hearing, consistent with the procedures in 34 CFR § 300.507, 300.508, and 300.510.

(b) Agency responsible for conducting the due process hearing.

The hearing described in paragraph (a) of this section must be conducted by the SEA or the public agency directly responsible for the education of the child, as determined under State statute, State regulation, or a written policy of the SEA.

(c) Impartial hearing officer.

(1) At a minimum, a **hearing officer**—

(i) **Must not be**—

(A) **An employee of the SEA or the LEA** that is involved in the education or care of the child; or

(B) **A person having a personal or professional interest that conflicts with the person's objectivity in the hearing;**

(ii) Must possess knowledge of, and the ability to understand, the provisions of the Act, Federal and State regulations pertaining to the Act, and legal interpretations of the Act by Federal and State courts;

(iii) Must possess the knowledge and ability to conduct hearings in accordance with appropriate, **standard legal practice**; and

(iv) Must possess the knowledge and ability to render and write decisions in accordance with appropriate, standard legal practice.

(2) A person who otherwise qualifies to conduct a hearing under paragraph (c)(1) of this section is not an employee of the agency solely because he or she is paid by the agency to serve as a hearing officer.

(3) Each public agency must keep a **list of the persons** who serve as hearing officers. The list must include a statement of the qualifications of each of those persons.

(d) Subject matter of due process hearings.

The party requesting the due process hearing **may not raise issues at the due process hearing** that were not raised in the due process complaint filed under 34 CFR § 300.508(b), unless the other party agrees otherwise.

(e) Timeline for requesting a hearing.

A parent or agency **must request an impartial hearing on their due process complaint within two years** of the date the parent or agency knew or should have known about the alleged action that forms the basis of the due process complaint, **or if the State** has an explicit time limitation for requesting such a due process hearing under this part, in the time allowed by that State law.

(f) Exceptions to the timeline.

The timeline described in paragraph (e) of this section does not apply to a parent if the parent was prevented from filing a due process complaint due to—

(1) **Specific misrepresentations** by the LEA that it had resolved the problem forming the basis of the due process complaint; or

(2) The LEA's **withholding of information** from the parent that was required under this part to be provided to the parent. (Authority: 20 U.S.C. 1415(f)(1)(A), 1415(f)(3)(A)–(D))

34 CFR § 300.512 Hearing rights.

(a) General.

Any party to a hearing conducted pursuant to 34 CFR § 300.507 through 300.513 or 34 CFR § 300.530 through 300.534, or an appeal conducted pursuant to 34 CFR § 300.514, has the right to—

(1) Be accompanied and advised by counsel and by individuals with special knowledge or training with respect to the problems of children with disabilities;

(2) **Present evidence and confront, cross-examine, and compel the attendance of witnesses;**

(3) **Prohibit the introduction of any evidence** at the hearing that has **not been disclosed** to that party **at least five business days** before the hearing;

(4) Obtain a written, or, at the option of the parents, electronic, verbatim record of the hearing; and

(5) Obtain written, or, at the option of the parents, electronic findings of fact and decisions.

(b) Additional disclosure of information.

(1) At least five business days prior to a hearing conducted pursuant to 34 CFR § 300.511(a), each party must disclose to all other parties all evaluations completed by that date and recommendations based on the offering party's evaluations that the party intends to use at the hearing.

(2) A hearing officer may bar any party that fails to comply with paragraph (b)(1) of this section from introducing the relevant evaluation or recommendation at the hearing without the consent of the other party.

(c) Parental rights at hearings. Parents involved in hearings must be given the right to—

(1) Have the child who is the subject of the hearing present;

(2) Open the hearing to the public; and

(3) Have the record of the hearing and the findings of fact and decisions described in paragraphs (a)(4) and (a)(5) of this section provided at no cost to parents. (Authority: 20 U.S.C. 1415(f)(2), 1415(h))

34 CFR § 300.513 Hearing decisions.

(a) Decision of hearing officer on the provision of FAPE.

(1) Subject to paragraph (a)(2) of this section, a hearing officer's determination of whether a child received FAPE must be based on **substantive grounds.**

(2) In matters alleging a **procedural violation**, a hearing officer may find that a child did not receive a FAPE **only if** the procedural inadequacies—

(i) **Impeded the child's right to a FAPE;**

(ii) **Significantly impeded the parent's opportunity to participate** in the decision-making process regarding the provision of a FAPE to the parent's child; or

(iii) **Caused a deprivation of educational benefit.**

(3) Nothing in paragraph (a) of this section shall be construed to preclude a hearing officer from ordering an LEA to comply with procedural requirements under 34 CFR § 300.500 through 300.536.

(b) Construction clause. Nothing in 34 CFR § 300.507 through 300.513 shall be construed to affect the right of a parent to file an appeal of the due process hearing decision with the SEA under 34 CFR § 300.514(b), if a State level appeal is available.

(c) Separate request for a due process hearing. Nothing in 34 CFR § 300.500 through 300.536 shall be construed to preclude a parent from filing a separate due process complaint on an issue s**eparate from a due process complaint already filed**.

(d) Findings and decision to advisory panel and general public. The public agency, after deleting any personally identifiable information, must—

(1) Transmit the findings and decisions referred to in 34 CFR § 300.512(a)(5) to the State advisory panel established under 34 CFR § 300.167; and

(2) Make those findings and decisions **available to the public**. (Authority: 20 U.S.C. 1415(f)(3)(E) and (F), 1415(h)(4), 1415(o))

34 CFR § 300.514 Finality of decision; appeal; impartial review.

(a) **Finality of hearing decision**. A decision made in a hearing conducted pursuant to 34 CFR § 300.507 through 300.513 or 34 CFR § 300.530 through 300.534 is final, except that any party involved in the hearing may appeal the decision **under the provisions of paragraph (b) of this section and 34 CFR § 300.516**.

(b) **Appeal of decisions; impartial review.**

(1) If the hearing required by 34 CFR § 300.511 is conducted by a public agency other than the SEA, any party aggrieved by the findings and decision in the hearing may appeal to the SEA.

(2) If there is an appeal, the **SEA must conduct an impartial review** of the findings and decision appealed. The official conducting the review must—

(i) Examine the entire hearing record;

(ii) Ensure that the procedures at the hearing were consistent with the requirements of due process;

(iii) Seek additional evidence if necessary. If a hearing is held to receive additional evidence, the rights in 34 CFR § 300.512 apply;

(iv) Afford the parties an opportunity for oral or written argument, or both, at the discretion of the reviewing official;

(v) Make an independent decision on completion of the review; and

(vi) Give a copy of the written, or, at the option of the parents, electronic findings of fact and decisions to the parties.

(c) **Findings and decision to advisory panel and general public**. The SEA, after deleting any personally identifiable information, must—

(1) Transmit the findings and decisions referred to in paragraph (b)(2)(vi) of this section to the State advisory panel established under 34 CFR § 300.167; and

(2) Make those findings and decisions available to the public.

(d) **Finality of review decision**. The decision made by the reviewing official is final **unless a party brings a civil action under 34 CFR § 300.516**. (Authority: 20 U.S.C. 1415(g) and (h)(4), 1415(i)(1)(A), 1415(i)(2))

34 CFR § 300.515 Timelines and convenience of hearings and reviews.

(a) The public agency must ensure that **not later than 45 days** after the expiration of the 30 day period under 34 CFR § 300.510(b), or the adjusted time periods described in 34 CFR § 300.510(c)

(1) A final decision is reached in the hearing; and

(2) A copy of the decision is mailed to each of the parties.

(b) The SEA must ensure that **not later than 30 days after the receipt of a request** for a review—

(1) A final decision is reached in the review; and

(2) A copy of the decision is mailed to each of the parties.

(c) **A hearing or reviewing officer may grant specific extensions of time** beyond the periods set out in paragraphs (a) and (b) of this section at the request of either party.

(d) Each hearing and each review involving oral arguments must be conducted at a time and place that is reasonably convenient to the parents and child involved. (Authority: 20 U.S.C. 1415(f)(1)(B)(ii), 1415(g), 1415(i)(1))

34 CFR § 300.516 Civil action.

(a) **General**. Any party **aggrieved by the findings and decision** made under 34 CFR § 300.507 through 300.513 or 34 CFR § 300.530 through 300.534 who does not have the **right to an appeal** under 34 CFR § 300.514(b), and any party aggrieved by the findings and decision under 34 CFR § 300.514(b), has the **right to bring a civil action** with respect to the due process complaint notice requesting a due process hearing under 34 CFR § 300.507 or 34 CFR § 300.530 through 300.532. The action may be brought in any State court of competent jurisdiction or in a district court of the United States without regard to the amount in controversy.

(b) **Time limitation**. The party bringing the action shall **have 90 days from the date of the decision** of the hearing officer or, if applicable, the decision of the State review official, to file a civil action, **or, if the State** has an explicit time limitation for bringing civil actions under Part B of the Act, in the time allowed by that State law.

(c) **Additional requirements**. In any action brought under paragraph (a) of this section, the court—

(1) Receives the records of the administrative proceedings;

(2) Hears additional evidence at the request of a party; and

(3) Basing its decision on the preponderance of the evidence, grants the relief that the court determines to be appropriate.

(d) Jurisdiction of district courts. The district courts of the United States have jurisdiction of actions brought under section 615 of the Act without regard to the amount in controversy.

(e) Rule of construction. Nothing in this part restricts or limits the rights, procedures, and remedies available under the Constitution, the Americans with Disabilities Act of 1990, title V of the Rehabilitation Act of 1973, or other Federal laws protecting the rights of children with disabilities, except that before the filing of a civil action under these laws seeking relief that is also available under section 615 of the Act, **the procedures under 34 CFR § 300.507 and 300.514 must be exhausted** to the same extent as would be required had the action been brought under section 615 of the Act. (Authority: 20 U.S.C. 1415(i)(2) and (3)(A), 1415(l))

34 CFR § 300.517 Attorneys' fees.

(a) In general.

(1) In any action or proceeding brought under section 615 of the Act, the court, in its discretion, **may award reasonable attorneys' fees** as part of the costs to—

(i) The prevailing party who is the parent of a child with a disability;

(ii) To a **prevailing party who is an SEA or LEA against the attorney of a parent** who files a complaint or subsequent cause of action that is **frivolous, unreasonable, or without foundation**, or against the attorney of a parent who **continued to litigate** after the litigation clearly became frivolous, unreasonable, or without foundation; or

(iii) To a **prevailing SEA or LEA against the attorney of a parent, or against the parent**, if the parent's **request** for a due process hearing or subsequent cause of action was presented for any **improper purpose, such as to harass, to cause unnecessary delay**, or to needlessly increase the cost of litigation.

(2) Nothing in this subsection shall be construed to affect section 327 of the District of Columbia Appropriations Act, 2005.

(b) Prohibition on use of funds.

(1) **Funds under Part B of the Act may not be used to pay attorneys' fees** or costs of a party related to any action or proceeding under section 615 of the Act and subpart E of this part.

(2) Paragraph (b)(1) of this section does not preclude a public agency from using funds under Part B of the Act for conducting an action or proceeding under section 615 of the Act.

(c) Award of fees. A court awards **reasonable attorneys' fees** under section 615(i)(3) of the Act consistent with the following:

(1) Fees awarded under section 615(i)(3) of the Act must be based on **rates prevailing in the community** in which the action or proceeding arose for the kind and quality of services furnished. No bonus or multiplier may be used in calculating the fees awarded under this paragraph.

(2)

(i) Attorneys' fees **may not be awarded and related costs may not be reimburse**d in any action or proceeding under section 615 of the Act for services performed **subsequent to the time of a written offer of settlement to a parent if**—

(A) The offer is made within the time prescribed by Rule 68 of the Federal Rules of Civil Procedure or, in the case of an administrative proceeding, at any time more than 10 days before the proceeding begins;

(B) The offer is not accepted within 10 days; and

(C) The court or administrative hearing officer finds that the relief finally obtained by the parents is not more favorable to the parents than the offer of settlement.

(ii) Attorneys' fees may not be awarded relating to any meeting of the IEP Team unless the meeting is convened as a result of an administrative proceeding or judicial action, or at the discretion of the State, for a mediation described in 34 CFR § 300.506.

(iii) A meeting conducted pursuant to 34 CFR § 300.510 shall not be considered—

(A) A meeting convened as a result of an administrative hearing or judicial action; or

(B) An administrative hearing or judicial action for purposes of this section.

(3) Notwithstanding paragraph (c)(2) of this section, an award of attorneys' fees and related costs may be made **to a parent who is the prevailing party** and who was substantially justified in rejecting the settlement offer.

(4) Except as provided in paragraph (c)(5) of this section, the court reduces, accordingly, the amount of the attorneys' fees awarded under section 615 of the Act, if the court finds that—

(i) The **parent, or the parent's attorney,** during the course of the action or proceeding, **unreasonably protracted the final resolution** of the controversy;

(ii) The amount of the attorneys' fees otherwise authorized to be awarded unreasonably exceeds the hourly rate prevailing in the community for similar services by attorneys of reasonably comparable skill, reputation, and experience;

(iii) The time spent and legal services furnished **were excessive** considering the nature of the action or proceeding; or

(iv) The attorney representing the parent did not provide to the LEA the **appropriate information in the due process request notice** in accordance with 34 CFR § 300.508.

(5) The provisions of paragraph (c)(4) of this section **do not apply** in any action or proceeding if the court finds that the State or local agency **unreasonably protracted the final resolution** of the action or proceeding or there was a violation of section 615 of the Act. (Authority: 20 U.S.C. 1415(i)(3)(B)–(G))

34 CFR § 300.518 Child's status during proceedings.

(a) Except as provided in 34 CFR § 300.533, **during the pendency of any administrative or judicial proceeding regarding a due process complaint notice** requesting a due process hearing under 34 CFR § 300.507, unless the State or local agency and the parents of the child agree otherwise, **the child** involved in the complaint must remain in his or her **current educational placement**.

(b) If the complaint involves an application for **initial admission** to public school, the child, with the consent of the parents, must be placed in the public school until the completion of all the proceedings.

(c) If the complaint involves an **application for initial services** under this part **from a child who is transitioning from Part C of the Act to Part B and is no longer eligible for Part C services** because the child has turned three, **the public agency is not required to provide the Part C services that the child had been receiving.** If the child is found eligible for special education and related services under Part B and the parent consents to the initial provision of special education and related services under 34 CFR § 300.300(b), **then the public agency must provide those special education and related services that are not in dispute between the parent and the public agency.**

(d) If the **hearing officer** in a due process hearing conducted by the SEA or a State review official in an administrative appeal **agrees** with the child's parents **that a change of placement is appropriate,** that placement must be treated as **an agreement** between the State and the parents for purposes of paragraph (a) of this section.[8]

34 CFR § 300.519 Surrogate parents.

(a) General. Each public agency must ensure that the rights of a child are protected when—

(1) No parent (as defined in 34 CFR § 300.30) can be identified;

(2) The public agency, after reasonable efforts, cannot locate a parent;

(3) The child is a ward of the State under the laws of that State; or

(4) The child is an unaccompanied homeless youth as defined in section 725(6) of the McKinney-Vento Homeless Assistance Act (42 U.S.C. 11434a(6)).

(b) Duties of public agency. The duties of a public agency under paragraph (a) of this section include the assignment of an individual to act as a surrogate for the parents. This must include a method—

(1) For determining whether a child needs a surrogate parent; and

---

8   This is usually applicable in a parentally placed private school tuition reimbursement *"Carter"* cases where the parents are seeking tuition reimbursement for the past expenses and prospective tuition for the future. **If the parents prevail, the LEA must immediately assume responsibility for the prospective tuition, even if the LEA appeals the case** to federal or state court. *See* this author's February 7, 2000 case against the Virginia Department of Education where the state refused to require the LEA to pay the past and prospective tuition after we prevailed at a due process hearing. This author requested a due process hearing against Virginia for the prospective, upcoming tuition. The Hearing Officer ordered the Commonwealth of Virginia to pay the tuition. The SEA appealed to federal court, lost, and the Judge ordered payment of tuition, attorney's fees, and dismissed the state's immunity claim. *See* https://www.wrightslaw.com/law/caselaw/VASEA_white.pdf

(2) For assigning a surrogate parent to the child.

(c) Wards of the State. In the case of a child who is a ward of the State, the surrogate parent alternatively may be appointed by the judge overseeing the child's case, provided that the surrogate meets the requirements in paragraphs (d)(2)(i) and (e) of this section.

(d) Criteria for selection of surrogate parents.

(1) The public agency may select a surrogate parent in any way permitted under State law.

(2) Public agencies must ensure that a person selected as a surrogate parent—

(i) Is not an employee of the SEA, the LEA, or any other agency that is involved in the education or care of the child;

(ii) Has no personal or professional interest that conflicts with the interest of the child the surrogate parent represents; and

(iii) Has knowledge and skills that ensure adequate representation of the child.

(e) Non-employee requirement; compensation.

A person otherwise qualified to be a surrogate parent under paragraph (d) of this section is not an employee of the agency solely because he or she is paid by the agency to serve as a surrogate parent.

(f) Unaccompanied homeless youth.

In the case of a child who is an unaccompanied **homeless youth**, appropriate staff of emergency shelters, transitional shelters, independent living programs, and street outreach programs may be appointed as temporary surrogate parents without regard to paragraph (d)(2)(i) of this section, until a surrogate parent can be appointed that meets all of the requirements of paragraph (d) of this section.

(g) Surrogate parent responsibilities. The **surrogate parent may represent the child in all** matters relating to—

(1) The identification, evaluation, and educational placement of the child; and

(2) The provision of FAPE to the child.

(h) SEA responsibility. The SEA must make reasonable efforts to ensure the assignment of a surrogate parent not more than **30 days** after a public agency determines that the child needs a surrogate parent. (Authority: 20 U.S.C. 1415(b)(2))

34 CFR § 300.520 Transfer of parental rights at age of majority.

(a) General. A State may provide that, when **a child with a disability reaches the age of majority** under State law that applies to all children (except for a child with a disability who has been determined to be incompetent under State law)—

(1)

(i) The public agency must provide any notice required by this part to both the child and the parents; and

(ii) All rights accorded to parents under Part B of the Act transfer to the child;

(2) All rights accorded to parents under Part B of the Act transfer to children who are incarcerated in an adult or juvenile, State or local correctional institution; and

(3) Whenever a State provides for the transfer of rights under this part pursuant to paragraph (a)(1) or (a)(2) of this section, the agency must notify the child and the parents of the transfer of rights.

(b) Special rule. A State **must establish procedures for appointing the parent of a child with a disability**, or, if the parent is not available, another appropriate individual, to represent the educational interests of the child throughout the period of the child's eligibility under Part B of the Act if, under State law, **a child who has reached the age of majority, but has not been determined to be incompetent,** can be determined not to have the ability to provide informed consent with respect to the child's educational program. (Authority: 20 U.S.C. 1415(m))

34 CFR § 300.521-300.529 [Reserved]

Discipline Procedures

34 CFR § 300.530 Authority of school personnel.

(a) Case-by-case determination.

School personnel may consider any unique circumstances on a case-by-case basis when determining whether a change in placement, consistent with the other requirements of this section, is appropriate for a child with a disability who violates a code of student conduct.

(b) General.

(1) School personnel under this section **may remove** a child with a disability who violates a code of student conduct from his or her current placement to an appropriate interim alternative educational setting, another setting, or suspension, for **not more than 10 consecutive school days** (to the extent those alternatives are applied to children without disabilities), and **for additional removals of not more than 10 consecutive school days** in that same school year for separate incidents of misconduct (**as long** as those removals do not constitute a change of placement under 34 CFR § 300.536).

(2) **After a child with a disability has been removed from his or her current placement for 10 school days in the same school year, during any subsequent days of removal the public agency must provide services to the extent required under paragraph (d) of this section.**

(c) Additional authority.

For disciplinary changes in placement that **would exceed 10 consecutive school days**, if the behavior that gave rise to the violation of the school code is **determined not to be a manifestation of the child's disability** pursuant to paragraph (e) of this section, school personnel may apply the relevant disciplinary procedures to children with disabilities in the same manner and for the same duration as the procedures would be applied to children without disabilities, except as provided in paragraph (d) of this section.

(d) Services.

(1) A child with a disability **who is removed from the child's current placement** pursuant to paragraphs (c), or (g) of this section must—

(i) **Continue to receive educational services**, as provided in 34 CFR § 300.101(a), so as to enable the child to continue to participate in the **general education curriculum**, although in another setting, and to **progress toward meeting the goals set out in the child's IEP**; and

(ii) Receive, as appropriate, a **functional behavioral assessment, and behavioral intervention services and modifications**, that are designed to address the behavior violation **so that it does not recur**.

(2) The services required by paragraph (d)(1), (d)(3), (d)(4), and (d)(5) of this section **may be provided in an interim alternative educational setting**.

(3) A public agency is **only required to provide services during periods of removal** to a child with a disability who has been removed from his or her current placement for **10 school days or less in that school year, if it provides services to a child without disabilities** who is similarly removed.

(4) After a child with a disability has been removed from his or her current placement **for 10 school days in the same school year**, if the current removal is for not more than 10 consecutive school days and is not a change of placement under 34 CFR § 300.536, school personnel, in consultation with at least one of the child's teachers, determine the extent to which services are needed, as provided in 34 CFR § 300.101(a), so as **to enable the child to continue to participate in the general education curriculum,** although in another setting, and to progress toward meeting the goals set out in the child's IEP.

(5) If the removal is a change of placement under 34 CFR § 300.536, the child's IEP Team determines appropriate services under paragraph (d)(1) of this section.

(e) Manifestation determination.

(1) **Within 10 school days** of any decision to change the placement of a child with a disability because of a violation of a code of student conduct, **the LEA, the parent, and relevant members of the child's IEP Team** (as determined by the parent and the LEA) must review all relevant information in the student's file, including the child's IEP, any teacher observations, and any relevant information provided by the parents to determine—

(i) If the **conduct in question was caused by, or had a direct and substantial relationship to**, the child's disability; or

(ii) If the conduct in question was the direct result of the **LEA's failure to implement the IEP**.

(2) The conduct **must be determined to be a manifestation** of the child's disability if the LEA, the parent, and relevant members of the child's IEP Team determine that **a condition in either** paragraph (e)(1)(i) or (1)(ii) of this section was met.

(3) If the LEA, the parent, and relevant members of the child's IEP Team determine the condition described in paragraph **(e)(1)(ii) of this section was met, the LEA must take immediate steps** to remedy those deficiencies.

(f) Determination that behavior was a manifestation. If the LEA, the parent, and relevant members of the IEP Team make the determination that the conduct was a manifestation of the child's disability, the IEP Team must—

(1) **Either**--

(i) Conduct a **functional behavioral assessment**, unless the LEA had conducted a functional behavioral assessment before the behavior that resulted in the change of placement occurred, and implement a behavioral intervention plan for the child; or

(ii) If a **behavioral intervention plan** already has been developed, **review** the behavioral intervention plan, **and modify it**, as necessary, to address the behavior; and

(2) Except as provided in paragraph (g) of this section, return the child to the placement from which the child was removed, **unless the parent and the LEA agree to a change of placement** as part of the modification of the behavioral intervention plan.

(g) Special circumstances. School personnel may remove a student to an interim alternative educational setting for not more than 45 school days **without regard to whether the behavior is determined to be a manifestation** of the child's disability, if the child—

(1) Carries a **weapon** to or possesses a weapon at school, on school premises, or to or at a school function under the jurisdiction of an SEA or an LEA;

(2) Knowingly possesses or uses **illegal drugs**, or sells or solicits the sale of a controlled substance, while at school, on school premises, or at a school function under the jurisdiction of an SEA or an LEA; or

(3) Has inflicted **serious bodily injury** upon another person while at school, on school premises, or at a school function under the jurisdiction of an SEA or an LEA.

(h) Notification. On the date on which the decision is made to make a removal that constitutes a change of placement of a child with a disability because of a violation of a code of student conduct, the LEA must notify the parents of that decision, and provide the parents the procedural safeguards notice described in 34 CFR § 300.504.

(i) Definitions. For purposes of this section, the following definitions apply:

(1) **Controlled substance** means a drug or other substance identified under schedules I, II, III, IV, or V in section 202(c) of the Controlled Substances Act (21 U.S.C. 812(c)).

(2) **Illegal drug** means a controlled substance; but does not include a controlled substance that is legally possessed or used under the supervision of a licensed health-care professional or that is legally possessed or used under any other authority under that Act or under any other provision of Federal law.

(3) **Serious bodily injury** has the meaning given the term "serious bodily injury" under paragraph (3) of subsection (h) of section 1365 of title 18, United States Code.

(4) **Weapon** has the meaning given the term "dangerous weapon" under paragraph (2) of the first subsection (g) of section 930 of title 18, United States Code. (Authority: 20 U.S.C. 1415(k)(1) and (7))

34 CFR § 300.531 Determination of setting.

The child's IEP Team determines the interim alternative educational setting for services under 34 CFR § 300.530(c), (d)(5), and (g). (Authority: 20 U.S.C. 1415(k)(2))

34 CFR § 300.532 Appeal.

(a) General. The parent of a child with a disability who **disagrees with any decision** regarding placement under 34 CFR § 300.530 and 300.531, **or the manifestation determination** under 34 CFR § 300.530(e), **or an LEA that believes that maintaining the current placement of the child is substantially likely to result in injury** to the child or others, **may appeal** the decision by requesting a hearing. The hearing is requested by **filing a complaint** pursuant to 34 CFR § 300.507 and 300.508(a) and (b).

(b) Authority of hearing officer.

(1) A hearing officer under 34 CFR § 300.511 hears, and makes a determination regarding an appeal under paragraph (a) of this section.

(2) In making the determination under paragraph (b)(1) of this section, the hearing officer **may**—

(i) **Return the child** with a disability to the placement from which the child was removed if the hearing officer determines that the removal was a violation of 34 CFR § 300.530 or that the child's behavior was a manifestation of the child's disability; or

(ii) **Order a change of placement** of the child with a disability to an appropriate interim alternative educational setting for **not more than 45 school days** if the hearing officer determines that maintaining the current placement of the child is substantially likely to result in injury to the child or to others.

(3) The procedures under paragraphs (a) and (b)(1) and (2) of this section may be repeated, if the LEA believes that returning the child to the original placement is substantially likely to result in injury to the child or to others.

(c) Expedited due process hearing.

(1) Whenever a hearing is requested under paragraph (a) of this section, the parents or the LEA involved in the dispute must have an opportunity for an impartial due process hearing consistent with the requirements of 34 CFR § 300.507 and 300.508(a) through (c) and 34 CFR § 300.510 through 300.514, except as provided in paragraph (c)(2) through (4) of this section.

(2) The SEA or LEA is responsible for arranging the **expedited due process hearing, which must occur within 20 school days** of the date the complaint requesting the hearing is filed. The hearing officer must make a determination within 10 school days after the hearing.

(3) Unless the parents and LEA agree in writing to waive the resolution meeting described in paragraph (c)(3)(i) of this section, or agree to use the mediation process described in 34 CFR § 300.506—

(i) A **resolution meeting must occur within seven days** of receiving notice of the due process complaint; and

(ii) The due process hearing may proceed unless the matter has been resolved to the satisfaction of both parties **within 15 days** of the receipt of the due process complaint.

(4) A State **may establish different State-imposed procedural rules for expedited due process hearings** conducted under this section than it has established for other due process hearings, but, except for the timelines as modified in paragraph (c)(3) of this section, the State must ensure that the requirements in 34 CFR § 300.510 through 300.514 are met.

(5) The decisions on expedited due process hearings are appealable consistent with 34 CFR § 300.514. (Authority: 20 U.S.C. 1415(k)(3) and (4)(B), 1415(f)(1)(A))

34 CFR § 300.533 Placement during appeals.

When an appeal under 34 CFR § 300.532 has been made by either the parent or the LEA, the child must remain in the interim alternative educational setting pending the decision of the hearing officer or until the expiration of the time period specified in 34 CFR § 300.530(c) or (g), whichever occurs first, unless the parent and the SEA or LEA agree otherwise. (Authority: 20 U.S.C. 1415(k)(4)(A))

34 CFR § 300.534 Protections for children not determined eligible for special education and related services.

(a) General. A child who has not been determined to be eligible for special education and related services under this part and who has engaged in behavior that violated a code of student conduct, **may assert any of the protections** provided for in this part **if the public agency had knowledge** (as determined in accordance with paragraph (b) of this section) that the child was a child with a disability before the behavior that precipitated the disciplinary action occurred.

(b) Basis of knowledge. A public agency must be deemed to have knowledge that a child is a child with a disability if before the behavior that precipitated the disciplinary action occurred—

(1) The parent of the child **expressed concern in writing** to supervisory or administrative personnel of the appropriate educational agency, or a teacher of the child, that the child is in need of special education and related services;

(2) The parent of the child **requested an evaluation** of the child pursuant to 34 CFR § 300.300 through 300.311; or

(3) The teacher of the child, or other personnel of the LEA, **expressed specific concerns** about a pattern of behavior demonstrated by the child directly to the director of special education of the agency or to other supervisory personnel of the agency.

(c) Exception. A public agency would not be deemed to have knowledge under paragraph (b) of this section if—

(1) The parent of the child—

(i) **Has not allowed an evaluation** of the child pursuant to 34 CFR § 300.300 through 300.311; or

(ii) **Has refused services** under this part; or

(2) The child has been evaluated in accordance with 34 CFR § 300.300 through 300.311 and determined to not be a child with a disability under this part.

(d) Conditions that apply if no basis of knowledge.

(1) If a public agency does not have knowledge that a child is a child with a disability (in accordance with paragraphs (b) and (c) of this section) prior to taking disciplinary measures against the child, the child may be subjected to the disciplinary measures applied to children without disabilities who engage in comparable behaviors consistent with paragraph (d)(2) of this section.

(2)

(i) If a **request is made for an evaluation** of a child during the time period in which the child is subjected to disciplinary measures under 34 CFR § 300.530, the evaluation must be conducted in an **expedited manner**.

(ii) Until the evaluation is completed, the child remains in the educational placement determined by school authorities, which can include suspension or expulsion without educational services.

(iii) If the child is determined to be a child with a disability, taking into consideration information from the evaluation conducted by the agency and information provided by the parents, the agency must provide special education and related services in accordance with this part, including the requirements of 34 CFR § 300.530 through 300.536 and section 612(a)(1)(A) of the Act. (Authority: 20 U.S.C. 1415(k)(5))

34 CFR § 300.535 Referral to and action by law enforcement and judicial authorities.

(a) Rule of construction. Nothing in this part prohibits an agency from reporting a crime committed by a child with a disability to appropriate authorities or prevents State law enforcement and judicial authorities from exercising their responsibilities with regard to the application of Federal and State law to crimes committed by a child with a disability.

(b) Transmittal of records.

(1) An agency reporting a crime committed by a child with a disability **must** ensure that copies of the special education and disciplinary records of the child are transmitted for consideration by the appropriate authorities to whom the agency reports the crime.

(2) An agency reporting a crime under this section **may** transmit copies of the child's special education and disciplinary records only to the extent that the transmission is permitted by the Family Educational Rights and Privacy Act. (Authority: 20 U.S.C. 1415(k)(6))

34 CFR § 300.536 Change of placement because of disciplinary removals.

(a) For purposes of removals of a child with a disability from the child's current educational placement under 34 CFR § 300.530 through 300.535, a change of placement occurs if—

(1) The removal is for more than 10 consecutive school days; or

(2) The child has been subjected to a series of removals that constitute a pattern—

(i) Because the series of removals total more than 10 school days in a school year;

(ii) Because the child's behavior is substantially similar to the child's behavior in previous incidents that resulted in the series of removals; and

(iii) Because of such additional factors as the length of each removal, the total amount of time the child has been removed, and the proximity of the removals to one another.

(b)

(1) The public agency determines on a case-by-case basis whether a pattern of removals constitutes a change of placement.

(2) This determination is subject to review through due process and judicial proceedings. (Authority: 20 U.S.C. 1415(k))

34 CFR § 300.537 State enforcement mechanisms.

Notwithstanding 34 CFR § 300.506(b)(7) and 300.510(d)(2), which provide for judicial enforcement of a written agreement reached as a result of mediation or a resolution meeting, there is nothing in this part that would prevent the SEA from using other mechanisms to seek enforcement of that agreement, provided that use of those mechanisms is not mandatory and does not delay or deny a party the right to seek enforcement of the written agreement in a State court of competent jurisdiction or in a district court of the United States. (Authority: 20 U.S.C. 1415(e)(2)(F), 1415(f)(1)(B))

34 CFR § 300.538–300.599 [Reserved]

Subpart F—Monitoring, Enforcement, Confidentiality, and Program Information Monitoring, Technical Assistance, and Enforcement

34 CFR § 300.600 State monitoring and enforcement.

(a) **The State must monitor the implementation of this part**, enforce this part in accordance with 34 CFR § 300.604(a)(1) and (a)(3), (b)(2)(i) and (b)(2)(v), and (c)(2), and annually report on performance under this part.

(b) The primary focus of the State's monitoring activities must be on—

(1) Improving educational results and functional outcomes for all children with disabilities; and

(2) Ensuring that public agencies meet the program requirements under Part B of the Act, with a particular emphasis on those requirements that are most closely related to improving educational results for children with disabilities.

(c) As a part of its responsibilities under paragraph (a) of this section, the State **must use quantifiable indicator**s and such qualitative indicators as are needed to adequately measure performance in the priority areas identified in paragraph (d) of this section, and the indicators established by the Secretary for the State performance plans.

(d) The State **must monitor the LEAs located in the State, using quantifiable indicators** in each of the following priority areas, and using such qualitative indicators as are needed to adequately measure performance in those areas:

(1) Provision of FAPE in the least restrictive environment.

(2) State exercise of general supervision, including child find, effective monitoring, the use of resolution meetings, mediation, and a system of transition services as defined in 34 CFR § 300.43 and in 20 U.S.C. 1437(a)(9).

(3) Disproportionate representation of racial and ethnic groups in special education and related services, to the extent the representation is the result of inappropriate identification. (Authority: 20 U.S.C. 1416(a))

34 CFR § 300.601 State performance plans and data collection.

(a) General. Not later than December 3, 2005, each State must have in place a performance plan that evaluates the State's efforts to implement the requirements and purposes of Part B of the Act, and describes how the State will improve such implementation.

(1) Each State must submit the State's performance plan to the Secretary for approval in accordance with the approval process described in section 616(c) of the Act.

(2) Each State must review its State performance plan at least once every six years, and submit any amendments to the Secretary.

(3) **As part of the State performance plan, each State must establish measurable and rigorous targets** for the indicators established by the Secretary under the priority areas described in 34 CFR § 300.600(d).

(b) Data collection.

(1) Each State must collect valid and reliable information as needed to report annually to the Secretary on the indicators established by the Secretary for the State performance plans.

(2) If the Secretary permits States to collect data on specific indicators through State monitoring or sampling, and the State collects the data through State monitoring or sampling, the State must collect data on those indicators for each LEA at least once during the period of the State performance plan.

(3) Nothing in Part B of the Act shall be construed to authorize the development of a nationwide database of personally identifiable information on individuals involved in studies or other collections of data under Part B of the Act. (Authority: 20 U.S.C. 1416(b))

34 CFR § 300.602 State use of targets and reporting.

(a) General. Each State must use the targets established in the State's performance plan under 34 CFR § 300.601 and the priority areas described in 34 CFR § 300.600(d) to analyze the performance of each LEA.

(b) Public reporting and privacy.

(1) Public report.

(i) Subject to paragraph (b)(1)(ii) of this section, **the State must—**

(A) **Report annually to the public on the performance of each LEA located in the State on the targets** in the State's performance plan; and

(B) Make the State's performance plan available through public means, including by posting on the Web site of the SEA, distribution to the media, and distribution through public agencies.

(ii) If the State, in meeting the requirements of paragraph (b)(1)(i) of this section, collects performance data through State monitoring or sampling, the State must include in its report under paragraph (b) (1)(i)(A) of this section the most recently available performance data on each LEA, and the date the data were obtained.

(2) State performance report. The State must report annually to the Secretary on the performance of the State under the State's performance plan.

(3) **Privacy**. The State must not report to the public or the Secretary any information on performance that would result in the disclosure of **personally identifiable information about individual children**, or where the available data are insufficient to yield statistically reliable information. (Authority: 20 U.S.C. 1416(b)(2)(C))

34 CFR § 300.603 Secretary's review and determination regarding State performance.

(a) Review. The **Secretary annually reviews the State's performance report** submitted pursuant to 34 CFR § 300.602(b)(2).

(b) Determination.

(1) General. Based on the information provided by the State in the State's annual performance report, information obtained through monitoring visits, and any other public information made available, the Secretary determines if the State—

(i) Meets the requirements and purposes of Part B of the Act;

(ii) Needs assistance in implementing the requirements of Part B of the Act;

(iii) Needs intervention in implementing the requirements of Part B of the Act; or

(iv) Needs substantial intervention in implementing the requirements of Part B of the Act.

(2) Notice and opportunity for a hearing.

(i) For determinations made under paragraphs (b)(1)(iii) and (b)(1)(iv) of this section, the Secretary provides reasonable notice and an opportunity for a hearing on those determinations.

(ii) The hearing described in paragraph (b)(2) of this section consists of an opportunity to meet with the Assistant Secretary for Special Education and Rehabilitative Services to demonstrate why the Department should not make the determination described in paragraph (b)(1) of this section. (Authority: 20 U.S.C. 1416(d))

34 CFR § 300.604 Enforcement.

(a) Needs assistance. If the Secretary determines, **for two consecutive years**, that a State needs assistance under 34 CFR § 300.603(b)(1)(ii) in implementing the requirements of Part B of the Act, the Secretary takes one or more of the following actions:

(1) Advises the State of available sources of technical assistance that may help the State address the areas in which the State needs assistance, which may include assistance from the Office of Special Education Programs, other offices of the Department of Education, other Federal agencies, technical assistance providers approved by the Secretary, and other federally funded nonprofit agencies, and requires the State to work with appropriate entities. Such technical assistance may include—

(i) The provision of advice by experts to address the areas in which the State needs assistance, including explicit plans for addressing the area for concern within a specified period of time;

(ii) Assistance in identifying and implementing professional development, instructional strategies, and methods of instruction that are based on scientifically based research;

(iii) Designating and using distinguished superintendents, principals, special education administrators, special education teachers, and other teachers to provide advice, technical assistance, and support; and

(iv) Devising additional approaches to providing technical assistance, such as collaborating with institutions of higher education, educational service agencies, national centers of technical assistance supported under Part D of the Act, and private providers of scientifically based technical assistance.

(2) Directs the use of State-level funds under section 611(e) of the Act on the area or areas in which the State needs assistance.

(3) **Identifies the State as a high-risk grantee and impose special conditions** on the State's grant under Part B of the Act.

(b) Needs intervention. If the Secretary determines, for three or more consecutive years, that a State needs intervention under 34 CFR § 300.603(b)(1)(iii) in implementing the requirements of Part B of the Act, the following shall apply:

(1) The Secretary may take any of the actions described in paragraph (a) of this section.

(2) The Secretary takes one or more of the following actions:

(i) Requires the State to prepare **a corrective action plan** or improvement plan if the Secretary determines that the State should be able to correct the problem within one year.

(ii) Requires the State to enter into a compliance agreement under section 457 of the General Education Provisions Act, as amended, 20 U.S.C. 1221 *et seq*. (GEPA), if the Secretary has reason to believe that the State cannot correct the problem within one year.

(iii) For each year of the determination, withholds not less than 20 percent and not more than 50 percent of the State's funds under section 611(e) of the Act, until the Secretary determines the State has sufficiently addressed the areas in which the State needs intervention.

(iv) Seeks to recover funds under section 452 of GEPA.

(v) Withholds, in whole or in part, any further payments to the State under Part B of the Act.

(vi) Refers the matter for appropriate enforcement action, which may include referral to the **Department of Justice.**

(c) Needs substantial intervention. Notwithstanding paragraph (a) or (b) of this section, at any time that the Secretary determines that a State **needs substantial intervention** in implementing the requirements of Part B of the Act or that there **is a substantial failure to comply** with any condition of an SEA's or LEA's eligibility under Part B of the Act, the Secretary takes one or more of the following actions:

(1) Recovers funds under section 452 of GEPA.

(2) Withholds, in whole or in part, any further payments to the State under Part B of the Act.

(3) Refers the case to the Office of the Inspector General at the Department of Education.

(4) Refers the matter for appropriate enforcement action, which may include referral to the **Department of Justice**.

(d) Report to Congress. The Secretary reports to the Committee on Education and the Workforce of the House of Representatives and the Committee on Health, Education, Labor, and Pensions of the Senate within 30 days of taking enforcement action pursuant to paragraph (a), (b), or (c) of this section, on the specific action taken and the reasons why enforcement action was taken. (Authority: 20 U.S.C. 1416(e)(1)-(e)(3), (e)(5))

34 CFR § 300.605 Withholding funds.

(a) Opportunity for hearing. Prior to withholding any funds under Part B of the Act, the Secretary provides reasonable notice and an opportunity for a hearing to the SEA involved, pursuant to the procedures in 34 CFR § 300.180 through 300.183.

(b) Suspension. Pending the outcome of any hearing to withhold payments under paragraph (a) of this section, the Secretary may suspend payments to a recipient, suspend the authority of the recipient to obligate funds under Part B of the Act, or both, after the recipient has been given reasonable notice and an opportunity to show cause why future payments or authority to obligate funds under Part B of the Act should not be suspended.

(c) Nature of withholding.

(1) If the Secretary determines that it is appropriate to withhold further payments under 34 CFR § 300.604(b)(2) or (c)(2), the Secretary may determine—

(i) That the withholding will be limited to programs or projects, or portions of programs or projects, that affected the Secretary's determination under 34 CFR § 300.603(b)(1); or

(ii) That the SEA must not make further payments under Part B of the Act to specified State agencies or LEAs that caused or were involved in the Secretary's determination under 34 CFR § 300.603(b)(1).

(2) Until the Secretary is satisfied that the condition that caused the initial withholding has been substantially rectified—

(i) Payments to the State under Part B of the Act must be withheld in whole or in part; and

(ii) Payments by the SEA under Part B of the Act must be limited to State agencies and LEAs whose actions did not cause or were not involved in the Secretary's determination under 34 CFR § 300.603(b)(1), as the case may be. (Authority: 20 U.S.C. 1416(e)(4), (e)(6))

34 CFR § 300.606 Public attention.

Any State that has received notice under 34 CFR § 300.603(b)(1)(ii) through (iv) must, by means of a public notice, take such measures as may be necessary to notify the public within the State of the pendency of an action taken pursuant to 34 CFR § 300.604. (Authority: 20 U.S.C. 1416(e)(7))

34 CFR § 300.607 Divided State agency responsibility.

For purposes of this subpart, if responsibility for ensuring that the requirements of Part B of the Act are met with respect to children with disabilities who are convicted as adults under State law and incarcerated in adult prisons is assigned to a public agency other than the SEA pursuant to 34 CFR § 300.149(d), and if the Secretary finds that the failure to comply substantially with the provisions of Part B of the Act are related to a failure by the public agency, the Secretary takes appropriate corrective action to ensure compliance with Part B of the Act, except that—

(a) Any reduction or withholding of payments to the State under 34 CFR § 300.604 must be proportionate to the total funds allotted under section 611 of the Act to the State as the number of eligible children with disabilities in adult prisons under the supervision of the other public agency is proportionate to the number of eligible individuals with disabilities in the State under the supervision of the SEA; and

(b) Any withholding of funds under 34 CFR § 300.604 must be limited to the specific agency responsible for the failure to comply with Part B of the Act. (Authority: 20 U.S.C. 1416(h))

34 CFR § 300.608 State enforcement.

(a) If an SEA determines that an LEA is not meeting the requirements of Part B of the Act, including the targets in the State's performance plan, **the SEA must prohibit the LEA from reducing the LEA's maintenance of effort** under 34 CFR § 300.203 for any fiscal year.

(b) Nothing in this subpart shall be construed to restrict a State from utilizing any other authority available to it to monitor and enforce the requirements of Part B of the Act. (Authority: 20 U.S.C. 1416(f); 20 U.S.C. 1412(a)(11))

34 CFR § 300.609 Rule of construction.

Nothing in this subpart shall be construed to restrict the Secretary from utilizing any authority under GEPA, including the provisions in 34 CFR parts 76, 77, 80, and 81 to monitor and enforce the requirements of the Act, including the imposition of special conditions under 34 CFR 80.12. (Authority: 20 U.S.C. 1416(g))

Confidentiality of Information

34 CFR § 300.610 Confidentiality.

The Secretary takes appropriate action, in accordance with section 444 of GEPA, to ensure the protection of the confidentiality of any personally identifiable data, information, and records collected or maintained by the Secretary and by SEAs and LEAs pursuant to Part B of the Act, and consistent with 34 CFR § 300.611 through 300.627. (Authority: 20 U.S.C. 1417(c))

34 CFR § 300.611 Definitions.

As used in 34 CFR § 300.611 through 300.625—

(a) **Destruction** means physical destruction or removal of personal identifiers from information so that the information is no longer personally identifiable.

(b) **Education records** means the type of records covered under the definition of "education records" in 34 CFR part 99 (the regulations implementing the <**Family Educational Rights and Privacy Act of 1974, 20 U.S.C. 1232g.**>

(c) **Participating agency** means any agency or institution that collects, maintains, or uses personally identifiable information, or from which information is obtained, under Part B of the Act. (Authority: 20 U.S.C. 1221e-3, 1412(a)(8), 1417(c))

34 CFR § 300.612 Notice to parents.

(a) The SEA must give notice that is adequate to fully inform parents about the requirements of 34 CFR § 300.123, including—

(1) A description of the extent that the notice is given in the native languages of the various population groups in the State;

(2) A description of the children on whom personally identifiable information is maintained, the types of information sought, the methods the State intends to use in gathering the information (including the sources from whom information is gathered), and the uses to be made of the information;

(3) A summary of the policies and procedures that participating agencies must follow regarding storage, disclosure to third parties, retention, and **destruction of personally identifiable information**; and

(4) A description of all of the rights of parents and children regarding this information, including the rights under FERPA and implementing regulations in 34 CFR part 99.[9]

(b) Before any major identification, location, or evaluation activity, the notice must be published or announced in newspapers or other media, or both, with circulation adequate to notify parents throughout the State of the activity. (Authority: 20 U.S.C. 1412(a)(8); 1417(c))

34 CFR § 300.613 Access rights.

(a) Each participating agency **must permit parents to inspect and review any education records relating to their children** that are collected, maintained, or used by the agency under this part. The agency must comply with a request without unnecessary delay **and before any meeting regarding an IEP**, or any hearing pursuant to 34 CFR § 300.507 or 34 CFR § 300.530 through 300.532, or resolution session pursuant to 34 CFR § 300.510, and in no case more than 45 days after the request has been made.

---

9   *See also* the <Protection of Pupil Rights Act at 20 U.S.C. § 1232h in Chapter 9.>

(b) The right to **inspect and review education records** under this section **includes—**

(1) The right to a response from the participating agency to reasonable **requests for explanations and interpretations** of the records;

(2) The right to request that the **agency provide copies** of the records containing the information if failure to provide those copies would effectively prevent the parent from exercising the right to inspect and review the records; and

(3) The **right to have a representative of the parent inspect** and review the records.

(c) An agency may **presume that the parent has authority to inspect and review records relating to his or her child unless** the agency has been advised that the parent does not have the authority under applicable State law governing such matters as guardianship, separation, and divorce. (Authority: 20 U.S.C. 1412(a)(8); 1417(c))

34 CFR § 300.614 Record of access.

Each participating agency **must keep a record of parties obtaining access to education records** collected, maintained, or used under Part B of the Act (except access by parents and authorized employees of the participating agency), including the name of the party, the date access was given, and the purpose for which the party is authorized to use the records. (Authority: 20 U.S.C. 1412(a)(8); 1417(c))

34 CFR § 300.615 Records on more than one child.

If any education record includes information on more than one child, the parents of those children have the right to inspect and review only the information relating to their child or to be informed of that specific information. (Authority: 20 U.S.C. 1412(a)(8); 1417(c))

34 CFR § 300.616 List of types and locations of information.

Each participating agency must provide parents on request a list of the types and locations of education records collected, maintained, or used by the agency. (Authority: 20 U.S.C. 1412(a)(8); 1417(c))

34 CFR § 300.617 Fees.

(a) Each participating agency may charge **a fee for copies of records** that are made for parents under this part if the fee does not effectively prevent the parents from exercising their right to inspect and review those records.

(b) A participating agency **may not charge a fee to search** for or to retrieve information under this part. (Authority: 20 U.S.C. 1412(a)(8); 1417(c))

34 CFR § 300.618 Amendment of records at parent's request.

(a) A parent who believes that information in the education records collected, maintained, or used under this part is inaccurate or misleading or violates the privacy or other rights of the child may request the participating agency that maintains the information to amend the information.

(b) The agency must decide whether to amend the information in accordance with the request within a reasonable period of time of receipt of the request.

(c) If the agency decides to refuse to amend the information in accordance with the request, it must inform the parent of the refusal and advise the parent of the **right to a hearing** under 34 CFR § 300.619. (Authority: 20 U.S.C. 1412(a)(8); 1417(c))

34 CFR § 300.619 Opportunity for a hearing.

The agency must, on request, **provide an opportunity for a hearing to challenge information in education records** to ensure that it is not inaccurate, misleading, or otherwise in violation of the privacy or other rights of the child. (Authority: 20 U.S.C. 1412(a)(8); 1417(c))

34 CFR § 300.620 Result of hearing.

(a) If, as a result of the hearing, the agency decides that the information is inaccurate, misleading or otherwise in violation of the privacy or other rights of the child, **it must amend the information** accordingly and so inform the parent in writing.

(b) If, as a result of the hearing, the agency decides that the information is not inaccurate, misleading, or otherwise in violation of the privacy or other rights of the child, it must inform the parent of the parent's right to place in the records the agency maintains on the child a statement commenting on the information or setting forth any reasons for disagreeing with the decision of the agency.

(c) Any explanation placed in the records of the child under this section must—

(1) Be maintained by the agency as part of the records of the child as long as the record or contested portion is

maintained by the agency; and

(2) If the records of the child or the contested portion is disclosed by the agency to any party, the explanation must also be disclosed to the party. (Authority: 20 U.S.C. 1412(a)(8); 1417(c))

34 CFR § 300.621 Hearing procedures.

A hearing held under 34 CFR § 300.619 must be conducted according to the procedures in 34 CFR 99.22. (Authority: 20 U.S.C. 1412(a)(8); 1417(c))

34 CFR § 300.622 Consent.

(a) **Parental consent** must be obtained before personally identifiable information is disclosed to parties, other than officials of participating agencies in accordance with paragraph (b)(1) of this section, unless the information is contained in education records, and the disclosure is authorized without parental consent under 34 CFR part 99.

(b)

(1) Except as provided in paragraphs (b)(2) and (b)(3) of this section, **parental consent is not required** before personally identifiable information is released to officials of participating agencies for purposes of meeting a requirement of this part.

(2) Parental consent, or the consent of an eligible child who has reached the age of majority under State law, must be obtained before personally identifiable information is released to officials of participating agencies providing or paying for transition services in accordance with 34 CFR § 300.321(b)(3).

(3) If a child is enrolled, or is going to enroll in a private school that is **not located in the LEA of the parent's residence**, parental consent must be obtained before any personally identifiable information about the child is released between officials in the LEA where the private school is located and officials in the LEA of the parent's residence. (Authority: 20 U.S.C. 1412(a)(8); 1417(c))

34 CFR § 300.623 Safeguards.

(a) Each participating agency must protect the confidentiality of personally identifiable information at collection, storage, disclosure, and destruction stages.

(b) **One official at each participating agency must assume responsibility for ensuring the confidentiality** of any personally identifiable information.

(c) All persons collecting or using personally identifiable information must receive training or instruction regarding the State's policies and procedures under 34 CFR § 300.123 and 34 CFR part 99.

(d) Each participating agency must maintain, for public inspection, a current listing of the names and positions of those employees within the agency who may have access to personally identifiable information. (Authority: 20 U.S.C. 1412(a)(8); 1417(c))

34 CFR § 300.624 Destruction of information.

(a) The public agency must inform parents when personally identifiable information collected, maintained, or used under this part is no longer needed to provide educational services to the child.

(b) The information must be destroyed at the request of the parents. However, a permanent record of a student's name, address, and phone number, his or her grades, attendance record, classes attended, grade level completed, and year completed may be maintained without time limitation. (Authority: 20 U.S.C. 1412(a)(8); 1417(c))

34 CFR § 300.625 Children's rights.

(a) The SEA must have in effect policies and procedures regarding the extent to which children are afforded rights of privacy similar to those afforded to parents, taking into consideration the age of the child and type or severity of disability.

(b) Under the regulations for FERPA in 34 CFR 99.5(a), **the rights of parents regarding education records are transferred to the student at age 18.**

(c) If the rights accorded to parents under Part B of the Act are transferred to a student who reaches the age of majority, consistent with 34 CFR § 300.520, the rights regarding educational records in 34 CFR § 300.613 through 300.624 must also be transferred to the student. However, the public agency must provide any notice required under section 615 of the Act to the student and the parents. (Authority: 20 U.S.C. 1412(a)(8); 1417(c))

34 CFR § 300.626 Enforcement.

The SEA must have in effect the policies and procedures, **including sanctions** that the State uses, to ensure that its policies and procedures consistent with 34 CFR § 300.611 through 300.625 are followed and that the requirements of the Act and the regulations in this part are met. (Authority: 20 U.S.C. 1412(a)(8); 1417(c))

34 CFR § 300.627 Department use of personally identifiable information.

If the Department or its authorized representatives collect any personally identifiable information regarding children with disabilities that is not subject to the Privacy Act of 1974, 5 U.S.C. 552a, the Secretary applies the requirements of 5 U.S.C. 552a(b)(1) and (b)(2), 552a(b)(4) through (b)(11); 552a(c) through 552a(e)(3)(B); 552a(e)(3)(D); 552a(e)(5) through (e)(10); 552a(h); 552a(m); and 552a(n); and the regulations implementing those provisions in 34 CFR part 5b. (Authority: 20 U.S.C. 1412(a)(8); 1417(c))

Reports - Program Information

34 CFR § 300.640 Annual report of children served—report requirement.

(a) The SEA must annually report to the Secretary on the information required by section 618 of the Act at the times specified by the Secretary.

(b) The SEA must submit the report on forms provided by the Secretary. (Authority: 20 U.S.C. 1418(a))

34 CFR § 300.641 Annual report of children served—information required in the report.

(a) For purposes of the annual report required by section 618 of the Act and 34 CFR § 300.640, the State and the Secretary of the Interior must count and report the number of children with disabilities receiving special education and related services on any date between October 1 and December 1 of each year.

(b) For the purpose of this reporting provision, a child's age is the child's actual age on the date of the child count.

(c) **The SEA may not report a child under more than one disability category**.

(d) If a child with a disability has **more than one disability**, the SEA must report that child in accordance with the following procedure:

(1) If a child has only two disabilities and those disabilities are deafness and blindness, and the child is not reported as having a developmental delay, that child must be reported under the category "deaf-blindness."

(2) A child who has **more than one disability** and is not reported as having deaf-blindness or as having a developmental delay **must be reported under the category "multiple disabilities."** (Authority: 20 U.S.C. 1418(a), (b))

34 CFR § 300.642 Data reporting.

(a) Protection of personally identifiable data. The data described in section 618(a) of the Act and in 34 CFR § 300.641 must be publicly reported by each State in a manner that does not result in disclosure of data identifiable to individual children.

(b) Sampling. The Secretary may permit States and the Secretary of the Interior to obtain data in section 618(a) of the Act through sampling. (Authority: 20 U.S.C. 1418(b))

34 CFR § 300.643 Annual report of children served—certification.

The SEA must include in its report a certification signed by an authorized official of the agency that the information provided under 34 CFR § 300.640 is an accurate and unduplicated count of children with disabilities receiving special education and related services on the dates in question. (Authority: 20 U.S.C. 1418(a)(3))

34 CFR § 300.644 Annual report of children served—criteria for counting children.

The SEA may include in its report children with disabilities who are enrolled in a school or program that is operated or supported by a public agency, and that—

(a) Provides them with both special education and related services that meet State standards;

(b) Provides them only with special education, if a related service is not required, that meets State standards; or

(c) In the case of children with disabilities enrolled by their parents in private schools, counts those children who are eligible under the Act and receive special education or related services or both that meet State standards under 34 CFR § 300.132 through 300.144. (Authority: 20 U.S.C. 1418(a))

34 CFR § 300.645 Annual report of children served—other responsibilities of the SEA.

In addition to meeting the other requirements of 34 CFR § 300.640 through 300.644, the SEA must—

(a) Establish procedures to be used by LEAs and other educational institutions in counting the number of children with disabilities receiving special education and related services;

(b) Set dates by which those agencies and institutions must report to the SEA to ensure that the State complies with 34 CFR § 300.640(a);

(c) Obtain certification from each agency and institution that an unduplicated and accurate count has been made;

(d) Aggregate the data from the count obtained from each agency and institution, and prepare the reports required under 34 CFR § 300.640 through 300.644; and

(e) Ensure that documentation is maintained that enables the State and the Secretary to audit the accuracy of the count. (Authority: 20 U.S.C. 1418(a))

34 CFR § 300.646 Disproportionality.

(a) **General**. Each State that receives assistance under Part B of the Act, and the Secretary of the Interior, **must provide for the collection and examination of data to determine if significant disproportionality based on race and ethnicity is occurring** in the State and the LEAs of the State with respect to—

(1) The identification of children as children with disabilities, including the identification of children as children with disabilities in accordance with a particular impairment described in section 602(3) of the Act;

(2) The placement in particular educational settings of these children; and

(3) The incidence, duration, and type of disciplinary actions, including suspensions and expulsions.

(b) **Review and revision of policies, practices, and procedures**. In the case of a determination of significant disproportionality with respect to the identification of children as children with disabilities, or the placement in particular educational settings of these children, in accordance with paragraph (a) of this section, the State or the Secretary of the Interior must—

(1) Provide for the review and, if appropriate revision of the policies, procedures, and practices used in the identification or placement to ensure that the policies, procedures, and practices comply with the requirements of the Act.

(2) Require any LEA identified under paragraph (a) of this section to reserve the maximum amount of funds under section 613(f) of the Act to provide comprehensive coordinated early intervening services to serve children in the LEA, particularly, but not exclusively, children in those groups that were significantly overidentified under paragraph (a) of this section; and

(3) Require the LEA to publicly report on the revision of policies, practices, and procedures described under paragraph (b)(1) of this section. (Authority: 20 U.S.C. 1418(d))

Subpart G - Authorization, Allotment, Use of Funds, and Authorization of Appropriations Allotments, Grants, and Use of Funds

34 CFR § 300.700 Grants to States.

(a) **Purpose of grants**. The Secretary makes grants to States, outlying areas, and freely associated States (as defined in 34 CFR § 300.717), and provides funds to the Secretary of the Interior, to assist them to provide special education and related services to children with disabilities in accordance with Part B of the Act.

(b) **Maximum amount**. The maximum amount of the grant a State may receive under section 611 of the Act is—

(1) For fiscal years 2005 and 2006—

(i) The number of children with disabilities in the State who are receiving special education and related services—

(A) Aged three through five, if the State is eligible for a grant under section 619 of the Act; and

(B) Aged 6 through 21; multiplied by—

(ii) Forty (40) percent of the average per-pupil expenditure in public elementary schools and secondary schools in the United States (as defined in 34 CFR § 300.717); and

(2) For fiscal year 2007 and subsequent fiscal years—

(i) The number of children with disabilities in the 2004–2005 school year in the State who received special education and related services—

(A) Aged three through five if the State is eligible for a grant under section 619 of the Act; and

(B) Aged 6 through 21; multiplied by

(ii) Forty (40) percent of the average per-pupil expenditure in public elementary schools and secondary schools in the United States (as defined in 34 CFR § 300.717);

(iii) Adjusted by the rate of annual change in the sum of—

(A) Eighty-five (85) percent of the State's population of children aged 3 through 21 who are of the same age as children with disabilities for whom the State ensures the availability of FAPE under Part B of the Act; and

(B) Fifteen (15) percent of the State's population of children described in paragraph (b)(2)(iii)(A) of this section who are living in poverty. (Authority: 20 U.S.C. 1411(a) and (d))

34 CFR § 300.701 Outlying areas, freely associated States, and the Secretary of the Interior.

  (a) Outlying areas and freely associated States.

    (1) Funds reserved. From the amount appropriated for any fiscal year under section 611(i) of the Act, the Secretary reserves not more than one percent, which must be used—

      (i) To provide assistance to the outlying areas in accordance with their respective populations of individuals aged 3 through 21; and

      (ii) To provide each freely associated State a grant in the amount that the freely associated State received for fiscal year 2003 under Part B of the Act, but only if the freely associated State—

        (A) Meets the applicable requirements of Part B of the Act that apply to States.

        (B) Meets the requirements in paragraph (a)(2) of this section.

    (2) Application. Any freely associated State that wishes to receive funds under Part B of the Act must include, in its application for assistance—

      (i) Information demonstrating that it will meet all conditions that apply to States under Part B of the Act.

      (ii) An assurance that, notwithstanding any other provision of Part B of the Act, it will use those funds only for the direct provision of special education and related services to children with disabilities and to enhance its capacity to make FAPE available to all children with disabilities;

      (iii) The identity of the source and amount of funds, in addition to funds under Part B of the Act, that it will make available to ensure that FAPE is available to all children with disabilities within its jurisdiction; and

      (iv) Such other information and assurances as the Secretary may require.

    (3) Special rule. The provisions of Public Law 95-134, permitting the consolidation of grants by the outlying areas, do not apply to funds provided to the outlying areas or to the freely associated States under Part B of the Act.

  (b) Secretary of the Interior. From the amount appropriated for any fiscal year under section 611(i) of the Act, the Secretary reserves 1.226 percent to provide assistance to the Secretary of the Interior in accordance with 34 CFR § 300.707 through 300.716. (Authority: 20 U.S.C. 1411(b))

34 CFR § 300.702 Technical assistance.

  (a) In general. The Secretary may reserve not more than one-half of one percent of the amounts appropriated under Part B of the Act for each fiscal year to support technical assistance activities authorized under section 616(i) of the Act.

  (b) Maximum amount. The maximum amount the Secretary may reserve under paragraph (a) of this section for any fiscal year is $25,000,000, cumulatively adjusted by the rate of inflation as measured by the percentage increase, if any, from the preceding fiscal year in the Consumer Price Index For All Urban Consumers, published by the Bureau of Labor Statistics of the Department of Labor. (Authority: 20 U.S.C. 1411(c))

34 CFR § 300.703 Allocations to States.

  (a) General. After reserving funds for technical assistance under 34 CFR § 300.702, and for payments to the outlying areas, the freely associated States, and the Secretary of the Interior under 34 CFR § 300.701 (a) and (b) for a fiscal year, the Secretary allocates the remaining amount among the States in accordance with paragraphs (b), (c), and (d) of this section.

  (b) Special rule for use of fiscal year 1999 amount. If a State received any funds under section 611 of the Act-for fiscal year 1999 on the basis of children aged three through five, but does not make FAPE available to all children with disabilities aged three through five in the State in any subsequent fiscal year, the Secretary computes the State's amount for fiscal year 1999, solely for the purpose of calculating the State's allocation in that subsequent year under paragraph (c) or (d) of this section, by subtracting the amount allocated to the State for fiscal year 1999 on the basis of those children.

  (c) Increase in funds. If the amount available for allocations to States under paragraph (a) of this section for a fiscal year is equal to or greater than the amount allocated to the States under section 611 of the Act for the preceding fiscal year, those allocations are calculated as follows:

    (1) Allocation of increase.

      (i) General. Except as provided in paragraph (c)(2) of this section, the Secretary allocates for the fiscal year—

        (A) To each State the amount the State received under this section for fiscal year 1999;

        (B) Eighty-five (85) percent of any remaining funds to States on the basis of the States' relative populations of children aged 3 through 21 who are of the same age as children with disabilities for whom the State ensures the availability of FAPE under Part B of the Act; and

        (C) Fifteen (15) percent of those remaining funds to States on the basis of the States' relative populations of children described in paragraph (c)(1)(i)(B) of this section who are living in poverty.

(ii) Data. For the purpose of making grants under this section, the Secretary uses the most recent population data, including data on children living in poverty, that are available and satisfactory to the Secretary.

(2) Limitations. Notwithstanding paragraph (c)(1) of this section, allocations under this section are subject to the following:

(i) Preceding year allocation. No State's allocation may be less than its allocation under section 611 of the Act for the preceding fiscal year.

(ii) Minimum. No State's allocation may be less than the greatest of—

(A) The sum of—

(1) The amount the State received under section 611 of the Act for fiscal year 1999; and

(2) One third of one percent of the amount by which the amount appropriated under section 611(i) of the Act for the fiscal year exceeds the amount appropriated for section 611 of the Act for fiscal year 1999;

(B) The sum of—

(1) The amount the State received under section 611 of the Act for the preceding fiscal year; and

(2) That amount multiplied by the percentage by which the increase in the funds appropriated for section 611 of the Act from the preceding fiscal year exceeds 1.5 percent; or

(C) The sum of—

(1) The amount the State received under section 611 of the Act for the preceding fiscal year; and

(2) That amount multiplied by 90 percent of the percentage increase in the amount appropriated for section 611 of the Act from the preceding fiscal year.

(iii) Maximum. Notwithstanding paragraph (c)(2)(ii) of this section, no State's allocation under paragraph (a) of this section may exceed the sum of—

(A) The amount the State received under section 611 of the Act for the preceding fiscal year; and

(B) That amount multiplied by the sum of 1.5 percent and the percentage increase in the amount appropriated under section 611 of the Act from the preceding fiscal year.

(3) Ratable reduction. If the amount available for allocations to States under paragraph (c) of this section is insufficient to pay those allocations in full, those allocations are ratably reduced, subject to paragraph (c)(2)(i) of this section.

(d) Decrease in funds. If the amount available for allocations to States under paragraph (a) of this section for a fiscal year is less than the amount allocated to the States under section 611 of the Act for the preceding fiscal year, those allocations are calculated as follows:

(1) Amounts greater than fiscal year 1999 allocations. If the amount available for allocations under paragraph (a) of this section is greater than the amount allocated to the States for fiscal year 1999, each State is allocated the sum of—

(i) 1999 amount. The amount the State received under section 611 of the Act for fiscal year 1999; and

(ii) Remaining funds. An amount that bears the same relation to any remaining funds as the increase the State received under section 611 of the Act for the preceding fiscal year over fiscal year 1999 bears to the total of all such increases for all States.

(2) Amounts equal to or less than fiscal year 1999 allocations.

(i) General. If the amount available for allocations under paragraph (a) of this section is equal to or less than the amount allocated to the States for fiscal year 1999, each State is allocated the amount it received for fiscal year 1999.

(ii) Ratable reduction. If the amount available for allocations under paragraph (d) of this section is insufficient to make the allocations described in paragraph (d)(2)(i) of this section, those allocations are ratably reduced. (Authority: 20 U.S.C. 1411(d))

34 CFR § 300.704 State-level activities.

(a) State administration.

(1) For the purpose of administering Part B of the Act, including paragraph (c) of this section, section 619 of the Act, and the coordination of activities under Part B of the Act with, and providing technical assistance to, other programs that provide services to children with disabilities—

(i) Each State may reserve for each fiscal year not more than the maximum amount the State was eligible to reserve for State administration under section 611 of the Act for fiscal year 2004 or $800,000 (adjusted in accordance with paragraph (a)(2) of this section), whichever is greater; and

(ii) Each outlying area may reserve for each fiscal year not more than five percent of the amount the outlying area receives under 34 CFR § 300.701(a) for the fiscal year or $35,000, whichever is greater.

(2) For each fiscal year, beginning with fiscal year 2005, the Secretary cumulatively adjusts—

(i) The maximum amount the State was eligible to reserve for State administration under section 611 of the Act for fiscal year 2004; and

(ii) $800,000, by the rate of inflation as measured by the percentage increase, if any, from the preceding fiscal year in the Consumer Price Index for All Urban Consumers, published by the Bureau of Labor Statistics of the Department of Labor.

(3) Prior to expenditure of funds under paragraph (a) of this section, the State must certify to the Secretary that the arrangements to establish responsibility for services pursuant to section 612(a)(12)(A) of the Act are current.

(4) Funds reserved under paragraph (a)(1) of this section may be used for the administration of Part C of the Act, if the SEA is the lead agency for the State under that Part.

(b) Other State-level activities.

(1) States may reserve a portion of their allocations for other State-level activities. The maximum amount that a State may reserve for other State-level activities is as follows:

(i) If the amount that the State sets aside for State administration under paragraph (a) of this section is greater than $850,000 and the State opts to finance a high cost fund under paragraph (c) of this section:

(A) For fiscal years 2005 and 2006, 10 percent of the State's allocation under 34 CFR § 300.703.

(B) For fiscal year 2007 and subsequent fiscal years, an amount equal to 10 percent of the State's allocation for fiscal year 2006 under 34 CFR § 300.703 adjusted cumulatively for inflation.

(ii) If the amount that the State sets aside for State administration under paragraph (a) of this section is greater than $850,000 and the State opts not to finance a high cost fund under paragraph (c) of this section—

(A) For fiscal years 2005 and 2006, nine percent of the State's allocation under 34 CFR § 300.703.

(B) For fiscal year 2007 and subsequent fiscal years, an amount equal to nine percent of the State's allocation for fiscal year 2006 adjusted cumulatively for inflation.

(iii) If the amount that the State sets aside for State administration under paragraph (a) of this section is less than or equal to $850,000 and the State opts to finance a high cost fund under paragraph (c) of this section:

(A) For fiscal years 2005 and 2006, 10.5 percent of the State's allocation under 34 CFR § 300.703.

(B) For fiscal year 2007 and subsequent fiscal years, an amount equal to 10.5 percent of the State's allocation for fiscal year 2006 under 34 CFR § 300.703 adjusted cumulatively for inflation.

(iv) If the amount that the State sets aside for State administration under paragraph (a) of this section is equal to or less than $850,000 and the State opts not to finance a high cost fund under paragraph (c) of this section:

(A) For fiscal years 2005 and 2006, nine and one-half percent of the State's allocation under 34 CFR § 300.703.

(B) For fiscal year 2007 and subsequent fiscal years, an amount equal to nine and one-half percent of the State's allocation for fiscal year 2006 under 34 CFR § 300.703 adjusted cumulatively for inflation.

(2) The adjustment for inflation is the rate of inflation as measured by the percentage of increase, if any, from the preceding fiscal year in the Consumer Price Index for All Urban Consumers, published by the Bureau of Labor Statistics of the Department of Labor.

(3) Some portion of the funds reserved under paragraph (b)(1) of this section must be used to carry out the following activities:

(i) For monitoring, enforcement, and complaint investigation; and

(ii) To establish and implement the mediation process required by section 615(e) of the Act, including providing for the costs of mediators and support personnel;

(4) Funds reserved under paragraph (b)(1) of this section also may be used to carry out the following activities:

(i) For support and direct services, including technical assistance, personnel preparation, and professional development and training;

(ii) To support paperwork reduction activities, including expanding the use of technology in the IEP process;

(iii) To assist LEAs in providing positive behavioral interventions and supports and mental health services for children with disabilities;

(iv) To improve the use of technology in the classroom by children with disabilities to enhance learning;

(v) To support the use of technology, including technology with universal design principles and assistive technology devices, to maximize accessibility to the general education curriculum for children with disabilities;

(vi) Development and implementation of transition programs, including coordination of services with agencies involved in supporting the transition of students with disabilities to postsecondary activities;

(vii) To assist LEAs in meeting personnel shortages;

(viii) To support capacity building activities and improve the delivery of services by LEAs to improve results for children with disabilities;

(ix) Alternative programming for children with disabilities who have been expelled from school, and services for children with disabilities in correctional facilities, children enrolled in State-operated or State-supported schools, and children with disabilities in charter schools;

(x) To support the development and provision of appropriate accommodations for children with disabilities, or the development and provision of alternate assessments that are valid and reliable for assessing the performance of children with disabilities, in accordance with sections 1111(b) and 6111 of the ESEA; and

(xi) To provide technical assistance to schools and LEAs, and direct services, including supplemental educational services as defined in section 1116(e) of the ESEA to children with disabilities, in schools or LEAs identified for improvement under section 1116 of the ESEA on the sole basis of the assessment results of the disaggregated subgroup of children with disabilities, including providing professional development to special and regular education teachers, who teach children with disabilities, based on scientifically based research to improve educational instruction, in order to improve academic achievement to meet or exceed the objectives established by the State under section 1111(b)(2)(G) of the ESEA.

(c) Local educational agency high cost fund.

(1) In general—

(i) For the purpose of assisting LEAs (including a charter school that is an LEA or a consortium of LEAs) in addressing the needs of high need children with disabilities, each State has the option to reserve for each fiscal year 10 percent of the amount of funds the State reserves for other State-level activities under paragraph (b)(1) of this section—

(A) To finance and make disbursements from the high cost fund to LEAs in accordance with paragraph (c) of this section during the first and succeeding fiscal years of the high cost fund; and

(B) To support innovative and effective ways of cost sharing by the State, by an LEA, or among a consortium of LEAs, as determined by the State in coordination with representatives from LEAs, subject to paragraph (c)(2) (ii) of this section.

(ii) For purposes of paragraph (c) of this section, local educational agency includes a charter school that is an LEA, or a consortium of LEAs.

(2)

(i) A State must not use any of the funds the State reserves pursuant to paragraph (c)(1)(i) of this section, which are solely for disbursement to LEAs, for costs associated with establishing, supporting, and otherwise administering the fund. The State may use funds the State reserves under paragraph (a) of this section for those administrative costs.

(ii) A State must not use more than 5 percent of the funds the State reserves pursuant to paragraph (c)(1)(i) of this section for each fiscal year to support innovative and effective ways of cost sharing among consortia of LEAs.

(3)

(i) The SEA must develop, not later than 90 days after the State reserves funds under paragraph (c)(1)(i) of this section, annually review, and amend as necessary, a State plan for the high cost fund. Such State plan must—

(A) Establish, in consultation and coordination with representatives from LEAs, a definition of a high need child with a disability that, at a minimum—

(1) Addresses the financial impact a high need child with a disability has on the budget of the child's LEA; and

(2) Ensures that the cost of the high need child with a disability is greater than 3 times the average per pupil expenditure (as defined in section 9101 of the ESEA) in that State;

(B) Establish eligibility criteria for the participation of an LEA that, at a minimum, take into account the number and percentage of high need children with disabilities served by an LEA;

(C) Establish criteria to ensure that placements supported by the fund are consistent with the requirements of 34 CFR § 300.114 through 300.118;

(D) Develop a funding mechanism that provides distributions each fiscal year to LEAs that meet the criteria developed by the State under paragraph(c)(3)(i)(B) of this section;

(E) Establish an annual schedule by which the SEA must make its distributions from the high cost fund each fiscal year; and

(F) If the State elects to reserve funds for supporting innovative and effective ways of cost sharing under paragraph (c)(1)(i)(B) of this section, describe how these funds will be used.

(ii) The State must make its final State plan available to the public not less than 30 days before the beginning of the school year, including dissemination of such information on the State Web site.

(4)

(i) Each SEA must make all annual disbursements from the high cost fund established under paragraph (c)(1)(i) of this section in accordance with the State plan published pursuant to paragraph (c)(3) of this section.

(ii) The costs associated with educating a high need child with a disability, as defined under paragraph (c)(3)(i) (A) of this section, are only those costs associated with providing direct special education and related services to the child that are identified in that child's IEP, including the cost of room and board for a residential placement determined necessary, consistent with 34 CFR § 300.114, to implement a child's IEP.

(iii) The funds in the high cost fund remain under the control of the State until disbursed to an LEA to support a specific child who qualifies under the State plan for the high cost funds or distributed to LEAs, consistent with paragraph (c)(9) of this section.

(5) The disbursements under paragraph (c)(4) of this section **must not be used to support legal fees**, court costs, or other costs associated with a cause of action brought on behalf of a child with a disability to ensure FAPE for such child.

(6) Nothing in paragraph (c) of this section—

(i) Limits or conditions the right of a child with a disability who is assisted under Part B of the Act to receive FAPE pursuant to section 612(a)(1) of the Act in the least restrictive environment pursuant to section 612(a)(5) of the Act; or

(ii) Authorizes an SEA or LEA to establish a limit on what may be spent on the education of a child with a disability.

(7) Notwithstanding the provisions of paragraphs (c)(1) through (6) of this section, a State may use funds reserved pursuant to paragraph (c)(1)(i) of this section for implementing a placement neutral cost sharing and reimbursement program of high need, low incidence, catastrophic, or extraordinary aid to LEAs that provides services to high need children based on eligibility criteria for such programs that were created not later than January 1, 2004, and are currently in operation, if such program serves children that meet the requirement of the definition of a high need child with a disability as described in paragraph (c)(3)(i)(A) of this section.

(8) Disbursements provided under paragraph (c) of this section must not be used to pay costs that otherwise would be reimbursed as medical assistance for a child with a disability under the State Medicaid program under Title XIX of the Social Security Act.

(9) Funds reserved under paragraph (c)(1)(i) of this section from the appropriation for any fiscal year, but not expended pursuant to paragraph (c)(4) of this section before the beginning of their last year of availability for obligation, must be allocated to LEAs in the same manner as other funds from the appropriation for that fiscal year are allocated to LEAs under 34 CFR § 300.705 during their final year of availability.

(d) **Inapplicability of certain prohibitions**. A State may use funds the State reserves under paragraphs (a) and (b) of this section without regard to—

(1) The prohibition on commingling of funds in 34 CFR § 300.162(b).

(2) The prohibition on supplanting other funds in 34 CFR § 300.162(c).

(e) **Special rule for increasing funds**. A State may use funds the State reserves under paragraph (a)(1) of this section as a result of inflationary increases under paragraph (a)(2) of this section to carry out activities authorized under paragraph(b) (4)(i), (iii), (vii), or (viii) of this section.

(f) **Flexibility in using funds for Part C**. Any State eligible to receive a grant under section 619 of the Act may use funds made available under paragraph (a)(1) of this section, 34 CFR § 300.705(c), or 34 CFR § 300.814(e) to develop and implement a State policy jointly with the lead agency under Part C of the Act and the SEA to provide early intervention services (which must include an educational component that promotes school readiness and incorporates preliteracy, language, and numeracy skills) in accordance with Part C of the Act to children with disabilities who are eligible for services under section 619 of the Act and who previously received services under Part C of the Act until the children enter, or are eligible under State law to enter, kindergarten, or elementary school as appropriate. (Authority: 20 U.S.C. 1411(e))

34 CFR § 300.705 Subgrants to LEAs.

(a) **Subgrants required**. Each State that receives a grant under section 611 of the Act for any fiscal year must distribute any funds the State does not reserve under 34 CFR § 300.704 to LEAs (including public charter schools that operate as LEAs) in the State that have established their eligibility under section 613 of the Act for use in accordance with Part B of the Act.

(b) **Allocations to LEAs**. For each fiscal year for which funds are allocated to States under 34 CFR § 300.703, each State shall allocate funds as follows:

(1) Base payments. The State first must award each LEA described in paragraph (a) of this section the amount the LEA would have received under section 611 of the Act for fiscal year 1999, if the State had distributed 75 percent of its grant for that year under section 611(d) of the Act, as that section was then in effect.

(2) Base payment adjustments. For any fiscal year after 1999—

(i) If a new LEA is created, the State must divide the base allocation determined under paragraph (b)(1) of this section for the LEAs that would have been responsible for serving children with disabilities now being served by the new LEA, among the new LEA and affected LEAs based on the relative numbers of children with disabilities ages 3 through 21, or ages 6 through 21 if a State has had its payment reduced under 34 CFR § 300.703(b), currently provided special education by each of the LEAs;

(ii) If one or more LEAs are combined into a single new LEA, the State must combine the base allocations of the merged LEAs; and

(iii) If, for two or more LEAs, geographic boundaries or administrative responsibility for providing services to children with disabilities ages 3 through 21 change, the base allocations of affected LEAs must be redistributed among affected LEAs based on the relative numbers of children with disabilities ages 3 through 21, or ages 6 through 21 if a State has had its payment reduced under 34 CFR § 300.703(b), currently provided special education by each affected LEA.

(3) Allocation of remaining funds. After making allocations under paragraph (b)(1) of this section, as adjusted by paragraph (b)(2) of this section, the State must—

(i) Allocate 85 percent of any remaining funds to those LEAs on the basis of the relative numbers of children enrolled in public and private elementary schools and secondary schools within the LEA's jurisdiction; and

(ii) Allocate 15 percent of those remaining funds to those LEAs in accordance with their relative numbers of children living in poverty, as determined by the SEA.

(c) **Reallocation of funds**. If an SEA determines that an LEA is adequately providing FAPE to all children with disabilities residing in the area served by that agency with State and local funds, the SEA may reallocate any portion of the funds under this part that are not needed by that LEA to provide FAPE to other LEAs in the State that are not adequately providing special education and related services to all children with disabilities residing in the areas served by those other LEAs. (Authority: 20 U.S.C. 1411(f))

34 CFR § 300.706 [Reserved]

Secretary of the Interior

34 CFR § 300.707 Use of amounts by Secretary of the Interior.

(a) **Definitions.** For purposes of 34 CFR § 300.707 through 300.716, the following definitions apply:

(1) Reservation means Indian Country as defined in 18 U.S.C. 1151.

(2) Tribal governing body has the definition given that term in 25 U.S.C. 2021(19).

(b) **Provision of amounts for assistance.**

The Secretary provides amounts to the Secretary of the Interior to meet the need for assistance for the education of children with disabilities on reservations aged 5 to 21, inclusive, enrolled in elementary schools and secondary schools for Indian children operated or funded by the Secretary of the Interior. The amount of the payment for any fiscal year is equal to 80 percent of the amount allotted under section 611(b)(2) of the Act for that fiscal year. Of the amount described in the preceding sentence, after the Secretary of the Interior reserves funds for administration under 34 CFR § 300.710, 80 percent must be allocated to such schools by July 1 of that fiscal year and 20 percent must be allocated to such schools by September 30 of that fiscal year.

(c) Additional requirement.

With respect to all other children aged 3 to 21, inclusive, on reservations, the SEA of the State in which the reservation is located must ensure that all of the requirements of Part B of the Act are implemented. (Authority: 20 U.S.C. 1411(h)(1))

34 CFR § 300.708 Submission of information.

The Secretary may provide the Secretary of the Interior amounts under 34 CFR § 300.707 for a fiscal year only if the Secretary of the Interior submits to the Secretary information that—

(a) Meets the requirements of section 612(a)(1), (3) through (9), (10)(B) through (C), (11) through (12), (14) through (16), (19), and (21) through (25) of the Act (including monitoring and evaluation activities);

(b) Meets the requirements of section 612(b) and (e) of the Act;

(c) Meets the requirements of section 613(a)(1), (2)(A)(i), (7) through (9) and section 613(i) of the Act (references to LEAs in these sections must be read as references to elementary schools and secondary schools for Indian children operated or funded by the Secretary of the Interior);

(d) Meets the requirements of section 616 of the Act that apply to States (references to LEAs in section 616 of the Act must be read as references to elementary schools and secondary schools for Indian children operated or funded by the Secretary of the Interior).

(e) Meets the requirements of this part that implement the sections of the Act listed in paragraphs (a) through (d) of this section;

(f) Includes a description of how the Secretary of the Interior will coordinate the provision of services under Part B of the Act with LEAs, tribes and tribal organizations, and other private and Federal service providers;

(g) Includes an assurance that there are public hearings, adequate notice of the hearings, and an opportunity for comment afforded to members of tribes, tribal governing bodies, and affected local school boards before the adoption of the policies, programs, and procedures related to the requirements described in paragraphs (a) through (d) of this section;

(h) Includes an assurance that the Secretary of the Interior provides the information that the Secretary may require to comply with section 618 of the Act;

(i)

> (1) Includes an assurance that the Secretary of the Interior and the Secretary of Health and Human Services have entered into a memorandum of agreement, to be provided to the Secretary, for the coordination of services, resources, and personnel between their respective Federal, State, and local offices and with the SEAs and LEAs and other entities to facilitate the provision of services to Indian children with disabilities residing on or near reservations.

> (2) The agreement must provide for the apportionment of responsibilities and costs, including child find, evaluation, diagnosis, remediation or therapeutic measures, and (where appropriate) equipment and medical or personal supplies, as needed for a child with a disability to remain in a school or program; and

(j) Includes an assurance that the Department of the Interior will cooperate with the Department in its exercise of monitoring and oversight of the requirements in this section and 34 CFR § 300.709 through 300.711 and 34 CFR § 300.713 through 300.716, and any agreements entered into between the Secretary of the Interior and other entities under Part B of the Act, and will fulfill its duties under Part B of the Act. The Secretary withholds payments under 34 CFR § 300.707 with respect to the requirements described in this section in the same manner as the Secretary withholds payments under section 616(e)(6) of the Act. (Authority: 20 U.S.C. 1411(h)(2) and (3))

34 CFR § 300.709 Public participation.

In fulfilling the requirements of 34 CFR § 300.708 the Secretary of the Interior must provide for public participation consistent with 34 CFR § 300.165. (Authority: 20 U.S.C. 1411(h))

34 CFR § 300.710 Use of funds under Part B of the Act.

(a) The Secretary of the Interior may reserve five percent of its payment under 34 CFR § 300.707(b) in any fiscal year, or $500,000, whichever is greater, for administrative costs in carrying out the provisions of 34 CFR § 300.707 through 300.709, 300.711, and 300.713 through 300.716.

(b) Payments to the Secretary of the Interior under 34 CFR § 300.712 must be used in accordance with that section. (Authority: 20 U.S.C. 1411(h)(1)(A))

34 CFR § 300.711 Early intervening services.

(a) The Secretary of the Interior may allow each elementary school and secondary school for Indian children operated or funded by the Secretary of the Interior to use not more than 15 percent of the amount the school receives under 34 CFR § 300.707(b) for any fiscal year, in combination with other amounts (which may include amounts other than education funds), to develop and implement coordinated, early intervening services, which may include interagency financing structures, for children in kindergarten through grade 12 (with a particular emphasis on children in kindergarten through grade three) who have not been identified as needing special education or related services but who need additional academic and behavioral support to succeed in a general education environment, in accordance with section 613(f) of the Act.

(b) Each elementary school and secondary school for Indian children operated or funded by the Secretary of the Interior that develops and maintains coordinated early intervening services in accordance with section 613(f) of the Act and 34 CFR § 300.226 must annually report to the Secretary of the Interior in accordance with section 613(f) of the Act. (Authority: 20 U.S.C. 1411(h) and 1413(f))

34 CFR § 300.712 Payments for education and services for Indian children with disabilities aged three through five.

(a) General. With funds appropriated under section 611(i) of the Act, the Secretary makes payments to the Secretary of the Interior to be distributed to tribes or tribal organizations (as defined under section 4 of the Indian Self-Determination and Education Assistance Act) or consortia of tribes or tribal organizations to provide for the coordination of assistance for special education and related services for children with disabilities aged three through five on reservations served by elementary schools and secondary schools for Indian children operated or funded by the Department of the Interior. The amount of the payments under paragraph (b) of this section for any fiscal year is equal to 20 percent of the amount allotted under 34 CFR § 300.701(b).

(b) Distribution of funds. The Secretary of the Interior must distribute the total amount of the payment under paragraph (a) of this section by allocating to each tribe, tribal organization, or consortium an amount based on the number of children with disabilities aged three through five residing on reservations as reported annually, divided by the total of those children served by all tribes or tribal organizations.

(c) Submission of information. To receive a payment under this section, the tribe or tribal organization must submit the figures to the Secretary of the Interior as required to determine the amounts to be allocated under paragraph (b) of this section. This information must be compiled and submitted to the Secretary.

(d) Use of funds.

(1) The funds received by a tribe or tribal organization must be used to assist in child find, screening, and other procedures for the early identification of children aged three through five, parent training, and the provision of direct services. These activities may be carried out directly or through contracts or cooperative agreements with the BIA, LEAs, and other public or private nonprofit organizations. The tribe or tribal organization is encouraged to involve Indian parents in the development and implementation of these activities.

(2) The tribe or tribal organization, as appropriate, must make referrals to local, State, or Federal entities for the provision of services or further diagnosis.

(e) Biennial report. To be eligible to receive a grant pursuant to paragraph (a) of this section, the tribe or tribal organization must provide to the Secretary of the Interior a biennial report of activities undertaken under this section, including the number of contracts and cooperative agreements entered into, the number of children contacted and receiving services for each year, and the estimated number of children needing services during the two years following the year in which the report is made. The Secretary of the Interior must include a summary of this information on a biennial basis in the report to the Secretary required under section 611(h) of the Act. The Secretary may require any additional information from the Secretary of the Interior.

(f) Prohibitions. None of the funds allocated under this section may be used by the Secretary of the Interior for administrative purposes, including child count and the provision of technical assistance. (Authority: 20 U.S.C. 1411(h)(4))

34 CFR § 300.713 Plan for coordination of services.

(a) The Secretary of the Interior must develop and implement a plan for the coordination of services for all Indian children with disabilities residing on reservations served by elementary schools and secondary schools for Indian children operated or funded by the Secretary of the Interior.

(b) The plan must provide for the coordination of services benefiting those children from whatever source, including tribes, the Indian Health Service, other BIA divisions, other Federal agencies, State educational agencies, and State, local, and tribal juvenile and adult correctional facilities.

(c) In developing the plan, the Secretary of the Interior must consult with all interested and involved parties.

(d) The plan must be based on the needs of the children and the system best suited for meeting those needs, and may involve the establishment of cooperative agreements between the BIA, other Federal agencies, and other entities.

(e) The plan also must be distributed upon request to States; to SEAs, LEAs, and other agencies providing services to infants, toddlers, and children with disabilities; to tribes; and to other interested parties. (Authority: 20 U.S.C. 1411(h)(5))

34 CFR § 300.714 Establishment of advisory board.

(a) To meet the requirements of section 612(a)(21) of the Act, the Secretary of the Interior must establish, under the BIA, an advisory board composed of individuals involved in or concerned with the education and provision of services to Indian infants, toddlers, children, and youth with disabilities, including Indians with disabilities, Indian parents or guardians of such children, teachers, service providers, State and local educational officials, representatives of tribes or tribal organizations, representatives from State Interagency Coordinating Councils under section 641 of the Act in States having reservations, and other members representing the various divisions and entities of the BIA. The chairperson must be selected by the Secretary of the Interior.

(b) The advisory board must—

(1) Assist in the coordination of services within the BIA and with other local, State, and Federal agencies in the provision of education for infants, toddlers, and children with disabilities;

(2) Advise and assist the Secretary of the Interior in the performance of the Secretary of the Interior's responsibilities described in section 611(h) of the Act;

(3) Develop and recommend policies concerning effective inter- and intra-agency collaboration, including modifications to regulations, and the elimination of barriers to inter- and intra-agency programs and activities;

(4) Provide assistance and disseminate information on best practices, effective program coordination strategies, and recommendations for improved early intervention services or educational programming for Indian infants, toddlers, and children with disabilities; and

(5) Provide assistance in the preparation of information required under 34 CFR § 300.708(h). (Authority: 20 U.S.C. 1411(h)(6))

34 CFR § 300.715 Annual reports.

(a) In general. The advisory board established under 34 CFR § 300.714 must prepare and submit to the Secretary of the Interior and to Congress an annual report containing a description of the activities of the advisory board for the preceding year.

(b) Availability. The Secretary of the Interior must make available to the Secretary the report described in paragraph (a) of this section. (Authority: 20 U.S.C. 1411(h)(7))

34 CFR § 300.716 Applicable regulations.

The Secretary of the Interior must comply with the requirements of 34 CFR § 300.103 through 300.108, 300.110 through 300.124, 300.145 through 300.154, 300.156 through 300.160, 300.165, 300.170 through 300.186, 300.226, 300.300 through 300.606, 300.610 through 300.646, and 300.707 through 300.716. (Authority: 20 U.S.C. 1411(h)(2)(A))

Definitions that Apply to this Subpart G

34 CFR § 300.717 Definitions applicable to allotments, grants, and use of funds.

As used in this subpart—

(a) **Freely associated States** means the Republic of the Marshall Islands, the Federated States of Micronesia, and the Republic of Palau;

(b) **Outlying areas** means the United States Virgin Islands, Guam, American Samoa, and the Commonwealth of the Northern Mariana Islands;

(c) **State** means each of the 50 States, the District of Columbia, and the Commonwealth of Puerto Rico; and

(d) **Average per-pupil expenditure in public elementary schools and secondary schools in the United States** means—

(1) Without regard to the source of funds—

(i) The aggregate current expenditures, during the second fiscal year preceding the fiscal year for which the determination is made (or, if satisfactory data for that year are not available, during the most recent preceding fiscal year for which satisfactory data are available) of all LEAs in the 50 States and the District of Columbia); plus

(ii) Any direct expenditures by the State for the operation of those agencies; divided by

(2) The aggregate number of children in average daily attendance to whom those agencies provided free public education during that preceding year. (Authority: 20 U.S.C. 1401(22), 1411(b)(1)(C) and (g))

Acquisition of Equipment and Construction or Alteration of Facilities

34 CFR § 300.718 Acquisition of equipment and construction or alteration of facilities.

(a) General. If the Secretary determines that a program authorized under Part B of the Act will be improved by permitting program funds to be used to acquire appropriate equipment, or to construct new facilities or alter existing facilities, the Secretary may allow the use of those funds for those purposes.

(b) Compliance with certain regulations. Any construction of new facilities or alteration of existing facilities under paragraph (a) of this section must comply with the requirements of—

(1) Appendix A of part 36 of title 28, Code of Federal Regulations (commonly known as the "Americans with Disabilities Accessibility Standards for Buildings and Facilities"); or

(2) Appendix A of subpart 101-19.6 of title 41, Code of Federal Regulations (commonly known as the "Uniform Federal Accessibility Standards"). (Authority: 20 U.S.C. 1404)

Subpart H—Preschool Grants for Children with Disabilities

34 CFR § 300.800 In general.

The Secretary provides grants under section 619 of the Act to assist States to provide special education and related services in accordance with Part B of the Act—

(a) To children with disabilities aged three through five years; and

(b) At a State's discretion, to two-year-old children with disabilities who will turn three during the school year. (Authority: 20 U.S.C. 1419(a))

34 CFR § 300.801-300.802 [Reserved]

34 CFR § 300.803 Definition of State.

As used in this subpart, State means each of the 50 States, the District of Columbia, and the Commonwealth of Puerto Rico. (Authority: 20 U.S.C. 1419(i))

34 CFR § 300.804 Eligibility.

A State is eligible for a grant under section 619 of the Act if the State—

(a) Is eligible under section 612 of the Act to receive a grant under Part B of the Act; and

(b) Makes FAPE available to all children with disabilities, aged three through five, residing in the State. (Authority: 20 U.S.C. 1419(b))

34 CFR § 300.805 [Reserved]

34 CFR § 300.806 Eligibility for financial assistance.

No State or LEA, or other public institution or agency, may receive a grant or enter into a contract or cooperative agreement under subpart 2 or 3 of Part D of the Act that relates exclusively to programs, projects, and activities pertaining to children aged three through five years, unless the State is eligible to receive a grant under section 619(b) of the Act. (Authority: 20 U.S.C. 1481(e))

34 CFR § 300.807 Allocations to States.

The Secretary allocates the amount made available to carry out section 619 of the Act for a fiscal year among the States in accordance with 34 CFR § 300.808 through 300.810. (Authority: 20 U.S.C. 1419(c)(1))

34 CFR § 300.808 Increase in funds.

If the amount available for allocation to States under 34 CFR § 300.807 for a fiscal year is equal to or greater than the amount allocated to the States under section 619 of the Act for the preceding fiscal year, those allocations are calculated as follows:

(a) Except as provided in 34 CFR § 300.809, the Secretary—

(1) Allocates to each State the amount the State received under section 619 of the Act for fiscal year 1997;

(2) Allocates 85 percent of any remaining funds to States on the basis of the States' relative populations of children aged three through five; and

(3) Allocates 15 percent of those remaining funds to States on the basis of the States' relative populations of all children aged three through five who are living in poverty.

(b) For the purpose of making grants under this section, the Secretary uses the most recent population data, including data on children living in poverty, that are available and satisfactory to the Secretary. (Authority: 20 U.S.C. 1419(c)(2)(A))

34 CFR § 300.809 Limitations.

(a) Notwithstanding 34 CFR § 300.808, allocations under that section are subject to the following:

(1) No State's allocation may be less than its allocation under section 619 of the Act for the preceding fiscal year.

(2) No State's allocation may be less than the greatest of—

(i) The sum of—

(A) The amount the State received under section 619 of the Act for fiscal year 1997; and

(B) One-third of one percent of the amount by which the amount appropriated under section 619(j) of the Act for the fiscal year exceeds the amount appropriated for section 619 of the Act for fiscal year 1997;

(ii) The sum of—

(A) The amount the State received under section 619 of the Act for the preceding fiscal year; and

(B) That amount multiplied by the percentage by which the increase in the funds appropriated under section 619 of the Act from the preceding fiscal year exceeds 1.5 percent; or

(iii) The sum of—

(A) The amount the State received under section 619 of the Act for the preceding fiscal year; and

(B) That amount multiplied by 90 percent of the percentage increase in the amount appropriated under section 619 of the Act from the preceding fiscal year.

(b) Notwithstanding paragraph (a)(2) of this section, no State's allocation under 34 CFR § 300.808 may exceed the sum of—

(1) The amount the State received under section 619 of the Act for the preceding fiscal year; and

(2) That amount multiplied by the sum of 1.5 percent and the percentage increase in the amount appropriated under section 619 of the Act from the preceding fiscal year.

(c) If the amount available for allocation to States under 34 CFR § 300.808 and paragraphs (a) and (b) of this section is insufficient to pay those allocations in full, those allocations are ratably reduced, subject to paragraph (a)(1) of this section. (Authority: 20 U.S.C. 1419(c)(2)(B) and (c)(2)(C))

34 CFR § 300.810 Decrease in funds.

If the amount available for allocations to States under 34 CFR § 300.807 for a fiscal year is less than the amount allocated to the States under section 619 of the Act for the preceding fiscal year, those allocations are calculated as follows:

(a) If the amount available for allocations is greater than the amount allocated to the States for fiscal year 1997, each State is allocated the sum of—

(1) The amount the State received under section 619 of the Act for fiscal year 1997; and

(2) An amount that bears the same relation to any remaining funds as the increase the State received under section 619 of the Act for the preceding fiscal year over fiscal year 1997 bears to the total of all such increases for all States.

(b) If the amount available for allocations is equal to or less than the amount allocated to the States for fiscal year 1997, each State is allocated the amount the State received for fiscal year 1997, ratably reduced, if necessary. (Authority: 20 U.S.C. 1419(c)(3))

34 CFR § 300.811 [Reserved]

34 CFR § 300.812 Reservation for State activities.

(a) Each State may reserve not more than the amount described in paragraph (b) of this section for administration and other State-level activities in accordance with 34 CFR § 300.813 and 300.814.

(b) For each fiscal year, the Secretary determines and reports to the SEA an amount that is 25 percent of the amount the State received under section 619 of the Act for fiscal year 1997, cumulatively adjusted by the Secretary for each succeeding fiscal year by the lesser of—

(1) The percentage increase, if any, from the preceding fiscal year in the State's allocation under section 619 of the Act; or

(2) The rate of inflation, as measured by the percentage increase, if any, from the preceding fiscal year in the Consumer Price Index for All Urban Consumers, published by the Bureau of Labor Statistics of the Department of Labor. (Authority: 20 U.S.C. 1419(d))

34 CFR § 300.813 State administration.

(a) For the purpose of administering section 619 of the Act (including the coordination of activities under Part B of the Act with, and providing technical assistance to, other programs that provide services to children with disabilities), a State may use not more than 20 percent of the maximum amount the State may reserve under 34 CFR § 300.812 for any fiscal year.

(b) Funds described in paragraph (a) of this section may also be used for the administration of Part C of the Act. (Authority: 20 U.S.C. 1419(e))

34 CFR § 300.814 Other State-level activities.

Each State must use any funds the State reserves under 34 CFR § 300.812 and does not use for administration under 34 CFR § 300.813—

(a) For support services (including establishing and implementing the mediation process required by section 615(e) of the Act), which may benefit children with disabilities younger than three or older than five as long as those services also benefit children with disabilities aged three through five;

(b) For direct services for children eligible for services under section 619 of the Act;

(c) For activities at the State and local levels to meet the performance goals established by the State under section 612(a)(15) of the Act;

(d) To supplement other funds used to develop and implement a statewide coordinated services system designed to improve results for children and families, including children with disabilities and their families, but not more than one percent of the amount received by the State under section 619 of the Act for a fiscal year;

(e) To provide early intervention services (which must include an educational component that promotes school readiness and incorporates preliteracy, language, and numeracy skills) in accordance with Part C of the Act to children with disabilities who are eligible for services under section 619 of the Act and who previously received services under Part C of the Act until such children enter, or are eligible under State law to enter, kindergarten; or

(f) At the State's discretion, to continue service coordination or case management for families who receive services under Part C of the Act, consistent with 34 CFR § 300.814(e). (Authority: 20 U.S.C. 1419(f))

34 CFR § 300.815 Subgrants to LEAs.

Each State that receives a grant under section 619 of the Act for any fiscal year must distribute all of the grant funds that the State does not reserve under 34 CFR § 300.812 to LEAs in the State that have established their eligibility under section 613 of the Act. (Authority: 20 U.S.C. 1419(g)(1))

34 CFR § 300.816 Allocations to LEAs.

(a) Base payments. The State must first award each LEA described in 34 CFR § 300.815 the amount that agency would have received under section 619 of the Act for fiscal year 1997 if the State had distributed 75 percent of its grant for that year under section 619(c)(3), as such section was then in effect.

(b) Base payment adjustments. For fiscal year 1998 and beyond—

(1) If a new LEA is created, the State must divide the base allocation determined under paragraph (a) of this section for the LEAs that would have been responsible for serving children with disabilities now being served by the new LEA, among the new LEA and affected LEAs based on the relative numbers of children with disabilities ages three through five currently provided special education by each of the LEAs;

(2) If one or more LEAs are combined into a single new LEA, the State must combine the base allocations of the merged LEAs; and

(3) If for two or more LEAs, geographic boundaries or administrative responsibility for providing services to children with disabilities ages three through five changes, the base allocations of affected LEAs must be redistributed among affected LEAs based on the relative numbers of children with disabilities ages three through five currently provided special education by each affected LEA.

(c) Allocation of remaining funds. After making allocations under paragraph (a) of this section, the State must—

(1) Allocate 85 percent of any remaining funds to those LEAs on the basis of the relative numbers of children enrolled in public and private elementary schools and secondary schools within the LEA's jurisdiction; and

(2) Allocate 15 percent of those remaining funds to those LEAs in accordance with their relative numbers of children living in poverty, as determined by the SEA.

(d) Use of best data. For the purpose of making grants under this section, States must apply on a uniform basis across all LEAs the best data that are available to them on the numbers of children enrolled in public and private elementary and secondary schools and the numbers of children living in poverty. (Authority: 20 U.S.C. 1419(g)(1))

34 CFR § 300.817 Reallocation of LEA funds.

If an SEA determines that an LEA is adequately providing FAPE to all children with disabilities aged three through five residing in the area served by the LEA with State and local funds, the SEA may reallocate any portion of the funds under section 619 of the Act that are not needed by that LEA to provide FAPE to other LEAs in the State that are not adequately providing special education and related services to all children with disabilities aged three through five residing in the areas the other LEAs serve. (Authority: 20 U.S.C. 1419(g)(2))

34 CFR § 300.818 Part C of the Act inapplicable.

Part C of the Act does not apply to any child with a disability receiving FAPE, in accordance with Part B of the Act, with funds received under section 619 of the Act. (Authority: 20 U.S.C. 1419(h))

End of IDEA Regulations

In Summation

This Chapter contained the full text of the IDEA 2004 Regulations published by the USDOE in Title 34, Part 300, of the Code of Federal Regulations, the first being 34 CFR § 300.1.

Chapter 7 includes portions of **six statutes** in the United States Code related to the Rehabilitation Act of 1973, **Section 504**, contained in Title 29, in the United States Code, specifically sections 701, 702, 705, 712, 794, and 794a. Those statutes are followed by the pertinent **regulations** issued by the USDOE, USDOJ, and other federal agencies. The regulations provide substantially more detail than the statutes and are the basis of public policy and legal decisions. Section 504 applies to entities receiving federal financial assistance, such as public schools.

End of Chapter 6 - IDEA Regulations

HyperLinks to Specific Sections in IDEA

20 U.S.C. § 1400	Findings and Purposes	20 U.S.C. § 1415	Procedural Safeguards
20 U.S.C. § 1401	Definitions	20 U.S.C. § 1415(b)(1)	Indep. Educ. Eval. IEE
20 U.S.C. § 1412	State Responsibilities	20 U.S.C. § 1415(f)	Due Process Hearing
20 U.S.C. § 1414(a)	Evaluations	20 U.S.C. § 1415(j)	Stay-Put / Pendency
20 U.S.C. § 1414(d)	IEPs	20 U.S.C. § 1415(k)	Discipline

Hyperlinks to Chapters

Ch. 01 Introduction	Ch. 06 IDEA Regulations
Ch. 02 History	Ch. 07 Section 504
Ch. 03 Overview of Law, Courts, Research	Ch. 08 ADA
Ch. 04 Overview of IDEA, Section 504, ADA	Ch. 09 Other laws
Ch. 05 IDEA (US Code)	Ch. 10 Selected Topics

CHAPTER 7

The Rehabilitation Act of 1973
Section 504 and Regulations[1]

29 U.S.C. Chapter 16 - General Provisions[2]

<§ 701 - Findings; purpose; policy>
§ 702 - Rehabilitative Services Administration
<§ 705 - Definitions>
§ 712 - Information clearinghouse

29 U.S.C. Chapter 16, Subchapter V - Rights and Advocacy[3]

<§ 794 - Nondiscrimination under Federal grants and programs>[4]
<§ 794a - Remedies and attorney fees>

Sections of the United States Code, Title 29

29 U.S.C. § 701 - Findings; purpose; policy

(a) **Findings.** Congress finds that--

(1) millions of Americans have one or more physical or mental disabilities and the number of Americans with such disabilities is increasing;

(2) individuals with disabilities constitute one of the most disadvantaged groups in society;

(3) disability is a natural part of the human experience and in no way diminishes the right of individuals to

(A) live independently;

---

1   Included in this chapter are statutes from Title 29 of the United States Code and regulations from Title 34, Part 104 of the Code of Federal Regulations that relate to educational issues.

2   There are 17 sections under the heading of "General Provisions." We have only included the 4 that relate to education issues.

3   There are 11 sections in **Subchapter V**, which is about **Rights and Advocacy**. Throughout this statute and regulations and the ADA statute and regulations, you will see a reference to "**Subchapter V.**" As with the prior portion, we have only included those that relate to education issues. The others are about employment, subminimum wages, architectural barriers, and funding for the "Protection and Advocacy" offices.

4   Technically, this is the specific "**Section 504**," which, in practice, spirit, and intent encompass all of these sections and federal regulations within **Subchapter V.**

(B) enjoy self-determination;

(C) make choices;

(D) contribute to society;

(E) pursue meaningful careers; and

(F) enjoy full inclusion and integration in the economic, political, social, cultural, and educational mainstream of American society;

(4) increased employment of individuals with disabilities can be achieved through implementation of statewide workforce development systems defined in section 3102 of this title that provide meaningful and effective participation for individuals with disabilities in workforce investment activities and activities carried out under the vocational rehabilitation program established under subchapter I, and through the provision of independent living services, support services, and meaningful opportunities for employment in integrated work settings through the provision of reasonable accommodations;

(5) **individuals with disabilities continually encounter various forms of discrimination** in such critical areas as employment, housing, public accommodations, **education**, transportation, communication, recreation, institutionalization, health services, voting, and public services; and

(6) **the goals of the Nation properly include** the goal of providing individuals with disabilities with the tools necessary to-

(A) make informed choices and decisions; and

(B) achieve **equality of opportunity, full inclusion and integration** in society, employment, independent living, and **economic and social self-sufficiency**, for such individuals; and

(7)

(A) a high proportion of students with disabilities is leaving secondary education **without being employed** in competitive integrated employment, **or being enrolled in postsecondary education**; and

(B) there is a substantial need to support such students as they transition from school to postsecondary life.[5]

(b) **Purpose.** The purposes of this chapter are--[6]

(1) to empower individuals with disabilities to **maximize employment, economic self-sufficiency,**[7] **independence, and inclusion and integration into society**, through--

(A) statewide workforce development systems defined in section 3102 of this title that include, as integral components, comprehensive and coordinated state-of-the-art programs of vocational rehabilitation;

(B) independent living centers and services;

(C) research;

(D) training;

(E) demonstration projects; and

(F) the guarantee of equal opportunity; and

(2) **to maximize opportunities for individuals with disabilitie**s, including individuals with significant disabilities, for competitive integrated employment;

(3) to ensure that the Federal Government **plays a leadership role** in promoting the employment of individuals with disabilities, especially individuals with significant disabilities, and in assisting States and

---

5   The 2004 revision of IDEA placed a greater emphasis on students with IEPs being able to transition to higher education.

6   This is the **mission statement and purpose of Section 504**. Compare it to the mission statement and "Purpose" of IDEA at 20 U.S.C. § 1400(d)(1)(A).

7   This term, **economic self-sufficiency,** is also included in the **"Findings"** portion of IDEA at 20 U.S.C. § 1400(c)(1).

providers of services in fulfilling the aspirations of such individuals with disabilities for meaningful and gainful employment and independent living;

(4) to increase employment opportunities and employment outcomes for individuals with disabilities, including through encouraging meaningful input by employers and vocational rehabilitation service providers on successful and prospective employment and placement strategies; and

(5) to ensure, to the greatest extent possible, that youth with disabilities and **students with disabilities who are transitioning from receipt of special education services under the Individuals with Disabilities Education Act (20 U.S.C. 1400 *et seq.*) and receipt of services under section 794** of this title[8] have opportunities for **postsecondary success**.[9]

(c) Policy. It is the policy of the United States that **all programs**, projects, and activities receiving assistance under this chapter shall be carried out in a manner consistent with the principles of--

(1) respect for individual dignity, personal responsibility, self-determination, and pursuit of meaningful careers, based on informed choice, of individuals with disabilities;

(2) respect for the privacy, rights, and **equal access** (including the use of accessible formats), of the individuals;

(3) inclusion, integration, and full participation of the individuals;

(4) support for the **involvement of an individual's representative** if an individual with a disability requests, desires, or needs such support; and

(5) support for individual and systemic advocacy and community involvement.

29 U.S.C. § 702 - Rehabilitative Services Administration

(a) There is **established in the Office of the Secretary in the Department of Education a Rehabilitation Services Administration** which shall be headed by a Commissioner (hereinafter in this chapter referred to as the "Commissioner") appointed by the President by and with the advice and consent of the Senate. Such Administration shall be the principal agency, and the Commissioner shall be the principal officer, of the Department for purposes of carrying out subchapters I, III, VI, and part B of subchapter VII.

The Commissioner shall be an individual with substantial experience in rehabilitation and in rehabilitation program management. In the performance of the functions of the office, **the Commissioner shall be directly responsible to the Secretary of Education** or to the Under Secretary or an appropriate Assistant Secretary of such Department, as designated by the Secretary. The functions of the Commissioner **shall not be delegated** to any officer not directly responsible, both with respect to program operation and administration, to the Commissioner.

Any reference in this chapter to duties to be carried out by the Commissioner shall be considered to be a reference to duties to be carried out by the **Secretary of Education acting through the Commissioner.** In carrying out any of the functions of the office under this chapter, the Commissioner **shall be guided by general policies of the National Council on Disability**[10] established under subchapter IV of this chapter.

(b) The **Secretary of Education** shall take whatever action is necessary to ensure that funds appropriated pursuant to this chapter are expended only for the programs, personnel, and administration of programs carried out under this chapter.

---

8   Section 794 of the Rehabilitation Act of 1973 is better known as **"Section 504 of the Rehabilitation Act."** They are the same.

9   See transition services in IDEA at 20 U.S.C. § 1401(34) and 1414(d)(1)(A)(i)(VIII)(d). In this statute, 20 U.S.C. § 794(b)(2)(A) refers to colleges, universities, and other institutions of higher education. Transitioning from public school to college / university.

10   In Spring, 2005, the **National Council on Disability** contracted with this author, Pete Wright, to write a paper on its behalf for subsequent filing with the pleadings in the U.S. Supreme Court's *Schaffer v. Weast*, burden of proof case. The URL for that comprehensive Policy Paper, titled **"Individuals with Disabilities Education Act - Burden of Proof: On Parents or Schools?"** is at https://www.wrightslaw.com/ncd/wright.burdenproof.pdf.

29 U.S.C. § 703 + 704[11] [not included]

29 U.S.C. § 705. Definitions[12]

For the purposes of this chapter:

. . . [13]

(3) Assistive Technology Terms[14]

(A) Assistive technology - The term "assistive technology" has the meaning given such term in section 3002 of this title.[15]

(B) Assistive technology **device** - The term "assistive technology device" has the meaning given such term in section 3002 of this title . . .

(C) Assistive technology **service** - The term "assistive technology service" has the meaning given such term in section 3002 of this title . . .

(9) Disability[16] - The term "disability" means[17]

(A) except as otherwise provided in subparagraph (B), a physical or mental impairment that constitutes or results in a substantial impediment to employment; or

(B) for purposes of sections 701, 711, and 712 of this title, and **subchapters** II, IV, *V*,[18] and VII, **the meaning given it in <section 12102 of title 42.>**

(16) Impartial hearing officer

(A) In general - The term "impartial hearing officer" means an individual—

(i) who is not an employee of a public agency (other than an administrative law judge, hearing examiner, or employee of an institution of higher education);

---

11   Sections 703 and 704 are not included in this book but are available on the Internet. For Section 703, go to https://www.law.cornell.edu/uscode/text/29/703.

12   This is the **"Definitions"** section of The Rehabilitation Act. You may want to compare the critical definitions in The Rehabilitation Act to the definitions in IDEA located at 20 U.S.C. § 1401 earlier in this book.

13   The 42 definitions listed in Section 705 are in strict alphabetical order, beginning with "administrative costs," and conclude with "youth with a disability." The URL for this complete section is at:
https://www.law.cornell.edu/uscode/text/29/705.

14   The **Assistive Technology Act** has been incorporated by reference into this statute. It begins at 29 U.S.C. § 3001. Section 3002 contains the definitions and is available at:
https://www.law.cornell.edu/uscode/text/29/3002.

15   The cited 29 U.S.C. § 3001 is the **"Assistive Technology Act"** and at 3001(b)(1)(B) it explains that the purpose of this federal law to is to "increase the ability of individuals with disabilities of all ages to **secure and maintain possession of assistive technology devices** as such individuals make the transition between services offered by educational or human service agencies or between settings of daily living (for example, between home and work)."

16   **This definition is actually provided by the Americans with Disabilities Act** in 42 U.S.C. § 12102 which has been incorporated by reference from the ADA into Section 504. Thus, if there is a later change in the ADA regarding this definition, it is automatically changed here. This 504 / ADA definition differs from the definition in IDEA of a "child with a disability" located at 20 U.S.C. § 1401(3). In IDEA, the child's disability must also adversely affect educational performance such that the child needs special education and related services. You will find the full text of that ADA definition in this book after the Section 504 regulations.

17   The definition as to whether a student qualifies for the protections of Section 504 of the Rehabilitation Act is found in the definitions of a disability listed here and in 29 U.S.C. § 705(9), (20), (21), (24), (37) **and also** in **42 U.S.C. § 12102 of the ADA**, incorporated here by reference. If a child has an IEP under IDEA, then the child also qualifies for the protections of Section 504.

18   **29 U.S.C. § 794 - this is "Section 504."**

(ii) who is not a member of the State Rehabilitation Council described in section 725 of this title;

(iii) who has not been involved previously in the vocational rehabilitation of the applicant or eligible individual;

(iv) who has knowledge of the delivery of vocational rehabilitation services, the State plan under section 721 of this title, and the Federal and State rules governing the provision of such services and training with respect to the performance of official duties; and

(v) who has no personal or financial interest that would be in conflict with the objectivity of the individual.

(B) Construction - An individual shall not be considered to be an employee of a public agency for purposes of subparagraph (A)(i) solely because the individual is paid by the agency to serve as a hearing officer.

(17) Independent living core services - The term "independent living core services" means—

(A) information and referral services;

(B) independent living skills training;

(C) peer counseling (including cross-disability peer counseling);

(D) individual and systems advocacy; and

(E) services that—

(i) facilitate the transition of individuals with significant disabilities from nursing homes and other institutions to home and community-based residences, with the requisite supports and services;

(ii) provide assistance to individuals with significant disabilities who are at risk of entering institutions so that the individuals may remain in the community; and

(iii) facilitate the transition of youth who are individuals with significant disabilities, who were eligible for **individualized education programs** under section 614(d) of the Individuals with Disabilities Education Act (20 U.S.C. 1414(d)), and who have completed their secondary education or otherwise left school, **to postsecondary life**.

(18) Independent living services - The term "independent living services" includes—

(A) independent living core services; and

(B)

(i) counseling services, including psychological, psychotherapeutic, **and related services**;

(ii) services related to securing housing or shelter, including services related to community group living, and supportive of the purposes of this chapter and of the subchapters of this chapter, and adaptive housing services (including appropriate accommodations to and modifications of any space used to serve, or occupied by, individuals with disabilities);

(iii) rehabilitation technology;

(iv) mobility training;

(v) services and training for individuals with cognitive and sensory disabilities, including life skills training, and interpreter and reader services;

(vi) personal assistance services, including attendant care and the training of personnel providing such services;

(vii) surveys, directories, and other activities to identify appropriate housing, recreation opportunities, and accessible transportation, and other support services;

(viii) consumer information programs on rehabilitation and independent living services available under this chapter, especially for minorities and other individuals with disabilities who have traditionally been unserved or underserved by programs under this chapter;

(ix) education and training necessary for living in a community and participating in community activities;

(x) supported living;

(xi) transportation, including referral and assistance for such transportation and training in the use of public transportation vehicles and systems;

(xii) physical rehabilitation;

(xiii) therapeutic treatment;

(xiv) provision of needed prostheses and other appliances and devices;

(xv) individual and group social and recreational services;

(xvi) training to develop skills specifically designed for youths who are individuals with disabilities to promote self-awareness and esteem, develop advocacy and self-empowerment skills, and explore career options;

(xvii) services for children;

(xviii) services under other Federal, State, or local programs designed to provide resources, training, counseling, or other assistance, of substantial benefit in enhancing the independence, productivity, and quality of life of individuals with disabilities;

(xix) appropriate preventive services to decrease the need of individuals assisted under this chapter for similar services in the future;

(xx) community awareness programs to enhance the understanding and integration into society of individuals with disabilities; and

(xxi) such other services as may be necessary and not inconsistent with the provisions of this chapter.

(20) Individual with a disability[19, 20]

(A) In general. Except as otherwise provided in subparagraph (B), the term "**individual with a disability**" means any individual who -

(i) has a physical or mental impairment which for such individual constitutes or results in a substantial impediment to employment; and

(ii) can benefit in terms of an employment outcome from vocational rehabilitation services provided pursuant to subchapter I, III, or VI of this chapter.

(B) Certain programs; limitations on major life activities. Subject to subparagraphs (C), (D), (E), and (F), **the term "individual with a disability" means,** for purposes of sections 701, 711, and 712 of this title, and subchapters II, IV, **V,**[21] and VII of this chapter, **any person who has a disability as defined in section 12102 of title 42.**[22]

(21) Individual with a significant disability

(A) In general - Except as provided in subparagraph (B) or (C), the term "individual with a significant disability" means an individual with a disability—

(i) who has a **severe** physical or mental impairment which seriously limits one or more functional capacities (such as mobility, communication, self-care, self-direction, interpersonal skills, work tolerance, or work skills) in terms of an employment outcome;

(ii) whose vocational rehabilitation can be expected to require multiple vocational rehabilitation services over an extended period of time; and

---

19 The term "**child with a disability**" is used in IDEA at 20 U.S.C. § 1401(3), and not the word "individual."

20 Subsections (20)(C) through (20)(G) are not included as they relate to drug abuse, alcoholism, "transvestism, transsexualism, pedophilia, exhibitionism, voyeurism, gender identity disorders not resulting from physical impairments, or other sexual behavior disorders, compulsive gambling, kleptomania, or pyromania" etc.

21 **Subchapter V is the beginning of the "Section 504" portion of this law**.

22 Again, the definition contained in the ADA is incorporated by reference here into The Rehabilitation Act.

(iii) who has one or more physical or mental disabilities resulting from amputation, arthritis, autism, blindness, burn injury, cancer, cerebral palsy, cystic fibrosis, deafness, head injury, heart disease, hemiplegia, hemophilia, respiratory or pulmonary dysfunction, intellectual disability, mental illness, multiple sclerosis, muscular dystrophy, musculo-skeletal disorders, neurological disorders (including stroke and epilepsy), paraplegia, quadriplegia, and other spinal cord conditions, sickle cell anemia, specific learning disability, end-stage renal disease, or another disability or combination of disabilities determined on the basis of an assessment for determining eligibility and vocational rehabilitation needs described in subparagraphs (A) and (B) of paragraph (2) to cause comparable substantial functional limitation.

(B) Independent living services and centers for independent living - For purposes of subchapter VII, the term "individual with a significant disability" means an individual with a severe physical or mental impairment whose ability to function independently in the family or community or whose ability to obtain, maintain, or advance in employment is substantially limited and for whom the delivery of independent living services will improve the ability to function, continue functioning, or move toward functioning independently in the family or community or to continue in employment, respectively.

(C) Research and training - For purposes of subchapter II, the term "individual with a significant disability" includes an individual described in subparagraph (A) or (B).

(D) Individuals with significant disabilities - The term "individuals with significant disabilities" means more than one individual with a significant disability.

(E) Individual with a most significant disability

(i) In general - The term "individual with a most significant disability", used with respect to an individual in a State, means an individual with a significant disability who meets criteria established by the State under section 721(a)(5)(C) of this title.[23]

(ii) Individuals with the most significant disabilities - The term "individuals with the most significant disabilities" means more than one individual with a most significant disability.

(22) Individual's representative; applicant's representative - The terms "individual's representative" and "applicant's representative" mean a parent, a family member, a guardian, an advocate, or an authorized representative of an individual or applicant, respectively.

(23) Institution of higher education - The term "institution of higher education" has the meaning given the term in section 1002 of title 20.

(37) Student with a disability

(A) In general - The term "student with a disability" means an individual with a disability who—

(i)

(I)(aa) is not younger than the earliest age for the provision of transition services under section 614(d)(1)(A)(i)(VIII) of the Individuals with Disabilities Education Act (20 U.S.C. 1414(d)(1)(A)(i)(VIII));[24] or

(bb) if the State involved elects to use a lower minimum age for receipt of pre-employment transition services under this chapter, is not younger than that minimum age; and

(II)(aa) is not older than 21 years of age; or

(bb) if the State law for the State provides for a higher maximum age for receipt of services under the Individuals with Disabilities Education Act (20 U.S.C. 1400 *et seq.*), is not older than that maximum age; and

---

23   Under this statute at 29 U.S.C. § 721(a)(5)(C), the State must "include an assurance that, in accordance with criteria established by the State for the order of selection, individuals with the most significant disabilities will be selected first for the provision of vocational rehabilitation services."

24   This section is a part of the law about IEPs in IDEA.

(ii)

(I) is eligible for, and receiving, special education or related services under part B of the Individuals with Disabilities Education Act (20 U.S.C. 1411 *et seq.*);[25] or

(II) is an individual with a disability, for purposes of section 794 of this title.

(B) Students with disabilities - The term "students with disabilities" means more than 1 student with a disability.

(42) Youth with a disability

(A) In general - The term "youth with a disability" means an individual with a disability who—

(i) is not younger than 14 years of age; and

(ii) is not older than 24 years of age.

(B) Youth with disabilities - The term "youth with disabilities" means more than 1 youth with a disability.

Wrightslaw Note: We did not include Sections 706 through 711 and Sections 713 through 718.[26] Section 712 is below.

29 U.S.C. § 712. Information clearinghouse[27]

(a) Establishment; information and resources for individuals with disabilities - The Secretary of Education shall establish a central clearinghouse for information and resource availability for individuals with disabilities which shall provide information and data regarding—

(1) the location, provision, and availability of services and programs for individuals with disabilities, including such information and data provided by State workforce development boards regarding such services and programs authorized under title I of such Act;

(2) research and recent medical and scientific developments bearing on disabilities (and their prevention, amelioration, causes, and cures); and

(3) the current numbers of individuals with disabilities and their needs.

The clearinghouse shall also provide any other relevant information and data which the Secretary of Education considers appropriate.

---

25   Part B of IDEA begins at Section 1411 and Part C, for "Infants and Toddlers with Disabilities" begins at 20 U.S.C. § 1431.

26   The omitted sections relate to funding, reports, allotments, nonduplication, technical assistance and other matters. To see those deleted sections, please go to

https://www.law.cornell.edu/uscode/text/29/chapter-16/level-general_provisions

then click on the specific section number to view each one.

27   We omitted subsections b, c, and d.

29 U.S. Code, Chapter 16, Subchapter V[28] - Rights and Advocacy[29]

29 U.S.C. § 794. Nondiscrimination under Federal grants and programs[30]

(a) Promulgation of rules and regulations. No otherwise qualified individual with a disability in the United States, as defined in section 705(20) of this title, **shall, solely**[31] **by reason of her or his disability, be excluded from the participation in, be denied the benefits of, or be subjected to discrimination** under any program or activity receiving Federal financial assistance[32] or under any program or activity conducted by any Executive agency or by the United States Postal Service. The head of each such agency shall promulgate such regulations as may be necessary to carry out the amendments to this section made by the Rehabilitation, Comprehensive Services, and Developmental Disabilities Act of 1978. Copies of any proposed regulation shall be submitted to appropriate authorizing committees of the Congress, and such regulation may take effect no earlier than the thirtieth day after the date on which such regulation is so submitted to such committees.

(b) "Program or activity" defined. For the purposes of this section, the term "program or activity" means all of the operations of-

(1)

(A) a department, agency, special purpose district, or other instrumentality of a State or of a local government; or

(B) the entity of such State or local government that distributes such assistance and each such department or agency (and each other State or local government entity) to which the assistance is extended, in the case of assistance to a State or local government;

(2)

(A) **a college, university, or other postsecondary institution, or a public system of higher education; or**

(B) **a local educational agency** (as defined in section 7801 of title 20), system of vocational education, or other school system;[33]

---

28   All of the statutes in Subsection V of the Act are available at this link -
https://www.law.cornell.edu/uscode/text/29/chapter-16/subchapter-V.

29   At this point we jump from the General Provisions portion of The Rehabilitation Act to Subchapter V which contains Section 504. When "The Act" was passed it contained sections of the Act. However, as with all laws, after it was passed by Congress, signed by the President and placed into the United States Code, those section numbers in the Act were changed to statutes in the United States Code. Section 504 of the Act was placed into the Code in Title 29, at Section 794. The specific statute known as Section 504 of the Rehabilitation Act of 1973 is cited as 29 U.S.C. § 794.

30   The "Section 504 statute," at Section 794, is quite short and is followed by the remedies and attorneys' fees statute in 794a. As noted earlier in Chapter 3, the Section 504 statute as compared to the IDEA statute, is quite short, but has extremely broad implications. The statute and the regulations do not have the detail included in IDEA. The accompanying regulations issued by the USDOE have more specificity than in the statute. The body of law that has built up about Section 504 primarily stems from Section 504 and ADA caselaw and USDOE and USDOJ policy positions.

31   While Section 504 requires "a plaintiff to show a denial of services 'solely by reason of' disability . . . [in Title II of the ADA] a plaintiff need show only that discrimination on the basis of disability was a 'motivating factor' for the decision." *KM v. Tustin Unif. Sch. Dist.*, 725 F.3d 1088 (9th Cir. 2013) In *Rogich v. Clark County Sch. Dist.* the Nevada federal judge found that the school district's "conduct satisfied the stricter *mens rea* standard of deliberate indifference under the Section 504 claim, [and] the Court incorporates its reasoning as to the Section 504 claim to find that Defendant violated Title II of the ADA." *Rogich* is on Wrightslaw at: https://www.wrightslaw.com/law/caselaw/2021/rogich.v.clark.county.nv.orton.gillingham.pdf

32   This "financial assistance" clause has been diminished because of ADA sections 42 U.S.C. §§ 12182(b)(2)(A)(ii) and 12181(7)(J). Courts have found private schools to be covered under the ADA and thus required to provide accommodations and modifications. The exception is a private school "**controlled**" by a religious organization. *See* 42 U.S.C. § 12187.

33   Title 20 of the United States Code contains the bulk of the federal laws about education. Section 7801 has 52 definitions and you might want to skim the terms and concepts defined in 20 U.S.C. § 7801 at:
https://www.law.cornell.edu/uscode/text/20/7801.

(3)

  (A) an entire corporation, partnership, or other private organization, or an entire sole proprietorship

    (i) if assistance is extended to such corporation, partnership, private organization, or sole proprietorship as a whole; or

    (ii) which is principally engaged in the business of providing education, health care, housing, social services, or parks and recreation; or

  (B) the entire plant or other comparable, geographically separate facility to which Federal financial assistance is extended, in the case of any other corporation, partnership, private organization, or sole proprietorship; or

(4) any other entity which is established by two or more of the entities described in paragraph (1), (2), or (3); any part of which is extended Federal financial assistance.

(c) Significant structural alterations by small providers. Small providers are not required by subsection (a) of this section to make significant structural alterations to their existing facilities for the purpose of assuring program accessibility, if alternative means of providing the services are available. The terms used in this subsection shall be construed with reference to the regulations existing on March 22, 1988.

(d) Standards used in determining violation of section. The standards used to determine whether this section has been violated in a complaint alleging employment discrimination under this section shall be the standards applied under **Title I of the Americans with Disabilities Act of 1990** (42 U.S.C. 12111 *et seq.*) and the provisions of sections 501 through 504, and 510, of the Americans with Disabilities Act of 1990 (42 U.S.C. 12201-12204 and 12210), as such sections relate to employment.

29 U.S.C. § 794a. Remedies and attorney fees[34]

(a)

(1) The remedies, procedures, and rights set forth in section 717 of the **Civil Rights Act of 1964** (42 U.S.C. 2000e-16), including the application of sections 706(f) through 706(k) (42 U.S.C. 2000e-5(f) through (k)), shall be available, with respect to any complaint under section 791 of this title, to any employee or applicant for employment aggrieved by the final disposition of such complaint, or by the failure to take final action on such complaint. In fashioning an equitable or affirmative action remedy under such section, a court may take into account the reasonableness of the cost of any necessary work place accommodation, and the availability of alternatives therefor or other appropriate relief in order to achieve an equitable and appropriate remedy.

(2) The remedies, procedures, and rights set forth in title VI of the Civil Rights Act of 1964 [42 U.S.C. 2000d *et seq.*] shall be available to any person aggrieved by any act or failure to act by any recipient of Federal assistance or Federal provider of such assistance under section 794 of this title.[35]

(b) In any action or proceeding to enforce or charge a violation of a provision of this subchapter, the court, in its discretion, may allow the prevailing party, other than the United States, a reasonable attorney's fee as part of the costs.

End of Title 29 United States (U.S.C.) Code portion of Section 504 of The Rehabilitation Act of 1973

---

34 For a couple of examples of Section 504 "remedies," see the *Ebonie S.* federal court complaint in Colorado, calculation of damages and subsequent 2.2 million dollar jury verdict for a child with multiple disabilities restrained in a chair.

See also the Order by a Judge in *Rogich v. Clark County Sch. Dist.*, finding, in part, that because the Nevada school district failed to consider the private evaluator's Orton-Gillingham recommendation, the district violated IDEA, Section 504, and the ADA. The child with dyslexia is entitled to compensatory education and parents entitled to private school tuition reimbursement. Links to all three files follow below:

https://www.wrightslaw.com/law/pleadings/CO.ebonie.amended.complaint.constitutionalviolation.pdf
https://www.wrightslaw.com/law/caselaw/2015/ebonie/2009.0911.ebonie.statement.of.damages.pdf
https://www.wrightslaw.com/law/pleadings/CO.ebonie.Jury.verdict.2.2m.pdf
https://www.wrightslaw.com/law/caselaw/2021/rogich.v.clark.county.nv.orton.gillingham.pdf

35 Remedies available for violations of the Civil Rights Act are incorporated by reference in this statute.

Title 34 of the Code of Federal Regulations, (CFR), Part 104 Follows

Wrightslaw Note: This is the end of the **two pertinent Section 504 statutes** in this book. As noted in the beginning of this chapter, the other omitted statutes are available on the Internet. Much of the USDOE and USDOJ policy and legal decisions are based on the Regulations provided below.

However, the Office for Civil Rights (OCR) of the USDOE[36] has issued a **"Notice of Proposed Rulemaking"** as the first step to issue new and revised regulations. Discussions about new regulations are available in a number of locations on the internet, such as

https://www.advocacyinstitute.org/blog/?p=1144
and
https://www.k12dive.com/news/disability-advocates-call-for-strengthening-section-504-regulations/626656/

Speculation is that the USDOE will issue specific detailed "Proposed Regulations" for public comment in 2023. After comments are received and reviewed by the USDOE staff, they will then publish Final Regulations, probably in 2024. As noted at the end of Chapter 1, after this book is published, any later changes in statutes or regulations will be posted on the Wrightslaw website at:

https://www.wrightslaw.com/lawbook.update/

To remain current about OCR's new investigations, findings of non-compliance, resolution agreements, regulations, and other events, we recommend that you periodically visit their "News Room" located at:

https://www2.ed.gov/about/offices/list/ocr/newsroom.html

Selected Regulations for Section 504 of the Rehabilitation Act of 1973, Code of Federal Regulations (CFR)

34 CFR PART 104 - Nondiscrimination on the Basis of Handicap in Programs or Activities receiving Federal Financial Assistance[37]

34 CFR Part 104, Subpart A - General Provisions
34 CFR § 104.1 - Purpose
34 CFR § 104.2 - Application
34 CFR § 104.3 - Definitions
34 CFR § 104.4 - Discrimination prohibited.
34 CFR § 104.5 - Assurances required
34 CFR § 104.6 - Remedial action
34 CFR § 104.7 - Responsible employee, Grievance procedures
34 CFR § 104.8 - Notice
34 CFR § 104.9 - Administrative requirements
34 CFR § 104.10 - Effect of state or local law

---

36   https://www.govinfo.gov/content/pkg/FR-2022-07-12/pdf/2022-13734.pdf

37   **Part 104 has seven subparts, A through G. The critical ones related to education are** A, D, and E.

34 CFR Part 104, Subpart C - Accessibility
34 CFR § 104.21 - Discrimination prohibited
34 CFR § 104.22 - Existing facilities

34 CFR Part 104, Subpart D - Preschool, Elementary, and Secondary Education[38]
34 CFR 104.31 Application of this subpart D.
34 CFR 104.32 Location and notification.
34 CFR 104.33 Free appropriate public education.
34 CFR 104.34 Educational setting.
34 CFR 104.35 Evaluation and placement.
34 CFR 104.36 Procedural safeguards.
34 CFR 104.37 Nonacademic services.
34 CFR 104.38 Preschool and adult education.
34 CFR 104.39 Private education.

34 CFR Part 104, Subpart E - Postsecondary Education[39]
34 CFR 104.41 Application of this subpart.
34 CFR 104.42 Admissions and recruitment.
34 CFR 104.43 Treatment of students; general.
34 CFR 104.44 Academic adjustments.
34 CFR 104.45 Housing.
34 CFR 104.46 Financial and employment assistance to students.
34 CFR 104.47 Nonacademic services.

34 CFR Part 104, Subpart F - Health, Welfare, and Social Services
34 CFR 104.51 Application of this subpart.
34 CFR 104.52 Health, welfare, and other social services.
34 CFR 104.53 Drug and alcohol addicts.
34 CFR 104.54 Education of institutionalized persons.

34 CFR Part 104, Subpart G - Procedures
34 CFR 104.61 Procedures.

Section 504 Regulations
34 CFR Part 104, Subpart A -- General Provisions[40]

34 CFR § 104.1 - Purpose
34 CFR § 104.2 - Application
34 CFR § 104.3 - Definitions
34 CFR § 104.4 - Discrimination prohibited.
34 CFR § 104.5 - Assurances required
34 CFR § 104.6 - Remedial action
34 CFR § 104.7 - Responsible employee, Grievance procedures
34 CFR § 104.8 - Notice
34 CFR § 104.9 - Administrative requirements
34 CFR § 104.10 - Effect of state or local law

---

38 This applies to public schools. Subpart E covers higher education.

39 This applies to higher education whereas Subpart D covers public schools.

40 **Wrightslaw Note:** This Subpart A provides the **purpose of this law** and establishes that an entity, public or private, which provides educational services are covered. As a condition, the private entity must be a recipient of "federal financial assistance." Very few institutions and educational settings escape liability under this clause. The definitions of those individuals protected are quite broad and include episodic conditions. Much of the Section 504 litigation is related to the definitions in Section 104.3.

34 CFR § 104.1 Purpose. -

The purpose of this part is to effectuate section 504 of the Rehabilitation Act of 1973, which is designed to eliminate discrimination on the basis of handicap in any program or activity receiving Federal financial assistance.

34 CFR § 104.2 Application. -

This part applies to each recipient of Federal financial assistance from the Department of Education and to the program or activity that receives such assistance.

34 CFR § 104.3 Definitions. - [41]

(a) The Act means the Rehabilitation Act of 1973, Pub. L. 93-112, as amended by the Rehabilitation Act Amendments of 1974, Pub. L. 93-516, 29 U.S.C. 794.

(b) Section 504 means section 504 of the Act.

(c) Education of the Handicapped Act means that statute as amended by the Education for all Handicapped Children Act of 1975, Pub. L. 94-142, 20 U.S.C. 1401 *et seq.*[42]

(d) Department means the Department of Education.

(e) Assistant Secretary means the Assistant Secretary for Civil Rights of the Department of Education.

(f) Recipient means any state or its political subdivision, any instrumentality of a state or its political subdivision, any public or private agency, institution, organization, or other entity, or any person to which Federal financial assistance is extended directly or through another recipient, including any successor, assignee, or transferee of a recipient, but excluding the ultimate beneficiary of the assistance.

(g) Applicant for assistance means one who submits an application, request, or plan required to be approved by a Department official or by a recipient as a condition to becoming a recipient.

(h) Federal financial assistance means any grant, loan, contract (other than a procurement contract or a contract of insurance or guaranty), or any other arrangement by which the Department provides or otherwise makes available **assistance in the form of**:

   (1) Funds;

   (2) Services of Federal personnel; or

   (3) Real and personal property or any interest in or use of such property, including:

      (i) Transfers or leases of such property for less than fair market value or for reduced consideration; and

      (ii) Proceeds from a subsequent transfer or lease of such property if the Federal share of its fair market value is not returned to the Federal Government.

(i) Facility means all or any portion of buildings, structures, equipment, roads, walks, parking lots, or other real or personal property or interest in such property.

(j) Handicapped person -

   (1) Handicapped person means any person who

      (i) has a physical or mental impairment which substantially limits one or more major life activities,

      (ii) has a record of such an impairment, or

      (iii) is regarded as having such an impairment.(2) As used in paragraph (j)(1) of this section, the phrase:[43]

---

41   *See also* the definitions in the 504 statute.

42   This statute is now known as the **Individuals with Disabilities Education Act (IDEA)**. The full text of that statute and its regulations are included in prior chapters of this book.

43   In Appendix A to these regulations, USDOE explained that "The definition does not set forth a list of specific diseases and conditions that constitute physical or mental impairments because of the difficulty of ensuring the comprehensiveness of any such list. The term includes, however, such diseases and conditions as orthopedic, visual, speech, and hearing impairments, cerebral palsy, epilepsy, muscular dystrophy, multiple sclerosis, cancer, heart disease, diabetes, intellectual disability, emotional illness, and, as discussed further, may include drug addiction and alcoholism."

(i) Physical or mental impairment means

    (A) any physiological disorder or condition, cosmetic disfigurement, or anatomical loss affecting one or more of the following body systems: neurological; musculoskeletal; special sense organs; respiratory, including speech organs; cardiovascular; reproductive, digestive, genito-urinary; hemic and lymphatic; skin; and endocrine; or

    (B) any mental or psychological disorder, such as intellectual disability, organic brain syndrome, emotional or mental illness, and specific learning disabilities.

(ii) Major life activities means functions such as caring for one's self, performing manual tasks, walking, seeing, hearing, speaking, breathing, learning, and working.

(iii) Has a record of such an impairment means has a history of, or has been misclassified as having, a mental or physical impairment that substantially limits one or more major life activities.

(iv) Is regarded as having an impairment means

    (A) has a physical or mental impairment that does not substantially limit major life activities but that is treated by a recipient as constituting such a limitation;

    (B) has a physical or mental impairment that substantially limits major life activities only as a result of the **attitudes of others** toward such impairment; or[44]

    (C) has none of the impairments defined in paragraph (j)(2)(i) of this section but is treated by a recipient as having such an impairment.[45, 46]

(k) Program or activity means all of the operations of-

    (1)

        (i) A department, agency, special purpose district, or other **instrumentality of a State or of a local government**; or

        (ii) The entity of such State or local government that distributes such assistance and each such department or agency (and each other State or local government entity) to which the assistance is extended, in the case of assistance to a State or local government;

    (2)

        (i) A college, university, or other postsecondary institution, or a public system of higher education; or

        (ii) A local educational agency (as defined in 20 U.S.C. 8801), system of vocational education, or other school system;

    (3)

        (i) An entire corporation, partnership, or other private organization, or an entire sole proprietorship -

            (A) If assistance is extended to such corporation, partnership, private organization, or sole proprietorship as a whole; or

            (B) Which is **principally engaged in the business of providing education**, health care, housing,

---

44   In litigation, if the defense is that the plaintiff does not truly have a disability that is covered by Section 504, the fact that the defendant or others, in the past, have believed that the plaintiff has a disability, then the defense of no disability is lost to the defendant, even if the plaintiff truly does not have a disability under Section 504. The ADA has the same clause.

45   In Appendix A, the USDOE also explains "The third part of the statutory and regulatory definition of handicapped person includes any person who is regarded as having a physical or mental impairment that substantially limits one or more major life activities. It includes many persons who are ordinarily considered to be handicapped but who do not technically fall within the first two parts of the statutory definition, such as persons with a limp. This part of the definition also includes some persons who might not ordinarily be considered handicapped, such as persons with disfiguring scars, as well as persons who have no physical or mental impairment but are treated by a recipient as if they were handicapped."

46   Appendix A to these regulations is located on the Internet at:
https://www.law.cornell.edu/cfr/text/34/appendix-A_to_part_104.

social services, or parks and recreation; or

(ii) The entire plant or other comparable, geographically separate facility to which Federal financial assistance is extended, in the case of any other corporation, partnership, private organization, or sole proprietorship; or

(4) Any other entity which is established by two or more of the entities described in paragraph (k)(1), (2), or (3) of this section; any part of which is extended Federal financial assistance.

(l) Qualified handicapped person[47] means:

(1) With respect to **employment**, a handicapped person who, with reasonable accommodation, can perform the essential functions of the job in question;

(2) With respect to **public preschool elementary, secondary, or adult educational services**, a handicapped person

(i) of an age during which nonhandicapped persons[48] are provided such services,

(ii) of any age during which it is mandatory under state law to provide such services to handicapped persons, or

(iii) to whom a state is required to provide a free appropriate public education under section 612 of the Education of the Handicapped Act; and

(3) With respect to **postsecondary** and vocational education services, a handicapped person who meets the academic and technical standards requisite to admission or participation in the recipient's education program or activity;

(4) With respect to other services, a handicapped person who meets the essential eligibility requirements for the receipt of such services.

(m) Handicap means any condition or characteristic that renders a person a handicapped person as defined in paragraph (j) of this section.

34 CFR § 104.4 Discrimination prohibited.

(a) General. No qualified handicapped person shall, on the basis of handicap, be excluded from participation in, be denied the benefits of, or otherwise be subjected to discrimination under any program or activity which receives Federal financial assistance.

(b) Discriminatory actions prohibited.

(1) A recipient, in providing any aid, benefit, or service, may not, **directly or through contractual, licensing, or other arrangements**, on the basis of handicap:

(i) **Deny** a qualified handicapped person **the opportunity** to participate in or benefit from the aid, benefit, or service;

(ii) Afford a qualified handicapped person an opportunity to participate in or benefit from the aid, benefit, or service **that is not equal to that afforded others**;

(iii) Provide a qualified handicapped person with an aid, benefit, or service that **is not as effective** as that provided to others;

(iv) **Provide different** or separate aid, benefits, or **services to handicapped persons** or to any class of handicapped persons **unless such action is necessary** to provide qualified handicapped persons with aid, benefits, or services that are as effective as those provided to others;

(v) **Aid or perpetuate discrimination** against a qualified handicapped person **by providing significant assistance** to an agency, organization, or person that discriminates on the basis of handicap in providing any aid, benefit, or service to beneficiaries of the recipients program or activity;

---

47 Per 42 U.S.C. § 12102(4) of the ADA, this "shall be construed in favor of **broad coverage**" and includes "episodic" conditions.

48 In other words, if services are provided to non handicapped children or adults, then those services are to be available, accessible and provided to handicapped children. This is a common problem with preschool and day care services for children with disabilities. *See* the preceding 34 CFR § 104.3(l).

(vi) Deny a qualified handicapped person the opportunity to participate as a member of planning or advisory boards; or

(vii) **Otherwise limit a qualified handicapped person** in the enjoyment of any right, privilege, advantage, or **opportunity enjoyed by others** receiving an aid, benefit, or service.

(2) For purposes of this part, aids, benefits, and services, to be equally effective, **are not required to produce the identical result or level of achievement** for handicapped and nonhandicapped persons, but **must afford handicapped persons equal opportunity** to obtain the same result, to gain the same benefit, or to reach the same level of achievement, in the most integrated setting appropriate to the person's needs.

(3) Despite the existence of separate or different aid, benefits, or services provided in accordance with this part, a recipient **may not deny** a qualified handicapped person **the opportunity to participate** in such aid, benefits, or services **that are not separate or different.**

(4) A recipient **may not,** directly or through contractual or other arrangements, **utilize criteria or methods of administ**ration

(i) that have the **effect of subjecting qualified handicapped persons to discrimination** on the basis of handicap,

(ii) that have the purpose or effect of defeating or substantially impairing accomplishment of the objectives of the recipient's program or activity with respect to handicapped persons, or

(iii) that **perpetuate the discrimination of another recipient** if both recipients are subject to common administrative control or are agencies of the same State.

(5) In determining the **site or location of a facility,** an applicant for assistance or a recipient may not make selections

(i) that have the effect of excluding handicapped persons from, denying them the benefits of, or otherwise subjecting them to discrimination under any program or activity that receives Federal financial assistance or

(ii) that have the purpose or effect of defeating or substantially impairing the accomplishment of the objectives of the program or activity with respect to handicapped persons.

(6) As used in this section, the aid, benefit, or service provided under a program or activity receiving Federal financial assistance **includes any aid, benefit, or ser**vice provided in or through a facility that has been constructed, expanded, altered, leased or rented, or otherwise acquired, in whole **or in part, with Federal financial assistance.**

(c) **Aid, benefits, or services limited by Federal law.** The **exclusion of nonhandicapped persons** from aid, benefits, or services limited by Federal statute or executive order to handicapped persons or the exclusion of a specific class of handicapped persons from aid, benefits, or services limited by Federal statute or executive order to a different class of handicapped persons **is not prohibited by this part**.

34 CFR § 104.5 Assurances required. (Not included in this book, but available on the Internet.)[49]

34 CFR § 104.6 Remedial action, voluntary action, and self-evaluation.

(a) **Remedial action.**

(1) If the Assistant Secretary finds that a recipient has discriminated against persons on the basis of handicap in violation of section 504 or this part, the recipient shall take such remedial action as the Assistant Secretary deems necessary to overcome the effects of the discrimination.

(2) Where a recipient is found to have discriminated against persons on the basis of handicap in violation of section 504 or this part and where another recipient exercises control over the recipient that has discriminated, the Assistant Secretary, where appropriate, may require either or both recipients to take remedial action.

---

49 "An applicant for Federal financial assistance . . . shall submit an assurance . . . that the program or activity will be operated in compliance with this part."

(3) The Assistant Secretary may, where necessary to overcome the effects of discrimination in violation of section 504 or this part, require a recipient to take remedial action (i) with respect to handicapped persons who are no longer participants in the recipient's program or activity but who were participants in the program or activity when such discrimination occurred or (ii) with respect to handicapped persons who would have been participants in the program or activity had the discrimination not occurred.

(b) Voluntary action. A recipient may take steps, in addition to any action that is required by this part, to overcome the effects of conditions that resulted in limited participation in the recipient's program or activity by qualified handicapped persons.

(c) Self-evaluation.[50]

(1) A recipient shall, within one year of the effective date of this part:

(i) **Evaluate**, with the **assistance of interested persons**, including handicapped persons or organizations representing handicapped persons, its current policies and practices and the effects thereof that do not or may not meet the requirements of this part;

(ii) Modify, after consultation with interested persons, including handicapped persons or organizations representing handicapped persons, any policies and practices that do not meet the requirements of this part; and

(iii) Take, after consultation with interested persons, including handicapped persons or organizations representing handicapped persons, appropriate remedial steps to eliminate the effects of any discrimination that resulted from adherence to these policies and practices.

(2) A recipient that employs fifteen or more persons shall, **for at least three years** following completion of the evaluation required under paragraph (c)(1) of this section, maintain on file, **make available for public inspection,** and provide to the Assistant Secretary upon request:

(i) A list of the interested persons consulted,

(ii) A description of areas examined and any problems identified, and

(iii) A description of any modifications made and of any remedial steps taken.

34 CFR § 104.7 Designation of responsible employee and adoption of grievance procedures.

(a) Designation of responsible employee. A recipient that employs fifteen or more persons **shall designate at least one person to coordinate its efforts** to comply with this part.

(b) Adoption of grievance procedures. A recipient that employs fifteen or more persons **shall adopt grievance procedures that incorporate appropriate due process standards** and that provide for the prompt and equitable resolution of complaints alleging any action prohibited by this part. Such procedures need not be established with respect to complaints from applicants for employment or from applicants for admission to postsecondary educational institutions.

34 CFR § 104.8 Notice.

(a) A recipient that employs fifteen or more persons shall take appropriate initial and continuing steps to notify participants, beneficiaries, applicants, and employees, including those with impaired vision or hearing, and unions or professional organizations holding collective bargaining or professional agreements with the recipient that it does not discriminate on the basis of handicap in violation of section 504 and this part. The notification shall state, where appropriate, that the recipient does not discriminate in admission or access to, or treatment or employment in, its program or activity. **The notification shall also include an identification of the responsible employee designated pursuant to § 104.7(a).** A recipient shall make the initial notification required by this paragraph within 90 days of the effective date of this part. Methods of initial and continuing notification may include the posting of notices, publication in newspapers and magazines, placement of notices in recipients' publication, and distribution of memoranda or other written communications.

---

50   *See also* 28 CFR § 35.105 - Assuming an initial self-evaluation was completed, this may not be necessary any longer.

(b) If a recipient publishes or uses recruitment materials or publications containing general information that it makes available to participants, beneficiaries, applicants, or employees, it shall include in those materials or publications a statement of the policy described in paragraph (a) of this section. A recipient may meet the requirement of this paragraph either by including appropriate inserts in existing materials and publications or by revising and reprinting the materials and publications.

34 CFR § 104.9 Administrative requirements for small recipients.

The Assistant Secretary may require any recipient with fewer than fifteen employees, or any class of such recipients, to comply with §§ 104.7 and 104.8, in whole or in part, when the Assistant Secretary finds a violation of this part or finds that such compliance will not significantly impair the ability of the recipient or class of recipients to provide benefits or services.

34 CFR § 104.10 Effect of state or local law or other requirements and effect of employment opportunities.

(a) The obligation to comply with this part is not obviated or alleviated by the existence of any state or local law or other requirement that, on the basis of handicap, imposes prohibitions or limits upon the eligibility of qualified handicapped persons to receive services or to practice any occupation or profession.

(b) The obligation to comply with this part is not obviated or alleviated because employment opportunities in any occupation or profession are or may be more limited for handicapped persons than for non handicapped persons.

34 CFR Part 104, Subpart B - Employment Practices (not included)[51]

34 CFR Part 104, Subpart C - Accessibility[52]

34 CFR § 104.21 - Discrimination prohibited.

No qualified handicapped person shall, because a recipient's facilities are inaccessible to or unusable by handicapped persons, be denied the benefits of, be excluded from participation in, or otherwise be subjected to discrimination under any program or activity to which this part applies.

34 CFR § 104.22 - Existing facilities

(a) Accessibility. A recipient shall operate its program or activity so that when each part is viewed in its entirety, it is readily accessible to handicapped persons. This paragraph **does not require** a recipient to make each of its existing facilities or every part of a facility accessible to and usable by handicapped persons.

(f) through (f) - [not included]

34 CFR § 104.23 - New Construction [not included]

---

51   Subpart B is not included in this book, but is available on the Internet at:
https://www.law.cornell.edu/cfr/text/34/part-104/subpart-B.

52   The omitted portions of Subpart C are available on the Internet at:
https://www.law.cornell.edu/cfr/text/34/part-104/subpart-C.

34 CFR Part 104, Subpart D - Preschool, Elementary, and Secondary Education[53]

34 CFR § 104.31 Application of this subpart.

Subpart D applies to **preschool, elementary, secondary, and adult education programs** or activities that receive Federal financial assistance and to recipients that operate, or that receive Federal financial assistance for the operation of, such programs or activities.

34 CFR § 104.32 Location and notification.

A recipient that operates a public elementary or secondary education program or activity shall annually:

(a) Undertake to **identify and locate every qualified handicapped person residing in the recipient's jurisdiction who is not receiving a public education;**[54] and

(b) Take appropriate steps to notify handicapped persons and their parents or guardians of the recipient's duty under this subpart.

34 CFR § 104.33 Free appropriate public education.[55]

(a) General. A recipient that operates a public elementary or secondary education program or activity **shall provide a free appropriate public education** to each **qualified handicapped person** who is in the recipient's jurisdiction, regardless of the nature or severity of the person's handicap.

(b) Appropriate education.

(1) For the purpose of this subpart, the provision of an appropriate education is the **provision of regular or special education and related aids and services** that

(i) **are designed to meet individual educational need**s of handicapped persons **as adequately**[56] as the needs of nonhandicapped persons are met and

(ii) are based upon adherence to procedures that satisfy the requirements of 104.34, 104.35, and 104.36.

(2) Implementation of an **Individualized Education Program**[57] developed in accordance with the Education of the Handicapped Act[58] is one means of meeting the standard established in paragraph (b)(1)(i) of this section.

---

53 **Wrightslaw Note:** Subpart D of Part 104 of the Section 504 regulations applies to "preschool, elementary, secondary, and adult education programs." Akin to that in IDEA, Section 504 includes "child find." A public school shall provide the eligible person with FAPE, much like IDEA, in the least restrictive environment. Before there is any significant change of placement, such as a school suspension for behavioral misconduct, there must be an evaluation. Like IDEA, it includes "Procedural Safeguards." Subpart E covers higher education.

54 This is similar to the law of **"Child Find"** in IDEA at 20 U.S.C. § 1412(a)(3).

55 "Free appropriate public education" known as FAPE, is in IDEA at 20 U.S.C. § 1401(9) and 20 U.S.C. § 1412(a)(1)(A). Its definition, in the context of IDEA, was the key issue in the two U.S. Supreme Court cases, *Rowley* in 1982 and *Andrew F.* in 2017.

56 **The phrase "as adequately" is different from the FAPE requirement contained in IDEA** which is spelled out in detail in Chief Justice Robert's decision in the 2017 *Andrew F.* decision. The full text of that decision and the transcript of his comments about the case are included in the 2017 edition of *Wrightslaw Year in Review.*

57 IDEA's IEP statute is located at 20 U.S.C. § 1414(d).

58 This is now known as the Individuals with Disabilities Education Act, i.e., IDEA.

(3) A recipient may place a handicapped person or refer such a person for aid, benefits, or services **other than those that it operates or provides** as its means of carrying out the requirements of this subpart. If so, the recipient remains responsible for ensuring that the requirements of this subpart are met with respect to any handicapped person so placed or referred.[59]

(c) Free education

(1) General. For the purpose of this section, the provision of a free education is the provision of educational and related services **without cost to the handicapped person or to his or her parents** or guardian, except for those fees that are imposed on non-handicapped persons or their parents or guardian. It may consist either of the provision of free services or, if a recipient places a handicapped person or refers such person for aid, benefits, or services not operated or provided by the recipient as its means of carrying out the requirements of this subpart, of payment for the costs of the aid, benefits, or services. Funds available from any public or private agency may be used to meet the requirements of this subpart. Nothing in this section shall be construed to relieve an insurer or similar third party from an otherwise valid obligation to provide or pay for services provided to a handicapped person.

(2) Transportation. If a recipient places a handicapped person or refers such person for aid, benefits, or services not operated or provided by the recipient as its means of carrying out the requirements of this subpart, the recipient **shall ensure that adequate transportation** to and from the aid, benefits, or services **is provided** at no greater cost than would be incurred by the person or his or her parents or guardian if the person were placed in the aid, benefits, or services operated by the recipient.

(3) Residential placement. If a public or private residential placement is necessary to provide a free appropriate public education to a handicapped person because of his or her handicap, **the placement, including non-medical care and room and board, shall be provided at no cost** to the person or his or her parents or guardian.

(4) Placement of handicapped persons by parents. If a recipient has made available, in conformance with the requirements of this section and § 104.34, a free appropriate public education[60] to a handicapped person and the person's parents or guardian choose to place the person in a private school, the recipient is not required to pay for the person's education in the private school. Disagreements between a parent or guardian and a recipient regarding whether the recipient has made a free appropriate public education available or otherwise regarding the question of financial responsibility are subject to the **due process procedures of § 104.36**.[61]

(d) Compliance. A recipient may not exclude any qualified handicapped person from a public elementary or secondary education after the effective date of this part. A recipient that is not, on the effective date of this regulation, in full compliance with the other requirements of the preceding paragraphs of this section shall meet such requirements at the earliest practicable time and in no event later than September 1, 1978.

34 CFR § 104.34 Educational setting.

(a) Academic setting. A recipient to which this subpart applies shall educate, or shall provide for the education of, each qualified handicapped person in its jurisdiction with persons who are not handicapped to the maximum extent appropriate to the needs of the handicapped person. **A recipient shall place a handicapped person in the regular educational environment operated by the recipient unless it is demonstrated by the recipient that the education of the person in the regular environment with the use of supplementary aids**

59   If a child eligible for protections under Section 504 needs aids or services other than those available within that agency's ability to provide, then that agency, in order to provide FAPE, is expected to contract out for that placement, or those aids, benefits or services.

60   If FAPE was provided by the school district and the parents placed the child into a private school, then, much like the requirements in IDEA, the school is not obligated to pay for the private placement. IDEA's statute also requires ten business days advance notice and an explanation "and concerns" about why the parent expects the public school district to pay for the private placement. *See* 20 U.S.C. § 1412(a)(10)(C).

61   These due process procedures in Section 504 are different from the due process procedures in IDEA at 20 U.S.C. § 1415(f).

and services cannot be achieved satisfactorily. Whenever a recipient places a person in a setting other than the regular educational environment pursuant to this paragraph, it shall take into account the proximity of the alternate setting to the person's home.[62]

(b) Nonacademic settings.[63] In providing or arranging for the provision of **nonacademic and extracurricular services and activities, including meals, recess periods,** and the services and activities set forth in **104.37(a) (2),** a recipient **shall ensure that handicapped persons participate** with nonhandicapped persons in such activities and services **to the maximum extent appropriate** to the needs of the handicapped person in question.

(c) Comparable facilities. If a recipient, in compliance with paragraph (a) of this section, operates a facility that is identifiable as being for handicapped persons, the recipient shall ensure that the facility and the services and activities provided therein **are comparable to the other facilities, services, and activities** of the recipient.

34 CFR § 104.35 Evaluation and placement.

(a) Preplacement evaluation. A recipient that operates a public elementary or secondary education program or activity **shall conduct an evaluation in accordance with the requirements of paragraph (b) of this section** of any person who, because of handicap, needs or is believed to need special education or related services **before taking any action with respect to the initial placement of the person** in regular or special education and any **subsequent significant change in placement.**[64]

(b) Evaluation procedures. A recipient to which this subpart applies shall establish standards and procedures for the evaluation and placement of persons **who, because of handicap, need or are believed to need special education or related service**s which ensure that:

(1) Tests and other evaluation materials have been validated for the specific purpose for which they are used[65] and are administered by trained personnel in conformance with the instructions provided by their producer;[66]

(2) Tests and other evaluation materials **include those tailored to assess specific areas of educational need** and **not merel**y those which are designed to provide a single general **intelligence quotient;** and[67]

(3) Tests are selected and administered so as best to ensure that, when a test is administered to a student with impaired sensory, manual, or speaking skills, **the test results accurately reflect the student's aptitude or achievement level** or whatever other factor the test purports to measure, rather than reflecting the student's impaired sensory, manual, or speaking skills (except where those skills are the factors that the test purports to measure).

---

62   This similar to the mainstreaming, **least restrictive environment (LRE)** mandate of IDEA at 20 U.S.C. § 1412(a)(5). *See also* IDEA's regulations about LRE beginning at 34 CFR § 300.114.

63   *See also* 34 CFR § 104.37 just below.

64   In **discipline** issues, a Section 504 "handicapped" child's removal from regular classes via an alternate placement, suspension, or expulsion can be a "significant change in placement" which mandates an evaluation "before taking any action." In the ADA, applicable here, the determination as to whether individual is covered, "shall be construed in favor of broad coverage" and includes "episodic" conditions and even someone who may not have a disability, but is "regarded as having a disability." *See* 42 U.S.C. § 12102(4). This regulation is critical in the discipline of a Section 504 youngster. For more, see <Selected Topics: Discipline in Chapter 10.>

65   Our book *"Wrightslaw: All About Tests, 2ⁿᵈ Ed."* includes names and descriptions of the most common assessment, evaluation measures of IQ, reading, writing, arithmetic, spelling, speech/language, social/behavioral and LD, ADHD, and assessment of English Language Learners (ELL). Educational achievement testing is necessary to determine the child's educational needs.

For more about educational needs, *see* IDEA at 20 U.S.C. §§ 1400(c)(2), 1414(a)(1)(C)(i)(II), 1414(b)(3)(C), 1414(b)(4)(A), 1414(c)(1)(B) (i), 1414(c)(4)(B)(i), and 1414(d)(1)(A)(i)(II)(bb).

In Section 504, *see* 34 CFR § 104.33(b)(1)(i). If you search the phrase "educational needs" in the adobe.pdf edition of this book, you will find 54 entries.

66   Websites of most test publishers provide the required evaluator qualifications.

67   Perhaps the most common deficit skill area that is across all types of disabilities relates to poor reading skills followed by poor written language skills which often directly impact the ability to write down and complete mathematical tasks. Administration of an IQ test alone does not comply with this statute.

(c) Placement procedures. In interpreting evaluation data and in making placement decisions, a recipient shall

(1) draw upon information from a variety of sources, including aptitude and achievement tests, teacher recommendations, physical condition, social or cultural background, and adaptive behavior,

(2) establish procedures to ensure that information obtained from all such sources is documented and carefully considered,

(3) ensure that the placement decision is made by a group of persons, including persons knowledgeable about the child, the meaning of the evaluation data, and the placement options, and

(4) ensure that the **placement decision is made in conformity** with § 104.34.[68]

(d) Reevaluation. A recipient to which this section applies shall establish procedures, in accordance with paragraph (b) of this section, for periodic reevaluation of students who have been provided special education and related services. A reevaluation procedure consistent with the Education for the Handicapped Act is one means of meeting this requirement.

34 CFR § 104.36 Procedural safeguards.

A recipient that operates a public elementary or secondary education program or activity **shall establish and implement**, with respect to actions regarding the identification, evaluation, or educational placement of persons who, because of handicap, need or are believed to need special instruction or related services, **a system of procedural safeguards** that includes notice, an opportunity for the parents or guardian of the person to examine relevant records, an impartial hearing with opportunity for participation by the person's parents or guardian and representation by counsel, and a review procedure.

Compliance with the procedural safeguards of section 615 of the Education of the Handicapped Act[69] is one means of meeting this requirement.

34 CFR § 104.37 Nonacademic services.

(a) General.

(1) A recipient to which this subpart applies **shall provide non-academic and extracurricular services and activities** in such manner as is necessary to afford handicapped students **an equal opportunity** for participation in such services and activities.

(2) Nonacademic and extracurricular services and activities **may include counseling services, physical recreational athletics, transportation, health services, recreational activities, special interest groups or clubs** sponsored by the recipients, referrals to agencies which provide assistance to handicapped persons, and employment of students, including both employment by the recipient and assistance in making available outside employment.

(b) Counseling services. A recipient to which this subpart applies that provides personal, academic, or vocational counseling, guidance, or placement services to its students **shall provide these services without discrimination on the basis of handicap.** The recipient shall ensure that qualified handicapped students **are not counseled toward more restrictive career objectives** than are nonhandicapped students with similar interests and abilities.

(c) Physical education and athletics.

(1) In providing physical education courses and athletics and similar aid, benefits, or services to any of its students, a recipient to which this subpart applies may not discriminate on the basis of handicap. A recipient that offers physical education courses or that operates or sponsors interscholastic, club, or intramural **athletics shall provide to qualified handicapped students an equal opportunity for participation.**

---

68   This includes the LRE mandate noted earlier.

69   This is the **"Procedural Safeguards"** statute in IDEA located at 20 U.S.C. § 1415. It addresses Independent Educational Evaluations (IEE), due process hearings, appeals, stay-put/pendency, discipline, and exhaustion of administrative remedies.

If a school district's IDEA evaluation, eligibility and dispute resolution procedures are in compliance with IDEA and the school district uses those same procedures in regard to Section 504 evaluations, eligibility, and dispute resolution, then the district is compliance with the Section 504 procedures.

(2) A recipient may offer to handicapped students physical education and athletic **activities that are separate or different** from those offered to nonhandicapped students **only if** separation or differentiation is consistent with the requirements of 104.34 and **only if no** qualified handicapped student is denied the opportunity to compete for teams or to participate in courses that are not separate or different.

34 CFR § 104.38 Preschool and adult education.

A recipient to which this subpart applies that **provides preschool education or day care** or adult education **may not**, on the basis of handicap, **exclude qualified handicapped persons** and shall take into account the needs of such persons in determining the aid, benefits, or services to be provided.

34 CFR § 104.39 Private education.

(a) A recipient that provides private elementary or secondary education may not, on the basis of handicap, exclude a qualified handicapped person if the person can, with minor adjustments, be provided an appropriate education, as defined in 104.33(b)(1), within that recipients program or activity.

(b) A recipient to which this section applies may not charge more for the provision of an appropriate education to handicapped persons than to nonhandicapped persons except to the extent that any additional charge is justified by a substantial increase in cost to the recipient.

(c) A recipient to which this section applies that provides special education shall do so in accordance with the provisions of 104.35 and 104.36. Each recipient to which this section applies is subject to the provisions of 104.34, 104.37, and 104.38.

34 CFR Subpart E - Postsecondary Education[70]

104.41 Application of this subpart.
104.42 Admissions and recruitment.
104.43 Treatment of students; general.
104.44 Academic adjustments.
104.45 Housing.
104.46 Financial and employment assistance to students.
104.47 Nonacademic services.

34 CFR § 104.41 Application of this subpart.

Subpart E applies to **postsecondary education programs or activities**, including postsecondary vocational education programs or activities, that receive Federal financial assistance and to recipients that operate, or that receive Federal financial assistance for the operation of, such programs or activities.

34 CFR § 104.42 Admissions and recruitment.

(a) General. Qualified handicapped persons **may not, on the basis of handicap, be denied admission** or be subjected to discrimination in admission or recruitment by a recipient to which this subpart applies.

(b) Admissions. In administering its admission policies, a recipient to which this subpart applies:

(1) **May not apply limitations upon the number or proportion of handicapped persons who may be admitted;**

(2) May not make use of any test or criterion for admission that has a **disproportionate, adverse effect on**

---

70 **Wrightslaw Note:** The following regulations in Subpart E explain that colleges and universities "may not make preadmission inquiry as to whether an applicant for admission is a handicapped person" and may not "exclude any qualified handicapped student from any course, course of study, or other part of its education program or activity."

Course modifications "may include changes in the length of time permitted for the completion of degree requirements, substitution of specific courses required for the completion of degree requirements, and adaptation of the manner in which specific courses are conducted." Course examinations shall represent "the student's achievement in the course, rather than reflecting the student's impaired sensory, manual" or speaking skills.

handicapped **persons** or any class of handicapped persons **unless**

(i) the test or criterion, as used by the recipient, has been validated as a predictor of success in the education program or activity in question and

(ii) alternate tests or criteria that have a less disproportionate, adverse effect are not shown by the Assistant Secretary to be available.

(3) Shall assure itself that

(i) admissions tests are selected and administered so as best to ensure that, when a test is administered to an applicant who has a handicap that impairs sensory, manual, or speaking skills, **the test results accurately reflect the applicant's aptitude or achievement level** or whatever other factor the test purports to measure, **rather than reflecting the applicant's impaired sensory, manual, or speaking skills** (except where those skills are the factors that the test purports to measure);

(ii) admissions tests that are designed for persons with impaired sensory, manual, or speaking skills are offered as often and in as timely a manner as are other admissions tests; and

(iii) admissions tests **are administered in facilities that, on the whole, are accessible** to handicapped persons; and

(4) Except as provided in paragraph (c) of this section, **may not make preadmission inquiry** as to whether **an applicant for admission is a handicapped person** but, after admission, may make inquiries on a confidential basis as to handicaps that may require accommodation.

(c) Preadmission inquiry exception. When a recipient is taking **remedial action to correct the effects of past discrimination** pursuant to § 104.6(a) or when a recipient is taking voluntary action to overcome the effects of conditions that resulted in limited participation in its federally assisted program or activity pursuant to § 104.6(b), the recipient may invite applicants for admission to indicate whether and to what extent they are handicapped, Provided, That:

(1) The recipient states clearly on any written questionnaire used for this purpose or makes clear orally if no written questionnaire is used that the information requested is intended for use solely in connection with its remedial action obligations or its voluntary action efforts; and

(2) The recipient states clearly that the information is being requested on a voluntary basis, that it will be kept confidential, that refusal to provide it will not subject the applicant to any adverse treatment, and that it will be used only in accordance with this part.

(d) Validity studies. For the purpose of paragraph (b)(2) of this section, a recipient may base prediction equations on first year grades, but **shall conduct periodic validity studie**s against the criterion of overall success in the education program or activity in question in order to monitor the general validity of the test scores.

34 CFR § 104.43 Treatment of students; general.

(a) No qualified handicapped student shall, on the basis of handicap, be excluded from participation in, be denied the benefits of, or otherwise be subjected to discrimination under any **academic**, research, occupational training, housing, health insurance, counseling, financial aid, physical education, athletics, recreation, transportation, other extracurricular, **or other postsecondary education aid, benefits, or services** to which this subpart applies.

(b) A recipient to which this subpart applies that considers participation by students in education programs or activities not operated wholly by the recipient as part of, or equivalent to, and education program or activity operated by the recipient **shall assure itself that the other education program or activity, as a whole, provides an equal opportunity** for the participation of qualified handicapped persons.

(c) A recipient to which this subpart applies **may not, on the basis of handicap, exclude a**ny qualified handicapped student from **any course, course of study, or other part** of its education program or activity.

(d) A recipient to which this subpart applies shall operate its program or activity in the most integrated setting appropriate.

34 CFR § 104.44 Academic adjustments.

(a) **Academic requirements.** A recipient to which this subpart applies shall make such modifications to its academic requirements as are necessary to ensure that such requirements do not discriminate or have the effect of discriminating, on the basis of handicap, against a qualified handicapped applicant or student. **Academic requirements that the recipient can demonstrate are essential to the instruction** being pursued by such student **or to any directly related licensing requirement** will not be regarded as discriminatory within the meaning of this section. Modifications may include changes in the length of time permitted for the completion of degree requirements, **substitution of specific courses** required for the completion of degree requirements, and adaptation of the manner in which specific courses are conducted.

(b) **Other rules.** A recipient to which this subpart applies may not impose upon handicapped students other rules, such as the **prohibition of tape recorders in classrooms or of dog guides**[71] in campus buildings, that have the effect of limiting the participation of handicapped students in the recipient's education program or activity.

(c) **Course examinations.** In its course examinations or other procedures for evaluating students' academic achievement, a recipient to which this subpart applies shall provide such methods for evaluating the achievement of students who have a handicap that impairs sensory, manual, or speaking skills as will best ensure that the results of the evaluation **represents the student's achievement in the course, rather than** reflecting the student's impaired sensory, manual, or speaking skills (except where such skills are the factors that the test purports to measure).

(d) **Auxiliary aids.**

(1) A recipient to which this subpart applies shall take such steps as are necessary to ensure that no handicapped student is denied the benefits of, excluded from participation in, or otherwise subjected to discrimination **because of the absence of educational auxiliary aids** for students with impaired sensory, manual, or speaking skills.

(2) **Auxiliary aids may include** taped texts, interpreters or other effective methods of making orally delivered materials available to students with hearing impairments, readers in libraries for students with visual impairments, classroom equipment adapted for use by students with manual impairments, and other similar services and actions. **Recipients need not provide attendants, individually prescribed devices, readers for personal use or study, or other devices or services of a personal nature**.

34 CFR § 104.45 Housing.

(a) **Housing provided by the recipient.** A recipient that provides housing to its nonhandicapped students shall provide **comparable**, convenient, and accessible housing to handicapped students **at the same cost as to other**. At the end of the transition period provided for in subpart C,[72] such housing shall be available in sufficient quantity and variety so that the scope of handicapped students' choice of living accommodations is, as a whole, comparable to that of nonhandicapped students.

(b) **Other housing.** A recipient that assists any agency, organization, or person in making housing available to any of its students shall take such action as may be necessary to assure itself that such housing is, as a whole, made available in a manner that does not result in discrimination on the basis of handicap.

34 CFR § 104.46 Financial and employment assistance to students.

(a) **Provision of financial assistance.**

(1) In providing financial assistance to qualified handicapped persons, a recipient to which this subpart applies **may not**,

---

71   See also the SCOTUS *Fry* case referenced elsewhere in this book.

72   Subpart C refers to accessibility of new and existing construction of buildings.

(i) On the basis of handicap, **provide less assista**nce than is provided to nonhandicapped persons, **limit eligibility** for assistance, or otherwise discriminate or

(ii) Assist any entity or person that provides assistance to any of the recipient's students in a manner that discriminates against qualified handicapped persons on the basis of handicap.

(2) A recipient may administer or assist in the administration of scholarships, fellowships, or other forms of financial assistance established under wills, trusts, bequests, or similar legal instruments that require awards to be made on the basis of factors that discriminate or have the effect of discriminating on the basis of handicap **only if the overall effec**t of the award of scholarships, fellowships, and other forms of financial assistance **is not discriminatory** on the basis of handicap.

(b) Assistance in making available outside employment. A recipient that assists any agency, organization, or person in providing employment opportunities to any of its students shall assure itself that such employment opportunities, as a whole, are made available in a manner that would not violate subpart B if they were provided by the recipient.

(c) Employment of students by recipients. A recipient that employs any of its students may not do so in a manner that violates subpart B.

34 CFR § 104.47 Nonacademic services.[73]

(a) Physical education and athletics.

(1) In providing physical education courses and athletics and similar aid, benefits, or services to any of its students, a recipient to which this subpart applies **may no**t discriminate on the basis of handicap. A recipient that offers physical education courses or that operates or sponsors intercollegiate, club, or intramural athletics shall provide to qualified handicapped students an equal opportunity for participation in these activities.

(2) A recipient may offer to handicapped students physical education and athletic activities that are separate or different **only if separation or differentiation is consistent with the requirements of § 104.43(d)** and only if no qualified handicapped student is denied the opportunity to compete for teams or to participate in courses that are not separate or different.

(b) Counseling and placement services. A recipient to which this subpart applies that provides personal, academic, or vocational counseling, guidance, or placement services to its students shall provide these services without discrimination on the basis of handicap. The recipient shall ensure that qualified handicapped students **are not counseled toward more restrictive career objectives than are nonhandicapped students with similar interests and abilities.** This requirement does not preclude a recipient from providing factual information about licensing and certification requirements that may present obstacles to handicapped persons in their pursuit of particular careers.

(c) Social organizations. A recipient that provides **significant** assistance to fraternities, sororities, or similar organizations shall assure itself that **the membership practices of such organizations do not permit discrimination** otherwise prohibited by this subpart.

---

73   *See also* <34 CFR § 104.37.>

34 CFR Part 104, Subpart F - Health, Welfare, and Social Services[74]

34 CFR § 104.51 Application of this subpart.

Subpart F applies to health, welfare, and other social service programs or activities that receive Federal financial assistance and to recipients that operate, or that receive Federal financial assistance for the operation of, such programs or activities.

34 CFR § 104.52 Health, welfare, and other social services.

(a) General. In providing health, welfare, or other social services or benefits, **a recipient may not**, on the basis of handicap:

(1) **Deny** a qualified handicapped person these benefits or services;

(2) Afford a qualified handicapped person an opportunity to receive benefits or services **that is not equal** to that offered nonhandicapped persons;

(3) Provide a qualified handicapped person with benefits or services that **are not as effective** (as defined in § 104.4(b)) as the benefits or services provided to others;

(4) Provide benefits or services in a manner that **limits** or has the effect of limiting **the participation** of qualified handicapped persons; or

(5) **Provide different or separate benefits or services** to handicapped persons except where necessary to provide qualified handicapped persons with benefits and services that are as effective as those provided to others.

(b) Notice. A recipient that provides notice concerning benefits or services or written material concerning waivers of rights or consent to treatment shall take such steps as are necessary to ensure that qualified handicapped persons, including those with impaired sensory or speaking skills, are not denied effective notice because of their handicap.

(c) Emergency treatment for the hearing impaired. A recipient hospital that provides health services or benefits **shall establish a procedure for effective communication with persons with impaired hearing** for the purpose of providing emergency health care.

(d) Auxiliary aids.

(1) A recipient to which this subpart applies that employs **fifteen or more persons shall provide** appropriate auxiliary aids to persons with **impaired sensory, manual, or speaking skills,** where necessary to afford such persons an equal opportunity to benefit from the service in question.

(2) The Assistant Secretary may require recipients with fewer than fifteen employees to provide auxiliary aids where the provision of aids would not significantly impair the ability of the recipient to provide its benefits or services.

(3) For the purpose of this paragraph, **auxiliary aids may include brailled and taped material, interpreters**, and other aids for persons with **impaired hearing or vision**.

34 CFR § 104.53 Drug and alcohol addicts.

A recipient to which this subpart applies that operates **a general hospital or outpatient facility** may not discriminate in admission or treatment against a drug or alcohol abuser or alcoholic who is suffering from a medical condition, **because of the person's drug or alcohol abuse or alcoholism.**

---

74 **Wrightslaw Note:** This explains that "health, welfare, and other social service programs . . . shall provide appropriate auxiliary aids to persons with impaired sensory, manual, or speaking skills, where necessary to afford such persons an equal opportunity to benefit from the service in question." They shall ensure that institutionalized individuals shall be "provided an appropriate education."

34 CFR § 104.54 Education of institutionalized persons.

A recipient to which this subpart applies and that operates or supervises a program or activity that provides aid, benefits or services for persons **who are institutionalized because of handicap** shall ensure that each qualified handicapped person, as defined in § 104.3(k)(2), in its program or activity **is provided an appropriate education**, as defined in § 104.33(b). Nothing in this section shall be interpreted as altering in any way the obligations of recipients under subpart D.

34 CFR Part 104, Subpart G - Procedures

34 CFR § 104.61 Procedures.

The procedural provisions applicable to title VI of the **Civil Rights Act of 1964** apply to this part.[75] These procedures are found in §§ 100.6-100.10 and part 101 of this title.

In Summation

In this Chapter 7, you were provided with portions of six **statutes** related to the Rehabilitation Act of 1973, **Section 504**, contained in Title 29, in the United States Code. Those statutes were followed by the pertinent **regulations** issued by the USDOE, USDOJ, and other federal agencies. The regulations provide substantially more detail than the statutes and are the basis of public policy and legal decisions. Section 504 applies to entities receiving federal financial assistance, such as public schools.

In **Chapter 8** you are provided with pertinent portions of the **Americans with Disabilities Act,** published in Title 42 of the United States Code, beginning at 42 U.S.C. § 12101 and the regulations issued by the USDOJ published in Title 28 of the Code of Federal Regulations. Title II, Public Services, such as Public Schools, is published in Part 35 of Title 28 (28 CFR Part 35). Title III, Public Accommodations and Private Entities, such as private schools, nursery schools, day care centers, etc., is published in Part 36 of Title 28 (28 CFR Part 36).

Entities that do not receive any form of federal funds, and private entities such as private schools, daycare centers. graduate schools, and other, non-public school educational facilities, although not impacted by Section 504,[76] may not discriminate based on Title III in the ADA and the ADA regulations in Part 36. Entities "**controlled**" by religious organizations **are exempt** from the ADA.

End of Chapter 7 - Section 504 and Regulations

Hyperlinks to Chapters

---

75 The phrase, "this part" refers to this "Part 104 - Nondiscrimination on the Basis of Handicap in Programs or Activities Receiving Federal Financial Assistance." *See* https://www.law.cornell.edu/cfr/text/34/part-104

76 Public schools are covered by Section 504, Title II in the ADA statute and the ADA regulations in Part 35

CHAPTER 8

Americans with Disabilities Act U.S.C. and CFR

U.S. Code Title 42 - The Public Health and Welfare
Chapter 126 - Equal Opportunity for Individuals with Disabilities

42 U.S.C. § 12101 - Findings and purpose
42 U.S.C. § 12102 - Definition of Disability
42 U.S.C. § 12103 - Additional definitions

<Title II - Public Services>
42 U.S.C. § 12131 - Definitions
42 U.S.C. § 12132 - Discrimination
42 U.S.C. § 12133 - Enforcement
42 U.S.C. § 12134 - Regulations

<Title III - Public Accommodations and Private Entities>
42 U.S.C. § 12181 - Definitions
42 U.S.C. § 12182 - Prohibition of discrimination by public accommodations
42 U.S.C. § 12187 - Exemptions for private clubs and religious organizations
42 U.S.C. § 12188 - Enforcement
42 U.S.C. § 12189 - Examinations and courses

<Title IV - Miscellaneous Provisions>
42 U.S. C. § 12201 - Construction
42 U.S.C. § 12202 - State immunity
42 U.S.C. § 12203 - Prohibition against retaliation and coercion
42 U.S.C. § 12205 - Attorney's fees
42 U.S.C. § 12212 - Alternative means of dispute resolution

Wrightslaw Note: Hyperlinks here for the <Part 35 regulations> of Title II and the <Part 36 regulations> of Title III.

THE AMERICANS WITH DISABILITIES ACT

42 U.S.C. § 12101 - Findings and Purpose

(a) Findings - The Congress finds that—

(1) physical or mental disabilities in no way diminish a person's right to fully participate in all aspects of society, yet many people with physical or mental disabilities have been precluded from doing so because of discrimination; others who have a record of a disability or are regarded as having a disability also have been subjected to discrimination;

(2) historically, society has tended to isolate and segregate individuals with disabilities, and, despite some improvements, such forms of discrimination against individuals with disabilities continue to be a serious and pervasive social problem;

(3) discrimination against individuals with disabilities persists in such critical areas as employment, housing, public accommodations, education, transportation, communication, recreation, institutionalization, health services, voting, and access to public services;

(4) unlike individuals who have experienced discrimination on the basis of race, color, sex, national origin, religion, or age, individuals who have experienced discrimination on the basis of disability have often had no legal recourse to redress such discrimination;

(5) individuals with disabilities continually encounter various forms of discrimination, including outright intentional exclusion, the discriminatory effects of architectural, transportation, and communication barriers, overprotective rules and policies, failure to make modifications to existing facilities and practices, exclusionary qualification standards and criteria, segregation, and relegation to lesser services, programs, activities, benefits, jobs, or other opportunities;

(6) census data, national polls, and other studies have documented that people with disabilities, as a group, occupy an inferior status in our society, and are severely disadvantaged socially, vocationally, economically, and educationally;

(7) the Nation's proper goals regarding individuals with disabilities are to assure equality of opportunity, full participation, independent living, and economic self-sufficiency for such individuals; and

(8) the continuing existence of unfair and unnecessary discrimination and prejudice denies people with disabilities the opportunity to compete on an equal basis and to pursue those opportunities for which our free society is justifiably famous, and costs the United States billions of dollars in unnecessary expenses resulting from dependency and nonproductivity.

(b) Purpose - It is the purpose of this chapter—

(1) to provide a clear and comprehensive **national mandate** for the elimination of discrimination against individuals with disabilities;

(2) to provide clear, strong, consistent, **enforceable standards addressing discrimination** against individuals with disabilities;

(3) to ensure that the Federal Government **plays a central role in enforcing the standard**s established in this chapter on behalf of individuals with disabilities; and

(4) to invoke the sweep of congressional authority, including the power to **enforce the fourteenth**[1] **amendment** and to regulate commerce, in order to address the major areas of discrimination faced day-to-day by people with disabilities.

---

1   14th Amendment to the U.S. Constitution is at the end of chapter 9.

42 U.S.C. § 12102 - Definition of Disability[2]

    (1) Disability - The term "disability" means, with respect to an individual—

        (A) a physical or mental impairment that substantially limits one or more major life activities of such individual;

        (B) a record of such an impairment; or

        (C) being regarded as having such an impairment (as described in paragraph (3)).

    (2) Major life activities

        (A) In general - For purposes of paragraph (1), major life activities include, but are not limited to, **caring for oneself, performing manual tasks, seeing, hearing, eating, sleeping, walking, standing, lifting, bending, speaking, breathing, learning,[3] reading, concentrating, thinking, communicating, and working.**

        (B) Major bodily functions - For purposes of paragraph (1), a major life activity **also includes** the operation of a major bodily function, including but not limited to, functions of the immune system, normal cell growth, digestive, bowel, bladder, neurological, brain, respiratory, circulatory, endocrine, and reproductive functions.

    (3) Regarded as having such an impairment - For purposes of paragraph (1)(C):

        (A) An individual meets the requirement of "being regarded as having such an impairment" if the individual establishes that he or she has been subjected to an action prohibited under this chapter because of an actual or perceived physical or mental impairment **whether or not the impairment limits** or is perceived to limit a major life activity.

        (B) Paragraph (1)(C) shall not apply to impairments that are transitory and minor. A transitory impairment is an impairment with an actual or expected duration of 6 months or less.

    (4) Rules of construction regarding the definition of disability - The definition of "disability" in paragraph (1) **shall be construed** in accordance with the following:

        (A) The definition of disability in this chapter shall be construed **in favor of broad coverage** of individuals under this chapter, to the maximum extent permitted by the terms of this chapter.

        (B) The term "substantially limits" shall be interpreted consistently with the findings and purposes of the **ADA Amendments Act of 2008.**

        (C) An impairment that substantially limits one major life activity need not limit other major life activities in order to be considered a disability.

        (D) An impairment that is **episodic[4]** or in remission **is a disability if** it would substantially limit a major life activity when active.

        (E)

            (i) The determination of whether an impairment substantially limits a major life activity shall be made **without regard to the ameliorative effects of mitigating measures** such as—

                (I) medication, medical supplies, equipment, or appliances, low-vision devices (which do not include ordinary eyeglasses or contact lenses), prosthetics including limbs and devices, **hearing aids**

---

2   The definition of a disability under Section 504 **incorporates by reference,** 42 U.S.C. § 12102, which contains the revised definition of a disability in the Americans with Disabilities Act Amendments Act. The definition of a disability in the ADA and in Section 504 is this in Section 12102.

3   If a child has an IEP under IDEA, then that child was found eligible under IDEA per 20 U.S.C. § 1401(3) and is eligible for these protections in Section 504 and the ADA.

4   Some examples of an **episodic** condition are allergies, arthritis, asthma, chronic fatigue syndrome, chronic pain, epilepsy, hepatitis C, HIV/AIDS, migraines, and some forms of cancer and mental illness and shall be "construed in favor of broad coverage."

and cochlear implants or other implantable hearing devices, mobility devices, or oxygen therapy equipment and supplies;

(II) use of **assistive technology**;

(III) **reasonable accommodations** or auxiliary aids or services; or

(IV) learned behavioral or adaptive neurological modifications.

(ii) The ameliorative effects of the mitigating measures of ordinary eyeglasses or contact lenses shall be considered in determining whether an impairment substantially limits a major life activity.

(iii) As used in this subparagraph—

(I) the term "ordinary eyeglasses or contact lenses" means lenses that are intended to fully correct visual acuity or eliminate refractive error; and

(II) the term "low-vision devices" means devices that magnify, enhance, or otherwise augment a visual image.

42 U.S.C. § 12103 - Additional definitions - As used in this chapter:

(1) Auxiliary aids and services - The term "auxiliary aids and services" includes—

(A) qualified interpreters or other effective methods of making aurally delivered materials available to individuals with hearing impairments;

(B) qualified readers, taped texts, or other effective methods of making visually delivered materials available to individuals with visual impairments;

(C) acquisition or modification of equipment or devices; and

(D) other similar services and actions.

(2) State - The term "State" means each of the several States, the District of Columbia, the Commonwealth of Puerto Rico, Guam, American Samoa, the Virgin Islands of the United States, the Trust Territory of the Pacific Islands, and the Commonwealth of the Northern Mariana Islands.

Title II - Public Services

42 U.S.C. § 12131 - Definitions - As used in this subchapter:

(1) Public entity - The term "public entity"[5] means -

(A) any State or local government;

(B) any department, agency, special purpose district, or other instrumentality of a State or States or local government; and

(C) the National Railroad Passenger Corporation, and any commuter authority (as defined in section 24102(4)[1] of title 49).

(2) Qualified individual with a disability

The term "qualified individual with a disability" means an individual with a disability who, with or without reasonable modifications to rules, policies, or practices, the removal of architectural, communication, or transportation barriers, or the provision of auxiliary aids and services, meets the essential eligibility requirements for the receipt of services or the participation in programs or activities provided by a public entity.

42 U.S.C. § 12132 - Discrimination[6]

Subject to the provisions of this subchapter, no qualified individual with a disability **shall**, by reason of such

---

5   School districts and state departments of education are public entities.

6   This Section 12132 was the basis for the SCOTUS ruling in **Olmstead v. L.C. by Zimring**, 527 U.S. 581 (1999) where the Court held that removal of discrimination "may require placement of persons with mental disabilities in community settings rather than in institutions." https://www.law.cornell.edu/supct/pdf/98-536P.ZO

disability,[7] **be excluded from participation in or be denied the benefits** of the services, programs, or activities of a public entity, **or be subjected to discrimination** by any such entity.[8]

42 U.S.C. § 12133 - Enforcement

The remedies, procedures, and rights set forth in section 794a of title 29 shall be the remedies, procedures, and rights this subchapter **provides to any person alleging discrimination** on the basis of disability in violation of section 12132 of this title.[9]

42 U.S.C. § 12134 - Regulations

(a) In general

Not later than 1 year after July 26, 1990, the Attorney General shall promulgate regulations in an accessible format that implement this part. Such regulations shall not include any matter within the scope of the authority of the Secretary of Transportation under section 12143, 12149, or 12164 of this title.

(b) Relationship to other regulations

Except for "program accessibility, existing facilities", and "communications", regulations under subsection (a) shall be consistent with this chapter and with the coordination regulations under part 41 of title 28, Code of Federal Regulations (as promulgated by the Department of Health, Education, and Welfare on January 13, 1978), applicable to recipients of Federal financial assistance under section 794 of title 29. With respect to "program accessibility, existing facilities", and "communications", such regulations shall be consistent with regulations and analysis as in part 39 of title 28 of the Code of Federal Regulations, applicable to federally conducted activities under section 794 of title 29.

(c) Standards

Regulations under subsection (a) shall include standards applicable to facilities and vehicles covered by this part, other than facilities, stations, rail passenger cars, and vehicles covered by part B. Such standards shall be consistent with the minimum guidelines and requirements issued by the Architectural and Transportation Barriers Compliance Board in accordance with section 12204(a) of this title.

Title III - Public Accommodations and Private Entities

42 U.S.C. § 12181 - Definitions[10]
As used in this subchapter:

(6) Private entity

The term "private entity" means **any entity other than a public entity** (as defined in section 12131(1) of this title).

---

7   The Ninth Circuit noted that the ADA standard to determine discrimination is that "a plaintiff need show only that discrimination on the basis of disability was a 'motivating factor' for the decision" and that the Section 504 discrimination standard of "solely by reason of" is "even stricter." *KM v. Tustin Unif. Sch. Dist.*, 725 F.3d 1088 (9th Cir. 2013)

8   This is the essence of the ADA.

9   This is also known as "Section 504 of The Rehabilitation Act of 1973" located at 29 U.S.C. § 794a and is incorporated by reference into the ADA by use of this language.

10   Section #'s 1-5, 8-11 are omitted. We have not included all definitions as they define "commerce, commercial facilities, demand responsive systems, fixed route systems, over the road buses, and rail and railroad transportation." The full text of Section 12181 is available at: https://www.law.cornell.edu/uscode/text/42/12181.

(7) Public accommodation - The following private entities[11] are considered public accommodations for purposes of this subchapter, if the operations of such entities affect commerce—

(D) an **auditorium, convention center, lecture hall,** or other place of public gathering;

(I) a park, zoo, amusement park, or other place of recreation;

(J) a nursery, elementary, secondary, undergraduate, or postgraduate private school, or other place of education;[12]

(K) a day care center,[13] senior citizen center, homeless shelter, food bank, adoption agency, or **other social service center establishment;** and

(L) a gymnasium, health spa, bowling alley, golf course, or other place of exercise or recreation.

42 U.S.C. § 12182 - Prohibition of discrimination by public accommodations

(a) General rule

No individual shall be discriminated against on the basis of disability **in the full and equal enjoyment of the goods, services, facilities, privileges, advantages, or accommodations** of any place of public accommodation by any person who owns, leases (or leases to), or operates a place of public accommodation.

(b) Construction

(1) General prohibition

(A) Activities

(i) Denial of participation

It shall be **discriminatory to subject an individual** or class of individuals on the basis of a disability or disabilities of such individual or class, directly, or through contractual, licensing, or other arrangements, **to a denial of the opportunity of the individual** or class **to participate in or benefit from** the goods, services, facilities, privileges, advantages, or accommodations of an entity.

(ii) Participation in unequal benefit

It shall be discriminatory to afford an individual or class of individuals, on the basis of a disability or disabilities of such individual or class, directly, or through contractual, licensing, or other arrangements with the opportunity to participate in or benefit from a good, service, facility, privilege, advantage, or accommodation **that is not equal** to that afforded to other individuals.

(iii) Separate benefit

It shall be discriminatory to provide an individual or class of individuals, on the basis of a disability or disabilities of such individual or class, directly, or through contractual, licensing, or other arrangements with a good, service, facility, privilege, advantage, or accommodation that is **different or separate from that provided to other individuals**, unless such action is necessary to provide the individual or class of individuals with a good, service, facility, privilege, advantage, or accommodation, or other opportunity that is as effective as that provided to others.

---

11   **Wrightslaw Note:** We have omitted a number of definitions including inn, restaurant, golf course, laundromat, etc.

12   Several ADA cases against institutions of higher education are in *Wrightslaw Year in Review*.

13   A day care program at a public school in Tennessee refused to enroll a disabled child because she was not toilet trained. On July 12, 2018, the Sixth Circuit in *Sophie G. v. Wilson Co. Sch.* (Case No. 17-6209) found that the day care program and the school district violated Section 504 and the ADA.

  On January 18, 2017 the US Dept. of Justice sued Nobel Learning Communities d/b/a Chesterbrook Academy, a day care facility in NJ, because they expelled a child with Down Syndrome who was not toilet trained within the program's desired timeframe. On November 13, 2019 the day care facility settled and paid $18k to the parents and $30k to DOJ. The complaint and settlement agreement are located on Wrightslaw at:

   https://www.wrightslaw.com/law/pleadings/ada/daycare/

(iv) Individual or class of individuals

For purposes of clauses (i) through (iii) of this subparagraph, the term "individual or class of individuals" **refers to the clients or customers** of the covered public accommodation that enters into the contractual, licensing or other arrangement.

(B) Integrated settings

Goods, services, facilities, privileges, advantages, and accommodations **shall be afforded** to an individual with a disability **in the most integrated setting appropriate** to the needs of the individual.[14]

(C) Opportunity to participate

Notwithstanding the existence of separate or different programs or activities provided in accordance with this section, an individual with a disability **shall not be denied the opportunity to participate** in such programs or activities that are not separate or different.

(D) Administrative methods - An individual or entity shall not, directly or through contractual or other arrangements, utilize standards or criteria or methods of administration—

(i) that have the effect of discriminating on the basis of disability; or

(ii) that perpetuate the discrimination of others who are subject to common administrative control.

(E) Association

It shall be discriminatory **to exclude or otherwise deny** equal goods, services, facilities, privileges, advantages, accommodations, or other opportunities to an individual or entity because of the known disability of an individual **with whom the individual** or entity **is known to have a relationship** or association.

(2) Specific prohibitions

(A) Discrimination - For purposes of subsection (a), **discrimination includes—**

(i) the imposition or **application of eligibility criteria that screen out** or tend to screen out an individual with a disability or any class of individuals with disabilities **from fully and equally enjoying any goods, services, facilities, privileges, advantages, or accommodations**, unless such criteria can be shown to be necessary for the provision of the goods, services, facilities, privileges, advantages, or accommodations being offered;

(ii) **a failure to make reasonable modifications** in policies, practices, or procedures, when such modifications are necessary to afford such goods, services, facilities, privileges, advantages, or accommodations to individuals with disabilities, **unless** the entity can demonstrate that making such modifications **would fundamentally alter the nature of such goods, services, facilities, privileges, advantages, or accommodations;**

(iii) a failure to take such steps as may be necessary to ensure that no individual with a disability is excluded, denied services, segregated or otherwise treated differently than other individuals because of the absence of auxiliary aids and services, unless the entity can demonstrate that taking such steps would fundamentally alter the nature of the good, service, facility, privilege, advantage, or accommodation being offered or would result in an undue burden;

(iv) a failure to remove architectural barriers, and communication barriers that are structural in nature, in existing facilities, and transportation barriers in existing vehicles and rail passenger cars used by an establishment for transporting individuals (not including barriers that can only be removed through the retrofitting of vehicles or rail passenger cars by the installation of a hydraulic or other lift), where such removal is readily achievable; and

---

14   Compare the "most integrated setting" to the Least Restrictive Environment (LRE) requirement in IDEA at 20 U.S.C. § 1412(a)(5) and in Section 504 at 34 CFR § 104.34.

(v) where an entity can demonstrate that the removal of a barrier under clause (iv) is not readily achievable, a failure to make such goods, services, facilities, privileges, advantages, or accommodations **available through alternative methods** if such methods are readily achievable.

(B) Fixed route system [not included] . . .

(C) Demand responsive system - [not included] . . .

(D) Over-the-road buses - [not included] . . .

(3) Specific construction

Nothing in this subchapter shall require an entity to permit an individual to participate in or benefit from the goods, services, facilities, privileges, advantages and accommodations of such entity **where such individual poses a direct threat to the health or safety of others.** The term "direct threat" means a significant risk to the health or safety of others that cannot be eliminated by a modification of policies, practices, or procedures or by the provision of auxiliary aids or services.

42 U.S.C. § 12187 - Exemptions for private clubs and religious organizations

The provisions of this subchapter shall not apply to private clubs or establishments exempted from coverage under title II of the Civil Rights Act of 1964 (42 U.S.C. 2000–a(e)) [42 U.S.C. 2000a *et seq.*] or **to religious organizations or entities controlled by religious organizations**, including places of worship.[15]

42 U.S.C. § 12188 - Enforcement

(a) In general

(1) Availability of remedies and procedures[16]

The remedies and procedures set forth in **section 2000a–3(a) of this title** are the remedies and procedures this subchapter provides to any person **who is being subjected to discrimination** on the basis of disability in violation of this subchapter or who has reasonable grounds for believing that such person **is about to be subjected to discrimination** in violation of section 12183[17] of this title. Nothing in this section shall require a person with a disability to engage in a futile gesture[18] if such person has actual notice that a person or organization covered by this subchapter does not intend to comply with its provisions.

(2) Injunctive relief

In the case of violations of sections 12182(b)(2)(A)(iv)[19] and section 12183(a) of this title, injunctive relief shall include an order to alter facilities to make such facilities readily accessible to and usable by individuals with disabilities to the extent required by this subchapter. Where appropriate, injunctive relief **shall also include requiring the provision of an auxiliary aid or service, modification of a policy, or provision of alternative methods,** to the extent required by this subchapter.

(b) Enforcement by Attorney General[20]

---

15   A private school that is **controlled by a religious organization** is exempt from the ADA. However, if that private school receives federal funds, Section 504 of the Rehabilitation Act may apply. Google scholar provides several cases where the significant issue was the word "control." Was the operation of the school truly controlled by a religious organization or not?

16   The legal procedures in the Civil Rights Act provide the enforcement procedures and remedies for violations of Title III of the ADA. However, per 42 U.S.C. § 12133, enforcement for Title II violations is pursuant to Section 504 at 29 U.S.C. § 794a.

17   This is related to construction.

18   Pursuant to 42 U.S.C. § 2000a–6(a), it is not necessary to exhaust your administrative remedies.

19   This is related to architectural barriers.

20   The Attorney General, i.e., U.S. Department of Justice shall unilaterally investigate a possible violation.

(1) Denial of rights

(A) Duty to investigate

(i) In general

The Attorney General **shall investigate** alleged violations of this subchapter, and shall undertake periodic reviews of compliance of covered entities under this subchapter.

(ii) Attorney General certification

On the application of a State or local government, the Attorney General may, in consultation with the Architectural and Transportation Barriers Compliance Board, and after prior notice and a public hearing at which persons, including individuals with disabilities, are provided an opportunity to testify against such certification, certify that a State law or local building code or similar ordinance that establishes accessibility requirements meets or exceeds the minimum requirements of this chapter for the accessibility and usability of covered facilities under this subchapter. At any enforcement proceeding under this section, such certification by the Attorney General shall be rebuttable evidence that such State law or local ordinance does meet or exceed the minimum requirements of this chapter.

(B) Potential violation - If the Attorney General has reasonable cause to believe that—

(i) any person or group of persons is engaged in a **pattern or practice of discrimination** under this subchapter; or

(ii) any person or group of persons has been discriminated against under this subchapter and such discrimination raises an issue of general public importance, the Attorney General **may commence a civil action in any appropriate United States district court.**[21]

(2) Authority of court - In a civil action under paragraph (1)(B), the court—

(A) may grant **any equitable relief that such court considers to be appropriate, including**, to the extent required by this subchapter—

(i) granting temporary, preliminary, or permanent relief;

(ii) providing an auxiliary aid or service, modification of policy, practice, or procedure, or alternative method; and

(iii) making facilities readily accessible to and usable by individuals with disabilities;

(B) **may award such other relief as the court considers to be appropriate, including monetary damages** to persons aggrieved when requested by the Attorney General; and

(C) may, to vindicate the public interest, **assess a civil penalty** against the entity in an amount—

(i) not exceeding $50,000 for a first violation; and

(ii) not exceeding $100,000 for any subsequent violation.

(3) Single violation

For purposes of paragraph (2)(C), in determining whether a first or subsequent violation has occurred, a determination in a single action, by judgment or settlement, that the covered entity has engaged in more than one discriminatory act shall be counted as a single violation.

(4) Punitive damages

For purposes of subsection (b)(2)(B), the term "monetary damages" and "such other relief" does not include punitive damages.

21　*See* the NJ day care case referenced earlier in this chapter. The federal court Complaint is located on Wrightslaw.

(5) Judicial consideration

In a civil action under paragraph (1)(B), the court, when considering what amount of civil penalty, if any, is appropriate, **shall give consideration to any good faith effort** or attempt to comply with this chapter by the entity. In evaluating good faith, the court shall consider, among other factors it deems relevant, whether the entity could have reasonably anticipated the need for an appropriate type of auxiliary aid needed to accommodate the unique needs of a particular individual with a disability.

42 U.S.C. § 12189 - Examinations and courses[22]

Any person that offers examinations or courses related to **applications, licensing, certification, or credentialing** for secondary or postsecondary **education, professional, or trade purposes** shall offer such examinations or courses in a place and **manner accessible to persons with disabilities or offer alternative accessible arrangements** for such individuals.[23]

Title IV - Miscellaneous Provisions[24]

42 U.S.C. § 12201 - Construction

(a) In general

Except as otherwise provided in this chapter, **nothing in this chapter shall be construed to apply a lesser standard than the standards applied under title V of the Rehabilitation Act of 1973** (29 U.S.C. 790 *et seq.*) or the regulations issued by Federal agencies pursuant to such title.

(b) Relationship to other laws

Nothing in this chapter shall be construed to invalidate or limit the remedies, rights, and procedures of any Federal law or law of any State or political subdivision of any State or jurisdiction that provides greater or equal protection for the rights of individuals with disabilities than are afforded by this chapter. Nothing in this chapter shall be construed to preclude the prohibition of, or the imposition of restrictions on, smoking in places of employment covered by subchapter I, in transportation covered by subchapter II or III, or in places of public accommodation covered by subchapter III.

(c) Insurance - (not included)

(d) Accommodations and services

Nothing in this chapter shall be construed to require an individual with a disability **to accept an accommodation**, aid, service, opportunity, or benefit which such individual chooses not to accept.

(e) Benefits under State worker's compensation laws

Nothing in this chapter alters the standards for determining eligibility for benefits under State worker's compensation laws or under State and Federal disability benefit programs.

---

22   This includes B**ar exams for attorneys** and **medical licensing exams** for prospective MD's. We have several such cases in the *Wrightslaw Year in Review* books. The famous "*Bartlett*" case that affected state bar exams nationwide is discussed on the Wrightslaw website at:

   https://www.wrightslaw.com/law/caselaw/case_Bartlett_Bar_2d_9809.htm.

See also the Ninth Circuit's ruling in *Enyart v. National Conference of Bar Examiners* (630 F.3d 1153 (9th Cir. 2011)) where the defendant was ordered to provide accommodations to a blind law student taking the Bar Exam.

23   The National Board of Medical Examiners for its licensing exam refused to provide Ramsay, a medical student (who has dyslexia and ADD) the same extended time reasonable accommodations provided to her by both her undergraduate university and medical school. Her federal court Complaint, the preliminary injunction ordering extra time and the Third Circuit's Order (published at 968 F.3d 251 (3d Cir. 2020)) upholding the earlier decision are on our Wrightslaw website at:

   https://www.wrightslaw.com/law/pleadings/ada/license/

24   We have only included five of the Title IV sections. Most are not education related. All sections - 42 U.S.C. §§ 12201-12213 are located and available at: https://www.law.cornell.edu/uscode/text/42/chapter-126/subchapter-IV.

(f) Fundamental alteration

Nothing in this chapter alters the provision of section 12182(b)(2)(A)(ii) of this title, specifying that reasonable modifications in policies, practices, or procedures shall be required, **unless** an entity can demonstrate that making such modifications in policies, practices, or procedures, including academic requirements in postsecondary education, **would fundamentally alter** the nature of the goods, services, facilities, privileges, advantages, or accommodations involved.

(g) Claims of no disability

Nothing in this chapter shall provide the basis for a claim by an individual without a disability that the individual was subject to discrimination because of the individual's lack of disability.

(h) Reasonable accommodations and modifications

A covered entity under subchapter I, a public entity under subchapter II, and any person who owns, leases (or leases to), or operates a place of public accommodation under subchapter III,[25] **need not provide a reasonable accommodation** or a reasonable modification to policies, practices, or procedures to an individual who meets the definition of disability in section 12102(1) of this title **solely under** subparagraph (C)[26] of such section.

42 U.S.C. § 12202 - State immunity

A State **shall not be immune** under the eleventh amendment to the Constitution of the United States from an action in Federal or State court of competent jurisdiction for a violation of this chapter. In any action against a State for a violation of the requirements of this chapter, remedies (including remedies both at law and in equity) are available for such a violation to the same extent as such remedies are available for such a violation in an action against any public or private entity other than a State.

42 U.S.C. § 12203 - Prohibition against retaliation and coercion

(a) Retaliation[27]

No person **shall discriminate against any individual because such individual has opposed any act** or practice made unlawful by this chapter or because such individual made a charge, testified, assisted, or participated in any manner in an investigation, proceeding, or hearing under this chapter.

(b) Interference, coercion, or intimidation

It shall be **unlawful to coerce, intimidate, threaten,** or interfere with any individual in the exercise or enjoyment of, or on account of his or her having exercised or enjoyed, or on account of his or her having **aided or encouraged any other individual** in the exercise or enjoyment of, any right granted or protected by this chapter.

(c) Remedies and procedures

The remedies and procedures available under sections 12117, 12133, and 12188 of this title shall be available to aggrieved persons for violations of subsections (a) and (b), with respect to subchapter I, subchapter II and subchapter III, respectively.[28]

42 U.S.C. § 12204 - Architectural Board Regulations [not included]

42 U.S.C. § 12205 - Attorney's fees

In any action or administrative proceeding commenced pursuant to this chapter, the court or agency, in its discretion, may allow the prevailing party, other than the United States, a reasonable attorney's fee, including litigation expenses, and costs, and the United States shall be liable for the foregoing the same as a private individual.

---

25 The referenced subchapters are the same as the "Titles" in the Act, i.e., Title I, II, and III.

26 42 U.S.C. § 12101(1)(C) references an individual who is "being regarded as having such an impairment" but may not, in fact, have an impairment.

27 This also protects against retaliation under Section 504.

28 This incorporates by reference all of the enforcement provisions in Title I, II, and III.

42 U.S.C. § 12212 - Alternative means of dispute resolution[29]

Where appropriate and to the extent authorized by law, the use of alternative means of dispute resolution, including settlement negotiations, conciliation, facilitation, mediation, factfinding, minitrials, and arbitration, is encouraged to resolve disputes arising under this chapter.

End of the United States Code portion of the Americans with Disabilities Act

Selected Regulations of the Americans with Disabilities Act

Code of Federal Regulations (CFR)

The "Nondiscrimination" Regulations for the ADA regarding to **Title II, Public Services,** such as Public Schools, are published in **Part 35 of Title 28 (28 CFR Part 35).**[30] The regulations for **Title III, Public Accommodations and Private Entities,** such as private schools, nursery schools, day care centers, etc., are published in <**Part 36 of Title 28 (28 CFR Part 36).**>[31] Critical portions of those regulations follow below.

In many instances, the regulations track, verbatim, the language in the U.S. Code. The regulations in **Part 35** are often **verbatim to those in Part 36. We have not included regulations that are unrelated to educational settings.** In some instances, but not all, we noted them with the phrase "[not included]" as that reference. All regulations in this book, including those we did not include, are available at the Cornell Law School's Legal Information Institute's website.[32]

28 CFR Part 35 - Public Services (Title II)

Part 35, also known as Title II, has seven Subparts, listed below:
Subpart A - General (§§ 35.101 - 35.108)
Subpart B - General Requirements (§§ 35.130 - 35.139)
Subpart C - Employment (§ 35.140)
Subpart D - Program Accessibility (§§ 35.149 - 35.152)
Subpart E - Communications (§§ 35.160 - 35.164)
Subpart F - Compliance Procedures (§§ 35.170 - 35.178)
Subpart G - Designated Agencies (§ 35.190)

Part 35 also has three Appendices listed below:
Appendix A to Part 35 - Guidance to Revisions to ADA Regulation on Nondiscrimination on the Basis of Disability in State and Local Government Services
Appendix B to Part 35 - Guidance on ADA Regulation on Nondiscrimination on the Basis of Disability in State and Local Government Services Originally Published July 26, 1991
Appendix C to Part 35 - Guidance to Revisions to ADA Title II and Title III Regulations Revising the Meaning and Interpretation of the Definition of "Disability" and Other Provisions in Order To Incorporate the Requirements of the ADA Amendments Act

---

29 This is known as ADR. In IDEA, there is a voluntary mediation section and, after initiation of a due process hearing request, a required "Resolution Session," which is a form of a mediation session. *See* 20 U.S.C. §§ 1415(e) and 1415(f).

30 Located on the Internet at: https://www.law.cornell.edu/cfr/text/28/part-35

31 Located on the Internet at: https://www.law.cornell.edu/cfr/text/28/part-36

32 https://www.law.cornell.edu/cfr/text/28/chapter-I

Pertinent portions of Part 35 - Public Services regulations we have included in the following pages are:

28 CFR Part 35, Subpart A - General (§§ 35.101 - 35.108)

28 CFR § 35.101 - Purpose and broad coverage

(a) **Purpose.** The purpose of this part is to implement subtitle A of title II of the Americans with Disabilities Act of 1990 (42 U.S.C. 12131-12134), as amended by the ADA Amendments Act of 2008 (ADA Amendments Act) (Pub. L. 110-325, 122 Stat. 3553 (2008)), which prohibits discrimination on the basis of disability by public entities.

(b) **Broad coverage.** The primary purpose of the ADA Amendments Act is to make it easier for people with disabilities to obtain protection under the ADA. Consistent with the ADA Amendments Act's purpose of reinstating a broad scope of protection under the ADA, the definition of "disability" in this part shall be construed broadly in favor of expansive coverage to the maximum extent permitted by the terms of the ADA. The primary object of attention in cases brought under the ADA should be whether entities covered under the ADA have complied with their obligations and whether discrimination has occurred, not whether the individual meets the definition of "disability." The question of whether an individual meets the definition of "disability" under this part should not demand extensive analysis.

28 CFR § 35.102 - Application

(a) Except as provided in paragraph (b) of this section, this part applies to all services, programs, and activities provided or made available by public entities.

(b) To the extent that public transportation services, programs, and activities of public entities are covered by subtitle B of title II of the ADA (42 U.S.C. 12141), they are not subject to the requirements of this part.

28 CFR § 35.103 - Relationship to other laws

(a) Rule of interpretation. Except as otherwise provided in this part, this part shall not be construed to apply a lesser standard than the standards applied under title V of the Rehabilitation Act of 1973 (29 U.S.C. 791) or the regulations issued by Federal agencies pursuant to that title.

(b) Other laws. This part does not invalidate or limit the remedies, rights, and procedures of any other Federal laws, or State or local laws (including State common law) that provide greater or equal protection for the rights of individuals with disabilities or individuals associated with them.

28 CFR § 35.104 - Definitions

For purposes of this part, the term -

1991 Standards means the requirements set forth in the ADA Standards for Accessible Design, originally published on July 26, 1991, and republished as Appendix D to 28 CFR part 36.

2004 ADAAG means the requirements set forth in appendices B and D to 36 CFR part 1191 (2009).[33]

2010 Standards means the **2010 ADA Standards for Accessible Design**, which consist of the 2004 ADAAG and the requirements contained in § 35.151.[34]

Act means the Americans with Disabilities Act (Pub. L. 101-336, 104 Stat. 327, 42 U.S.C. 12101-12213 and 47 U.S.C. 225 and 611).

Assistant Attorney General means the Assistant Attorney General, Civil Rights Division, United States Department of Justice.

Auxiliary aids and services includes -

(1) **Qualified interpreters** on-site or through video remote interpreting (VRI) services; notetakers; real-time computer-aided transcription services; written materials; exchange of written notes; telephone handset amplifiers; assistive listening devices; assistive listening systems; telephones compatible with hearing aids; closed caption decoders; open and closed captioning, including real-time captioning; voice, text, and video-based telecommunications products and systems, including text telephones (TTYs), videophones, and captioned telephones, or equally effective telecommunications devices; videotext displays; accessible electronic and information technology; or other effective methods of making aurally delivered information available to individuals who are deaf or hard of hearing;

(2) **Qualified readers;** taped texts; audio recordings; Brailled materials and displays; screen reader software; magnification software; optical readers; secondary auditory programs (SAP); large print materials; accessible electronic and information technology; or other effective methods of making visually delivered materials available to individuals who are blind or have low vision;

(3) **Acquisition or modification of equipment** or devices; and

(4) Other similar services and actions.

---

33 This refers to the Accessibility Guidelines and the Architectural Barriers Act. *See* 36 CFR Part 1191, url at: https://www.law.cornell.edu/cfr/text/36/part-1191.

34 28 CFR § 35.151 refers to "New Construction and Alterations" and is not included in this book. URl is https://www.law.cornell.edu/cfr/text/28/35.151.

Complete complaint means a written statement that contains the complainant's name and address and **describes the public entity's alleged discriminatory action in sufficient detail** to inform the agency of the nature and date of the alleged violation of this part. It shall be signed by the complainant or by someone authorized to do so on his or her behalf. Complaints filed on behalf of classes or third parties shall describe or identify (by name, if possible) the alleged victims of discrimination.

Current illegal use of drugs means illegal use of drugs that occurred recently enough to justify a reasonable belief that a person's drug use is current or that continuing use is a real and ongoing problem.

Designated agency means the Federal agency designated under subpart G of this part to oversee compliance activities under this part for particular components of State and local governments.

Direct threat means a **significant risk** to the health or safety of others that cannot be eliminated by a modification of policies, practices or procedures, or by the provision of auxiliary aids or services as provided in § 35.139.

Disability. The definition of disability can be found at § 35.108.

Drug means a controlled substance, as defined in schedules I through V of section 202 of the Controlled Substances Act (21 U.S.C. 812).

Existing facility means a facility in existence on any given date, without regard to whether the facility may also be considered newly constructed or altered under this part.

Facility means **all or any portion** of buildings, structures, sites, complexes, equipment, rolling stock or other conveyances, roads, walks, passageways, parking lots, or other real or personal property, including the site where the building, property, structure, or equipment is located.

Historic preservation programs means programs conducted by a public entity that have preservation of historic properties as a primary purpose.

Historic Properties means those properties that are listed or eligible for listing in the National Register of Historic Places or properties designated as historic under State or local law.

Housing at a place of education means housing operated by or on behalf of an elementary, secondary, undergraduate, or postgraduate school, or other place of education, including dormitories, suites, apartments, or other places of residence.

Illegal use of drugs means the use of one or more drugs, the possession or distribution of which is unlawful under the Controlled Substances Act (21 U.S.C. 812). The term illegal use of drugs does not include the use of a drug taken under supervision by a licensed health care professional, or other uses authorized by the Controlled Substances Act or other provisions of Federal law.

Individual with a disability means a person who has a disability. The term individual with a disability **does not include** an individual who is currently engaging in the illegal use of drugs, when the public entity acts on the basis of such use.

Other power-driven mobility device means any mobility device powered by batteries, fuel, or other engines - whether or not designed primarily for use by individuals with mobility disabilities - that is used by individuals with mobility disabilities for the purpose of locomotion, including golf cars, electronic personal assistance mobility devices (EPAMDs), such as the Segway® PT, or any mobility device designed to operate in areas without defined pedestrian routes, but that is not a wheelchair within the meaning of this section. This definition does not apply to Federal wilderness areas; wheelchairs in such areas are defined in section 508(c)(2) of the ADA, 42 U.S.C. 12207(c)(2).

Public entity means -

> **(1) Any State or local government; (2) Any department, agency, special purpose district, or other instrumentality of a State or States or local government; and (3)**The National Railroad Passenger Corporation, and any commuter authority (as defined in section 103(8) of the Rail Passenger Service Act).

Qualified individual with a disability means an individual with a disability who, with or without reasonable modifications to rules, policies, or practices, the removal of architectural, communication, or transportation barriers, or the provision of auxiliary aids and services, meets the essential eligibility requirements for the receipt of services or the participation in programs or activities provided by a public entity.

Qualified interpreter means an interpreter who, via a video remote interpreting (VRI) service or an on-site appearance, is able to interpret effectively, accurately, and impartially, both receptively and expressively, using any necessary specialized vocabulary. Qualified interpreters include, for example, sign language interpreters, oral transliterators, and cued-language transliterators.

Qualified reader means a person who is able to read effectively, accurately, and impartially using any necessary specialized vocabulary.

Section 504 means section 504 of the Rehabilitation Act of 1973 (Pub. L. 93-112, 87 Stat. 394 (**29 U.S.C. 794**)), as amended.

Service animal means any dog that is individually trained to do work or perform tasks for the benefit of an individual with a disability, including a physical, sensory, psychiatric, intellectual, or other mental disability. Other species of animals, whether wild or domestic, trained or untrained, are not service animals for the purposes of this definition.

The work or tasks performed by a service animal **must be directly related to the individual's disability.** Examples of work or tasks include, but are not limited to, assisting individuals who are blind or have low vision with navigation and other tasks, alerting individuals who are deaf or hard of hearing to the presence of people or sounds, providing non-violent protection or rescue work, pulling a wheelchair, assisting an individual during a seizure, alerting individuals to the presence of allergens, retrieving items such as medicine or the telephone, providing physical support and assistance with balance and stability to individuals with mobility disabilities, and helping persons with psychiatric and neurological disabilities by preventing or interrupting impulsive or destructive behaviors. The crime deterrent effects of an animal's presence and the provision of emotional support, well-being, comfort, or companionship do not constitute work or tasks for the purposes of this definition.

State means each of the several States, the District of Columbia, the Commonwealth of Puerto Rico, Guam, American Samoa, the Virgin Islands, the Trust Territory of the Pacific Islands, and the Commonwealth of the Northern Mariana Islands.

Video remote interpreting (VRI) service means an interpreting service that uses video conference technology over dedicated lines or wireless technology offering high-speed, wide-bandwidth video connection that delivers high-quality video images as provided in § 35.160(d).

Wheelchair means a manually-operated or power-driven device designed primarily for use by an individual with a mobility disability for the main purpose of indoor or of both indoor and outdoor locomotion. This definition does not apply to Federal wilderness areas; wheelchairs in such areas are defined in section 508(c)(2) of the ADA, 42 U.S.C. 12207(c)(2).

28 CFR § 35.105 - Self-evaluation

(a) A public entity **shall**, within one year of the effective date of this part, evaluate its current services, policies, and practices, and the effects thereof, that do not or may not meet the requirements of this part and, to the extent modification of any such services, policies, and practices is required, the public entity shall proceed to make the necessary modifications.

(b) A public entity **shall provide an opportunity to interested persons, including individuals with disabilities** or organizations representing individuals with disabilities, **to participate in the self-evaluation process** by submitting comments.

(c) A public entity that employs 50 or more persons **shall, for at least three years** following completion of the self-evaluation, maintain on file and make available for public inspection:

(1) A list of the interested persons consulted;

(2) A description of areas examined and any problems identified; and

(3) A description of any modifications made.

(d) If a public entity has already complied with the self-evaluation requirement of a regulation implementing section 504 of the Rehabilitation Act of 1973, then the requirements of this section shall apply **only to those policies and practices that were not included** in the previous self-evaluation.

28 CFR § 35.106 - Notice

A public entity **shall make available to applicants, participants, beneficiaries,** and other interested persons information regarding the provisions of this part and its applicability to the services, programs, or activities of the public entity, and make such information available to them in such manner as the head of the entity finds necessary to apprise such persons of the protections against discrimination assured them by the Act and this part.

28 CFR § 35.107 - Designation of responsible employee and adoption of grievance procedures

(a) Designation of responsible employee. A public entity that employs 50 or more persons shall designate at least one employee to coordinate its efforts to comply with and carry out its responsibilities under this part, including any investigation of any complaint communicated to it alleging its noncompliance with this part or alleging any actions that would be prohibited by this part. The public entity shall make available to all interested individuals the name, office address, and telephone number of the employee or employees designated pursuant to this paragraph.

(b) Complaint procedure. A public entity that employs 50 or more persons shall adopt and publish grievance procedures providing for prompt and equitable resolution of complaints alleging any action that would be prohibited by this part.

28 CFR § 35.108 - Definition of "disability"

(a)

(1) Disability means, with respect to an individual:

(i) A physical or mental impairment that substantially limits one or more of the major life activities of such individual;

(ii) A record of such an impairment; or

(iii) Being regarded as having such an impairment as described in paragraph (f) of this section.

(2) Rules of construction.

(i) The definition of "disability" **shall be construed broadly** in favor of expansive coverage, to the maximum extent permitted by the terms of the ADA.

(ii) An individual may establish coverage under any one or more of the **three prongs** of the definition of "disability" in paragraph (a)(1) of this section, the **"actual disability"** prong in paragraph (a)(1)(i) of this section, the **"record of"** prong in paragraph (a)(1)(ii) of this section, or the **"regarded as"** prong in paragraph (a)(1)(iii) of this section.

(iii) Where an individual is not challenging a public entity's failure to provide reasonable modifications under § 35.130(b)(7), it is generally unnecessary to proceed under the "actual disability" or "record of" prongs, which require a showing of an impairment that substantially limits a major life activity or a record of such an impairment. In these cases, the evaluation of coverage can be made solely under the "regarded as" prong of the definition of "disability," which does not require a showing of an impairment that substantially limits a major life activity or a record of such an impairment. An individual may choose, however, to proceed under the "actual disability" or "record of" prong regardless of whether the individual is challenging a public entity's failure to provide reasonable modifications.

(b)

(1) Physical or mental impairment means:

(i) Any physiological disorder or condition, cosmetic disfigurement, or anatomical loss affecting one or more body systems, such as: neurological, musculoskeletal, special sense organs, respiratory (including speech organs), cardiovascular, reproductive, digestive, genitourinary, immune, circulatory, hemic, lymphatic, skin, and endocrine; or

(ii) Any mental or psychological disorder such as intellectual disability, organic brain syndrome, emotional or mental illness, and **specific learning disability**.

(2) Physical or mental impairment **includes, but is not limited to,** contagious and noncontagious diseases and conditions such as the following: orthopedic, visual, speech, and **hearing impairments, and cerebral palsy, epilepsy,** muscular dystrophy, multiple sclerosis, cancer, heart disease, **diabetes, intellectual disability**, emotional illness, **dyslexia and other specific learning disabilities, Attention Deficit Hyperactivity Disorder,** Human Immunodeficiency Virus infection (whether symptomatic or asymptomatic), tuberculosis, drug addiction, and alcoholism.

(3) Physical or mental impairment does not include homosexuality or bisexuality.

(c)

(1) Major life activities include, but are not limited to:

(i) Caring for oneself, performing manual tasks, seeing, hearing, eating, sleeping, walking, standing, sitting, reaching, lifting, bending, **speaking, breathing, learning, reading, concentrating, thinking, writing, communicating, interacting with others,** and working; **and**

(ii) The operation of a major bodily function, such as the functions of the immune system, special sense organs and skin, normal cell growth, and digestive, genitourinary, bowel, bladder, neurological, brain, respiratory, circulatory, cardiovascular, endocrine, hemic, lymphatic, musculoskeletal, and reproductive systems. The operation of a major bodily function includes the operation of an individual organ within a body system.

(2) Rules of construction.

(i) In determining whether an impairment substantially limits a major life activity, the term major shall not be interpreted strictly to create a demanding standard.

(ii) Whether an activity is a major life activity is not determined by reference to whether it is of central importance to daily life.

(d) Substantially limits -

(1) Rules of construction. The following rules of construction apply when determining whether an impairment **substantially limits** an individual in a major life activity.

(i) The term "substantially limits" shall be **construed broadly in favor of expansive coverage, to the maximum extent permitted by the terms of the ADA.** "Substantially limits" is not meant to be a demanding standard.

(ii) **The primary object of attention** in cases brought under title II of the ADA **should be whether public entities have complied** with their obligations and whether discrimination has occurred, not the extent to which an individual's impairment substantially limits a major life activity. Accordingly, the **threshold issue** of whether an impairment substantially limits a major life activity should not demand extensive analysis.

(iii) An impairment that substantially limits one major life activity does not need to limit other major life activities in order to be considered a substantially limiting impairment.

(iv) An impairment that is **episodic or in remission is a disability** if it would substantially limit a major life activity when active.

(v) An impairment is a disability within the meaning of this part if it substantially limits the ability of an individual to perform a major life activity **as compared to most people** in the general population. An impairment does not need to prevent, or significantly or severely restrict, the individual from performing a major life activity in order to be considered substantially limiting. Nonetheless, not every impairment will constitute a disability within the meaning of this section.

(vi) The determination of whether an impairment substantially limits a major life activity **requires an individualized assessment**. However, in making this assessment, the term "substantially limits" shall be interpreted and applied to require a degree of functional limitation that is lower than the standard for substantially limits applied prior to the ADA Amendments Act.

(vii) The **comparison of an individual's performance** of a major life activity to the performance of the same major life activity **by most people** in the general population usually **will not require scientific, medical, or statistical evidence.** Nothing in this paragraph (d)(1) is intended, however, to prohibit or limit the presentation of scientific, medical, or statistical evidence in making such a comparison where appropriate.[35]

(viii) The determination of whether an impairment substantially limits a major life activity shall be made **without regard to the ameliorative effects of mitigating measures.** However, the ameliorative effects of ordinary eyeglasses or contact lenses shall be considered in determining whether an impairment substantially limits a major life activity. Ordinary eyeglasses or contact lenses are lenses that are intended to fully correct visual acuity or to eliminate refractive error.

(ix) The six-month "transitory" part of the "transitory and minor" exception in paragraph (f)(2) of this section does not apply to the "actual disability" or "record of" prongs of the definition of "disability." The effects of an impairment lasting or expected to last less than six months can be substantially limiting within the meaning of this section for establishing an actual disability or a record of a disability.

(2) **Predictable assessments.**

(i) The principles set forth in the **rules of construction** in this section are intended to provide for **more generous coverage and application** of the ADA's prohibition on discrimination through a framework that is predictable, consistent, and workable for all individuals and entities with rights and responsibilities under the ADA.

(ii) Applying these principles, the individualized assessment of some types of impairments will, in virtually all cases, result in a determination of coverage under paragraph (a)(1)(i) of this section (the "actual disability" prong) or paragraph (a)(1)(ii) of this section (the "record of" prong). Given their inherent nature, these types of impairments will, as a factual matter, virtually always be found to impose a substantial limitation on a major life activity. Therefore, with respect to these types of impairments, the necessary individualized assessment should be particularly simple and straightforward.

(iii) For example, applying these principles it should easily be concluded that the types of impairments set forth in paragraphs (d)(2)(iii)(A) through (K) of this section will, at a minimum, substantially limit the major life activities indicated. The types of impairments described in this paragraph may substantially limit additional major life activities (including major bodily functions) not explicitly listed in paragraphs (d)(2)(iii)(A) through (K).

(A) Deafness substantially limits hearing;

(B) Blindness substantially limits seeing;

---

35   Virginia ADA litigation attorney, Nick Simopoulos, Esq., asserts that the language about comparison "to most people" in the above subsections is a "tricky" issue of evidence and proof.

(C) Intellectual disability substantially limits brain function;

(D) Partially or completely missing limbs or mobility impairments requiring the use of a wheelchair substantially limit musculoskeletal function;

(E) Autism substantially limits brain function;

(F) Cancer substantially limits normal cell growth;

(G) Cerebral palsy substantially limits brain function;

(H) Diabetes substantially limits endocrine function;

(I) Epilepsy, muscular dystrophy, and multiple sclerosis each substantially limits neurological function;

(J) Human Immunodeficiency Virus (HIV) infection substantially limits immune function; and

(K) Major depressive disorder, bipolar disorder, post-traumatic stress disorder, traumatic brain injury, obsessive compulsive disorder, and schizophrenia each substantially limits brain function.

(3) Condition, manner, or duration.

(i) At all times taking into account the principles set forth in the rules of construction, in determining whether an individual is substantially limited in a major life activity, it may be useful in appropriate cases to consider, as compared to most people in the general population, the conditions under which the individual performs the major life activity; the manner in which the individual performs the major life activity; or the duration of time it takes the individual to perform the major life activity, or for which the individual can perform the major life activity.

(ii) Consideration of facts such as condition, manner, or duration may include, among other things, **consideration of the difficulty, effort or time required to perform a major life activity;** pain experienced when performing a major life activity; the length of time a major life activity can be performed; or the way an impairment affects the operation of a major bodily function. In addition, the non-ameliorative effects of mitigating measures, such as **negative side effects of medication** or burdens associated with following a particular treatment regimen,[36] may be considered when determining whether an individual's impairment substantially limits a major life activity.

(iii) In determining whether an individual has a disability under the "actual disability" or "record of" **prongs of the definition of "disability," the focus is on how a major life activity is substantially limited,** and not on what outcomes an individual can achieve. For example, someone with a learning disability may achieve a high level of academic success, but may nevertheless be substantially limited in one or more major life activities, including, but not limited to, reading, writing, speaking, or learning because of the additional time or effort he or she must spend to read, write, speak, or learn compared to most people in the general population.

(iv) Given the rules of construction set forth in this section, it may often be unnecessary to conduct an analysis involving most or all of the facts related to condition, manner, or duration. This is particularly true with respect to impairments such as those described in paragraph (d)(2)(iii) of this section, which by their inherent nature should be easily found to impose a substantial limitation on a major life activity, and for which the individualized assessment should be particularly simple and straightforward.

---

36 Children with brain cancer suffer from the chemotherapy, radiation, and or surgery used in treatment.

(4) Mitigating measures include, but are not limited to:

(i) **Medication**, medical supplies, equipment, appliances, low-vision devices (defined as devices that magnify, enhance, or otherwise augment a visual image, but not including ordinary eyeglasses or contact lenses), prosthetics including limbs and devices, **hearing aid(s) and cochlear implant(s)** or other implantable hearing devices, mobility devices, and oxygen therapy equipment and supplies;

(ii) Use of assistive technology;

(iii) Reasonable modifications or auxiliary aids or services as defined in this regulation;

(iv) Learned behavioral or adaptive neurological modifications; or

(v) Psychotherapy, behavioral therapy, or physical therapy.

(e) Has a record of such an impairment.

(1) An individual has a record of such an impairment if the individual has a history of, or has been misclassified as having, a mental or physical impairment that substantially limits one or more major life activities.

(2) Broad construction. Whether an individual has a record of an impairment that substantially limited a major life activity **shall be construed broadly to the maximum extent permitted by the ADA and should not demand extensive analysis**. An individual will be considered to fall within this prong of the definition of "disability" if the individual has a history of an impairment that substantially limited one or more major life activities when compared to most people in the general population, or was misclassified as having had such an impairment. In determining whether an impairment substantially limited a major life activity, the principles articulated in paragraph (d)(1) of this section apply.

(3) Reasonable modification. An individual with a record of a substantially limiting impairment may be entitled to a reasonable modification if needed and related to the past disability.

(f) Is regarded as having such an impairment. The following principles apply under the "regarded" as prong of the definition of "disability" (paragraph (a)(1)(iii) of this section):

(1) Except as set forth in paragraph (f)(2) of this section, an individual is "regarded as having such an impairment" if the individual is subjected to a prohibited action because of an actual or perceived physical or mental impairment, **whether or not that impairment substantially limits, or is perceived to substantially limit**, a major life activity, even if the public entity asserts, or may or does ultimately establish, a defense to the action prohibited by the ADA.

(2) **An individual is not "regarded as having such an impairment" if** the public entity demonstrates that the impairment is, objectively, both **"transitory" and "minor."** A public entity may not defeat "regarded as" coverage of an individual simply by demonstrating that it subjectively believed the impairment was transitory and minor; rather, the public entity must demonstrate that the impairment is (in the case of an actual impairment) or would be (in the case of a perceived impairment), objectively, both "transitory" and "minor." For purposes of this section, "transitory" is defined as lasting or expected to last six months or less.

(3) Establishing that an individual is "regarded as having such an impairment" does not, by itself, establish liability. Liability is established under title II of the ADA only when an individual proves that a public entity discriminated on the basis of disability within the meaning of title II of the ADA, 42 U.S.C. 12131-12134.

(g) Exclusions. The term "disability" does not include -

(1) Transvestism, transsexualism, pedophilia, exhibitionism, voyeurism, gender identity disorders not resulting from physical impairments, or other sexual behavior disorders;

(2) Compulsive gambling, kleptomania, or pyromania; or

(3) Psychoactive substance use disorders resulting from current illegal use of drugs.

28 CFR Part 35, Subpart B - General Requirements (§§ 35.130 - 35.139)

28 CFR § 35.130 - General prohibitions against discrimination

(a) No qualified individual with a disability shall, on the basis of disability, be excluded from participation in or be denied the benefits of the services, programs, or activities of a public entity, or be subjected to discrimination by any public entity.

(b)

(1) A public entity, in providing any aid, benefit, or service, may not, directly or through contractual, licensing, or other arrangements, on the basis of disability -

(i) Deny a qualified individual with a disability the opportunity to participate in or benefit from the aid, benefit, or service;

(ii) Afford a qualified individual with a disability an opportunity to participate in or benefit from the aid, benefit, or service that is not equal to that afforded others;

(iii) Provide a qualified individual with a disability with an aid, benefit, or service that is not as effective in affording equal opportunity to obtain the same result, to gain the same benefit, or to reach the same level of achievement as that provided to others;

(iv) Provide different or separate aids, benefits, or services to individuals with disabilities or to any class of individuals with disabilities than is provided to others unless such action is necessary to provide qualified individuals with disabilities with aids, benefits, or services that are as effective as those provided to others;

(v) Aid or perpetuate discrimination against a qualified individual with a disability by providing significant assistance to an agency, organization, or person that discriminates on the basis of disability in providing any aid, benefit, or service to beneficiaries of the public entity's program;

(vi) Deny a qualified individual with a disability the opportunity to participate as a member of planning or advisory boards;

(vii) Otherwise limit a qualified individual with a disability in the enjoyment of any right, privilege, advantage, or opportunity enjoyed by others receiving the aid, benefit, or service.

(2) **A public entity may not deny** a qualified individual with a disability the opportunity to participate in services, programs, or activities that are not separate or different, despite the existence of permissibly separate or different programs or activities.

(3) A public entity may not, directly or through contractual or other arrangements, utilize criteria or methods of administration:

(i) That have the effect of subjecting qualified individuals with disabilities to discrimination on the basis of disability;

(ii) That have the purpose or effect of defeating or substantially impairing accomplishment of the objectives of the public entity's program with respect to individuals with disabilities; or

(iii) That perpetuate the discrimination of another public entity if both public entities are subject to common administrative control or are agencies of the same State.

(4) A public entity may not, in determining the site or location of a facility, make selections -

(i) That have the effect of excluding individuals with disabilities from, denying them the benefits of, or otherwise subjecting them to discrimination; or

(ii) That have the purpose or effect of defeating or substantially impairing the accomplishment of the objectives of the service, program, or activity with respect to individuals with disabilities.

(5) A public entity, in the selection of procurement contractors, may not use criteria that subject qualified individuals with disabilities to discrimination on the basis of disability.

(6) A public entity **may not administer a licensing or certification program** in a manner that subjects qualified individuals with disabilities to discrimination on the basis of disability, nor may a public entity establish requirements for the programs or activities of licensees or certified entities that subject qualified individuals with disabilities to discrimination on the basis of disability. The programs or activities of entities that are licensed or certified by a public entity are not, themselves, covered by this part.

(7)

(i) A public entity **shall make reasonable modifications in policies, practices, or procedures** when the modifications are necessary to avoid discrimination on the basis of disability, unless the public entity can demonstrate that making the modifications would **fundamentally alter** the nature of the service, program, or activity.

(ii) A public entity is not required to provide a reasonable modification to an individual who meets the definition of "disability" solely under the "regarded as" prong of the definition of "disability" at § 35.108(a)(1)(iii).

(8) A public entity **shall not impose or apply eligibility criteria** that screen out or tend to screen out an individual with a disability or any class of individuals with disabilities from fully and equally enjoying any service, program, or activity, **unless** such criteria can be shown to be necessary for the provision of the service, program, or activity being offered.

(c) Nothing in this part prohibits a public entity from providing benefits, services, or advantages to individuals with disabilities, or to a particular class of individuals with disabilities beyond those required by this part.

(d) A public entity shall administer services, programs, and activities **in the most integrated setting** appropriate to the needs of qualified individuals with disabilities.

(e)

(1) **Nothing in this part shall be construed to require an individual with a disability to accept an accommodation, aid, service, opportunity, or benefit** provided under the ADA or this part which such individual chooses not to accept.

(2) Nothing in the Act or this part authorizes the representative or guardian of an individual with a disability to decline food, water, medical treatment, or medical services for that individual.

(f) A public entity **may not place a surcharge on a particular individual with a disability** or any group of individuals with disabilities to cover the costs of measures, such as the provision of auxiliary aids or program accessibility, that are required to provide that individual or group with the nondiscriminatory treatment required by the Act or this part.

(g) A public entity shall not exclude or otherwise deny equal services, programs, or activities to an individual or entity because of the known disability of an individual with whom the individual or entity is known to have a relationship or association.

(h) A public entity may impose legitimate safety requirements necessary for the safe operation of its services, programs, or activities. However, the public entity must ensure that its safety requirements are based on actual risks, not on mere speculation, stereotypes, or generalizations about individuals with disabilities.

(i) Nothing in this part shall provide the basis for a claim that an individual without a disability was subject to discrimination because of a lack of disability, including a claim that an individual with a disability was granted a reasonable modification that was denied to an individual without a disability.

28 CFR § 35.134 - Retaliation or coercion

(a) No private or public entity shall discriminate against any individual because that individual has opposed any act or practice made unlawful by this part, or because that individual made a charge, testified, assisted, or participated in any manner in an investigation, proceeding, or hearing under the Act or this part.

(b) No private or public entity shall coerce, intimidate, threaten, or interfere with any individual in the exercise or enjoyment of, or on account of his or her having exercised or enjoyed, or on account of his or her having aided or encouraged any other individual in the exercise or enjoyment of, any right granted or protected by the Act or this part.

28 CFR § 35.135 - Personal devices and services

This part does not require a public entity to provide to individuals with disabilities personal devices, such as wheelchairs; individually prescribed devices, such as prescription eyeglasses or hearing aids; readers for personal use or study; or services of a personal nature including assistance in eating, toileting, or dressing.

28 CFR § 35.136 - Service animals

(a) **General.** Generally, a public entity shall modify its policies, practices, or procedures to permit the use of a service animal by an individual with a disability.[37]

(b) **Exceptions.** A public entity may ask an individual with a disability to remove a service animal from the premises if -

    (1) The animal is out of control and the animal's handler does not take effective action to control it; or

    (2) The animal is not housebroken.

(c) **If an animal is properly excluded.** If a public entity properly excludes a service animal under § 35.136(b), it shall give the individual with a disability the opportunity to participate in the service, program, or activity without having the service animal on the premises.

(d) **Animal under handler's control.** A service animal shall be under the control of its handler. A service animal shall have a harness, leash, or other tether, unless either the handler is unable because of a disability to use a harness, leash, or other tether, or the use of a harness, leash, or other tether would interfere with the service animal's safe, effective performance of work or tasks, in which case the service animal must be otherwise under the handler's control (e.g., voice control, signals, or other effective means).

(e) **Care or supervision.** A public entity is not responsible for the care or supervision of a service animal.

(f) **Inquiries.** A public entity shall not ask about the nature or extent of a person's disability, but may make two inquiries to determine whether an animal qualifies as a service animal. A public entity may ask if the animal is required because of a disability and what work or task the animal has been trained to perform. A public entity shall not require documentation, such as proof that the animal has been certified, trained, or licensed as a service animal. Generally, a public entity may not make these inquiries about a service animal when it is readily apparent that an animal is trained to do work or perform tasks for an individual with a disability (e.g., the dog is observed guiding an individual who is blind or has low vision, pulling a person's wheelchair, or providing assistance with stability or balance to an individual with an observable mobility disability).

(g) **Access to areas of a public entity.** Individuals with disabilities shall be permitted to be accompanied by their service animals in all areas of a public entity's facilities where members of the public, participants in services, programs or activities, or invitees, as relevant, are allowed to go.

(h) **Surcharges.** A public entity shall not ask or require an individual with a disability to pay a surcharge, even if people accompanied by pets are required to pay fees, or to comply with other requirements generally not applicable to people without pets. If a public entity normally charges individuals for the damage they cause, an individual with a disability may be charged for damage caused by his or her service animal.

---

37   <Service animal is defined> in 28 CFR § 35.104.

(i) Miniature horses.

    (1) Reasonable modifications. A public entity shall make reasonable modifications in policies, practices, or procedures to permit the use of a miniature horse by an individual with a disability if the miniature horse has been individually trained to do work or perform tasks for the benefit of the individual with a disability.

    (2) Assessment factors. In determining whether reasonable modifications in policies, practices, or procedures can be made to allow a miniature horse into a specific facility, a public entity shall consider -

        (i) The type, size, and weight of the miniature horse and whether the facility can accommodate these features;

        (ii) Whether the handler has sufficient control of the miniature horse;

        (iii) Whether the miniature horse is housebroken; and

        (iv) Whether the miniature horse's presence in a specific facility compromises legitimate safety requirements that are necessary for safe operation.

    (3) Other requirements. Paragraphs 35.136(c) through (h) of this section, which apply to service animals, shall also apply to miniature horses.

28 CFR Part 35, Subpart C - Employment (§ 35.140) [*not included*]

28 CFR Part 35, Subpart D - Program Accessibility (§§ 35.149 - 35.152)

28 CFR § 35.149 - Discrimination prohibited

Except as otherwise provided in § 35.150,[38] no qualified individual with a disability shall, because a public entity's facilities are inaccessible to or unusable by individuals with disabilities, be excluded from participation in, or be denied the benefits of the services, programs, or activities of a public entity, or be subjected to discrimination by any public entity.

28 CFR Part 35, Subpart E - Communications (§§ 35.160 - 35.164)

28 CFR § 35.160 - General

(a)

    (1) A public entity shall take appropriate steps to ensure that communications with applicants, participants, members of the public, and companions with disabilities **are as effective as communications with others**.

    (2) For purposes of this section, "companion" means a family member, friend, or associate of an individual seeking access to a service, program, or activity of a public entity, who, along with such individual, is an appropriate person with whom the public entity should communicate.

(b)

    (1) A public entity **shall furnish appropriate auxiliary aids and services** where necessary to afford individuals with disabilities, including applicants, participants, companions, and members of the public, an equal opportunity to participate in, and enjoy the benefits of, a service, program, or activity of a public entity.

    (2) The type of auxiliary aid or service necessary to ensure effective communication will vary in accordance with the method of communication used by the individual; the nature, length, and complexity of the communication involved; and the context in which the communication is taking place. In determining what types of auxiliary aids and services are necessary, a public entity shall give primary consideration to the

---

38   28 CFR § 35.150 relates to usability and structural changes to existing facilities and is not included in this book.

requests of individuals with disabilities. In order to be effective, auxiliary aids and services must be provided in accessible formats, in a timely manner, and in such a way as to protect the privacy and independence of the individual with a disability.

(c)

(1) A public entity shall not require an individual with a disability to bring another individual to interpret for him or her.

(2) **A public entity shall not rely on an adult accompanying an individual with a disability to interpret** or facilitate communication except -

(i) In an emergency involving an imminent threat to the safety or welfare of an individual or the public where there is no interpreter available; or

(ii) Where the individual with a disability specifically requests that the accompanying adult interpret or facilitate communication, the accompanying adult agrees to provide such assistance, and reliance on that adult for such assistance is appropriate under the circumstances.

(3) A public entity shall not rely on a minor child to interpret or facilitate communication, except in an emergency involving an imminent threat to the safety or welfare of an individual or the public where there is no interpreter available.

(d) Video remote interpreting (VRI) services. A public entity that chooses to provide qualified interpreters via VRI services shall ensure that it provides -

(1) Real-time, full-motion video and audio over a dedicated high-speed, wide-bandwidth video connection or wireless connection that delivers high-quality video images that do not produce lags, choppy, blurry, or grainy images, or irregular pauses in communication;

(2) A sharply delineated image that is large enough to display the interpreter's face, arms, hands, and fingers, and the participating individual's face, arms, hands, and fingers, regardless of his or her body position;

(3) A clear, audible transmission of voices; and

(4) Adequate training to users of the technology and other involved individuals so that they may quickly and efficiently set up and operate the VRI.

28 CFR § 35.164 - Duties

This subpart **does not require a** public entity to take any action that it can demonstrate would result in a **fundamental alteration** in the nature of a service, program, or activity or in undue financial and administrative burdens. In those circumstances where personnel of the public entity believe that the proposed action would fundamentally alter the service, program, or activity or would result in undue financial and administrative burdens, a public entity has the burden of proving that compliance with this subpart would result in such alteration or burdens.

The decision that compliance would result in such alteration or burdens must be made by the head of the public entity or his or her designee after considering all resources available for use in the funding and operation of the service, program, or activity and must be accompanied by a written statement of the reasons for reaching that conclusion. If an action required to comply with this subpart would result in such an alteration or such burdens, a public entity shall take any other action that would not result in such an alteration or such burdens but would nevertheless ensure that, to the maximum extent possible, individuals with disabilities receive the benefits or services provided by the public entity.

28 CFR Part 35, Subpart F - Compliance Procedures (§§ 35.170 - 35.179)

28 CFR § 35.170 - Complaints

(a) **Who may file.** An individual who believes that he or she or a specific class of individuals has been subjected to discrimination on the basis of disability by a public entity may, by himself or herself or by an authorized representative, file a complaint under this part.

(b) **Time for filing.** A complaint **must be filed not later than 180 days**[39] from the date of the alleged discrimination, unless the time for filing is extended by the designated agency for good cause shown. A complaint is deemed to be filed under this section on the date it is first filed with any Federal agency.

(c) **Where to file.** An individual may file a complaint with any agency that he or she believes to be the appropriate agency designated under subpart G of this part, or with any agency that provides funding to the public entity that is the subject of the complaint, **or with the Department of Justice** for referral as provided in § 35.171(a)(2).

28 CFR § 35.171 - Acceptance of complaints

(a) **Receipt of complaints.**

(1)

(i) Any Federal agency that receives a complaint of discrimination on the basis of disability by a public entity **shall promptly review the complaint to determine whether it has jurisdiction over the complaint under section 504.**

(ii) If the agency does not have section 504 jurisdiction, it shall promptly determine whether it is the designated agency under **subpart G of this part** responsible for complaints filed against that public entity.

(2)

(i) If an agency other than the Department of Justice determines that it does not have section 504 jurisdiction and is not the designated agency, **it shall promptly refer the complaint** to the appropriate designated agency, the agency that has section 504 jurisdiction, or the Department of Justice, **and so notify the complainant.**

(ii) When the Department of Justice receives a complaint for which it does not have jurisdiction under section 504 and is not the designated agency, **it may exercise jurisdiction pursuant to § 35.190(e)** or refer the complaint **to an agency that does have jurisdiction under section 50**4 or to the appropriate agency designated in subpart G of this part or, in the case of an employment complaint that is also subject to title I of the Act, to the Equal Employment Opportunity Commission.

(3)

(i) If the agency that receives a complaint has section 504 jurisdiction, it shall process the complaint according to its procedures for enforcing section 504.

(ii) If the agency that receives a complaint does not have section 504 jurisdiction, but is the designated agency, it shall process the complaint according to the procedures established by this subpart.

(b) **Employment complaints.**

(1) If a complaint alleges employment discrimination subject to title I of the Act, and the agency has section 504 jurisdiction, the agency shall follow the procedures issued by the Department of Justice and the Equal Employment Opportunity Commission under section 107(b) of the Act.

---

39 This is a 180 day statute of limitations!

(2) If a complaint alleges employment discrimination subject to title I of the Act, and the designated agency does not have section 504 jurisdiction, the agency shall refer the complaint to the Equal Employment Opportunity Commission for processing under title I of the Act.

(3) Complaints alleging employment discrimination subject to this part, but not to title I of the Act shall be processed in accordance with the procedures established by this subpart.

(c) Complete complaints.

(1) A designated agency shall accept all complete complaints under this section and shall promptly notify the complainant and the public entity of the receipt and acceptance of the complaint.

(2) If the designated agency receives a complaint that is not complete, it shall notify the complainant and specify the additional information that is needed to make the complaint a complete complaint. If the complainant fails to complete the complaint, the designated agency shall close the complaint without prejudice.

28 CFR § 35.172 - Investigations and compliance reviews

(a) The designated agency shall investigate complaints for which it is responsible under § 35.171.

(b) The designated agency may conduct compliance reviews of public entities in order to ascertain whether there has been a failure to comply with the nondiscrimination requirements of this part.

(c) Where appropriate, the designated agency shall attempt informal resolution of any matter being investigated under this section, and, if resolution is not achieved and a violation is found, issue to the public entity and the complainant, if any, a Letter of Findings that shall include -

(1) Findings of fact and conclusions of law;

(2) A description of a remedy for each violation found (including compensatory damages where appropriate); and

(3) Notice of the rights and procedures available under paragraph (d) of this section and §§ 35.173 and 35.174.

(d) At any time, the complainant may file a private suit pursuant to section 203 of the Act, 42 U.S.C. 12133, whether or not the designated agency finds a violation.

28 CFR § 35.173 - Voluntary compliance agreements

(a) When the designated agency issues a **noncompliance Letter of Findings**, the designated agency **shall** -

(1) Notify the Assistant Attorney General by forwarding a copy of the Letter of Findings to the Assistant Attorney General; and

(2) Initiate negotiations with the public entity to secure compliance by voluntary means.

(b) Where the designated agency is able to secure **voluntary compliance**, the voluntary compliance agreement shall -

(1) Be in writing and signed by the parties;

(2) Address each cited violation;

(3) Specify the corrective or remedial action to be taken, within a stated period of time, to come into compliance;

(4) Provide assurance that discrimination will not recur; and

(5) Provide for enforcement by the Attorney General.

28 CFR § 35.174 - Referral

If the public entity **declines to enter into voluntary compliance** negotiations or if negotiations are unsuccessful, the designated agency shall refer the matter to the Attorney General with a recommendation for appropriate action.

28 CFR § 35.175 - Attorney's fees

In any action or administrative proceeding commenced pursuant to the Act or this part, the court or agency, in its discretion, may allow the prevailing party, other than the United States, a reasonable attorney's fee, including litigation expenses, and costs, and the United States shall be liable for the foregoing the same as a private individual.

28 CFR § 35.176 - Alternative means of dispute resolution

Where appropriate and to the extent authorized by law, the use of alternative means of dispute resolution, including settlement negotiations, conciliation, facilitation, mediation, factfinding, minitrials, and arbitration, is encouraged to resolve disputes arising under the Act and this part.

28 CFR § 35.177 - Effect of unavailability of technical assistance

A public entity shall not be excused from compliance with the requirements of this part because of any failure to receive technical assistance, including any failure in the development or dissemination of any technical assistance manual authorized by the Act.

28 CFR § 35.178 - State immunity

A State shall not be immune under the eleventh amendment to the Constitution of the United States from an action in Federal or State court of competent jurisdiction for a violation of this Act. In any action against a State for a violation of the requirements of this Act, remedies (including remedies both at law and in equity) are available for such a violation to the same extent as such remedies are available for such a violation in an action against any public or private entity other than a State.

28 CFR Part 35, Subpart G - Designated Agencies

28 CFR § 35.190 - Designated agencies

(a) The Assistant Attorney General shall coordinate the compliance activities of Federal agencies with respect to State and local government components, and shall provide policy guidance and interpretations to designated agencies to ensure the consistent and effective implementation of the requirements of this part.

(b) The Federal agencies listed in paragraph (b) (1) through (8) of this section shall have responsibility for the implementation of subpart F of this part for components of State and local governments that exercise responsibilities, regulate, or administer services, programs, or activities in the following functional areas.

(1) Department of Agriculture: All programs, services, and regulatory activities relating to farming and the raising of livestock, including extension services.

(2) **Department of Education:** All programs, services, and regulatory activities relating to the operation of **elementary and secondary education systems** and institutions, **institutions of higher education** and vocational education (other than schools of medicine, dentistry, nursing, and other health-related schools), and libraries.

(3) **Department of Health and Human Services:** All programs, services, and regulatory activities relating to the provision of health care and social services, **including schools of medicine, dentistry, nursing, and other health-related schools,** the operation of health care and social service providers and institutions, including "grass-roots" and community services organizations and programs, and **preschool and daycare programs.**

(4) Department of Housing and Urban Development: All programs, services, and regulatory activities relating to state and local public housing, and housing assistance and referral.

(5) Department of Interior: All programs, services, and regulatory activities relating to lands and natural resources, including parks and recreation, water and waste management, environmental protection, energy, historic and cultural preservation, and museums.

(6) Department of Justice: All programs, services, and regulatory activities relating to law enforcement, public safety, and the administration of justice, including courts and correctional institutions; commerce and industry, including general economic development, banking and finance, consumer protection, insurance, and small business; planning, development, and regulation (unless assigned to other designated agencies); state and local government support services (e.g., audit, personnel, comptroller, administrative services); all other government functions not assigned to other designated agencies.

(7) Department of Labor: All programs, services, and regulatory activities relating to labor and the work force.

(8) Department of Transportation: All programs, services, and regulatory activities relating to transportation, including highways, public transportation, traffic management (non-law enforcement), automobile licensing and inspection, and driver licensing.

(c) Responsibility for the implementation of subpart F of this part for components of State or local governments that exercise responsibilities, regulate, or administer services, programs, or activities relating to functions not assigned to specific designated agencies by paragraph (b) of this section may be assigned to other specific agencies by the Department of Justice.

(d) If two or more agencies have apparent responsibility over a complaint, the Assistant Attorney General shall determine which one of the agencies shall be the designated agency for purposes of that complaint.

(e) When the Department receives a complaint directed to the Attorney General alleging a violation of this part that may fall within the jurisdiction of a designated agency or another Federal agency that may have jurisdiction under section 504, the Department may exercise its discretion to retain the complaint for investigation under this part.

End of 28 CFR Part 35[40]

---

40   <Click here to return to the beginning of 28 CFR § 35.>

28 CFR Part 36 - Nondiscrimination on the Basis of Disability by Public Accommodations and in Commercial Facilities (Title III)

Part 36, also known as Title III, has the following Subparts and Sections. We have only included those regulations related to education and day care centers.

Subpart A - General (§§ 36.101 - 36.105)
Subpart B - General Requirements (§§ 36.201 - 36.213)
Subpart C - Specific Requirements (§§ 36.301 - 36.311)
Subpart D - New Construction and Alterations (§§ 36.401 - 36.406)
Subpart E - Enforcement (§§ 36.501 - 36.508)
Subpart F - Certification of State Laws or Local Building Codes (§§ 36.601 - 36.607)

Following the Subparts are six Appendices[41] that provide **guidance** and detail.

Appendix A to Part 36 - Guidance on Revisions to ADA Regulation on Nondiscrimination on the Basis of Disability by Public Accommodations and Commercial Facilities
Appendix B to Part 36 - Analysis and Commentary on the 2010 ADA Standards for Accessible Design
Appendix C to Part 36 - Guidance on ADA Regulation on Nondiscrimination on the Basis of Disability by Public Accommodations and in Commercial Facilities originally published on July 26, 1991
Appendix D to Part 36 - 1991 Standards for Accessible Design as Originally Published on July 26, 1991
Appendix E to Part 36 - Guidance to Revisions to ADA Title II and Title III Regulations Revising the Meaning and Interpretation of the Definition of "disability" and Other Provisions in Order To Incorporate the Requirements of the ADA Amendments Act
Appendix F to Part 36 - Guidance and Section-by-Section Analysis

The Part 36 - Public Accommodations (Title III) regulations we have included in this book are:
28 CFR Part 36, Subpart A - In General
28 CFR § 36.101 - Purpose and broad coverage
28 CFR § 36.102 - Application
28 CFR § 36.103 - Relationship to other laws
28 CFR § 36.104 - Definitions
28 CFR § 36.105 - Definition of "disability"

28 CFR Part 36, Subpart B - General Requirement
28 CFR § 36.201 - General
28 CFR § 36.202 - Activities
28 CFR § 36.203 - Integrated Settings
28 CFR § 36.204 - Administrative methods
28 CFR § 36.205 - Association
28 CFR § 36.206 - Retaliation or Coercion
28 CFR § 36.207 - Public Accommodations
28 CFR § 36.208 - Direct Threat
28 CFR § 36.211 - Maintenance of Accessible Features
28 CFR § 36.213 - Relationship of Subpart B to C and D

---

41   These appendices are available at: https://www.law.cornell.edu/cfr/text/28/part-36.

28 CFR Part 36, Subpart C - Specific Requirements
28 CFR § 36.301 - Eligibility Criteria
28 CFR § 36.302 - Modifications in Policies
28 CFR § 36.303 - Auxiliary Aids and Services
28 CFR § 36.304 - Removal of Barriers
28 CFR § 36.305 - Alternatives to Barrier Removal
28 CFR § 36.306 - Personal Devices and Services
28 CFR § 36.307 - Accessible or Special Goods
28 CFR § 36.308 - Setting in Assembly Areas
28 CFR § 36.309 - Examinations and Courses
28 CFR § 36.311 - Mobility Devices

28 CFR Part 36, Subpart E - Enforcement
28 CFR § 36.501 - Private suits
28 CFR § 36.502 - Investigations and compliance reviews
28 CFR § 36.503 - Suit by the Attorney General
28 CFR § 36.504 - Relief
28 CFR § 36.505 - Attorneys fees
28 CFR § 36.506 - Alternative means of dispute resolution
28 CFR § 36.507 - Effect of unavailability of technical assistance

28 CFR Part 36, Subpart A - General

28 CFR § 36.101 - Purpose and broad coverage

(a) Purpose. The purpose of this part is to implement subtitle A of title III of the Americans with Disabilities Act of 1990 (42 U.S.C. 12181-12189), as amended by the ADA Amendments Act of 2008 (ADA Amendments Act) (Pub. L. 110-325, 122 Stat. 3553 (2008)), which prohibits discrimination on the basis of disability by covered public accommodations and requires places of public accommodation and commercial facilities to be designed, constructed, and altered in compliance with the accessibility standards established by this part.

(b) Broad coverage. The primary purpose of the ADA Amendments Act is to make it easier for people with disabilities to obtain protection under the ADA. Consistent with the ADA Amendments Act's purpose of reinstating a broad scope of protection under the ADA, the definition of "disability" in this part shall be construed broadly in favor of expansive coverage to the maximum extent permitted by the terms of the ADA. The primary object of attention in cases brought under the ADA should be whether entities covered under the ADA have complied with their obligations and whether discrimination has occurred, not whether the individual meets the definition of "disability." The question of whether an individual meets the definition of "disability" under this part should not demand extensive analysis.

28 CFR § 36.102 - Application

(a) General. This part applies to any -

(1) Public accommodation;

(2) Commercial facility; or

(3) Private entity that offers examinations or courses related to applications, licensing, certification, or credentialing for secondary or postsecondary education, professional, or trade purposes.

(b) Public accommodations.

(1) The requirements of this part applicable to public accommodations are set forth in subparts B, C, and D of this part.

(2) The requirements of subparts B and C of this part obligate a public accommodation only with respect to the operations of a place of public accommodation.

(3) The requirements of subpart D of this part obligate a public accommodation only with respect to -

(i) A facility used as, or designed or constructed for use as, a place of public accommodation; or

(ii) A facility used as, or designed and constructed for use as, a commercial facility.

(c) Commercial facilities. The requirements of this part applicable to commercial facilities are set forth in subpart D of this part.

(d) Examinations and courses. The requirements of this part applicable to private entities that offer examinations or courses as specified in paragraph (a) of this section are set forth in § 36.309.

(e) Exemptions and exclusions. This part does not apply to any private club (except to the extent that the facilities of the private club are made available to customers or patrons of a place of public accommodation), or to any religious entity or public entity.

28 CFR § 36.103 - Relationship to other laws

(a) Rule of interpretation. Except as otherwise provided in this part, this part shall not be construed to apply a lesser standard than the standards applied under title V of the Rehabilitation Act of 1973 (29 U.S.C. 791) or the regulations issued by Federal agencies pursuant to that title.

(b) Section 504. This part does not affect the obligations of a recipient of Federal financial assistance to comply with the requirements of section 504 of the Rehabilitation Act of 1973 (29 U.S.C. 794) and regulations issued by Federal agencies implementing section 504.

(c) Other laws. This part does not invalidate or limit the remedies, rights, and procedures of any other Federal laws, or State or local laws (including State common law) that provide greater or equal protection for the rights of individuals with disabilities or individuals associated with them.

28 CFR § 36.104 - Definitions[42]

Place of public accommodation means a facility operated by a private entity whose operations affect commerce and fall within at least one of the following categories -

(8) A museum, library, gallery, or other place of public display or collection;

(9) A park, zoo, amusement park, or other place of recreation;

(10) A nursery, elementary, secondary, undergraduate, or postgraduate private school, or other place of education;

(11) A day care center, senior citizen center, homeless shelter, food bank, adoption agency, or other social service center establishment; and

(12) A gymnasium, health spa, bowling alley, golf course, or other **place of exercise or recreation**.

Public entity means -

(1) Any State or local government;

(2) Any department, agency, special purpose district, or other instrumentality of a State or States or local government; and . . .

Private entity means a person or entity other than a public entity.

Undue burden means significant difficulty or expense. In determining whether an action would result in an undue burden, factors to be considered include . . .

28 CFR § 36.105 - Definition of "disability"

(a)

(1) Disability means, with respect to an individual:

(i) A physical or mental impairment that **substantially limits** one or more of the major life activities of such individual;

(ii) A **record** of such an impairment; or

(iii) **Being regarded as having such an impairment** as described in paragraph (f) of this section.

(2) Rules of construction.

(i) The definition of "disability" shall be **construed broadly** in favor of expansive coverage, to the maximum extent permitted by the terms of the ADA.

(ii) An individual may establish coverage under any one or more of the three prongs of the definition of "disability" in paragraph (a)(1) of this section, the "actual disability" prong in paragraph (a)(1)(i) of this section, the "record of" prong in paragraph (a)(1)(ii) of this section, or the "regarded as" prong in paragraph (a)(1)(iii) of this section.

(iii) Where an individual is not challenging a public accommodation's failure to provide reasonable modifications under § 36.302, it is generally unnecessary to proceed under the "actual disability" or "record of" prongs, which require a showing of an impairment that substantially limits a major life activity or a record of such an impairment. In these cases, the evaluation of coverage can be made solely under the "regarded as" prong of the definition of "disability," which does not require a showing of an impairment that substantially limits a major life activity or a record of such an impairment. An individual may choose, however, to proceed under the "actual disability" or "record of" prong regardless

---

42   Many definitions are not included. This regulation repeats many of the regulations contained in Section 35.104 of Title II, with some additional definitions of numerous terms contained in the ADA, including but not limited to a qualified interpreter, qualified reader, service animal, and wheelchair. The full regulation is available at: https://www.law.cornell.edu/cfr/text/28/36.104.

of whether the individual is challenging a public accommodation's failure to provide reasonable modifications.

(b)

(1) Physical or mental impairment means:

(i) Any physiological disorder or condition, cosmetic disfigurement, or anatomical loss affecting one or more body systems, such as: Neurological, musculoskeletal, special sense organs, respiratory (including speech organs), cardiovascular, reproductive, digestive, genitourinary, immune, circulatory, hemic, lymphatic, skin, and endocrine; or

(ii) Any mental or psychological disorder such as **intellectual disability**, organic brain syndrome, emotional or mental illness, and **specific learning disability.**

(2) Physical or mental impairment **includes, but is not limited to,** contagious and noncontagious diseases and conditions such as the following: Orthopedic, visual, speech and hearing impairments, and cerebral palsy, epilepsy, muscular dystrophy, multiple sclerosis, cancer, heart disease, diabetes, intellectual disability, emotional illness, **dyslexia and other specific learning disabilities, Attention Deficit Hyperactivity Disorder,** Human Immunodeficiency Virus infection (whether symptomatic or asymptomatic), tuberculosis, drug addiction, and alcoholism.

(3) Physical or mental impairment does not include homosexuality or bisexuality.

(c)

(1) Major life activities include, but are not limited to:

(i) Caring for oneself, performing manual tasks, seeing, hearing, eating, sleeping, walking, standing, sitting, reaching, lifting, bending, speaking, breathing, learning, reading, concentrating, thinking, writing, communicating, interacting with others, and working; and

(ii) The operation of a major bodily function, such as the functions of the immune system, special sense organs and skin, normal cell growth, and digestive, genitourinary, bowel, bladder, neurological, brain, respiratory, circulatory, cardiovascular, endocrine, hemic, lymphatic, musculoskeletal, and reproductive systems. The operation of a major bodily function includes the operation of an individual organ within a body system.

(2) Rules of construction.

(i) In determining whether an impairment substantially limits a major life activity, the term major shall not be interpreted strictly to create a demanding standard.

(ii) Whether an activity is a major life activity is not determined by reference to whether it is of central importance to daily life.

(d) Substantially limits -

(1) Rules of construction. The following rules of construction apply when **determining whether an impairment substantially limits an individual in a major life activity.**

(i) The term "substantially limits" **shall be construed broadly** in favor of expansive coverage, to the maximum extent permitted by the terms of the ADA. "Substantially limits" is not meant to be a demanding standard.

(ii) The primary object of attention in cases brought under title III of the ADA should be whether public accommodations have complied with their obligations and whether discrimination has occurred, not the extent to which an individual's impairment substantially limits a major life activity. Accordingly, the threshold issue of **whether an impairment substantially limits a major life activity should not demand extensive analysis.**

(iii) An impairment that substantially limits one major life activity does not need to limit other major life activities in order to be considered a substantially limiting impairment.

(iv) An impairment that is **episodic or in remission is a disability** if it would substantially limit a major life activity **when active**.

(v) An impairment is a disability within the meaning of this part if it substantially limits the ability of an individual to perform a major life activity as compared to most people in the general population. An impairment does not need to prevent, or significantly or severely restrict, the individual from performing a major life activity in order to be considered substantially limiting. Nonetheless, not every impairment will constitute a disability within the meaning of this section.

(vi) The determination of whether an impairment substantially limits a major life activity requires an individualized assessment. However, in making this assessment, the term "substantially limits" shall be interpreted and applied to require a degree of functional limitation that is lower than the standard for substantially limits applied prior to the ADA Amendments Act.

(vii) The comparison of an individual's performance of a major life activity to the performance of the same major life activity by most people in the general population **usually will not require scientific, medical, or statistical evidence**. Nothing in this paragraph (d)(1) is intended, however, to prohibit or limit the presentation of scientific, medical, or statistical evidence in making such a comparison where appropriate.

(viii) The determination of whether an impairment substantially limits a major life activity shall be made **without regard to the ameliorative effects of mitigating measures**. However, the ameliorative effects of ordinary eyeglasses or contact lenses shall be considered in determining whether an impairment substantially limits a major life activity. Ordinary eyeglasses or contact lenses are lenses that are intended to fully correct visual acuity or to eliminate refractive error.

(ix) The six-month "transitory" part of the "transitory and minor" exception in paragraph (f)(2) of this section **does not apply to the "actual disability" or "record of" prongs of the definition of "disability."** The effects of an impairment lasting or expected to last less than six months can be substantially limiting within the meaning of this section for establishing an actual disability or a record of a disability.

(2) Predictable assessments.

(i) The principles set forth in the rules of construction in this section are intended to provide for more generous coverage and application of the ADA's prohibition on discrimination through **a framework that is predictable, consistent, and workable** for all individuals and entities with rights and responsibilities under the ADA.

(ii) Applying these principles, the individualized assessment of some types of impairments will, in virtually all cases, result in a determination of coverage under paragraph (a)(1)(i) of this section (the "**actual disability**" prong) **or** paragraph (a)(1)(ii) of this section (the "**record of**" prong). Given their inherent nature, these types of impairments will, as a factual matter, virtually always be found to impose a substantial limitation on a major life activity. Therefore, with respect to these types of impairments, the necessary individualized assessment should be particularly simple and straightforward.

(iii) For example, applying these principles it should easily be concluded that the types of impairments set forth in paragraphs **(d)(2)(iii)(A) through (K)** of this section will, at a minimum, substantially limit the major life activities indicated. The types of impairments described in this paragraph may substantially limit additional major life activities (including major bodily functions) not explicitly listed in paragraphs (d)(2)(iii)(A) through (K).

(A) Deafness substantially limits hearing;

(B) Blindness substantially limits seeing;

(C) Intellectual disability substantially limits brain function;

(D) Partially or completely missing limbs or mobility impairments requiring the use of a wheelchair substantially limit musculoskeletal function;

(E) Autism substantially limits brain function;

(F) Cancer substantially limits normal cell growth;

(G) Cerebral palsy substantially limits brain function;

(H) Diabetes substantially limits endocrine function;

(I) Epilepsy, muscular dystrophy, and multiple sclerosis each substantially limits neurological function;

(J) Human Immunodeficiency Virus (HIV) infection substantially limits immune function; and

(K) Major depressive disorder, bipolar disorder, post-traumatic stress disorder, traumatic brain injury, obsessive compulsive disorder, and schizophrenia each substantially limits brain function.

(3) Condition, manner, or duration.

(i) At all times taking into account the principles set forth in the rules of construction, in determining whether an individual is substantially limited in a major life activity, it may be useful in appropriate cases to consider, as compared to most people in the general population, the conditions under which the individual performs the major life activity; the manner in which the individual performs the major life activity; or the duration of time it takes the individual to perform the major life activity, or for which the individual can perform the major life activity.

(ii) Consideration of facts such as condition, manner, or duration may include, among other things, consideration of the difficulty, effort or time required to perform a major life activity; pain experienced when performing a major life activity; the length of time a major life activity can be performed; or the way an impairment affects the operation of a major bodily function. In addition, the non-ameliorative effects of mitigating measures, such as negative side effects of medication or burdens associated with following a particular treatment regimen, may be considered when determining whether an individual's impairment substantially limits a major life activity.

(iii) In determining whether an individual has a disability under the "actual disability" or "record of" prongs of the definition of "disability," the focus is on how a major life activity is substantially limited, and not on what outcomes an individual can achieve. For example, someone with a learning disability may achieve a high level of academic success, but may nevertheless be substantially limited in one or more major life activities, including, but not limited to, reading, writing, speaking, or learning because of the additional time or effort he or she must spend to read, write, speak, or learn compared to most people in the general population.

(iv) Given the rules of construction set forth in this section, it may often be unnecessary to conduct an analysis involving most or all of the facts related to condition, manner, or duration. This is particularly true with respect to impairments such as those described in paragraph (d)(2)(iii) of this section, which by their inherent nature should be easily found to impose a substantial limitation on a major life activity, and for which the individualized assessment should be particularly simple and straightforward.

(4) Mitigating measures include, but are not limited to:

(i) Medication, medical supplies, equipment, appliances, low-vision devices (defined as devices that magnify, enhance, or otherwise augment a visual image, but not including ordinary eyeglasses or contact lenses), prosthetics including limbs and devices, **hearing aid(s) and cochlear implant(s)** or other implantable hearing devices, mobility devices, and oxygen therapy equipment and supplies;

(ii) Use of **assistive technology;**

(iii) Reasonable modifications or auxiliary aids or services as defined in this regulation;

(iv) Learned behavioral or adaptive neurological modifications; or

(v) Psychotherapy, behavioral therapy, or physical therapy.

(e) Has a record of such an impairment.

(1) An individual has a record of such an impairment if the individual has **a history of, or has been misclassified** as having, a mental or physical impairment that substantially limits one or more major life activities.

(2) Broad construction. Whether an individual has a record of an impairment that substantially limited a major life activity shall be construed broadly to the maximum extent permitted by the ADA and should not demand extensive analysis. An individual will be considered to fall within this prong of the definition of "disability" if the individual has a history of an impairment that substantially limited one or more major life activities when compared to most people in the general population, or was misclassified as having had such an impairment. In determining whether an impairment substantially limited a major life activity, the principles articulated in paragraph (d)(1) of this section apply.

(3) Reasonable modification. An individual with a record of a substantially limiting impairment may be entitled to a reasonable modification if needed and related to the past disability.

(f) Is regarded as having such an impairment. The following principles apply under the "regarded as" prong of the definition of "disability" (paragraph (a)(1)(iii) of this section):

(1) Except as set forth in paragraph (f)(2) of this section, an individual is "regarded as having such an impairment" if the individual is subjected to a prohibited action because of an actual or perceived physical or mental impairment, whether or not that impairment substantially limits, or is perceived to substantially limit, a major life activity, even if the public accommodation asserts, or may or does ultimately establish, a defense to the action prohibited by the ADA.

(2) An individual is not "regarded as having such an impairment" if the public accommodation demonstrates that the impairment is, objectively, both "transitory" and "minor." A public accommodation may not defeat "regarded as" coverage of an individual simply by demonstrating that it subjectively believed the impairment was transitory and minor; rather, the public accommodation must demonstrate that the impairment is (in the case of an actual impairment) or would be (in the case of a perceived impairment), objectively, both "transitory" and "minor." For purposes of this section, "transitory" is defined as lasting or expected to last six months or less.

(3) Establishing that an individual is "regarded as having such an impairment" does not, by itself, establish liability. Liability is established under title III of the ADA only when an individual proves that a public accommodation discriminated on the basis of disability within the meaning of title III of the ADA, 42 U.S.C. 12181-12189.

(g) Exclusions. The term **"disability" does not include** -

(1) Transvestism, transsexualism, pedophilia, exhibitionism, voyeurism, gender identity disorders not resulting from physical impairments, or other sexual behavior disorders;

(2) Compulsive gambling, kleptomania, or pyromania; or

(3) Psychoactive substance use disorders resulting from current illegal use of drugs.

28 CFR Part 36, Subpart B - General Requirements

28 CFR § 36.201 - General

(a) Prohibition of discrimination. No individual shall be discriminated against on the basis of disability in the full and equal enjoyment of the goods, services, facilities, privileges, advantages, or accommodations of any place of public accommodation by any private entity who owns, leases (or leases to), or operates a place of public accommodation.

(b) Landlord and tenant responsibilities. Both the landlord who owns the building that houses a place of public accommodation and the tenant who owns or operates the place of public accommodation are public accommodations subject to the requirements of this part. As between the parties, allocation of responsibility for complying with the obligations of this part may be determined by lease or other contract.

(c) Claims of no disability. Nothing in this part shall provide the **basis for a claim that an individual without a disability was subject to discrimination** because of a lack of disability, including a claim that an individual with a disability was granted a reasonable modification that was denied to an individual without a disability.

28 CFR § 36.202 - Activities

(a) Denial of participation. A public accommodation shall not subject an individual or class of individuals on the basis of a disability or disabilities of such individual or class, directly, or through contractual, licensing, or other arrangements, to a denial of the opportunity of the individual or class to participate in or benefit from the goods, services, facilities, privileges, advantages, or accommodations of a place of public accommodation.

(b) Participation in unequal benefit. A public accommodation shall not afford an individual or class of individuals, on the basis of a disability or disabilities of such individual or class, directly, or through contractual, licensing, or other arrangements, with the opportunity to participate in or benefit from a good, service, facility, privilege, advantage, or accommodation that is not equal to that afforded to other individuals.

(c) Separate benefit. A public accommodation shall not provide an individual or class of individuals, on the basis of a disability or disabilities of such individual or class, directly, or through contractual, licensing, or other arrangements with a good, service, facility, privilege, advantage, or accommodation that is different or separate from that provided to other individuals, unless such action is necessary to provide the individual or class of individuals with a good, service, facility, privilege, advantage, or accommodation, or other opportunity that is as effective as that provided to others.

(d) Individual or class of individuals. For purposes of paragraphs (a) through (c) of this section, the term "individual or class of individuals" refers to the clients or customers of the public accommodation that enters into the contractual, licensing, or other arrangement.

28 CFR § 36.203 - Integrated settings

(a) General. A public accommodation shall afford goods, services, facilities, privileges, advantages, and accommodations to an individual with a disability in the most integrated setting appropriate to the needs of the individual.

(b) Opportunity to participate. Notwithstanding the existence of separate or different programs or activities provided in accordance with this subpart, a public accommodation shall not deny an individual with a disability an opportunity to participate in such programs or activities that are not separate or different.

(c) Accommodations and services.

(1) Nothing in this part shall be construed to require an individual with a disability **to accept an accommodation**, aid, service, opportunity, or benefit available under this part that such individual chooses not to accept.

(2) Nothing in the Act or this part authorizes the representative or guardian of an individual with a disability to decline food, water, medical treatment, or medical services for that individual.

28 CFR § 36.204 Administrative methods

A public accommodation **shall not**, directly or through contractual or other arrangements, **utilize standards or criteria or methods** of administration that **have the effect of discriminating** on the basis of disability, or that perpetuate the discrimination of others who are subject to common administrative control.

28 CFR § 36.205 Association

A public accommodation shall not exclude or otherwise deny equal goods, services, facilities, privileges, advantages, accommodations, or other opportunities to an individual or entity because of the known disability of an individual with whom the individual or entity is known to have a relationship or association.

28 CFR § 36.206 Retaliation or coercion

(a) No private or public entity shall discriminate against any individual because that individual **has opposed any act or practice** made unlawful by this part, or because that individual made a charge, testified, assisted, or participated in any manner in an investigation, proceeding, or hearing under the Act or this part.

(b) No private or public entity shall **coerce, intimidate, threaten, or interfere** with any individual in the exercise or enjoyment of, or on account of his or her having exercised or enjoyed, or on account of his or her having aided or encouraged any other individual in the exercise or enjoyment of, any right granted or protected by the Act or this part.

(c) Illustrations of conduct prohibited by this section **include, but are not limited to:**

(1) Coercing an individual to deny or limit the benefits, services, or advantages to which he or she is entitled under the Act or this part;

(2) Threatening, intimidating, or interfering with an individual with a disability who is seeking to obtain or use the goods, services, facilities, privileges, advantages, or accommodations of a public accommodation;

(3) Intimidating or threatening any person because that person is assisting or encouraging an individual or group entitled to claim the rights granted or protected by the Act or this part to exercise those rights; or

(4) Retaliating against any person because that person has participated in any investigation or action to enforce the Act or this part.

28 CFR § 36.207 Places of public accommodation located in private residences

(a) When a place of public accommodation is **located in a private residence,** the portion of the residence used exclusively as a residence is not covered by this part, but that portion used exclusively in the operation of the place of public accommodation or **that portion used both** for the place of public accommodation and for residential purposes **is covered** by this part.

(b) The portion of the residence covered under paragraph (a) of this section extends to those elements used to enter the place of public accommodation, **including the homeowner's front sidewalk**, if any, the door or entryway, and hallways; and those portions of the residence, interior or exterior, available to or used by customers or clients, including restrooms.

28 CFR § 36.208 Direct threat

(a) This part does not require a public accommodation to permit an individual to participate in or benefit from the goods, services, facilities, privileges, advantages and accommodations of that public accommodation when that individual poses a direct threat to the health or safety of others.

(b) In determining whether an individual poses a direct threat to the health or safety of others, a public accommodation must make an individualized assessment, based on reasonable judgment that relies on current medical knowledge or on the best available objective evidence, to ascertain: The nature, duration, and severity of the risk; the probability that the potential injury will actually occur; and whether reasonable modifications of policies, practices, or procedures or the provision of auxiliary aids or services will mitigate the risk.

28 CFR § 36.211 Maintenance of accessible features[43]

(a) A public accommodation shall maintain in operable working condition those features of facilities and equipment that are required to be readily accessible to and usable by persons with disabilities by the Act or this part.

(b) This section does not prohibit isolated or temporary interruptions in service or access due to maintenance or repairs.

(c) If the 2010 Standards reduce the technical requirements or the number of required accessible elements below the number required by the 1991 Standards, the technical requirements or the number of accessible elements in a facility subject to this part may be reduced in accordance with the requirements of the 2010 Standards.

28 CFR § 36.213 Relationship of subpart B to subparts C and D of this part

Subpart B of this part sets forth the **general principles of nondiscrimination** applicable to all entities subject to this part. Subparts C and D of this part provide guidance on the application of the statute to **specific situation**s. The **specific provisions**, including the limitations on those provisions, **control over the general provisions** in circumstances where both specific and general provisions apply.

28 CFR Part 36, Subpart C - Specific Requirements

28 CFR § 36.301 Eligibility criteria

(a) General. A public accommodation shall not impose or apply eligibility criteria that screen out or tend to screen out an individual with a disability or any class of individuals with disabilities from fully and equally enjoying any goods, services, facilities, privileges, advantages, or accommodations, unless such criteria can be shown to be necessary for the provision of the goods, services, facilities, privileges, advantages, or accommodations being offered.

(b) Safety. A public accommodation **may impose legitimate safety requirement**s that are necessary for safe operation. Safety requirements must be based on actual risks and not on mere speculation, stereotypes, or generalizations about individuals with disabilities.

(c) Charges. A public accommodation **may not impose a surcharge** on a particular individual with a disability or any group of individuals with disabilities to cover the costs of measures, such as the provision of auxiliary aids, barrier removal, alternatives to barrier removal, and reasonable modifications in policies, practices, or procedures, that are required to provide that individual or group with the nondiscriminatory treatment required by the Act or this part.

28 CFR § 36.302 Modifications in policies, practices, or procedures

(a) General. A public accommodation shall make reasonable modifications in policies, practices, or procedures, when the modifications are necessary to afford goods, services, facilities, privileges, advantages, or accommodations to individuals with disabilities, unless the public accommodation can demonstrate that making the modifications would fundamentally alter the nature of the goods, services, facilities, privileges, advantages, or accommodations.

(b) through (g) [not included][44]

28 CFR § 36.303 Auxiliary aids and services

(a) General. A public accommodation shall take those steps that may be necessary to ensure that no individual with a disability is excluded, denied services, segregated or otherwise treated differently than other individuals because of the absence of auxiliary aids and services, unless the public accommodation can demonstrate that taking those steps would fundamentally alter the nature of the goods, services, facilities, privileges, advantages,

---

43 **Wrightslaw Note:** We omitted three regulations relating to smoking, drug usage, and insurance. (Sections 36.209, 210, and 212.).

44 Available at: https://www.law.cornell.edu/cfr/text/28/36.302.

or accommodations being offered or would result in an undue burden, i.e., significant difficulty or expense.[45]

(b) Examples. The term "auxiliary aids and services" includes -

(1) Qualified interpreters on-site or through video remote interpreting (VRI) services; notetakers; real-time computer-aided transcription services; written materials; exchange of written notes; telephone handset amplifiers; assistive listening devices; assistive listening systems; telephones compatible with hearing aids; closed caption decoders; open and closed captioning, including real-time captioning; voice, text, and video-based telecommunications products and systems, including text telephones (TTYs), videophones, and captioned telephones, or equally effective telecommunications devices; videotext displays; accessible electronic and information technology; or other effective methods of making aurally delivered information available to individuals who are deaf or hard of hearing;

(2) Qualified readers; taped texts; audio recordings; Brailled materials and displays; screen reader software; magnification software; optical readers; secondary auditory programs (SAP); large print materials; accessible electronic and information technology; or other effective methods of making visually delivered materials available to individuals who are blind or have low vision;

(3) Acquisition or modification of equipment or devices; and

(4) Other similar services and actions.

(c) Effective communication.

(1) A public accommodation **shall furnish appropriate auxiliary aids and services** where necessary to ensure effective communication with individuals with disabilities. This includes an obligation to provide effective communication to companions who are individuals with disabilities.

(i) For purposes of this section, "companion" means a family member, friend, or associate of an individual seeking access to, or participating in, the goods, services, facilities, privileges, advantages, or accommodations of a public accommodation, who, along with such individual, is an appropriate person with whom the public accommodation should communicate.

(ii) The type of auxiliary aid or service necessary to ensure effective communication will vary in accordance with the method of communication used by the individual; the nature, length, and complexity of the communication involved; and the context in which the communication is taking place. A public accommodation should consult with individuals with disabilities whenever possible to determine what type of auxiliary aid is needed to ensure effective communication, but the ultimate decision as to what measures to take rests with the public accommodation, provided that the method chosen results in effective communication. In order to be effective, auxiliary aids and services must be provided in accessible formats, in a timely manner, and in such a way as to protect the privacy and independence of the individual with a disability.

(2) A public accommodation shall not require an individual with a disability to bring another individual to interpret for him or her.

(3) A public accommodation shall not rely on an adult accompanying an individual with a disability to interpret or facilitate communication, except -

(i) In an emergency involving an imminent threat to the safety or welfare of an individual or the public where there is no interpreter available; or

(ii) Where the individual with a disability specifically requests that the accompanying adult interpret or facilitate communication, the accompanying adult agrees to provide such assistance, and reliance on that adult for such assistance is appropriate under the circumstances.

(4) A public accommodation shall not rely on a minor child to interpret or facilitate communication, except

---

45   Undue burden has a more expansive definition in 28 CFR § 104.4.

in an emergency involving an imminent threat to the safety or welfare of an individual or the public where there is no interpreter available.

(d) Telecommunications. [not included]

(e) Closed caption decoders. Places of lodging that provide televisions in five or more guest rooms and hospitals that provide televisions for patient use shall provide, upon request, a means for decoding captions for use by an individual with impaired hearing.

(f) Video remote interpreting (VRI) services. A public accommodation that chooses to provide qualified interpreters via VRI service shall ensure that it provides -

(1) Real-time, full-motion video and audio over a dedicated high-speed, wide-bandwidth video connection or wireless connection that delivers high-quality video images that do not produce lags, choppy, blurry, or grainy images, or irregular pauses in communication;

(2) A sharply delineated image that is large enough to display the interpreter's face, arms, hands, and fingers, and the participating individual's face, arms, hands, and fingers, regardless of his or her body position;

(3) A clear, audible transmission of voices; and

(4) Adequate training to users of the technology and other involved individuals so that they may quickly and efficiently set up and operate the VRI.

(g) Movie theater captioning and audio description - not included

(h) Alternatives. If provision of a particular auxiliary aid or service by a public accommodation would result in a fundamental alteration in the nature of the goods, services, facilities, privileges, advantages, or accommodations being offered or in an undue burden, i.e., significant difficulty or expense, the public accommodation shall provide an alternative auxiliary aid or service, if one exists, that would not result in an alteration or such burden but would nevertheless ensure that, to the maximum extent possible, individuals with disabilities receive the goods, services, facilities, privileges, advantages, or accommodations offered by the public accommodation.

28 CFR § 36.304 Removal of barriers

(a) General. A public accommodation shall remove architectural barriers in existing facilities, including communication barriers that are structural in nature, where such removal is readily achievable, i.e., easily accomplishable and able to be carried out without much difficulty or expense.

(b) Examples. Examples of steps to remove barriers include, but are not limited to, the following actions -

(1) Installing ramps;

(2) Making curb cuts in sidewalks and entrances;

(3) Repositioning shelves;

(4) Rearranging tables, chairs, vending machines, display racks, and other furniture;

(5) Repositioning telephones;

(6) Adding raised markings on elevator control buttons;

(7) Installing flashing alarm lights;

(8) Widening doors;

(9) Installing offset hinges to widen doorways;

(10) Eliminating a turnstile or providing an alternative accessible path;

(11) Installing accessible door hardware;

(12) Installing grab bars in toilet stalls;

(13) Rearranging toilet partitions to increase maneuvering space;

(14) Insulating lavatory pipes under sinks to prevent burns;

(15) Installing a raised toilet seat;

(16) Installing a full-length bathroom mirror;

(17) Repositioning the paper towel dispenser in a bathroom;

(18) Creating designated accessible parking spaces;

(19) Installing an accessible paper cup dispenser at an existing inaccessible water fountain;

(20) Removing high pile, low density carpeting; or

(21) Installing vehicle hand controls.

Subsections (c) and (d) [not included]

28 CFR § 36.305 Alternatives to barrier removal

(a) General. Where a public accommodation can demonstrate that barrier removal is not readily achievable, the public accommodation shall not fail to make its goods, services, facilities, privileges, advantages, or accommodations available through alternative methods, if those methods are readily achievable.

(b) Examples. Examples of alternatives to barrier removal include, but are not limited to, the following actions -

(1) Providing curb service or home delivery;

(2) Retrieving merchandise from inaccessible shelves or racks;

(3) Relocating activities to accessible locations;

(c) Multiscreen cinemas. [not included'

28 CFR § 36.306 - Personal devices and services

This part does not require a public accommodation to provide its customers, clients, or participants with personal devices, such as wheelchairs; individually prescribed devices, such as prescription eyeglasses or hearing aids; or services of a personal nature including assistance in eating, toileting, or dressing.

28 CFR § 36.307 - Accessible or special goods

(a) This part does not require a public accommodation to alter its inventory to include accessible or special goods that are designed for, or facilitate use by, individuals with disabilities.

(b) A public accommodation shall order accessible or special goods at the request of an individual with disabilities, if, in the normal course of its operation, it makes special orders on request for unstocked goods, and if the accessible or special goods can be obtained from a supplier with whom the public accommodation customarily does business.

(c) Examples of accessible or special goods include items such as Brailled versions of books, books on audio cassettes, closed-captioned video tapes, special sizes or lines of clothing, and special foods to meet particular dietary needs.

28 CFR § 36.308 - Seating in assembly areas

A public accommodation **shall ensure that wheelchair spaces and companion seats are provided** in each specialty seating area that provides spectators with distinct services or amenities that generally are not available to other spectators. If it is not readily achievable for a public accommodation to place wheelchair spaces and companion seats in each such specialty seating area, it shall provide those services or amenities to individuals with disabilities and their companions at other designated accessible locations at no additional cost. The number of wheelchair spaces and companion seats provided in specialty seating areas shall be included in, rather than in addition to, wheelchair space requirements set forth in table 221.2.1.1 in the 2010 Standards.

28 CFR § 36.309 - Examinations and courses

(a) General. Any private entity that offers examinations or courses related to applications, licensing, certification, or credentialing for secondary or postsecondary education, professional, or trade purposes shall offer such examinations or courses in a place and manner accessible to persons with disabilities or offer alternative accessible arrangements for such individuals.

(b) Examinations.

(1) **Any private entity offering an examination** covered by this section must assure that -

(i) The examination is selected and administered so as to best ensure that, when the examination is administered to an individual with a disability that impairs sensory, manual, or speaking skills, the examination results accurately reflect the individual's aptitude or achievement level or whatever other factor the examination purports to measure, rather than reflecting the individual's impaired sensory, manual, or speaking skills (except where those skills are the factors that the examination purports to measure);

(ii) An examination that is designed for individuals with impaired sensory, manual, or speaking skills is offered at equally convenient locations, as often, and in as timely a manner as are other examinations; and

(iii) The examination is administered in facilities that are accessible to individuals with disabilities or alternative accessible arrangements are made.

(iv) Any request for documentation, if such documentation is required, is reasonable and limited to the need for the modification, accommodation, or auxiliary aid or service requested.

(v) When considering requests for modifications, accommodations, or auxiliary aids or services, the entity gives considerable weight to documentation of past modifications, accommodations, or auxiliary aids or services received in similar testing situations, as well as such modifications, accommodations, or related aids and services provided in response to an Individualized Education Program (IEP) provided under the Individuals with Disabilities Education Act or a plan describing services provided pursuant to section 504 of the Rehabilitation Act of 1973, as amended (often referred to as a Section 504 Plan).

(vi) The entity responds in a timely manner to requests for modifications, accommodations, or aids to ensure equal opportunity for individuals with disabilities.

(2) **Required modifications to an examination** may include changes in the length of time permitted for completion of the examination and adaptation of the manner in which the examination is given.

(3) **A private entity offering an examination covered by this section shall provide** appropriate auxiliary aids for persons with impaired sensory, manual, or speaking skills, **unless that private entity** can demonstrate that offering a particular auxiliary aid would fundamentally alter the measurement of the skills or knowledge the examination is intended to test or would result in an **undue burden**. Auxiliary aids and services required by this section may include taped examinations, interpreters or other effective methods of making orally delivered materials available to individuals with hearing impairments, Brailled or large print examinations and answer sheets or qualified readers for individuals with visual impairments or learning disabilities, transcribers for individuals with manual impairments, and other similar services and actions.

(4) Alternative accessible arrangements may include, for example, provision of an examination at an individual's home with a proctor if accessible facilities or equipment are unavailable. Alternative arrangements must provide comparable conditions to those provided for nondisabled individuals.

(c) Courses.

(1) Any private entity that offers a course covered by this section must make such modifications to that course as are necessary to ensure that the place and manner in which the course is given are accessible to individuals with disabilities.

(2) Required modifications **may include changes in the length of time permitted** for the completion of the course, **substitution of specific requirements,** or adaptation of the manner in which the course is conducted

or course materials are distributed.

(3) **A private entity that offers a course** covered by this section **shall provide** appropriate auxiliary aids and services for persons with impaired sensory, manual, or speaking skills, unless the private entity can demonstrate that offering a particular auxiliary aid or service would fundamentally alter the course or would result in an undue burden. Auxiliary aids and services required by this section may include taped texts, interpreters or **other effective methods of making orally delivered materials available to individuals with hearing impairments**, Brailled or large print texts or qualified readers for individuals with visual impairments and learning disabilities, classroom equipment adapted for use by individuals with manual impairments, and other similar services and actions.

(4) Courses must be administered in facilities that are accessible to individuals with disabilities or alternative accessible arrangements must be made.

(5) Alternative accessible arrangements may include, for example, provision of the course through videotape, cassettes, or prepared notes. Alternative arrangements must provide comparable conditions to those provided for nondisabled individuals.

28 CFR § 36.310 - Transportation provided by public accommodations (not included)

28 CFR § 36.311 Mobility devices

(a) Use of wheelchairs and manually-powered mobility aids. A public accommodation shall permit individuals with mobility disabilities to use wheelchairs and manually-powered mobility aids, such as walkers, crutches, canes, braces, or other similar devices designed for use by individuals with mobility disabilities in any areas open to pedestrian use.

(b)

(1) Use of other power-driven mobility devices. A public accommodation shall make reasonable modifications in its policies, practices, or procedures to permit the use of other power-driven mobility devices by individuals with mobility disabilities, unless the public accommodation can demonstrate that the class of other power-driven mobility devices cannot be operated in accordance with legitimate safety requirements that the public accommodation has adopted pursuant to § 36.301(b).

(2) Assessment factors. In determining whether a particular other power-driven mobility device can be allowed in a specific facility as a reasonable modification under paragraph (b)(1) of this section, a public accommodation **shall consider** -

(i) The type, size, weight, dimensions, and speed of the device;

(ii) The facility's volume of pedestrian traffic (which may vary at different times of the day, week, month, or year);

(iii) The facility's design and operational characteristics (e.g., whether its business is conducted indoors, its square footage, the density and placement of stationary devices, and the availability of storage for the device, if requested by the user);

(iv) Whether legitimate safety requirements can be established to permit the safe operation of the other power-driven mobility device in the specific facility; and

(v) Whether the use of the other power-driven mobility device creates a substantial risk of serious harm to the immediate environment or natural or cultural resources, or poses a conflict with Federal land management laws and regulations.

(c)

(1) **Inquiry about disability.** A public accommodation **shall not ask an individual** using a wheelchair or other power-driven mobility device **questions** about the nature and extent of the individual's disability.

(2) Inquiry into use of other power-driven mobility device. A public accommodation **may ask a** person using an other power-driven mobility device **to provide a credible assurance that the mobility device is required** because of the person's disability. A public accommodation that permits the use of an other power-driven mobility device by an individual with a mobility disability shall accept the presentation of a valid, State-issued disability parking placard or card, or State-issued proof of disability, as a credible assurance that the use of the other power-driven mobility device is for the individual's mobility disability. In lieu of a valid, State-issued disability parking placard or card, or State-issued proof of disability, a public accommodation shall accept as a credible assurance a verbal representation, not contradicted by observable fact, that the other power-driven mobility device is being used for a mobility disability. A "valid" disability placard or card is one that is presented by the individual to whom it was issued and is otherwise in compliance with the State of issuance's requirements for disability placards or cards.

28 CFR Part 36, Subpart D - New Construction [*not included*][46]

28 CFR Part 36, Subpart E - Enforcement

28 CFR § 36.501 - Private suits

(a) General. Any person who is being subjected to discrimination on the basis of disability in violation of the Act or this part or who has reasonable grounds for believing that such person is about to be subjected to discrimination in violation of section 303 of the Act or subpart D of this part **may institute a civil action** for preventive relief, including an application for a permanent or temporary injunction, restraining order, or other order. Upon timely application, the court may, in its discretion, permit the Attorney General to intervene in the civil action if the Attorney General or his or her designee **certifies that the case is of general public importance.** Upon application by the complainant and in such circumstances as the court may deem just, the court **may appoint an attorney** for such complainant and may authorize the commencement of the civil action without the payment of fees, costs, or security. Nothing in this section shall require a person with a disability to engage in a futile gesture if the person has actual notice that a person or organization covered by title III of the Act or this part does not intend to comply with its provisions.

(b) Injunctive relief. In the case of violations of § 36.304, §§ 36.308, 36.310(b), 36.401, 36.402, 36.403, and 36.405 of this part, injunctive relief shall include an order to alter facilities to make such facilities readily accessible to and usable by individuals with disabilities to the extent required by the Act or this part. Where appropriate, injunctive relief shall also include requiring the provision of an auxiliary aid or service, modification of a policy, or provision of alternative methods, to the extent required by the Act or this part.

28 CFR § 36.502 - Investigations and compliance reviews

(a) The Attorney General shall investigate alleged violations of the Act or this part.

(b) Any individual who believes that he or she or a specific class of persons has been subjected to discrimination prohibited by the Act or this part may request the Department to institute an investigation.

(c) Where the Attorney General has reason to believe that there may be a violation of this part, he or she may initiate a compliance review.

28 CFR Section § 36.503 - Suit by the Attorney General

Following a compliance review or investigation under § 36.502, or at any other time in his or her discretion, the Attorney General **may commence a civil actio**n in any appropriate United States district court if the Attorney General has reasonable cause to believe that -

(a) Any person or group of persons is engaged in a pattern or practice of discrimination in violation of the Act or this part; or

(b) Any person or group of persons has been discriminated against in violation of the Act or this part and the discrimination raises an issue of general public importance.

---

46   Available at: https://www.law.cornell.edu/cfr/text/28/part-36/subpart-D.

28 CFR § 36.504 - Relief

(a) Authority of court. In a civil action under § 36.503, the court -

(1) May grant any **equitable relief that such court considers to be appropriate**, including, to the extent required by the Act or this part -

(i) Granting temporary, preliminary, or permanent relief;

(ii) Providing an auxiliary aid or service, modification of policy, practice, or procedure, or alternative method; and

(iii) Making facilities readily accessible to and usable by individuals with disabilities;

(2) May award other relief as the court considers to be appropriate, **including monetary damages** to persons aggrieved when requested by the Attorney General; and

(3) May, to vindicate the public interest, assess a civil penalty against the entity in an amount

(i) Not exceeding $50,000 for a first violation occurring before September 29, 1999, and not exceeding $55,000 for a first violation occurring on or after September 29, 1999, and before April 28, 2014, and not exceeding $75,000 for a first violation occurring on or after April 28, 2014, except that, for civil penalties assessed after August 1, 2016, for a first violation occurring after November 2, 2015, the civil penalty shall not exceed the applicable amount set forth in 28 CFR 85.5.

(ii) Not exceeding $100,000 for any subsequent violation occurring before September 29, 1999, and not exceeding $110,000 for any subsequent violation occurring on or after September 29, 1999, and before April 28, 2014, and not exceeding $150,000 for any subsequent violation occurring on or after April 28, 2014, except that, for civil penalties assessed after August 1, 2016, for any subsequent violation occurring after November 2, 2015, the civil penalty shall not exceed the applicable amount set forth in 28 CFR 85.5.

(b) **Single violation.** For purposes of paragraph (a) (3) of this section, in determining whether a first or subsequent violation has occurred, a determination in a single action, by judgment or settlement, that the covered entity has engaged in more than one discriminatory act shall be counted as a single violation.

(c) **Punitive damages.** For purposes of paragraph (a)(2) of this section, the terms "monetary damages" and "such other relief" do not include punitive damages.

(d) **Judicial consideration.** In a civil action under § 36.503, the court, when considering what amount of civil penalty, if any, is appropriate, shall give consideration to any good faith effort or attempt to comply with this part by the entity. In evaluating good faith, the court shall consider, among other factors it deems relevant, whether the entity could have reasonably anticipated the need for an appropriate type of auxiliary aid needed to accommodate the unique needs of a particular individual with a disability.

28 CFR § 36.505 - Attorneys fees

In any action or administrative proceeding commenced pursuant to the Act or this part, the court or agency, in its discretion, may allow the prevailing party, other than the United States, a reasonable attorney's fee, including litigation expenses, and costs, and the United States shall be liable for the foregoing the same as a private individual.

28 CFR § 36.506 - Alternative means of dispute resolution

Where appropriate and to the extent authorized by law, the use of alternative means of dispute resolution, including settlement negotiations, conciliation, facilitation, mediation, factfinding, minitrials, and arbitration, is encouraged to resolve disputes arising under the Act and this part.

28 CFR § 36.507 - Effect of unavailability of technical assistance

A public accommodation or other private entity shall not be excused from compliance with the requirements of this part because of any failure to receive technical assistance, including any failure in the development or dissemination of any technical assistance manual authorized by the Act.

28 CFR § 36.508 - Effective date. [not included]

28 CFR Part 36, Subpart F - Certification of State Laws or Local Building Codes [not included]

End of 28 CFR Part 36[47]

28 CFR Part 41, Implementation of Executive Order 12250 - Nondiscrimination on the basis of handicap in federally assisted programs

28 CFR Part 41 has three subparts,[48] **listed below:**
Subpart A - Federal Agency Responsibilities (§§ 41.1 - 41.7)
Subpart B - Standards for Determining Who Are Handicapped Persons (§§ 41.31 - 41.32)
Subpart C - Guidelines for Determining Discriminatory Practices (§§ 41.51 - 41.58)
Included below are two of the regulations -

28 CFR § 41.5 - Enforcement.

(a) Each agency shall establish a system for the enforcement of section 504 and its implementing regulation with respect to the programs and activities to which it provides assistance. The system shall include:

(1) The enforcement and hearing procedures that the agency has adopted for the enforcement of title VI of the Civil Rights Act of 1964, and

(2) A requirement that recipients sign assurances of compliance with section 504.

(b) Each agency regulation shall also include requirements that recipients:

(1) Notify employees and beneficiaries of their rights under section 504,

(2) Conduct a self-evaluation of their compliance with section 504, with the assistance of interested persons, including handicapped persons or organizations representing handicapped persons, and

(3) Otherwise consult with interested persons, including handicapped persons or organizations representing handicapped persons, in achieving compliance with section 504.

28 CFR § 41.51 General prohibitions against discrimination.

(a) No qualified handicapped person, shall, on the basis of handicap, be excluded from participation in, be denied the benefits of, or otherwise be subjected to discrimination under any program or activity that receives or benefits from federal financial assistance.

(b) [not included]

(c) [not included]

(d) Recipients shall administer programs and activities in the **most integrated setting** appropriate to the needs of qualified handicapped persons.

(e) Recipients shall take appropriate steps to ensure that communications with their applicants, employees, and beneficiaries are available to persons with impaired vision and hearing.

---

47   <Click here to return to the beginning of 28 CFR § 36.>

48   All of the Part 41 regulations are available here: https://www.law.cornell.edu/cfr/text/28/part-41

In Summation

In this Chapter 8, you learned about the Americans with Disabilities Act and its relationship with Section 504, Like Section 504, much of the basis of the ADA is in the regulations. While Part 35 (Title II) is similar to Section 504, Part 36 (Title III) covers private entities, even if they do not receive federal financial assistance. This includes private schools, daycare centers, licensing boards, but not entities controlled by religious organization.

In **Chapter 9**, you will learn about the **Family Educational and Rights and Privacy Act (FERPA)**. We omitted the statute since the bulk is in the "regulations" which are provided in an FAQ format located in 34 CFR Part 99.

Included in the chapter is the **McKinney-Vento Homeless Assistance Act** (42 U.S.C. § 11431) which mandates that homeless children have "equal access to the same free, appropriate public education" as children who are not homeless and that school districts shall make decisions in the best interest of the child.

We have included **other federal statutes** from Title 28 that are present from time to time in special education issues. The statutes are Federal Question, Civil Rights, Removal of case to federal court, Creation of remedy, and Further relief (Sections 1331, 1343, 1441, 2201, and 2202) and 42 U.S.C. § 1983 - Civil action for deprivation of rights.

In the next chapter are a few of the Federal Rules of Civil Procedure (FRCP) and portions of the United States Constitution that are frequently referenced in caselaw.

End of Chapter 8 - ADA Statute and Regulations

Hyperlinks to Chapters

Ch. 01 Introduction	Ch. 06 IDEA Regulations
Ch. 02 History	Ch. 07 Section 504
Ch. 03 Overview of Law, Courts, Research	Ch. 08 ADA
Ch. 04 Overview of IDEA, Section 504, ADA	Ch. 09 Other laws
Ch. 05 IDEA (US Code)	Ch. 10 Selected Topics

CHAPTER 9

Family Educational Rights and Privacy Act
McKinney-Vento Homeless Assistance Act
Other Federal Statutes
Federal Rules of Civil Procedure
U.S. Constitution

You may recall in Chapter 5, we refer to Section 1412 of the Individuals with Disabilities Act as the "catch-all statute" because it covers many topics, from child find, least restrictive environment, unilateral placements, reimbursement, and to assessments, by states and districts.

Chapter 9 is the "catch-all chapter" of this book. This chapter includes portions of two statutes that often affect the education of children with disabilities. They are the **Family Educational Rights and Privacy Act (FERPA)** and the **McKinney-Vento Homeless Assistance Act**.

Chapter 9 also has portions of the **United States Code** and the **Federal Rules of Civil Procedure (FRCP)** that are frequently referenced in federal court special education and disability cases. Finally, because many education and disability-related cases include allegations that the defendant violated Article VI, and/or the First, Fourth, Fifth, and Fourteenth Amendments, this chapter ends with text from the U.S. Constitution.

Family Educational Rights and Privacy Act (FERPA)
20 U.S.C. § 1232g / 34 CFR Part 99

The **Family Educational Rights and Privacy Act of 1974 (FERPA)**[1] deals with education records, privacy and confidentiality, parent access to education records, parent amendment of records, and destruction of records. The purpose of this statute and the next, **Protection of Pupil Rights Amendment (PPRA),**[2] is to protect the privacy of students and parents. FERPA applies to all agencies and institutions that receive federal funds, including elementary and secondary schools, colleges, and universities.

Immediately following FERPA (§1232g) is the "**Protection of Pupil Rights**" statute (§1232h), which establishes that parents have the right to inspect instructional materials, including teacher's manuals and other materials and that students are not required to reveal any information about either their own or their parent's political or religious practices and beliefs.[3] In consultation with parents, school districts shall develop and adopt policies in regard to

---

1   20 U.S.C. § 1232g is available at: https://www.law.cornell.edu/uscode/text/20/1232g

2   20 U.S.C. § 1232h is available at: https://www.law.cornell.edu/uscode/text/20/1232h

3   20 U.S.C. § 1232h(b)

inspection of instructional materials and student privacy,[4] and provide notice to the parents in regard to any "substantive change in such policies."[5]

The **Family Educational Rights and Privacy Act of 1974 (FERPA)** is in the United States Code at 20 U.S.C. 1232g. The regulations are in the Code of Federal Regulations at 34 C.F.R. Part 99 in an FAQ format. FERPA has been amended several times since 1974. For more about the history, *see* the article by the "Electronic Privacy Information Center" (EPIC.org).[6] Key concepts in FERPA relate to the definition of education records, the rights to inspect and review such records, confidentiality, disclosure of personally identifiable information, and destruction of the records.

Education records

Education records means, "those records, files, documents, and other materials which (i) contain information directly related to a student; and (ii) are maintained by an educational agency or institution or by a person acting for such agency or institution." Personal notes and memory aids that are used only by the person who made them are not education records. They do not include **records that "are in the sole possession** of the maker thereof and which are not accessible or revealed" to others.[7] If the notes are shared with or disclosed to another individual, they become education records.

In addition to FERPA, pursuant to PPRA, "**All instructional materials**, including teacher's manuals, films, tapes, or other supplementary material which will be used in connection with any survey, analysis, or evaluation as part of any applicable program **shall be available for inspection** by the parents or guardians of the children."[8]

Test materials, including **test protocols** are education records and must be disclosed. In *Newport-Mesa Unified v. State of CA Dept of Ed.*, 371 F. Supp. 2d 1170 (CA 2005)[9] publishers of the Wechsler IQ test and the Woodcock-Johnson educational achievement test[10] were joined as "intervenors" in the litigation. The Court held that parents have a right to inspect and review their child's test protocols. See also the Wrightslaw YouTube video about the parent's right to review test protocols[11] and the *Newport-Mesa* federal case against the California DOE.

Right to Inspect and Review Education Records

Parents have a right to **inspect and review** all education records relating to their child. This right includes the right to have copies of records and to receive explanations and interpretations from school officials. Agencies must comply with requests to inspect and review records **within forty-five days**.[12]

The school must provide copies of records to the parent if the failure to do so would prevent the parent from exercising the right to view records. Schools may charge reasonable copying fees unless the fee would "effectively prevent" the parent or student from exercising the right to inspect and review the records. Fees may not be charged for searching and retrieving records.

---

4   20 U.S.C. § 1232h(c)(1)

5   20 U.S.C. § 1232h(c)(2)(A)

6   https://epic.org/family-educational-rights-and-privacy-act-ferpa/

7   20 U.S.C. § 1232g(4)(A+B) - personal notes not shared with another are excluded.

8   https://www.law.cornell.edu/uscode/text/20/1232h(a)

9   https://www.wrightslaw.com/law/caselaw/05/2005.CA.dist.court.newport-mesa.test.protocols.pdf

10   For more information about the Wechsler IQ test (WISC-V), the Wechsler Individual Achievement Test (WIAT), the Woodcock-Johnson's Tests of educational achievement and cognitive abilities, see our book - *Wrightslaw: All About Tests and Assessments, 2nd Ed*. available in our online store at: https://www.wrightslaw.com/store/

11   https://youtu.be/RxQoiMDpNuY

12   Some states have shorter timelines. Check your own state regulations. This issue might not be addressed in a state's special education regulations but instead the more global education regulations for your state.

"If circumstances effectively prevent the parent or eligible student from exercising the right to inspect and review the student's education records, the educational agency or institution, or SEA or its component, shall (1) Provide the parent or eligible student with a copy of the records requested; or (2) Make other arrangements for the parent or eligible student to inspect and review the requested records".[13]

If a parent believes their child's educational record contains inaccurate or misleading information, the parent may ask the agency to amend the record. The parent may also request a hearing to correct or challenge misleading or inaccurate information.[14]

Confidentiality and Personally Identifiable Information

Personally identifiable information may not be disclosed without written consent or pursuant to a court order or subpoena. Personal information is defined as **individually identifiable** information that includes, but is not limited to: (i) a student or parent's first and last name; (ii) a home or other physical address (including street name and the name of the city or town); (iii) a telephone number; or (iv) a Social Security identification number."[15]

The Privacy Technical Assistance Center and the Student Privacy Policy Office of the USDOE provides a website titled *Protecting Student Privacy*. That website contains instructions and videos about FERPA along with the form to file a FERPA / PPRA complaint online.[16]

Disclosure and Destruction of Records

Records may be released without consent to "other school officials, including teachers within the educational institution or local educational agency, who have been determined by such agency or institution to have legitimate educational interests". Records may be released to "officials of other schools or school systems in which the student seeks or intends to enroll, upon condition that the student's parents be notified of the transfer, receive a copy of the record if desired, and have an opportunity for a hearing to challenge the content of the record . . ."[17]

Directory information may be released without consent. Disclosures may be made without consent in health and safety emergencies. Law enforcement agencies and monitoring agencies have access to confidential records. The agency must maintain a log of all disclosures without parental consent. Consent for disclosure must be signed and dated and include information about the recipients of information.[18]

FERPA statute, 20 U.S.C. § 1232g

The FERPA statute, Section 1232g, includes subsections "a" through "j." Many of the statutes open with "**No funds shall be made available** under any applicable program to any educational agency or institution which has a policy or practice of . . ." and then lists and details the procedures that **should not be done,** such as denying an individual the right to inspect and view their records. The rest of FERPA and the **Protection of Pupil Rights** in Section 1232h, **are not reproduced in this book**.[19] FERPA contains ten subsections as follows:

(a) Conditions for availability of funds to educational agencies or institutions; inspection and review of education records; specific information to be made available; procedure for access to education records; reasonableness of time for such access; hearings; written explanations by parents; definitions

(b) Release of education records; parental consent requirement; exceptions; compliance with judicial orders and subpoenas; audit and evaluation of federally-supported education programs; recordkeeping

---

13 34 CFR § 99.10

14 20 U.S.C. § 1232g(a)(2)

15 20 U.S.C. § 1232h(c)(6)(E)

16 https://studentprivacy.ed.gov/file-a-complaint

17 20 U.S.C. § 1232g(b)(1)

18 20 U.S.C. § 1232g(b)

19 The complete FERPA statute is available at: https://www.law.cornell.edu/uscode/text/20/1232g

(c) Surveys or data-gathering activities; regulations

(d) Students' rather than parents' permission or consent

(e) Informing parents or students of rights under this section

(f) Enforcement; termination of assistance

(g) Office and review board; creation; functions

(h) Disciplinary records; disclosure

(i) Drug and alcohol violation disclosures

(j) Investigation and prosecution of terrorism

FERPA Regulations - Frequently Asked Questions[20]

We originally planned to include the full text of the FERPA statute and regulations in this book. After formatting the statute and regulations, we realized that they were very long and would increase the size, weight, and printing cost. We decided to convert the formatted regulations into an Adobe PDF file and upload the file to the Wrightslaw website. You can download the formatted FERPA regulations from our website.[21]

The regulations were revised in 2008 and again in 2012. The FERPA directory on the Wrightslaw website's includes an analysis we provided about the 2008 revisions.[22] The FERPA index page has numerous links to additional information.[23]

The **FERPA regulations** are written in a "Frequently Asked Questions" **FAQ format** with 41 questions and answers, with five subparts, A through E. Hyperlinks to each subpart are in the footnotes. The questions are categorized under each subpart and each question and answer is its own regulation. The FAQ format of the regulations is quite unlike IDEA, Section 504, and the ADA regulations. Following is a list of the 41 questions.

34 CFR Part 99, Subpart A - General[24]

§ 99.1 To which educational agencies or institutions do these regulations apply?

§ 99.2 What is the purpose of these regulations?

§ 99.3 What definitions apply to these regulations?

§ 99.4 What are the rights of parents?

§ 99.5 What are the rights of students?

§ 99.6 [Reserved]

§ 99.7 What must an educational agency or institution include in its annual notification?

§ 99.8 What provisions apply to records of a law enforcement unit?

34 CFR Part 99, Subpart B - What Are the Rights of Inspection and Review of Education Records?[25]

§ 99.10 What rights exist for a parent or eligible student to inspect and review education records?

§ 99.11 May an educational agency or institution charge a fee for copies of education records?

§ 99.12 What limitations exist on the right to inspect and review records?

34 CFR Part 99, Subpart C - What Are the Procedures for Amending Education Records?[26]

§ 99.20 How can a parent or eligible student request amendment of the student's education records?

§ 99.21 Under what conditions does a parent or eligible student have the right to a hearing?

§ 99.22 What minimum requirements exist for the conduct of a hearing?

20   The complete FERPA statute is available at: https://www.law.cornell.edu/uscode/text/20/1232g

21   https:www.wrightslaw.com/law/ferpa/ferpa.regs.pdf

22   https://www.wrightslaw.com/law/ferpa/finalrule.sec.analysis.08.pdf

23   https://www.wrightslaw.com/info/ferpa.index.htm

24   https://www.law.cornell.edu/cfr/text/34/part-99/subpart-A

25   https://www.law.cornell.edu/cfr/text/34/part-99/subpart-B

26   https://www.law.cornell.edu/cfr/text/34/part-99/subpart-C

34 CFR Part 99, Subpart D - May an Educational Agency or Institution Disclose Personally Identifiable Information From Education Records?[27]

§ 99.30 Under what conditions is prior consent required to disclose information?

§ 99.31 Under what conditions is prior consent not required to disclose information?

§ 99.32 What recordkeeping requirements exist concerning requests and disclosures?

§ 99.33 What limitations apply to the redisclosure of information?

§ 99.34 What conditions apply to disclosure of information to other educational agencies or institutions?

§ 99.35 What conditions apply to disclosure of information for Federal or State program purposes?

§ 99.36 What conditions apply to disclosure of information in health and safety emergencies?

§ 99.37 What conditions apply to disclosing directory information?

§ 99.38 What conditions apply to disclosure of information as permitted by State statute adopted after November 19, 1974, concerning the juvenile justice system?

§ 99.39 What definitions apply to the nonconsensual disclosure of records by postsecondary educational institutions in connection with disciplinary proceedings concerning crimes of violence or non-forcible sex offenses?

34 CFR Part 99, Subpart E - What Are the Enforcement Procedures?[28]

§ 99.60 What functions has the Secretary delegated to the Office and to the Office of Administrative Law Judges?

§ 99.61 What responsibility does an educational agency or institution, a recipient of Department funds, or a third party outside of an educational agency or institution have concerning conflict with State or local laws?

§ 99.62 What information must an educational agency or institution or other recipient of Department funds submit to the Office?

§ 99.63 Where are complaints filed?

§ 99.64 What is the investigation procedure?

§ 99.65 What is the content of the notice of investigation issued by the Office?

§ 99.66 What are the responsibilities of the Office in the enforcement process?

§ 99.67 How does the Secretary enforce decisions?

FERPA Caselaw[29]

Two SCOTUS decisions are viewed as landmark cases about FERPA: *Owasso Ind. Sch. Dist. v. Falvo*, 534 U.S. 426 (2002) and *Gonzaga University v. Doe*, 536 U.S. 273 (2002). Recent cases protect the right of Protection and Advocacy agencies to access education records in investigations of abuse. In non-special education matters, the right to sue for a violation of confidentiality is limited.

In *Owasso Ind. Sch. Dist. v. Falvo*, 534 U.S. 426 (2002)[30] SCOTUS addressed FERPA and student grading. Kristja Falvo had three children who attended a public school in the Owasso Independent School District in Tulsa, Oklahoma. She asked the school to stop peer grading in classrooms because it embarrassed her children. When the school refused her request, Falvo filed a lawsuit in federal district court, claiming that peer grading violated FERPA.

The school district argued that the law only covered records that would go in a student's permanent file such as final grades, grade point averages, standardized test scores, attendance records, counseling records, and disciplinary records; not scores on individual assignments.

The district court held that peer-graded papers were not education records and not protected by FERPA. On appeal, the Tenth Circuit held that peer-graded papers were education records and protected by FERPA. Owasso appealed.

---

27 https://www.law.cornell.edu/cfr/text/34/part-99/subpart-D

28 https://www.law.cornell.edu/cfr/text/34/part-99/subpart-E

29 *See also* the *Newport-Mesa v. CA DOE* test protocol case discussed at the beginning of this chapter.

30 https://supreme.justia.com/cases/federal/us/534/426/

In a **unanimous opinion, SCOTUS held** that the practice of peer-grading tests and calling out grades did not violate student privacy under the Family Educational Rights and Privacy Act of 1974.

That decision was issued on February 19, 2002. Four months later, SCOTUS issued its decision in ***Gonzaga Univ. v. Doe***[31, 32] which addressed the question of **whether individuals can bring civil suits against schools** for violations of FERPA. John Doe, a student at Gonzaga University, planned to be a teacher after graduating from college. Under Washington state law, colleges had to provide an affidavit of "good moral character" when education students graduated.

The teacher in charge of certifying affidavits overheard a conversation about sexual misconduct by Doe i.e. a "date rape," so she refused to provide an affidavit. Doe was denied a teaching certificate. Doe sued the University and staff under 42 U.S.C. § 1983, claiming they violated his confidentiality rights under FERPA.

Doe prevailed in a state court jury trial and was awarded damages. Gonzaga appealed. In trial transcripts, the alleged victim "denied she made many of the statements that Gonzaga personnel attributed to her . . . John Doe testified he found 'a lot of lies' when he read statements of Gonzaga personnel. John Doe said Gonzaga destroyed his career in teaching, his goals, and his dreams."

On appeal to SCOTUS, Gonzaga was represented by **attorney John Roberts.**[33] **The issue on appeal was whether a student can sue an educational institution or faculty because they violated FERPA.**

In a 7-2 decision, SCOTUS held that "FERPA's confidentiality provisions **create no rights enforceable under §1983** . . . and clearly does not confer the sort of individual entitlement that is enforceable under §1983." Unlike the IDEA,[34] Section 504, and the ADA, **FERPA does not provide any private right of action to sue for a violation of the FERPA** confidentiality requirements. **The only remedy for a student or parent complaining of a FERPA violation is to file a complaint with the USDOE,** a slow, ineffective process. The USDOE **may** withhold funds.[35]

A National Center for Education Statistics webpage provides information about the **relationship between FERPA and HIPPA**. It explains that HIPPA is not always applicable, especially in regard to an IDEA child.

> Technically, schools and school systems that provide health care services to students may qualify as "covered entities" under HIPAA. However, the final regulations for the HIPAA Privacy Rule **exclude** information considered **"education records"** under FERPA from HIPAA privacy requirements. This includes student health records and immunization records maintained by an education agency or institution, or its representative; as "education records" subject to FERPA, these files **are not subject to HIPAA privacy** requirements. In addition, school nurse or other health records maintained on students receiving services under the Individuals with Disabilities Education Act (IDEA) are considered "education records" and also subject to that Act's confidentiality provisions. Consequently, these records are subject to FERPA and not the HIPAA Privacy Rule.[36]

END of FERPA

McKinney-Vento Homeless Assistance Act
42 U.S.C. § 11431 *et seq.*

In this section, you will learn about powerful rights in the McKinney-Vento Homeless Assistance Act. States are responsible for ensuring that homeless children receive a free, appropriate public education.

The McKinney-Vento Homeless Assistance Act requires all school districts to ensure that all children whose fam-

---

31   https://supreme.justia.com/cases/federal/us/536/273/

32   *Gonzaga Univ. v. Doe*, 536 US 273, 122 S.Ct. 2268, 153 L. Ed. 2d 309 (2002)

33   John Roberts is now the Chief Justice of the U.S. Supreme Court.

34   However, a violation of confidentiality regarding a child with an IEP, can be a violation of IDEA. See the **"Confidentiality of Information"** IDEA regulations beginning at <34 CFR § 300.610> in Chapter 6.

35   https://studentprivacy.ed.gov/sites/default/files/resource_document/file/FERPA_Enforcement_Notice_2018.pdf

36   https://nces.ed.gov/pubs2006/stu_privacy/healthrecords.asp

ilies are homeless have access to school. The statute begins at 42 U.S.C. § 11431.[37] There are **no Code of Federal Regulations (CFR) for this law,** only "Guidelines" from the USDOE.[38] Public Law 100-77[39] was passed in 1987[40] and provides funding to states to ensure that homeless children have **"equal access to the same free, appropriate public education"**[41] as provided to other children who are not homeless.

The McKinney-Vento Homeless Assistance Act includes this Statement of Policy:

> Each state shall ensure that each child of a homeless individual and each homeless youth has **equal access** to the same free, appropriate public education, including a public preschool education, as provided to other children and youths . . . to ensure that homeless children and youths are afforded the same free, appropriate public education as provided to other children and youths.[42]

States are **prohibited from segregating** ". . . homeless children in separate schools or separate programs within a school, based on the child's status as homeless."[43] A child's "**school district of origin**" is the district the child last attended or was entitled to attend when the child became homeless.[44]

Definition of "Homeless Children and Youth"

A child is homeless if the child lacks "a fixed, regular, and adequate nighttime residence . . . and includes children and youth who are sharing the housing of other persons due to loss of housing, economic hardship . . . are living in motels, hotels, trailer parks, or camping grounds . . . in emergency or transitional shelters; are abandoned in hospitals; or are awaiting foster care placement . . . are living in cars, parks, public spaces, abandoned buildings, substandard housing, bus or train stations, or similar settings; and migratory children."[45]

Schools Are Required to Immediately Enroll

School districts are required **to immediately enroll** homeless children,[46] even if medical, academic and residency records are not available. The school shall immediately contact the last school attended to obtain relevant records. If the child needs immunizations or medical records, the school shall immediately refer the parent or guardian to the school district liaison who shall assist in obtaining the necessary immunizations or medical records.[47]

Much like the IDEA,[48] McKinney-Vento has **stay-put / pendency** that "If a dispute arises [the child] shall be immediately enrolled in the school in which enrollment is sought, pending final resolution of the dispute, including all available **appeals**.[49]

---

37   https://www.law.cornell.edu/uscode/text/42/11431

38   In lieu of Regulations, at 42 U.S.C. § 11434(g), Congress instructed the USDOE to "develop, issue, and publish in the Federal Register, not later than 60 days after December 10, 2015, guidelines . . ."

39   https://www.govinfo.gov/content/pkg/STATUTE-101/pdf/STATUTE-101-Pg482.pdf

40   Note: Title 42, "Public Health and Welfare," has 163 Chapters in which Chapter 119 is titled "Homeless Assistance." Subchapter VI is titled "Education and Training" which has Parts A through F. Part B addresses the "Education for Homeless Children and Youth." See https://www.law.cornell.edu/uscode/text/42 and continue to https://www.law.cornell.edu/uscode/text/42/chapter-119/subchapter-VI

41   42 U.S.C. § 11431(1), compare to FAPE under IDEA

42   42 U.S.C. § 11432(g)(3)(B)

43   42 U.S.C. § 11432(e)(3)(A)

44   42 U. S. C. § 11432(g)(3)(A)(i) + (g)(3)(B)

45   42 U. S. C. § 11432(a)(2)

46   42 U. S. C. § 11432(g)(3)(C) + (g)(3)(E)

47   42 U. S. C. § 11432(g)(3)(C)

48   20 U.S.C. § 1415(j)

49   42 U. S. C. § 11432(g)(3)(E)

Transportation

Transportation is a common problem for homeless children. Is transportation provided by the school district (LEA) where the school of origin is located? Or is transportation provided by the new school in a different school district? McKinney-Vento advises that the former LEA and the new LEA where the child is currently -

> . . . living shall agree upon a method to apportion the responsibility and costs for providing the child or youth with transportation to and from the school of origin. If the local educational agencies are unable to agree upon such method, the responsibility and costs for transportation shall be **shared equally**.[50]

McKinney-Vento requires all school districts to have a **liaison to assist homeless children**.[51] States must have a plan to ensure that homeless children who are "separated from public schools are identified and accorded equal access to appropriate secondary education and support services, including by identifying and removing barriers."[52] Resolution of transportation issues is one of the initial problems in need of immediate resolution.

In the "Best Interest of the Child"

School districts shall make decisions in the best interest of the child.[53] In determining the "best interest of the child," schools shall:

- Keep a homeless child or youth in the school of origin except when doing so is contrary to the wishes of the child's parent or guardian . . .

- Provide a written explanation, including a statement regarding the right to appeal to the parent or guardian if the school district sends a child to a school other than the school of origin or a school requested by the parent or guardian . . .

- Ensure that the liaison helps make placement and enrollment decisions for an unaccompanied youth.[54]

Comparable Services

"Each homeless child or youth to be assisted under this part shall be provided services comparable to services offered to other students in the school selected . . ." Barriers to full participation in these services must be eliminated. This includes access to academic and extracurricular activities, including magnet school, summer school, career and technical education, advanced placement, online learning, and charter school programs. It also includes Special Education, Transportation, School Meal Programs, Pre-School, Head Start, Title I Services, Gifted and Talented Programs, Vocational and Technical Education, GED Programs, Online/Distance Education, and Sports.[55]

Notice of Educational Rights

McKinney-Vento requires that a "notice of the educational rights of homeless children and youths is disseminated where such children and youths receive services . . . such as schools, family shelters, and soup kitchens . . . and that the parent or guardian . . . is fully informed of all transportation services . . ."[56]

Child Find and Surrogate Parents

When IDEA was reauthorized in 2004, the Child Find requirements that school districts must identify, evaluate, and provide services to all children with disabilities were specifically extended to homeless children.[57] The law also

50   42 U.S.C. § 11432(g)(1)(J)(II)(iii)

51   42 U.S.C. § 11432(g)(6)

52   42 U.S.C. § 11432(g)(1)(F)

53   20 U. S. C. § 11432(g)(3)(A)

54   42 U. S. C. § 11432(g)(3)(B)(iv)

55   42 U.S.C. §11432(g)(4) + (g)(1)(F)(iii)

56   42 U. S. C. § 11432(g)(6)(A

57   20 U.S.C. § 1412(a)(3)(A)

requires that an "unaccompanied youth" (i.e., a homeless adolescent who is not accompanied by a parent or guardian) have a surrogate parent appointed. If the child is living in a homeless shelter, an employee of the shelter may serve as a temporary surrogate.[58]

Resources

Wrightslaw.com has a topics page **Educating Homeless Children**[59] that includes legal information about education rights, organizations, and local support systems for community members.

In response to the displacement of so many families and children during and after Hurricanes Katrina and Harvey, followed by Irma, and Ian, we posted an article by special education attorney, Michael O'Connor. *The Education Rights of Homeless Children Displaced by Hurricane Harvey* that includes links to several useful resources.[60]

To find your state's plan, procedures and resources, Google YourStateName and McKinney-Vento. In some instances, the law is referred to as the Education for Homeless Children and Youth (EHCY) so you may also want to use those words and acronym in your search. In a search for Virginia,[61] we found a page that includes changes in the McKinney-Vento Act that went into effect on October 1, 2016.

The relevant text from McKinney-Vento begins below. We omitted portions of McKinney-Vento and noted these omissions with [not included] or by inserting ellipsis or both. The full text with the omissions begins at § 11431 and continues through § 11435 and is available here.[62]

McKinney-Vento Homeless Assistance Act / 42 U.S.C. § 11431

42 U.S. Code § 11431 - Statement of policy

The following is the policy of the Congress:

(1) Each State educational agency **shall ensure** that each child of a homeless individual and each homeless youth **has equal access** to the same **free, appropriate public education,** including a public preschool education, as provided to other children and youths.

(2) In any State where compulsory residency requirements or other requirements, in laws, regulations, practices, or policies, may act as a barrier to the identification of, or the enrollment, attendance, or success in school of, homeless children and youths, the State educational agency and local educational agencies in the State will review and undertake steps to revise such laws, regulations, practices, or policies to ensure that homeless children and youths are afforded the same free, appropriate public education as provided to other children and youths.

(3) Homelessness is not sufficient reason to separate students from the mainstream school environment.

(4) Homeless children and youths should have access to the education and other services that such children and youths need to ensure that such children and youths have an opportunity to meet the same challenging State academic standards to which all students are held.

42 U.S.C. § 11432 - Grants for State and local activities for the education of homeless children and youths

(a) General authority

The Secretary is authorized to make grants to States . . .

(b) Grants from allotments

The Secretary shall make the grants to States from the allotments made under subsection (c)(1).

---

58   *See also* IDEA regulation 34 CFR § 300.519(f)

59   https://www.wrightslaw.com/info/homeless.index.htm

60   https://www.wrightslaw.com/info/homeless.educate.htm

61   https://www.doe.virginia.gov/administrators/superintendents_memos/2017/126-17a.pdf

62   https://www.law.cornell.edu/uscode/text/42/11431

(c) Allocation and reservations [not included]

(d) Activities - Grants under this section **shall be used for the following**:

(1) To carry out the policies set forth in section 11431 of this title in the State.

(2) To **provide services and activities** to improve the identification of homeless children and youths (including preschool-aged homeless children) and enable such children and youths to enroll in, attend, and succeed in school, including, if appropriate, in preschool programs.

(3) To establish or designate in the State educational agency an Office of the Coordinator for Education of Homeless Children and Youths that can sufficiently carry out the duties described for the Office in this part in accordance with subsection (f).

(4) + (5) [not included]

(e) State and local subgrants

(1) Minimum disbursements by States [not included]

(2) Use by State educational agency [not included]

(3) Prohibition on segregating homeless students

(A) In general

Except as provided in subparagraph (B) and section 11433(a)(2)(B)(ii) of this title, in providing a free public education to a homeless child or youth, **no State receiving funds under this part shall segregate such child** or youth **in a separate school, or in a separate program within a school**, based on such child's or youth's status as homeless.

(B) Exception [not included]

(C) School requirements [not included][63]

(D) School ineligibility [not included]

(E) Local educational agency requirements

For the State to be eligible to receive the funds described in subparagraph (B), the local educational agency described in subparagraph (B)(ii) **shall**—

(i) implement a coordinated system for **ensuring that homeless children** and youths—

(I) **are advised of the choice of schools** provided in subsection (g)(3)(A);

(II) **are immediately enrolled**, in accordance with subsection (g)(3)(C), in the school selected under subsection (g)(3)(A); and

(III) are promptly provided necessary services described in subsection (g)(4), **including transportation,** to allow homeless children and youths to exercise their choices of schools under subsection (g)(3)(A);

(ii) document that written notice has been provided—

(I) in accordance with subparagraph (C)(i) for each child or youth enrolled in a separate school under subparagraph (B); and

(II) in accordance with subsection (g)(6)(A)(vi);

(iii) **prohibit schools** within the agency's jurisdiction **from referring homeless children** or youths to, or **requiring homeless children** and youths to enroll in or attend, **a separate school** described in subparagraph (B);

(iv) identify and **remove any barriers** that exist in schools within the agency's jurisdiction that may have contributed to the creation or existence of separate schools described in subparagraph (B); and

---

63 Schools are required to provide a written notice of rights, no requirement that the child attend a separate school, entitlement to comparable services, and school staff shall not stigmatize the child for being homeless.

(v) **not use funds** received under this part **to establish—**

    (I) new or additional **separate schools** for homeless children or youths; or

    (II) new or additional sites for separate schools for homeless children or youths, other than the sites occupied by the schools described in subparagraph (B) in fiscal year 2000.

(F) Report [not included]

(G) Definition [not included]

(f) Functions of the Office of the Coordinator - The Coordinator for Education of Homeless Children and Youths established in **each State shall—** [not included] . . .

(g) State plan[64]

(1) In general

For any State desiring to receive a grant under this part, the State educational agency **shall submit** to the Secretary **a plan** to provide for the education of homeless children and youths within the State. **Such plan shall include the following:** [not included are subsections A through I] . . .

    (J) **Assurances** that the following will be carried out:

        (i) **The State educational agency and local educational agencies in the State will adopt policies and practices to ensure that homeless children and youths are not stigmatized or segregated on the basis of their status as homeless.**

        (ii) The local educational agencies will designate an appropriate staff person, able to carry out the duties described in paragraph (6)(A), who may also be a coordinator for other Federal programs, as a **local educational agency liaison** for homeless children and youths.

        (iii) The State and the local educational agencies in the State will adopt policies and practices to ensure that **transportation is provided**, at the request of the parent or guardian (or in the case of an unaccompanied youth, the liaison), **to and from the school of origin** (as determined under paragraph (3)), in accordance with the following, as applicable:

            (I) If the child or youth continues to live in the area served by the local educational agency in which the school of origin is located, the child's or youth's transportation to and from the school of origin **shall be provided or arranged by the local educational agency in which the school of origin is located**.

            (II) If the child's or youth's living arrangements in the area served by the local educational agency of origin terminate and the child or youth, though continuing the child's or youth's education in the **school of origin, begins living in an area served by another local educational agency,** the local educational agency of origin and the local educational agency in which the child or youth is living **shall agree upon a method to apportion the responsibility and costs** for providing the child or youth **with transportation to and from the school of origin**. If the local educational agencies are unable to agree upon such method, the responsibility and costs for transportation shall be shared equally.

        (iv) The State and the local educational agencies in the State will adopt policies . . .

    (K) A description of how youths described in section 11434a(2) of this title will receive assistance from counselors to advise such youths, and prepare and improve the readiness of such youths for college.

(2) Compliance

(A) In general

Each plan adopted under this subsection shall also describe how the State will ensure that local educational agencies in the State **will comply** with the requirements of paragraphs (3) through (7).

(B) Coordination [not included]

---

64   The state plan submitted by Virginia is at: https://oese.ed.gov/files/2021/09/Virginia-ARP-HCY-State-Plan.pdf

(3) Local educational agency requirements

(A) In general

The local educational agency serving each child or youth to be assisted under this part **shall, according to the child's or youth's best interest—**[65]

(i) continue the child's or youth's education in the **school of origin** for the duration of homelessness—

(I) in any case in which a family becomes homeless between academic years or during an academic year; and

(II) for the remainder of the academic year, if the child or youth becomes permanently housed during an academic year; or

(ii) **enroll the child or youth in any public school** that nonhomeless students who live in the attendance area in which the child or youth is actually living are eligible to attend.

(B) School stability

In determining **the best interest of the child** or youth under subparagraph (A), the local educational agency shall—

(i) **presume** that keeping the child or youth in the school of origin is in the child's or youth's best interest, except when doing so is contrary to the request of the child's or youth's parent or guardian, or (in the case of an unaccompanied youth) the youth;

(ii) consider **student-centered factors** related to the child's or youth's best interest, including factors related to the impact of mobility on achievement, education, health, and safety of homeless children and youth, **giving priority to the request of the child's or youth's parent** or guardian or (in the case of an unaccompanied youth) the youth;

(iii) if, **after conducting the best interest determination** based on consideration of the **presumption** in clause (i) and the **student-centered factors** in clause (ii), the local educational agency determines that it is not in the child's or youth's best interest to attend the school of origin or the school requested by the parent or guardian, or (in the case of an unaccompanied youth) the youth, **provide** the child's or youth's parent or guardian or the unaccompanied youth with a **written explanation** of the reasons for its determination, in a manner and form understandable to such parent, guardian, or unaccompanied youth, **including information regarding the right to appeal under subparagraph (E)**; and

(iv) in the case of an unaccompanied youth, ensure that the local educational agency liaison designated under paragraph (1)(J)(ii) assists in placement or enrollment decisions under this subparagraph, gives **priority to the views of such unaccompanied youth**, and provides notice to such youth of the right to appeal under subparagraph (E).

(C) Immediate enrollment

(i) In general

The school selected in accordance with this paragraph **shall immediately enroll** the homeless child or youth, **even if the child** or youth—

(I) **is unable to produce records normally required for enrollment**, such as previous academic records, records of immunization and other required health records, proof of residency, or other documentation; or

(II) **has missed application or enrollment deadlines** during any period of homelessness.

(ii) Relevant academic records

The enrolling school **shall immediately contact the school last attended** by the child or youth to obtain relevant academic and other records.

---

65 The **best interest of the child is a standard that far exceeds the requirements** of FAPE in IDEA and the "as adequately" standard in Section 504 and the ADA. *See* 20 U.S.C. § 1401(9) for IDEA and 34 CFR § 104.33 for Section 504.

(iii) Relevant health records

If child or youth needs to obtain immunizations or other required health records, the enrolling school **shall the immediately refer the parent** or guardian of the child or youth, or (in the case of an unaccompanied youth) the youth, **to the local educational agency liaison d**esignated under paragraph (1)(J)(ii), **who shall assist in obtaining necessary immunizations** or screenings, or immunization or other required health records, in accordance with subparagraph (D).

(D) Records

Any record ordinarily kept by the school, including immunization or other required health records, academic records, birth certificates, guardianship records, and evaluations for special services or programs, regarding each homeless child or youth **shall be maintained**—

(i) so that the records involved are available, in a timely fashion, when a child or youth enters a new school or school district; and

(ii) in a manner consistent with section 1232g of title 20.[66]

(E) Enrollment disputes

If a dispute arises over eligibility, or school selection or enrollment in a school—

(i) the child or youth **shall be immediately enrolled** in the school in which enrollment is sought, **pending final resolution of the dispute, including all available appeals;**

(ii) the parent or guardian of the child or youth or (in the case of an unaccompanied youth) the youth shall be provided with a **written explanation of any decisions** related to school selection or enrollment made by the school, the local educational agency, or the State educational agency involved, including **the rights** of the parent, guardian, or unaccompanied youth **to appeal such decisions;**

(iii) the parent, guardian, or unaccompanied youth shall be referred to the **local educational agency liaison** designated under paragraph (1)(J)(ii), **who shall carry out the dispute resolution process as described in paragraph (1)(C)**[67] as expeditiously as possible after receiving notice of the dispute; and

(iv) in the case of an unaccompanied youth, **the liaison shall ensure that the youth is immediately enrolled in the school in which the youth seeks** enrollment pending resolution of such dispute.

(F) Placement choice

The choice regarding placement shall be made regardless of whether the child or youth lives with the homeless parents or has been temporarily placed elsewhere.

(G) Privacy

Information about a homeless child's or youth's living situation shall be treated as a **student education record, and shall not be deemed to be directory information,** under section 1232g of title 20.

(H) Contact information

Nothing in this part shall prohibit a local educational agency from requiring a parent or guardian of a homeless child or youth to submit contact information.

(I) School of origin defined

In this paragraph:

(i) In general

The term **"school of origin" means** the school that a child or youth attended when permanently housed or the school in which the child or youth was last enrolled, including a preschool.

---

66   FERPA, earlier in this chapter, is 20 U.S.C. § 1232g.

67   This is located in paragraph (1)(C) under the preceding subsection g, about "state plans." Your state's plan should have more detailed information about the appellate process.

(ii) Receiving school

When the child or youth completes the final grade level served by the school of origin, as described in clause (i), the term "school of origin" shall include the designated receiving school at the next grade level for all feeder schools.

(4) Comparable services

Each homeless child or youth to be assisted under this part **shall be provided services comparable**[68] **to services offered to other students** in the school selected under paragraph (3), including the following:

(A) Transportation services.

(B) Educational services for which the child or youth meets the eligibility criteria, such as services provided under title I of the Elementary and Secondary Education Act of 1965 (20 U.S.C. 6301 *et seq.*)[69] or similar State or local programs, **educational programs for children with disabilities**, and educational programs for English learners.

(C) Programs in career and technical education.

(D) Programs for **gifted and talented** students.

(E) School nutrition programs.

(5) Coordination[70]

(A) In general

Each local educational agency serving homeless children and youths that receives assistance under this part **shall coordinate**—

(i) the provision of services under this part with **local social services agencies** and other agencies or entities providing services to homeless children and youths and their families, including services and programs funded under the **Runaway and Homeless Youth Act** (42 U.S.C. 5701 *et seq.*); and

(ii) transportation, transfer of school records, and other interdistrict activities, with other local educational agencies.

(B) Housing assistance

If applicable, each State educational agency and local educational agency that receives assistance under this part **shall coordinate with State and local housing agencies** responsible for developing the comprehensive housing affordability strategy described in section 12705 of this title to minimize educational disruption for children and youths who become homeless.

(C) Coordination purpose

The coordination required under subparagraphs (A) and (B) shall be designed to—

(i) ensure that all homeless children and youths **are promptly identified**;

(ii) ensure that all homeless children and youths **have access to**, and are in reasonable proximity to, available **education and related support services**; and

(iii) raise the awareness of school personnel and service providers of the effects of short-term stays in a **shelter and other challenges associated with homelessness.**

---

68 This is similar to the "comparable services" requirement in IDEA when a child, with an IEP, moves from one jurisdiction to another. Comparable is defined in the Commentary as similar or equivalent. See <20 U.S.C. § 1414(d)(2)(C)(i)> and footnotes.

69 This is the Elementary and Secondary Education Act of 1965, now known as Every Student Succeeds Act.

70 A McKinney-Vento Homeless case against NYC was filed in NY Federal District Court and, after a December 30, 2020 ruling adverse to NY, the case was settled. It involved the failure to adequately **coordinate with homeless shelters** and failure to provide the homeless child with access to the internet and be educated online. **The Complaint and Settlement Agreement are on our website at**: https://www.wrightslaw.com/law/caselaw/covid/.

(D) Homeless children and youths with disabilities

For children and youths who are to be assisted both under this part, and under the **Individuals with Disabilities Education Ac**t (20 U.S.C. 1400 *et seq.*) or section 794 of title 29, each **local educational agency shall coordinate** the provision of services under this part with the provision of programs for children with disabilities served by that local educational agency and other involved local educational agencies.

(6) Local educational agency liaison[71]

(A) Duties

Each local educational agency liaison for homeless children and youths, designated under paragraph (1)(J)(ii), **shall ensure** that—

(i) homeless children and youths **are identified** by school personnel through outreach and coordination activities with other entities and agencies;

(ii) homeless children and youths **are enrolled in, and have a full and equal opportunity** to succeed in, schools of that local educational agency;

(iii) homeless families and homeless children and youths have **access to and receive educational services** for . . .

(iv) . . . [and receive] referrals to **health care services, dental services,** mental health and substance abuse services, **housing services,** and other appropriate services;

(v) [and] . . . are informed of the educational and related opportunities available . . .

(vi) **public notice of the educational rights** of homeless children and youths is disseminated . . .

(vii) enrollment disputes are mediated in accordance with **paragraph (3)(E);**[72]

(viii) the parent or guardian of a homeless child or youth, and any unaccompanied youth, is **fully informed of all transportation services**, including transportation to the school of origin, as described in paragraph (1)(J)(iii), and is assisted in accessing transportation to the school that is selected under paragraph (3)(A);

(ix) school personnel providing services under this part receive professional development and other support; and

(x) unaccompanied youths—

(I) **are enrolled in school;**

(II) have opportunities to meet the same challenging State academic standards as the State establishes for other children and youth, including through implementation of the procedures under paragraph (1)(F)(ii); and

(III) are informed of their status as **independent students** under section 1087vv of title 20[73] and that the youths may obtain assistance from the local educational agency liaison to receive verification of such status for purposes of the **Free Application for Federal Student Aid** described in section 1090 of title 20.

(B) Notice [not included]

(C) Local and State coordination [not included]

(D) Homeless status [not included]

---

71   Each school district must have a designated **liaison who is required to assist** the family.

72   Section 11432(g)(3)(E) mandates that the "liaison shall ensure that the youth is **immediately enrolled** in the school in which the youth seeks enrollment pending resolution of such dispute."

73   See 20 U.S.C. § 1087vv(d) which defines an "independent student."
https://www.law.cornell.edu/uscode/text/20/1087vv

(7) Review and revisions

(A) In general [not included] . . .

(B) Consideration [not included] . . .

(C) Special attention

Special attention shall be given to ensuring the identification, enrollment, and attendance of homeless children and youths **who are not currently attending school**.

42 U.S.C. § 11433 - Local educational agency subgrants for the education of homeless children and youths

(a) General authority

(1) In general

The State educational agency shall, in accordance with section 11432(e) of this title, and from amounts made available to such agency under section 11435 of this title, **make subgrants to local educational agencies** for the purpose of facilitating **the identification, enrollment, attendance, and success** in school of homeless children and youths.

(2) Services

(A) In general

Services under paragraph (1)—

(i) may be provided through programs on school grounds or at other facilities;

(ii) shall, to the **maximum extent practicable**, be provided through existing programs and mechanisms that **integrate homeless children and youths with nonhomeless children** and youths; and

(iii) shall be designed to expand or improve services provided as part of a school's regular academic program, but not to replace such services provided under such program.

(B) Services on school grounds

If services under paragraph (1) are provided on school grounds, the related schools—

(i) **may use funds under this part** to provide the same services to other children and youths who are determined by the local educational agency to be at risk of failing in, or dropping out of, school, subject to the requirements of clause (ii); and

(ii) except as otherwise provided in section 11432(e)(3)(B) of this title, **shall not provide services** in settings within a school that **segregate homeless children** and youths from other children and youths, except as necessary for short periods of time—

(I) for health and safety emergencies; or

(II) to provide temporary, special, and supplementary services to meet the unique needs of homeless children and youths.

(3) Requirement

Services provided under this section shall **not replace the regular academic program** and shall be designed to expand upon **or improve services** provided as part of the school's regular academic program.

(4) Duration of grants.

Subgrants made under this section shall be for terms of not to exceed 3 years.

(b) Application - A local educational agency that **desires to receive a subgrant** under this section **shall submit an application** to the State educational agency [not included] . . .

(c) Awards [not included] . . .

(d) Authorized activities . . . [not included][74]

---

74 Funds are available for use **off school grounds**, such as purchasing supplies for homeless shelters, renovation of space, **tutoring, supplemental instruction, expedited evaluations**, medical, dental, mental, and other health services, excess cost of transportation, specialized instructional support services and more.

42 U.S.C. § 11434 - Secretarial responsibilities[75]

(g) Guidelines[76]

The Secretary **shall develop, issue, and publish in the Federal Register,**[77] not later than 60 days after December 10, 2015, **guidelines** concerning ways in which a State—

(1) may assist local educational agencies to implement the provisions related to homeless children and youths amended by that Act; and

(2) may review and revise State policies and procedures that may present barriers to the identification of homeless children and youths, and the enrollment, attendance, and success of homeless children and youths in school.[78]

(h) Information

(1) In general

From funds appropriated under section 11435 of this title, the Secretary shall, directly or through grants, contracts, or cooperative agreements, periodically collect and disseminate data and information regarding—

(A) the **number and primary nighttime residence** of homeless children and youths in all areas served by local educational agencies;

(B) the education and related services such children and youths receive;

(C) the extent to which the needs of homeless children and youths are being met; and

(D) such other data and information as the Secretary determines to be necessary and relevant to carry out this part.

(2) Coordination

The Secretary shall coordinate such collection and dissemination with other agencies and entities that receive assistance and administer programs under this part.

(i) Report[79] [not included]

42 U.S.C. § 11434a - Definitions

For purposes of this part:

(1) The terms "enroll" and "enrollment" include attending classes and participating fully in school activities.

(2) The term "homeless children and youths"—

(A) means individuals who **lack a fixed, regular, and adequate nighttime residence** (within the meaning of section 11302(a)(1) of this title); **and**

---

75   **Subsections a through f,** such as the responsibility to review state plans, provide technical assistance etc., **are not included.**

76   Unlike IDEA, Section 504, the ADA, and FERPA, Congress did not instruct the USDOE to issue regulations. There are no McKinney-Vento **regulations published in the CFR**. However, per the footnote below, the USDOE has issued guidelines.

77   On March 17, 2016 in the Federal Register, Vol. 81 # 52, at page 11432 issued **Guidelines** (5 pages) about compliance with McKinney-Vento, URL is: https://www.govinfo.gov/content/pkg/FR-2016-03-17/pdf/2016-06073.pdf.

78   On **July 27, 2017** the USDOE issued a comprehensive 54 page document titled *Education for Homeless Children and Youths Program - Non-Regulatory Guidance*. It was updated on July 28, 2018 and is located at:
https://oese.ed.gov/files/2020/07/160240ehcyguidanceupdated082718.pdf.

79   In **October, 2020** the USDOE issued its "Report to the President and Congress" about implementation this law and its impact on the Education for Homeless Children and Youth. (EHCY). It is located at:
https://oese.ed.gov/files/2020/10/Report-to-Congress-re-Implementation-of-EHCY-Program_October-2020.pdf.

(B) includes—

(i) children and youths who are **sharing the housing of other persons** due to loss of housing, economic hardship, or a similar reason; are **living in motels, hotels, trailer parks, or camping grounds** due to the lack of alternative adequate accommodations; are living in emergency or transitional **shelters**; or are abandoned in hospitals;

(ii) children and youths who have **a primary nighttime residence** that is a public or private place not designed for or ordinarily used as a regular sleeping accommodation for human beings (within the meaning of section 11302(a)(2)(C) [1] of this title);

(iii) children and youths who are **living in cars, parks, public spaces, abandoned buildings,** substandard housing, bus or train stations, or similar settings; and

(iv) **migratory** children (as such term is defined in section 6399 of title 20) who qualify as homeless for the purposes of this part because the children are living in circumstances described in clauses (i) through (iii).

(3) The terms "local educational agency" and "State educational agency" have the meanings given such terms in section 7801 of title 20.

(4) The term "Secretary" means the Secretary of Education.

(5) The term "State" means each of the 50 States, the District of Columbia, and the Commonwealth of Puerto Rico.

(6) The term "unaccompanied youth" includes a homeless child or youth not in the physical custody of a parent or guardian.

42 U.S.C. § 11435. Authorization of appropriations

There are authorized to be appropriated to carry out this part $85,000,000 for each of fiscal years 2017 through 2020.

End of McKinney-Vento

Overview: Federal Rules of Civil Procedure (FRCP), Other U.S. Code Statutes, U.S. Constitution

The United States Code (U.S.C.) contains the laws of the United States arranged into 54 broad titles[80] by subject matter. The Titles in this book are listed in chronological order. Title 20 is Education and includes IDEA and FERPA. Title 28 focuses on Judicial Procedures for the federal courts. Title 29 includes Vocational Rehabilitation with Section 504 of the Rehabilitation Act. Title 42 is Public Health and Welfare, "Equal Opportunity for Individuals with Disabilities" and includes the ADA.

Wrightslaw: Special Education Law, 3rd Edition includes portions of the **Federal Rules of Civil Procedure (FRCP)** for cases filed in federal courts, including appeals of special education due process decisions under the **IDEA** and civil rights cases filed under **Section 504, ADA, and Section 1983.** Certain statutes in the United States Code (U.S.C.) restrict or expand the jurisdiction of the court to proceed with a case. Legal decisions issued by federal judges often begin with a discussion of the legal basis for the decision, whether the court has jurisdiction, and whether the defendant's motion to dismiss should be granted or denied.

---

80 https://www.law.cornell.edu/uscode/text

Federal Question[81] and Removal

After a due process decision is issued, the losing party may appeal to federal or state court. The issue is often whether the school district did or did not provide the child with a free appropriate public education. If the case is filed initially in state court by the parents or the school district, the defendant can petition the federal court to remove the case to federal court.[82]

Since "free appropriate public education" is defined in the IDEA,[83] a federal statute, the case involves a "Federal Question."[84] If the federal judge makes a finding that the case involves a "federal question," the case is removed from state court to federal court. Because of the absolute right to petition for removal of a case to federal court, most special education due process appeals are filed in federal court, not in state court.

Federal Rules of Civil Procedure (FRCP)

A lawsuit in federal court begins when the plaintiff files a Complaint. In most scenarios, the defendant's initial "responsive pleading" will be a "Motion to Dismiss." A Motion to Dismiss, also known as a "12(b)(6) Motion" pursuant to Federal Rule 12 of the FRCP, alleges that the plaintiff's complaint failed "to state a claim upon which relief can be granted."

12(b)(6) Motion to Dismiss

Let's look at an example to see how this can play out. Assume a parent alleged that the IEP prepared for their child is not appropriate, or that after an initial evaluation, the school district found that the child was not eligible for special education and related services. Assume the parent did not request and proceed with a special education due process hearing. The parent filed a lawsuit in federal court.

In a "12(b)(6) Motion," the court is required to assume that all facts alleged in the parent's complaint are true. The school district is likely to file a Motion to asserting that even if all facts were true and the IEP was not appropriate, or if the child should have been found eligible for services, the court cannot go forward with the case because the court cannot grant any relief at this point. Before filing suit, the parent is required to comply with IDEA's exhaustion of administrative remedies statute.[85]

The "exhaustion of administrative remedies statute" required the parent to request a special education due process hearing. If the parent requested a due process hearing but did not prevail, the parent could then file in federal court.

When you read a decision from a U.S. District Court that upholds or denies a 12(b)(6) Motion to Dismiss, you will see the Judge's statement that the court accepted all factual allegations in the complaint as true, construed the complaint in the light most favorable to the plaintiff, and is tasked with determining whether, under any reasonable reading of the complaint, the plaintiff may be entitled to relief. The court will often write that, in order "to survive a Rule 12(b)(6) Motion to Dismiss, the complaint must contain sufficient factual allegations to raise the plaintiff's right to relief above the speculative level, so the claim 'is plausible on its face.'"[86]

---

81   This statute consists of a single sentence but establishes that a state court lawsuit that includes a "Federal Question," as whether IDEA, Section 504 or the ADA were violated, the defendant has an automatic right to petition for removal of the case from state court to federal court. But on February 3, 2020, in a Virginia public school personal injury case on behalf of a child with Cerebral Palsy who fell and was injured at school and filed a lawsuit in state court, the school district attempted to remove the case to federal court pursuant to 28 U.S.C. § 1441. The federal court refused to permit removal. The Court held that the "mere presence of a federal issue in a state cause of action is not enough to confer jurisdiction. Instead, federal question jurisdiction exists only where a federal question is necessarily raised and actually disputed by the parties; [and] the question is substantial." *C.F.S. v. Dickenson County Pub. Sch.* (Case No. 2:19CV00044, Western District, Virginia)

82   28 U.S.C. § 1441

83   FAPE in IDEA is at: <20 U.S.C. § 1401(9)>

84   28 U.S.C. § 1331

85   See the <SCOTUS *Fry*> case and <20 U.S.C. § 1415(l).>

86   *Ashcroft v. Iqbal*, 556 U.S. 662, 678 (2009)

Let's change the facts. The case is an appeal of a due process decision and the plaintiff filed the Complaint after the 90-day statute of limitations[87] had passed. The defendant's "12(b)(6) Motion" would assert a violation of the statute of limitations as a defense and allege that the court has no jurisdiction to hear the case.

Change the facts again. The adverse due process decision was not a final decision, but an interim, interlocutory decision. The plaintiff filed suit prematurely, before fully exhausting[88] their administrative remedies. In these two scenarios, the federal court would typically grant the defendant's "12(b)(6)" motion and dismiss the case.

Rule 56 Motion for Summary Judgment

If a case is not dismissed at an early point, it will continue with both parties filing briefs that provide the rationale or basis for upholding or reversing the earlier due process decision which is now on appeal. At that point, the parties will usually file a Rule 56 Motion for Summary Judgment, or, depending on the pending issues, a Rule 57 Motion for Declaratory Judgment. In some instances, to allow a quick settlement, or to reduce the issues, a party may submit a Rule 68 Offer of Judgment to the opposing party.

In an appeal of a due process decision about whether an IEP is adequate, after the court denies a 12(b)(6) motion, the court will review the decision issued by the Hearing Officer / Administrative Law Judge and will often review the exhibits and testimony to determine whether the school district's proposed IEP did provide a free appropriate public education (FAPE) under IDEA. The judge may or may not accept the conclusions of the HO / ALJ, depending on whether those conclusions are supported by the record. However, courts are cautioned that they must not "substitute their own notions of sound educational policy for those of the school authorities which they review."[89]

Civil Rights Statutes / U.S. Constitution

Some **education related civil rights cases** may be filed directly in federal court without exhausting administrative remedies. One example is the SCOTUS *Fry v. Napoleon* case where a school district refused to allow a child with severe cerebral palsy to be accompanied in school by her service dog. The child's parents sought dollar damages under Section 504 and the ADA and filed suit. SCOTUS ruled in favor of the child and service dog.

Education cases that are not special education due process appeals often allege violations of Section 504 and the ADA, violations of an individual's civil rights pursuant to several statutes provided below, and violations of Article VI, and or the First, Fourth, Fifth and Fourteenth Amendments of the <**U.S. Constitution.**>

The Federal Rules of Civil Procedure govern federal court cases. Court procedures stem from the guarantees of due process in the Fifth and the Fourteenth Amendments. These Amendments contain the Due Process Clause which states that no one shall be "deprived of life, liberty or property without due process of law."

Other Federal Statutes

28 U.S.C. § 1331 - Federal Question

28 U.S.C. § 1343 - Civil rights and elective franchise

28 U.S.C. § 1441 - Removal of civil actions

28 U.S.C. § 2201 - Creation of remedy

28 U.S.C. § 2202 - Further relief

42 U.S.C. § 1983 - Civil action for deprivation of rights

---

87   20 U.S.C. § 1415(i)(2)

88   20 U.S.C. § 1415(l)

89   *Bd. of Educ. of Hendrick Hudson Cent. Sch. Dist. v. Rowley*, 458 U.S. 176, 206 (1982)

28 U.S.C. § 1331 - Federal Question

The district courts shall have **original jurisdiction of all civil actions** arising under the Constitution, laws, or treaties of the United States.[90]

28 U.S.C. § 1343 - Civil rights and elective franchise

(a) The district courts shall have **original jurisdiction** of any civil action authorized by law to be commenced by any person:

(1) **To recover damages for injury** to his person or property, or because of the deprivation of any right or privilege of a citizen of the United States, by **any act done in furtherance of any conspiracy mentioned in section 1985 of Title 42;**[91]

(2) To recover damages from any person **who fails to prevent or to aid in preventing any wrongs** mentioned in section 1985 of Title 42 which he had knowledge were about to occur and power to prevent;

(3) To redress **the deprivation, under color of any State law, statute, ordinance, regulation, custom or usage, of any right, privilege or immunity secured by the Constitution** of the United States or by any Act of Congress providing for equal rights of citizens or of all persons within the jurisdiction of the United States;[92]

(4) To recover damages or to secure equitable or other relief under any Act of Congress providing for the protection of civil rights, including the right to vote.

(b) For purposes of this section—

(1) the District of Columbia shall be considered to be a State; and

(2) any Act of Congress applicable exclusively to the District of Columbia shall be considered to be a statute of the District of Columbia.

28 U.S.C. § 1441 - Removal of civil actions

(a) Generally.—

Except as otherwise expressly provided by Act of Congress, any civil action brought in a State court of which the district courts of the United States have original jurisdiction, **may be removed**[93] **by the defendant** or the defendants, to the district court of the United States for the district and division embracing the place where such action is pending.

---

90   In 1987, in Virginia, I prevailed in two special education due process cases, one against Amelia County and the other against Henrico County. Both school districts appealed to the state courts for their counties. The school districts' state court complaints did not mention the federal special education law. All legal references were to Virginia's statute and regulations. Pursuant to the removal statute, 28 U.S.C. § 1441, I filed a petition citing a "Federal Question" to remove each case to federal court. "Because identical issues and arguments have been presented in the two cases, the Court consolidates them for purposes of these motions only." The federal district court judge joined both cases together, denied the removal petition, and remanded both cases back to the respective state courts, explaining that: "Because it is abundantly clear that Virginia does meet the minimum federal requirements, the preemption prong of the "artful pleading" doctrine has not been met, and the "well-pleaded complaint" rule governs. Consequently, plaintiffs are the masters of their claims, and can rightly pursue those claims in state court under state law." *Amelia County School Bd. v. Virginia Bd. of Educ.*, 661 F. Supp. 889 (E.D. Va. 1987), available at: https://cite.case.law/f-supp/661/889/

In retrospect, I should have found a reason to file a cross-appeal and alleged violations of federal law, thus keeping the case in federal court with a more neutral forum, rather than in the local state county court. I followed that approach in another case a few years later with the same federal judge and same opposing counsel and prevailed with the court writing a comprehensive favorable opinion in the first extended school year (ESY) case in Virginia.

91   42 U.S.C. § 1985 is the statute that authorizes lawsuits against two or more individuals who conspire to violate the plaintiff's civil rights.

92   A number of cases in the *Wrightslaw Year in Review* books allege violations of constitutional rights as the basis of jurisdiction.

93   The "Notice of Removal" must be filed with the state court, the federal court and provided to all parties within 30 or less days pursuant to 28 U.S.C. § 1446 or it may be lost.

(b) Removal Based on Diversity of Citizenship.[94] [not included]

(c) Joinder of Federal Law Claims and State Law Claims.

(1) If a civil action **includes**—

(A) a claim arising under the Constitution, laws,[95] or treaties of the United States (within the meaning of section 1331[96] of this title), and

(B) a claim not within the original or supplemental jurisdiction[97] of the district court or a claim that has been made nonremovable by statute, **the entire action may be remove**d if the action would be removable **without the inclusion of the claim** described in subparagraph (B).[98]

(2) Upon removal of an action described in paragraph (1), the district court shall sever from the action all claims described in paragraph (1)(B) and shall remand the severed claims to the State court from which the action was removed. Only defendants against whom a claim described in paragraph (1)(A) has been asserted are required to join in or consent to the removal under paragraph (1).

(d) Actions Against Foreign States.[99] . . .

(e) Multiparty, Multiforum Jurisdiction.[100] . . .

(f) Derivative Removal Jurisdiction.—

The court to which a civil action is removed under this section is not precluded from hearing and determining any claim in such civil action because the State court from which such civil action is removed did not have jurisdiction over that claim.

28 U.S.C. § 2201 - Creation of remedy[101]

(a) In a case of actual controversy within its jurisdiction . . . any court of the United States, upon the filing of an appropriate pleading, **may declare the rights** and other legal relations of any interested party seeking such declaration, whether or not further relief is or could be sought. Any such declaration shall have the force and effect of a final judgment or decree and shall be reviewable as such.[102]

28 U.S.C. § 2202 - Further relief

Further necessary or proper relief based on a declaratory judgment or decree may be granted, after reasonable notice and hearing, against any adverse party whose rights have been determined by such judgment.

---

94   In this scenario, the plaintiff and defendant are citizens/corporations located in different states, thus have a "diversity of citizenship." This is not a usual issue in special education/disability litigation.

95   A special ed claim under our laws usually alleges that, under IDEA, a school district failed to provide FAPE to the child with a disability, a "Federal Question", the parent has "exhausted their administrative remedies," and now files in federal court.

96   This is the **Federal Question** statute.

97   Assume a parent alleges that a school employee abused and assaulted their child, a violation of state law, and, in addition, did not provide the child with FAPE—a state law claim of assault and a federal question about FAPE. If it is proven that FAPE was provided, the sole state law claim of assault would likely cause the case to be remanded back to the state court.

98   Lawsuits filed by or on behalf of individuals with disabilities, alleging federal questions, typically include violations of state civil rights laws and may include state "tort" claims. For example, a lawsuit filed by a parent on behalf of their child with a disability, may allege a violation of one or more of those "federal question" statutes and allege a state law tort of assault by a school district employee. In that scenario, the federal judge or federal court jury can hear and rule on the complete case. However, if the federal court judge finds that there was no federal question, no violation of those preceding federal statutes, that federal district court judge can dismiss the federal claims and "remand" the case back to the state court for further proceedings. Since the right to remove to federal court exists with almost all special education disability types of cases, most such cases are initially filed in federal court.

99   Subsection (d) involves lawsuits against foreign countries and is not included in this book..

100   Subsection (e) involves a scenario resulting in 75 or more deaths pursuant to an accident and is not included in this book.

101   This section authorizes issuance of a **"Declaratory Judgment."**

102   Subsection (b) relates to patent actions about drugs and cosmetics and is not included in this book.

42 U.S.C. § 1983 - Civil action for deprivation of rights[103, 104, 105]

Every person who, under color of any statute, ordinance, regulation, custom, or usage, of any State or Territory or the District of Columbia, **subjects, or causes to be subjected**, any citizen of the United States or other person within the jurisdiction thereof **to the deprivation of any rights, privileges, or immunities secured by the Constitution and laws,** shall be liable to the party injured in an action at law, suit in equity, or other proper proceeding for redress, except that in any action brought against a judicial officer for an act or omission taken in such officer's judicial capacity, injunctive relief shall not be granted unless a declaratory decree was violated or declaratory relief was unavailable. For the purposes of this section, any Act of Congress applicable exclusively to the District of Columbia shall be considered to be a statute of the District of Columbia.

End of Other Federal Statutes

Overview About Federal Rules of Civil Procedure (FRCP)

The **Federal Rules of Civil Procedure** (FRCP)[106] included are:

Rule 12 - Motion to Dismiss
Rule 56 - Motion for Summary Judgment
Rule 57 - Declaratory Judgment
Rule 68 - Offer of Judgment

---

103   To prevail in a section 1983 case, the plaintiff must prove that (1) he was deprived of a federally protected right (2) by a "person" (3) acting under color of state law. Section 1983 liability attaches where the deprivation of constitutional rights was caused by an official policy, custom, or practice.

104   **Wrightslaw Note:** Section 1983 authorizes private suits against any person acting under color of law who deprives the plaintiff of rights "secured by the Constitution and laws." At the time this book was published, a Section 1983 case is pending in which the **special education administrator and the school district's attorney are defendants**. In *C.B. v. Chicago Public Schools, Wagman and Mock*, (Case # 20-cv-00586) the Complaint, filed in the Northern District, Eastern Division of the federal court in Illinois, alleges that attorney Wagman "unilaterally made decisions that should have been made by an Individualized Education Program team . . .[and] was the actual primary decision maker in C.B.'s education for the 2017-18 and 2018-19 school years."

The plaintiff is seeking a jury trial and dollar damages against Chicago and two individuals. The defendant's motion also seeks dismissal based upon **qualified immunity**. Government officials are entitled to qualified immunity under § 1983 unless (1) they violated a federal statutory or constitutional right, and (2) the unlawfulness of their conduct was clearly established at the time. . . this doctrine gives government officials breathing room to make reasonable but mistaken judgments, and protects all but the plainly incompetent or those who knowingly violate the law. . . . For their claim to survive a motion to dismiss, the Does' complaint must allege that (1) they engaged in constitutionally protected conduct, (2) they were subjected to an adverse action by the defendant, and (3) the protected conduct was a substantial or motivating factor in the adverse action."

The U.S. District Court Judge denied the FRCP 12(b)(6) Motion to Dismiss based on *Stanek v. St. Charles Comm. Unit Sch. Dist. 783 F.3d 634 (7th Cir. 2015)*, a Seventh Circuit ruling that permits Section 1983 actions in IDEA cases, explaining that although the "overwhelming weight of authority finding that the IDEA does not authorize individual liability . . . the law of this Circuit is that Section 1983 can be used for IDEA claims" and the individuals defendants may be liable. The court denied the defendant's qualified immunity defense. Defendants have filed an answer. On November 28, 2022 the Court ordered that discovery must be completed by February 27, 2023.

105   The Federal court Complaint and later Memorandum and Order in *CB v. Chicago Public Sch.* et al. are located at:
https://www.wrightslaw.com/law/pleadings/cb.v.chicago.1983.complaint.pdf and
https://www.wrightslaw.com/law/caselaw/2022/2022.0826.opinion.cb.v.chicago.wagman.mock.pdf

106   https://www.law.cornell.edu/rules/frcp

The federal courts have rules about appeals, evidence, criminal procedure and civil procedure. Links to the full text of each are located at the U.S. Courts website[107] and Cornell's Legal Information Institute's website.[108] District courts and the Courts of Appeals typically also have local rules. The rules are revised occasionally. Failure to follow the federal and local rules of court can result in dismissal of a case.

In most special education due process cases that are appealed to federal court, **no new evidence is permitted**. The judge reviews the due process decision, testimony, exhibits, briefs, and rules on that administrative record. If there are Section 504 and ADA issues or "after discovered evidence," there may be additional issues with subsequent discovery depositions and affidavits. Prior to that stage and after discovery, the parties will usually file Motions to Dismiss, Motions for Summary Judgment, or a Motion for Judgment on the Administrative Record.

The court's ruling on the motion(s) often begins with:

> The defendants have filed a motion to dismiss pursuant to **Rule 12(b)(1)** of the Federal Rules of Civil Procedure for lack of subject matter jurisdiction and a motion to dismiss pursuant to **Rule 12(b)(6)** for failure to state a claim upon which relief may be granted.[109]

> In deciding a Rule 12(b)(6) motion to dismiss for failure to state a claim, the court accepts all well-pleaded facts as true, viewing them in the light most favorable to the plaintiff. While the complaint attacked by a Rule 12(b)(6) motion does not need detailed factual allegations in order to avoid dismissal, the plaintiff's factual allegations must be enough to raise a right to relief above the speculative level. The court need not accept as true conclusory allegations or allegations stating a legal conclusion. The complaint must contain sufficient facts to state a claim for relief that is plausible on its face.

> Both parties have relied upon the administrative record, testimony and exhibits in the previous due process hearing and depositions and affidavits filed in this proceeding. The Court finds . . ."

At this point, the Judge will discuss the facts and law of the case. In the beginning or at the end, the court will provide rationale for dismissing all or portions of the plaintiff's case or denying the defendant's motions.

Federal Rules of Civil Procedure (FRCP)[110]

FRCP Rule 12 - Defenses and Objections: When and How Presented; Motion for Judgment on the Pleadings; Consolidating Motions; Waiving Defenses; Pretrial Hearing[111]

(a) Time to Serve a Responsive Pleading . . .

(b) **How to Present Defenses.** Every defense to a claim for relief in any pleading must be asserted in the responsive pleading if one is required. But a party may assert the following defenses by motion:

> (1) lack of subject-matter jurisdiction;
> (2) lack of personal jurisdiction;
> (3) improper venue;
> (4) insufficient process;
> (5) insufficient service of process;

---

107   https://www.uscourts.gov/rules-policies/current-rules-practice-procedure

108   https://www.law.cornell.edu/rules

109   For application of a "12(b)(6) Motion to Dismiss," see the preceding *CB v. Chicago, et al.* case in the Section 1983 discussion.

110   In the following Rules, this notation ". . ." means that the full text of the Rule is not included, see the full text at either:
       https://www.law.cornell.edu/rules/frcp   or   https://www.uscourts.gov/rules-policies/current-rules-practice-procedure

111   https://www.law.cornell.edu/rules/frcp/rule_12

(6) failure to state a claim upon which relief can be granted;[112] **and**

(7) failure to join a party under Rule 19.

A motion asserting any of these defenses must be made before pleading if a responsive pleading is allowed. If a pleading sets out a claim for relief that does not require a responsive pleading, an opposing party may assert at trial any defense to that claim. No defense or objection is waived by joining it with one or more other defenses or objections in a responsive pleading or in a motion.

(c) Motion for Judgment on the Pleadings. After the pleadings are closed—but early enough not to delay trial—a party may move for judgment on the pleadings.

(d) Result of Presenting Matters Outside the Pleadings. If, on a motion under Rule 12(b)(6) or 12(c), matters outside the pleadings are presented to and not excluded by the court, the motion must be treated as one for summary judgment under Rule 56. All parties must be given a reasonable opportunity to present all the material that is pertinent to the motion.

(e) Motion for a More Definite Statement. A party may move for a more definite statement of a pleading to which a responsive pleading is allowed but which is so vague or ambiguous that the party cannot reasonably prepare a response. The motion . . .

(f) Motion to Strike. The court may strike from a pleading an insufficient defense or any redundant, immaterial, impertinent, or scandalous matter. The court may act . . .

(g) Joining Motions . . .

(h) Waiving and Preserving Certain Defenses . . .

(i) Hearing Before Trial . . .

FRCP Rule 56 - Motion for Summary Judgment[113]

(a) Motion for Summary Judgment or Partial Summary Judgment. A party may move for summary judgment, identifying each claim or defense — or the part of each claim or defense — on which summary judgment is sought. The court **shall grant summary judgment** if the movant shows that there is **no genuine dispute as to any material fact and the movant is entitled to judgment as a matter of law.** The court should state on the record the reasons for granting or denying the motion.

(b) Time to File a Motion. Unless a different time is set by local rule or the court orders otherwise, a party may file a motion for summary judgment at any time **until 30 days after** the close of all discovery.

(c) Procedures.

(1) Supporting Factual Positions. A party asserting that a fact cannot be or is genuinely disputed must support the assertion by:

(A) citing to particular parts of materials in the record, including depositions, documents, electronically stored information, affidavits or declarations, stipulations (including those made for purposes of the motion only), admissions, interrogatory answers, or other materials; or

(B) showing that the materials cited do not establish the absence or presence of a genuine dispute, or that an adverse party cannot produce admissible evidence to support the fact.

(2) and (3) [not included]

(4) Affidavits or Declarations. An affidavit or declaration used to support or oppose a motion must be made on personal knowledge, set out facts that would be admissible in evidence, and show that the affiant or declarant is competent to testify on the matters stated.

(d) and (e) [not included]

---

112   This is known as a **"Rule 12(b)(6) Motion to Dismiss."**

113   https://www.law.cornell.edu/rules/frcp/rule_56

(f) Judgment Independent of the Motion. After giving notice and a reasonable time to respond, the court may:

(1) grant summary judgment for a nonmovant;

(2) grant the motion on grounds not raised by a party; or

(3) consider summary judgment on its own[114] after identifying for the parties material facts that may not be genuinely in dispute.

(g) Failing to Grant All the Requested Relief. If the court does not grant all the relief . . . it may enter an order . . . treating the fact as established in the case.

(h) Affidavit or Declaration Submitted in Bad Faith. If satisfied that an affidavit or declaration under this rule is submitted in bad faith or solely for delay, the court . . . may order the submitting party to pay the other party the reasonable expenses, including attorney's fees, . . . [who] may also be held in contempt or subjected to other appropriate sanctions.

FRCP Rule 57 - Declaratory Judgment[115]

These rules govern the procedure for obtaining a **declaratory judgment under 28 U.S.C. §2201**. Rules 38 and 39 govern a demand for a jury trial. The existence of another adequate remedy does not preclude a declaratory judgment that is otherwise appropriate. **The court may order a speedy hearing of a declaratory-judgment action.**

FRCP Rule 68 - Offer of Judgment[116]

(a) Making an Offer; Judgment on an Accepted Offer. At least 14 days before the date set for trial, a party defending against a claim may serve on an opposing party an offer to allow judgment on specified terms, with the costs then accrued. If, within 14 days after being served, the opposing party serves written notice accepting the offer, either party may then file the offer and notice of acceptance, plus proof of service. The clerk must then enter judgment.

(b) Unaccepted Offer. An unaccepted offer is considered withdrawn, but it does not preclude a later offer. Evidence of an unaccepted offer is not admissible except in a proceeding to determine costs.

(c) Offer After Liability is Determined. When one party's liability to another has been determined but the extent of liability remains to be determined by further proceedings, the party held liable may make an offer of judgment. It must be served within a reasonable time—but at least 14 days—before the date set for a hearing to determine the extent of liability.

(d) Paying Costs After an Unaccepted Offer. If the judgment that the offeree finally obtains is not more favorable than the unaccepted offer, the offeree must pay the costs incurred after the offer was made.

End of Federal Rules of Civil Procedure (FRCP)

---

114 In 1980, another attorney, without having first requested a special education due process hearing, filed a lawsuit on behalf of McGovern against Chesterfield County Public Schools Superintendent Sullins. The school allegedly failed to provide the child with special education services. That attorney then moved out of Virginia and this author began representing the parents. It was my first case ever in federal court. For reasons now lost to memory, the school board attorney and I both agreed that "exhaustion" was not necessary as it was "futile." However, the District Court Judge, *sua sponte*, on his own Motion, dismissed the case for failure to exhaust administrative remedies. We appealed and the Fourth Circuit upheld the dismissal. *McGovern v. Sullins*, 676 F.2d 98 (4th Cir. 1982).

115 https://www.law.cornell.edu/rules/frcp/rule_57

116 https://www.law.cornell.edu/rules/frcp/rule_68

United States Constitution[117]

Many education and disability related disputes involve allegations that the defendant violated the U.S. Constitution. Portions generally referenced in such litigation are:

Article VI[118]

"This Constitution, and the Laws of the United States . . . shall be the **supreme Law of the Land**; and the Judges in every State shall be bound thereby. . . ."

First Amendment

"Congress shall make no law . . . abridging the freedom of speech . . ."

Fourth Amendment

"The right of the people to be secure in their persons, houses, papers, and effects, against unreasonable searches and seizures, shall not be violated . . ."

Fifth Amendment

"No person shall be . . . deprived of life, liberty, or property, **without due process of law** . . ."

Fourteenth Amendment

"All persons born or naturalized in the United States, and subject to the jurisdiction thereof, are citizens of the United States and of the state wherein they reside. No state shall make or enforce any law which shall abridge the privileges or immunities of citizens of the United States; nor shall any state deprive any person of life, liberty, or property, **without due process of law; nor deny** to any person within its jurisdiction **the equal protection** of the laws."

In Summation

In this Chapter 9, you learned about the Family Educational and Rights and Privacy Act (FERPA). the McKinney-Vento Homeless Assistance Act, other relevant federal statutes, and portions of the United States Constitution that are frequently referenced in special education caselaw.

Coming up next - **Chapter 10** contains **24 Selected Topics** that generate many questions. A few of these are Bullying, Child Find, COVID and Compensatory Education, Discipline, FAPE, LRE, Military children, Section 504 Plans v IEP, and Transition.

End of Chapter 9 - Miscellaneous Statutes + Rules

---

117   https://www.law.cornell.edu/constitution/index.html

118   This is known as the Supremacy Clause.

Hyperlinks to Chapters

CHAPTER 10

Selected Topics

When you have a question about IDEA, Section 504, or the ADA, you can expect to receive misinformation, confusing advice, and conflicting opinions. The answer to your question will often depend on whether the question arises under IDEA, Section 504, and/or the ADA.

Because some topics generate so much confusion and bad advice, we included a chapter about some of these issues. In the Table below, you'll find the **Selected Topics.** Each **is hyperlinked** to the discussion about it in this chapter.

Three federal laws protect children with disabilities: the Individuals with Disabilities Education Act (IDEA), Section 504 of the Rehabilitation Act of 1973 (Section 504), and the American with Disabilities Act of 1990 (ADA). Because these laws have different purposes and are enforced differently, this can lead to confusion and consternation.

IDEA[1] is not a complicated statute. It is not written in "legalese" and is relatively easy to understand. **Section 504,**[2] the civil rights law that protects individuals with disabilities, is short. The essence of Section 504 is in the regulations. The **Americans with Disabilities Act**[3] prohibits discrimination against individuals with disabilities and extends the protections beyond the entities covered by Section 504, such as private day care and nursery schools, private schools, colleges and universities, graduate schools, and professional licensing exams.

Selected Topics

Academic Content Standards	Enforcement	Placement, Change of
Assistive Technology	Evaluations	Placement, Continuum
Bullying & Harassment	FAPE	Related Services
Charter Schools	Grades	Restraint and Seclusion
Child Find	Individualized Health Care Plans	Section 504 v IEP
COVID & Compensatory Ed.	Least Restrictive Environment	Supplementary Aids & Services
Discipline	Military children	Transition
Eligibility	PE/Adaptive PE	Transition to Higher Ed.

---

1 The full text of IDEA is in <Chapter 5.> Its regulations are in <Chapter 6.>

2 Critical portions of Section 504 and its regulations are in <Chapter 7.>

3 Critical portions of the Americans with Disabilities Act and its regulations are in <Chapter 8.>

Academic Content Standards

IDEA defines "special education" as "**specially designed instruction**, at no cost to the parents to meet the unique needs of the child with a disability . . ."[4]

The IDEA regulations expand the concept of **specially designed instruction** which

"means adapting, as appropriate to the needs of an eligible child, the content, methodology, or delivery of instruction-

(i) to address the **unique needs** of the child that result from the child's disability and

(ii) **to ensure access of the child to the general curriculum, so that the child can meet the educational standards within the jurisdiction of the public agency that apply to all children.**"[5]

While addressing the child's unique needs and adapting the content, methodology and delivery of instruction, the IEP must be designed to enable the child to be involved in and make progress in the general education curriculum.

Your State academic content standards describe what your state determined that **all students** need to know and be able to do in each grade – what schools will teach each child – **including children with disabilities**.

Because the IEP must be aligned to the State's academic content standards for the grade in which the child is enrolled, the IEP team must develop a plan of specialized instruction to teach these academic content standards. The IEP must include:

"a statement of the special education and related services and supplementary aides and services . . . to enable the child to be **involved in and make progress in the general education curriculum** . . ."[6]

"a statement of measurable annual goals, including academic and functional goals, designed to meet the child's needs . . . to enable the child to be **involved in and make progress in the general education curriculum** . . ."[7]

"a statement of any individual appropriate accommodations that are necessary **to measure the child's academic achievement** and functional performance on State and districtwide assessments . . ."[8]

When you review the state academic content standards for your child's grade and the IEP, you should know if your child is involved in and making progress in the general education curriculum.

In *Closing the Gap: Academic Content Standards and FAPE (OSERS, 2015)*,[9] the Office of Special Education and Rehabilitative Services (OSERS) published guidance to clarify that IEPs must be aligned with grade level academic content standards:

IEP Teams must ensure that annual IEP goals are aligned with the State academic content standards for the grade in which the child is enrolled;

The IEP must include the specially designed instruction needed to address the child's unique needs that result from the child's disability;

The IEP must ensure that the child has access to the general education curriculum, so the child can meet the State academic content standards that apply to all children;

The IEP must provide support services and program modifications or supports for school personnel that will enable the child to advance appropriately toward attaining the annual goals.[10]

---

4   <20 U.S.C. §1401(29)>

5   <34 C.F.R. §300.39(b)(3)>

6   20 U. S. C. § 1414(d)(1)(A)(IV)(bb)

7   20 U. S. C. § 1414(d)(1)(A)(II)(aa)

8   20 U. S. C. § 1414(d)(1)(A)(VI)(aa)

9   *Closing the Gap: Academic Content Standards and FAPE* (OSERS, 2015) at:
      https://www.wrightslaw.com/law/osers/2015.fape.acad.content.close.gap.pdf

10 *Id.*

Assistive Technology Devices and Services[11]

An **assistive technology device** is "any item, piece of equipment, or product system, whether acquired commercially off the shelf, modified, or customized, that is used to increase, maintain, or improve functional capabilities of a child with a disability."[12]

An **assistive technology service** is "any service that directly assists a child with a disability in the selection, acquisition, or use of an assistive technology device" and may include an assistive technology evaluation; training for the child, family members, and teachers in how to use a device; and modifying or customizing a device. An assistive technology evaluation may include a functional evaluation of the child at school and/or at home.[13]

Under **IDEA**, if a child is eligible for special education and related services, the IEP team is **required to determine if the child needs assistive technology**[14] to receive a free and appropriate public education (FAPE). Schools are to use assistive technology devices and services "to maximize accessibility for children with disabilities."[15]

Under **Section 504,** the **failure to provide an assistive technology service or device is discriminatory** because this denies a "qualified handicapped person . . . an opportunity to participate in or benefit from the aid, benefit, or service that is not equal to that afforded others . . ."[16] The **ADA** regulations focus on "appropriate auxiliary aids and services" to "provide effective communication" to "persons with impaired vision and hearing."[17]

When an IEP team determines that a child needs assistive technology device(s) and services, the school is responsible for providing these and cannot use lack of availability or cost as an excuse. IDEA also requires schools to provide **assistive technology training** for the child's teachers, the child, and the child's family.

All assistive technology devices and services, including evaluations and training for parents and staff, should be written into the child's IEP.[18]

IDEA includes a section about <"special factors"> in IEPs. These special factors address the unique needs of children who are deaf or hard of hearing, children who are blind or visually impaired, children with communication disorders, and children who need assistive technology.[19] For additional information, please check the **Wrightslaw Assistive Technology** topic page.[20]

Bullying and Harassment

Bullying is a fact of life for many children and adolescents with disabilities. Children with disabilities are often targets of bullying at school.[21]

Bullying takes many forms, from physical behavior, verbal, emotional, and blatant aggression to subtle and covert behaviors. Cyberbullying[22] refers to bullying through electronic technology and includes offensive text messages, e-mails, rumors, or embarrassing photos posted on social networking sites, and fake online profiles. Most states have laws, regulations, and policies that define bullying, children who are common targets of bullying, requirements for school district policies, and state maps of "Anti-Bullying Laws and Policies."[23]

---

11   See also the <Assistive Technology Act at starting at 29 U.S.C. § 3001.>

12   20 U.S.C. § 1401(1)

13   20 U.S.C. § 1401(2)

14   20 U.S.C. § 1414(d)(3)(B)(v)

15   20 U.S.C. § 1400(c)(5)(H)

16   34 CFR § 104.4(b)(ii)

17   28 CFR §§ 35.104., 35.160, 36.303, 41.51, and 34 CFR § 104.33

18   20 U.S.C. §1401(2)(E) & (F)

19   20 U.S.C. § 1414(d)(3)(B)

20   https://www.wrightslaw.com/info/atech.index.htm

21   https://dev.aacap.org/AACAP/Families_and_Youth/Facts_for_Families/FFF-Guide/Bullying-080.aspx

22   https://www.stopbullying.gov/cyberbullying/what-is-it

23   https://www.stopbullying.gov/resources/laws

When bullying is directed at a child with a disability and creates a hostile environment at school, this is "disability harassment." Under **Section 504** and **Title II of the ADA**, schools are required to address disability harassment.[24]

In **2010**, the Office for Civil Rights and the U.S. Department of Education issued "Dear Colleague" guidance for school staff that peer harassment based on disability "is sufficiently serious that it creates a hostile environment and such harassment is encouraged, tolerated, **not adequately addressed, or ignored by school employees," this is a violation of Section 504 and the ADA**.[25]

In **2013**, the Office of Special Education and Rehabilitative Services (OSERS) issued another "Dear Colleague" guidance letter about bullying, harassment and IDEA.[26]

> Bullying of a student with a disability that results in the student not receiving meaningful educational benefit constitutes a denial of FAPE under the IDEA and must be remedied . . . even when situations do not rise to a level that constitutes a denial of FAPE, bullying can undermine a student's ability to achieve his or her **full academic potential**.

> [I]t is also **intolerable for teachers and school staff** to be party to school bullying and disability harassment (i.e., **being active participants in bullying), or observers to school bullying without taking action** to address the behavior.

In **2014**, the Office for Civil Rights issued another guidance letter to clarify that when a child who receives services under IDEA or Section 504 is bullied, this results in a **disability-based harassment violation** and a **denial of FAPE**.[27]

> A school is **responsible for addressing harassment incidents** about which it knows or reasonably should have known. In some cases, harassment may be in plain sight, widespread, or well-known. In these cases, the obvious signs of the harassment are sufficient to **put the school on notice**. In other cases, the school may become aware of misconduct, triggering an **investigation** that leads to the discovery of additional incidents that, taken together, may constitute a hostile environment."

> When a student who receives **IDEA FAPE services or Section 504 FAPE services** has experienced bullying resulting in a disability-based harassment violation, however, there is a strong likelihood that the **student was denied FAPE**. This is because when bullying is sufficiently serious to create **a hostile environment** and the school **fails to respond appropriately**, there is a strong likelihood both that the effects of the bullying included an impact on the student's receipt of FAPE and that the school's failure to remedy the effects of the bullying included its **failure to address these FAPE-related concerns** . . .the school should . . . **promptly convene the IEP team or the Section 504 team** to determine whether, and to what extent:

> (1) the student's educational needs have changed;

> (2) the bullying impacted the student's receipt of IDEA FAPE services or Section 504 FAPE services; and

> (3) additional or different services, if any, are needed, and to ensure any needed changes are made promptly. By doing so, the school will be in the best position to ensure the student's ongoing receipt of FAPE.[28]

The **Wrightslaw Bullying and Harassment Page**[29] is a comprehensive source of information about effective strategies for responding to bullying and harassment, legal decisions and settlements, training programs, and resources to end bullying and harassment of children.

---

24   https://www.stopbullying.gov/bullying/special-needs

25   https://www2.ed.gov/about/offices/list/ocr/letters/colleague-201010.pdf

26   https://www.wrightslaw.com/info/bully.osep.letter.2013.0820.pdf

27   https://www.wrightslaw.com/info/bully.ocr.letter.2014.1021.pdf

28   https://www.wrightslaw.com/info/bully.ocr.letter.2014.1021.pdf

29   https://www.wrightslaw.com/info/harassment.index.htm

Charter Schools

Charter schools are publicly funded, independently run schools. Some public charter schools operate as LEAs and are supervised by their State Education Department. Other charter schools operate within an existing LEA that is their supervising entity. The USDOE has issued guidance about rights and **responsibilities of charter schools under IDEA**[30] **and Section 504.**[31]

Children with disabilities who attend charter schools have the same rights under IDEA, Section 504, and the ADA as nondisabled children.[32] Charter schools must serve children with disabilities who attend charter schools in the same manner as public schools serve children with disabilities.

Child Find

"Child Find" applies to public schools under **IDEA** and **Section 504**.

IDEA requires schools to ensure that:

All children with disabilities residing in the State, including children with disabilities who are homeless children or are wards of the State, and children with disabilities attending private schools, regardless of the severity of their disabilities, and who are in need of special education and related services, are identified, located, and evaluated and a practical method is developed and implemented to determine which children with disabilities are currently receiving needed special education and related services.[33]

Section 504 requires that schools **shall**:

[I]dentify and locate every qualified handicapped person residing in the recipient's jurisdiction who is not receiving a public education; and . . . notify handicapped persons and their parents or guardians of . . . [their rights and] . . .[34]

[P]rovide a free appropriate public education to each qualified handicapped person who is in the recipient's jurisdiction, regardless of the nature or severity of the person's handicap.[35]

IDEA requires that public schools consult with private school staff and parents about "the design and development of special education and related services for the children . . ."[36] See also the **Wrightslaw Child Find topic page**.[37]

Compensatory Education, COVID, and Caselaw

When the COVID-19 pandemic closed public schools in March 2020, millions of children with disabilities did not receive the in-person special education and related services and evaluations in their IEPs and Section 504 Plans. In some school districts, this failure to provide appropriate services continued for years, causing special needs children to fall further behind their peers. The pandemic did not relieve schools of the responsibility to provide special needs children with the appropriate services and evaluations in their IEPs and Section 504 Plans.

On March 12, 2020, within days of school closures, the USDOE issued guidance to clarify that schools were required to make individualized determinations about providing **compensatory education services** to children with IEPs and 504 Plans, including helping the children make up for the knowledge and skills lost or never learned.

If a child does not receive services after an extended period of time, a school must make an individualized determination about whether and to what extent **compensatory services** may be needed, consistent with applicable requirements, including to make up for any skills that may have been lost.[38]

---

30 https://sites.ed.gov/idea/files/policy_speced_guid_idea_memosdcltrs_faq-idea-charter-school.pdf

31 https://www2.ed.gov/about/offices/list/ocr/docs/dcl-faq-201612-504-charter-school.pdf

32 20 U.S.C. § 1413(a)(5); 34 CFR § 300.209

33 20 U.S.C. § 1412(a)(3)

34 34 CFR § 104.32

35 34 CFR § 104.33

36 34 CFR § 300.134

37 https://www.wrightslaw.com/info/child.find.index.htm

38 https://www.wrightslaw.com/covid/2020.0312.USDOE.QandA.Services.pdf

The position of U.S. Department of Education and the Office for Civil Rights has been consistent in the years since school closures. In September 2021, the USDOE published the *Return to School Roadmap* clarifying that:

> If a student with a disability did not receive appropriate evaluations or services, including the services that the school had previously determined they were entitled to, **the school must convene** a group of persons knowledgeable about the student to make an **individualized determination whether, and to what extent, compensatory services are required.**[39]

In February 2022, the Office for Civil Rights published guidance for parents and schools about how to **determine a child's needs for compensatory education**:[40]

> The compensatory services inquiry **requires looking backwards** to determine the educational and other benefits that likely would have accrued from services the student should have received in the first place.

> Compensatory services are **required to remedy educational or other deficits** that result from the student not receiving the evaluations or services to which they were entitled. **Providing compensatory services . . .** is a remedy that recognizes the **reality that students experience injury** when they do not receive appropriate and timely initial evaluations, reevaluations, or services, including the services that the school had previously determined they were entitled to, **regardless of the reason.**

> The **individualized determinations** of whether and to what extent, compensatory services are required must be made by a group of persons knowledgeable about the student, including school nurses, teachers, counselors, psychologists, school administrators, social workers, doctors and/or family members.

> Ideally, the team of knowledgeable persons will come to a mutually acceptable decision regarding compensatory services to mitigate the impact of the COVID-19 pandemic on the child's receipt of services.

Several **factors** may be relevant for the group of knowledgeable persons to consider in determining the **appropriate type and amount of compensatory services**:

- the frequency and duration of missed instruction and related services;
- whether special education and/or related services that were provided during the pandemic were appropriate based on the student's individual needs;
- the student's present levels of performance and the results of updated evaluations;
- whether evaluations were delayed; and any other relevant information.[41]

If a parent or guardian believes their child did not receive FAPE, did not have equal access to other services provided by the school, or did not receive appropriate compensatory services, they may seek a hearing under either the IDEA or Section 504 due process procedures or file a complaint with OCR.[42]

Compensatory education is not specifically addressed in IDEA, Section 504, the Code of Federal Regulations, or in state statutes and regulations. Compensatory education was created and evolved through case law. To learn more about "comp ed," *see Compensatory Education Case Law from the Beginning Through Draper in 2008*.[43]

The **COVID Compensatory Education pages on Wrightslaw**[44] have articles about compensatory education, directives from the USDOE and the Office for Civil Rights, guidance from legal and advocacy organizations, and selected cases about compensatory education and COVID.

---

[39] See 34 CFR 104.35; *cf,. "Return to School Roadmap:* (September 2021) at: https://sites.ed.gov/idea/files/rts-iep-09-30-2021.pdf

[40] https://www2.ed.gov/about/offices/list/ocr/docs/factsheet-504.html

[41] *"Providing Students with Disabilities FAPE During the COVID-19 Pandemic and Addressing the Need for Compensatory Services Under Section 504"* (February, 2022) at:
https://www2.ed.gov/about/offices/list/ocr/docs/factsheet-504.html
https://www2.ed.gov/about/offices/list/ocr/docs/fape-in-covid-19.pdf

[42] For a discussion of these procedures, see the *Parent and Educator Resource Guide to Section 504 in Public Elementary and Secondary Schools* at p 35; see also 34 C.F.R. § 104.36

[43] https://www.wrightslaw.com/info/comp.ed.law.htm

[44] https://www.wrightslaw.com/info/covid.index.htm

Discipline

In **IDEA** discipline issues, concerns often relate to "manifestation determination" and whether, pursuant to the law about "Special Factors" in IEPs,[45] the school conducted a Functional Behavior Assessment (FBA) and developed a Behavioral Intervention Plan (BIP). If a child with a disability violates a code of student conduct, the school may remove the child from the current placement to an interim alternative placement for **no more than 10 days**.[46]

IDEA addresses disciplinary placements in alternative educational settings, manifestation determinations, appeals, and the authority of the hearing officer.[47] Most discipline cases are about specific issues:

- Did the school **use suspension and/or expulsion to remove a child** who violated a code of student conduct or other misbehavior from school and place the child in an **alternative educational setting?**

- Was the child's misbehavior caused by or have a direct relationship to the child's disability (**manifestation determination**) or was the misbehavior a result of the school's **failure to implement the IEP?**[48]

- Did the school perform a **Functional Behavior Assessment (FBA)** and develop and implement a **Behavior Intervention Plan** as required by the law about "special factors" in IEPs?[49]

- Did the school **provide the child with FAPE**, including **behavioral intervention services and modifications** to address the behavior violation, so the behavior does not reoccur?[50]

Under IDEA, when a school suspends or expels a child from school, the **child is still entitled to FAPE**.[51] This requirement means the school **shall** continue to provide educational services that enable the child to participate in the general education curriculum, make progress on the IEP goals, and receive "a functional behavioral assessment, behavioral intervention services and modifications designed to address the behavior violation so it does not recur.[52]

Because Congress was concerned about the inappropriate use of **zero-tolerance** policies in schools, they added new language to the discipline statute requiring that school personnel consider "**any unique circumstance on a case-by-case basis** when determining . . . a change in placement for a child with a disability who violates a code of student conduct."[53]

Under **Section 504**, the school district "**shall conduct an evaluation** . . . before taking any action with respect to the **initial placement . . . and any subsequent significant change in placement**."[54] The language about "change of placement" for the Section 504 youngster is considered by many to provide greater rights in discipline.

The **OCR Resource Guide**[55] at page 22 explains that Section 504:

- requires schools to conduct periodic reevaluations of students with disabilities and conduct **reevaluations prior to significant changes in placement**

- considers excluding a child from the educational program (for example, an out-of-school suspension) for more than 10 consecutive school days to be a significant change in placement

- considers a series of short-term exclusions (each 10 school days or less) from the educational program to be

---

45   20 U.S.C. § 1414(d)(3)(B)(i)

46   20 U.S.C. § 1412(a)(1)(A)

47   20 U.S.C. § 1415(k)

48   20 U.S.C. § 1415(k)(1)(E)

49   20 U. S. C. § 1414(d)(3)(B)

50   20 U. S. C. § 1415(k)(1)(D)

51   *Id.*

52   20 U. S. C. § 1415(k)(1)(D)

53   <20 U.S.C. § 1415 (k)(1)(A)>

54   34 CFR § 104.35

55   https://www2.ed.gov/about/offices/list/ocr/docs/504-resource-guide-201612.pdf, and
https://www.wrightslaw.com/law/ocr/sec504.guide.ocr.2016.pdf

a significant change in placement and if short-term exclusions total more than 10 school days, this creates a pattern of removal

- requires schools to have "a system of **procedural safeguards** that includes notice, . . . an impartial hearing, . . . representation by counsel, and a review procedure."[56]

Consider this scenario: *Salim is a student with a disability and he has a Section 504 plan. At the start of the spring semester, he received an* **out-of-school suspension for 12 consecutive school days**. *Is the school required to reevaluate Salim?* [57]

Answer from OCR: Yes. Section 504 requires schools to conduct reevaluations periodically, and **before a significant change in placement.** OCR considers an exclusion from the educational program of more than 10 consecutive school days to be a **significant change in placement.**[58] In this example, the school must reevaluate Salim, prior to imposing the 11th day of suspension, to determine whether his misconduct is caused by or related to his disability (manifestation determination), and if so to further evaluate to determine if his **current placement is appropriate**.[59]

Because of concerns about schools' **overuse of suspension, expulsion and zero tolerance policies** and the negative costs of these policies, the USDOE issued a "Key Policy Letter" on this subject.

> The **widespread overuse of suspensions and expulsions** has **tremendous costs**. . . . Suspended students are less likely to graduate on time and more likely to be suspended again, repeat a grade, drop out of school, and become involved in the juvenile justice system.
>
> When carried out in connection with zero-tolerance policies, such practices can **erode trust between students and school staff**, and undermine efforts to create the positive school climates needed to engage students in a well-rounded and rigorous curriculum. In fact, research indicates an association between **higher suspension rates and lower schoolwide academic achievement and standardized test scores**. Schools and taxpayers also bear the steep direct and indirect costs from the associated grade retention and elevated school dropout rates.[60]

Resources:

"The Framework for Effective School Discipline" published by the **National Association of School Psychologists (NASP).**[61]

"Discipline: Suspensions, Expulsions & IEPs by Massachusetts attorney, Robert K. Crabtree.[62]

"Wrightslaw Game Plan: How to Deal with Discipline & Behavior Problems[63]

You'll find information about behavior and discipline, Functional Behavior Assessments and Behavior Intervention Plans, and Caselaw on the **Wrightslaw Behavior and Discipline Page**.[64]

Eligibility

Eligibility for special education and related services under IDEA is different from eligibility for protections and services under Section 504 / ADA.

IDEA requires the school to evaluate to determine if the child is a "child with a disability" and is eligible for an IEP. IDEA defines a 'child with a disability' as "a child (i) with . . . [specific disabilities listed here] **and** (ii) who, **by rea-**

---

56   34 CFR § 104.36

57   This is "scenario # 7" at page 23 from the OCR's *Resource Guide.*

58   *See* the discussion about <Placement> later in this chapter.

59   *Parent Educator Resource Guide to Section 504*, page 23, explaining impact of 34 CFR § 104.35(a).

60   https://www2.ed.gov/policy/elsec/guid/secletter/140108.html

61   https://www.nasponline.org/assets/Documents/Resources%20and%20Publications/Discipline-Framework-Document%20(1).pdf

62   https://www.wrightslaw.com/info/discipl.suspend.crabtree.htm

63   https://www.wrightslaw.com/info/discipl.plan.expulsion.htm

64   https://www.wrightslaw.com/info/discipl.index.htm

son thereof, **needs special education and related services."**[65] The <regulations defining a "child with a disability"> include more specifics.[66] The initial evaluation and determination of eligibility must be completed within **60 calendar days**[67] of receiving parent consent [68] **unless** a state law or regulation permits a shorter or longer timeline.[69]

IDEA requires "a team of qualified professionals and the child's parent" to determine the child's eligibility and educational needs and that "a copy of the evaluation report and documentation of eligibility **shall** be given to the parent."[70] IDEA also **requires the school to evaluate** before determining that a child is no longer eligible for services **unless** the child has graduated with a regular diploma or "aged out" of eligibility.[71]

Section 504 requires a group of people, including people who are knowledgeable about evaluation data and placement options, to determine eligibility. **The child's parent is not a required member of this group.** The group must draw from a variety of sources, including aptitude and achievement tests, teacher recommendations, physical condition, social and cultural background, and adaptive behavior.[72]

IDEA does not require that a child be classified by a disability before receiving services through an IEP "so long as . . . [the] child . . . has a disability listed in Section 1401."[73]

Section 504 requires school districts to provide a free appropriate public education (FAPE) to children who

- have a physical or mental impairment that substantially limits one or more major life activities, regardless of the nature or severity of the disability; or
- have a record of such an impairment; or
- are regarded as having such an impairment.

The determination about who is covered and protected under Section 504 and the ADA is to be "broadly construed." Individuals with episodic conditions and individuals whose disability is mitigated with hearing aids, medication, or other means are covered. Examples of episodic conditions include allergies, arthritis, asthma, chronic fatigue syndrome, chronic pain, diabetes, epilepsy, hepatitis C, HIV/AIDS, migraines, some forms of cancer, and mental illness. Examples of mitigating measures are hearing aids, cochlear implants, low vision devices, prosthetics, mobility devices, assistive technology, reasonable accommodations, and more.

The definitions of "disability" in **Section 504**[74] and the **ADA**[75] are the same,[76] and include children with IEPs, Section 504 Plans, children in public and private daycare centers and nursery schools, private schools, and institutions of higher education. Schools and other entities **"controlled"** by religious organizations **are exempt** from the ADA.[77]

---

65 20 U.S.C. § 1401(3)

66 34 CFR § 300.8

67 <20 U.S.C. § 1414(a)(1)(C)(i)>

68 It is not the date of the request, but the **date of consent to evaluate** that starts the clock to run. Parents requesting an evaluation should do so in writing and provide the basis for the request using facts, data, and observations, not opinions, and note that the letter is the request and is also the **consent to evaluate.**

69 20 U.S.C. § 1414(a)(1)(B)

70 20 U.S.C. § 1414(b)(4)

71 20 U.S.C. § 1414(b)(5)

72 34 CFR § 104.35(c)(3)

73 20 U.S.C. § 1412(a)(3)(B)

74 29 U.S.C. § 705(9) and (20). Under Section 504, the definition of a disability is the definition written into the ADA and, for a student with an IEP, also incorporates by reference, IDEA.

75 42 U.S.C. § 12102

76 Definitions at 29 U.S.C. 705(37)(A)(ii)(I) explains that the term "'student with a disability' means an individual with a disability who (I) is eligible for, and receiving, special education or related services under part B of the Individuals with Disabilities Education Act; . . . or (II) is an individual with a disability, for purposes of section 794 of this title."

77 42 U.S.C. § 12187

Determinations by courts about whether an individual is protected are inconsistent. Eligibility for protections under Section 504 and the ADA is an area of developing caselaw.

Enforcement of IDEA, Section 504 and ADA

Three federal statutes protect children with disabilities: the Individuals with Disabilities Education Act (IDEA), Section 504 of the Rehabilitation Act of 1973 (Section 504), and the American with Disabilities Act of 1990 (ADA). Each law is enforced differently.

The **Individuals with Disabilities Education Act (IDEA)** provides federal funds to the states to help defray the costs of special education and related services. To receive funding, State Education Agencies (SEAs) and school districts (LEAs) are required to provide all children with disabilities with a free appropriate public education (FAPE) in the least restrictive environment (LRE).

The **Office of Special Education Programs (OSEP)** at the USDOE is responsible for monitoring how states implement IDEA. State Education Agencies are responsible for monitoring school districts' implementation of the law. The IDEA statute and regulations provide actions OSEP may take to enforce the law. When a state refuses to comply with the law, OSEP may refer the case to the U.S. Department of Justice (USDOJ) for enforcement, although OSEP has never referred a case to the USDOJ to enforce IDEA.

OSEP does not provide a formal process through which an individual can file a complaint about IDEA violations. Although OSEP receives phone calls and written communications of complaints, it has no written process about how it handles these complaints (unlike the written state complaint process described in IDEA federal regulations).

Typically, enforcement of IDEA violations are handled by parents who file administrative complaints with the SEA or request special education due process hearings against the LEA.

In 2000, the National Council on Disability (NCD) published *Back to School on Civil Rights*, their first report on IDEA Enforcement and Compliance since the law was enacted.[78] NCD found that "efforts to enforce the law over several Administrations have been **inconsistent, ineffective, and lacking any real teeth** . . . **Every State was out of compliance** with IDEA requirements to some degree . . . noncompliance persisted over many years."[79]

> Although the Education Department is responsible for enforcing IDEA, the DOE has **never required states to enforce the law** . . . (and) consistently **fail to impose sanctions** on states that refuse to comply with the law.[80]
>
> **Enforcing the law is the burden of parents** who must invoke . . . expensive and time-consuming litigation to obtain the appropriate services that their children are entitled to under the law . . . Even parents with significant resources are hard-pressed to prevail over state education agencies and school districts when they, or their publicly financed attorneys, choose to be resistant.[81]

The NCD recommended that Congress provide the Department of Justice with **independent authority** to investigate and litigate against school districts or states where pattern and practice violations exist. "As an agency that specializes primarily in enforcing the law, DOJ's first responsibility is to those protected by the laws it enforces."[82] When Congress reauthorized IDEA in 2004, they did not add teeth to the enforcement provisions.

In 2018, the NCD issued *The Individuals with Disabilities with Education Act Report,* a five-part series about unresolved enforcement problems, new topics since IDEA was reauthorized in 2004, and recommendations about how to resolve these issues.[83]

---

78 National Council on Disability, *Back to School on Civil Rights* (Washington, DC: Author, 2000), at:
   https://ncd.gov/publications/2000/Jan252000
   and
   https://www.wrightslaw.com/law/reports/IDEA_Compliance_overview.htm

79 https://www.wrightslaw.com/news/2000/NCD_IDEA_Report_00_0125.htm

80 https://www.wrightslaw.com/law/reports/IDEA_Compliance_9.htm

81 https://www.wrightslaw.com/law/reports/IDEA_Compliance_1.htm#Parents

82 https://www.wrightslaw.com/law/reports/IDEA_Compliance_6.htm

83 https://ncd.gov/publications/2018/individuals-disabilities-education-act-report-series-5-report-briefs

The five reports are:

- *Broken Promises: The Underfunding of IDEA;*[84]
- *English Learners and Students from Low-Income Families;*[85]
- *Federal Monitoring and Enforcement of IDEA Compliance;*[86]
- *Every Student Succeeds Act and Students with Disabilities;*[87] and
- *The Segregation of Students with Disabilities.*[88]

The NCD reported that the Office of Special Education Programs (OSEP) continued to pass the buck on enforcing IDEA.[89] For example, OSEP does not:

- use its authority to withhold funds when states do not comply with the law;
- refer cases to the Department of Justice for enforcement;
- have a formal process for parents to file complaints about IDEA violations;
- require states to provide information about their findings of school district non-compliance.

In their annual report on IDEA Enforcement for 2020, the USDOE reported that fewer than half the states were in compliance with the federal special education law. *USA Today* published ***Most states fail education obligations to special needs students: So, what else is new?*** by John M. McLaughlin who laid out the facts about the USDOE's failure to enforce the law:

> Foot dragging, slow walking, using the law to delay, and running out the clock are common tactics schools use to postpone services, especially for students with complex issues or assertive and informed parents. But school districts are not the only shirkers of responsibility.
>
> ***Rules not enforced breed contempt.*** School districts avoid compliance with the law for the simple reason that there are no real consequences to districts for ignoring the law . . . no one loses a license, no one pays a fine, no one goes to jail.
>
> Only the children and their families pay the consequences . . . The Individuals with Disabilities Education Act is effectively ***the only parentally-enforced federal law on the books.***[90]

Section 504 of the Rehabilitation Act of 1973 is the federal law designed to protect the rights of people with disabilities in programs and activities that receive federal financial assistance. Section 504 requires schools to provide appropriate educational services that meet the individual educational needs of students with disabilities to the same extent that the needs of students without disabilities are met.

The **Office for Civil Rights (OCR)** enforces Section 504. OCR receives and investigates complaints from parents, students, and advocates, conducts compliance reviews, and provides technical assistance to school districts, parents, and advocates. OCR also provides guidance through Dear Colleague Letters (DCLs) and other published materials.

When a parent and school district cannot resolve an issue, they can utilize a Section 504 due process hearing. OCR offers an early complaint resolution process, negotiates corrective action agreements, and has an appeals process for complainants. If OCR cannot accomplish voluntary compliance with Section 504, the agency may initiate admin-

---

84   https://ncd.gov/sites/default/files/NCD_BrokenPromises_508.pdf

85   https://ncd.gov/sites/default/files/NCD_EnglishLanguageLearners_508.pdf

86   https://ncd.gov/sites/default/files/NCD_Monitoring-Enforcement_Accessible.pdf

87   https://ncd.gov/sites/default/files/NCD_ESSA-SWD_Accessible.pdf

88   https://ncd.gov/sites/default/files/NCD_Segregation-SWD_508.pdf

89   National Council on Disability, *Federal Monitoring and Enforcement of IDEA* (Washington, DC: Author, 2018) https://ncd.gov/sites/default/files/NCD_Monitoring-Enforcement_Accessible.pdf

90   "Most states fail education obligations to special needs students: So, what else is new?" by John M. McLaughlin in *USA Today* (August 10, 2020)
   https://www.usatoday.com/story/opinion/voices/2020/08/08/disability-rights-states-fail-obligation-special-needs-students/3318292001/

istrative proceedings to terminate financial assistance to the school district or refer the case to the Department of Justice for judicial proceedings.[91]

The **Americans with Disabilities Act (ADA)** is broader than Section 504, especially in specific disability-related areas. The law includes a mandate to **eliminate discrimination** against people with disabilities. The ADA prohibits discrimination against individuals with disabilities in many settings, including public schools, private schools, child care centers, restaurants, lodging, transportation, and more, whether or not the entity receives federal funds.

The enforcement provisions in Title II and Title III of the ADA are different. Title II of the ADA prohibits discrimination on the basis of disability by state and local governments, regardless of whether they receive federal funds. When Title II provides greater protections than Section 504, entities must also comply with Title II. The Office for Civil Rights and the Department of Justice share enforcement of Title II of the ADA.

Title III of the ADA prohibits discrimination by entities that do not receive federal funds, including private schools, daycare centers, graduate schools, and other non-public school educational facilities."[92] Parents may find daycare centers that refuse to accept their children with disabilities. If the parent files a complaint with the Department of Justice, the doors of that daycare center will generally swing open. Enforcement of **Title III against private schools** is through the statutory provisions in the Civil Rights Act.[93]

Schools and other entities **"controlled"** by religious organizations **are exempt** from the ADA.[94] Private clubs are also exempt.

Parents can file suit for violations of these statutes. In suits against public schools, parents must ensure that they are not required to exhaust their administrative remedies under IDEA, even if their child does not have an IEP.[95]

In an **enforcement action**, the plaintiff must establish that:

(1) the student is a qualified individual with a disability within the meaning of Section 504 of the Rehabilitation Act or the ADA;

(2) the student was excluded from participation in, or was denied benefits of, services, programs, or activities for which the school district is responsible;

(3) the exclusion, denial of benefits, or discrimination was by reason of the disability; and

(4) the exclusion, denial of benefits, or discrimination was intentional or pursuant to deliberate indifference.

In a claim that a school district **failed to make reasonable accommodations** for a child's disability, the plaintiff must show that:

(1) the child's disability and limitations were known by the school district;

(2) the school failed to make reasonable accommodations for the known limitations; and

(3) the failure was intentional or that there was deliberate indifference.

The USDOE, OCR, and the USDOJ rarely become involved in violations of IDEA.

In Chapter 5, at the beginning of <20 U.S.C. § 1416,> the enforcement statute for IDEA, we explain that the U.S. "Department of Education has a minimal focus on whether schools and districts were teaching children with disabilities to read, write, spell, do arithmetic and prepare the children for further education, employment, independent living." We have seen no evidence that the recommendations from the NCD have been given serious consideration by the USDOE, the USDOJ, or Congress.

---

91   *Id.*

92   28 CFR §§ 35.103 and 36.103

93   <42 U.S.C. § 12188> and 42 U.S.C. § 2000a through 2000a-6, the latter located at:
    https://www.law.cornell.edu/uscode/text/42/chapter-21/subchapter-II

94   42 U.S.C. § 12187

95   20 U.S.C. § 1415(l) / *See also* the 2017 *Fry* SCOTUS case and our discussion about "Exhaustion."

It is our belief that the USDOE does not want to give up its power and the USDOJ does not want to assume more responsibility. Thus, with regard to IDEA, children who are eligible for IEPs and their parents will continue to suffer from these enforcement failures.

When individuals and the USDOJ file lawsuits for violations of Section 504 and the ADA, the subsequent jury trials and dollar damage verdicts and settlement agreements appear to have greater impact in creating change.

Evaluations

IDEA and **Section 504** have similar legal requirements for evaluations (see the Eligibility topic in this chapter).

IDEA and Section 504 require the school to obtain parental consent for initial evaluations. If the parent refuses to provide consent, the school district may request a due process hearing to over-ride the parent's denial of consent.[96]

IDEA and Section 504 require the school to evaluate the child before classifying the child as having a disability, before providing the child with special education services, or making an initial placement or a significant change of placement.[97]

The IDEA and Section 504 requirements for evaluations are **nearly identical.**[98] Tests and other evaluation materials must be selected to evaluate specific areas of educational need, must be validated for the purpose for which they are used, and must be administered by appropriately trained personnel.[99]

IDEA requires schools to "use a variety of assessment tools and strategies to gather relevant functional, developmental, and academic information" and "technically sound instruments that may assess physical or developmental factors and cognitive and behavioral factors . . ." Assessments must be selected "to yield accurate information on what the child knows and can do academically, developmentally, and functionally" and be "administered by trained and knowledgeable personnel."[100]

Section 504 requires that tests and other evaluation materials must be selected to evaluate specific areas of educational need, must be validated for the purpose for which they are used, and must be administered by appropriately trained personnel.[101] Tests and evaluation materials must be "tailored to assess specific areas of educational need and not merely those which are designed to provide a single general intelligence quotient."[102]

When "interpreting evaluation data and making placement decisions," the school shall "draw upon information from a variety of sources," and ensure that the obtained information "is documented and carefully considered."[103]

The **Section 504 regulation** about evaluations was discussed in the Eligibility topic. The regulation about placement decisions states that before the school district takes any action about an "initial placement" or a "subsequent significant change in placement," (example - discipline), the district must evaluate the child.[104]

IDEA and Section 504 require **reevaluations.** Using the reevaluation procedures in IDEA is one way to meet this requirement.[105]

---

96   https://www2.ed.gov/about/offices/list/ocr/504faq.html#placement

97   20 U.S.C. § 1414(b)(2)-(3)

98   20 U.S.C. § 1414(b)(2)-(3)

99   20 U.S.C § 1414(b)

100   20 U.S.C § 1414(b)

101   20 U.S.C. § 1414(b)

102   34 CFR § 104.35(b)(2)

103   34 CFR § 104.35(c)

104   34 CFR § 104.35

105   20 U.S.C § 1414(a)(2)

FAPE - Free Appropriate Public Education

Although **IDEA and Section 504** require public schools to provide children with disabilities with a "free appropriate public education," these laws define "FAPE" differently.

IDEA defines FAPE as "special education and related services that

(A) have been provided at public expense, under public supervision and direction, and without charge;

(B) meet the standards of the State educational agency;

(C) include an **appropriate** preschool, elementary school, or secondary school education in the State involved; and

(D) are provided in conformity with the individualized education program required under Section 1414(d)."[106]

After IDEA was enacted, Courts disagreed about what constituted an "appropriate" special education program. The Supreme Court attempted to clarify the meaning of "appropriate" in two cases, *Rowley*[107] in 1982 and *Endrew F.*[108] in 2017.

In *Rowley*, SCOTUS held that an IEP was appropriate if it was "reasonably calculated to enable the child to receive educational benefits." FAPE was not the best program, nor did it require a school to develop a program to maximize a child's potential.

After the *Rowley* decision, Courts disagreed about the definition of "educational benefit." Some held that educational benefit must be "meaningful" while others defined it as "some benefit, merely more than "*de minimis*." The Supreme Court agreed to hear the *Endrew F.* case to resolve the split among circuits about the *Rowley* standard of "some educational benefit."

In 2017, the Supreme Court issued a unanimous decision in *Endrew F.* and rejected the "*de minimis*" standard and adopted a standard that is "markedly more demanding than the 'merely more than *de minimis*' test applied by the 10th Circuit."[109] The decision in *Endrew F.* focused on the **child's potential** and **providing opportunities to meet challenging objectives**:

> An IEP is not a form document. It is constructed only after **careful consideration of the child's present levels of achievement, disability, and potential for growth.**

> A focus on the particular child is at the core of the IDEA. The instruction offered must be **specially designed to meet a child's unique needs** through an **individualized education program.**[110]

See Chapter 2 for a discussion about the *Endrew F.* decision. The full text of the decision[111] and analysis[112] are available on the Wrightslaw website and in the 2017 edition of *Wrightslaw Year in Review*.[113]

Section 504 defines a "free appropriate public education" (FAPE) as "regular or special education and related aids and services that . . . are designed to **meet individual educational needs** of handicapped persons **as adequately as the needs of nonhandicapped persons are met.**"[114] The key concept is "**as adequately as** the needs of nonhandicapped are met."[115]

---

106   20 U.S.C. § 1401(9)

107   *Board of Education v. Rowley*, 458 U.S. 176 (1982)

108   *Endrew F. v. Douglas County*, 580 U.S. __ (2017), 137 S. Ct. 988; 197 L. Ed. 2d 335

109   https://www.wrightslaw.com/law/caselaw/2017/ussupct.endrew.douglas.15-827.pdf

110   Chief Justice Roberts was quoting a portion of the definition of special education located 20 U.S.C. § 1401(29).

111   https://www.wrightslaw.com/law/caselaw/2017/ussupct.endrew.douglas.15-827.pdf

112   https://www.wrightslaw.com/law/art/endrew.douglas.scotus.analysis.htm

113   https://www.wrightslaw.com/store/2017law.html

114   34 CFR § 104.33

115   *See* the OCR publication *Protecting Students with Disabilities* - https://www2.ed.gov/about/offices/list/ocr/504faq.html

Unlike IDEA, if a child only needs related services, the 504 regulation requires the school to provide the related services.[116, 117]

The 2016 edition of *Wrightslaw Year in Review* featured *AG v. Paradise Valley Unif. Sch. Dist.*,[118] as a "Case of the Year" because it clarified the meaning of FAPE under IDEA and Section 504.[119] FAPE in the 504 setting "means that the child receives education and services **as adequately** [as provided to non-special ed children.]" . . . A plaintiff bringing suit under section 504 or Title II of the ADA must show she was **denied a reasonable accommodation** that [she] needs to enjoy **meaningful access** to the benefits of public services."

In *Rogich v. Clark County Sch. Dist.*,[120] a Nevada federal district court held that a school district's failure to use the Orton-Gillingham approach to provide remediation to a child with dyslexia was a **denial of FAPE under IDEA, Section 504, and the ADA.**

The court held that the Rogich child "**needed a methodology** in order to 'enjoy **meaningful access**' to a public school education . . . the record establishes **Defendant's deliberate indifference** . . . [because the defendant was aware of the child's dyslexia] and need for the identification and implementation of a methodology, and Defendant failed to act despite knowing that O.R. would be **deprived of educational opportunity** without adequate programming."[121, 122]

The decision in the *Rogich v. Clark County* case shows how violations of the requirement to provide FAPE can occur under IDEA and Section 504 simultaneously.

Grades

Grades are meant to report students academic knowledge and skills. But teachers give grades based on factors not related to learning, which leads to grade inflation. Some teachers allow students to improve on their grades by doing extra credit work. Others base grades on class participation, a good attitude, or citizenship. Many teachers give a student a grade because they believe the child is trying hard to do good work.

In the federal court complaint[123] filed in *Miguel Perez v. Sturgis Public Schools*,[124] at page 7, it is alleged that:

"Sturgis awarded Miguel A's in nearly all his classes." - Paragraph 41

"In fact, during the four years that Miguel spent at Sturgis Public High School, he was on the Honor Roll every single semester or trimester." - Paragraph 42

"The grades that Sturgis awarded Miguel misrepresented the extent to which Miguel had no access whatsoever to what was taught in class." - Paragraph 43

"Additionally, Miguel cannot read or write. He had so little access to English classes at Sturgis that, by May of 2016, he still did not know the words for many of the foods he regularly ate." - Paragraph 46

Many parents report that the school team says their child cannot be evaluated and found eligible for an IEP or Section 504 Plan because the child is receiving passing grades. This is wrong!

IDEA states that a child does not have to fail or be retained to be eligible for special education and related services. The school must provide special education to an eligible child with a disability "even though the child has not failed or been retained in a course or grade, **and is advancing from grade to grade.**[125]

---

116   34 CFR § 300.8(a)(2)(ii)

117   *See* the discussion about <**Related Services**> in this chapter.

118   *AG v. Paradise Valley Unif. Sch. Dist.* 815 F.3d 1195 (9th Cir. 2016)

119   *AG v. Paradise Valley Unif. Sch. Dist.* 815 F.3d 1195 (9th Cir. 2016)

120   *Rogich v. Clark County Sch. Dist.*, Case 2:17-cv-01541 page 15-16.

121   *Id.*

122   https://www.wrightslaw.com/law/caselaw/2021/rogich.v.clark.county.nv.orton.gillingham.pdf

123   https://www.wrightslaw.com/law/scotus/sturgis/2018.1002.complaint.by.perez.us.district.ct.pdf

124   Oral argument before the U.S. Supreme Court is scheduled for January 18, 2023. An article about the case, the argument and decision is at: https://www.wrightslaw.com/law/art/2022.perez.sturgis.scotus.htm

125   34 CFR § 300.101(c)

The *Section 504 Resource Guide*[126] offers similar guidance:

> School staff should note that a student may have a disability and be eligible for Section 504 services, including modifications, **even if the student earns good grades**. This is because the student's impairment may substantially limit a major life activity regardless of whether the student performs well academically... For example, a student who has dyslexia and is substantially limited in reading finds it challenging to read the required class material in a timely manner."

School districts sometimes rely on a student's average, or better-than-average, classroom grades or grade point average (GPA) and, as a result, make inappropriate decisions. For example, a school district might wrongly assume that a student with an above-average GPA does not have a disability and fail to conduct a Section 504 evaluation of that student, even if the school suspects that the student has ADHD or the school is aware that the student has been diagnosed with ADHD outside of school.

A student with a disability may achieve a high level of academic success but may nevertheless be substantially limited in a major life activity due to the student's impairment because of the additional time or effort the student must spend to read, write, or learn compared to others.

Individualized Health Care Plans (IHCPs)

Individualized Health Care Plans (IHCPs) are often developed for children with significant and / or chronic physical and mental health conditions, including allergies, seizures, feeding tubes, medication management, ADHD, PANDAS, and other health conditions. A child with diabetes may have a Diabetes Medical Management Plan (DMMP).[127] In school settings, IHCPs and DMMPs are similar to nursing care plans.

IHCPs and DMMPs are not mentioned in IDEA or Section 504 and **do not provide a child with any of the rights, protections, or procedural safeguards available under IDEA or Section 504.** To protect a child with medical or health conditions, **request an IEP and / or 504 Plan**. Contact the school to request the name and contact information for the school's Section 504 coordinator to make this request.

To ensure that the child has the rights, protections, and procedural safeguards from IDEA, Section 504 and ADA, the child's IEP or Section 504 Plan should expressly reference the IHCP or DMMP as a part of the school document, incorporated by reference in it, and attached to the IEP or written Section 504 Plan.

To learn about ICHPs, see two references in the footnotes: a Resolution Agreement between OCR and Memphis, TN City Schools (January 19, 2012)[128] and *Ask the Expert*, a monograph[129] prepared by this author for use in a **Wrightslaw Special Education Law Training**[130] for the Food Allergy Network's (FARE)[131] annual conference.

Least Restrictive Environment (LRE)

Least Restrictive Environment (LRE) is a core concept in IDEA, Section 504, and the ADA.[132]

IDEA states that "children with disabilities . . . are educated with children who are not disabled . . . [and] removal of children with disabilities from the regular educational environment **occurs only when** the nature or severity of the disability of a child is such that education in regular classes with the use of **supplementary aids and services cannot be achieved satisfactorily.**"[133]

---

126   https://www.wrightslaw.com/law/ocr/sec504.guide.ocr.2016.pdf

127   https://www.diabetes.org/tools-support/know-your-rights/safe-at-school-state-laws/written-care-plans/diabetes-medical-management-plan

128   https://www.wrightslaw.com/info/allergy/case.2012.OCR.v.Memphis.TN.IHCPv504.pdf

129   https://www.wrightslaw.com/info/allergy/FARE.Wright.Ask.the.Expert.IHCP.QandA.pdf

130   https://www.wrightslaw.com/speak/schedule.htm

131   https://www.foodallergy.org/

132   The two core concepts in IDEA are the child's right to a free appropriate public education (FAPE) in the least restrictive environment (LRE).

133   20 U.S.C. § 1412(a)(5)

Section 504 requires schools to educate the student "with persons who are not handicapped to the **maximum extent appropriate** to the needs of the handicapped person." Like IDEA, it allows for a more restrictive setting if the "use of supplementary aids and services cannot be achieved satisfactorily."[134]

The **ADA** requires that "services, facilities, privileges, advantages, and accommodations shall be afforded to an individual with a disability in the **most integrated setting** appropriate to the needs of the individual."[135] In 1999, the Supreme Court ruled on this issue in ***Olmstead v. L.C. by Zimring***,[136] 527 U.S. 581 (1999),[137] and required that individuals with mental disabilities be placed into community settings.

Military Children with Special Needs

Military families move often and face unique financial, medical and legal issues, especially during a deployment or a Permanent Change of Station (PCS). Family stress increases when a parent is deployed to a war zone. The challenges are greater when the family has a "special needs child."

Most military children attend between six and nine different schools between Kindergarten and 12th grade.[138] Military children experience transitions more than twice as high during high school, when disruptions are most likely to create significant stress and academic problems.[139] Parents of children with disabilities need to be familiar with the law about their child's entitlement to a comparable IEP when preparing to move to a new school district.

Colonel (retired) Elizabeth L. Schuchs-Gopaul advocates for military families with special needs children. As the parent of a child with special needs, she provides parents with a road map to secure FAPE for their children.

"Twelve Things Every JAG Should Know! Legal Issues Facing Military Families with Special Needs Children"[140]

"Want to Find a Special Education Program That Meets Your Child's Needs Before You Move? Go Shopping."[141]

Most military children attend locally operated public schools in the same jurisdictional area as the military base. Some local education agencies have public schools on the military base. In other states, the school on the military base is operated by DoDEA and is not affiliated with the local school district or state department of education. As the special education website[142] for DoDEA explains:

> The purpose of special education is to enable students to successfully develop to their fullest potential by providing a free appropriate public education in compliance with the Individuals with Disabilities Education Act (IDEA) as implemented by DoD Instruction 1342.12, "Provision of Early Intervention and Special Education Services to Eligible DoD Dependents.

The **Military Interstate Children's Compact Commission (MIC3)**[143] is an excellent resource for special needs parents, educators and advocates:

> Through the Interstate Compact, MIC3 addresses key educational transition issues encountered by children of military families . . . . The Compact deals with the challenges of military children and their frequent relocations. It allows for uniform treatment as military children transfer between school districts in member states.

---

134 34 CFR § 104.34

135 42 U.S.C. § 12182(b)(1)(B)

136 Jonathan Zimring is an attorney in Georgia who also represented the parents in the Cobb County IEE case discussed in Chapter 5 in conjunction with the IEE statute.

137 https://www.law.cornell.edu/supct/pdf/98-536P.ZO

138 https://mic3.net/assets/2018_parents_guide.pdf

139 *id.*

140 https://www.wrightslaw.com/info/mil.parents.12things.pdf

141 https://www.wrightslaw.com/info/move.schls.shop.gopaul.htm

142 https://www.dodea.edu/Curriculum/SpecialEducation/index.cfm

143 https://www.mic3.net

Resources

The MIC3 site publishes a "***Guide for Parents, School Officials and Public Administrators***" that addresses the transfer of records, course sequencing, redundant or missed entrance/exit testing, and other issues that affect military children.[144]

Good resources for military families with special needs children are provided by MilitaryOneSource[145] and the Exceptional Family Member Program (EFMP) operated by each military branch. The EFMP of one military branch has JAG attorneys who assist parents with special education issues. We understand that JAG attorneys in other branches are being trained in special education law.

Wrightslaw - The Military Child, PCS, DoDI's, MIC3[146] is a YouTube video about what the law requires in "comparable IEPs," Department of Defense Education Activity Schools (DoDEA),[147] and differences between the Department of Defense Instructions (DoDI)[148] in 32 CFR Part 57[149] and USDOE special education regulations.

Physical Education (PE) and Adapted PE (APE)

IDEA requires that "**physical education services, specially designed or adapted if necessary** be available **for every child with a disability to receive FAPE.**"[150] If a child has a disability and an IEP, the school **must provide physical education** as part of the child's special education program[151] unless the school district "does not provide physical education to children without disabilities in the same grades."[152]

Although many children with disabilities can safely participate in general physical education, with or without accommodations and supports, other children benefit from **specially designed or adapted physical education**. Content in adapted physical education should mirror the general physical education curriculum to the greatest extent possible.

"Physical education" means –

   (i) The development of –

      (A) Physical and motor skills;

      (B) Fundamental motor skills and patterns; and

      (C) Skills in aquatics, dance, and individual and group games and sports (including intramural and lifetime sports); and

   (ii) Includes special physical education, adapted physical education, movement education, and motor development.[153]

"Physical education" includes regular physical education, special physical education, and education in separate facilities."[154] If the child's IEP includes specially designed physical education, the school district must provide the

---

144   https://mic3.net/assets/2018_parents_guide.pdf

145   https://www.militaryonesource.mil/family-relationships/special-needs/special-education-and-childcare/special-education-programs-and-resources/

146   https://youtu.be/ulrzR4o02Vc

147   https://www.dodea.edu

148   https://www.wrightslaw.com/info/dodi.regs.2015.pdf

149   https://www.law.cornell.edu/cfr/text/32/part-57

150   <34 § CFR § 300.39(b)(2)> and <34 CFR § 300.108>

151   <20 U.S.C. 1401(29)>

152   34 CFR § 300.108(a)

153   34 CFR § 300.39(b)(2)

154   34 CFR § 300.108

services directly or arrange for the services to be provided through other public or private programs.[155] Physical education services **are special education services**, not related services like physical therapy and occupational therapy.

If the child needs a specially designed or adapted PE service, this service should be written into the IEP and may be described as **"specially designed"** or **"adapted PE" (APE)**. Content in adapted physical education should mirror the general physical education curriculum to the greatest extent possible. If the child receives specially designed physical education, the child's general and/or adapted physical education teacher should be on the child's IEP team.

Professor Garth Tymeson[156] wrote to the Office of Special Education Programs (OSEP) about a child who was transitioning from an elementary school to a middle school that did not have a qualified APE teacher. The school district had a policy of replacing Adapted PE with physical therapy (a related service) in IEPs. The USDOE clarified that pursuant to IDEA, "special education" includes "special physical education [and] adapted physical education" pursuant to 34 CFR § 300.39(b)(2)(i), and that they are not considered to be a "related service."[157, 158]

The **Section 504** regulations explain that "qualified handicapped students" must be provided "**an equal opportunity for participation**" in interscholastic, club, and intramural athletics,[159] and **shall not "be excluded from participation** in . . . physical education, athletics, recreation . . . other extracurricular, or other postsecondary education aid, benefits, or services."[160]

Resources

The **Adapted Physical Education National Standards (APENS)** provide adapted physical education standards, the national certification exam and study guide, and alternative methods for becoming a nationally certified adapted physical educator (CAPE).[161] A basic tenet of APENS is that Physical Educators who teach students in integrated or segregated environments must be able to **demonstrate basic instructional competencies.**[162]

The **Wrightslaw PE/ APE for Students with Disabilities Page**[163] has information about legal requirements for PE and APE, eligibility for adapted PE services, APE certification for teachers, adapted PE information for parents and school staff from State Departments of Education, adapted PE videos, and free information about PE and adapted PE.

Placement: Change of Placement and Discipline

Discipline cases often lead to a **change of placement**.

Under IDEA, when a school **suspends or expels a child** from school, the child is still **entitled to FAPE**.[164] If the child is removed from school "for more than **10 consecutive school days** . . . [or] is subjected to a series of removals that constitute a pattern . . . [and] the series of removals total **more than 10 school days in a school year**" then a "**change of placement**" has occurred under IDEA.[165] Depending on the disciplinary process at that time, stay-put/pendency may **not apply.**[166]

---

155   34 CFR §300.108(d)

156   Professor Emeritus, Adapted Physical Education Programs, University of Wisconsin-La Crosse, Department of Exercise and Sport Science

157   https://sites.ed.gov/idea/files/osep-letter-to-tymeson-05-12-2021.pdf

158   See also 34 CFR § 300.108 and 20 U.S.C. § 1401(29)

159   34 CFR § 104.37(c)(1)

160   34 CFR § 104.43(a)

161   https://www.ncpeid.org/apens-15-standards

162   *See also* https://www.shapeamerica.org/standards/adapted/ and https://www.ncpeid.org/governance

163   https://www.wrightslaw.com/info/pe.index.htm

164   20 U.S.C. § 1412(a)(1)(A)

165   34 CFR § 300.536(a)

166   20 U.S.C. § 1415(j)

As discussed in the preceding topic about Discipline, under **Section 504**, the school district "**shall conduct an evaluation** . . . before taking any action with respect to the **initial placement . . . and any subsequent significant change in placement.**"[167] The language about "change of placement" for the Section 504 youngster is considered by many special education attorneys to provide **greater protections** than those provided by IDEA for the child with an IEP.

The Office for Civil Rights (OCR) considers an **exclusion from the educational program** (for example, an out-of-school suspension) for **more than 10 consecutive school days** to be a significant change in placement. OCR also views a series of short-term exclusions (each 10 school days or fewer) from the educational program to be a significant change in placement, if the short-term exclusions total **more than 10 school days and create a pattern of removal.**[168]

The IDEA and Section 504 regulations about placement are nearly identical:

A recipient shall place a handicapped person in the **regular educational environment** . . . **unless** it is demonstrated by the recipient that the **education of the person in the regular environment** with the use of **supplementary aids and services cannot be achieved** satisfactorily.[169] Whenever a recipient places a person in a setting other than the regular educational environment . . . it shall take into account the **proximity of the alternate setting to the person's home.**[170]

Section 504 requires school districts to conduct **periodic reevaluations** of students with disabilities and requires school districts to conduct reevaluations prior to a significant change in placement.

• OCR considers an exclusion from the educational program (for example, an out-of-school suspension) for **more than 10 consecutive school days** to be a significant change in placement.

• OCR also considers a series of short-term exclusions (each 10 school days or fewer) from the educational program to be a significant change in placement, if the short-term exclusions total **more than 10 school days and create a pattern of removal.**[171]

Placement - Continuum of Alternative Placements

IDEA requires schools to provide a free appropriate public education (FAPE) in the least restrictive environment (LRE).[172] The LRE requirement means schools "must ensure that a **continuum of alternative placements** is available to meet the needs of children with disabilities for special education and related services."[173]

This **continuum of placements must include** instruction in regular classes, special classes, special schools, home instruction, and instruction in hospitals and institutions and provide **supplementary services** (such as resource room or itinerant instruction) in conjunction with regular class placement.[174]

When "interpreting evaluation data and making placement decisions," the school shall "draw upon information from a variety of sources," and ensure that the obtained information "is documented and carefully considered."[175]

Before the IEP team can determine a child's placement, the team must ensure that the **placement decision**:

---

167   34 CFR § 104.35

168   *Parent and Educator Guide to Section 504* at
https://www2.ed.gov/about/offices/list/ocr/docs/504-resource-guide-201612.pdf

169   Compare to last sentence of 20 U.S.C. § 1414(a)(5)(A) - identical language.

170   34 CFR § 104.34(a)

171   *Parent and Educator Guide to Section 504*

172   <20 U.S.C. § 1412(a)(5)>

173   34 CFR § 300.115

174   <34 CFR § 300.115>

175   34 CFR § 104.35(c)

(a)(1) Is made by a group of persons, **including the parents**, and other persons knowledgeable about the child, the meaning of the evaluation data, and the placement options; and (2) Is made in conformity with the LRE provisions of this subpart, including 34 CFR § 300.114 through 300.118; and

(b) The child's **placement** (1) Is determined at least annually; (2) Is based on the child's IEP; and (3) **Is as close as possible to the child's home;**

(c) Unless the IEP of a child with a disability requires some other arrangement, the **child is educated in the school that he or she would attend if nondisabled**; and . . .

(e) the child with a disability **is not removed from education in age-appropriate regular classrooms** solely because of needed modifications in the general education curriculum.

After the IEP team determines a child's placement, the school may decide to change the child's placement. **Changing the location** where services are delivered **is not usually viewed as a change of placement**. Here's why.

Assume an child with an IEP is placed in an LD self-contained (LDSC) program at the East End Middle School. The school district decides to move the LDSC program to the West End Middle School for the next school year. The parent objects. Most courts would rule that moving or relocating the program is not a change of placement. But if the school changes the child's program from an LD self-contained to an LD Resource program in the same school or a different school, this is a change of placement.

If the school proposes to change a child's program, *i.e.*, a change in the nature of and / or delivery of services, and the parent does not consent, the school must provide <"Prior Written Notice" (PWN).>[176] The parent can utilize the **stay-put / pendency statute** that "during the pendency of any proceedings conducted pursuant to this section . . . the child shall remain in the then-current educational placement . . ."[177]

See *Introduction to Procedural Safeguards by NICHY*,[178] *Prior Written Notice is a Powerful Tool When Skillfully Used* by Jeff Martin, Esq.,[179] and *Surviving Due Process: When Parents and the School Board Disagree - Stephen Jeffers v. School Board* (DVD)[180]

Related Services

The **IDEA** statute[181] and regulations[182] contain a long, non-inclusive list of related services. Related services include "**transportation**, and such **developmental, corrective, and other supportive services** . . . designed to enable a child with a disability **to receive a free appropriate public education** as described in the individualized education program of the child, as may be required to assist a child with a disability **to benefit from special education** . . ."[183]

The child's IEP must include "a **statement of the special education and related services and supplementary aids and services** . . . and **a statement of the program modifications or supports for school personnel** that will be provided to enable the child . . . to advance appropriately toward attaining the annual goals . . . to be involved in and make progress in the general education curriculum . . . and to participate in extracurricular and other nonacademic activities; and to be educated and participate with other children . . ."[184]

---

176   20 U.S.C. § 1415(c)(1)

177   <20 U.S.C. § 1415(j)>

178   https://www.parentcenterhub.org/partb-module17/

179   https://www.wrightslaw.com/info/pwn.refusal.martin.htm

180   https://www.wrightslaw.com/bks/dvddp/index.htm

181   20 U.S.C. § 1401(26)

182   34 CFR § 300.34

183   <20 U.S.C. § 1401(26)> and <34 CFR § 300.34>

184   <34 CFR § 300.320(a)(4)>

For a "child with a disability" to be eligible for an IEP under IDEA, the child must **need** special education and related services.[185] What happens if a child with a disability needs related services but does not need special education services?

Section 504 allows this child to receive related aids and services without receiving special education services. Section 504 defines FAPE as "is the provision of regular or special education **and related aids and services** that (i) are designed to meet individual educational needs of handicapped persons **as adequately** as the needs of nonhandicapped persons are met . . ."[186]

Section 504 describes **independent living services** as "counseling services, including psychological, psychotherapeutic, and **related services**."[187]

Restraint and Seclusion

Although restraint and seclusion of children with disabilities are long-standing problems, these practices are not addressed directly in **IDEA, Section 504**, the **ADA**, or other federal laws.[188] The only federal law that expressly limits seclusion and restraints is the U.S. Constitution although several states, including North Carolina, have laws that restrict their use.

In 2012, the USDOE issued *"Restraint and Seclusion: Resource Document,"* a comprehensive 40-page report on restraint and seclusion in public schools that begins with this statement:

> There is **no evidence that using restraint or seclusion is effective in reducing** the occurrence of the **problem behaviors** that frequently precipitate the use of such techniques. Physical restraint or seclusion should not be used except in situations where the **child's behavior poses imminent danger of serious physical harm to self or others** and restraint and seclusion should be avoided to the greatest extent possible without endangering the safety of students and staff. **Schools should never use mechanical restraints** to restrict a child's freedom of movement.
>
> . . .
>
> **Restraint or seclusion should not be used as routine school safety measures** . . . they should not be implemented except in situations where **a child's behavior poses imminent danger of serious physical harm to self or others** and not as a routine strategy implemented to address instructional problems or inappropriate behavior (e.g., disrespect, noncompliance, insubordination, out of seat), as a means of coercion or retaliation, or as a convenience.[189]

The Office for Civil Rights has a *"Discipline, Restraint and Seclusion"*[190] website that opens with this statement:

> Data from the Civil Rights Data Collection (CRDC) illustrate that **students with disabilities (served by IDEA) are treated far more harshly** than their peers without disabilities; for example, they are **twice as likely to receive an out-of-school suspension (13%) as are students without disabilities (6%).** Moreover, students with disabilities represent 12% of students in public schools but 58% of students placed in seclusion or involuntary confinement. They are also **75% of students physically restrained** at school and make up 25% of students arrested and referred to law enforcement.
>
> **Resolution agreements in Section 504 discipline cases** include remedies **requiring the institution to develop a protocol** to ensure that manifestation determination reviews (MDR protocol) occur as required by Section 504, provide training to school and district staff, and monitor the implementation of the MDR protocol. Remedies in cases of inappropriate restraint or seclusion include implementation of new policies, dissemination

---

185   <20 U.S.C. § 1401(3)>

186   <34 CFR § 104.33(a) and (b)>

187   <29 U.S.C. § 705(18)(B)(i)>

188   On May 6, 2022, the Office for Civil Rights announced that they are revising the Section 504 regulations to address the many disability discrimination issues we face today.

189   https://www2.ed.gov/policy/seclusion/restraints-and-seclusion-resources.pdf

190   https://www2.ed.gov/about/offices/list/ocr/frontpage/pro-students/issues/dis-issue02.html

of policies to staff and parents, and training for staff on these policies . . . **compensatory educational services may also be required**, especially in cases where the student missed class time as a result of the action. OCR closely reviews proposed remedies in such cases to make the determination whether or not compensatory services are necessary.[191]

In September 2020, the Education Law Center (ELC) issued a report on *"Restraint and Seclusion Information Sheet"* to answer this question: **What is the Relationship between Restraint and Seclusion and FAPE?**

Restraint or seclusion may have **a traumatic effect on a studen**t, potentially resulting **in new academic or behavioral difficulties** or **increased school absences resulting in a denial of FAPE**. Repeated and extended periods of seclusion, moreover, may have the cumulative effect of denying the student the instructional time and related services needed to provide FAPE.

The **disproportionate use of restraint and seclusion on students with disabilities raises disability discrimination issues** under Section 504 of the Rehabilitation Act and Title II of the Americans with Disabilities Act.

Parents may initiate an IEP meeting or Section 504 team meeting to:

(1) address the behavior that led to restraint or seclusion;

(2) determine if current interventions are being properly implemented;

(3) consider the need for additional interventions and supports, including positive behavioral supports; and

(4) revise the student's IEP or 504 plan accordingly. Parents may also request new evaluations of the student if needed.[192]

In September 2019, the **Wake County Public Schools Board of Education in North Carolina** settled a teacher abuse, seclusion, and restraint case with parents for **$450,000.00**.[193] After the parents requested a special education due process hearing, the case was settled before the litigation began.

In **Georgia**, a para-professional punished a child "for failing to comply with his verbal commands by hanging him [by his belt loop] from the chalk board in his classroom, while his teacher and other students made fun of him."[194] The judge took evidence about the intentional infliction of emotional distress, and subsequently awarded the plaintiff **$267,000.00**.[195, 196] However, on April 28, 2022, in *Cummings v. Premier Rehab Keller*, the Supreme Court of the United States held that damages for emotional distress are not recoverable in a Section 504 case.[197]

If you are the parent of a child with an IEP or a 504 Plan and concerned about the school's use of restraint and / or seclusion of your child, you can **file a complaint** with the Office for Civil Rights (OCR) or the U.S. Department of Justice (USDOJ).[198]

A **Sample "No Restraint" Letter** to restrict the school's use of restraints is available from Bridges4Kids and the "Respect ABILITY Law Center."[199]

---

191   https://www2.ed.gov/about/offices/list/ocr/frontpage/pro-students/issues/dis-issue02.html

192   https://edlawcenter.org/assets/files/pdfs/publications/RESTRAINT_AND_SECLUSION_INFORMAT.pdf

193   https://www.wrightslaw.com/law/art/settle.wcpss.teach.abuse.htm

194   See Complaint, page 11 - https://www.wrightslaw.com/law/caselaw/ga/ga.complaint.belt.loop.pdf

195   https://www.wrightslaw.com/law/caselaw/ga/ga.judgment.beltloop.267k.pdf

196   Pursuant to a telephone call with plaintiff's attorney, Kamau Mason. (https://www.kamaumasonlaw.com/)

197   https://www.supremecourt.gov/opinions/21pdf/20-219_1b82.pdf

198   https://www2.ed.gov/about/offices/list/ocr/complaintform.pdf // https://civilrights.justice.gov/

199   https://www.bridges4kids.org/IEP/NoRestraintLetter.html

Section 504 Plan vis-à-vis an IEP

Many parents have questions about whether their child needs an IEP or a Section 504 Plan. When a child is found "not eligible" for an IEP, the school district may offer a Section 504 Plan as a "consolation prize."

Is a Section 504 Plan really a prize? There are pros and cons for Section 504 Plans and IEPs. The correct answer will depend on your child's needs and the willingness of the school to meet those needs.

The U.S. Code for Section 504 and the Code of Regulations do not provide a legal definition for a "Section 504 Plan." Section 504 Plans are described in publications, books, and articles, including publications by the USDOE and the Office for Civil Rights. In most cases, Section 504 Plans describe the specific accommodations that will be provided to a child.[200]

We encourage you to download two publications issued by the OCR of the USDOE that will answer many of your questions about special education rights and responsibilities under Section 504. Consider printing and filing both publications in a handy 3 ring binder. As you read, use a highlighter and make notes.

Parent and Educator Resource Guide to Section 504 in Public Elementary and Secondary Schools[201]

Protecting Students With Disabilities: Frequently Asked Questions About Section 504 and the Education of Children with Disabilities[202]

Review the **"Selected Topics"** at the beginning of this chapter. You'll see that most topics discuss how IDEA and Section 504 apply.

In **Section 504**, FAPE means providing regular or special education and related aids and services designed to **meet the child's individual educational needs as adequately as the needs of nondisabled students are met**.

- A Section 504 Plan should document the child's needs, the regular and / or special education and related aids and services the child needs and the school will provide, and the setting where the child will receive these services in a written plan that is shared with the parent. A written plan helps all parties avoid misunderstandings or confusion about the services the school offered the child. **But Section 504 does not require a written plan.**[203]

- **Section 504** requires schools to **evaluate** any student who needs or is believed to need special education or related services in a **timely manner.** But Section 504 does not define "timely manner" or provide an amount of time for the school to complete the evaluation.

- Section 504 requires **tests and evaluations** to be selected and administered in a way that ensures the test results accurately reflect the child's aptitude or achievement, measure areas of educational need, and be administered by trained personnel. But Section 504 does not require tests and evaluations to meet specifc standards.

- Section 504 requires schools to consider information from a **variety of sources** when interpreting evaluation data and making placement decisions. But Section 504 does not clarify whether evaluation data may include an independent evaluation of the child by an individual in the private sector.

- Section 504 requires schools to **reevaluate students periodically** and to reevaluate before making a significant change in placement. But Section 504 does not define "periodically."

- Section 504 requires that a child who qualifies as having a disability and **needs a related service** (i.e. speech therapy) receive the related service, without receiving special education services.

---

200   In May 2022, the Office for Civil Rights announced their plan to revise the Section 504 regulations.

201   *The Parent and Educator Resource Guide to Section 504 in Public Elementary and Secondary Schools* is available at:
https://www2.ed.gov/about/offices/list/ocr/docs/504-resource-guide-201612.pdf
and
https://www.wrightslaw.com/law/ocr/sec504.guide.ocr.2016.pdf

202   https://www2.ed.gov/about/offices/list/ocr/504faq.html

203   When this book was published, Section 504 did not require a written plan.

- Section 504 requires **placement decisions**[204] to be made by a group of "knowledgeable persons" including individuals who are knowledgeable about the child, the meaning of the evaluation data, and placement options, But Section 504 does not require a parent to be involved in educational decision-making.

Under **IDEA, eligible students with disabilities with an IEP are not required to have a Section 504 Plan,** although they still are protected under Section 504 and the ADA.[205]

IDEA requires that the **Individualized Education Program (IEP) comply with specific requirements.** The child's **parent is a member of any team that makes educational decisions.**[206] IEPs must be completed within **30 days** after the child is found eligible for special education services. An IEP must include **present levels** of academic achievement and functional performance and **measurable goals.** The IEP must address the "Special Factors" including the child's communication needs and behavior issues, Functional Behavioral Assessments (FBAs) and Behavioral Intervention Plans (BIPs).

An IEP is written for **the child and staff** because it includes "a statement of the **program modifications or supports for school personnel . . ."**[207] IEP **progress reports** are to be provided to the child's parents at regular intervals.

An IEP must be **reviewed and revised as needed, at least once a year** and must be in place **before the school year begins**.

When a child with an IEP moves from one jurisdiction to another, the receiving school must provide the child with **a "comparable IEP"** until the receiving school develops a new IEP.[208] If a child with a 504 Plan moves to a new jurisdiction, the Section 504 regulations do not address whether the child is entitled to a "comparable" Section 504 Plan.

An IEP does not terminate or "discontinue" because an IEP meeting has not been held within a required timeline.

Under IDEA, the school may not remove or exit a child from special education or discontinue the IEP unless the school has completed a new evaluation.

Under IDEA, **parents are members of the IEP Team** and parental participation is a key element.[209] *See* the Wrightslaw Youtube video[210] about the Ninth Circuit's ***Doug C. v. Hawaii*** case where the school convened an IEP meeting in the parent's absence - a major procedural violation."

There is no clear answer to the question of which is better - an IEP or a Section 504 Plan. Many factors affect what is better for a particular child.

If a child has an IEP, the child has all Section 504 protections. If a child has a Section 504 Plan, the child is not entitled to the rights and protections available under IDEA.

The answer to a question about which is better, an IEP or a Section 504 Plan is based on the child's educational needs and what the school can provide. For example, too often schools lower their expectations for children with dyslexia by providing Section 504 modifications and accommodations, but fail to teach the child how to read pursuant to an IEP.

---

204 <34 CFR § 104.35(c)>

205 See <42 U.S.C. § 12102>

206 20 U.S.C. § 1414(d)(1)(B)

207 20 U.S.C. § 1414(d)(1)(A)(i)(IV)

208 <20 U.S.C. § 1414(d)(2)(C)>

209 20 U.S.C. § 1414(d)(1)(B)(i)

210 https://youtu.be/Hf7vqsmK_ZM

Supplementary Aids and Services

Supplementary aids and services enable children with disabilities to be educated with other "nondisabled" children and participate in school activities and learning opportunities with their classmates.[211]

Supplementary aids and services means "aids, services, and other supports that are provided in regular education classes, other educational settings, and in extracurricular and nonacademic settings, to enable children with disabilities to be educated with nondisabled children to the maximum extent appropriate . . ."[212]

The child's IEP must include:

> a statement of the special education and related services and **supplementary aids and services**, based on peer-reviewed research to the extent practicable, to be provided to the child, or on behalf of the child, and a statement of the program modifications or **supports for school personnel** that will be provided for the child.[213]

The school district must "afford children with disabilities **an equal opportunity" to participate in "nonacademic and extracurricular services**," which "may include counseling services, athletics, transportation, health services, recreational activities, special interest groups or clubs sponsored by the public agency,"[214]

Transition

You know the purpose of IDEA is "to ensure that all children with disabilities have available to them a free appropriate public education that emphasizes special education and related services designed to meet their unique needs and prepare them for further education, employment, and independent living."[215]

The IEP team is **required to develop a transition plan** that is based on "age-appropriate transition assessments related to training, education, employment, and, where appropriate, independent living skills . . . and facilitate the child's movement from school to post-school activities . . . [and] **prepare the child for further education, employment, and independent living.**"[216]

Transition assessments should be selected to identify the child's needs and clarify the child's strengths, preferences, and interests related to training, education, employment, and independent living skills" and "the transition services (including courses of study) to assist the child in reaching these goals."[217]

A transition plan with measurable goals and services, including "courses of study," must be included in the IEP that is in effect when the child turns 16 (in general, the IEP developed when the child is 15). Some states require transition plans at age 14 or earlier so it's essential to know your state's requirements. The transition plan should include services to "improve the academic and functional achievement of the child with a disability . . . facilitate the child's movement from school to post-school activities . . ." [and] "prepare the child for further education, employment, and independent living."[218]

Transition services include:

- post-secondary education, vocational education;
- employment and integrated employment, supported employment;
- continuing education and adult education;

---

211   20 U.S.C. § 1401(33); 34 C.F.R. § 300.42

212   34 CFR § 300.42

213   < 20 U.S.C. § 1414(d)(1)(A)(IV) >

214   34 CFR § 300.107

215   20 U.S.C. § 1400(d)(1)

216   Purpose of IDEA - 20 U.S.C. § 1400(d)

217   20 U.S.C. § 1414(d)(1)(A)(VIII)

218   20 U.S.C. § 1401(34)(A)

- post-school adult living and community participation;
- independent living and daily living skills; and
- a functional vocational evaluation.[219]

The IEP team is required to invite the child to all IEP meetings when the team will consider or discuss transition goals and plans.

Transition to Higher Education

As you learned in the Overview of IDEA in Chapter 4, and in the prior topic, transition services[220] must begin "not later than the first IEP to be in effect when the child is 16, and updated annually thereafter . . . [and include] **appropriate measurable postsecondary goals** based upon age appropriate transition assessments related to training, education, employment, and, where appropriate, independent living skills . . . and the transition services (including **courses of study**)[221] needed to assist the child in reaching these goals."[222]

In some states, the special education regulations require the IEP team to address transition by the child's 14th birthday. Some high school students with IEPs and Section 504 Plans are able to take courses at institutions of higher education and receive college credits for these courses. In other cases, students who took Advanced Placement (AP) courses in high school received waivers for that college course.

Families of children with disabilities with IEPs and 504 Plans need to do their homework before enrolling their children in an institution of higher education. When a child **graduates with a regular high school diploma**, the special education services, accommodations and modification in the child's **Section 504 Plan or IEP end**.

Colleges and universities are **not required** to accept specific documents to determine if a student is eligible for the protections and accommodations of Section 504 and the ADA. Colleges and universities develop their own policies for reviewing **disability documentation**, determining barriers to education, and providing needed accommodations. Elizabeth Cohen Hamblet,[223] an expert in transition, advises that IEPs and Section 504 Plans "end at graduation from high school. Although colleges may use these plans in decision making, they are not required to follow the requirements of these plans."[224] Documentation about whether a college student is entitled to the protections and accommodations of Section 504 and the ADA vary from one institution of higher education to another.

Hamblet referenced guidance from The Association on Higher Education And Disability (AHEAD)[225] published in "*Supporting Accommodation Requests: Guidance on Documentation Practices.*"[226] This publication is a standard reference used to request accommodations:

> Disability documentation should be current and relevant but not necessarily "recent." Disabilities are typically stable, lifelong conditions. Therefore, historic information, supplemented by interview of self-report, is often sufficient to describe how the condition impacts the student at the current time and in the current circumstances. Institutions should not establish blanket statements that limit the age of acceptable external documentation.[227]

---

219   20 USC 1401(34)(A); 34 CFR 300.34(a)(1) + (2)

220   *Id.*

221   In The Commentary, this phrase includes **Advanced Placement** courses. 71 Fed. Reg. 46668 (August 14, 2006) https://www.wrightslaw.com/idea/comment/46661-46688.reg.320-328.ieps.pdf

222   20 U.S.C. § 1414(d)(1)(A)(i)(VIII)

223   Hamblet has written a unique step-by-step guide that is an essential resource for college-bound students, their families, and the special educators and school counselors who work with them. https://ldadvisory.com/

224   https://www.wrightslaw.com/info/trans.college.accoms.hamblet.htm

225   https://www.ahead.org/

226   AHEAD. *Supporting accommodation requests: guidance on documentation practices.* (October 2012). Huntersville, NC: Association on Higher Education and Disability.

227   https://www.ahead.org/professional-resources/accommodations/documentation

AHEAD's guidance document explains that "documentation for substantiating a student's disability and request for particular accommodations can take a variety of forms" and recommends using three sources of information:[228]

- Primary Documentation: Student's Self-report;
- Secondary Documentation: Observation and Interaction; and
- Tertiary documentation: Information from External or Third-Parties.

All institutions of higher education do not follow AHEAD's approach.

In 2021, the Learning Disabilities Association published a "special issue" of *Journal*[229] (2021, Vol. 26, No. 2) to address concerns about disability documentation in higher education institutions. "*Postsecondary Disability Documentation: What Have We Learned Ten Years After the ADAAA?*" describes concerns about AHEAD's approach and current research.

For more information about disability documentation and higher education, read *Do Colleges Have to Follow IEPs or 504 Plans?*"[230] To learn how to build a strong foundation in high school, anticipate the challenges of college, and find the right college, you may want to obtain a copy of *From High School to College: Steps to Success for Students with Disabilities,*[231] a unique step-by-step guide for college-bound students, their families, and the educators and counselors who work with them.

Before enrolling in a college or university, families and students with IEPs and Section 504 Plans need to learn about the practices and climate of the schools they are considering. The articles on LDAdvisory.com[232] provide advice on college topics for students with learning disabilities and ADHD and their families.

In Summation

Chapter 10 focused on 24 **"Selected Topics"** that generate misinformation, confusing advice, and conflicting opinions. Each topic provides you with an overview so that you can read statutes, regulations, and cases to assist in finding the best answer to a legal question you may have.

End of Chapter 10 - Selected Topics

Hyperlinks to Chapters

Ch. 01 Introduction	Ch. 06 IDEA Regulations
Ch. 02 History	Ch. 07 Section 504
Ch. 03 Overview of Law, Courts, Research	Ch. 08 ADA
Ch. 04 Overview of IDEA, Section 504, ADA	Ch. 09 Other laws
Ch. 05 IDEA (US Code)	Ch. 10 Selected Topics

228   In the "Background" portion; AHEAD explained that "No legislation or regulations require that documentation be requested or obtained in order to demonstrate entitlement to legal protections because of disability and seek reasonable accommodations. The regulations acknowledge that postsecondary institutions may request a reasonable level of documentation."

229   *Learning Disabilities: A Multidisciplinary Journal* (2021, Volume 26, No. 2) Individual copies available from Sagamore-Venture at: https://www.sagamorepub.com

230   https://ldadvisory.com/college_no_iep_504/

231   https://www.wrightslaw.com/bks/trans/transition.htm
and
https://ldadvisory.com/book/

232   https://ldadvisory.com/families_students

Acknowledgments

We were fortunate to receive assistance from a number of individuals who gave their time to read large portions of the manuscript.

Missy Alexander is the Director of Education at The Parents' Place of **Maryland**, which serves as Maryland's Parent Training and Information Center[233] and Family-to-Family Health Information Center. She is parent of a daughter on the autism spectrum. and is a former Chair of the **Council of Parent Attorneys and Advocates (COPAA)**[234] and is on their Board of Directors. We have had a close friendship with Missy since the late 1990's.

Abra "Abbe" Allexenberg, a **Massachusetts** attorney, earned her Human Services Degree, Specialization in Early Intervention, a Minor in Psychology, and interned at the Pediatric Burns Unit of The Boston Shriners Hospital for Children, the Cerebral Palsy Association, and a first grade classroom in Bradford, England. Later she earned her JD at New England School of Law. She handled a variety of cases and now represents children with disabilities.[235]

Roy T. Atwood, the father of a child with Down syndrome, has been practicing law in **Texas** since 1988. He is a frequent speaker on litigation and special education-related topics, teaches trial skills. He is the past president of the board of trustees of LaunchAbility, which helped people with developmental disabilities lead fulfilling lives through workplace employment. After it merged with My Possibilities, Roy now serves on its Board of Directors. He has assisted many parents navigate special education from development of the IEP, to LRE issues, due process hearings, and court appeals.[236]

Ashley Barlow taught students in nearly every grade from Kindergarten to seniors in college. After becoming an attorney in **Kentucky**, her second child was born with Down Syndrome. She expanded her practice to include special education law and advocacy "after nearly six months of meetings, data collection, phone calls, and correspondence" with the school district. She has developed a strong presence in social media, and provides online courses on her website. She started Ashley Barlow Co.[237] to empower and inspire IEP team members and special education advocates, to form a community of like-minded advocates, and to teach people to empathetically advocate within the framework of the law. She is the Director of Education at the National Down Syndrome Congress.[238]

Juliet Barraza has been a Bilingual Education Advocate in **California** with the PTI Center with the Disability Rights Education & Defense Fund (DREDF) since 2005 where she provides training, technical assistance and attends IEP Meetings. She is the parent of two young men, one of whom has developmental disabilities and epilepsy. Using her language skills, she supports and assists Latino Spanish–speaking families focusing on race, culture, poverty and language barriers. She is an active member of the COPAA and holds an Advanced Training Certificate.[239]

Lynn Brogan is "Senior Instructional Faculty" in special education at the Western Governors University. She has taught there and at Pierce College for over ten years teaching about special education, special education law and project management. She has developed hybrid, online and face-to-face training programs. She earned her doctorate in Administrative Leadership from Columbia University and has been teaching and training since 1988.[240]

Dr. Roseann Capanna-Hodge is a **Connecticut** Certified School Psychologist, a Licensed Professional Counselor (LPC), Certified Integrative Medicine Mental Health Provider (CMHIMP), and a Board Certified Neurofeedback Provider (BCN). She is a media personality, having appeared on dozens of media outlets. She is the author of the

---

233   https://www.ppmd.org/

234   https://www.copaa.org/

235   https://www.allexenberglaw.com

236   http://atwoodgameros.com/

237   https://ashleybarlowco.com/

238   https://www.ndsccenter.org

239   https://dredf.org/about-us/people/juliet-barraza/

240   https://www.pierce.ctc.edu/staff-directory/lynn-brogan

first ever book on teletherapy activities for child and adolescent therapists, "Teletherapy Toolkit™" and It's Gonna be OK!™ and gives parents step-by-step solutions for their struggling kids with her books, Raising Successful Kids Community and remote neurofeedback program.[241]

Daphne Corder is a licensed clinical social worker in Austin, **Texas** and has over 25 years of experience working with children and families in the areas of Early Childhood Intervention, Counseling, Foster Care, and Special Education Advocacy. She has an active advocacy practice and is characterized as an "Education Advocate & Dyslexia Specialist" with a special interest in helping military families.[242]

Stacey Gahagan, a **North Carolina** attorney, has been practicing education law exclusively since 2012 when she graduated with honors from the University of North Carolina School of Law. Prior to law school, Stacey spent 19 years working as a public school educator and administrator. In 2014, Stacey started The Gahagan Law Firm representing students with disabilities. In 2019, she merged with Ann Paradis to create Gahagan Paradis, PLLC the largest firm in the state that focuses on representing parents in special education disputes.[243]

Dr. Harry L. Gewanter is a Richmond, **Virginia** pediatrician and pediatric rheumatologist and a cofounder and Medical Director of Medial Home Plus, Inc., a nonprofit agency that provides information and resource coordination to families of children with special health care need and the professionals that serve them. He is an active member of the American Academy of Pediatrics, Arthritis Foundation and other organizations, nationally, regionally and locally, including being a board member of the Disability Law Center of Virginia Foundation and the Friendship Circle of Virginia, among others. Dr. Gewanter was a faculty member of William and Mary School of Law Institute for Special Education Advocacy (ISEA) and is a Clinical Associate Professor of Pediatrics at the VCU School of Medicine and the recipient of a variety of awards for his leadership and advocacy activities. The father of 4 children, 3 of whom had IEP's, his passion for improving the lives of all children and youth with special health care needs and their families is driven by his personal and professional experiences.[244]

Danielle Green began practicing law in **Massachusetts** in 2007. As a result of her own experience with her son and the school district, she developed a passion for special education advocacy, believing that a "collaborative approach between teachers, administrators, and parents is the best place to start in this process, but in certain circumstances having legal support is necessary."[245]

Jaclyn Knapp, in **Utah**, is the Director of Special Education for the Park City School District. Knapp has worked as a consultant for the Utah State Office of Education and as a school psychologist for Davis School District. She received an Education Specialist degree in psychology and a master's degree in psychology from Utah State University, and a bachelor's degree in psychology from Weber State University.[246]

Calvin Luker has been an attorney in **Michigan** since 1981 and concentrates exclusively on issues related to people with disabilities. For ten years he worked with Michigan's Protection and Advocacy Service. His practice is limited to special education; end of life issues; fair housing law; guardianship/ conservatorship law; juvenile justice; and other legal areas when they directly impact his clients with disabilities.

Patricia Luker developed her expertise in special education, community supports and parent advocacy in 1975. She has been the Director of Training at Michigan Protection and Advocacy Service, the Director of Family Services for Michigan's Parent Training and Information Center, Senior Advocate for The Arc of Oakland County and created and managed parent training programs for the Epilepsy Foundation of Michigan. The Lukers created the

241   https://drroseann.com/

242   https://www.daphnecorder.com/

243   https://www.ncgplaw.com/staff/stacey-gahagan

244   https://www.dlcv.org/dlcv-board-of-directors/dlcv-board-members

245   https://forexceptionalchildren.com

246   https://www.pcschools.us/

The Respect ABILITY Law Center[247] in 2001 to advance the civil, service and support rights of and for people with disabilities and their families. The Center is a founding member of the Alliance to Prevent Aversive Intervention and Seclusion [APRAISE], a national organization dedicated to the enactment and implementation of national legislation to eliminate the use of seclusion, restraint and aversives in all schools.

Rosemary Palmer, began practicing law in 1987 in Utah, later moved to Florida, and has been practicing law in Tallahassee, **Florida** for almost 30 years. Her focus is on matters involving civil rights and special education. She is a member of the Education Law Committee of the Florida Bar Association. For many years, through her frequent posts on the COPAA listserv, she has provided excellent advice and guidance to attorneys, lay advocates, related service professionals and parents of children with special needs.

Benjamin Powers is the Headmaster of The Southport School,[248] (formerly known as Eagle Hill) in Southport, **Connecticut**. The Southport School is for children in grades 2nd-8th who struggle with language-based learning differences, like dyslexia, and ADHD. He is known as an educator with deep experience in language-based learning disabilities.

He trains educators and professionals in three specialized training programs: Structured Literacy / Orton-Gillingham, Executive Functioning, and Assistive Technology. In 2012, when Ben was the Head of The Kildonan School, founded by Pete's Orton-Gillingham tutor in the early 1950's Diana Hanbury King,[249] Pete provided the Founder's Day speech.

Ellen Saideman represents individuals with disabilities in **Rhode Island** and **Massachusetts** and is counsel in the pending SCOTUS *Perez v. Sturgis Public Schools* case from Michigan. She has been practicing since 1988 and assists the Council of Parent Attorneys and Advocates (COPAA) with many of their numerous amicus briefs.[250]

Sona Schmidt-Harris is a freelance writer based in **Utah**. She has been writing since she was a child and her first work was published when she was in the third grade. She owns MUSE Enterprises, LLC,[251] where she provides freelance writing, editing, and paralegal services. As a paralegal, she has worked on issues involving government, criminal defense, insurance defense, corporate, and intellectual property litigation law in New York City and Salt Lake City.

Nick Simopoulos is an experienced trial attorney in **Virginia.** His state wide practice is focused on civil rights, education law, employment law, and personal injury matters. He has had several high profile ADA cases against colleges and universities in Virginia. Prior to starting Simopoulos Law, Nick served as a Senior Assistant Attorney General for the Virginia Attorney General's Office and as the Manager of the Office's General Civil Trial Unit, he handled many of Virginia's complex and high-profile civil cases. He is an Adjunct Professor of Law at William & Mary School of Law, where he teaches Advanced Civil Pretrial Practice and Legal Writing.[252]

Wayne and Cheryl Steedman practice special education law in **Maryland**. Wayne has practiced law for more than 30 years and has an MSW degree. He has handled cases in Delaware, Pennsylvania, Virginia, New Jersey, New York, and Florida and is active with COPAA[253] and is a Wrightslaw speaker. link.[254] Cheryl has been practicing law with her husband since 2012. Prior to that she worked with children as a mental health therapist and then became a paralegal focusing on children, disabilities, and mental health.[255]

247 http://www.respectabilitylawcenter.com/

248 https://www.southportschool.org/

249 https://www.wrightslaw.com/info/king.diana.tribute.htm

250 https://www.facebook.com/profile.php?id=100039658640832&referrer=services_landing_page

251   https://www.museenterprisesllc.com/

252 https://simopouloslaw.com/

253 https://www.copaa.org

254 https://www.wrightslaw.com/speak/steedman/bio.htm

255 https://steedmanlaw.net/

Chan Stroman is the Research Director of ParSEC **Wisconsin**, (Parent and Student Equity Connections)[256] which conducts independent research and analysis, and engages in pro bono consulting and advisory work, on education equity issues for students. ParSEC emphasizes practical advocacy and legal literacy for students, their families, and others who support them, with a focus on students with disabilities and students of color. For more than 30 years, she has also represented clients in commercial real estate acquisitions, dispositions, financings, and lease transactions for Class A commercial properties located nationwide, including metropolitan areas of the West and East coasts and the Midwest, Southeast and Southwest regions of the United States.

Brett Tingley, a parent in **Ohio**, is the principal force behind the award winning, documentary film *"Our Dyslexic Children,"*[257] the story of a successful struggle to transform the Upper Arlington School District into one of the best school districts in the country for children with disabilities. This film was made to provide a roadmap for parents to learn how advocate on behalf of all children.[258] It tells the story of parents who filed a systemic, group complaint with the Ohio DOE, prevailed, as the district was found in violation on all three allegations. The parents then formed a partnership with the district and now all special education teachers are trained in the Orton-Gillingham Approach in contrast with the severe problems present in the late 1980's to early 1990's.[259]

Susie van der Vorst is the Head of Camp Spring Creek[260] located in **North Carolina**. It is one of three camps, nationwide, for children with dyslexia. It's focus is on learning by using the Orton-Gillingham Approach. Suzie is a Fellow of the Academy of Orton-Gillingham Practitioners and Educators,[261] one of fewer than 200 professionals worldwide to achieve this distinction. An educator for over 25 years, Susie trained with esteemed teacher and Pete's tutor, Diana Hanbury King[262] at the Kildonan School and Camp Dunnabeck. Susie is a nationally recognized teacher trainer who presents frequently at dyslexia conferences. She's passionate about helping children become self-confident, independent readers and learners.

Kelly Walker is a professor of exceptional student education at Broward College in **Florida**. She spent more than 14 years in the public school system teaching and coordinating services for students with special needs prior to becoming a professor at Broward in 2010. In addition to teaching a full course load at Broward,[263] she presents frequently on the impact of accelerated curriculum on student achievement, student effectiveness and educational issues that concern students ages 3-21 who have disabilities or who are gifted.

Suzanne Whitney of Manchester, New Hampshire, is the Research Editor for Wrightslaw and the co-author, with Pam and Pete Wright, of *Wrightslaw: No Child Left Behind*. Sue writes about creative advocacy strategies in her column, Doing Your Homework, which appears in The Special Ed Advocate Newsletter and on Wrightslaw.com. Sue, Pete, and Pam have been friends for over 30 years.[264]

Index begins on the next page

---

256 https://parsecwi.com/

257 https://youtu.be/oJ7xa6meD2Q

258 https://parentsforreadingjustice.org/

259 See Cameron James 1996 "Letter to the Stranger" at: https://www.wrightslaw.com/advoc/ltrs/strngr.joejames.htm

260 https://campspringcreek.org/

261 https://www.ortonacademy.org/

262 https://www.wrightslaw.com/info/king.diana.tribute.htm

263 https://start.broward.edu/directory/faculty.aspx?UserName=KWALKER1

264 https://www.wrightslaw.com/speak/whitney/bio.htm

Index